THINK
SOCIAL PROBLEMS

JOHN D. CARL
Rose State College

PEARSON

Boston   Columbus   Indianapolis   New York   San Francisco   Upper Saddle River
Amsterdam   Cape Town   Dubai   London   Madrid   Milan   Munich   Paris   Montreal   Toronto
Delhi   Mexico City   Sao Paulo   Sydney   Hong Kong   Seoul   Singapore   Taipei   Tokyo

Editorial Director: Craig Campanella
Editor-in-Chief: Dickson Musslewhite
Editorial Project Manager: Maggie Barbieri
Publisher: Karen Hanson
Editorial Assistant: Alyssa Levy
Director of Marketing: Brandy Dawson
Executive Marketing Manager: Kelly May
Marketing Assistant: Gina Lavagna
Full-Service Project Management: Lauren Pecarich,
    Adam Noll, Matt Gardner, Shannon McCarthy/Words & Numbers
Senior Production Project Manager: Elizabeth Gale Napolitano
Manufacturing Buyer: Debbie Rossi
Line Art Illustrations: Words & Numbers
Manager of Design Development: John Christiana

Manager, Visual Research: Beth Brenzel
Photo Researchers: Words & Numbers, Kathy Ringrose
Manager, Rights and Permissions: Zina Arabia
Image Permission Coordinator: Debbie Hewitson
Manager, Cover Visual Research and Permissions: Karen Sanatar
Front Cover Art: Diamondlypse/istockphoto.com
Back Cover Art: Skip O'Donnell/istockphoto.com
Media Director: Karen Scott
Lead Media Project Management: Melanie McFarlane
Supplements Editor: Mayda Bosco
Composition: Words & Numbers
Printer/Binder: Courier/Kendallville
Cover Printer: Lehigh-Phoenix Color/Hagerstown

To Keven: Thanks for everything you do.
I love you.

This book was set in 8.5/12 Helvetica Neue Light.

Credits and acknowledgments for material borrowed from other sources and reproduced, with permission, in this textbook appear on page 333.

Library of Congress Cataloging-in-Publication Data
CIP data not available at time of publication.

10 9 8 7 6 5 4 3 2 1   CIN   13 12 11 10 09

Prentice Hall
is an imprint of

www.pearsonhighered.com

ISBN 10:   0-205-73309-3
ISBN 13:   978-0-205-73309-5
Exam Copy ISBN-10:   0-205-73311-5
Exam Copy ISBN-13:   978-0-205-73311-8

BRIEF CONTENTS

CONTENTS

13

CRIME 180

14

CRIMINAL JUSTICE 194

15

SOCIAL PROBLEMS OF MARRIAGE AND FAMILY 208

16

URBANIZATION: SOCIAL PROBLEMS FROM THE GROWTH OF CITIES 222

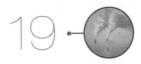

While my name is under the title of this book, it should be obvious to everyone that no single person could create a piece of work like this on his own. I would like to thank the many people involved for their support and assistance.

I am a very fortunate man. I have many friends and family who, throughout this life and the process of writing this book, have provided me with love and support. I first wish to thank my wife and life partner, Keven, for all she has done to allow me the hours of work time needed to complete this project. My children, Sara and Caroline, have also sacrificed their time with me for this as well. You all are the BEST! I am also grateful to my father and sisters for their continued support of my many activities.

I have many friends whose love and support make life so much richer. So many times, they would ask how things were going on the book, just at the time I needed it most. Such kindness is truly a blessing. Thanks to you all!

The vast majority of my colleagues both at Rose State and at the University of Oklahoma have given me a great deal of support during this project. Thanks to you all! I am also grateful to President Britton and the administration of Rose State College for their support of faculty goals and continued scholarship. I am indebted to you for your leadership and support.

The team of professionals who bring you this text are an amazing group of people who are almost too numerous to mention. However, special thanks go to the group at Pearson including Dickson Musslewhite, Karen Hanson, Maggie Barbieri, and Nancy Roberts, and the people at Words & Numbers: Lauren Pecarich, Kristen Intlekofer, Adam Noll, Salimah Perkins, Shannon McCarthy, Matt Gardner, and Luz Aranda. Each of you helped shape this text and I am grateful for that assistance. Few people understand that each chapter of this book went through an extensive review process. I am grateful to the members of my editorial review board for their work to make sure that the information in this book is both accurate and up to date. Special thanks go to:

Richard Ball, Ferris State University
Deborah Burris-Kitchen, Tennessee State University
Donna Chaffee, State University of New York at New Paltz
Sister Nancy DeCesare, Ph.D., Chestnut Hill College
Anna Hall, Delgado Community College
Brian Hawkins, University of Colorado at Boulder
Judith Hennessy, Central Washington University
Ann Marie Hickey, UMKC
Kimberly Johanek, Boise State University
Peter Phipps, State University of New York at Dutchess
Bonni Raab, Dominican College
Annette Schwabe, Florida State University
Kelly Smith, University of Arizona
Brooke Strahn-Koller, Kirkwood Community College
Eric Strayer, Hartnell College
Linda Whitman, Johnson County Community College

Finally, I wish to thank the students and faculty who took a chance on *THINK Sociology*, which resulted in the opportunity for this book. It is my hope that this book will teach students to think more clearly about social problems, and assist faculty who are engaged in the noble art of teaching. You all are the future, and sociological thinking can make it bright!

Sincerely,
John Carl, Ph.D.

ABOUT THE AUTHOR

JOHN D. CARL holds a Ph.D. in Sociology from the University of Oklahoma. His work history includes not only colleges but also hospitals, schools, churches, and prisons. John is the author of *THINK Sociology*, an introductory text for college level sociology courses. This is the second book he has written for Prentice Hall.

Sociology remains a passion for John, as does his teaching. Primarily focusing his efforts on class and online education, he continues to teach Social Problems every semester. "I enjoy the writing, but it is teaching that I love," says John.

The goal of this book is rather simple: To teach students to view social problems critically and to use sociological thinking to help them do that.

John lives in Oklahoma with his wife Keven, and daughters Sara and Caroline. In his free time, John plays golf, gardens, throws pottery, and plays his guitar in the church choir. He also provides consulting to non-profit organizations in order to help them better achieve their goals through effective leadership and management. "Sociology has so much to say about how to live in a world and make it better. I hope that this book about social problems gives students some insights into some of the big issues of our day, and ways in which we might go about decreasing their severity."

John welcomes your comments and suggestions about this THINK SOCIAL PROBLEMS book at jcthinksociology@gmail.com

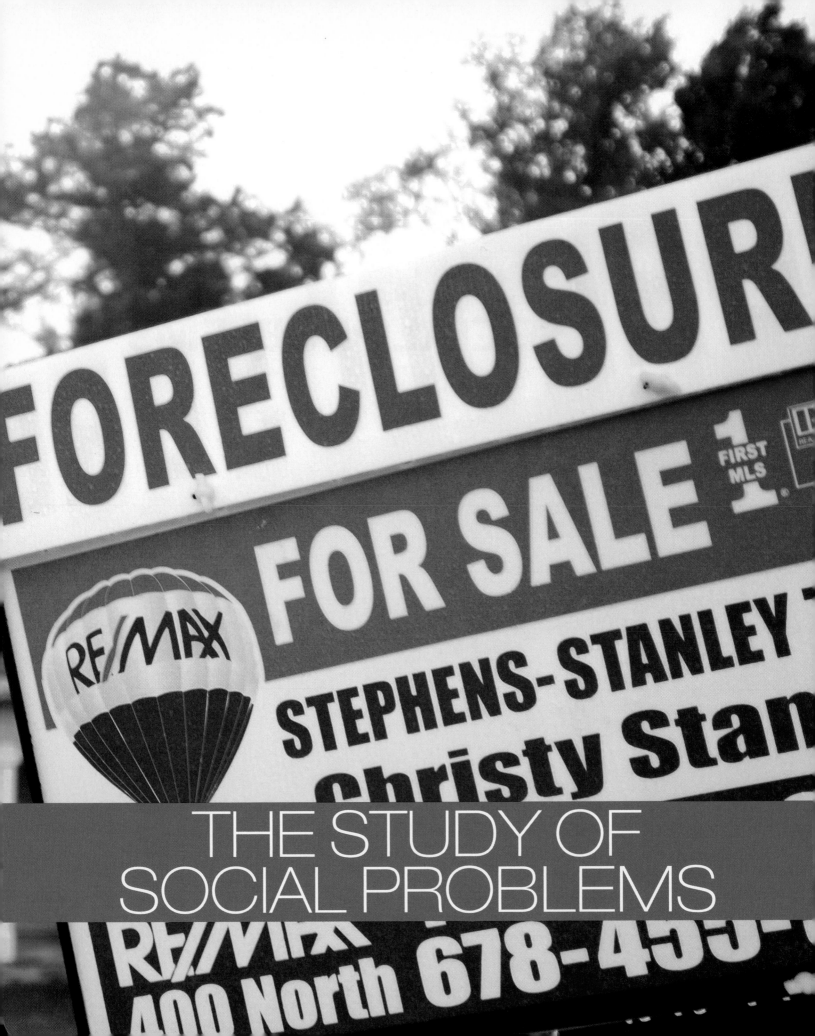

THE STUDY OF
SOCIAL PROBLEMS

WHAT IS A SOCIAL PROBLEM?
HOW DO SOCIOLOGISTS USE
    THEORETICAL PARADIGMS TO FRAME
    THEIR THINKING?
WHAT IS THE ROLE OF RESEARCH AND
    SOCIAL POLICY IN UNDERSTANDING
    SOCIAL PROBLEMS?

If asked

to make a list of the social problems in the world, most of us would be able to produce pages and pages. After all, what *isn't* wrong with our society? Violent crimes dominate the news, masses of people are out of work, and both teen pregnancy and drug use seem to be on the rise. Around the world, poverty leaves families on the brink of starvation, while genocide threatens millions of lives. When you look at the misery and violence that surrounds us, it's easy to believe the declaration of British politician David Cameron: *Society is broken*.

Not everyone agrees, however. Critics of Cameron point out that his views are not new; although we often think of the past as the "good old days," claims of broken society can be traced back all the way to the 1st century BCE. The Roman poet Juvenal lamented the moral downfall of the human race as thieves roamed the streets, men married men, and women were allowed to step outside of their traditional female roles. "It is difficult not to write satire," he explained of his profession, "when you look at broken society."

Few would dispute the fact that we've made great strides since then, particularly in the fields of science and medicine. The human life expectancy is longer than it's ever been, and it continues to increase. We have made key advancements in tolerance and respect for all people regardless of race, sexual preference, gender, or religion. Medical break-throughs such as penicillin and the polio vac-cine have made our lives safer, and instant communication through technology such as the Internet have transformed us into a tightly knit global community. Could it be that the "good old days" of the past really weren't that good at all?

Modern society is no more broken than that of Juvenal's time. While David Cameron may be correct in his identification of today's social issues, his claim fails to take into account the bigger picture. How does poverty arise? Why do nations declare war? What steps can we take to minimize crime? The first step in preventing these problems is under-standing their cause. Is a car thief immoral, or does he need the money to pay medical bills? Is a sexual deviant mentally ill, or is she just expressing her individuality? Certainly, there are social problems in the world today, but society is not one of them.[1]

---David Cameron is a conservative politician in Great Britain who regularly views social problems as a sign that society is falling apart. Family breakdown, murder, and social unrest always seem to be popular topics for politicians to bring up.

In Britain, the conservative party has been out of power for more than 10 years, so discussing social instability sends a clear message, "We didn't cause it, but we can fix it." Such ideas are often present in the United States as well. Political leaders are quick to lay blame and shirk responsibility. Claims of corruption and moral breakdown provide fuel to a fire that many feel will consume our society. Issues such as poverty, crime, and drug abuse all make for great debating points, but are these problems really any worse today than they were 100 years ago?

What makes something a social problem? When I was in college, a social problem meant I didn't have a date on Friday night. To a sociologist, a **social problem** is an issue that negatively affects a person's state of being in a society. Often, social problems raise considerable debate and controversy. How can we understand the problems of society? What can we do about these problems? Can we do this objectively without letting political ideology influence our point of view? These are the core questions that this chapter strives to answer.

Certainly, the idea of a broken society is nothing new to anyone who has turned on the television. But can we trust the media or our political leaders to provide a perspective from which we can truly investigate these issues? This book seeks to investigate the area of social problems from the point of view of sociology. Like any other science, sociology is thorough, orderly, and logical. It engages in the task objectively, without bias. The American Sociological Association defines **sociology** as "the study of social life, social change, and the social causes and consequences of human behavior."[2]

get the topic: WHAT IS A SOCIAL PROBLEM?

SOCIAL PROBLEM is an issue that negatively affects a person's state of being in a society.

SOCIOLOGY refers to a systematic and objective science that investigates human behavior in the social environment.

SOCIOLOGICAL IMAGINATION is the ability to look beyond the individual as the cause for success and failure and see how one's society influences the outcome.

MACRO is a large-scale point of view.

MICRO is a small-scale reference.

The Sociological Imagination

We're tuned into the news and we've heard the reports: The recent financial crisis is the worst global recession since the Great Depression. News reports are filled with headlines of the housing collapse, the credit crunch, banks in trouble, and the Big Three automakers' bankruptcy. It's likely that you or someone you know has been directly affected by the economic downturn through job loss or bankruptcy. What other social problems do you think will develop as a result of the current recession?

Consider this: You pull up to an intersection and notice a man with a makeshift sign; he's holding out an empty coffee can to the windows of stopped cars. He looks weary, but certainly strong enough to work. At first glance, do you immediately assume that his situation is entirely a consequence of drug addiction or laziness?

Prominent American sociologist C. Wright Mills (1916–1962) argued that people must understand how extraneous factors contribute to individual situations. To do this, we must practice **sociological imagination**—the ability to look beyond the individual as the only cause of success and failure and see how society influences a person's outcome.[3] Mills noted that this **macro** (large-scale) point of view helps us understand how history and social structure affect people. Mills noted that we often see social issues from our personal viewpoints only, interpreting actions at face value—a **micro** (small-scale) view. Using only a micro point of view is detrimental to a clear understanding of the world and can negatively influence our perception of events.

Instead of assuming the worst, we should use our sociological imagination and pause to consider that the man on the corner might be there for a number of reasons. Maybe he really is a drug addict or simply lazy. Then again, he may be a victim of recent layoffs. Perhaps he's a casualty of globalization, as his former employer downsized staff to hire cheap overseas labor. He may even be mentally ill and unable to hold a job. Can we really assume that we understand a person merely from seeing him on the side of the road? As Mills argued, the goal of sociology is to move beyond our own perceptions and toward a sociological imagination. Without connecting what we know about society to the individual, we run the risk of wrongly placing blame and misconstruing the way we interpret events. In everyday life, we make this mistake regularly, but sociological study is not the same as our everyday "common sense."

∧
∧   We often claim to know the cause of
∧   events based on our own assumptions.

Is this woman practicing sociological imagination or imposing personal beliefs?

The Essential Elements of a Social Problem

THE OBJECTIVE CONDITION

An **objective condition** is any aspect of society that can be viewed without bias. The recorded number of violent crimes in Britain, the conditions in which people live in a certain region of the United States, or the number of mass layoffs at an auto plant because of the recent economic crisis are examples of objective conditions. All can be quantifiably measured, and generally are not arguable. For example, according to the U.S. Bureau of Labor Statistics, 5.7 million jobs have been lost since the recession began in December 2007.[4] Take a look at the table below to see the difference in rate of unemployment between 2007 and 2008.

Overall, men experienced a slightly larger increase in unemployment than women. By April 2009, the total national unemployment rate for men and women combined was 8.9 percent, compared to 8.5 percent the prior month, and 5 percent total in 2008.[5]

What are some of the objective effects of this? According to a study conducted by the Association for Health Services, there is a relationship

Men (16 years and older)		Women (16 years and older)	
2007	2008	2007	2008
4.7%	6.1%	4.5%	5.4%

U.S. Unemployment Rates between 2007 and 2008

Source: Data from the U.S. Bureau of Labor Statistics, Labor Force Statistics from the Current Population Survey, CPS Table 24, "Unemployed persons by marital status, race, Hispanic or Latino ethnicity, age, and sex."

OBJECTIVE CONDITION is any aspect of society that can be viewed without bias.

SUBJECTIVITY refers to making judgments based on personal feelings and opinions rather than external facts.

between job loss and individual health problems. The results indicate that displaced workers, in relation to their continuously employed counterparts, exhibit poorer physical functioning and higher levels of depression. The study also found that job displacement in the later stages of a worker's career can result in more negative health effects.[6]

SUBJECTIVE CONCERNS

Most of my students approach the study of sociology with subjective concerns. Is the depletion of Social Security resources really a problem for those in their early 20s? As a student of mine once said, "It's not a social problem if it doesn't affect me." This is a perfect example of **subjectivity**, a judgment based on personal feelings and opinions rather than external facts. Subjectivity often appears in my classes when students rely on personal experiences. Every semester it seems, a student claims to know a rich welfare mom who sucks the taxpayers dry while riding around in her new Cadillac Escalade. This usually leads the student to make the erroneous conclusion that all welfare recipients are freeloaders. Is that really possible?

We can use the social imagination as a tool to step outside of our subjectivity, or "biography," and look at the big picture, which includes both the objective facts and the historical background of the situation. This does not mean that the subjective is not important, only that it must be balanced against the objective reality of a situation. According to C. Wright Mills, "[It is] by means of the sociological imagination that men now hope to grasp what is going on in the world, and to understand what is happening in themselves as minute points of the intersections of biography and history within society."[7]

Factors that Define a Social Problem

What is and is not considered a social problem can vary a great deal over time. As you continue through this course, you will see that social problems are common to all societies, and they often are latent results from efforts to deal with certain social situations. For example, the idea that people should take care of themselves leads to limited government involvement in housing, jobs, and other aspects of people's lives. This can result in members of the population being unemployed, homeless, and/or living in substandard housing. Are such things socially caused? Perhaps, but what is certain is that they have social consequences for us all. For example, whether or not you care about the argument for a more generous social service program, you'll be dealing with the results of that decision, either by encountering more beggars on the street or paying higher federal taxes to fund the program.

Of course, not everyone agrees that such things are social problems. In my years of teaching, I've found that students are more eager to classify the things that directly affect them as social problems, while discounting the importance of things that do not affect them. For something to be considered a legitimate social problem, however, it must be agreed that it is a problem, and that something can be done about it.

Other a factors influence how we define social problems as well. Let's take look at those now in more detail.

Five Cultural Values Affected by a Global Recession

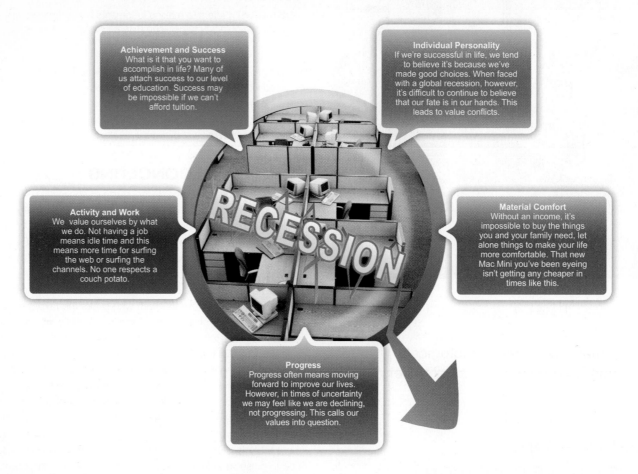

Achievement and Success
What is it that you want to accomplish in life? Many of us attach success to our level of education. Success may be impossible if we can't afford tuition.

Individual Personality
If we're successful in life, we tend to believe it's because we've made good choices. When faced with a global recession, however, it's difficult to continue to believe that our fate is in our hands. This leads to value conflicts.

Activity and Work
We value ourselves by what we do. Not having a job means idle time and this means more time for surfing the web or surfing the channels. No one respects a couch potato.

Material Comfort
Without an income, it's impossible to buy the things you and your family need, let alone things to make your life more comfortable. That new Mac Mini you've been eyeing isn't getting any cheaper in times like this.

Progress
Progress often means moving forward to improve our lives. However, in times of uncertainty we may feel like we are declining, not progressing. This calls our values into question.

RECESSION

VALUES are a part of a society's nonmaterial culture that represent cultural standards by which we determine what is good, bad, right, or wrong.

CULTURAL UNIVERSALS are aspects of one's social life that are common to all societies.

HISTORY

History changes the definition of social problems. The issues that society considered major in the past are often not that important in the present. For example, at one point in history, a major concern in the United States was horse theft—obviously, this is no longer an issue. Many of the problems we encounter today may also go the way of the horse thief. For instance, high gasoline prices and fear of an oil shortage may seem laughable 50 years from now when electric or magnetic motors are the norm.

Of course, history is often written by the powerful, and this influences how we view the problems of the past. We've been taught "In 1492, Columbus sailed the ocean blue," and he discovered the New World. But according to political scientist Howard Zinn, no textbook accounts for the torture, slave labor, or murder of approximately half of the 250,000 natives that occurred as well.[8] At the time, Columbus and the subsequent European explorers probably felt that what they were doing was "right." And yet nowadays, killing, enslaving, and forcing people into religious conversions would certainly be viewed differently.

CULTURAL VALUES

Just as history defines social problems, so do values. **Values** are a part of society's nonmaterial culture that represent standards by which we determine what is good, bad, right, or wrong. As we've mentioned before, one of the country's largest current social problems is unemployment. But why do you suppose this is? According to noted American sociologist Robin Murphy Williams Jr., there are certain dominant values held by people in the United States.[9] In the diagram above, you can see five of these values, and how they relate to the recent economic crisis.

Societies tend to define social problems according to their cultural values. For example, in countries where women's education is devalued, it's not seen as a social problem for girls to be illiterate. In our nation, this would be shocking. Values matter.

CULTURAL UNIVERSALS

A **cultural universal** is any aspect of one's social life that is common to all societies. All societies experience births, deaths, crime, war, and a host of other issues. In response to these issues, they create social customs to deal with them. For example, think back to a wedding you may have attended or viewed on TV. Most likely, it was similar to all the others you've seen: fancy clothes, lots of food, and friends and family gathered in celebration. Although the color of the dress or the wording of the vows may differ, people from all over the world still deal with the same issue: How do two people leave their childhood behind them and step into their new, adult lives? Wedding ceremonies help make this important step official—and fun.

From this perspective, social problems are also cultural universals. In other words, every society has social problems, but how societies deal with these problems can vary a great deal from place to place. For example, when I lived in Mexico, I remember my friends having a big celebration on November 2, The Day of the Dead. As they explained, it's a traditional Mexican day to remember loved ones who have passed away. In the United States, many people use Memorial Day as an occasion to pay their respects to fallen soldiers and departed relatives. Both cultures honor their dead; they simply have different dates and rituals by which to do it.

AWARENESS

The last factor that defines a social problem is awareness. **Awareness** is the ability of a person or group to bring a problem into public recognition. This often happens only after years of conflict. The battle for women's suffrage, for example, lasted about 150 years before women finally achieved the right to vote in the United States.[10]

Awareness can lead people to start **social movements**—activities that support or protest social change. These often start as grassroots movements formed by non-government organizations. For example, the Civil Rights Movement started in churches in the South, as leaders worked to increase the awareness of racial discrimination.

Charles Tilly, a 20th-century American sociologist, identified three elements common to all social movements. The first involves **campaigns**, organized and ongoing efforts that make claims targeting a specific authority in society. For example, at the outbreak of the war in Iraq, peaceful protestors marched on Washington, hoping to demonstrate enough negative public response to end the war. Campaigns tend to focus on one specific issue. Recently, a campaign to begin curbside recycling was successful in my hometown. Citizens voted for higher tax rates in order to be able to decrease the amount of waste that goes into landfills and began to put recycling bins in their driveways.

A **repertoire** is the second element of a social movement. According to Tilly, this step involves the actions used to promote interest and participation within the movement. Anti-war campaigners might lobby, protest,

or march to advertise their opinions. Depending on the situation, different strategies may be more useful. The recyclers in my neighborhood used direct mail and door-to-door visits to promote their cause. Their campaign was successful because of these efforts.

The third element of a social movement encompasses the **worthiness, unity, numbers, and commitments (WUNC)** of the individuals involved. Social movements must be seen by the public as "worthy" of action. Recycling seemed worthy of action in my town, but carpooling has not. Unity refers to the idea that all members of the movement must agree on what they are trying to accomplish—the message must be focused. Furthermore, the movement must have enough people involved to avoid looking like a small "splinter group." Finally, members must be committed to the social change. Having WUNC gives the movement a fighting chance for success. A social movement typically goes through several conventional stages of development: emergence, coalescence, bureaucratization, and decline.[11]

AWARENESS is the ability of a person or group to bring a problem into public recognition.

SOCIAL MOVEMENTS are activities that support or protest social issues organized by non-governmental organizations.

CAMPAIGNS are organized and ongoing efforts that make claims targeting a specific authority in the society.

REPERTOIRE is the actions used to promote interest and participation within the movement.

WUNC refers to worthiness, unity, numbers, and commitments, which are the characteristics shown by members of a social movement.

∨
∨
∨ **Charles Tilly noted that** all social movements travel through four stages: emergence, coalescence, bureaucratization, and decline. **He also argued that all movements involve campaigns, repertoire, and WUNC.**

The Four Stages of Social Movements

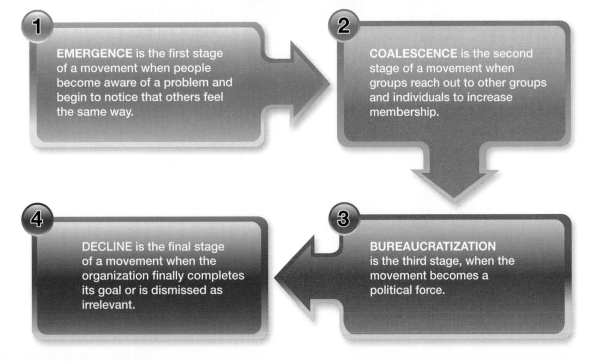

1 EMERGENCE is the first stage of a movement when people become aware of a problem and begin to notice that others feel the same way.

2 COALESCENCE is the second stage of a movement when groups reach out to other groups and individuals to increase membership.

3 BUREAUCRATIZATION is the third stage, when the movement becomes a political force.

4 DECLINE is the final stage of a movement when the organization finally completes its goal or is dismissed as irrelevant.

think social problems: HOW DO SOCIOLOGISTS USE THEORETICAL PARADIGMS TO FRAME THEIR THINKING?

> **PARADIGMS** are theoretical frameworks through which scientists study the world.
>
> **FUNCTIONALISM** is a theoretical framework that defines society as a system of interrelated parts.
>
> **CONFLICT THEORY** is a theoretical framework that views society as being in a constant struggle over scarce resources.

The Three Major Paradigms of Sociology

The issues that we define as social problems are complex in nature, and because of the increase in globalization and media outlets, they do not remain confined to one institution or geographic area. For this reason, sociologists must look carefully at a problem to see all its parts. So, how do we begin to approach thinking about social problems? Historically, sociologists use either macro or micro **paradigms**, the theoretical frameworks through which scientists study the world. These include three major paradigms that we'll be focusing on in this text: functionalism, conflict theory, and symbolic interactionism. Sociologists from each school of thought analyze similar issues, but the manner in which they reach conclusions differs. Let's explore each of these paradigms a little further.

FUNCTIONALISM

Functionalism is a theoretical framework that defines society as a system of interrelated parts. Because functionalism focuses on the entire social system and not just the individual, it's considered a macro approach to sociological study. If something happens to one component of a social structure, the other components will automatically step in to help restore balance. Think about an automatic HVAC (heating, ventilating, and air-conditioning) system. Some warehouses manufacture products that must be stored at a certain temperature and humidity. If the temperature and humidity outside goes up or down, so do the conditions inside the warehouse. But if an HVAC system has been installed, it can be switched on to maintain a stable temperature and humidity level. Social structures operate in the same manner. If problems occur, society automatically acts in ways to offset these issues. Functionalism treats society as relatively secure—everything that occurs has a purpose in the preservation of stability.

Functionalists believe that the best way to understand society as a whole is to understand how social institutions (such as family, education, and the economy) are interrelated. Each institution has an impact no matter how small it may seem; because

everything is connected, a butterfly effect occurs. Here's an example: When the economy does poorly, it doesn't just affect your wallet. Companies fold, jobs are lost, families go hungry, and children do poorly in school. Because society's balance is reliant on each of its components, functionalism suggests that all social structures must agree on values and norms. These values and norms create society's rules and laws, thus regulating the relationships between institutions.

Let's take a quick look at a few prominent functionalists from history and their beliefs.

Functionalists:

- **Herbert Spencer (1820–1903)** Society can be considered a living organism in which some are more apt to deal with social dynamics and, therefore, adapt better to changes in the environment.[12]

- **Emile Durkheim (1858–1917)** Social integration and social control hold society together. People view themselves as unified wholes, which helps them stay within the boundaries of their social structure's rules and laws.[13]

- **Talcott Parsons (1902–1979)** Society is a grand interrelated system in which each individual is instrumental in keeping the system functional. If one individual falters, society as a whole will suffer.[14]

- **Robert Merton (1910–2003)** Every action in society has manifest functions (factors that lead to an expected consequence) and latent functions (factors that lead to an unforeseen or unexpected consequence).[15]

CONFLICT THEORY

Conflict theory is a theoretical framework that views society as being in a constant struggle over a limited amount of resources. Similar to functionalism, this theory also uses a macro approach because it deals with the interaction of multiple groups fighting to gain power. For example, conflict theorists would examine how and why the rift between the rich and the poor affects the quality of education, health care, and living conditions of those groups. The wealthy can afford better housing and tend to live near people of the same status. Because of this, the values of these homes increase, and the poor who originally lived there are forced into separate areas. It's no surprise

∧∧∧ **Auguste Comte (1798–1857)** coined the term *sociology* and proposed the **basic principles of functionalism.**

that individuals who can afford to live in more expensive neighborhoods can also afford better schools for their children, thereby increasing the chances that their offspring will also be more successful. Conflict theorists suggest that once inequality begins to take root, those at the top are unlikely to push for social change. This is because the elite set standards and rules that benefit themselves, not the individuals or groups below them. These standards also help keep the wealthy and powerful in prominent positions.

Conflict theory can be applied to many institutions, not just social class. Conflict theorists apply their principles to age, gender, race, religion . . . any social construct in which inequality can be viewed as a social problem. Take a look at the list below to see the different ways in which conflict theorists approach this paradigm:

Conflict Theorists:

- **Harriet Martineau (1802–1876)** A society's actions are often quite different from the values expressed by that society. For example, despite boasts of freedom and democracy in the United States, only men had the right to vote until 1920.[16]

- **Karl Marx (1818–1883)** Capitalism breeds conflict between the rich and the poor. The pursuit of wealth corrupts society and will ultimately destroy it. Economic power should not lie in the hands of the elite few, but in the hands of all people.

- **W. E. B. Du Bois (1868–1963)** Social equality is impossible to achieve in corrupt social systems. The past strongly influences the present, such as the connection between past and present discrimination against African Americans and all disadvantaged groups.[17]

- **John Bellamy Foster (1953–Present)** Social unrest is a result of unequal distribution of power and wealth. Capitalism cannot continue as is; the process of seeking short-term rewards and avoiding long-term consequences must be stopped if society is to continue.[18]

∧
∧ Symbolic interactionists are interested in
∧ people's reactions to cultural symbols.

How do you think someone from Nigeria would respond to these images?

SYMBOLIC INTERACTIONISM

Symbolic interactionism is a theoretical framework that focuses on how individual interactions between people influence their behavior and how these interactions can impact society. Unlike functionalism and conflict theory, this paradigm is a micro approach because it deals with individuals, not groups or institutions. Symbolic interactionists analyze how social interactions influence, create, and sustain human relationships. They believe that symbols such as body language, words, gestures, and images affect communication. Humans interact with one another according to the meanings of these symbols.

How did you first learn your name? Early on in your life, your parents called you something, and you learned to respond to it. Now if someone calls you by another name, you're unlikely to even move your head. Why? Because somewhere in your mind, you use this symbol to help form your sense of self. It is this identity that you carry with you your entire life and use in interactions with others to create a social world.

We also learn the meaning behind symbols within social contexts. For example, a photo of Chinese revolutionary Mao Zedong probably has little or no meaning to you, whereas a picture of George Washington might bring forth thoughts of freedom and rebellion. Despite both men being revolutionary leaders, your cultural context influences how you view each photo.

Symbolic Interactionists:

- **George Herbert Mead (1863–1931)** Society is made up of symbols that teach us to understand the world. We use these symbols to develop a sense of self, or identity. We then take this identity into the world to interact with other identities to create society.

- **Herbert Blumer (1900–1987)** An individual's behavior depends on the meanings we've already created through experience and interaction. We use an interpretive process to handle and alter these meanings.

- **Erving Goffman (1922–1982)** Social interactions are the building blocks of society. Individuals alter their behavior constantly, requiring a complex series of actions and reactions.

- **Howard Becker (1928–Present)** Social interactions can lead to self-fulfilling prophecies that limit a person's outcomes. We place labels on people in society; individuals then feel as though they must embody those labels.[19]

What Types of Questions Do Sociologists Ask?

Understanding the three paradigms can be confusing, especially when applying them to complicated social problems. Use the table on the following page as a reference to help you remember the basic ideas behind each theory. Often, the types of questions sociologists ask give clues to their school of thought.

The Three Paradigms—How Are They Interrelated?

Often, the lines between microanalysis and macroanalysis blur. Most sociologists I know follow in the footsteps of Max Weber (VAY-bur), a famous social scientist who, in many ways, defied being put into any one of these categories. Like conflict theorists, Weber asserted that social class is one of the most important influences in the outcome of our lives. Power disparities between the classes often dictate who succeeds in a society and who does not. However, he also took a more functionalist approach, arguing that society at its most efficient will naturally run like a bureaucracy: One leader presides over a group of smaller organizations that all share a common goal. At the same time, Weber incorporated symbolic interaction into his theories, noting that values influence people's goals and behaviors. Weber understood that sociologists aren't naturally immune to personal biases, and he urged his colleagues to separate their private values from their professional work.

Like Weber, modern sociologists often find themselves taking on the roles of functionalist, conflict theorist, and symbolic interactionist interchangeably to best analyze today's social problems. Few of us are purists; can you think of ways these theories overlap?

Emerging Paradigms

Other paradigms exist, apart from the major three. Let's take a look at some of the more modern approaches to sociological theory.

FEMINIST THEORY

Feminist theory is a female-centered, interdisciplinary approach that seeks to demonstrate how women fit into the social world. Feminists often ask questions such as "Why is the social world the way that it is?" and "Can we change the social world to make it a fair place for all people?" Feminists are also interested in how race, ethnicity, social class, and age interact with gender to determine the outcomes for individuals. There are three prominent feminist theories:

- **Gender-inequality theories:** Women's experiences of the social world are not equal to those of men. Such theories focus on sexist patterns that limit women's opportunities for work, education, and other social needs.

- **Theories of gender oppression:** Men purposefully maintain control over women through discrimination and the use of power; this leads to oppression.

- **Structural oppression theories:** Women's oppression is rooted in capitalism; patriarchies keep women on the margins of the social world.

EXCHANGE THEORY

Exchange theorists suggest that our social experiences consist of a series of costs and rewards. People inherently seek to maximize their rewards and minimize their costs, resulting in social action. Exchange theory often appeals to thinkers on a micro level—for example, why do we choose one mate over another? If you're dating someone and the effort you're exerting makes the relationship feel like the cost is higher than the reward, you're likely to end the relationship. But exchange theory also has a macro point of view. For example, do you suppose it's in the best interest of a country to export all manufacturing jobs to other nations that can provide cheaper labor? In calculating the value of the exchange, we must consider not only the short-term reward (the immediate profit, in this case), but also the potential long-term costs (economic collapse when transportation of goods is interrupted, for example).

ENVIRONMENTAL THEORY

Environmental theory is the most recent paradigm to emerge in sociology. This theory combines social thought and ecological principles to discover how environmental policies influence society and how attitudes toward the environment have changed over time. Environmental theorists often attempt to understand how societies adjust to ecological changes. For example, how many people can live in a specific area? This amount is known as carrying capacity. Often we believe that humans are an exception to the ecological limits of carrying capacity. However, for environmental sociologists, humans are merely one type of organism sharing the same ecological space with other organisms. How do societies adapt to these limits? If they fail to adapt, will they continue to survive? These types of questions are at the center of environmental theory.

Core Questions of the Three Paradigms			
	Functionalists	Conflict Theorists	Symbolic Interactionists
Approach to Analysis	Macro	Macro	Micro
Core Questions	1. What are the components of society? 2. How do these components relate to each other? 3. What keeps society in balance? 4. What are the expected and unexpected consequences of an event?	1. How are wealth, power, opportunities, and resources divided within society? 2. How do individuals or groups maintain their wealth and power? 3. Which groups thrive in society and why?	1. What influence do individuals have on the creation of a social structure? 2. In what manner does social interaction impact human relationships? 3. Do individuals alter their behavior depending on setting? If so, why?

WRAP YOUR MIND AROUND THE THEORY

Sometimes, **it takes a financial collapse to remind consumers to spend responsibly,** but functionalists trust that society will rectify its own misdoings. **What are some other ways in which society seeks to restore balance?**

FUNCTIONALISM

From a functionalist point of view, society can't be "broken." Systems evolve due to needs that must be met, and social structures exist to balance society. The housing collapse triggered financial instability in many areas, but people and institutions create reforms to counterbalance volatility. For example, after years of heavy borrowing, consumers will now begin to adopt practices of net saving. Social problems that exist are the result of dysfunctions of the system; however, these dysfunctions do not indicate that society is "broken," as David Cameron insists. To a functionalist, fixing society merely involves tinkering with it.

CONFLICT THEORY

Modern conflict theorists look at social problems, often focusing on how inequality affects the lives of people, as well as the different structures of society. If one were to argue, like David Cameron, that society seems broken, a conflict theorist would likely suggest that those with the most money and power broke it, or that they somehow benefit from those problems. In short, social problems such as these are the result of those in power using their dominance to benefit themselves, ignoring the pain it causes others.

IS SOCIETY BROKEN?

SYMBOLIC INTERACTIONISM

A symbolic interactionist might ask, "What does 'broken' mean?" The definition will change depending on your social status. If you're poor, it's likely that one of your concerns is having enough food to feed your family. If you're rich and powerful, odds are you won't think twice about obtaining your next meal. Before we define and/or deal with social problems, we must first acknowledge their existence. The next step is to find new ways to view the situation so that these same problems will be avoided in the future.

Conflict theory suggests **that there is an ongoing struggle for wealth and power creating inequality.** How might the housing collapse advance classism in the United States?

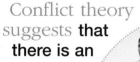

In order for everyone to agree on whether or not society is broken, we would all have to have a common understanding of what society is supposed to be. **Do we all share the same ideas?**

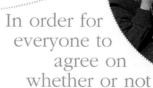

discover solutions to social problems:
WHAT IS THE ROLE OF RESEARCH AND SOCIAL POLICY IN UNDERSTANDING SOCIAL PROBLEMS?

RESEARCH METHODS are scientific procedures that sociologists use to conduct research and develop knowledge about a particular topic.

OBJECTIVITY refers to the ability to conduct research without allowing the influence of personal biases or prejudices.

Research Methods

Sociology is more than a school of thought or a philosophy of life. It is a science that attempts to discover facts and connections between people and the social world in which they live. The only way in which sociologists can truly understand and solve social problems is by studying and conducting scientific research. Like all science, however, sociology has its limits. It provides tools to help us study the social world, but many of these must be fully understood in order to avoid false conclusions.

This section will familiarize you with the various aspects of sociological research. **Research methods** are the scientific procedures that sociologists use to conduct studies and develop knowledge about a particular topic. Was David Cameron thinking like a sociologist when he hypothesized that society was broken? What does "broken" mean? How would

you go about measuring a society's "brokenness?" What would society look like if it were "fixed?" What would "fixing" it mean? Anyone can comment on society, but it takes a lot more effort to solve its problems. The first step is to understand the specific terms and research methods that sociologists use.

OBJECTIVITY

For sociologists, **objectivity** is the ability to conduct research without allowing the influence of personal biases or prejudices. As Max Weber first advised, sociologists must set aside all private values and preconceived notions to study a subject objectively. Personal experiences and political affiliations are two major biases that most of us find hardest to keep in check. Do you think you could objectively analyze the war in Iraq if your son was stationed in Baghdad? Could you study pedophiles impartially if your child was victimized by one? Objectivity is difficult, but essential to sociological research.

So, how do we think objectively? According to Weber, the only way to draw accurate conclusions is to completely detach yourself from the subject. When you do this successfully, you're able to accomplish *verstehen*, an understanding of the action from the actor's point of view.[20]

The Six Steps of Social Research

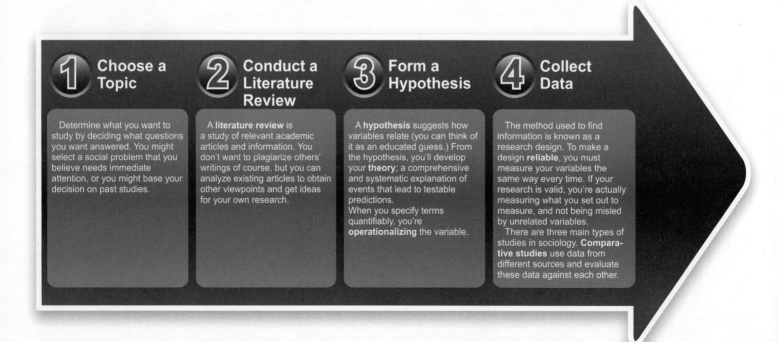

1 Choose a Topic

Determine what you want to study by deciding what questions you want answered. You might select a social problem that you believe needs immediate attention, or you might base your decision on past studies.

2 Conduct a Literature Review

A **literature review** is a study of relevant academic articles and information. You don't want to plagiarize others' writings of course, but you can analyze existing articles to obtain other viewpoints and get ideas for your own research.

3 Form a Hypothesis

A **hypothesis** suggests how variables relate (you can think of it as an educated guess.) From the hypothesis, you'll develop your **theory**; a comprehensive and systematic explanation of events that lead to testable predictions. When you specify terms quantifiably, you're **operationalizing** the variable.

4 Collect Data

The method used to find information is known as a research design. To make a design **reliable**, you must measure your variables the same way every time. If your research is valid, you're actually measuring what you set out to measure, and not being misled by unrelated variables.

There are three main types of studies in sociology. **Comparative studies** use data from different sources and evaluate these data against each other.

Source: Earl Babbie, *The Practice of Social Research, 8th edition* (Belmont, CA: Wadsworth Publishing Company, 1998).

VARIABLES

Once you train yourself to view social problems objectively, the next step is to determine the variables in the situation. Variables are simply things we want to know about. For example, we may want to know if having a college degree affects the likelihood of having a job. But we may also want to know if the findings vary depending on a person's degree choice, race, or gender. Each of these is a variable.

There are two main types of variables in sociological research: independent and dependent. **Independent variables** are factors that are deliberately manipulated in an experiment, and **dependent variables** are the response. So, the dependent variable *depends* on the independent variable. In our previous example, having a college degree is the independent variable, whereas employment status is the dependent one. This is

INDEPENDENT VARIABLES are variables that are deliberately manipulated to test the response in an experiment.

DEPENDENT VARIABLES are the responses to the manipulated variable.

<<< Shows such as Campbell Brown's *No Bias, No Bull*—a self-proclaimed non-partisan newscast of CNN—is increasingly more popular amid the flurry of highly opinionated news commentaries, such as *The Daily Show* and *The O'Reilly Factor.* Ironically, the show begins with a detailed news summary, which is immediately followed by Brown's opinion, followed by other analysts' opinions. Is it possible to get a completely objective news report?

 **Collect Data**

Cross-sectional studies focus on a single event in time. **Longitudinal studies** include data from observations over time, and consistently use the same groups of people (known to sociologists as **cohorts**).

Sociologists also collect data by conducting **surveys**, investigations of the opinions or experiences of people, usually obtained through questioning. **Field research** is also useful, since it allows researchers to carry out their experiments in natural, social settings.

5 Analyze the Results

This step involves interpreting data, so understanding the basics of statistical data is important. In statistics, the numbers inside a group of numbers are called the **central tendency**. There are three measures of central tendency. The **mean** is the sum of a series of numbers divided by the amount of numbers. The **median** is the midpoint in a distribution of numbers arranged in order of size. The **mode** is the number in the group that occurs most frequently.

6 Share and Publish the Results

Sociologists rely on the data and trends of other researchers when attempting to understand and solve social problems.

In the sociological world, everyone must abide by specific guidelines when publishing their work. A good resource to look into is the American Sociological Association style guide.

> **CONTROL VARIABLES** are variables that are kept constant to accurately test the impact of an independent variable.
>
> **CAUSAL RELATIONSHIPS** are relationships in which a condition or variable leads to a certain consequence.
>
> **CAUSATION** is the relationship between cause and effect.
>
> **CORRELATION** is an indication that one factor *might* be the cause for another factor.
>
> **POSITIVE CORRELATION** involves two variables moving in a parallel.

because we believe that employment depends on education. Of course, such a study would be rather simple. Do teachers and engineers have the same unemployment rates as social workers and art history majors? Probably not.

To determine what effect, if any, a college degree has on a person's employment status, you must control for other variables that might influence the results and lead to false conclusions. **Control variables** are factors that are kept constant to accurately test the impact of an independent variable. If you compare the rate of unemployment of people with college degrees to the rate of unemployment of people without college degrees, you must be sure that other factors such as race and gender are equivalent. In short, control variables take into account other features that might influence the outcome.

CAUSE AND CORRELATION

Perhaps one of the most misunderstood concepts in research is the difference between cause and correlation. In common speech, we frequently claim causality when it doesn't exist. It's common to remark that a person "made me mad" when in fact it was you choosing to get angry. In sociological research, a **causal relationship** is one in which a condition or variable leads directly to a certain consequence. Such a finding is rare in sociology; some have even argued that it's impossible. Why? This is explored in the sections that follow.

Causation

Causation is the relationship between cause and effect. For example, the H1N1 virus, a subtype of the swine influenza, causes flu-like symptoms. Therefore, if you catch swine flu, you must have caught the virus. But being exposed to someone with the virus doesn't necessarily mean that you will get sick. Why? Because, just like with any common cold, being around a sick person does not mean you will necessarily catch his or her disease. The virus causes the illness; being around someone doesn't cause the illness. Of course, if you hang around with people who have the flu, you're likely to catch it yourself. Being around an infected person is correlated with catching the disease.

Correlation

Unlike causation, **correlation** is an indication that a factor *might* be connected to another factor. What does this mean for us in sociology? Correlation tells us that the variables we're studying are related in some way. In sociological research, we have numerous correlations and almost no causations. Let's say, for example, that those people who have college degrees are more likely to have jobs than those who don't attain such high levels of education. In this example, there is a correlation between education and employment rates. However, this doesn't mean that having a college degree means automatic employment (especially in the current U.S. economy). There are many other factors we must consider, such as age, race, location, and so forth.

Correlations exist in three forms: positive, negative, and spurious.

1 A **positive correlation** involves two variables moving in a parallel. In other words, the variables must increase or decrease *together*. For example, it's likely that a family who defaults on its mortgage payments will lose its home to foreclosure. Although both variables have a negative impact, they show a positive correlation because they both move in the same direction.

2 A **negative correlation** occurs when the variables move in opposite directions. If a community spays or neuters *more* of their

Cloud Computing Activities by Different Age Cohorts				
Internet users in each age group who do the following online activities (%)				
	18–29	30–49	50–64	65+
Use webmail services such as Hotmail, Gmail, or Yahoo! mail	77	58	44	27
Store personal photos	50	34	26	19
Use online applications such as Google Documents or Adobe Photoshop Express	39	28	25	19
Store personal videos	14	6	5	2
Pay to store computer files online	9	4	5	3
Back up hard drive to an online site	7	5	5	4
Have done at least <u>one</u> activity	87	71	59	46
Have done at least <u>two</u> activities	59	39	31	21

N=1,553 Internet users. Margin of error is ±3%.

Source: Pew Internet & American Life Project April-May 2008 Survey.

pets, the community members would notice *fewer* strays wandering the streets. This situation results in a positive result, but it's still a negative correlation because the variables move in different directions.

3 The third form of correlation is *spurious*, meaning not genuine or authentic. A **spurious correlation** occurs when two variables appear to be related, but actually have separate causes. For example, the number of violent crimes generally increases in summer months. The consumption of ice cream also increases in summer months. Does this mean that ice cream causes violence? Certainly not. It could be the warm weather, the longer days, or one of many other factors. As you work your way through this course, be careful to avoid making spurious correlations.

INTERPRETING TABLES

You're likely to encounter many tables and graphs when you're evaluating statistical data. This type of information is helpful because it means someone has already taken the time to collect and organize the information for you; all *you* have to do is interpret it. Even if you've had experience with scientific tables before, here are some tips to help you interpret data faster and more accurately. Take some time to walk through the steps below.

1 Read the table and figure out why someone created it—what is the information trying to tell you? In this example, the researcher wants to convey that use of the Internet varies between age groups. What else might this tell you?

2 Pay attention to subheadings; they often exist to present new information necessary for analyzing the contents of the table. In this case, the subtitle clarifies that the data represent the percent of Internet users in multiple age groups who participate in the following online activities.

3 Read any information printed below the table. This is where you'll find the source of the original material and any other information the author wants you to understand. In this table, you'll note that the number (N) of people surveyed was 1,553 and that the study was published in early 2008. The source information also tells us exactly where to find the original data.

ETHICAL CONCERNS

Sociological research, especially when it deals with social problems, is often a snapshot of society at its worst. You may be discouraged to learn that not many sociologists spend their time researching the dining trends of rich, healthy, happily married couples. In sociology, we need to study the worst problems in society to be able to solve them. Sometimes, our research involves sensitive topics such as prostitution or drug abuse. Sociologists must approach these issues ethically and with delicacy. **Ethics** is a system of values or principles that guide one's behavior. The American Sociology Association provides five universal principles that all sociologists must adhere to in their studies.

Researchers must be *professionally competent*, limiting their studies to areas in which they've had previous experience. Personal beliefs and opinions must be ignored because all sociologists have a *professional and scientific responsibility*. They must also show *integrity* and never coerce their subjects into telling them what they want to hear. Likewise, scientists need to show *respect for people's rights, dignity, and diversity*. Discrimination is detrimental to any form of research and goes against the

NEGATIVE CORRELATION occurs when the variables move in opposite directions.

SPURIOUS CORRELATION occurs when two variables appear to be related, but actually have separate causes.

ETHICS refers to a system of values or principles that guide one's behavior.

QUANTITATIVE DATA refer to data based on numbers and used for macroanalysis.

QUALITATIVE DATA refer to information that may include words, pictures, photos, or any other type of information that comes to the researcher in a non-numerical form.

TRIANGULATION is the process of using multiple approaches to study a phenomenon.

very foundations of sociology. Last, researchers have a *social responsibility* to mankind. Sociologists must remember that the work they do affects real human lives.

Why so many rules? Because research subjects shouldn't have to be worried about their safety while being studied. If they have concerns, it won't be long before no one will want to participate in sociological research.

Quantitative and Qualitative Methods

There are two categories of research that sociologists use. Neither of them is necessarily linked to functionalism, conflict theory, or symbolic interactionism. There are no set rules about which methods must be applied to each of the theories, but sociologists have found that each framework uses data in different ways. Quantitative and qualitative data are the foundation for these differences.

QUANTITATIVE METHODS

The term **quantitative data** refers to data based on numbers and used for macroanalysis. Physicians often ask their patients to rate their pain on a scale of 1 to 10. The patient's response would be an example of this type of data. Another type of quantitative data are research numbers, such as the number of recent arrests involving domestic violence. Methods of quantitative analysis include participant observation, case studies, and ethnographies.

QUALITATIVE METHODS

Qualitative data may include interviews, pictures, photos, or any other type of information that comes to the researcher in a non-numerical form. These data tend to be used for microanalysis. A good example is content analysis, a type of research in which sociologists look for common words or themes in newspapers, books, or structured interviews. Methods of qualitative analysis include cross-sectional, comparative, and longitudinal studies, as well as surveys and experiments.

Triangulation

Think back to our discussion of overlapping theories. We learned that sociologists often frame their thinking by borrowing ideas from the three major paradigms. Similarly, sociologists sometimes use both qualitative and quantitative methods to collect data from different angles, providing a larger picture of an issue or event. **Triangulation** is the process of using multiple methods to study a phenomenon. For example, perhaps you want to study the influence of after-school recreation on high school students. First, you'd want to look at quantitative data such as the number of students who are and aren't involved in after-school activities. Then, you'd conduct a qualitative study that looks into what these students do during their free time and how the activity, or lack thereof, influences their education and grades. The idea is that if you can't gather the information you need from one type of data, the others will help fill in the gaps.

Social Policy and Statistics

SOCIAL POLICY

Social policies refer to deliberate attempts on the part of society to solve social problems. For example, unemployment insurance is a social policy designed to help people survive until they regain employment. In times of economic hardship, such policies keep many people from losing their homes.

CIVIC ENGAGEMENT

Students in my classes always seem to ask the same question, "What can we do?" Throughout this book, we'll address this issue in the Social Policy section of each chapter. One simple thing you can do to help research and understanding of your own country is to comply with the U.S. Census Bureau's population survey. The census is important because it tracks data about changes in communities, which aids social policy efforts. For example, a census might indicate that the number of senior citizens in a specific area has doubled since the last survey was conducted, or that the number of children under five years old has decreased dramatically. Planning committees use this information to allocate resources accordingly, such as building new retirement communities

in lieu of day care centers or elementary schools. It also makes sure that your community receives its equal share of government funding, and it determines your area's representation in Congress.

The Census Bureau has made major changes to the 2010 census survey to ensure accuracy of the population's socioeconomic status. As of 2010, every home will receive a short form to tally the number of residents; these ask only for very basic demographic information. But another affiliated poll—the American Community Survey—will capture detailed socioeconomic data every year, instead of every 10 years. A small sample of the population will receive this survey on a rotating basis. If the process works, no home will receive the survey more than once in five years. Similar to the Bureau's "long form," The American Community Survey is important because it aids government in determining which areas need resources for issues such as health care, education, transportation, and regional improvements. Why is the U.S. Census Bureau making this change? Cost savings are the main reason. Sampling a population is extremely expensive and difficult to do, but if the sample is taken accurately, the advantages are well worth the cost. One way you can aid public policy research is by filling out this survey when it arrives at your door.

STATISTICS

Social policies are often hotly debated. People on all sides seem to have statistics to back up their points of view. But are all statistics equal? Take a look at a few pointers below to help you determine the value of the statistics you read.

Five Pitfalls of Statistical Analysis

✓ **Be cautious of headlines.** Newspapers and newscasts will do anything they can to sell their story. Sometimes they present faulty information in their attempts to form concise reports. For example, "Eye Drops off Shelf," "Man Struck by Lightning Faces Battery Charge," and "Lack of Brains Hinders Research" are all examples of actual published headlines. These are comical, but you can imagine how you could be misinformed if you took headlines at face value without researching further.

Types of Field Reseach

Participant Observation: Research in which the sociologist poses as a citizen of the environment he or she is studying. In the mid-1900s, Canadian researcher Erving Goffman joined the staff of a mental hospital, posing as an assistant athletic director. By getting to know the patients in an uninhibited, natural environment, he was able to study them as they really were.

Case Studies: Research investigating a person or event in detail in order to study a complex issue through an individual case. In 2006, Stanford University conducted a study on Facebook CEO (and Harvard dropout) Mark Zuckerberg to investigate the growing influence of technology and social networking in today's society.

Ethnographies: Research aimed at a particular group of people. In his book Appalachian Valley, author George Hicks describes how he moved to the Appalachian Valley to study the culture of the local people. Over the years, Hicks learned—in his own words—"the hidden principles of another way of life."

Secondary Data Analysis: The process of using and analyzing data others have collected. The Internet contains many data sources for contemporary sociologists such as census data, crime statistics, and journal entries.

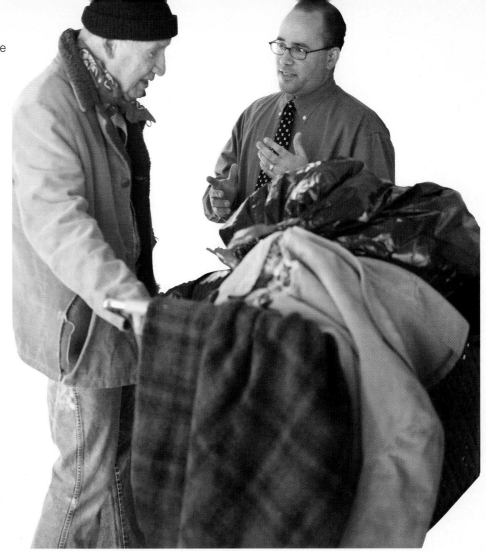

✓ **Double-check the definition of terms.** Be cautious of studies that include terms that may be interpreted in various ways. For example, two researchers may not identically define the term *biracial*. Barack Obama's mother was a white woman of English descent, and his father was a black man from Kenya—yet he is considered the first African American to be elected president. Of course, he embraces this label, but some might dispute its accuracy.

✓ **Investigate the source.** It's important to find out who has stake in the study you're researching. The agencies that fund projects are often affected by the outcomes. It's no surprise that the tobacco industry has funded and published multiple studies "disproving" the harmful effects of smoking.

✓ **Beware of selective causes.** Be sure that the results of the data are actually attributable to the outlined causes. Remember our discussion on independent and dependent variables; has the researcher taken into account all applicable explanations?

✓ **Watch out for hidden agendas.** Politicians and policymakers have timetables and goals. Be cautious of statistics and claims presented as facts—those people with an agenda may manipulate or adjust data to benefit themselves.[21]

∧
∧   **Sociologists can only collect so much data** through studies, surveys, and experiments.
∧   **Sometimes, the best way to understand society is to study it in action.**

From Classroom to Community │ Poverty

Aaron was a sophomore at King's College in New York City. He had worked hard in high school and received several scholarships that allowed him the chance at higher education. His family had lived in poverty as long as he could remember, and he often wondered why no one on the outside was doing anything to help them. The memories of his childhood were still very vivid in his mind, so it was no surprise that he chose the topic of poverty for his Social Problems final paper. When they met during office hours, his professor asked him exactly what he was planning to do in his assignment. Aaron replied, "Solve poverty. No one really cares about it, and obviously no one's doing anything about it."

The professor provided Aaron with a copy of *The End of Poverty*, by Jeffrey Sachs, and suggested that he start by researching individual people's opinions.

Over the course of a month, Aaron's project led him to investigate local attitudes toward the poor. To his surprise, he found that the majority of students surveyed shared similar views about the causes and nature of poverty, and had many of the same ideas about how to solve it. Claiming that "no one cares" is the same as declaring that "society is broken"—it doesn't tell the whole story. "Poverty,"

Aaron wrote in his paper, "is not an individually caused event, but a result of collective decisions made by many different independent actors. However, poverty does have many implications to the individuals trapped within. If society is serious about ending such social problems, it must first look into the issue of inequality." When handing back the papers, the professor remarked that he had the makings of a conflict theorist. Aaron simply replied, "Power to the people."

01

WHAT IS A SOCIAL PROBLEM?   4

any condition that affects the quality of life for an individual or society as a whole; social problems are defined by history, cultural values, cultural universals, and awareness

HOW DO SOCIOLOGISTS USE THEORETICAL PARADIGMS TO FRAME THEIR THINKING?   8

macro theories such as functionalism and conflict theory help sociologists understand how individuals affect society as a whole; symbolic interactionism—a micro paradigm—helps explain how events or circumstances affect how individuals interact with each other

WHAT IS THE ROLE OF RESEARCH AND SOCIAL POLICY IN UNDERSTANDING SOCIAL PROBLEMS?   12

sociologists develop solutions to social problems through specific research methods and organized steps; social policy functions when people become aware of problems and take the initiative to solve them

get the topic: WHAT IS A SOCIAL PROBLEM?

Theory

CONFLICT THEORY   8

- looks at how society's structures contribute to conflict, such as the "broken" economic system of the United States
- those in power use their dominance to benefit themselves and ignore the pain inflicted on others

FUNCTIONALISM   8

- the system evolves due to some need that must be met
- people create social structures to meet these needs and balance society; society isn't "broken"; we just need a "tune-up"

SYMBOLIC INTERACTIONISM   9

- asks "What does 'broken' mean?"; definitions vary for different socioeconomic groups
- acknowledges that social definitions are always in flux
- to define and/or deal with social problems requires that we first acknowledge their existence and, secondly, find new ways to view the situation so that they will be avoided in the future

Key Terms

social problem is an issue that negatively affects a person's state of being in a society.   *4*

sociology refers to a systematic and objective science that investigates human behavior in the social environment.   *4*

sociological imagination is the ability to look beyond the individual as the cause for success and failure and see how one's society influences the outcome.   *4*

macro is a large-scale point of view.   *4*

micro is a small-scale reference.   *4*

objective condition is any aspect of society that can be viewed without bias.   *5*

subjectivity refers to making judgments based on personal feelings and opinions rather than external facts.   *5*

values are a part of a society's nonmaterial culture that represent cultural standards by which we determine what is good, bad, right, or wrong.   *6*

cultural universal is any aspect of one's social life that is common to all societies.   *6*

awareness is the ability of a person or group to bring a problem into public recognition.   *7*

social movements are activities that support or protest social issues organized by non-governmental organizations.   *7*

campaigns are organized and ongoing efforts that make claims targeting a specific authority in the society.   *7*

repertoire is the second element of a social movement. *7*

WUNC refers to worthiness, unity, numbers, and commitments, which are the characteristics shown by members of a social movement. *7*

paradigms are theoretical frameworks through which scientists study the world. *8*

functionalism is a theoretical framework that defines society as a system of interrelated parts. *8*

conflict theory is a theoretical framework that views society as being in a constant struggle over scarce resources. *8*

symbolic interactionism is a theoretical framework that focuses on how individual interactions between people influence their behavior and how these interactions can impact society. *9*

gender-inequality theories focus on sexist patterns that limit women's opportunities for work, education, and other social needs. *10*

theories of gender oppression refer to a situation in which men purposefully maintain control over women through discrimination and the use of power, leading to oppression. *10*

structural oppression theories refer to the fact that women's oppression is rooted in capitalism; patriarchies keep women on the margins of the social world. *10*

research methods are scientific procedures that sociologists use to conduct research and develop knowledge about a particular topic. *12*

objectivity refers to the ability to conduct research without allowing personal biases or prejudices to influence them. *12*

independent variables are variables that are deliberately manipulated to test the response in an experiment. *13*

dependent variables are the responses to the manipulated variable. *13*

control variables are variables that are kept constant to accurately test the impact of an independent variable. *14*

causal relationships are relationships in which a condition or variable leads to a certain consequence. *14*

causation is the relationship between cause and effect. *14*

correlation is an indication that one factor *might* be the cause for another factor. *14*

positive correlation involves two variables moving in a parallel. *14*

negative correlation occurs when the variables move in opposite directions. *15*

spurious correlation occurs when two variables appear to be related, but actually have separate causes. *15*

ethics refers to a system of values or principles that guide one's behavior. *15*

quantitative data refer to data based on numbers and used for macroanalysis. *15*

qualitative data refer to information that may include words, pictures, photos, or any other type of information that comes to the researcher in a non-numerical form. *15*

triangulation is the process of using multiple approaches to study a phenomenon. *15*

social policies refer to deliberate attempts on the part of society to solve social problems. *16*

Sample Test Questions

These multiple-choice questions are similar to those found in the test bank that accompanies this textbook.

1. Which of the following is an example of an objective condition?
   a. Poverty affects education.
   b. Society is broken in Britain.
   c. The unemployment rate is higher than it was two years ago.
   d. Society is responsible for displaced workers and the homeless.

2. Geoff was an employee of the Chrysler Corporation for 40 years. Last June he was laid off, causing his family to lose their home. Geoff is upset, but he understands that Chrysler's bankruptcy will ultimately lead to a stronger overall economy. Geoff is approaching his crisis through
   a. subjectivity.
   b. functionalism.
   c. a sociological imagination.
   d. a conflict theorist point of view.

3. A negative correlation exists when
   a. variables increase or decrease together.
   b. a variable is not able to be measured.
   c. two variables move in the opposite direction.
   d. one factor directly causes a negative effect.

4. Which of the following is *not* an example of conflict theory?
   a. the powerful exploiting the common citizen
   b. homelessness as a sign of inequality in a society
   c. the upper class controlling a community's wealth
   d. society thinking of the homeless as bums because the upper class has labeled them as such

5. A symbolic interactionist might try to discern the expected and unexpected consequences of an event.
   a. true
   b. false

ESSAY

1. Do you agree or disagree with David Cameron's assessment that society is broken? On what factors do you base your opinion?
2. What are the most pressing social problems in your community? What action is your community taking to solve these issues?
3. Suppose that you wanted to study the causes of the recent housing collapse. What research methods would you use and why?
4. Howard Becker believes that the labels assigned to a person often lead to self-fulfilling prophecies. What labels do you believe society has placed on you? Have you taken on these identities?
5. Considering what you now know of the three major paradigms—functionalism, conflict theory, and symbolic interactionism—which do you use most often to view the world around you? Why?

WHERE TO START YOUR RESEARCH PAPER

For a wide range of information on labor economics and statistics, go to http://www.bls.gov/

For a guide to sociological Internet sources, check out http://www.socioweb.com/

To read an in-depth sociology dictionary, go to http://www.webref.org/sociology/sociology.htm

To review an abbreviated version of the American Sociological Association (ASA) style guide, go to http://www.asanet.org/

For U.S. Census facts and information, go to http://www.census.gov

To learn more about social policy, see http://www.un.org/esa/socdev/

ANSWERS: 1. c; **2.** b; **3.** c; **4.** d; **5.** b

Remember to check www.thethinkspot.com **for additional information, downloadable flashcards, and other helpful resources.**

INEQUALITY: POVERTY AND WEALTH

WHAT IS INEQUALITY, AND HOW DOES IT
AFFECT PEOPLE?
HOW DO SOCIOLOGISTS VIEW
INEQUALITY?
WHAT SOCIAL POLICIES ADDRESS
ECONOMIC INEQUALITY?

It's another

Saturday morning in Pennsylvania, and Rick and Sheyda Belli dream of getting rich quick. Like many families suffering in this soft economy, the Bellis spend money on lottery games.

"I look at it as a shot, a chance, a ray of hope," said Sheyda Belli, 38. "People say you're wasting your money, could put it in a savings account, but, you know, somebody wins every day."

Every Saturday morning, they head off looking for that pot of lottery gold, driving past the doughnut shop they used to visit.

"That was about $40 a week. Just trying to cut back everywhere that we can really, but still not giving up playing my lottery," Sheyda said, laughing.

The drive to the Beaver Valley Mall is a family ritual in which their kids, 2-year-old Cheyenne, 4-year-old Alexander, and 6-year-old Amber, ride the tiny train for $2 a ticket.

With what's left in Rick's wallet, mom and dad head for the kiosk that peddles powerful fantasies: the chance at $640,000 in the Cash 5 jackpot and the $52 million Powerball prize.

Sheyda plays both games and also buys a scratch-off ticket, for total winnings of $24. The scratch-off cards provide the satisfaction of an instant answer, but nothing else.

The odds against those winning big-money games are astronomical. Cash 5 players have a one in 962,958 chance of winning the top prize, and the Powerball odds are even worse (one out of more than 146 million) . . .

. . . Yale psychologist Emily Haisley said one study suggested that buying a lotto ticket counteracts any negative feelings that come from feeling poor or financially behind.

"The purchase of the lottery ticket can temporarily take them away from that negative feeling and let them have the hope of winning big," she said.

The Bellis spend up to $100 a week on the lottery, amounting to about $5,200 a year. It's a lot of money considering that Rick recently lost his job, cutting the family's annual income by nearly half to $67,000.

But on the very day that Rick, 39, got "downsized," he said he stopped on the way home and bought a lottery ticket.

"And it worked!" Rick said. "I bought a $10 lottery ticket and won $100." . . .

. . . Every weekend, the family gathers together to watch the results. One weekend in late October the Cash 5 game was not a complete loss.

"I think I got my money back, if not some more," Sheyda said.

Much later that night, the Powerball drawing offered one last glimmer of possibility. But in the end, they weren't winners.

"We'll just need better luck next time," Sheyda said. "Oh well."

It was another disappointment, but for the Bellis hope springs eternal.

"Sometimes that's all you have when everything else has fallen down around you. When you're down, the only way to go is up. So, hopefully, that will be us," Sheyda explained.

In the Belli household, hard times are simply no match for sweet dreams.[1]

CHAPTER 02

---More than 30 states have lotteries. Lotto slogans scream from billboards around the country: "Let Yourself Play!"

The lottery, in effect, becomes a voluntary tax often used to support essential state functions such as education. However, lotteries do not necessarily result in increased funds for those projects.[2] Although some states earmark lottery revenues directly for programs like education, others send the money to a general fund for the legislature to use as it sees fit.[3]

Who plays state lotteries? Regular gamblers account for the majority of players. Men are more likely to play than women are, with adults between the ages of 25 and 65 years falling within the most-likely-to-play age category. A higher level of education also appears to affect how likely someone is to play the lottery.[4] As a person becomes more educated, he or she is less likely to play.

How much do people spend on lotto tickets? The average lottery expense is about the same for households earning between $10,000 and $60,000 per year. Households with income levels higher than $60,000, however, have lower levels of play.[5]

In particular, in light of the current downturn in the U.S. economy, should the government be coaxing people to gamble away their money? Is a tax on the desperate really an effective way to fund government services? Or are there other means of financing essential social programs that would create less of a burden on the poor and the working class?

As we take a look at the issues of income inequality in the United States, some fundamental questions will arise. How much inequality is there? Are we all living in a "land of opportunity?" What can we do, if anything, to ensure that everyone has the same chance?

get the topic: WHAT IS INEQUALITY, AND HOW DOES IT AFFECT PEOPLE?

SOCIAL STRATIFICATION is the ranking of people and the rewards they receive based on objective criteria, often including wealth, power, and/or prestige.

INCOME is the money received for work or through investments.

WEALTH is all of an individual's material possessions, including income.

MEDIAN is the midpoint of a group of numbers ranked from lowest to highest.

Defining Economic Inequality

SOCIAL STRATIFICATION

Human beings have a tendency to categorize or rank things. Whether it's the "Top Ten" songs for a given week or the "Five Best Cities" in which to raise your kids, people enjoy the distinction of knowing that the city, song, or book that they have chosen is well ranked by their peers. Sociologists apply the same process to people and use **social stratification** to rank individuals based on objective criteria, often wealth, power, and/or prestige. Social stratification naturally creates inequality, as some people are "haves" and some are "have-nots." This inequality causes many social conflicts, which lead to greater social problems.

Each society has its own way to rank, or stratify, the population, but the level of stratification can vary greatly.[6] In certain societies, political power may be used to separate people. For example, in Cuba, members of the Communist party often have preferential housing and access to better schools, while people with different political affiliations often live in poverty.[7] Wealth and income are other means by which societies stratify people into social classes; generally in the United States, the wealthier you are, the more important others consider you. Other societies use birth status and family origins as a way to divide people. In these societies, privileged positions may be available only to families regarded as "nobility." For example, if you're a member of the Dubai royal family, you're probably living well. That is, you have excellent health care, the trendiest cars, the finest wardrobe, and the choicest foods, among other things.

In the United States, people are often divided by their access to wealth, income, or both. **Income** refers to the money received for work or through investments. It may be the paycheck you receive every month or the dividends you receive from the stock market. **Wealth**, on the other hand, refers to all of your material possessions including income. You could probably raise a considerable sum that would be more than your monthly paychecks if you were to take everything you owned—your car, your electronics, your clothes—and place these items on eBay to sell at a fair market value. Let's look further at the distribution of wealth and income in the United States.

INCOME DISTRIBUTION

As you've probably noticed, the U.S. workplace is home to a wide range of salaries. Many families today have experienced a painful transformation in their economic situations. After an unexpected layoff, a middle-class family may go from owning a large and comfortable home in suburbia to renting a one-bedroom apartment in the bad part of town. Income earners in the United States can range from struggling workers making minimum wage to high-powered executives with six- or seven-figure salaries.

The figure to the right provides a visual representation of incomes in the United States. It divides the entire income of the country into five groups, each with the same number of households in it. The poorest three-fifths of working people in the United States are the most likely to play the state lottery. Yet, this group (which includes about 60 percent of Americans), receives less than 27 percent of the nation's income. Meanwhile, the wealthiest fifth of the population receive nearly 50 percent of the money.[8] If the country's income was divided equally, each group would receive 20 percent, but as you can see, this is not the case. If this figure represented a pie from your favorite bakery, which slice would you want?

Although the percentages are telling, it might be easier to understand the disparities between these groups if you were presented with the real dollar amounts. Looking at the figure above, what salary level would put someone in the bottom 20 percent of income earners? The poorest fifth of the population earns less than $20,300 each year.[9] This means that one in every five households in the United States earns less than this amount. On the other end of the spectrum, if your household income exceeds $100,000, then your family is among the top fifth of income earners in the country.[10] The difference between income levels grows even larger when it comes to the top 5 percent of the population (not included in the figure), who earn over $177,000 a year.[11]

Another important measurement is the income median. Remember, the **median** of a distribution is the midpoint of all

Share of Total U.S. Income

Lowest fifth
3.4%
($0+)

Highest fifth
49.7%
($100,000+)

Second fifth
8.7%
($20,300+)

Middle fifth
14.8%
($39,100+)

Fourth fifth
23.4%
($62,000+)

Sources: Data from Carmen DeNavas-Walt, Bernadette D. Proctor, and Jessica C. Smith, U.S. Census Bureau, Current Population Reports, P60-235, Income, Poverty, and Health Insurance Coverage in the United States: 2007, U.S. Government Printing Office, Washington, DC, 2008; U.S. Census Bureau, Current Population Survey, Annual Social and Economic Supplement, Table HINC-05: Percent Distribution of Households, by Selected Characteristics Within Income Quintile and Top 5 Percent in 2007.

the numbers ranked from lowest to highest. In 2007, the median income of all households in the United States was $50,233.[12] In other words, half of American households earned less than that amount.

In the United States, income inequality has increased over time. The chart at the bottom of the page provides income data across 55 years. As you review the chart, you'll notice that the poorest fifth of the population is actually earning less of the total U.S. income each year. At their peak in 1975, this group earned 5.6 percent of the nation's income, but their share of the "pie" has declined steadily ever since. Meanwhile, the wealthiest fifth of the population has been increasing its share of total U.S. income since 1975.[13]

Is the income gap widening between the wealthy and the poor? The numbers show that it is. Over time, the top fifth of the population has been earning an increasing share of the total U.S. income.[14] The graph on page 24 shows income change over the last 30 years. During this period, the pretax incomes for the bottom 90 percent of Americans actually dropped 0.1 percent.[15] At the same time, incomes grew for those people in the top 10 percent of the population. To put it another way, people in the top 5- to 10-percent

Income Change Over Time

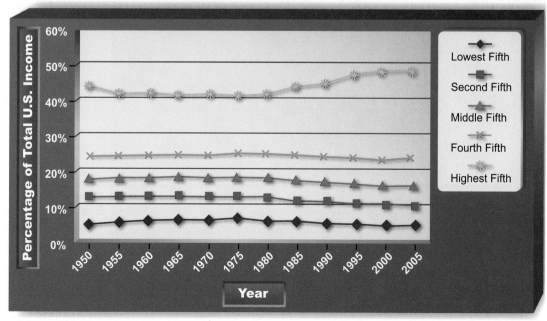

Source: DeNavas-Walt, 2006, U.S. Census Bureau

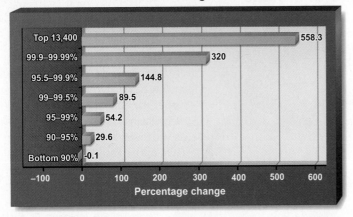

U.S. Income Change 1970–2000

Group	Percentage change
Top 13,400	558.3
99.9–99.99%	320
95.5–99.9%	144.8
99–99.5%	89.5
95–99%	54.2
90–95%	29.6
Bottom 90%	-0.1

Source: Data from David Cay Johnson, *Perfectly Legal: The Covert Campaign to Rig Our Tax System to Benefit the Super Rich and Cheat Everybody Else* (New York: Penguin Group Inc., 2003).

income group saw their pay increase almost 30 percent.[16] Those households in the top 95–99% of incomes saw an even greater increase of just over 54 percent.[17] The top 13,400 households in the country experienced the biggest gain. Over 30 years, this group's income increased over 558 percent.[18] That means that if a person had a household income of $5 million in 1970, then his or her income would have increased to $27.9 million by 2000!

During the 2008 presidential election, Democratic candidate Barack Obama and Republican candidate John McCain often debated the role of government in dealing with income inequality. Both agreed that wealthy people needed to pay a higher percentage of their income in taxes, but they did not agree as to what that percentage should be. One thing is certain however: if the government is going to fund itself, the money has to be generated from somewhere.

The famous sociologist Max Weber suggests that when we stratify people in society, we should do so based on their wealth, power, and prestige. In other words, your rank in society won't change a great deal just because your income rises or falls temporarily. Lasting rank in society is determined by accumulated wealth and property, level of prestige, and amount of power to do what one wants.[19]

WEALTH

Wealth includes income and assets. It can consist of stocks, bonds, real estate, cash, and a host of other items. As you review the pie chart on page 25, you might at first believe that it represents a relatively equal distribution. However, taking a closer look, you'll see that each piece does not represent the same number of people. Astonishingly, the top 1 percent of wealth holders in the United States has more total wealth than the entire bottom 90 percent of the population.[20]

To better illustrate this point, here's an example that I've often used in class. Let's say I have 100 students, and start out with 100 Tootsie Rolls. I give 34 pieces of candy to one person and 37 pieces to the next 9 people (averaging about 4 pieces per person). To the remaining 90 people, I give 29 pieces to divide, meaning that each person gets one-third of a piece of candy. The disparity is much easier to see when viewed this way. At the end of the demonstration, one student is left with a majority of the wealth (in this case, 34 Tootsie Rolls), whereas 90 percent of the students are left with one-third of a Tootsie Roll each.

POWER

Income and wealth often bring with them power or access to power. Power is discussed in a variety of ways. First, we can address it as a coercive element in society that manipulates people to do things that they might not otherwise do. According to this line of thinking, **power** is the ability to get people to do what you want without having to make them do so. Sometimes, however, others may not do what you want unless you coerce them. When a professor makes a course so difficult that the only way a student can receive a passing grade is to help her with her research, she is using coercion. On the other hand, **force** is a type of power that occurs when you make someone do something against his or her will. Dictators often use force or the threat of force to make people follow orders.

Persuasive power means that you use direct or indirect methods to get what you want. It is much easier to get people to follow along if they believe it is in their best interests. Oprah Winfrey is considered to be one of the most powerful women in the media today because of her ability to persuade her audience. Books selected for her Book Club often skyrocket to *The New York Times*' best sellers list.

It is very difficult to convince someone that his or her long-standing ideas about an issue are not necessarily true. For example, most of my students

∧
∧ For the majority of Americans, **owning their own car**
∧ **and home is a big step toward the achievement of the**
American dream.

Percentage Total Wealth, 2004

Bottom 90% of Wealth holders 28.7%

Top 1% of Wealth holders 34.3%

Next 9% of Wealth holders (91–98%) 36.9%

Source: Data from Lawrence Mishel, Jared Bernstein, and Sylvia Allegretto, *State of working America 2006/2007* (Ithaca, New York: Cornell University Press, 2006).

believe that the social class structure in the United States is entirely fair, making chapters such as this one difficult to swallow. That's because if you believe that everyone has an equal chance to succeed, then you are persuaded to keep the system unchanged.[21]

PRESTIGE

Prestige refers to the level of esteem associated with our status and social standing. As I'm sure you've noticed, different jobs have different levels of prestige. Occupations are generally ranked on a scale from 0 to 100, with

POWER is the ability to carry out your will and impose it on others.

FORCE is a type of power that occurs when you make someone do something against his or her will.

PERSUASIVE POWER refers to using direct or indirect methods to get what you want.

PRESTIGE is the level of esteem associated with one's status and social standing.

0 as the lowest. Doctors and lawyers, as you might suspect, are on the high end of the scale with ratings of 86 and 75, whereas janitors rank a 22. Generally speaking, the less a job pays, the less prestige it carries. Not only do low-wage workers have to struggle financially, they must struggle to earn respect in society as well.

A prestigious job has benefits other than the obvious monetary ones. For example, you might be inclined to take career advice from a successful airline pilot, but it's doubtful that the advice of a minimum-wage service station attendant would merit your respect. Naturally, you don't expect someone who pumps gas for a living to be able to give you great advice on how to build a successful career. Occupational prestige varies according to the job and reflects which work a society respects the most.

Few parents look at their children and dream of them becoming burger flippers rather than engineers, because an engineer attains more occupational prestige in our society. A combination of wealth, power, and prestige form the stratification and class systems used to characterize the population of the United States.

Occupational Prestige Rankings

Occupation	Prestige Rating	Occupation	Prestige Rating
Physician	86	Housewife	51
Lawyer	75	Manager of a supermarket	48
College professor	74	Secretary	46
Airline pilot	73	Insurance agent	46
Engineer	71	Bank teller	43
Medical technician	68	Househusband	36
Clergy	67	Assembly line worker	35
Registered nurse	66	Housekeeper	34
Accountant	65	Cook in a restaurant	34
Elementary school teacher	64	Sales person in a store	31
Police	61	Garbage collector	28
Journalist	60	Bartender	25
Farm owner	53	Janitor	22
Firefighter	53	Service station attendant	21
Social worker	52	Grocery bagger	18
Electrician	51	Street-corner drug dealer	13

Source: Data from Keiko Nakao and Judith Treas, "Updating Occupational Prestige and Socioeconomic Scales: How the New Measures Measure Up." *Sociological Methodology*, 1994. 24: 1–72.

How Does Inequality Affect the Lives of People?

CLASS IN AMERICA

Ask yourself this: When it comes to social class, where do you stand? When asked to identify themselves in the social class scheme, most people claim to be part of the middle class.[22] But are these claims accurate?

Sociologists have varying opinions on how many classes exist and what the distinctions between each class are. For example, Karl Marx suggested that there are two: the proletariat and the bourgeois. Others, like Max Weber, suggest that there are more. But regardless of how many classes one believes there to be, the lower you are on the social class ladder, the more social problems you're likely to experience. For the purposes of this chapter, we'll take a look at five different social classes that exist in the United States: upper class, upper middle class, middle class, working class, and lower class.

Upper or Elite Class

The **upper** or **elite class** is very small in number and holds significant wealth. Approximately 3 million of the 300 million people in the country are considered upper class. Who are these people? Many are considered "old money"; their class standing comes from wealth, power, and prestige.[23] Others are entertainers or professional athletes who have generally earned, not inherited, their wealth. In his studies on the upper class, sociologist G. William Domhoff found that prerequisites for membership in this class may include attendance at an exclusive prep school, belonging to exclusive social clubs, and being born into a wealthy or powerful family.[24]

Upper Middle Class

The **upper middle class** consists of high-income members of society who are well educated but do not belong to the elite membership of the super wealthy. They tend to occupy professional positions with high prestige and hold places of authority in the workplace.[25] Their income usually exceeds $100,000 a year—enough for them to live comfortably—and they own property or other outside investments. Owning a small business, having a professional career, or holding a high-status job often guides a person into the upper middle class.[26] This group makes up about 15 percent of the U.S. population.

Social Class in the United States

Upper/Elite Class

Middle Class

Working Class

Urban Underclass

Middle Class

As mentioned above, most Americans claim to belong to the middle class. If you're not rich and you're not poor, you should fall somewhere in the middle, right? Sociologists, however, have a more complex definition.

In general, **middle-class** people have moderate incomes. They vary from low-paid white-collar workers (e.g., teachers, policemen) to well-paid blue-collar workers (e.g., restaurant managers, factory foremen). Middle-class workers may be skilled laborers (e.g., plumbers), but they are generally not manual laborers. Members of the middle class have at least a high school diploma, and many have trade school or college experience. The middle class makes up approximately 34 percent of the U.S. population, and incomes of members in this group range from $40,000 to $80,000 per year.[27] The Bellis, as mentioned in the news article at the beginning of this chapter, transitioned from the upper middle class to the middle class because of Rick's layoff. However, they're still seeking that elusive lucky lotto ticket that could propel them, at least monetarily, into the upper class.

Working Class

The **working class** makes up about 30 percent of the population and comprises people who have completed high school and lower levels of education[28]. Most of its members hold jobs that require manual labor or clerical skills such as construction workers and bank tellers. Unlike those in higher classes, working-class citizens earn an hourly wage instead of a salary. Unfortunately, there are very limited opportunities for job improvement because they work by the hour and lack a formal education.

Lower Class

Those in the **lower class** are the ones who truly feel the effects of poverty. In the United States, close to 37 million people are in this category.[29] Members often live paycheck to paycheck, if they are employed at all. More than two-thirds of African Americans and 60 percent of Hispanics in the nation live near or below the poverty line.[30] Almost half of the children in the United States live in or near poverty, along with 10 percent of senior citizens.[31]

The Urban Underclass

The homeless and the chronically unemployed are classified as the **urban underclass**. Truly impoverished, they often live in substandard housing in neighborhoods with poor schools, high crime, and heavy drug use.[32] Some are lucky enough to receive financial assistance from the government. Members of this class rarely have health care coverage and often lack a high school education. The jobs they find are usually minimum-wage positions that propel them no higher than the low end of the working class. Despite all these disadvantages, sociologist William J. Wilson notes that both their lack of vision and lack of role models are what make it difficult for many to imagine any other way of life.[33] Yes, they are disadvantaged, experiencing broken homes, poor schools, and substandard housing, but what makes them truly disadvantaged is that they know of almost nothing else. This perpetuates the situation, as the young have very few positive role models that can show them how to escape poverty. This leads them to live their entire lives mired in many social problems without viable solutions.

THE EFFECTS OF SOCIAL CLASS

Neighborhoods

In recent studies, sociologists have observed how people's behavior is influenced by the quality of the neighborhoods they live in. Results show that over time, poor people tend to settle in areas already populated by their own class. The same can be said of the affluent. Think of the Main Line in Philadelphia or Manhattan's Upper East Side.[34] Interestingly enough, people who change classes (e.g., if the Bellis really did strike it rich in the lottery) tend to move into areas where people of their new class can be found.[35]

So, how does growing up in a wealthy neighborhood affect a child? Studies have shown that children from these areas do better in school, have a lower risk of teen pregnancies, and have higher standardized test scores. In contrast, children who grow up in disadvantaged communities have lower birth weights, poorer health, and lower levels of education.[36]

Health

When you're sick, do you go to the doctor? Studies find that poor women with children, who frequently have insufficient diets, suffer from higher rates of mental depression and worse physical health than their wealthier counterparts.[37] Poverty influences access to food, and food influences both physical and mental health. A great body of research supports the notion that poor people generally have poor health.[38] This may be associated with a lack of medical care as well as other environmental factors. A poor child living in a home with broken windows may suffer from more colds than a child living in a middle-class neighborhood, for example.

UPPER or **ELITE CLASS** is a social class that is very small in number and holds significant wealth.

UPPER MIDDLE CLASS is a social class that consists of high-income members of society who are well educated but do not belong to the elite membership of the super wealthy.

MIDDLE CLASS is a social class that consists of those who have moderate incomes.

WORKING CLASS is a social class generally made up of people with a high school diploma and a lower level of education.

LOWER CLASS is a social class living in poverty.

URBAN UNDERCLASS is a social class living in disadvantaged neighborhoods that are characterized by four components: poverty, family disruption, male unemployment, and lack of individuals in high-status occupations.

Health and socioeconomic status (SES) have been found to be linked; those with a greater SES tend to enjoy better health, whereas those with a lower SES tend to have poorer health. Furthermore, poor health has been shown to have direct and significant effects on other issues as well. The outlook for educational attainment of sick children is not as promising as for healthy ones. Sick children grow into adults who have less education and earn less than their healthy counterparts. An individual's health influences his social stratification across a lifetime.[39]

Family

There are a variety of factors that differentiate families, but a particularly important one is social class. Are there predictable patterns of income directly related to the composition of families?

The U.S. Census Bureau has found correlations between family form and poverty rates. For example, female-headed households have poverty rates that are nearly three times higher than the national rate for all families.[40] Female poverty rates are also higher than the rates for households headed by single men.[41] Thus, family composition appears to be a main factor that affects whether or not children live in poverty. Since the 1970s, the poverty rate for children under 18 years old has been higher than the poverty rate for any other age bracket.[42] In fact, in 2007, children represented almost 36 percent of all the people in

Poverty Rates by Age in 2007

Source: Data from Carmen DeNavas-Walt, Bernadette D. Proctor, and Jessica C. Smith, U.S. Census Bureau, Current Population Reports, P60-235, Income, Poverty, and Health Insurance Coverage in the United States: 2007, U.S. Government Printing Office, Washington, DC, 2008.

poverty, even though only 25 percent of the total population were children.[43] In recent years, the federal government has attempted to aggressively address this issue by attempting to curb non-marital pregnancy rates and stressing the importance of children's growing up in two-parent households.[44] However, is the difference in family composition appropriately linked to an increase in the rates of women giving birth outside of marriage?

In a 2006 article, Molly A. Martin discusses the history of family structure and its impact on social inequality.[45] She finds that two-parent households have the highest income levels, and female-headed households have the lowest. But, she asks, what are the reasons for female-headed households and how are these households perceived? Three possible reasons a woman might be raising children without a husband are divorce, death of spouse, or a conscious decision not to marry. The most common reason that children live in single-parent households is divorce. Children raised in homes in which their mother and father never married suffer not only from higher rates of poverty, but they also experience greater levels of social stigmatization. Families headed by widows have the highest social standing among mother-only families, whereas those headed by divorced women are somewhere in the middle. Martin notes that non-marital fertility is on the rise in the United States and remains an important contributing factor to the likelihood of children growing up poor.[46]

Education

It's true that, in the United States, a free 12-year education is available to every child regardless of family or class. However, not all educational opportunities are the same. In a two-year study of public schools, Jonathan Kozol found that the schools he visited in urban communities frequently lacked basic educational supplies. In some cases, chemistry labs didn't have beakers or test tubes and students were forced to share textbooks.[47] Meanwhile, suburban schools often had a surplus of supplies and staff.

What accounts for such dramatic differences? Kozol found that the answer lay in the very structure of the system. Because local taxes fund schools, places with higher property taxes receive more educational funding. Children living in poor urban areas need more help but actually get less. Therefore, he concluded that educational equality does not exist in United States.[48] Because poor neighborhoods lack access to high-quality education, most residents are denied opportunities to overcome poverty.

Social Mobility

Those of us who are lucky enough to win big at Mega Millions or invest in the right stock at the right time might soar quickly to upper-class standing. In a poor economy, however, we might as easily be laid off

V Is life just a game of Chutes and Ladders? **As long as social mobility is possible, our lives**
V
V **can always take a turn for the better—or for the worse.**

What Is Social Mobility?

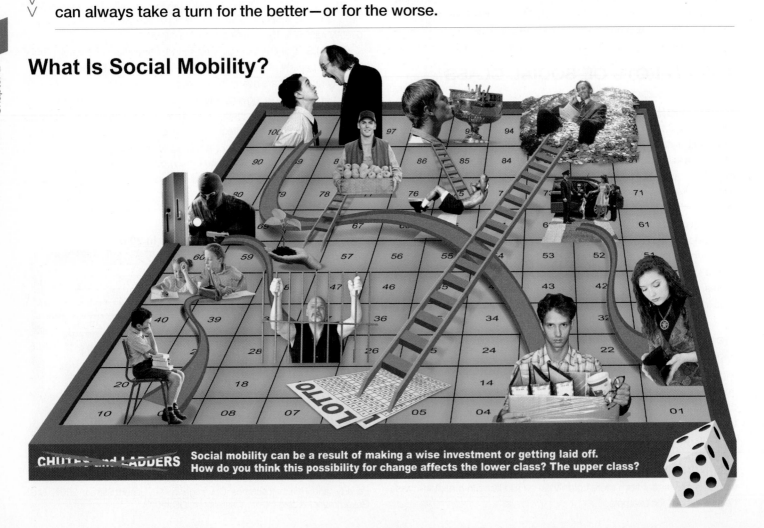

CHUTES and LADDERS Social mobility can be a result of making a wise investment or getting laid off. How do you think this possibility for change affects the lower class? The upper class?

and subsequently plunge into poverty. These are examples of **social mobility**, a term that describes the ability to change social classes. If you've ever played the board game *Chutes and Ladders*, you know that players can climb ladders to the top or slide down chutes to the bottom, depending on the number they roll. Social mobility works in much the same way. According to sociologists, different patterns of social mobility occur.

Horizontal mobility refers to moving within the same status category. For example, a paralegal who leaves one law firm for a position at another law firm across town experiences horizontal mobility. In this example, the paralegal is earning the same amount of money and performing the same tasks, she is simply employed at a different firm in a different location. **Vertical mobility** involves moving from one social status to another. For example, if the same paralegal completed law school and passed the bar exam to become a lawyer, this exemplifies vertical mobility because, with her passing the bar exam, she has entered a higher social status.

Intragenerational mobility occurs when an individual changes social standing, especially in the workforce. An employee who works his way up from the mail room to senior executive is experiencing intragenerational mobility.

Intergenerational mobility refers to the change that family members make from one social class to the next through generations. Many of your relatives probably immigrated to the United States as members of the lower class and never dreamed of ever being able to achieve the level of education that you have achieved. If you hope to some day live a better life than your parents did, you too are hoping for upward intergenerational mobility.

Structural mobility occurs when social changes cause many people to change social status simultaneously. Whether you're a member of the upper or lower class, there's always a chance that something could happen that would drastically change your status. Think of the recent economic slump. Large numbers of workers have been laid off, and the job market is more competitive than in previous years, causing large groups to shift in social class. Both long-time employees and entry-level students are finding it hard to make enough money, and those with families find that the change affects the entire household as well.

The concept of **exchange mobility** suggests that within the United States, each social class contains a relatively fixed number of people. As some families move into a higher class, others must move down. The data we saw earlier on the changes in income over time support the idea that social stratification levels change very little. However, they don't tell us whether the people who make up each layer have stayed there or exchanged places in the meantime.

What Do Societies Do About This?
HISTORY OF POVERTY

Throughout human history, there have always been people who are poor. The roots of the popular U.S. viewpoint of poverty have their origins in European, particularly British, ideals. The system of welfare and care for the needy arose from the religious concepts of charity and compassion for the less fortunate.

The Elizabethan "Poor Law" of 1601 was the first real law dealing with "welfare and poverty" in Britain.[49] What was the reason behind this? It was simply that churches could no longer adequately handle the job. The Elizabethan Poor Law attempted to accomplish four

SOCIAL MOBILITY is the ability to change social classes.

HORIZONTAL MOBILITY refers to moving within the same status category.

VERTICAL MOBILITY refers to moving from one social status to another.

INTRAGENERATIONAL MOBILITY occurs when an individual changes social standing, especially in the workforce.

INTERGENERATIONAL MOBILITY is the change that family members make from one social class to the next through generations.

STRUCTURAL MOBILITY is when social changes affect large numbers of people.

EXCHANGE MOBILITY is a concept suggesting that, within the United States, each social class contains a relatively fixed number of people.

things: separate the church from the delivery of social services, eliminate begging and crime in the streets, bring social assistance under government control, and set standards to determine those eligible to receive help and the amount of help they should receive.[50] Since that time, a great many changes in policies toward the poor have occurred both in Britain and the United States. However, both countries share an ideology for welfare and a "Protestant work ethic" of hard work, thrift, and individualism.[51]

From the time of the colonies through the Civil War, welfare in the United States was largely left up to the local areas. However, because of large numbers of injured soldiers and increases in immigration, the need to help the poor became greater than many localities could handle. Two welfare ideas arose. The first was the settlement house movement. Neighborhood centers already provided educational, social, and cultural activities, but the settlement houses provided social services and financial assistance. Settlement houses were based on three key concepts: Social change could occur, social class distinctions could be narrowed through information and education, and change could only come when social workers immersed themselves in the neighborhoods they served.[52]

The second movement was the Charity Organization Society. They held that a foundation of "moral beliefs" was essential to combat poverty and that individuals were personally responsible for their plight and could overcome it.[53]

Perhaps the key historical event in the United States in a discussion of poverty is the Great Depression of 1929. The country experienced massive unemployment, with millions seeking assistance from volunteer organizations and completely overwhelming the system. President Franklin D. Roosevelt's New Deal was the answer to the devastated United States. This was a revolutionary, wide-reaching plan to save the economy. The main focus was on aiding struggling farmers, reforming questionable financial and business practices, and promoting the recovery of the economy. Later, the Social Security Act of 1935 further alleviated poverty in the ranks of the elderly, widowed, unemployed, and disabled.[54]

The Great Society and War on Poverty of the 1960s and 1970s attempted to address poverty with the formation of new social programs, which included the Peace Corps, Job Corps, Head Start, and Volunteers in Service to America (VISTA). Additional enhanced and expanded programs included Medicare, Medicaid, the Older Americans Act, and the Food Stamp Act.[55]

TRANSITIONAL POVERTY refers to a temporary state of poverty that occurs when someone goes without a job for a short period of time.

MARGINAL POVERTY refers to a state of poverty that occurs when a person lacks stable employment.

RESIDUAL POVERTY refers to chronic and multigenerational poverty.

ABSOLUTE POVERTY refers to poverty so severe that one lacks resources to survive.

RELATIVE POVERTY is a state of poverty that occurs when we compare ourselves to those around us.

HOW DOES THE UNITED STATES DEFINE POVERTY?

"Are you poor?" I often ask my students. Most immediately say yes, and then they pull out their iPhones to text their friends during class. But what does it mean to be poor? Sociologists often divide poverty into five separate categories. **Transitional poverty** is a temporary state that occurs when someone goes without a job for a short period of time. **Marginal poverty** occurs when a person lacks stable employment. A handyman bouncing between jobs is experiencing marginal poverty. The next, more serious level, is **residual poverty**. This type is chronic and multigenerational. A family living in residual poverty will pass the poverty on to their children, who will pass it to their children, and on and on down the line. People who experience **absolute poverty** are so poor that they don't have the resources necessary to survive. Farmers starving to death in the Orissa region of India are living in absolute poverty. **Relative poverty** is a state that occurs when we compare our financial standing and material possessions to those around us. You might experience relative poverty if your friend pulls out the latest smartphone, and you're still using a flip phone. You feel poor because you're comparing yourself to others who have more than you, when, in fact, neither of you is really poor. On the flip side, if you live in a poor neighborhood but drive a fancy car, your neighbors are experiencing relative poverty.

The U.S. government has different standards for defining poverty. Using a benchmark known as the poverty line, the government can determine what services are needed by whom. If you fall below the poverty line, you're eligible to receive health care, food, and career aid from the government. If your income is above the poverty line, however, you receive little or no government assistance.[56]

U.S. Department of Health and Human Services Poverty Guidelines, 2009

Number of Persons in Family	Poverty Guideline
1	$10,830
2	14,570
3	18,310
4	22,050
5	25,790
6	29,530
7	33,270
8	37,010
For each additional person, add	3,740

Source: *Federal Register*, Vol. 74, No. 14, January 23, 2009, pp. 4199–4201, http://aspe.hhs.gov/poverty/09fedreg.shtml

The poverty line dates from 1963–1964, when Mollie Orshansky, an analyst at the Social Security Administration, developed the official U.S. poverty thresholds. The thresholds, now updated for inflation, were originally calculated by multiplying three times the cost of an economy food plan. These calculations were made based on the assumption that people spend about one-third of their income on food.[57] But what are the actual dollar amounts? In the United States, how low does your yearly income have to be for you to be living below the poverty line? The table above provides this information.

Can you predict any problems associated with this system? For one, using a national standard for poverty can be misleading. Living in a beautiful 2,500-square-foot house in a suburb in Texas can easily cost less than living in a cramped Manhattan apartment. Because the poverty line is identical in 48 states, cost-of-living issues aren't accounted for.[58]

Gender issues also come into play, since women are more likely to be poor than men. Even in this day and age, a woman still earns three-quarters of what a man who hold the same job makes.[59] As a result, poverty in the United States is mostly concentrated in female-run households.[60] In Chapter 4, we'll discuss the effect known as *feminization of poverty* in more detail.

▶▶ GO GL⊕BAL

Decline in Global Income Inequality

In their article titled "Accounting for the Recent Decline in Global Income Inequality," Glenn Firebaugh and Brian Goesling argue that global inequality is on the decline.[61] Historically, we have had a great diversity of global inequality, and yet we know that this is changing. Globalization is connected to this change. The old adage "The rising tide raises all boats" appears to be true. Inequality between countries is narrowing. However, inequality within countries has generally gotten worse. As in the United States, the wealthy throughout the world have greatly benefited from globalization and the profits it generates, while the poor have not.

The conclusions reached in the article suggest that this is in large part demographic. The industrialization of India and China mean that now 40 percent of the world's population has experienced an increase in income, which means a massive change in the measurement of income inequality internationally *between* nations.[62] The sheer size of those two nations accounts for a great deal of the cause of the change.

think social problems: HOW DO SOCIOLOGISTS VIEW INEQUALITY?

Functionalism

According to functionalists Kingsley Davis and Wilbert Moore, every system tends toward equilibrium, and so the inequality of the United States is inevitable—even essential—for society to function smoothly.[63] We need janitors and garbage collectors as well as surgeons and astronauts. But why do janitors make so much less than doctors?

Society has various positions that need to be filled; the more important the position is, the rarer the skill or the longer the training period required for it. Generally, these jobs have greater rewards in order to entice people to take them. Thus, the occupations that are greatly rewarded in our society are the ones that require the most skills. This idea suggests that the United States is a meritocracy, a country in which people can rise to the top if they have special skills and/or abilities. The **meritocracy argument** states that those who get ahead in society do so based on their own merit.

Conflict Theory

You will recall from Chapter 1 that conflict theorists generally follow the ideas of Karl Marx, noting that stratification occurs because the proletariat (workers) are exploited by the bourgeoisie (owners). How does the meritocracy argument hold up against this line of thinking? Sociologist Melvin Tumin argued against Davis and Moore, offering a different point of view. Few things affect a person as much as his or her social class. Being born into a wealthy family opens doors to high-quality education and college degrees (the necessary training) that establish a person for a life of affluence. I know a family with three generations of medical doctors. Do they have the "doctor gene," or are their children socialized to think about going to medical school? Tumin also questions the logic that important jobs must necessarily offer high pay to get people to do them. Not so. Consider why kindergarten teachers, soldiers, and firefighters are paid so little. Is there some other type of reward, perhaps social respect, that these people might receive? Why does it have to be money? Furthermore, don't we need soldiers more than we need professional baseball players? Yet who reaps the monetary rewards from society? Something doesn't quite fit the meritocracy argument here. Tumin suggests that we reward certain occupations because we're forced to. We want to watch pro baseball, so

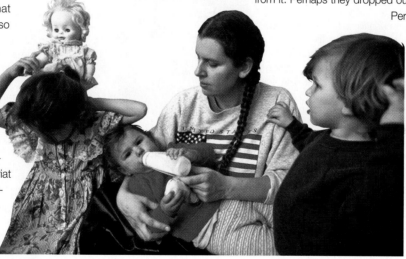

∧∧∧ Contrary to stereotypes, **families on welfare are not living easy on government money.**

teams fight for the best hitters and pitchers. We need heart surgeons, but they are so rare that they can demand high salaries. Those who receive proper training are also rare. Many people cannot afford college. Does that mean they can't be doctors? Probably not.

Symbolic Interactionism

Interactionists often look at the meaning behind social problems. Does social class really matter? Look around a college campus. Can you distinguish working-class students from upper middle-class students by their clothing or cell phones? Some of my students who come from homes with higher SESes aren't forced to make the tough financial decisions that students from working-class families have to make. It is not uncommon for a student to ask me, "Will I really need the book?" Usually, this student comes from a working-class family and frequently struggles with success in college.

William Ryan suggests that when people look at inequality, they tend to view those at the bottom as creators or co-creators of their problem. He refers to this as **blaming the victim**. In short, it involves blaming those who suffer from a social problem for that problem. So, if you consider the issue of poverty, it is often easy to make assumptions about why people suffer from it. Perhaps they dropped out of school at a young age. Perhaps they waste money on lottery tickets. Maybe they have a drug or alcohol problem. Part of the process of blaming the victim involves saying any of these issues are the *cause* of poverty. Students who support such a claim often say, "If they'd just stop drinking, they'd be able to keep a job," as if getting over an addiction is as easy as turning off a light switch. Furthermore, we know that the cause of any social problem is far more complex than any simple statement, but that doesn't stop our habit of blame. Ryan believes that such a process ignores the structural problems of the society, such as lack of good jobs, low pay, and preexisting inequalities.[64] Sociologist William J. Wilson (2009) suggests that this mentality of blaming the victim prevents us from actually seeing the social structural problems that lead to inequality. Certainly, many who are poor have made poor choices, yet it's not fair to say all poor people have done so.[65]

In her book *So You Think I Drive a Cadillac?*, author Karen Seccombe investigates the social stigma associated with female welfare recipients and suggests that some of them even blame themselves. Of the women she interviews, many use denial as a way of coping with the negative feelings associated with being on welfare.

Author J. K. Rowling was a single mother on welfare before the success of the *Harry Potter* series. **What factors might have contributed to her rise in society?**

FUNCTIONALISM

Functionalism is based on the idea that stratification is a natural and necessary process in society. As the old saying goes, "The cream rises to the top." Thus, some suggest that your starting position on the economic ladder is not important—those who get ahead in society do so because of the decisions they make and the skills they possess. According to functionalists, the social class you start in has no lasting effect on the rest of your life.

WHY DO SOCIETIES HAVE DIFFERENT SOCIAL CLASSES?

CONFLICT THEORY

Conflict theory focuses on the struggle between those who have wealth and power and those who don't. To theorists such as Tumin, those born without the proverbial silver spoon will likely never obtain it. The rich do the best they can to stay rich, and their luxuries are passed on to the next generation. Wealthier families can provide their children with music lessons, private tutoring, and workplace connections, all of which contribute to a child's eventual success.

SYMBOLIC INTERACTIONISM

The better off a person is, the less he or she tends to perceive the effects of social class. To those in need, however, there is great shame in being poor. Society often frowns upon government aid, and those who qualify for Section Eight housing or welfare are looked down upon even by their peers.[66] Unfortunately, children raised in poor households set lower expectations for themselves than middle- or upper-class children do. Instead of "reaching for the stars," poor children grow up to find themselves trapped in a lifestyle similar to that of their parents.

Both George H. W. Bush and George W. Bush served as presidents of the United States. **How might the younger George Bush's upbringing have steered him toward this career choice?**

Begging for food or money **is a social stigma** in our society. **In what sort of environment do you think this man was raised?**

discover solutions to social problems:
WHAT SOCIAL POLICIES ADDRESS ECONOMIC INEQUALITY?

The Welfare System

As mentioned earlier, there is a harsh social stigma associated with those who receive welfare. As one of my students once put it, "I have to work, and they get to drive around in Hummers and live off the government!" Many people equate welfare with sitting at home living on the taxpayers' dime. Others insist that women at the poverty level have more children to increase benefits. However, few people take the time to understand the recent welfare reform and its results on the lower-class community.

Until 1996, the U.S. welfare system was run as an entitlement program. To demonstrate this, picture a burglar breaking into your house in the middle of the night. When you call the police, you expect them to come and help you no matter who you are, where you live, or how many times you've called the police before. In 1996, however, President Bill Clinton signed the Personal Responsibility and Work Opportunity Reconciliation Act. This act created the Temporary Assistance to Needy Families (TANF) program, which changed the welfare system drastically.

Let's say a burglar breaks into your house again and you call the police. However, this time you are told that you've already used up your two police requests and from now on, you're on your own. This is how the present welfare system works. Through the TANF program, a person is only allowed to receive government assistance for a total of five years total and only up to two years at a time. Among other ramifications, this means that that person's children will not receive aid throughout their childhood.

This restriction prevents freeloaders from living off of the system for years, right? Recent data show that two-thirds of those who were on Aid to Families with Dependent Children (the program in effect before TANF) were never on the program longer than two years. Less than 15

> **RESIDUAL WELFARE** is a temporary system of relief when a person's job or family has failed to be enough to support them.
>
> **INSTITUTIONAL WELFARE** is a preventive "first line of defense" against poverty. There is no time limit, and no social stigma is associated with receiving this aid.

percent were continuous users of the system.[67] It seems that before TANF was put into place, most were already living by its rules. Now, however, there is no support for the less than 15 percent of the population who are truly desperate.

One of the driving forces behind TANF was the emphasis on job training for the poor. It makes sense that higher education and increased skills translate into better paying jobs. However, because TANF assistance only lasts for two years at a time, long-term training options, such as obtaining a college degree, are impossible. Data show that the transition from welfare to work usually results in jobs that don't pay a living wage.[68] Spending the summer sweeping up popcorn or serving food for only $7.25 per hour may seem exasperating, but imagine doing it for the rest of your life. About 79 percent of minimum-wage workers are older than 25 years of age.[69]

There are actually two separate philosophies that guide the U.S. welfare system; we'll call them residual and institutional. What we have been discussing up until now is the former. **Residual welfare** is a system of relief intended for people with jobs whose earnings are not enough to support them. As we have seen, this aid is temporary, only used in emergencies and handed out as infrequently as possible. TANF is of this sort.

Alternatively, **institutional welfare** is part of the first line of defense against poverty. Assistance is offered on a preventive basis, and no time

MAKE CONNECTIONS

What Else Might Affect Social Inequality?

As Chapter 6 will explain, income equality is not shown in the media. We see wealthy stars living in luxurious mansions and owning million-dollar yachts. Actors on TV shows have lifestyles that would be impossible to afford on their characters' real-world salaries. The media seems to portray life in the United States as easy and effortless.

In the next few chapters, we'll discuss gender and race. As you'll learn, studies consistently show that women and certain minority groups such as blacks and Latinos have lower general incomes than their white male counterparts. In Chapter 5, we'll discuss aging and the startling fact that children and young adults make up the majority of the poor.

>>> **Kramer from the hit show *Seinfeld* never held down a real job, and yet was able to enjoy a life of eccentric luxury.** Characters on TV shows often live financially impossible lives.

limit is imposed. Unlike residual welfare, no social stigma is attached. Because the money comes from the government and all citizens receive some form of governmental aid, it's seen as no more embarrassing than a tax deduction. Public schools, for example, qualify for institutional welfare. When I ask my students, "Who's on welfare?" only a few of them raise their hands. I then point out that because they attend a state college, their tuition is subsidized by taxpayers, and, in fact, all of them receive a form of institutional welfare. After hearing this, they become aware of the immediacy and relevance of welfare to their lives.

Taxation

Despite how it sometimes feels, having to pay taxes is not a punishment. Taxes pay for roads, parks, schools, firefighters, and even military protection. They're essential for successfully functioning in society.

The United States makes use of two separate forms of taxation: **progressive taxation** and **regressive taxation**. Generally, the country operates on a progressive tax

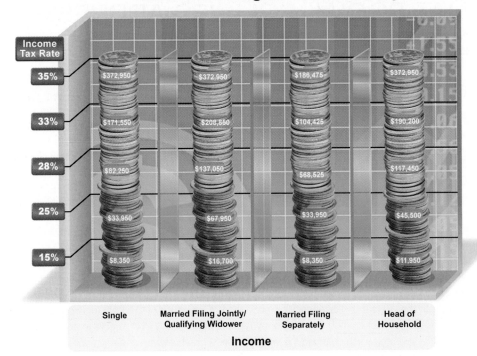

Income Tax Rates: What Percentage do the Poor Pay? What Percentage do the Rich Pay?

Income Tax Rate	Single	Married Filing Jointly/ Qualifying Widower	Married Filing Separately	Head of Household
35%	$372,950	$372,950	$186,475	$372,950
33%	$171,550	$208,850	$104,425	$190,200
28%	$82,250	$137,050	$68,525	$117,450
25%	$33,950	$67,950	$33,950	$45,500
15%	$8,350	$16,700	$8,350	$11,950

Income

Source: "2009 Federal Income Tax Rates And Tax Brackets, Official IRS Tax Schedule." http://www. moolanomy.com/1772/2009-federal-income-tax-brackets-official-irs-tax-rates/ Accessed July 28, 2009.

From Classroom to Community } Rags to Riches

As mentioned in the introduction to this chapter, purchasing a lottery ticket can often eliminate the feeling of poverty, if only temporarily. However, although the purchase brings hope, it drags many people deeper into debt. As a part of her sorority's community service requirement, Eva volunteered at a human services office downtown where she witnessed this behavior with her own eyes.

"Once a week, this girl about my age would come in with two young boys to collect her check. One day she came to my window, and I commented on her adorable little brothers. She looked at me oddly and told me they were her sons.

"From then on, I got to know Alexia a little better. Over time, she told me about her life: How her mother had died when she was younger, how her boyfriend had left when she was pregnant with their second son, and how

her father worked the graveyard shift as a security guard to support the family. My parents had divorced when I was 13, but that felt like nothing compared to Alexia's story.

"On my way home one night, I stopped at the 7-Eleven for a soda. I was standing in line when I noticed Alexia at the front with some friends. She had a stack of lotto tickets in her hands. I was in shock. There must have been over $100 there. I knew from her checks that she couldn't afford to throw away a single dime.

"Alexia turned and saw me. She seemed surprised, but greeted me cheerfully. I asked her how she could afford the tickets.

"Alexia rolled her eyes at me. 'Girl, you can't win it if you're not in it! My boys might have a millionaire mommy.'

"She left, and I walked home alone, that silly slogan from the state lotto commer-

cials still ringing in my head. *You can't win it if you're not in it!* I realized she must have been buying tickets whenever she got the money to do so. It seemed like such a waste.

"Eventually, I was able to place myself in Alexia's shoes. I imagined living every day in poverty, seeing movie stars on TV and wishing I could live like them. With a lottery ticket, there was a small chance to escape into the good life. It gave people like Alexia hope, and blended the lines between the rich and the poor if only for a few moments of hopeful suspense.

"I saw Alexia a couple more times, and then she was gone. I asked around, and someone said she was living with her ex after her father kicked her out. Someone else said he'd seen her on the street. I never did find out what became of her, but every time I see a figure hunched over on the sidewalk, shaking a metal can, I can't help but think sadly, *You can't win it if you're not in it!*"

system. People who earn more pay higher taxes. Even though your boss makes more than you, her income tax is higher than yours.

Regressive taxation technically charges everyone the same percentage of money, however this actually means that the poor pay a higher percentage than the rich do. If you go shopping with your wealthy friend, both of you will pay a 7 percent sales tax on the jeans you buy. Regressive taxes may seem fairer because everyone is charged equally; however, consider the example below:

	Aiden	Rachel	Stephen
Monthly income	$1,000	$5,000	$10,000
Price per gallon of gasoline	$4	$4	$4
Gallons used in a month	40	40	40
7% sales tax paid in dollars	$11.20	$11.20	$11.20
Percent of monthly income	1.12%	0.224%	0.112%

Aiden ends up paying 10 times more of his monthly income than Stephen does. Although all three individuals are paying the same amount of monthly tax, its effect is much greater on Aiden. Generally, sales taxes on necessities are regressive.

With mandatory taxes in place, you wouldn't think people would volunteer to pay more. However, that's exactly what lottery games such as Powerball and Mega Millions are—volunteer taxes. Only part of the money goes to the winner. The rest is used to fund education, protect natural resources, and support the state government, just like regular taxes. Those who don't play the lottery are essentially providing themselves with tax breaks. Because trends show that the frequency of playing the lottery goes down as income levels go up, this once again negatively affects the lower class.

Those who receive most of their income from dividends and capital gains are also receiving huge tax breaks. Large companies like to treat their stockholders well, especially if the stock isn't moving up at the moment. Because of this, major stockholders will often receive dividends in the form of cash, property, or more stock, bypassing tax laws. People who live off capital gains make their money selling items (usually stock) for a higher price than they paid for them. The law on the books only requires these individuals to pay taxes when they sell their stock, not while they own it. Because capital gain taxes rise and fall over time, most investors sell when the tax is low, guaranteeing that they make the highest profit possible.

Pro & Con

Progressive Taxes

Progressive taxes tax the wealthy at a higher rate than the poor. Is this a system the United States should continue?

Pro

- Progressive taxes are "fairer," allowing the less fortunate to pay less.
- This arrangement evens out the playing field, closing the gap between the rich and the poor.
- The system promotes political stability, since most of the nation's money isn't concentrated in the hands of a wealthy few.[70]
- Even with the current system of progressive taxes in place, the rich still pay nearly half what middle-class Americans do.[71] Stricter progressive taxes may need to be instituted.

Con

- More complex tax laws lead to more bureaucracy.
- The majority (middle to lower class) might continue to vote for higher taxes for the minority (higher classes). This is called "soaking the rich."
- Even though Congress passes these higher tax rates, it also approves exclusions and deductions that give tax shelters to the rich, rendering the higher rates ineffective.[72]
- Economically, progressive taxes are inefficient, since they discourage the upper classes to work and invest, thus reducing the productivity of society.[73]
- Some studies argue that these taxes don't aid in redistribution of money, since the gap between the rich and the poor remains as wide as ever.

<<< **Warren Buffett may be the second richest man in the world, but he's the number one advocate of progressive taxes.** In 2007, Buffett made news when he traveled to Washington to convince Congress not to repeal a number of taxes on the rich, including a 55 percent estate tax. **"I see nothing wrong with those who have been blessed by this society to give a larger portion of their income to the society than somebody that's working very, very hard to make ends meet," Buffett said.**[74]

WHAT IS INEQUALITY, AND HOW DOES IT AFFECT PEOPLE? 22

the difference in income, wealth, power, and prestige that leads to social stratification in society

HOW DO SOCIOLOGISTS VIEW INEQUALITY? 31

functionalists: inequality is necessary for society to function smoothly
conflict theorists: social inequality begins at birth because of the struggle for limited resources; we reward certain professions (such as doctors) because we have no choice
symbolic interactionists: there is a social stigma associated with being poor, and children growing up in poor households set lower expectations for themselves than children from affluent families; the wealthier a person is, the less that person perceives social inequality

WHAT SOCIAL POLICIES ADDRESS ECONOMIC INEQUALITY? 33

welfare programs such as the Temporary Assistance to Needy Families; residual welfare temporarily aids citizens while institutional welfare acts as a first line of defense against poverty

get the topic: WHAT IS INEQUALITY, AND HOW DOES IT AFFECT PEOPLE?

Theory

FUNCTIONALISM 31

- different positions need to be filled in society, from busboys to marine biologists
- social inequality is necessary for a civilization to function properly
- the meritocracy argument claims that certain people get ahead in society because of their personal skills and drive

CONFLICT THEORY 31

- there are limited resources in the world that we all must compete for
- social inequality begins at birth, and mobility is limited

- we reward professions that are vital to our society (such as surgeons) because we're forced to do so

SYMBOLIC INTERACTIONISM 31

- the wealthier a person is, the less he or she perceives social class inequalities
- the poor are stigmatized in our society
- in general, poor children set lower expectations for themselves than higher-class children do

Key Terms

social stratification is the ranking of people and the rewards they receive based on objective criteria, often including wealth, power, and/or prestige. *22*

income is the money received for work or through investments. *22*

wealth is all of an individual's material possessions, including income. *22*

median is the midpoint of a group of numbers ranked from lowest to highest. *23*

power is the ability to carry out your will and impose it on others. *24*

force is a type of power that occurs when you make someone do something against his or her will. *24*

persuasive power refers to using direct or indirect methods to get what you want. *24*

prestige is the level of esteem associated with one's status and social standing. *25*

upper or **elite class** is a social class that is very small in number and holds significant wealth. *26*

upper middle class is a social class that consists of high-income members of society who are well educated but do not belong to the elite membership of the super wealthy. *26*

middle class is a social class that consists of those who have moderate incomes. *26*

working class is a social class generally made up of people with a high school diploma and a lower level of education. *26*

lower class is a social class living in poverty. *27*

urban underclass is a social class living in disadvantaged neighborhoods that are characterized by four components: poverty, family disruption, male unemployment, and lack of individuals in high-status occupations. *27*

social mobility is the ability to change social classes. *29*

horizontal mobility refers to moving within the same status category. *29*

vertical mobility refers to moving from one social status to another. *29*

intragenerational mobility occurs when an individual changes social standing, especially in the workforce. *29*

intergenerational mobility is the change that family members make from one social class to the next through generations. *29*

structural mobility is when social changes affect large numbers of people. *29*

exchange mobility is a concept suggesting that, within the United States, each social class contains a relatively fixed number of people. *29*

transitional poverty refers to a temporary state of poverty that occurs when someone goes without a job for a short period of time. *30*

marginal poverty refers to a state of poverty that occurs when a person lacks stable employment. *30*

residual poverty refers to chronic and multigenerational poverty. *30*

absolute poverty refers to poverty so severe that one lacks resources to survive. *30*

relative poverty is a state of poverty that occurs when we compare ourselves to those around us. *30*

meritocracy argument states that those who get ahead in society do so according to their own merit. *31*

blaming the victim refers to the act of accusing those who suffer from a social problem for that problem. *31*

residual welfare is a temporary system of relief when a person's job or family has failed to be enough to support them. *33*

institutional welfare is a preventive "first line of defense" against poverty. There is no time limit, and no social stigma is associated with receiving this aid. *33*

progressive taxation is a system in which people who earn more pay higher taxes. *34*

regressive taxation is a system that taxes everyone the same percentage of money, but results in the poor paying a higher percentage than the rich. *34*

Sample Test Questions

These multiple-choice questions are similar to those found in the test bank that accompanies this textbook.

1. A lawyer moving to another law firm downtown is an example of
   a. exchange mobility.
   b. transitional mobility.
   c. horizontal mobility.
   d. stratified mobility.

2. Joe works hard in college and graduates at the top of his class. However, due to the bad economy, he can only find work as a gas station attendant. How would a functionalist account for this?
   a. Because he was previously successful, Joe set low goals for the future.
   b. Joe does not have the skills or drive necessary to find a higher-paying job.
   c. Being a student is not a vital position in our society, and Joe is now experiencing the effects of wasted time.
   d. This situation is to be expected due to the limited resources of a poor economy.

3. A migrant worker would most likely experience
   a. marginal poverty.
   c. residual poverty.
   b. absolute poverty.
   d. relative poverty.

4. Which is an example of progressive taxation?
   a. The wealthy paying estate taxes
   b. A sales tax on imported products
   c. Your poor friend being taxed the same percentage of money as you
   d. A tax increase to spur the economy

5. The lottery can best be described as
   a. an easy opportunity for vertical mobility.
   b. a practice that promotes hopelessness in the lower class.
   c. a tax on the poor.
   d. a source of income for the rich.

ESSAY

1. How would both a functionalist and a conflict theorist explain occupational prestige?

2. Do you think a person living off capital gains would support progressive taxation or regressive taxation?

3. Do you believe that the income gap is increasing? Take into account the concept of exchange mobility and the graph of U.S. income change that appears in this chapter.

4. How might a person in marginal poverty view TANF?

5. Knowing what you do now, would you still consider yourself "middle class?" Why or why not?

WHERE TO START YOUR RESEARCH PAPER

For more information on the U.S. poverty line, go to
http://aspe.hhs.gov/poverty/09poverty.shtml

For information about social policies in place to alleviate poverty, go to
http://www.whitehouse.gov/issues/poverty/

For more information about the U.S. welfare system, go to
http://www.welfareinfo.org/

To view how the progressive rate has varied over time, go to
http://www.treasury.gov/education/fact-sheets/taxes/ustax.shtml

ANSWERS: 1. c; 2. b; 3. a; 4. a; 5. c

Remember to check www.thethinkspot.com for additional information, downloadable flashcards, and other helpful resources.

RACE AND IMMIGRATION

IS RACIAL AND ETHNIC INEQUALITY
A SOCIAL PROBLEM?
WHY DOES RACIAL AND ETHNIC
INEQUALITY STILL EXIST IN THE
UNITED STATES?
HOW CAN SOCIETY ADDRESS RACIAL AND
ETHNIC INEQUALITY?

It popped

out casually, a throwaway line as he talked to reporters about finding the right puppy for his young daughters.

But with just three offhanded words in his first news conference as president-elect, Barack Obama reminded everyone how thoroughly different his administration—and inevitably, this country—will be.

"Mutts like me."

By now, almost everyone knows that Obama's mother was white and father was black, putting him on track to become the nation's first African-American president. But there was something startling, and telling, about hearing his self-description—particularly in how offhandedly he used it.

The message seemed clear—here is a president who will be quite at ease discussing race, a complex issue as unresolved as it is uncomfortable for many to talk about openly. And at a time when whites in the country are not many years from becoming the minority.

Obama made the remark as he revealed his thinking in what is becoming one of the highest-profile issues of this transition period: What kind of puppy will he and his wife, Michelle, get for their daughters as they move into the White House.

Because Malia, 10, has allergies, the family wants a low-allergy dog. But Obama said they also want to adopt a puppy from an animal shelter, which could make it harder to find a breed that wouldn't aggravate his daughter's problem.

"Obviously, a lot of shelter dogs are mutts like me," Obama said with a smile. "So whether we're going to be able to balance those two things, I think, is a pressing issue on the Obama household."

In his first post-election news conference, the man who will be president in just over two months described himself as a mutt as casually as he may have poked fun at his jump shot.

If he thought nothing of such a remark in his first news conference, doesn't that signal that over the next four years, the country is likely to hear more about race from the White House—and from the perspective of a black man—than it ever has before?

It's not necessarily that he will make a crusade about the issue once he takes office. There was little sign of that in his election campaign, in which he ran on issues like the economy with a broad appeal to all Americans.

But it does underscore that the president-elect clearly does not see race as a subject best sidestepped or discussed in hushed tones. To Obama, race in all its complications has long been a defining part of his life, and he is comfortable talking about it.[1]

CHAPTER 03

---Oprah Winfrey is famous for getting guests to pour out their hearts while perched on her yellow leather couches. So it's not surprising that in 1997 Tiger Woods confessed to Oprah that he is "a Cablinasian."[2]

With these words, Tiger Woods, like Barack Obama, sparked a discussion about race. Woods, who expressed dismay at being classified as just an African American, coined the term "Cablinasian" to define his caucasian, black, American Indian, and Asian roots.[3] While most people would say that Tiger Woods is black, Woods shows us that it's nearly impossible to use skin color to define a person's race.

So what *is* race if it has little to do with skin color? In ***The Race Myth: Why We Pretend Race Exists in America***, evolutionary biologist Joseph L. Graves uses science to prove that the biological differences that exist between people are negligible. Thus, race is purely a social construct, not a biological one.[4] Most genetic differences occur within a single race, and not between one race and another.[5] For example, it's likely that two Chinese people will have the same amount of genetic differences as a Chinese person and a person from Kenya.

In fact, factors such as migration and intermarriage have further complicated the notion that people can be placed in strict racial categories. President Barack Obama's casual comment about animal shelter dogs being "mutts like me" is an example of how people are increasingly refusing to limit their identity to society's idea of race. And yet, why is it that a man whose father was black and whose mother was white is referred to as the nation's first black president?

get the topic: IS RACIAL AND ETHNIC INEQUALITY A SOCIAL PROBLEM?

> **RACE** is the division of people based on certain physical characteristics.
>
> **ETHNICITY** is the classification of people who share a common cultural, linguistic, or ancestral heritage.

Defining Race and Ethnicity

One question to consider is this: Is the very idea of race a social problem, or is the dominant majority's response to different races the problem? In general, this chapter seeks to look at the latter question.

To understand inequality based on race and ethnicity, we must first define what these two terms mean. Generally speaking, **race** refers to the divisions of people based on certain physical characteristics. Often, we categorize people on a superficial basis, such as the color of their skin or the texture of their hair. The U.S. Census Bureau outlines six different racial categories. When you fill out the census, you will be given the following choices: white, black or African American, American Indian or Alaska Native, Asian, Native Hawaiian or other Pacific Islander, or some other race.[6] The Census Bureau does not classify Hispanic or Latino as a race, but as an ethnicity. Those of Hispanic or Latino background are left with the option of choosing one of the previously mentioned groups, or "some other race." Persons such as President Obama must choose a race, or "two or more races." Which race do they choose? Does their choice matter?

Ethnicity is different from race because it links a person's culture to his or her identity. Often, this includes a common language, ancestry, and geography. Ethnicity includes a sense of belonging. For example, I am ethnically German, Bohemian, and Swedish. However, I have no strong ties to any of these ethnicities. If, for example, I started speaking any of these languages or began attending celebrations for my heritage, I might claim those cultures as my ethnicity. In this sense, ethnicity is both objective and subjective. It's objective in that you have concrete facts about where your family is from (e.g., Germany, Sweden), and it's subjective in that you can choose whether you want to officially identify with one of those ethnicities.

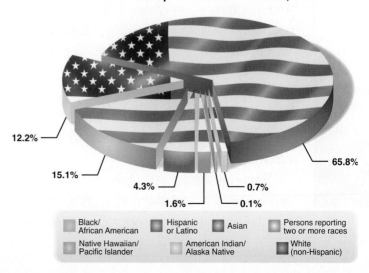

Racial Makeup of the United States, 2007

12.2%

15.1%

4.3%

1.6%

0.1%

0.7%

65.8%

- Black/African American
- Hispanic or Latino
- Asian
- Persons reporting two or more races
- Native Hawaiian/Pacific Islander
- American Indian/Alaska Native
- White (non-Hispanic)

With immigration, population growth, and intermarriage, physical traits may no longer be relied upon so heavily to determine one's identity. Even so, sociological questions regarding race do not focus solely on differences in looks. Instead, these questions deal with how society interprets racial and ethnic differences and how those interpretations, in turn, affect an individual's opportunities.

MAJORITY AND MINORITY GROUPS

Different racial and ethnic groups can be further classified as majority or minority groups. For example, in 2007, whites made up 65.8 percent of the U.S. population.[7] This makes them a **majority group** that not only has a greater numerical representation in society but also holds significant power and privilege. A **minority group** refers to any group that holds less power than the majority group. Minorities often experience unequal treatment compared to the dominant group, giving them a collective sense of being discriminated against.[8]

With the aid of migration patterns, minority groups are gaining greater representation within the U.S. population. Over the next 40 years, percentages of Hispanic Americans and Asian Americans are projected to nearly double, whereas the percentage of whites will decline by about 19 percent.[9]

RACISM

Do you think the changing demographics in the United States will result in more racism or less racism? **Racism** is a prejudice that asserts that members of one race are inferior to another, thus making them less worthy of fair treatment. Often, racism leads to discrimination. In addition to discrim-

MAJORITY GROUP is the group that has the largest population in society and holds significant power and privilege.

MINORITY GROUP is a group that has a smaller population and less power than the majority group.

RACISM is a prejudice that asserts one race is inferior to another, thus making them less worthy of fair treatment.

GENOCIDE is the attempt to destroy or exterminate a people based on their race and/or ethnicity.

ination, racism also involves intergroup privilege, power, and oppression. According to Graves, racism in the United States is based on three assumptions: (1) Races exist; (2) each race has distinct genetic differences; and (3) racial inequality is due to those differences. Graves goes on to define five pillars of racist thought that are prevalent in the United States.

1. Biological races exist in the human species.
2. Races have genetic differences that determine their intelligence.
3. Races have genetically determined differences that produce unique diseases and cause them to die at different rates.
4. Races have genetically determined sexual appetites and reproductive capacities.
5. Races have genetically determined differences in athletic and musical ability.

<<< **Hate groups include white supremacists,** Neo-Nazis, and others who advocate hate against immigrants, gays, and other minorities.

▶▶▶ GO GL🌐BAL

Armenian Genocide

An extreme example of racism is the use of **genocide**, the attempt to destroy or exterminate a people based on their race or ethnicity. Beginning in 1915, the Ottomans expanded their empire into modern-day Turkey, killing more than one million Armenians in their effort to take control. To this day, the Turkish government denies the genocide. Many Armenian activists have spent years protesting this denial.

Armenian American protesters received recognition during the 2008 election campaign when presidential hopeful Barack Obama pledged to officially recognize the genocide if he was elected. But when April 24, the Armenian

Remembrance Day, came and went without official U.S. recognition of the genocide, many protesters were upset. Although President Obama delivered a statement in which he spoke of the *meds yeghem* ("great calamity") of the Armenian people, he did not use the word genocide, which would be offensive to the Turkish government.

Whereas some protesters expressed disappointment at the fact that the U.S. government did not officially recognize the genocide, others were satisfied that President Obama made a public statement about the massacres, lamenting them as a great tragedy.[13]

∧
∧ **Armenians urge Turkey to recognize the genocide of 1915** in a demonstration outside European Union headquarters.

HATE GROUPS are organizations that promote hostility or violence toward others based on race and other factors.

PREJUDICE refers to rigid generalizations, often negative, about an entire category of people.

STEREOTYPES are simplified and extreme perceptions of an entire group of people that are usually based on false assumptions.

DISCRIMINATION is the deliberate and unfair treatment of people based on a prejudice.

INSTITUTIONAL DISCRIMINATION maintains the advantage for the dominant group, while providing the appearance of fairness to all.

SCAPEGOAT means making an unfair accusation against a person or group as the cause of a problem.

DOUBLE CONSCIOUSNESS is the sense that a person must keep a foot in two worlds, one in the majority group's world and one in the minority group's world.

In the United States, racism has long been used to justify mistreatment of certain groups of people, from Native Americans to African Americans to immigrant laborers. For example, in the early 1800s, the U.S. government became involved in the forced relocation of the Cherokee, Chickasaw, Choctaw, Creek, and Seminole tribes from the south to what is now modern-day Oklahoma. What is now known as the Trail of Tears resulted in thousands of deaths.[10] African Americans, on the other hand, faced years of discrimination in the form of slavery, lynchings, segregation, and Jim Crow laws. Likewise, many Chinese and Mexican immigrants who came to the United States as migrant workers were also mistreated and discriminated against. Although the Chinese railroad workers of the late 1800s and the Mexican *braceros* of the 1940s were initially welcomed as a source of cheap labor, the dominant group eventually began to view them as unwelcome competition.

Such extreme racism is not entirely in the past, either. The blatant racism displayed by some during the 2008 presidential election is one example. Obama's campaign volunteers and other supporters sometimes encountered racial slurs or had doors slammed in their faces when they were canvassing for votes. The night before the state primary elections, Obama's Vincennes, Indiana, campaign headquarters was vandalized.[11] **Hate groups**, or organizations that promote hostility or violence toward others based on race and other factors, perpetuate this type of behavior. In 2008, there were 926 active hate groups in the United States.[12]

PREJUDICE VS. DISCRIMINATION

Minority groups often face prejudice from the dominant group. **Prejudice** usually refers to rigid generalizations, often negative, about an entire category of people. These prejudices are often reinforced by **stereotypes**: simplified and extreme perceptions people have of an entire group, usually based on false assumptions. These attitudes, if left unchecked, may lead to **discrimination,** or the deliberate and unfair treatment of people based on a prejudice.

The 2006 film *Glory Road*, which retells the true story of the first NCAA basketball team with an all black starting line-up, is a perfect example of how prejudiced attitudes can lead to discrimination. In the movie, prejudiced attitudes—based on negative stereotypes about blacks in general—lead to mistreatment of the black players. The black players are beaten up, treated unfairly by the referees, and tormented and taunted by the fans because of the color of their skin. You see a portrayal of prejudice and discrimination based on overly simplistic stereotypes.

INSTITUTIONAL DISCRIMINATION IN THE UNITED STATES

Sometimes, personal biases can carry over into the structures of society and often go unnoticed by others who don't even hold those views. When this happens, social institutions end up supporting racial and ethnic inequality. This **institutional discrimination** maintains the advantage for the dominant group while providing the appearance of fairness to others.

Historically, institutional discrimination in the United States was evidenced by the Jim Crow laws of the early to mid-1900s. These laws, which required "separate but equal" facilities for blacks and whites, caused disparities in institutions such as education and housing. Although these institutions were separate, they were not equal. Jim Crow laws have been struck down; however, institutional discrimination continues to exist to this day. For example, as you can see in the table on page 43, minority groups are more likely to be poor than the white majority. This could be related to the fact that poorer children are less likely to attend quality schools.[14] Perhaps it is due to the fact that economic changes in the United States have shipped many jobs for low-skilled workers overseas; many of the jobs that remain are in suburbs away from the areas where poorer minorities live. Couple this with the fact that many cities lack adequate public transportation to transport people to jobs, and you can see why minorities have lost ground economically over the last 30 years.[15] The high rates of poverty lead poorer people—and by extension minorities—to live in environmentally dangerous areas. This takes the form of *environmental racism*. One recent example of environmental racism occurred in the town of Norco, Louisiana. Even before the devastation brought on by Hurricanes Katrina and Rita, poor, black residents of Norco struggled against environmental hazards from a local Shell Chemical plant. These residents suffered from health problems and even fought to be relocated from their neighborhoods.[16]

CAUSES FOR PREJUDICE AND DISCRIMINATION

So, if race is purely an invention of society, why does discrimination happen at all? John Dollard suggests that frustration leads to prejudice.[17] In situations in which we feel powerless, we tend to **scapegoat**, or unfairly accuse, another group as being the cause of our problem. Blaming a racial or ethnic minority for issues such as poverty or unemployment won't increase your salary, but it does keep you from having to accept any blame for your situation.

Generally, studies support the notion that prejudice is learned. However, assuming prejudice is a learned behavior, it can also be unlearned.[18]

MINORITY SUCCESS

Of course, many minorities, despite suffering from prejudice and discrimination, become successful. In her book *Assimilation Blues: Black Families in a White Community*, Beverly Tatum investigates what it means to be black and middle class in a mostly white neighborhood. She finds that the parents of middle-income black families are generally happy with their choice to move into mostly white areas. The most common reason for moving is the improved public schools offered in such neighborhoods. Of course, these better schools are also the places where the children and parents say they have experienced the most overt racism.

Despite this racism, the families are generally happy with their choice and yet must deal with the conflicts of feeling isolated from others of their race. Often, this includes their own family members, many of whom have not achieved the same degree of economic success. In many ways, the families experience what W.E.B. DuBois called **double consciousness**. They must live in a white and black world and be able to keep these worlds separate. (The idea of double consciousness will be discussed in more detail later in this chapter.)

Ellis Cose found similar issues when interviewing successful African Americans in his book *The Rage of the Privileged Class*. Cose discusses a number of issues that even the most successful African Americans must confront, such as these:

1 Inability to fit in. There is an unexamined assumption that whites, simply because they are white, are likely to fit in, while African American and other minority group members are not.

2 Lack of respect. African American professionals constantly must prove they are worthy of respect.

3 Low expectations. Low expectations by employers frequently allow African American employees little or no room to grow.

4 Faint praise. Compliments such as "It's too bad there aren't more blacks like you" often anger African American professionals. Such statements are often taken to mean that many blacks lack the intellect to fit in with whites.

5 Identity troubles. Achieving success in a career may be at the expense of one's African American identity. Even modest attempts at advocacy may result in being typecast as an undesirable. Thus, disassociating oneself from any hint of a racial agenda may result in other blacks in the company labeling the person an Uncle Tom; their achievements, however, bring about enough pleasure to balance out the pain of not being "black."

6 Self-censorship and silence. Many blacks find it best to be silent when sensitive issues are raised. There's a painful awareness that "whites don't want you to be angry."

7 Collective guilt. This occurs when law-abiding blacks feel responsible for the behavior of black criminals. Cose notes that whites rarely have to answer for the actions of white criminals. Rejecting this burden of blame for "misbehaving blacks" isn't always an option.

8 Exclusion from the club. Although many African Americans have made great efforts to get the right education, acquire the right accent, and dress in proper attire, they still find that the doors of many private social clubs (in both a real and symbolic sense) are closed to them.

The end result of these conditions is the continuation of a racial gap that Cose concludes "will never be completely closed; not as long as blacks and whites in America live fundamentally different lives."[19]

RACIAL STRATIFICATION IN THE UNITED STATES

We live in a free society that claims to be equal, yet there are still significant disparities between racial groups. This racial gap can be seen in areas such as poverty levels, income, and education. Take a look at the chart below to see the numbers.

As the numbers clearly show, some minorities tend to be overrepresented in poverty statistics, particularly African Americans, American Indians, and Hispanics. This is, in part, due to the **cycle of poverty**, which makes it difficult for people to break into the middle class if their parents were poor.[20]

It follows that the same three minority groups that have the greatest numbers of people living below the poverty level would also have the lowest median income. One recent study found that although incomes are rising among black and white families, they are not increasing at the same rate. In a study comparing parents' incomes to the incomes of their grown children three decades later, two-thirds of white children earned more than their parents but only one-third of black children earned higher incomes than their parents.[21]

> **CYCLE OF POVERTY** is a generational barrier that prevents poor people from breaking into middle and upper classes.

Racial Stratification by Poverty, Income, and Educational Attainment			
Racial–Ethnic Group	Percentage Living Below the Poverty Line	Median Household Income	Percentage with a Bachelor's Degree or Higher
Black or African American	24.7%	$34,001	17.3%
American Indian and Alaska Native	25.3%	$35,343	12.7%
Asian	10.6%	$66,935	49.4%
Native Hawaiian and Other Pacific Islander	15.7%	$55,273	14.7%
Hispanic or Latino	20.7%	$40,766	12.6%
White	9%	$55,096	30.4%

Source: U.S. Census Bureau, 2007 American Community Survey

One of the most important factors in determining income is education. The lack of a proper education forces people into low-paying jobs and the cycle of poverty continues. In contrast, people who have advanced degrees earn the most money. But who exactly is earning these advanced degrees? Data show that one of the means of increasing one's income—namely higher education—continues to be stratified by race.[22] Only small percentages of the American Indian and Hispanic populations receive bachelor's degrees, whereas much higher percentages of whites and Asians earn advanced degrees.

Based on these data, it is no surprise that minorities made up only 15 percent of faculty members in U.S. colleges and universities in 2003.[23] In fact, at the college where I teach, when searching for new professors, we often have no minority candidates apply. Why is this so? As the numbers show, only a small percentage of doctoral degrees are awarded to minorities in the United States.

Doctoral Degrees Earned by Race/Ethnicity in 2006

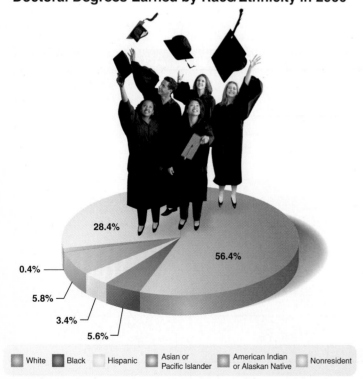

28.4%

56.4%

0.4%

5.8%

3.4%

5.6%

■ White   ■ Black   ■ Hispanic   ■ Asian or Pacific Islander   ■ American Indian or Alaskan Native   ■ Nonresident

Source: Data from Table 289, "Degrees Earned by Level and Race/Ethnicity: 1990 to 2006," U.S. Census Bureau, The 2009 Statistical Abstract.

Immigration

As we've already discussed, interracial conflict is as old as history itself. But how did all this get started? Immigration is one issue that can create racial and ethnic tension. **Voluntary immigration** refers to the willing movement of people from one society to another. People may choose to migrate because they are seeking a better life or more freedom. **Involuntary immigration** refers to the forced movement of people from one society to another. Bringing millions of Africans as enslaved people against their will and forcing Native Americans onto reservations are examples of involuntary immigration in U.S. history.[24]

∧
∧ **In the United States, the first large voluntary**
∧ **internal migration** arose from 1910–1940 when blacks from the South began to move to midwestern and northern cities seeking non-farm labor jobs. **Often known as the "Great Migration,"** millions left the South and settled in cities such as Chicago, Detroit, and New York.[25]

WHO MIGRATES AND WHY?

People migrate for different reasons. Several different categories of immigrants include the following:

- **Labor immigrants**—both legal and undocumented—migrate because they are seeking work.[26] Often, labor immigrants are discussed as a problem even though they provide significant support to the economy.

- **Professional immigrants**, such as doctors and engineers, possess some skill or profession needed in the United States.[27] One drawback to professional immigration is the "brain drain," in which the best and brightest of poorer nations leave their countries to live in the United States.

- **Entrepreneurial immigrants** seek to own their own businesses.[28] For example, small businesses related to ethnic food or culture are common in areas such as New York City's Chinatown.

- **Refugees** are people seeking safety and freedom. Since 1980, the United States has granted asylum to people who have a fear of persecution or physical harm in their own country.[29]

IS IMMIGRATION A SOCIAL PROBLEM?

In a nation of immigrants, is immigration truly a social problem? Immigrants have been coming to the United States for hundreds of years; immigration is nothing new. In 2007, the U.S. foreign-born population was 38.1 million, according to the U.S. Census Bureau.[30] And yet, each major wave of new immigrants experiences a backlash from the dominant group in society. The mistreatment and eventual deportation of many Chinese laborers in the late 1800s is one example. Although they were at first welcomed as a source of cheap labor for building the railroads of the West, the Chinese became targets of anti-immigrant sentiment, suffering violence at the hands of vigilante groups and being driven out of town or out of the country altogether.[31]

Anti-immigrant sentiment in the United States is evidenced by the number of anti-immigration groups that are currently active. These organized anti-immigration groups include openly racist groups, such as the European-American Unity and Rights Organization (EURO). Members of EURO believe that "Ultimately, massive Third World immigration will destroy the character and heritage of America and put the European American population at risk."[32] At the other end of the spectrum are more moderate groups, such as NumbersUSA. This organization strives toward a goal of "setting a fair level of immigration . . . protecting and enhancing the United States' unique experiment in democracy for all Americans, including recent immigrants, regardless of their particular ethnicity."[33] Immigration has always been a source of conflict; the current debate over illegal immigration is just one example. In the next few sections, we will explore how people deal with those who are different from themselves.

ETHNOCENTRISM

Anti-immigrant sentiment is often justified through ethnocentric thinking. **Ethnocentrism** is thinking about or defining another culture on the basis of your own. Most of us are in some way ethnocentric. We view the world from our point of view and generally see groups with greater differences from us more negatively.

ETHNIC ENCLAVES

Facing discrimination often encourages a sense of solidarity among members of a single racial or ethnic group. In a sense, being "outsiders" bonds people together. Minority groups tend to cluster together in **ethnic enclaves** (neighborhoods where people from similar cultures live together) for three

> **ETHNOCENTRISM** is thinking about or defining another culture on the basis of your own.
>
> **ETHNIC ENCLAVES** are neighborhoods where people from similar cultures live together and assert cultural distinction from the dominant group.

main reasons: (1) Their differences from the dominant group often lead to discrimination; (2) the shared values of similar people make adjustment easier; and (3) their social capital increases their chances of success.[34]

This means that a person who enters a new country with very little money, few resources, and limited knowledge of the new culture can increase his or her chances of success by living in an enclave. This has always been the case in the United States as new immigrants seek out locations with others from their same country. For example, all of my ancestors came from Europe and found farming communities made up of people from their home country.

> ∧ ∧ ∧ **As a result of discrimination,** minority groups often bond together in ethnic enclaves. **These neighborhoods allow immigrants** to more easily adjust to a new society without forsaking their **cultural values or practices.**

Of course, belonging to a group that looks like the dominant group tends to decrease discrimination. Yet, many groups who are now considered "white" initially suffered from discrimination. Groups such as Italians, Germans, Poles, and Russians were all at one time or another singled out for discrimination. In response to this, such people often let go of their ethnic heritage because their appearance makes it easier to assimilate into the dominant culture.

History of Immigration to the United States

•1600s–early 1700s
There were no significant immigration restrictions for free white men. Most immigrants came from the British Isles, with English, Scottish, Welsh, and Ulster Irish groups gravitating toward different colonies and regions. Additionally, some immigrants came from France, Netherlands, and other areas.

•1820–1880
About 15 million immigrants entered the United States, many to work in agriculture in the American Midwest. Generally, immigrants came from Northern Europe and Ireland.

•1880–1920
The largest single mass-migration in U.S. history occurred during this time, with most immigrants traveling from southern Europe, Russia, and Poland. These immigrants mostly found work in cities.

•1960s–present
During the Cold War, many refugees fleeing communism entered the United States. These included Cuban, Vietnamese, Chinese, and Russian immigrants. Latino immigration rose as well during this period, including immigrants with or without proper documentation.

Source: Data from Hasia Diner, "Immigration and U.S. History," America.gov, February 13, 2008, http://www.america.gov/st/diversity-english/2008/February/20080307112004ebyessedo0.1716272.html, Accessed April 28, 2009; Alejandro Portes and Ruben G. Rumbaut, Immigrant America (Berkeley, CA: University of California Press, 1996); United States. Department of Homeland Security. Yearbook of Immigration Statistics: 2007. Washington, D.C.: U.S. Department of Homeland Security, Office of Immigration Statistics, 2008.

think social problems: WHY DOES RACIAL AND ETHNIC INEQUALITY STILL EXIST IN THE UNITED STATES?

COLOR-BLIND RACISM is the idea that racism still exists in society in more subtle ways.

You've seen the data showing the disparities that exist between racial and ethnic groups in society. But why do these disparities exist in the United States, where society proclaims the importance of equality? Several sociological schools of thought have differing explanations for why racial and ethnic inequality exists in our society.

Symbolic Interactionism: Color-blind Racism

Symbolic interactionists stress the importance of symbolism and language in the creation of society. In the United States, although overtly racist language has become socially unacceptable, **color-blind racism**—the idea that racism still exists in more subtle ways—remains a part of U.S. society to this day.

As the opening article discussed, Barack Obama's election to the presidency has brought down some, but not all, racial barriers. It is no longer acceptable to make overtly racist comments. As Obama's "mutts like me" comment indicates, he sees himself as biracial, and just a part of the American mix. Yet have we really let go of racism?

There is no doubt that many people of color in the United States remain in disadvantaged positions—they are poorer, achieve lower educational outcomes, live shorter lives,[35] attend underfunded schools,[36] experience problems with assimilation, and generally believe that the police and other social institutions work to increase their disadvantage.[37] Despite these facts, though, many claim these outcomes have nothing to do with racism. Eduardo Bonilla-Silva suggests that color-blind racism occurs when whites use a series of excuses to justify the status quo and keep the races separate. For example, white people may tell a racist joke but before they do so, they first assert that "some of my best friends are black" or label the behavior as "racist, but funny." Before the election, I received an e-mail with a photo-shopped picture of what Air Force One would look like if Obama won. The sender of the e-mail wrote: "This is so racist, but it's hilarious." I was shocked to see a photo of a plane with watermelon and fried chicken painted on the side of it. When confronted, the sender became indignant that he was not racist; it was "just a joke." Color-blind racism excuses our racist tendencies under the guise that we are color blind. It occurs in an environment with four key factors:

1. First, whites tend to hold onto ideals such as equality, individualism, and choice in an effort to explain why racial groups are disadvantaged.[38] In other words, people are only poor because they made bad choices, not because of some historical or cultural connection that supports racism.

2. Second, white people often use cultural stereotypes to rationalize racial inequality. Rather than understand the source of the problem, too many people simply latch onto stereotypes to explain the issue.

3. The third factor is the false belief that segregation is a personal choice. The suggestion is that it's natural for racial groups to prefer "their own kind." Often, this attitude prevents white people from understanding the complex role institutionalized racism has on "segregated" communities.

4. Finally, many whites in the United States simply believe that racism is a thing of the past and deny that it has any impact on minorities' lives today. Such thinking serves to defend the way things are, and excuses the dominant group from any responsibility to make things better.

Despite the obvious structural problems of the poor and minorities in this country, many suggest it is "their problem." This can be termed *laissez-faire racism*, the notion that blacks are responsible for their own problems, particularly economic ones; therefore, they no longer deserve government help and support.[39] Of course we understand that the choices people make occur within a social context. Do negative environments influence these choices, or do the choices keep a person in such environments?

Functionalism: The Interaction of Culture and Structure

Sociologist William J. Wilson admits that overt racism has declined in the United States, although forms of institutional racism continue to affect schools, jobs, health care, and other aspects of the lives of the poor and minority members of this country. In other words, one cannot ignore the reality of structural racism, and yet out of these structures have sprung cultures that can lead the individual to poor choices and negative outcomes. If you consider, poor, inner-city, racially segregated neighborhoods, you can see that such areas are shaped not only by race and poverty but also by the responses of people who live in poverty and suffer from racial discrimination. Wilson suggests that, often, inner-city youths develop cultural values that are counterproductive to them achieving success.[40]

Elijah Anderson referred to this as the "code of the street" in his book *Code of the Street: Decency, Violence and the Moral Life of the Inner City*. Wilson agrees with Anderson that inner-city youths often adopt this code, which is an alternative to pro-social paths to success, focusing on things such as appearing tough, having the "right" look, and talking in the "right" way. Wilson suggests—and Anderson agrees—that inner-city youths frequently develop negative attitudes toward authority, police, and education. As a result, these attitudes clearly hinder the ability of a person to assimilate into the larger culture.

According to Wilson, there is a reciprocal process going on here. The social structures of poverty, crime, and joblessness help to create the "code of the street" culture. And this culture tends to support the preexisting stereotypes that allow the poverty in the first place. Poor minorities hurt their own cause when their responses to poverty provide justification to the majority that individual causes of poverty have some validity. Their behavior can even reinforce ideas such as laissez-faire racism, which tends to ignore the structural component to race relations, and simply blames blacks for their plight. For example, someone who thinks this way might say something like, "Obama made it, so why can't you?" One must remember, however, that the behavior of inner-city minorities arose as a result of years of social policies that failed to support their schools, their jobs, and their housing.

According to Wilson, racism is rooted in the structures of society, and a change in those structures is required to attack it. However, the change will not occur quickly because a culture and code of the street now works to reify that poverty. The election of a "black" president may go a long way toward combating negative stereotypes, but the process of change is likely to be slow.

Conflict Theory

Although racism is not as overt as it once was, that doesn't mean the problem has been eradicated. Accusations of racial prejudice are common in many areas of society—from the world of business to politics to entertainment. The popular viewer-voting show *American Idol* is one example. For several years, there have been claims that the voters and the show itself are racist. In 2004, Elton John famously criticized the show after Jennifer Hudson and two other black female contestants received the lowest number of phoned-in votes and landed in the bottom three. Although she had received praise from the show's judges, Hudson was later forced out of the competition by voters. "I don't know what it was based on, but it wasn't talent," Hudson commented.[41] However, the show's producer and others have denied accusations of racism, referring to the show's previous winners—two of whom are African American and one who is biracial—as evidence supporting their claim.[42]

W.E.B. DuBois suggested that African Americans will always be faced with a dominant majority that wants to exploit them. In order to survive, they develop a double consciousness, making a distinction between two worlds: one white and one black.[43] As a result, minorities may unconsciously adopt the racist attitudes held by the dominant group. For example, in a study on people's responses to strangers, researchers found that whites were more likely to fear black strangers than white strangers. However, in cases where the stranger was a young black male, blacks were just as likely as whites to fear the stranger.[44] Due to a sense of double-consciousness, the blacks who participated in the study had adopted the common fear of the dominant group, accepting the belief that young black men pose a threat.

DuBois's classical ideas also apply to the study of other minority groups, including Hispanics and women.[45] Generally, sociologists find that members of the dominant group do not think much about race, but as one student put it, "When you're a minority, race is always a factor."

V
V
V Rosie O'Donnell and Elton John both famously questioned the fairness of the popular viewer-voting show *American Idol.* **What do you think--**are viewer-voting shows racially biased? If so, how can this be avoided?

WRAP YOUR MIND AROUND THE THEORY

When immigrants move to ethnic enclaves, **they strengthen their in-group connections, and also improve their odds of successfully adapting to the new country.** Can voluntary segregation be functional for both the minority and majority? How?

FUNCTIONALISM

Racism supports in-group biases, thus causing groups that see themselves as alike to unite strongly. The ability of these groups to unite ties them together. In this way, self segregation helps immigrants and minorities. Of course there are latent consequences of this. Self-segregation can be dysfunctional when societies limit the opportunities of minority groups, and thereby miss recognizing strengths that could help improve society.

CONFLICT THEORY

Conflict theory deals with racial and ethnic divisions within society, and shows how these divisions also relate to social class. According to conflict theorists, racism potentially creates a willing "underclass" to provide cheap labor to the elites. Consider racial stratification in terms of education, income and poverty, and opportunities. Conflict theorists might view the inequalities experienced by minority groups as a way for the powerful majority to keep racial and ethnic minorities in a subordinate position. For example, in the United States, business owners may be tempted to hire undocumented immigrant workers who are willing to work for a lower wage. Factors such as low wages, inferior education, and lack of access to public assistance keep many immigrants in subordinate positions. As a result, business owners have a constant supply of cheap labor.

HOW DOES SOCIAL THEORY VIEW THE EFFECTS OF RACISM?

SYMBOLIC INTERACTIONISM

Symbolic interactionists look at the micro interactions of daily life and how they either support or attack an issue. For example, consider the prevalence of racial slurs 100 years ago versus today. Years ago, teachers may have been willing and able to utter racial slurs in the classroom. But today, a teacher who did so would most likely be reprimanded and could even lose his or her job. What has changed? Over time, society's tolerance for racial slurs has decreased dramatically. Symbolic interactionists would suggest that by changing the acceptable terms, we can change the reality. Perhaps we can eliminate racial slurs altogether.

According to conflict theory, those with power often use it to dominate others. **How does the dominant group benefit by keeping minorities in a subordinate position?**

Interactionists suggest that eliminating racial slurs puts the world on more equal terms. **Over the last hundred years,** we have made strides toward creating a more equal society. **How much of this progress is due to the fact that racial slurs are no longer socially acceptable?**

discover solutions to social problems:
HOW CAN SOCIETY ADDRESS RACIAL AND ETHNIC INEQUALITY?

Whether racial and ethnic inequality persists due to color-blind racism, institutional discrimination, or a combination of many factors, the fact remains that it continues to exist in the United States. What social policies can society use to address and eventually correct this type of inequality?

> **SEGREGATION** is enforced separation from the dominant group based on factors such as race, gender, or ethnicity.
>
> **MULTICULTURALISM** is a concept that supports the inherent value of different cultures within society.

Social Problems and Racial Segregation

People who are discriminated against are often separated from the dominant group in terms of housing, workplace, and social settings. This enforced separation is called **segregation** when factors such as race, gender, or ethnicity are involved. Although the "separate but equal" facilities of the 1960s and earlier are no longer legal, issues such as unofficial segregation continue to this day.

In a study of housing segregation, Massey and Denton show that blacks of various income levels experience similar segregation from whites. They note that racial segregation is linked to a number of factors, including personal choice. Sometimes, minorities prefer to live in areas that are populated by their own groups; however, their research shows that whites tend to prefer neighborhoods that are almost completely white.[46] This explains the phenomenon known as "white flight," the housing pattern that occurs when many white people move out of a neighborhood in response to blacks or other people of color moving in.

To help prevent housing segregation based on discrimination, the U.S. Department of Housing and Urban Development formed the Office of Fair Housing and Equal Opportunity (FHEO). The FHEO's mission is as follows: "To create equal housing opportunities for all persons living in America by administering laws that prohibit discrimination in housing on the basis of race, color, religion, sex, national origin, disability, and familial status."[47]

Immigration Control and Immigration Issues

Before the 1800s, immigration to the United States was hardly controlled. Anyone could come to the states—particularly free white men. However, the passing of the Chinese Exclusion Act in 1882 ushered in a new era of immigration control.

A current issue facing the United States is illegal immigration. U.S. Customs and Border Protection (CBP) is tasked with securing the nation's borders between Canada, Mexico, and other coastal areas. CBP employs a law enforcement air force, a marine fleet, and uniformed officers on the ground to protect and patrol between ports of entry into the United States. However, CBP is also responsible for safely processing international travelers through U.S. Customs. In 2008, CBP welcomed more than 400 million people into the United States.[48] What is the best way for immigrants to adapt?

MULTICULTURALISM AND ASSIMILATION

One possible solution to the problem of racial and ethnic conflict is the rise of **multiculturalism,** a concept that supports the inherent value of different cultures within society. Proponents of multiculturalism think that immigrants should maintain links to their original culture—such as language, cultural beliefs and traditions, and religion—while also integrating into their new culture. However, opponents of multiculturalism worry that this practice keeps groups from adapting to the dominant culture.

MAKE CONNECTIONS

Racism and Immigration

As you have seen in this chapter, racism and immigration are closely related. New immigrants are often treated as scapegoats for social problems when they are merely doing what millions did before—moving to a new country in search of opportunity.

Chapter 2 of this book discussed social inequality in terms of the poverty rate and low-wage jobs. As you learned, greater percentages of minorities live below the poverty level than of the dominant group. Minority groups also have the lowest median incomes. This provides an example of the racial stratification that exists in the United States. Furthermore, welfare reform, also discussed in Chapter 2, limits the ability of undocumented immigrants from obtaining any federal assistance.

Chapter 18 shows how the issues of racism and immigration intertwine on a global scale, as the world's population continues to increase. Today, most immigrants to the United States come from Central America and Asia, particularly India, Pakistan, and China. These are all areas of the world with rapidly growing populations, where finding work is often difficult. As you learned in this chapter, one of the ways immigrant groups assimilate to a new society is by forming ethnic enclaves. In these enclaves, immigrants seek to avoid discrimination by the dominant group, adjust more easily to the new culture, and have a greater chance of success in their new country.

ASSIMILATION is the process by which minority groups adopt the patterns of the dominant culture.

RAPID ASSIMILATION occurs when a minority group completely abandons its previous culture in favor of a new one.

SEGMENTED ASSIMILATION is the idea that there is more than one way to adopt a new land and become economically and social successful.

Assimilation is the process by which minority groups adopt the patterns of the dominant culture. Assimilation can be voluntary, but it can also be enforced by social policies. "English Only" laws are an example of one such policy. In recent years, several states have adopted these laws, which range from merely declaring English as the official state language to limiting government services in languages other than English.

Rapid assimilation occurs when a minority group completely abandons its previous culture in favor of a new one. One method by which the U.S. government tried to force rapid assimilation involved taking Native American children from their parents and placing them in boarding schools to teach them "white ways." However, many Native American students left the boarding schools unprepared to live in either the dominant culture or their own culture.[49]

The fact is that most immigrant groups practice **segmented assimilation,** which means that there is more than one way to adapt to a new land and become economically and socially successful. Traditional thought has held that the faster immigrants become acculturated to the United States (that is, give up the culture of their home country), the faster they will achieve successful assimilation. Alejandro Portes argues that this is not necessarily so. He states that the cultural elements to which immigrants are exposed are of particular importance.[50] That is, successful assimilation depends on being exposed to the *right* elements of a new culture, not just *any* elements of a new culture. For example, poor immigrants who are acculturated to the culture of poor inner-city residents do not learn a culture that leads to successful assimilation. However, poor immigrants who are exposed to the culture of the poor have a better chance of success if they maintain a close connection with the culture of their home countries—such as the connections established through ethnic enclaves. This connection protects immigrants from a culture that is detrimental, and is an alternative path to assimilation. By taking this path, immigrants are able to develop the social capital necessary to achieve social and economic success without giving up traditional cultural practices.

Proponents of "English Only" laws say these policies encourage assimilation. The American Civil Liberties Union, however, argues that such laws harm immigrants by restricting or cutting funding for multilingual programs that some U.S. residents can't do without, such as health services, voting assistance, and driver's licensing tests[48]

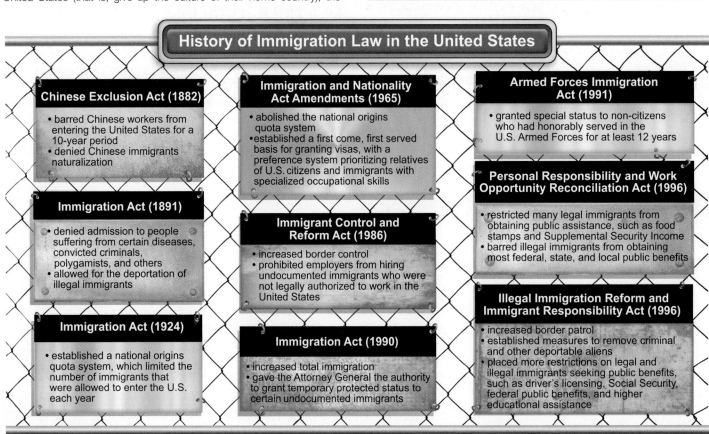

History of Immigration Law in the United States

Chinese Exclusion Act (1882)
- barred Chinese workers from entering the United States for a 10-year period
- denied Chinese immigrants naturalization

Immigration Act (1891)
- denied admission to people suffering from certain diseases, convicted criminals, polygamists, and others
- allowed for the deportation of illegal immigrants

Immigration Act (1924)
- established a national origins quota system, which limited the number of immigrants that were allowed to enter the U.S. each year

Immigration and Nationality Act Amendments (1965)
- abolished the national origins quota system
- established a first come, first served basis for granting visas, with a preference system prioritizing relatives of U.S. citizens and immigrants with specialized occupational skills

Immigrant Control and Reform Act (1986)
- increased border control
- prohibited employers from hiring undocumented immigrants who were not legally authorized to work in the United States

Immigration Act (1990)
- increased total immigration
- gave the Attorney General the authority to grant temporary protected status to certain undocumented immigrants

Armed Forces Immigration Act (1991)
- granted special status to non-citizens who had honorably served in the U.S. Armed Forces for at least 12 years

Personal Responsibility and Work Opportunity Reconciliation Act (1996)
- restricted many legal immigrants from obtaining public assistance, such as food stamps and Supplemental Security Income
- barred illegal immigrants from obtaining most federal, state, and local public benefits

Illegal Immigration Reform and Immigrant Responsibility Act (1996)
- increased border patrol
- established measures to remove criminal and other deportable aliens
- placed more restrictions on legal and illegal immigrants seeking public benefits, such as driver's licensing, Social Security, federal public benefits, and higher educational assistance

Source: Data from "Immigration Legal History," U.S. Citizenship and Immigration Services, U.S. Department of Homeland Security, http://www.uscis.gov/portal/site/uscis/menuitem.eb1d4c2a3e5b9ac89243c6a7543f6d1a/?vgnextoid=dc60e1df53b2f010VgnVCM1000000ecd190aRCRD&vgn extchannel=dc60e1df53b2f010VgnVCM1000000ecd190aRCRD, Accessed May 12, 2009.

Pro & Con

"English Only" Laws

Social policies dealing with assimilation, such as the so-called "English Only" laws, draw passionate responses from both sides of the issue. What does each side have to say?

Pro

- Having an official language unites the country by giving us commonality.

- Having an official language provides an incentive for new immigrants to assimilate.

- New immigrants will assimilate more quickly because they will be forced to learn the English language.

- "English Only" laws potentially save costs because government documents will no longer need to be printed in multiple languages.

- With waves of immigration, such laws ensure that the history of the country, and its language, remains intact.

- Such laws are unnecessary—people must learn English in order to work, shop, and interact with society anyway.

Con

- "English Only" laws are anti-immigrant because they make it harder for immigrants to obtain driver's licenses, find work, and so forth.

- The fear of losing English as the national language is unfounded. U.S. Census Bureau projections suggest that by 2050, approximately 24 percent of the U.S. population will be Latinos (the largest immigrant group).[51] Even if all these people were to speak only Spanish, it still means that almost three-fourths of Americans would speak English.

- Such laws can be used to weaken the educational opportunities of non–English-speaking children.

From Classroom to Community | Anti-immigration Legislation

In 1994, the state of California passed Proposition 187, a law that was designed to limit public services to illegal immigrants. Once in effect, the proposition would keep undocumented immigrants from obtaining access to public education, health care, and food stamps, among other forms of assistance.[52] Although the proposition was barred from being implemented within days and eventually voided by a federal judge, several states have since signed into law bills that similarly limit public assistance to illegal immigrants.

Nicole saw these effects firsthand when she student-taught at an elementary school in her home state. Nicole had studied Spanish for several years and was excited to put her skills to the test in the classroom.

"The school where I student-taught wasn't incredibly diverse, although there was one little boy in my second-grade class who spoke Spanish as a first language—José. He was so attentive. Most second graders have pretty short attention spans, but José was incredibly focused and always seemed so eager to learn.

"One day, José came to school and complained that his stomach was hurting him. The teacher took him to the nurse's office, but, because he didn't have a fever or any other symptoms, there wasn't much she could do. José eventually said he felt better and asked if he could go back to the classroom. This happened several days in a row—José just wasn't his usual eager self.

"The teacher finally spoke with José's mother the next day when she picked him up from school. When the teacher voiced her concerns to José's mother, she looked worried and quietly explained that she couldn't take José to the doctor because she couldn't risk deportation. In the past, when one of her children was sick or injured, she would take him to the emergency room. The wait was long, but it was her only option because she didn't have health insurance. But now she was afraid to go even there because of a new state law. Her neighbor had told her that the new law required all doctors to report undocumented immigrants to the authorities.

"I didn't know the details of the law, so I went home and did some research that night. I found out that the law does limit certain health benefits to undocumented immigrants, but not all. In some of the articles I read, state health officials expressed their concern that illegal immigrants might forgo all health benefits—even those for their children—for fear of being reported.

"The next day, the teacher and I spoke with José's mother again and tried to explain to her that the new law doesn't apply to emergency care. She didn't seem convinced. José had stopped complaining about his stomach and seemed back to normal, so the teacher let it go. But I worry about the next time José gets sick.

"This law was supposed to discourage undocumented immigrants from entering the state, and maybe it has. But, whether intentional or not, this law has definitely harmed some of the illegal immigrants who were already here, especially the children. Do these kids deserve to be punished because they and their parents are here illegally?"

IS RACIAL AND ETHNIC INEQUALITY A SOCIAL PROBLEM?   40

yes, because it adversely affects minorities in terms of poverty, income, and educational attainment.

WHY DOES RACIAL AND ETHNIC INEQUALITY STILL EXIST IN THE UNITED STATES?   46

because of concealed forms of racism, such as color-blind racism laissez-faire racism, racial stereotypes, and belief that segregation is a personal choice, belief that racism is a thing of the past, which denies its impact on minorities.

HOW CAN SOCIETY ADDRESS RACIAL AND ETHNIC INEQUALITY? 49

through government agencies such as the Office of Fair Housing and Equal Opportunity; by enacting laws that protect rather than reduce immigrants' rights; through encouraging multiculturalism and segmented assimilation

get the topic: IS RACIAL AND ETHNIC INEQUALITY A SOCIAL PROBLEM?

Theory

FUNCTIONALISM   46

- racism supports in-group biases, causing groups that see themselves as alike to unite strongly
- this can be dysfunctional when societies limit the opportunities of minority groups, and thereby miss recognizing strengths that could help improve society

CONFLICT THEORY   47

- conflict theory relates racial and ethnic divisions to social class
- racism potentially creates a willing "underclass" to provide cheap labor to the elites

- the powerful majority has a social and economic interest in keeping racial and ethnic minorities in a subordinate position

SYMBOLIC INTERACTIONISM   46

- by changing what is acceptable in society, we change reality
- racial slurs that were acceptable 100 years ago are highly discouraged today
- acceptable terms lead to what is said and thought in society

Key Terms

race is the division of people based on certain physical characteristics.   40

ethnicity is the classification of people who share a common cultural, linguistic, or ancestral heritage.   40

majority group is the group that has the largest population in society and holds significant power and privilege.   41

minority group is a group that has a smaller population and less power than the majority group.   41

racism is a prejudice that asserts one race is inferior to another, thus making them less worthy of fair treatment.   41

genocide is the attempt to destroy or exterminate a people based on their race and/or ethnicity.   41

hate groups are organizations that promote hostility or violence toward others based on race and other factors.   42

prejudice refers to rigid generalizations, often negative, about an entire category of people.   42

stereotypes are simplified and extreme perceptions of an entire group of people that are usually based on false assumptions.   42

discrimination is the deliberate and unfair treatment of people based on a prejudice.   42

institutional discrimination maintains the advantage for the dominant group, while providing the appearance of fairness to all.   42

scapegoat means making an unfair accusation against a person or group as the cause of a problem.   42

double consciousness is the sense that a person must keep a foot in two worlds, one in the majority group's world and one in the minority group's world. *42*

cycle of poverty is a generational barrier that prevents poor people from breaking into middle and upper classes. *43*

voluntary immigration is the willing movement of people from one society to another. *44*

involuntary immigration is the forced movement of people from one society to another. *44*

labor immigrants are those who migrate to a new country because they are seeking work. *44*

professional immigrants are those who migrate to a new country because they possess some skill or profession. *44*

entrepreneurial immigrants are people who migrate because they seek to own their own businesses. *44*

refugees are people who migrate because they are seeking safety and freedom. *44*

ethnocentrism is thinking about or defining another culture on the basis of your own. *45*

ethnic enclaves are neighborhoods where people from similar cultures live together and assert cultural distinction from the dominant group. *45*

color-blind racism is the idea that racism still exists in society in more subtle ways. *46*

segregation is enforced separation from the dominant group based on factors such as race, gender, or ethnicity. *49*

multiculturalism is a concept that supports the inherent value of different cultures within society. *49*

assimilation is the process by which minority groups adopt the patterns of the dominant culture. *50*

rapid assimilation occurs when a minority group completely abandons its previous culture in favor of a new one. *50*

segmented assimilation is the idea that there is more than one way to adopt a new land and become economically and social successful. *50*

Sample Test Questions

These multiple-choice questions are similar to those found in the test bank that accompanies this textbook.

1. What type of group often experiences unequal treatment compared to the dominant group, creating a collective sense of being discriminated against?

  a. Hate group

  b. Minority group

  c. Majority group

  d. Immigrant group

2. What is the largest minority group currently in the United States?

  a. Black

  b. White

  c. Hispanic

  d. Biracial

3. Discrimination is

  a. the unfair treatment of people based on a prejudice.

  b. a negative attitude toward an entire category of people.

  c. a simplified perception of an entire group of people that is usually based on false assumptions.

  d. All of the above

4. Alejandro Portes argues that

  a. multiculturalism keeps groups from adapting to the dominant culture.

  b. "English Only" laws will encourage new immigrants to adapt to U.S. culture more quickly.

  c. the faster immigrants give up the culture of their home country, the faster they will achieve successful assimilation.

  d. successful assimilation depends on being exposed to the right elements of a new culture, not just any elements of a new culture.

5. Conflict theorists would suggest that by changing the acceptable terms, we can change the reality.

  a. True

  b. False

ESSAY

1. What are your thoughts about President Obama's "mutts like me" comment? Is the statement offensive? Why or why not?

2. Consider the effects "English Only" laws would have on you if you were a recent immigrant who did not speak English. How would your life be different?

3. What defines your identity most: your race, your language, or your social class? Explain.

4. Consider Anderson's idea about the "code of the street." Are Wilson and Anderson simply blaming the victim?

5. Sometimes, politicians equate immigration with "invasion"—as the conservative pundit Pat Buchanan famously did in 2006.[53] Does this idea have racial overtones? Why or why not?

WHERE TO START YOUR RESEARCH PAPER

For U.S. Census facts and information, go to http://www.census.gov

For more information about the ways in which the United States helps immigrants who are entering the country, go to http://www.usimmigrationsupport.org/

To view an interactive presentation on the illusion of race, go to http://www.pbs.org/race/000_General/000_00-Home.htm

To learn more about immigrants' rights in the United States, go to http://www.aclu.org/immigrants/index.html

To locate information on active U.S. hate groups, go to http://www.splcenter.org/intel/map/hate.jsp

ANSWERS: 1. b; 2. c; 3. a; 4. d; 5. b

Remember to check www.thethinkspot.com for additional information, downloadable flashcards, and other helpful resources.

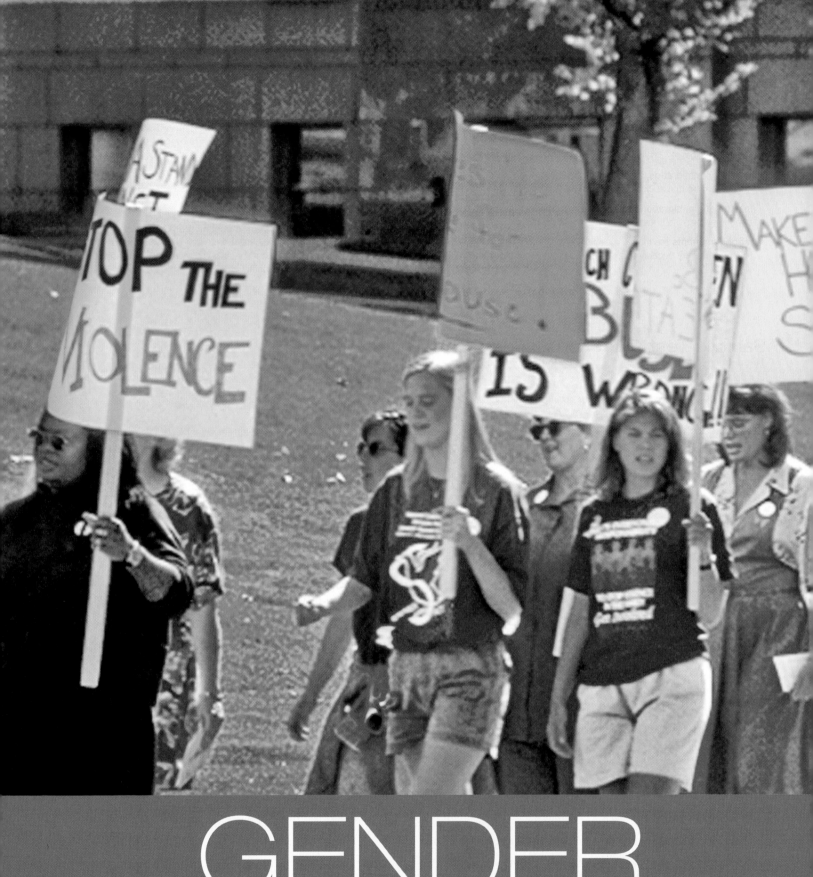

GENDER

HOW DOES A SOCIETY DEAL WITH
GENDER?
WHAT ARE THE THEORIES OF GENDER
RELATED TO SOCIAL PROBLEMS?
WHAT SOCIAL POLICIES ARE IN PLACE TO
PREVENT DOMESTIC VIOLENCE?

A shocking

new ad starring actress Keira Knightley created to call attention to the issue of domestic violence draws criticism for being too violent.

Some say it is too graphic and crosses a line, but victims of domestic violence call it a realistic depiction of the abuse many suffer.

The ad shows actress Keira Knightley coming home after a long day of work. A jealous boyfriend, waiting at home, asks angrily, "Did you have a good time with your leading man?"

He starts to hit her. Then the ad shows the actress on a movie set, with no one around.

So, the boyfriend continues hitting her and kicking her in the stomach.

That graphic depiction of violence has turned the stomach of some critics, such as advertising executive Jerry Della Femina.

"Couldn't they just show his face while he's kicking? No. It went too far, and I question the motives," Della Femina said.

"A lot of advertising people take on these PSAs because they think, 'Hey, I'm going to win an award,'" he continued. "This was a little movie. I think people think it was ugly, violent. It was horrible, and I don't think it's going to help anybody."

And that's the heart of the matter. Would the ad encourage a domestic abuse victim to get help, or would it force her to turn away?

Roughly one in four women in this country and one in nine men become victims of domestic violence at some point in their lives, according to the National Coalition Against Domestic Violence.

ABC News showed the ads to a domestic abuse survivor, whom we agreed not to identify.

"I think that it was really well done," she told us. "We have a responsibility to see the PSA, be moved by it, and do something action-oriented to stop domestic violence."

Bea Hanson, who works for Safe Horizon, the largest provider of domestic violence services in the country, said the ad reflected reality.

"It's real in many women's lives," Hanson said.

Do the means justify the ends? She says as difficult as ads like this are to watch, they bring benefits.

"We've done ad campaigns in the past with graphic images of women who've been abused, and our call volume goes way up, so we know there is an impact," said Hanson.[1]

---If you flip your TV channel to the Spike network and catch an episode of *The Ultimate Fighter*, you'll witness an entire hour devoted to two men kicking, punching, and grappling with each other.

If you change the channel to VH1 and catch an episode of *Rock of Love*, you're likely to see two women scratching, clawing, and pulling at each other's hair—all in an effort to prove their love to rock star Bret Michaels. Most people watch these shows because they find this kind of violence entertaining. But when the same kicking, punching, and hair pulling was aired in a public service announcement (PSA) to raise awareness for domestic violence, audiences were anything but entertained—they were outraged.

So, why is it that the violence on reality shows is entertaining, whereas the violence in the opening PSA was considered too graphic? It may be that the fights on TV seem to be consensual, with no clear victim. But what if the participants were not of the same gender? Would audiences still feel comfortable watching a man and a woman fight, especially if the woman seemed to receive most of the blows? Our feelings toward violent acts change when gender becomes a factor; in fact, our feelings toward a lot of situations change when gender is called into play.

get the topic: HOW DOES A SOCIETY DEAL WITH GENDER?

> **GENDER** refers to the behavioral, cultural, and psychological traits associated with being male or female.
>
> **SEX** is the biological makeup of males or females, especially in regard to their reproductive organs and physical structures.

Core Concepts

THE DIFFERENCE BETWEEN GENDER AND SEX

When filling out a survey, form, or application, you may be asked to fill in a box titled "gender" or "sex." In this case, the two terms are asking you for the same thing—are you male or female?—but in sociology, the terms *gender* and *sex* have two very different meanings. **Gender** is the behavioral, cultural, and psychological traits associated with being male or female. Immediately after birth, these traits are applied to individuals. For example, it's common for parents to dress their infant girls in pink, whereas clothes for infant boys often come in shades of blue. **Sex**, however, refers strictly to the biological makeup of males and females, especially in terms of their reproductive organs and bodily structures.

It's difficult to find significant differences between baby boys and girls, especially right after birth. Beyond the obvious biological dissimilarities, female infants appear to be less reactive to stressors and less likely to die in infancy. Baby boys, on the other hand, tend to be longer and slightly stronger.[2] As children grow, other differences arise. Between the ages of one and two, most children show a preference for same-sex playmates and enjoy separate types of toys based on gender.[3] Despite this, young boys and girls are still far more similar than they are different.

It's not until early childhood that the gap between genders widens. Although intelligence scores show no differences, girls have a strong tendency to be more verbal. Boys exhibit more aggression and independence, whereas their female counterparts tend to be more compliant and empathetic. As toddlers, both genders hit, bite, and throw tantrums, but girls generally cease these behaviors earlier than boys do. Some studies suggest that socialization is part of the cause; in American society, such behaviors are considered far less "female" appropriate. Given fewer rewards in the socialization process, girls tend to stop these behaviors faster than boys do.[4]

The process of learning gender roles continues throughout childhood and into adolescence. Consider the gifts that children receive. Boys get action figures and BB guns, whereas girls receive stuffed animals and makeup kits. Girls obtain rewards when they're passive and submissive to authority figures, and as they age, they're watched more closely than their parents than a son would be. This leaves boys with higher amounts of unsupervised free time, allowing them to engage in risky, thrill-seeking behaviors. This may contribute to the generally higher rate of crime committed by males.[5]

GENDER CONSTRUCTION AND IDENTITY

The "Mr. Mom" concept has been a Hollywood staple for many years. From films such as *Daddy Daycare* to TV shows like *Daddio*, this husband-as-a-homemaker dynamic follows the same set formula: A man stays home to take care of the house and children while his wife goes to work; the man—who is incapable of doing domestic work, of course—ultimately screws up and hilarity ensues. As a former "Mr. Mom" myself, I find such characterizations to be rather demeaning to men, although they are often funny. Why is a man in a domestic position such a fish-out-of-water story? Shouldn't a man be just as capable of taking care of children and doing housework as a woman?

The idea regarding what is and is not "normal" for a particular gender isn't based on a biological set of traits; it is the product of social behavior. Childhood is the primary time for developing and understanding these standards; children follow the cultural rules and try to meet the expectations of the gender that they perceive themselves to be. By doing so, they form a **gender identity**. Once children learn to project the "appropriate" behavior, they are more likely to fit in with their peers and be accepted by their parents and other authority figures.[6]

Sociologists West and Zimmerman propose that there is a difference between "doing gender" and "having gender."[7] Just because a child "has" a gender doesn't mean he or she is biologically forced to "do" that gender. "Doing gender" refers to the act of matching one's behavior to a certain set of gender-related standards (for example, a boy might roughhouse with friends because that's what he thinks boys are supposed to do).[8] "Having gender" refers to simply being male or being female. We all have a gender, but the way we carry it out is the doing of gender. When a little girl puts on her mother's makeup, or a little boy picks up his father's tools, they're learning to do gender.

These constructs can become so fixed that children who don't fit the mold are often ostracized. Think back to your childhood. Was there a girl you knew who liked sports more than playing make-believe? Perhaps it was a boy who wore pink and played with dolls. Most likely, that child experienced negative feedback from his or her peers. The study of gender often includes a discussion of how social expectations of doing gender affect different people in society. In Chapter 11, we'll discuss sexual identity in greater detail.

PATRIARCHY

"Wait until your father gets home!" Even if you haven't had that statement directed at you, you still know what it means: When the supreme authority

GENDER IDENTITY is our perception of ourselves as male or female.

PATRIARCHY is a social system in which men control a majority of the power and exert authority over women and children.

MATRIARCHY is a social system in which women are the main authority and hold power over men.

SEXISM is the belief that one sex is superior to the other.

figure of the family—the father—returns home, a severe punishment will be handed out. This threat has been used to strike fear into children for decades. In fact, it was the title of an animated TV show that aired for two years during the 1970s. But the statement indicates that a mother has less influence than a father on the behavior of children and reinforces an enduring stereotype that the man is the dominant one in the family.

This type of family dynamic is common in a **patriarchy**, a social system in which men control a majority of the power and exert authority over women and children. In a patriarchy, men manage public institutions such as government, business, religion, and education. No pure **matriarchies** exist in the world, even though some women may seem to have more influence than men. In most cultures, there are clear lines of male dominance in the social system, and women in general have less power in society.

SEXISM

These types of systems often result in **sexism**, the belief that one sex is superior to the other. In a patriarchy, women are typically viewed as weak and incapable of matching a man's physical or intellectual prowess. In early 2009, a new law in Afghanistan made headlines because of its extreme patriarchal bias. This law required a woman to seek her husband's approval

▶▶▶ GO GL◉BAL

Female Circumcision

In some of the world's most patriarchal societies, women are subjected to strong male pressures that, over time, become deep-rooted cultural and religious customs. Female circumcision, also referred to as female genital mutilation (FGM), is one such practice.[9] The procedure consists of the alteration or removal of parts of the female genital organs for no purpose other than to keep women sexually "pure." Without the normal sensory nerves, women are considered more likely to remain virgins until marriage and less likely to commit infidelity afterward. In extreme cases, FGM procedures ensure that sexual activity will not take place until a second operation allowing access to reproductive organs is performed after marriage.[10]

Women who undergo FGM not only risk death from infection or blood loss, but may suffer from a number of long-term medical consequences including recurrent urinary tract infections, infertility, and increased risk of childbirth complications.[11] The practice is most common

in the western, eastern, and northeastern regions of Africa, as well as parts of Asia and the Middle East, and certain immigrant communities in Europe and North America.[12] It's estimated that between 100 and 140 million girls worldwide have undergone and are currently living with this mutilation.[13] Cultural traditions about proper sexual behavior maintain this practice, subjecting new generations of female children to a painful and dangerous operation. Although FGM is rooted in cultural traditions, the World Health Organization (WHO) has classified it a "violation of

human rights," as well as "an extreme form of discrimination against women."[14] Along with the United Nations and volunteers around the world, WHO is working to end this widespread practice of gender inequality.

<<< Viewers of the popular reality show *America's Next Top Model* were able to connect a face to the brutal affects of FGM when **contestant Fatima Siad revealed that she had been circumcised as a child** in her hometown of Mogadishu, Somalia.[15] **Her experience struck a chord with audience members and exposed this brutal tradition to thousands of young viewers.**

before leaving the house and submit to his sexual demands every four days unless critically ill.[16]

Even in societies that give women the same civil rights as men, there are still different standards placed on women. One example is income inequality. Despite years of fighting for women's rights in the United States, women still make less money than men do. A man graduating with a bachelor's degree will make an average of $54,000 a year, whereas a woman will make $35,000. With a doctorate, men average $90,000 to women's $61,000.[17]

The Lolita Effect

In August 2009, Disney pop star Miley Cyrus appeared in a controversial set of photos in the fashion magazine *Elle*. Images included the 16-year old reclining sensuously in thigh-high leather boots, stretching backward on the floor to expose her chest to the camera, and posing seductively on the magazine cover in a tight black bustier. Parents and youth advocacy groups were outraged. They claimed the photos were too racy and that *Elle* was promoting an overly sexual depiction of a young teen star.

Dr. M. Gigi Durham addresses this issue in her book *The Lolita Effect: The Media Sexualization of Young Girls and What We Can Do About It*. According to Durham, there are five common myths about sex and sexuality in our society.[18] They are as follows:

1. Girls don't choose boys. Boys choose girls, but only sexy ones.

2. There is only one kind of sexy—having a slender yet curvy body, preferably Caucasian.

3. Girls should work to be that type of sexy.

4. The younger a girl is, the sexier she is (as long as she isn't prepubescent).

5. Sexual violence is sexy.

These myths are believed to be true by many impressionable girls, leading them to think that being attractive is the most important attribute a woman can have. The Lolita effect can damage girls' self-confidence, cause self-destructive behaviors, and inadvertently promote sex crimes. Durham does believe that sexuality is a normal and healthy part of life. However, she argues that the selective, narrowly defined image of sexuality portrayed in the media is ultimately unhealthy for young girls and boys.[19]

GENDER ROLES

Do you ever find yourself using phrases such as "female police officer" or "male nurse"? Today, there are plenty of females in law enforcement and numerous males in mid-level health care, but certain occupations still carry strong connotations to gender. These associations are due to **gender roles**, society's expectations of how males and females should think and act. Men are assumed to be tough and authoritarian (policemen, politicians, businessmen), whereas women are nurturing and tolerant (nurses, social workers, housewives). Although we've seen the rigidity of these roles loosen over the years—studies have even shown a recent increase in social aggression among girls—our society still imposes gender roles on children.[20] For example, toy manufacturers still market fashion dolls to girls and action figures to boys, and parents buy them as such. Although this trend may seem harmless, children's toys are an example of the indoctrination of gender roles at a young age.

How Culture Affects Gender Roles

Anthropologist Margaret Mead conducted provocative research in 1935. She focused on three native tribes in New Guinea: the Arapesh, the Mundgumor, and the Tchambuli.[21] The men and women of the Arapesh tribe exhibited characteristics that would be considered feminine by our standards. The Mundgumor men and women were aggressive and violent, possessing generally masculine qualities. In the Tchambuli tribe, the men accepted domestic positions at home with the children, and women took on the responsibility of providing for the family.[22] This study drew much criticism, however, as many accused Mead of doctoring her results to show what she had hoped to find—that gender is culturally constructed.[23]

Other studies have found that in most societies, traditional gender roles have degrees of variation. In 1937, anthropologist George Murdock studied more than 200 societies and found that women performed tasks such as farming and construction in almost as many societies as men did. Although not all cultures share the same customs, Murdock's findings showed definite cross-cultural similarities in the roles of men and women.[24]

History of Gender Differences
ROOTED IN RELIGION

Throughout the world, gender differences and stratification often have their roots in religion. Recall that early Christians blamed Eve for the fall of man because, as the story goes, she tempts Adam into eating fruit from the Tree of Knowledge. Over time, Christianity transferred this belief to society, as philosophers and theologians often blamed women for the problems of men. In the 15th century, for example, women were considered to be prone to becoming witches because of their weak nature.[25] For most of history, Christian women were seen as inferior to men because they were beings that could tempt men away from God.[26] Gender inequality stems from and contributes to religious beliefs around the world.

PRESENT IN THE EARLY COLONIES

Many of these same themes followed women to the colonization of the Americas. Although women were important to the functioning of the new society (and, indeed, the early colonies didn't become stable until the formation of family units), they were still treated as second-class citizens who couldn't own property or inherit land. Colonization was a small step toward female rights, however, as all hands were needed to survive and prosper. Women and men worked the land together, becoming partners in the settlement of the United States.

EFFECTS OF THE FEMINIST MOVEMENT

Feminism is a philosophy based on the political, social, and economic equality of the sexes, specifically a woman's right to have the same opportunities as a man. The term typically refers to the collection of social movements and theories regarding gender differences. The first milestone in the feminist movement was Mary Wollstonecraft's publication of *A Vindication of the Rights of Woman* in 1792. Her manifesto, one of the earliest examples of feminist thought, argued for a woman's right to an education. Wollstonecraft's work set off a surge of other forms of feminist thought, which emerged in three distinct "waves."

1 The first wave was started by the progressive thinking of early feminists such as Susan B. Anthony and Elizabeth Cady

Stanton. The women of this era protested legal inequality. Their efforts helped lead to passage of the 19th Amendment (women's suffrage), which was ratified in 1920.

2 The second wave of feminism began in the 1960s with the rise of the women's liberation movement. It was characterized by feminist thinkers such as Betty Friedan, who, in her book *The Feminine Mystique*, introduced the idea that a woman could and should seek personal fulfillment outside the home and family. This era also brought to light other controversial issues such as women's reproductive rights and domestic violence.

3 The third wave of feminism began in the early 1990s and branched out to protect the rights of minorities and underprivileged women. Feminist leaders such as Maxine Hong Kingston, Gloria Anzaldua, bell hooks (née Gloria Jean Watkins), and Audre Lorde are typically associated with the third wave. These women called attention to how race, capitalism, and gender affect the lives of women throughout the world.[27]

Does Gender Make a Difference?
EDUCATION

It's a decades-old strategy: A guy signs up for a women's studies course in college—knowing he will be completely outnumbered by girls—in an effort to improve his odds of getting a date. This is a clever idea, but generally unnecessary in today's educational environment. As the number of female college students continues to climb, a guy may find himself outnumbered by girls in most courses, not just those with the words *women* or *feminist* in the title. As you can see in the graph on the next page, 52 percent of college graduates are women. Women outnumber men when it comes to master's degrees as well, and they are less likely to drop out of school at an early age.[28]

Women from the Silent Generation or even baby boomers would find these statistics mind-boggling. Sixty years ago, higher education was still trying to break out of the old boy's club mentality. Even women who did attend college found their education vastly different from that of their male peers. Women were encouraged to pursue more "feminine" fields such as

> ⋁ Studying different religions has taught us that **gender inequality is not only an ancient tradition, but a universal one as well.**

The History of Women in Religion

Judaism

The primary role of the woman was to act as wife and keeper of the house. Women were discouraged from pursuing higher education and religious studies because of the effect it might have on their "duties." Their participation in synagogue life was strictly limited, allowing men to dominate public life.

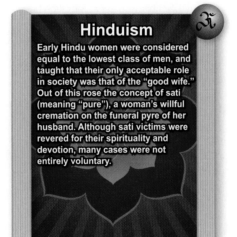

Hinduism

Early Hindu women were considered equal to the lowest class of men, and taught that their only acceptable role in society was that of the "good wife." Out of this rose the concept of sati (meaning "pure"), a woman's willful cremation on the funeral pyre of her husband. Although sati victims were revered for their spirituality and devotion, many cases were not entirely voluntary.

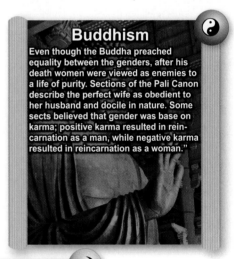

Buddhism

Even though the Buddha preached equality between the genders, after his death women were viewed as enemies to a life of purity. Sections of the Pali Canon describe the perfect wife as obedient to her husband and docile in nature. Some sects believed that gender was base on karma; positive karma resulted in reincarnation as a man, while negative karma resulted in reincarnation as a woman."

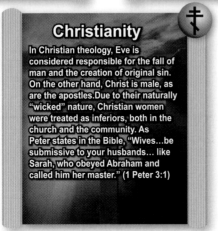

Christianity

In Christian theology, Eve is considered responsible for the fall of man and the creation of original sin. On the other hand, Christ is male, as are the apostles. Due to their naturally "wicked" nature, Christian women were treated as inferiors, both in the church and the community. As Peter states in the Bible, "Wives...be submissive to your husbands... like Sarah, who obeyed Abraham and called him her master." (1 Peter 3:1)

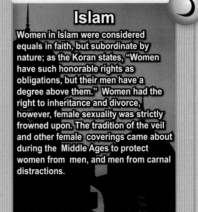

Islam

Women in Islam were considered equals in faith, but subordinate by nature; as the Koran states, "Women have such honorable rights as obligations, but their men have a degree above them." Women had the right to inheritance and divorce, however, female sexuality was strictly frowned upon. The tradition of the veil and other female coverings came about during the Middle Ages to protect women from men, and men from carnal distractions.

Source: Sen, Mala. *Death by fire: sati, dowry, death, and female infanticide in modern India*. London: Weidenfeld & Nicolsen, Ltd., 2001; de Silva, Swarna, "The Place of Women in Buddhism: A Talk given to the Midlands Buddhist Society (UK) on Sanghamittâ Day 1988," June 1994, http://www.enabling.org/ia/vipassana/Archive/D/DeSilva/WomenInBuddhism/womenInBuddhismSwarnaDeSilva.html#chap3; (1 Peter 3:1 New International Version); (Sura 2:228) (Qur'an 2:228)

INCOME GAP is the difference in earnings between different demographics.

teaching, nursing, or art, whereas males were encouraged to study more scientific and logic-based subjects. The same way of thinking still exists today, as men earn the majority of science and engineering degrees.[29]

If women are achieving better educations than before, why are women's salaries still significantly lower than men's? Census data show that the **income gap**—the difference in earnings between different demographics—between men and women actually becomes wider with higher levels of educational background. Can it be that a woman's education is not valued as much as a man's?

WORK

The income gap between men and women has created a great divide in the workplace. Currently, women earn just $0.77 for every $1 that a male counterpart makes. That means that if a male project manager at an accounting firm makes $75,000 per year, a female worker with the same position in the same metropolitan area might only make $57,750 per year.[30] With 58.6 percent of women aged 16 years or older currently employed, that results in a lot of missing wages.[31] This gap isn't only a financial burden; it stifles a woman's career advancement and devalues her efforts. The choices that women make in the workplace do have an effect on how much they're paid. Many women choose positions that offer flexibility rather than a high salary, and avoid extensive overtime or business travel because they have responsibilities at home with their children or aging parents. They also tend to take breaks in their work careers due to maternity leave or child-rearing duties. In a 2007 study conducted by sociologists at Cornell University, researchers found that mothers are often penalized in the workplace. The researchers found that working mothers are perceived by employers as less competent and are generally offered lower starting salaries than equally qualified childless women. Men, however, aren't similarly penalized for being parents.[32]

POLITICS

Actress Glenn Close portrayed the vice president of the United States in the movie *Air Force One*, and Geena Davis portrayed the president in the short-lived TV series *Commander in Chief*, but we have yet to see a female fill either role in real life. Lately, we've come close. The 2008 presidential election was groundbreaking on many levels, but besides the realization of the first African American president, there was also the potential for the first female president or vice president of the United States. Although Hillary Clinton lost the Democratic nomination to Barack Obama, Clinton made political strides by becoming the first female to be a viable candidate. And like Geraldine Ferraro, Walter Mondale's running mate in the 1984 election, Sarah Palin also had a chance at the vice presidency.

Discrepancies exist outside of the executive branch as well. Currently, only 17 of the 100 members of the Senate are women; in the House of Representatives, women also account for only 17 percent.[33] These statistics could be due to the myth that women, by nature, are uninterested in politics. However, voting records have shown that this isn't true.[34] There's also the belief that the structure of a woman's life (that is, her responsibility to her family) doesn't lend itself to the rigors of political office. This impression assumes that male politicians don't have similar obligations to their families. Why was Governor Palin seen by some as unfit for office because of her infant, whereas President Obama is fit to be both a father and the Commander in Chief? Unfortunately, women must face the same double standard in politics as they do in educational institutions, social settings, and the workplace.

Education Attainment of the Population by Gender

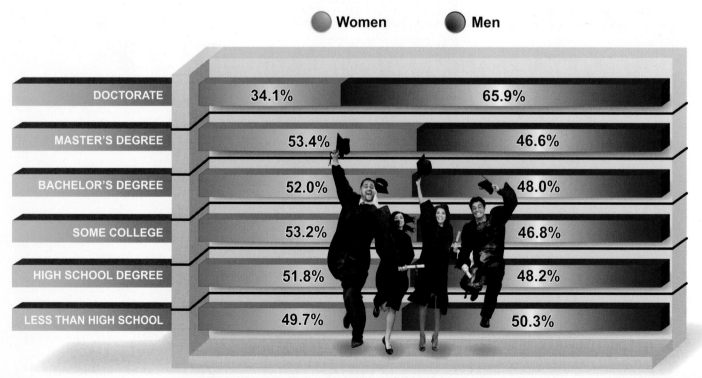

● Women   ● Men

	Women	Men
DOCTORATE	34.1%	65.9%
MASTER'S DEGREE	53.4%	46.6%
BACHELOR'S DEGREE	52.0%	48.0%
SOME COLLEGE	53.2%	46.8%
HIGH SCHOOL DEGREE	51.8%	48.2%
LESS THAN HIGH SCHOOL	49.7%	50.3%

Source: U.S. Census Bureau, "Educational Attainment in the United States: 2008,"http://www.census.gov/population/www/socdemo/education/cps2008.html.

History of Women in Politics

Martha Washington becomes First Lady during her husband's presidency in 1789 and remains in the White House until 1797.

Mary Wollstonecraft writes *A Vindication of the Rights of Woman* in 1792.

Victoria Woodhull is the first woman to run for president in 1872. She runs on the Equal Rights ticket.

In 1917, Jeannette Rankin (R-MT) becomes the first female member of the U.S. House of Representatives.

In 1981, President Reagan appoints Sandra Day O'Connor to be the first female Supreme Court Judge. She serves in this position until her retirement in 2006.

In 1984, Geraldine Ferraro (D-NY) becomes the first woman to win a vice presidential nomination on a major party ticket.

Senator Hilary Clinton competes with current President Barack Obama for the Democratic nomination; for the first time, a woman has an actual chance of becoming president. Clinton now serves as the U.S. Secretary of State.

Governor Sarah Palin runs for Vice President on Senator John McCain's ticket during the 2008 presidential election. Once again, however, a woman falls short of attaining office in the White House.

[Source: "Milestones in Politics for American Women" February 13, 2008, http://uspolitics.about.com/od/usgovernment/a/women_milestone.htm, Accessed June 18, 2009.]

∧
∧ Although you might not think it from election results, **women account for 56 percent of**
∧ **registered voters,** making them a demographic worth paying attention to. **If so many women vote, why are there so few in political positions?**

HEALTH

As the inequalities between men and women illustrate, being male can be an advantage in society. However, females have one major benefit—a longer life expectancy. On average, women have a life expectancy seven year longer than men. Is it a healthier lifestyle, safer types of work, or some biological advantage? Answers vary, but the fact is that women start to outnumber men by around age 35, and the gap continues to grow with age. Older women greatly outnumber older men in most countries, making the health and socioeconomic problems of the elderly essentially the problems of women.[35]

Despite a longer life expectancy, women often suffer from health disadvantages. Heart disease is the number-one killer of women in the United States, the causes of which may not be completely biological. According to a study conducted by the American Heart Association's Council on Clinical Cardiology, female patients are not always given the same aggressive treatment that their male counterparts receive for heart attacks. This is due in part to the faulty idea that women are not as susceptible to heart attacks as men are. This, coupled with the fact that their symptoms often appear to be less severe, causes many deaths because of lack of proper treatment.[36]

think social problems: WHAT ARE THE THEORIES OF GENDER RELATED TO SOCIAL PROBLEMS?

Feminist Theory

Feminist theory examines how gender affects the experiences and opportunities of men and women. Feminists seek to achieve the following: (1) greater equality in the workplace and in schools; (2) equal opportunities for men and women; (3) a world in which rights, opportunities, and income are no longer stratified by gender; and (4) an end to sexual violence.

Although the central theme of feminism is equality for all people, there are different types of feminism that have specific goals or methods for achieving equality. Feminism can be separated into many different categories; for now we'll focus on the two major groups—radical feminism and liberal feminism.

Liberal feminists tend not to stray from the primary focus of feminism: equal rights. They believe that women should receive equal pay for equal work, have the right to hold political office, be given the same educational and professional opportunities as men, and be safe from domestic violence. Liberal feminists share an overarching philosophy for how women should expect to be treated.

Radical feminists are just that—radical. They believe in the same core concepts as liberal feminists, but add new ideals to the philosophy. They point out the division between men and women in all societies and see men as the social dominators. Radical feminists blame the firmly rooted patriarchal system for all forms of oppression in society, including class oppression and racial oppression. Their views lead them to believe that radical action must be taken as well. Some suggest that women should avoid taking on any traditional roles through marriage or childbearing; others suggest that women should avoid participating in capitalism because its structure favors men. As it stands, there are far more liberal feminists than radical ones.

WRAP YOUR MIND AROUND THE THEORY

Gender roles can be rigid, but **often complement each other.** Does this **help or hinder the lives of men and women?**

According to conflict theory, those with power often use it to dominate others. Even in today's world, the majority of societal power still lies in the hands of men. **Can men benefit by keeping women in a subordinate position?**

FUNCTIONALISM

Functionalists view society as a system of many parts working together to form a whole. When studying gender, functionalists examine how different gender roles complement each other and help society run smoothly. If Mom washes the dishes and Dad patches up the drywall, the house remains in good shape. Children watch and learn from their parents and step into these roles early on in life. Girls are often expected to help their mothers with domestic chores, whereas boys are primed to work outside the house, as their fathers do.[37]

FEMINIST THEORY

Women are treated differently than men because society in general views women as physically, mentally, and emotionally weak. This gives rise to the belief that women are incapable of performing selected tasks or of making certain accomplishments. Women also suffer from a "glass ceiling," which keeps them from rising to the top of the corporate world, and experience an income gap regardless of ability or education.

CONFLICT THEORY

Conflict theorists are interested in the struggle for power between groups, especially economic power. In general, women are more likely to be poor than their male counterparts, a trend referred to as the "feminization of poverty." This is a result of the job and wage discrimination present in the system. One of the earliest theorists to note this oppression was Friedrich Engels, who suggested that women were actually the first group to be oppressed.

WHAT ARE THE SOCIAL PROBLEMS ASSOCIATED WITH GENDER?

SYMBOLIC INTERACTIONISM

Symbolic interactionists look at the micro-interactions of daily life and how they influence the ways in which we perceive an issue. Do we define certain tasks as "men's" or "women's" work? As I write this, I'm preparing dinner for my family—does that make me less of a man? In today's society we're far more fluid with our gender role definitions than we were 50 years ago. What's changed? Over time, societal views on household labor have been modified. How does this affect the lives of present-day men and women?

Indra Nooyi is the CEO of PepsiCo, a Fortune 500 company. Even so, **only two other women are on the PepsiCo board of directors.** How can women break through the corporate glass ceiling?

How we define the roles of men and women determines how they act in society. What does it mean if a man stays home while his wife goes to work?

discover solutions to social problems:
WHAT SOCIAL POLICIES ARE IN PLACE TO PREVENT DOMESTIC VIOLENCE?

Preventing Domestic Violence

When oppression starts to cause physical, emotional, sexual, or psychological harm, that oppression becomes abuse. A 2000 survey by The National Institute of Justice and the Centers for Disease Control and Prevention found that a large number of these crimes go unreported. Generally, only one fifth of rapes, one quarter of physical assaults, and one half of stalking committed against women by their intimate partners are reported.[38] Unfortunately, some victims do not understand enough about domestic abuse to know to seek help.

Victims should know that abuse is about power and control, and it can come in many forms. Some abusers use intimidation to harm their victim. This may not be by physical assault, but through words or phrases that suggest that something bad will happen if the victim does not follow the abuser's commands. Whether or not the abuser actually follows through with the threats doesn't matter—the threat itself is abuse. If there are children involved in the relationship, they may be used as pawns in the struggle. Threats can be made against the children, and sometimes the children themselves can be used to relay threats to the victim. Abuse can occur through no contact at all, simply by isolating the victim and making her feel insecure and alone. And of course, any physical attack is considered abuse. Whether the physical interaction is meant to be playful or harmful, if it is unwanted, it is abuse.[39]

Resources are available to help the victims, but victims are often too scared or ashamed to come forward or don't understand that what they're experiencing is illegal and undeserved. In response to the rising concern about these crimes, offenders are receiving longer sentences. In addition, law enforcement and community organizations have initiated campaigns against sexual assault and domestic violence. Shelters for battered women give victims a safe place to recuperate, and counseling services help them with self-esteem issues as well as other psychological trauma brought on by abuse. It is important to help men, women, and families suffering from abuse because damages extend far beyond bruises.

> **TITLE IX** is a 1972 educational amendment that prohibits the exclusion of any person from participation in an education program on the basis of gender.

Title IX

In 1972, the Patsy T. Mink Equal Opportunity in Education Act, commonly known as **Title IX**, was passed in Congress. A revolutionary document, Title IX prohibits the exclusion of any person from participation in an educational program on the basis of gender. The most extreme effect, and the one that gave the act its controversial reputation, was the allocation of funding to female extracurricular activities, specifically sports.

Before 1972, very few girls were involved in sports, partly because very few organized athletic programs existed for them. My wife, who attended school in the 1970s, points out that girls at her school had only track and field available to them. Today, it's very different. In the decades since Title IX was passed, the number of female athletes has skyrocketed.

Even though women's participation in athletics has increased, the goal of equality has still not been met. Although girls have more

MAKE CONNECTIONS

Sexism, Discrimination, and Gender Roles

Chapter 11 discusses sexuality, which is a factor in gender roles. Our perceptions of what is sexually appropriate are determined by social customs and expectations of gender. For example, society finds it acceptable for boys to flaunt their conquests. They are admired by their peers for showing sexual confidence, whereas if a girl brags about her partners, she is considered promiscuous. In general, women are viewed as objects that should not have control or power over sexual actions. This double standard is reinforced in the media, especially in the music industry.

Songs such as Necro's "Who's Ya Daddy?" make it seem cool and manly to treat women as sexual objects.

Woman in general experience oppression and discrimination in many parts of their lives. For women who are of a minority race, the oppression and discrimination is compounded by the challenges they face as a person of color, as you learned in Chapter 3. African American women have been referred to as the "mules of the world" because they have to carry so many burdens that society has placed on them. Other minority women face similar difficulties as they attempt to overcome the obstacles put in front of them due to their gender and race.

Women are constantly battling the glass ceiling. They have been able to achieve higher levels in business, political, and educational institutions, but many of the top positions are still held by men. There are few female CEOs in corporate America, and we have yet to elect a female president. The fact that a woman is limited to a certain level of success is worsened by the fact that women only earn $0.77 for every dollar a man earns. This income inequality, which is also discussed in Chapter 2, is especially burdensome for single mothers who provide the only source of income for their families.

Changes in Women's Athletic Participation

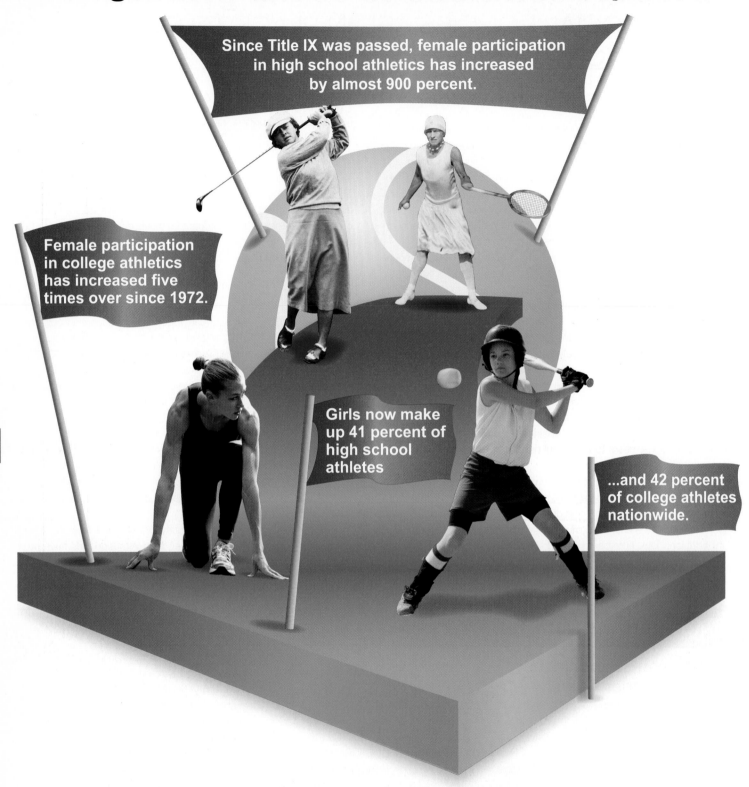

Since Title IX was passed, female participation in high school athletics has increased by almost 900 percent.

Female participation in college athletics has increased five times over since 1972.

Girls now make up 41 percent of high school athletes

...and 42 percent of college athletes nationwide.

Sources: NWLC: National Women's Law Center, "Title IX and Women's Athletic Opportunity: A Nation's Promise Yet to be Fulfilled," July 2008, http://www.nwlc.org/pdf/Nation's%20Promise%20July%202008.pdf; NWLC: National Women's Law Center, "The Battle for Gender Equality in Athletics in Elementary and Secondary Schools," June 2008, http://www.nwlc.org/pdf/Battle%20final.pdf.

∧
∧ **The Patsy T. Mink Equal Opportunity in Education Act,** otherwise known as Title IX, **has
∧ provided girls with the funds needed to increase their participation in school sports.** What might the future hold for female athletes?

Title IX

In college sports, women usually play against women and men usually play against men. But when university funds become an issue, sometimes men and women have to compete against each other in order to get their equal share. What does each side have to say?

Pro

- More funds mean more opportunities for female athletes, which increase women's chances of pursuing a college education. In addition, female student athletes are more likely to stay in school and achieve higher grades than women who do not play sports.[42]
- Equal funding is an equal right. Women make up 42 percent of Division I varsity college athletes; thus, financial support should equal their presence.[43]
- Title IX has led to more women and girls participating in sports. Increased athletic participation has been proven to decrease risk of developing certain health problems; women and girls who play sports also have higher levels of self-esteem.[44]

Con

- Title IX takes away money from men's sports, which are the ones people want to watch.
- Women's sports should follow the same guidelines as men's sports and become self-supporting.
- Equal opportunities and equal funding do not necessarily mean the same thing. Women's sports have the same fund-raising opportunities as men's sports; they just cannot reach their goals.

<<< Before Title IX, men's and women's sports did not receive equal funding. **Does equal funding mean equal rights?**

opportunities now than they did 40 years ago, they still fail to receive equal funding for sports programs in their schools. Even though women outnumber men on college campuses, they receive 45 percent of Division I scholarship money and only 32 percent of recruiting dollars, on average.[40] Why? Because, although Title IX requires equal treatment of male and female teams, it does not require schools to spend equal amounts of money on male and female athletes.[41] Many schools are wary of investing in sports that so few members of the public have historically been interested in. Every dollar that's given to a female sports team has to be taken away from a male one. Both sides of this argument are discussed in more detail in the Pro & Con feature above.

From Classroom to Community Volunteering for the Abused

Renee was inspired by a project in her graduate sociology class and decided to do some volunteer work at a local metropolitan shelter for female victims of domestic violence. Although the volunteer work was part of her master's degree, this subject hit close to home for Renee. Walking into the shelter and seeing the battered women brought back painful memories of abuse from her ex-husband.

"I got married when I was 19 to a man I thought I loved at the time . . . he was charming, but had a terrible temper. I put up with his abuse for three years, but once he started abusing our daughter, I'd had enough and we went to a women's shelter."

For Renee, staying at the shelter was a life-changing experience. Her counselor there worked with her to sort out the issues that had led her to stay with an abusive husband for so long. "My counselor opened my eyes to the fact that I deserved better treatment than I got from him, and helped me understand the causes of my low self-esteem and ways to improve it."

While volunteering, Renee answered phone calls from women in abusive households, served meals, and filed intake paperwork. She also got to spend time with the women and share her personal experience. This was the most rewarding part for her.

"I made a real connection with some of the women in the shelter, and I really hope that sharing my experience with domestic abuse and my recovery from it made a difference to them . . . if I can touch just one woman's life by showing her that she deserves better treatment, I'll be satisfied."

HOW DOES A SOCIETY DEAL WITH GENDER? 56

gender is the behavioral, cultural, and psychological traits associated with being male or female; stratification exists in many areas of society as a result of gender differences and how society perceives those differences

WHAT ARE THE THEORIES OF GENDER RELATED TO SOCIAL PROBLEMS? 61

feminist theory: gender affects the experiences and opportunities of men and women; inequalities in areas such as work, education, opportunities, and income are based on gender

functionalism: society places men and women in different roles; these differences help maintain society

conflict theory: capitalism is intertwined with patriarchy; women, who tend to make less money than men, are locked in a cycle that keeps them subservient

symbolic interactionism: men and women's perceptions of gender—that is, "doing gender—cause them to self-select certain "gender-appropriate" roles and careers

WHAT SOCIAL POLICIES ARE IN PLACE TO PREVENT DOMESTIC VIOLENCE? 63

shelters, counseling services, campaigns against domestic violence, and stricter sentencing for those who are convicted of domestic abuse

get the topic: HOW DOES A SOCIETY DEAL WITH GENDER?

Theory

FEMINIST THEORY 62

- women are typically treated differently than men because society as a whole views women as physically, mentally, and emotionally weak
- women are seen as incapable of performing particular tasks or of accomplishing certain goals
- women have trouble getting on the frontlines of the corporate battlefield; they are too emotional for the cutthroat nature of corporate business

FUNCTIONALISM 62

- functionalists examine how gender roles affect society
- we tend to view men and women as two separate species; they are each given roles that play to their traditional strengths
- a woman who wants to pursue a career in law enforcement may find it hard to prove that she can be just as "tough" as a man; a male hairdresser may likewise find it difficult to overcome established gender roles

CONFLICT THEORY 62

- when it comes to the struggle between men and women, conflict theorists see men as the victors. Their role as the providers gives them power and control
- even when women do provide financial assistance, they tend to make less money than their husbands, and so continue to play the subordinate role in the family
- Engels argued that women were actually the first group to be oppressed

SYMBOLIC INTERACTIONISM 62

- today, women seem to prefer to have a career in addition to having a family
- society has come to view "homemaker" as an oppressed position
- by no longer fulfilling that position, women are no longer oppressed

Key Terms

gender refers to the behavioral, cultural, and psychological traits associated with being male or female. *56*

sex is the biological makeup of males or females, especially in regard to their reproductive organs and physical structures. *56*

gender identity is our perception of ourselves as male or female. *57*

patriarchy is a social system in which men control a majority of the power and exert authority over women and children. *57*

matriarchy is a social system in which women are the main authority and hold power over men. *57*

sexism is the belief that one sex is superior to the other. *57*

gender roles are society's expectations of how males and females should think and act. *58*

feminism is a philosophy based on the political, social, and economic equality of the sexes, specifically a woman's right to have the same opportunities as a man. *58*

income gap is the difference in earnings between different demographics. *60*

Title IX is a 1972 educational amendment that prohibits the exclusion of any person from participation in an education program on the basis of gender. *63*

Sample Test Questions

These multiple-choice questions are similar to those found in the test bank that accompanies this textbook.

1. Which of the following is *most likely* a driving force behind cases of domestic abuse?

   a. Because of the Lolita effect, some men see violence as "sexy."
   b. Certain men have a need for power and control.
   c. Most women do not seek help until oppression has turned to violence.
   d. Women often see themselves as subservient and provoke men into asserting their dominance.

2. Choose the situation that *best* demonstrates "doing gender."

   a. A boy learning to cook pancakes
   b. A boy and girl playing "house" together
   c. A girl playing hopscotch with her friends
   d. A boy being teased for wearing pink

3. Which of the statements below is *not* an argument against Title IX?

   a. Equal opportunities are not the same as equal funding.
   b. Both men's and women's sports should be self-supporting.
   c. Women and men who play sports both report high levels of self-esteem.
   d. The amendment takes money away from sports that more people want to watch.

4. What is the percentage of matriarchies to patriarchies in the world?

   a. 60% to 40%
   b. 20% to 80%
   c. 15% to 85%
   d. 0% to 100%

5. According to conflict theorists,

   a. poverty is primarily a female problem.
   b. gender roles are necessary for society to run smoothly.
   c. women suffer from a "glass ceiling" in the corporate world.
   d. children associate themselves with their parents early on in life.

ESSAY

1. What is your perspective on Title IX? Does equal funding mean equal opportunities?

2. Compare female oppression in places such as Egypt and Somalia with that in the United States. How are women treated mentally and/or physically like objects?

3. Think of some examples of the Lolita effect in today's media. How might idolization of these stars affect a child's gender role formation?

4. Was the ad campaign staring Keira Knightley too over-the-top? How do you think victims of domestic violence might view the commercial?

5. People rarely talk about reverse sexism. Do you think the current emphasis on feminism in our society has had a negative effect on men?

WHERE TO START YOUR RESEARCH PAPER

For information on legislation that expands opportunities for girls and women, visit http://www.nwlc.org/

To view the controversial domestic violence ad featuring actress Keira Knightley, go to http://www.guardian.co.uk/media/video/2009/apr/02/womens-aid-keira-knightley-ad

To learn more about how to prevent domestic violence, visit http://www.domesticviolence.org/

For additional links about domestic violence, go to http://www.nlm.nih.gov/medlineplus/domesticviolence.html

For facts about female genital mutilation and the international response to this practice, go to the World Health Organization's site at http://www.who.int/mediacentre/factsheets/fs241/en/

ANSWERS: 1. b; 2. c; 3. c; 4. d; 5. a

Remember to check www.thethinkspot.com for additional information, downloadable flashcards, and other helpful resources.

AGING: SOCIAL PROBLEMS OF GROWING OLD

WHO ARE THE AGING POPULATION, AND WHAT DOES AGEISM MEAN IN OUR CULTURE?

WHAT THEORIES EXIST ABOUT THE AGING PROCESS?

HOW DOES SOCIETY DEAL WITH SPECIFIC PROBLEMS OF AGING?

Americans

are changing the game plan for retirement, with millions laboring right past the traditional retirement age and working into their late 60s and beyond.

While the average retirement age remains 63, that standard may soon be going the way of the gold watch — a trend expected to accelerate as baby boomers close in on retirement without sufficient savings . . .

. . . [F]or Melissa Fodor, a retired travel agent who works part-time as a caregiver for the elderly, the extra work "keeps my head above water" and there's no end in sight to that financial need at age 68.

Although the work is satisfying, she confides, "Financially I'm kind of scared most of the time. Because what should happen if my health and my body fail?"

Fodor says that "to work is to have dignity." But she has little choice but to keep laboring because otherwise she couldn't pay her bills.

Growing evidence documents that people are working longer as they live longer. Twenty-nine percent of people in their late 60s were working in 2006, up from 18 percent in 1985, according to the Bureau of Labor Statistics. Nearly 6 million workers last year were 65 or over. Over the next decade, the number of 55-and-up workers is expected to rise at more than five times the rate of the overall workforce, the BLS reported. A slowing economy and stock market, squeezing funds set aside for retirement, also are contributing. In an April survey conducted for AARP, 27 percent of workers age 45 and over, and 32 percent of those 55–64 said they had pushed back their planned retirement date because of the economic downturn . . .

. . . [F]odor ended her more than three-decade career as a travel agent when work dried up following the 9/11 attacks, but hasn't stopped working through her 60s. First she sold paint at a home improvement store for seven years. Now she puts in 17 hours a week as a certified nursing assistant and another 10 to 15 hours walking dogs and pet sitting.

Divorced and with no children, she says she will have to work "forever" to make up for a lack of savings since Social Security doesn't go far enough to make ends meet. Caring for seniors, a job she loves, pays just $9 an hour and dog walking pays less. Squeezed by rising prices and still $20,000 in debt on her condo, she stopped buying meat, beer and pricier vegetables and cheeses this year and is making other cutbacks. "I feel blessed with the good health that I have. But I'm a little bit bitter because I don't think I should be scared financially at 68," she said, adding that she blames only herself for not saving more.

What disturbs her even more than her situation is all the men in their 60s, 70s, and even 80s that still have to work at Lowe's.

After losing their jobs as engineers and scientists, they now stock shelves just to survive. But they hide when fellow retirees come in, she said, because they don't want people they knew from their country clubs and higher-income jobs to see them.

When people work out of desperation and not choice, in other words, it carries little dignity. "That's just not right," she said. "That hurts me to see that. Some of these people are supporting their grandchildren."[1]

---One reason I like the idea of being a college professor is that it's a job that I can do for a long time.

And the good news is, people are living longer and enjoying better health than ever. If I take care of myself, I will get to teach my classes for years to come. From 1982 to 1999, the percentage of senior citizens who had chronic disabilities dropped from 26 percent to less than 20 percent. People experience chronic illnesses such as lung and heart disease and arthritis about 10 to 25 years later than they used to. Even the onset of dementia seems to be receding.[2] This means that retirees have time to embrace the freedom of old age. They can travel or take up new hobbies. Some may just want to sit back, relax in a hammock, and sip lemonade. However they choose to spend their time, they've worked hard and earned the right to enjoy their golden years.

Unfortunately, this is not the reality for many retired people. The problems facing seniors are multifaceted, and financial instability often lies at the source. Many seniors must return to work, or remain working, for much longer than they had planned. They simply can't sustain themselves on their pensions and Social Security income alone. Family responsibilities also hinder seniors, with some grandparents taking on the role of parents once again. It's difficult to take a golf trip to the Florida Keys when you're stuck at home watching your grandchild so his parents can work a second job. According to the U.S. Census Bureau, 2.4 million grandparents were the primary caregivers for their grandchildren in 2000.[3] The number of grandparents residing with their families is also increasing. The bottom line is that older adults must battle a greater variety of obstacles nowadays than generations of seniors have in the past.

get the topic: WHO ARE THE AGING POPULATION, AND WHAT DOES AGEISM MEAN IN OUR CULTURE?

AGEISM is prejudice and discrimination based solely on age.

Demographics

The increasing size of the aging population affects many aspects of our society, challenging families, health care providers, and policymakers to meet the needs of aging individuals. So, who makes up the aging population of the United States?

The U.S. Census Bureau defines the elderly population as 65 and older. In 2000, this demographic made up 12 percent of the total U.S. population. As you learned in Chapter 1, the U.S. Census tracks the population every 10 years; imagine how the numbers will have changed by the 2010 survey. Let's take a look at some interesting projections provided by the Bureau:

- The nation will be more racially and ethnically diverse, as well as much older, by the mid-21st century.

- In 2030, when all of the baby boomers (babies born from approximately 1946 to 1964) are 65 or older, nearly one in five U.S. residents will be considered elderly. This age group will increase to 88.5 million in 2050, more than doubling since 2008 (38.7 million).[4]

- The 85-and-older population will more than triple from 5.4 million to 19 million between 2008 and 2050.[5]

Why the big changes? The most obvious reason is that people are living longer than they once did. In 1900, the combined life expectancy for men and women in the United States was 47 years. In 2005, it was greater than 77 years.[6] How might the prospect of living a longer life influence a person? Historically, people did important things at much earlier ages. For example, Thomas Jefferson was 33 years old when he wrote the Declaration of Independence, and Napoleon Bonaparte was 30 when he led a coup d'état and took over the reins of France.[7] Today, it is not uncommon for people to make major decisions and changes later in life. For example, one student of mine came back to college at the age of 55. She said, "I've got 20 years left to work, and I want to be a teacher."

When sociologists talk about the elderly, they generally divide the group into different categories: the "young old" and the "old old." The young old are people who range in age from 65 to 75. This group is generally healthy and comprise an active group of senior citizens. As a group, the young old tend to have fewer social problems than the old old. The old old are those over the age of 75. Although some in this group remain vibrant and active, others suffer from serious health concerns. Still others have problems with maintaining their daily functioning and living independently. The "old old" tend to have more problems and need more social support.

How might factors such as increased longevity and increasing numbers of older people influence our society? What are some social problems that can you see on the horizon?

Ageism

We all know a little something about the "isms" in society: capitalism, communism, atheism, and so on. "Isms" represent systems of beliefs and usually encompass stereotypes as well. We're about to discuss the next big "ism" creeping to the forefront of social stereotypes: ageism. **Ageism**—prejudice and discrimination based solely on age—is likely to become more prevalent due in part to the growing

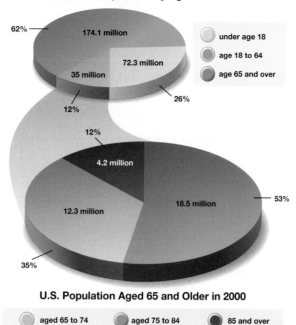

The Aging Population of America
Total U.S. Population by Age in 2000

62% — 174.1 million
72.3 million
35 million
26%
12%
12%
4.2 million
18.5 million — 53%
12.3 million
35%

- under age 18
- age 18 to 64
- age 65 and over

U.S. Population Aged 65 and Older in 2000

- aged 65 to 74
- aged 75 to 84
- 85 and over

Sources: Julie Meyer, "Age: 2000," *Census 2000 Brief*, U.S. Census Bureau, http://www.census.gov/prod/2001pubs/c2kbr01-12.pdf, Accessed June 20, 2009; Yvonne J. Gist and Lisa I. Hetzel, "We the People: Aging in the United States," Economics and Statistics Administration, U.S. Census Bureau, Census 2000 Special Reports, Issued December 2004.

population of older individuals. If older workers are fired strictly because they are old, they are the victims of ageism. If you believe in stereotypes such as "old people can't drive," you're participating in ageism. However, with increasing numbers of elderly people in the United States, we can't take them or their position in society for granted.

According to David Certner, legislative policy director for the American Association of Retired Persons, "We have people who are healthier, who are living longer, and have more economic reasons to stay in the workforce. On the employment side, you have greater demand for *experienced* (older) workers."[8] So, does experience counter ageism? Probably not, since America is a country that values youth—the millions of dollars spent every year on cosmetic surgery alone are a good indicator.[9] According to the American Society of Plastic Surgeons, in 2008 there were more than 3 million cosmetic procedures performed in the United States to people 55 years and older; more than 90 percent of the patients were women. How does one grow old in a culture dedicated to preserving youth?

▶▶ GO GL◉BAL

International Life Expectancy

In the United States, most of us believe that we will inevitably live into our 70's and 80's. The common belief is that medical advances have increased our life expectancy. However, research suggests that this is largely a myth. In fact, studies show that medical science accounts for only three percent of the increase in life expectancy from 1900 to 1970.[15] So, if medical science is *not* the cause of longer life, what is? Researcher Thomas McKeown argues that the increase in life expectancy is mostly due to two factors: First, improvements in the standard of living that provide better housing and food for people; and second, improvements in hygiene that decrease the spread of disease. Although vaccines and other medical procedures have contributed some, the greatest cause of extended longevity is related to these other factors.[16]

Thus, as we look around the globe, we see that in nonindustrialized nations which

are less able to provide these two important improvements, life expectancy remains quite low. In 28 nations around the world, people have less than a 50 percent chance of living to their 60th birthday. The populations of 70 nations have a 50–80 percent chance of living to 60. You may be surprised to hear that the United States ranks 147th of 198 nations in life expectancy—in other words, people in 41 nations are more likely to live past 60 than people in the United States are. Iceland, China, Sweden, and Japan have the highest life expectancies, whereas Zimbabwe, Zambia, and Lesotho have the lowest.[17] Historically, poverty and HIV/AIDS are to blame. But recent figures show a slight decline in the HIV/AIDS epidemic in Zimbabwe and neighboring nations. The key reason now for low life expectancy is an increasingly lower standard of living prompted by the recent economic crisis.[19] Such despairing figures might change your perspective on what it means to grow old—perhaps it's less a chore and more a privilege.

∨
∨
∨ **Many blame Zimbabwe's socioeconomic devastation and low life expectancy rating on the militant actions and polices of Robert Mugabe,** presidential incumbent and head of the Zimbabwe African National Union-Patriotic Front

What Are the Problems That Face an Aging Population?

With an increasingly older population, a host of problems arise. Let's consider some of the major issues.

CURRENT INFLUENCES ON AGEISM

Considering society's infatuation with the young and the beautiful, the media—especially TV—has a huge impact on the spread of ageism. In recent years, reality TV shows have flooded the market due to the fact that they are cheaper to produce than scripted shows.[10] Offhand, you'd probably be able to name at least 10 different programs, but ask yourself this: How many participants over the age of 50 can you name? The cast of most shows are young. When the older generation is included in other TV shows, they're often depicted as hunched-over and wrinkled, with gray hair and liver spots. Such depictions reinforce the negative stereotypes that lead to ageism and distort our perceptions of growing older. Recently I took my elderly father to the doctor. I noticed a distinct difference in the way in which we were treated. Often, nurses and the doctor would ask me questions about his health, rather than him. Since he has no impairment, I found this odd. But this subtle type of ageism is widely used when we assume the elderly to be senile, sick, or unable to function. In fact, sociologist Erdman Palmore suggests that medical professionals frequently engage in subtle ageism when they view the symptoms as simply a matter of being old.[11]

THE HISTORY OF AGEISM

Contemporary ageism is a social problem because of the current socioeconomic implications. But the real problem of aging is rooted in history. According to Thomas R. Cole, author of *The Journey of Life*, we can trace the roots of ageism to the late 1700s and early 1800s. Cole writes that the "revolt against hierarchical authority and the rise of Victorian morality" cultivated a negative view of aging.[12] Only those individuals with the strictest control over their bodies and minds were seen as virtuous; thus, the less an elderly person showed his or her old age, the better he or she was as a human being.

Cole also points out that ageism is a product of mid-19th century health reformers who believed that individuals were healthy by nature and that disease was caused by some offense of natural law. According to Cole, this philosophy "harbored evasive and hostile attitudes about the realities of aging," leaving many middle-class Americans with feelings of indignity and failure as they grew older.[13] Between 1909 and 1935, reformers continued to press the idea that old people were sick, poor, and in need of care in order to support their legislative agendas. Middle-class Americans latched onto this stereotype because of their own fears of aging.[14] It was almost as if old age, poverty, and disease were synonymous *and* contagious, and growing old became "taboo."

Elderly People Living in Poverty

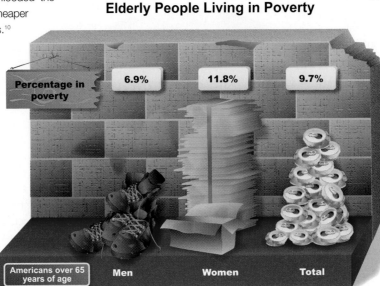

Percentage in poverty

6.9%   11.8%   9.7%

Americans over 65 years of age

Men   Women   Total

Source: U.S. Census Bureau, Current Population Survey, March 2000 Internet Release

INCOME AND POVERTY

It comes as no surprise that as we age, it becomes more difficult to work, and therefore our ability to support ourselves through income decreases. In fact, about one in ten seniors currently lives in poverty. Social Security is one of the main reasons why this percentage is as low as it is; we will explore this more later in the chapter. Income shortfall is no small problem for the elderly. In 2007, 16.1 percent of the elderly lived at 125 percent of the poverty threshold, meaning they were just barely above the poverty line. Clearly, age stratification is a problem for a society with an increasing number of elderly members. How might we provide financial support?

SAFETY AND SECURITY

One problem related to aging is elder abuse. Most of us are aware of child abuse, but not many hear about abuse of the elderly. Elder abuse comes in many forms:

- Physical—deliberate infliction of physical harm

- Sexual—any sexual activity with a person who doesn't consent or isn't capable of providing consent

- Psychological—deliberate infliction of mental or emotional harm, such as insults, verbal assaults, threats, humiliation, or intimidation

- Financial—misuse or theft of material possessions or monetary assets

- Neglect—intentional or unintentional failure of the caregiver to meet the physical, social, or emotional needs of the older person

- Abandonment—desertion[20]

We'll never know the exact number of elder abuse incidents because many cases go unreported. Mental impairment is often the reason why many victims do not report their abuse. Other victims are dependent on the abuser who is often a family member. Women are more at risk than men in regard to abuse, and people over the age of 80 are at the greatest risk of neglect. Research also indicates that the most common perpetrators of elder abuse are family members.[21]

There are no federal guidelines for structuring elder abuse laws, and only some states mandate reporting procedures.[22] However, there are actions you can take if you suspect a caregiver or facility is abusing an elderly person. Adult Protective Services is a state-managed organization that works in conjunction with police to investigate, intervene, and prosecute cases of elder abuse. Elder abuse hotlines exist for the same purpose. National information and help is available through The Administration of Aging and the National Center on Elder Abuse. Check out the links provided at the end of this chapter for more information on these programs.

HOUSING AND RESIDENTIAL CARE

Owning a home is part of the American dream, and if current trends in home ownership continue, most people will live in a home they own when they are elderly. Some may choose to "downsize," meaning that they will sell their larger home and move into one that is smaller, often with a smaller yard. However, most seniors decide to stay in their own homes, a trend referred to as "aging in place." Are those who choose to remain in their homes doing so out of habit or a desire to remain active and involved in their communities? Research is mixed, but it suggests that seniors are far from ready to be "put out to pasture" merely because they've gotten old.[23]

Yet, we know that, at times, the elderly simply cannot take care of themselves at home. As a solution to this problem, other residential options exist to support the elderly who require more assistance. These elderly individuals depend on residential care such as independent living apartments, assisted living programs, and nursing homes.

Senior Care: Behind Closed Doors

The quality of care generally varies depending on who funds the nursing home. The state runs some nursing homes (non-profit facilities), whereas private insurers or residents fund other facilities (for-profit facilities). Historically, state-funded homes provide poorer care than those that are privately funded.[24] In 1987, the government enacted the Nursing Home Reform Act (NHRA) after studies highlighted the abuse and neglect of residents in nursing homes across the United States. Since the NHRA, conditions in nursing homes have improved.[25] Still, we are a long way from an ideal situation. In 1999, the General Accounting Office reported that 25 percent of nursing homes were cited for quality problems that would either harm residents or put them at risk of death. Follow-up inspections showed that nearly half of the homes did not make efforts to improve their care.[26]

>>> **Not all nursing homes abuse, ignore,** administer incorrect (or no) medication, **or unnecessarily restrain their patients.**

Levels of Residential Care

High Level of Care

NURSING HOMES...
- are for seniors who are in poor health.
- provide complete care, including feeding, bathing, and medication administration.
- are staffed with medical personnel on a 24-hour basis.
- accept Medicare, Medicaid, and private insurance.

Mid Level of Care

ASSISTED LIVING COMMUNITIES...
- are for seniors who require more care and are less mobile.
- accommodate tenants who need physical help with daily tasks such as shopping and cooking.
- work in conjunction with nursing homes and hospitals to meet physical needs.
- occasionally accept some types of insurance to cover costs.

Low Level of Care

INDEPENDENT LIVING COMMUNITIES...
- are created with seniors in mind and usually require residents to be at least 65.
- include amenities such as walk-in showers, wide doorways for wheelchair access, and door-to-door garbage pick-up.
- have easy access to parking.
- do not accept Medicare or private insurance.

Lowest Level of Care

INDEPENDENT OR LIVING WITH RELATIVES...
- Many seniors are independent or living with relatives. These seniors typically require the lowest level of care.

Levels of Residential Care Available to the Aging Population

SPECIAL PROBLEMS FOR THE ELDERLY

When you get sick at home, does your mother take care of you? Who will take care of your mother when she's sick and alone? All seniors face a similar problem. What measures have been put in place for elders who don't have anyone to turn to?

Home-Health Care

One type of short-term aid is **home-health care**, medical care provided for patients who cannot leave their homes but have the possibility of improving. For example, an active 75-year-old who has been living alone and managing her chores easily might require short-term aid after sustaining an injury, such as a fractured leg. After surgery, she will recover with time and a prescribed therapy regimen. This patient would be the perfect candidate for home-health care because she is likely to recover fully and return to her daily routine.

Hospice Care

Hospice care is also short-term aid, but only available to patients with six months or less to live. Hospice care does not take measures to prolong life nor does it try to prematurely end a person's life. It simply provides comfort measures to assist the dying person with physical and emotional issues. It works to keep a dying person at home or in a facility of his/her choosing.

For three years, I worked in hospice care. I saw repeatedly what current research seems to confirm—most people wait too long before using hospice services. For example, physicians recommend that patients use hospice for six months prior to death. But studies indicate that most patients actually use the aid for a third of this time or less.[27] The causes for this discrepancy may be due to consumer attitudes, cultural barriers, financial limitations, geography, or awareness. According to a study on the end-of-life experiences of 3,357 terminally ill patients, family members reported that 40 percent were in severe pain prior to their death, and 25 percent experienced moderate to great anxiety or depression before they died.[28] The study found that very few of these patients received hospice care prior to their death. Many of the families felt that hospice would have significantly reduced their own distress, as well as the distress of their loved ones, if they had known about the service.[29] My own experience shows that hospice care can be a respectful way to console people and allow them to die as comfortably as possible.

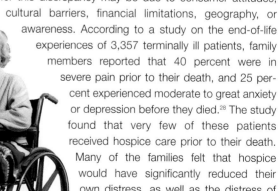

think social problems: WHAT THEORIES EXIST ABOUT THE AGING PROCESS?

DISENGAGEMENT THEORY states that reduced interaction between elderly persons and other members of society is unavoidable, mutual, and acceptable.

ACTIVITY THEORY states that life satisfaction depends on maintaining social involvement by developing new interests, hobbies, roles, and relationships.

CONTINUITY THEORY states that older people seek out familiar areas of their lives and strive to keep those constant as they age, which becomes a strategy for adaptation to the challenges of growing old.

Functionalism: Disengagement Theory

What is the outcome of growing older? What problems arise? Functionalists tend to view aging as a natural shifting of roles. **Disengagement theory** suggests that reduced interaction between elderly persons and other members of society is unavoidable, mutual, and acceptable.[30] To avoid disrupting the social system, society disengages aging individuals, making room for younger people to fill their roles. Disengagement theory also suggests that this ensures that the remaining members of society are freed from regularly having to see the painful side of aging, death, and dysfunction. By disengaging the elderly, society can move forward. Some theorists argue that this process is desirable for not only the young, but also for aging people because it allows these older individuals to prepare themselves for the end of their lives, while at the same time freeing them from the expectations of their previous life. [31]

Critics of disengagement theory dispute that the process is as functional as we might think. For example, do all seniors willingly retire, or are some "forced out"? Furthermore, is it really a good idea to segregate seniors from the rest of the population? Does society pay the cost of losing their wisdom?[32]

Symbolic Interactionism: Activity Theory

Symbolic interactionists believe that each individual will experience the process of aging differently depending on how the envi-

ronment and individual relationships affect him or her. For example, does an aging woman see herself as wise, or just *old*? According to sociologist Charles H. Cooley,[33] people develop a sense of "self" through personal interactions with others. We get a sense of who we are by seeing how others react to us. This developmental process continues until we die; therefore, social interaction is still important for seniors.

In this line of thinking, successful aging is a "multifaceted phenomenon that encompasses not only health but also psychological well-being, role integration, and social engagement."[34] **Activity theory** captures this idea; it states that life satisfaction depends on maintaining societal involvement by developing new interests, hobbies, roles, and relationships. Some sociologists argue that seniors who are still engaged in some form of work are the happiest and have the greatest expressed life satisfaction.[35] Sixty-four-year-old retiree John Lee works as a contractual IT technical support specialist. According to John, he is not working because of financial difficulty. Rather, he likes feeling needed and uses the extra cash to travel and visit his grandchildren.[36]

Growing old is a difficult transition for many seniors. It's a time when they may be losing their freedom, homes, jobs, spouses, or friends. These events could understandably cause depression or dissatisfaction in anyone's life. Robert Atchley suggests that older persons will strive for continuity in their lives. His **continuity theory** argues that older people seek out familiar areas of their lives and strive to keep those constant as they age. This becomes a strategy for adaptation to the challenges of growing old. A person can continue to define his or her self similarly if able to maintain continuity.[37]

Perhaps nowhere is the continuity of values so obvious as it is in the spiritual life of the elderly. Research suggests that spirituality serves to help people adapt and cope with the problems of aging. Atchley finds that keeping routines and having a strong spiritual life help the elderly face the negative aspects of aging, including their ultimate mortality.[38]

∧
∧ Remaining involved in family affairs keeps
∧ seniors active. **Babysitting grandchildren, providing temporary housing, and offering advice can be gratifying and increase overall life satisfaction. These activities are now more prevalent than ever due in part to the "sandwiched" generation;** today's baby boomers find themselves taking care of both their children and their elderly parents.

WRAP YOUR MIND AROUND THE THEORY

According to functionalism, each interrelated part of society works together to serve as a whole. **As older workers retire, they are replaced by younger workers,** which assures a smooth transition to the next generation. **How might this worldview be optimal to everyone except retirees?**

FUNCTIONALISM

Functionalists view society in its entirety; any action that aids the progress of "the whole" is justified. This includes retirement. From a functionalist point of view, retirement makes room for the next generation of workers. Technology is constantly changing and altering the way companies function. Instead of teaching old workers new methods and new technology, companies find that it's easier to replace them with new employees who are seen as more flexible. New employees might also be entering the job with tools already in hand; in other words, learning to switch from a manual system to a computerized system is probably much harder for a 60-year-old than it is for a 20-year-old. New ideas and innovative thinking, provided by younger generations, move society forward. Functionalists have an opinion on retirement as well, viewing it as a buffer from death. If older employees were to stay in the workplace until they died, their passing would hinder workflow and overall morale. To functionalists, retirement is necessary to keep the workforce running with optimal efficiency.

CONFLICT THEORY

Conflict theory suggests that those with power often use it to their advantage, exploiting those with few options. Think back to Melissa Fodor, the retired travel agent who now works as a caregiver and part-time dog walker. In the opening article, she commented on the embarrassment she sees in fellow retirees who now work at Lowe's just to maintain financial stability.[39] Companies that pay close to minimum wage will hire retirees because they can pay them low wages, but receive the work experience of a person who has a long history of maintaining a job. To conflict theorists, situations like these potentially exploit the elderly. This form of ageism penalizes the old and desperate. In this same vein, retirement allows companies to save money by replacing older, more expensive workers with a younger, cheaper workforce. As Fodor remarks, "When people work out of desperation and not choice, it carries little dignity."[40]

WHY DO WE HAVE RETIREMENT?

SYMBOLIC INTERACTIONISM

Symbolic interactionists argue that a retiree has the ability to remain in society. Depending on how retirees interact with others, their lives after retirement have the potential to be full and satisfying. The four core components measuring the satisfaction of life for seniors are physical status, emotional health, social support, and locus of control. The findings determine that physical health is the most important indicator of overall satisfaction.[41] It makes sense that retirement should be a time to pursue hobbies and continue interacting with peers, all while focusing on staying healthy and active. Seniors must move on by redefining their purpose and setting new norms by which to live. Retiring may mean the end of life for some, but to others who have redefined their purpose, it illuminates new paths.

Wealth and power are two major concerns for conflict theorists. **How might corporate heads use ageism to gain the upper hand in a work environment?**

Symbolic interactionists believe that society is fluid and in a constant state of change. **In what ways might retirees approach change and redefine their norms?**

discover solutions to social problems:
HOW DOES SOCIETY DEAL WITH SPECIFIC PROBLEMS OF AGING?

Social Security

Social Security is a government-run social insurance program paid to retired workers. The government mandates Social Security, and the American workforce funds it through payroll taxes. Overall, Social Security has been successful and beneficial to our nation's retirees. Lately, however, with a large number of workers preparing for retirement, questions about the system's lack of sustainability are rampant. We've already discussed earlier in the chapter the alarming rate at which the elderly population is continuing to grow. According to the Social Security Administration, without major changes to the system, it will no longer be able to pay benefits in full by the year 2037. Because it will only be able to pay approximately 76 percent of the current rate, the administration warns citizens to save for retirement through other avenues as well.[42]

Medicare

Medicare is a government-run social insurance program that provides health coverage for people 65 and older. Similar to Social Security, projections of continuing coverage for future generations look problematic. In 2008, Medicare began paying out more than it was collecting.[46] The Social Security and Medicare Boards of Trustees claim that the problems facing Medicare are actually more severe than those of Social Security because of the rising costs of medical care. Thus, the depletion of funds will occur sooner for the health care system than for Social Security. Although the growing population affects both systems, Medicare must also contend with the increasing cost of health care that continues to spiral ever faster.[47]

So you can see that on the horizon there are large numbers of retirees, and the government's own estimates for both SSA and Medicare show that we cannot support them. What do you think will happen? How can we fund our seniors? What social problems might result if we do nothing?

Death and Dying

The complex subject of aging broaches many issues, not all of them financial. Most of us wish our death to be quick, peaceful, and free of pain. This is not always the case.

MEDICARE is a government-run social insurance program that provides health coverage for people 65 and older.

One topic of worldwide debate centers on physician-assisted suicide (PAS) and euthanasia. In PAS, terminally ill residents receive prescriptions for self-administered lethal medications from their physicians (thus, "physician assisted"). Euthanasia is divided into two subgroups—*passive*, or allowing a person to die, and *active*, or doing something to assist suicide. Taking away a patient's life-sustaining medication, for example, is passive euthanasia. When a physician directly administers a lethal medication to a patient, we consider it active assistance.

EUTHANASIA IN ACTION

Some European nations, such as the Netherlands and Belgium, allow forms of euthanasia, but the terms are ambiguous and problematic. According to an article by Maurice A. M. de Wachter, director of the Maastricht Institute for Bioethics, although active euthanasia is technically illegal in the Netherlands, physicians are protected as long as they adhere to three conditions.[48] These conditions are:

- Voluntariness: The patient's request must be persistent, conscious, and freely made. In the Netherlands, "involuntary euthanasia" is a contradiction of terms.

- Unbearable suffering: The patient's suffering (including but not limited to physical pain) cannot be relieved by any other means. Both the physician and patient must consider the patient's condition to be beyond recovery or improvement.

- Consultation: The attending physician must consult with a colleague regarding the patient's condition and the genuineness and appropriateness of the request for euthanasia.

According to Dr. Borst-Eilers, former medical director of the Academic Hospital at the University of Utrecht, the overall incidence of euthanasia in 1990 was probably between 4,000 and 6,000 cases annually—a massive increase from 1989. This makes up approximately about four percent of all deaths in the Netherlands.[49] In 1990, the Institute for Bioethics in Maastricht assembled a conference to discuss the topic of euthanasia for its Canadian, American, and British visitors.[50] The conference was eye opening for many attendants, but invited further ethical scrutiny.

MAKE CONNECTIONS

Aging, Poverty, and Population Growth

The Social Security slump affects some demographics more than others. As you learned in Chapter 3, African Americans, American Indians, and Hispanics have the lowest median income and the greatest numbers of people living below the poverty level. The U.S. Census Bureau expects minorities, now roughly one-third of the U.S. population, to become the majority in 2042, with the nation projected to be 54 percent minority in 2050.[43] If the system remains unchanged, it is likely that those who need Social Security the most will have the least support.[44]

Chapter 18 discusses the social problems connected to population growth worldwide. The United States is not the only nation in which the graying population is multiplying faster than its resources. According to a report by the U.S. Census Bureau and the National Institute on Aging, the world's population is growing by about 800,000 people a month.[45] As the aging population around the world continues to grow, demands will be placed on all support systems for the elderly.

DEATH WITH DIGNITY

When I was a child, our dog developed an incurable heart condition, and the vet said he should be "put down." As a child, I can remember not wanting that to happen, but my mother said that we were being merciful. This is fine for dogs, but active euthanasia is still illegal in the United States for people. In 1997, however, Oregon endorsed the Death with Dignity Act, which states that terminally ill patients may seek physician-assisted suicide. According to this act, patients can voluntarily self-administer a lethal drug prescribed by their physician. Under the act, physicians and patients must first provide full disclosure to the Oregon Department of Human Services, which use these data to produce an annual statistical report.[51]

According to the 2008 annual report, 401 patients died under the act. The majority of patients were between 55 and 84 years old, white, well educated, had some form of cancer, and died in their homes. Of the 401 cases, 88 patients died in 2008, an increase from 24 patients in 1997.[52] The number of cases is small, but steadily increasing.

The state of Washington passed a similar law in November 2008. To many residents, the law was overdue. However, even now, few physicians are willing to follow through with the procedure. According to the Washington State Department of Health, as of June 2009, the department received only 13 written requests for medication and only four death notices from attending physicians.[53]

A universal stigma attached to death and dying weighs heavily on society today. Laws such as Death with Dignity are slow to be legislated. However, according to a 2005 opinion poll of 1,010 U.S. adults, 79 percent of those surveyed were in favor of a law that would "allow doctors to comply with the wishes of a dying patient in severe distress who asks to have his or her life ended."[54] Is the stigma changing?

Pro & Con

Active Euthanasia

Death is still taboo; this, coupled with legal and ethical considerations, makes for heated debate on the subject of euthanasia. Let's take a look at a few points from both sides:

Pro

- The state should not interfere with a patient's right to choose when or how he or she dies.
- Euthanasia is an act of mercy for patients in severe pain and emotional turmoil.
- Medical advancements that prolong the lives of the terminally ill are against natural law, so euthanasia should be a valid option, too.
- It costs much more to keep patients alive (through medicine, treatment, etc.) than to let them die.

Con

- Euthanasia is murder and, depending on the situation, suicide. It breaches spiritual and religious boundaries, resulting in dire moral consequences.
- In some cases, the family or medical personnel would have to decide when the patient dies, not the patient.
- Euthanasia is against natural law.
- If euthanasia were made legal, the cost of monitoring and legal interferences would be greater than the cost of heath care to keep patients alive.

>>> Although Jack Kevorkian spent eight years in prison for participating in multiple assisted suicides, his views on the subject haven't changed.[55] **What do you think: Is euthanasia murder, or is it a final act of mercy?**

From Classroom to Community | Back to Work

Ageism is a societal concern, now exacerbated by the tight labor market, making it difficult for older people to get jobs. Those who are able to find jobs often take massive pay cuts. Melissa Fodor, who went from working as a travel agent to dog walking, is just one example.

Stories like Fodor's exist everywhere. Jessica saw this for herself when she worked part-time at her university's administration office.

"The job didn't pay much, but it was a breeze. I answered the same questions every day, and what I didn't know, I could quickly look up in the office database. It was an easy job."

She had fun with her co-workers, who were all undergraduates—all except for Ms. Verna.

"At first I thought Verna was a middle-aged snob. When she wasn't brown-nosing in the supervisor's office, she kept to herself at her corner station, or went on break. She must have taken twenty breaks a day."

One day, Jessica heard the woman crying in the ladies' room. She hated to see anyone upset, so she asked what was wrong.

"As it turns out, Verna wasn't 'brown-nosing' in the supervisor's office at all. She was confused by her work and embarrassed to ask us for help. Instead, she directed her questions to our supervisor or went out in the hall to call her 20-year-old daughter for computer help."

At first, Jessica was baffled as to why an older woman like Verna would want to work in an office with college kids at a job in which she had no experience.

Verna then explained that she had been a professor of religious studies at a nearby university until her department had to make major cutbacks. She was laid off and left to find any job she could. Her husband was ill, and had left his job 10 years before he was able to draw a full pension. Even with Social Security, the couple was nearly starving.

"Verna's situation was a wake-up call. Until that point, I guess I really didn't understand the current state of the economy. I was also ashamed of myself and my co-workers for belittling a woman of her stature. A world-traveled scholar such as herself shouldn't have been stuck in an office, embarrassed that she never learned Microsoft Excel."

WHO ARE THE AGING POPULATION, AND WHAT DOES AGEISM MEAN IN OUR CULTURE? 70

there were 35 million people aged 65 and over in 2000; ageism is discrimination based solely on age, and it is becoming more apparent as the older generation either remains in or returns to the workforce

WHAT THEORIES EXIST ABOUT THE AGING PROCESS? 74

functionalism: reduced interaction between older people and society is acceptable, and makes for an easy transition of roles while keeping society functioning as it should

symbolic interactionism: aging people should maintain some form of activity to continue the growth process and maintain life satisfaction

HOW DOES SOCIETY DEAL WITH SPECIFIC PROBLEMS OF AGING? 76

government assistance such as Social Security and Medicare in addition to progressive ways to approach suffering and death, such as the Death with Dignity Act

get the topic: WHO ARE THE AGING POPULATION, AND WHAT DOES AGEISM MEAN IN OUR CULTURE?

Theory

FUNCTIONALISM 74

- to avoid disrupting the social system, society disengages aging individuals from important roles
- reducing interaction between society and the aging is both inevitable and necessary to assure a smooth transition as the younger generation takes over the roles of their aging counterparts

SYMBOLIC INTERACTIONISM 74

- to maintain a healthy mind set, seniors must remain physically and mentally active; individuals young and old should engage in social interaction since the process of developing the sense of self is an ongoing process

CONFLICT THEORY 75

- ageism creates an unjust system in which the workplace does not provide fair opportunities
- the powerful majority has a social and economic interest in removing older people from their roles

Key Terms

ageism is prejudice and discrimination based solely on age. *71*

home-health care is provided for patients who cannot leave their homes but have the possibility of improving. *73*

hospice care is short-term care, but only available to patients with six months or less to live. *73*

disengagement theory states that reduced interaction between elderly persons and other members of society is unavoidable, mutual, and acceptable. *74*

activity theory states that life satisfaction depends on maintaining social involvement by developing new interests, hobbies, roles, and relationships. *74*

continuity theory states that older people seek out familiar areas of their lives and strive to keep those constant as they age, which becomes a strategy for adaptation to the challenges of growing old. *74*

Medicare is a government-run social insurance program that provides health coverage for people 65 and older. *76*

Sample Test Questions

These multiple-choice questions are similar to those found in the test bank that accompanies this textbook.

1. Which of the following is an example of ageism?
   a. The Social Security Administration will reduce benefits to seniors by the year 2037.
   b. Home Depot hires a 70-year-old man and pays him minimum wage.
   c. A nursing home straps an old woman to her bed for several days at a time.
   d. General Motors fires a 50-year-old woman and replaces her with a 25-year-old employee with less experience.

2. Hospice is a service that
   a. prepares patients for physician-assisted suicide.
   b. aids seniors who require short-term care after surgery.
   c. aids terminally ill patients with palliative (comfort) care.
   d. provides for old people who can no longer care for themselves.

3. Maurice is retired and financially secure. Lately, however, he's been feeling unneeded and depressed. Maurice's physician recommends that he volunteer at the local food bank to remain engaged with society and improve his outlook on life. This suggestion best alludes to an example of
   a. ageism.
   b. functionalism.
   c. conflict theory.
   d. symbolic interactionism.

4. According to the Death with Dignity Act, physicians may
   a. discontinue life support for a patient who is terminally ill and physically suffering.
   b. provide a prescription for a lethal medication to a patient who is suffering and requests to die.
   c. administer a lethal medication to a patient who is terminally ill, suffering, and requests to die.
   d. end the life of a terminally ill patient who is physically suffering and in a coma after consulting with the patient's family.

5. When Social Security and Medicare funds deplete, the poverty rate of men will rise more than that of women because men have more health problems than women.
   a. True
   b. False

ESSAY

1. How has the nation's economic crisis affected the aging population, and how is this connected to ageism?
2. What experiences do you have with ageism at school? At your job?
3. Functionalists believe that society needs to force old people out of their roles to make room for younger generations with new ideas. What are the positive and negative consequences of this?
4. Why is your generation in jeopardy of not receiving Social Security benefits by the time it retires? What consequences will this have on society?
5. Imagine that the U.S. government mandates physician-assisted suicide in every state. What are some of the potential outcomes?

WHERE TO START YOUR RESEARCH PAPER

For U.S. Census facts and information, go to http://www.census.gov

To learn more about elder abuse, go to http://www.aoa.gov/ and http://www.ncea.aoa.gov

To locate more information about Social Security and future trends, go to http://www.ssa.gov/

For more information on hospice care, visit http://www.hospicenet.org/

For information on the Death with Dignity National Center, go to http://www.deathwithdignity.org/

To explore the pros and cons of euthanasia, go to http://euthanasia.procon.org/

Remember to check www.thethinkspot.com for additional information, downloadable flashcards, and other helpful resources.

MEDIA AND TECHNOLOGY

After a

lifetime of working for newspapers and radio, Kevin Klose will take on an entirely new challenge: rethinking journalism's future as technology transforms traditional media.

Klose will be the next dean of the nearly 600-student Philip Merrill College of Journalism at the University of Maryland. At 68, he has covered everything from street crime to the former Soviet Union for The Washington Post, written books, overseen U.S. radio broadcasts to foreign countries, and led National Public Radio through a decade of dramatic audience growth and fund-raising success.

He comes to the school at a time when journalism is changing rapidly. It is decentralizing from traditional sources to the hands of countless individuals able to record video or send text with cell phones and BlackBerrys. Newspapers are closing, and many media outlets are sharply downsizing as readers move online.

"Everyone is looking at it in horror," interim dean Lee Thornton said of the layoffs and newspaper closures. "It's just a drumbeat, isn't it? It's frightening. Yet our applications here at Merrill are up. Students want to come to journalism."

Klose said he doesn't know yet where people will get their news in coming years. "It's like the early days of radio," he said. "There was a tremendous amount of feverish invention, trial and error that went on in the 1920s and 1930s. . . . The outlets or platforms are unclear now—they're being invented."

When he joins the school in mid-April, Klose will jump into what he described as the ongoing experiment to find formats for the independent journalism a democracy needs.

What will endure, he said, are the standards of accurate, ethical reporting. "There's still going to be, and always will be, a need for edited, fact-checked, archived, verifiable journalism," he said.

He'll bring his grounding in traditional newspaper journalism—Klose worked at The Post from 1967 to 1992—as well as his experiences as president of NPR, where he ushered in the switch from tape to digital and other technological advances. He restructured Radio Free Europe for the post–Cold War world.

"I'm good at setting a transformational course," Klose said.[1]

CHAPTER 06

---If you were born after 1990, you probably can't remember a time before computers. While people only one generation older than you struggle to understand basic concepts such as e-mail or Web searches, working with digital technology comes almost as naturally to you as walking or breathing.

Why do computers seem to stump older people?

The truth is, it's not just computers; it's happened before. Most people in your parents' generation can't remember a time before color TV. And most of your grandparents probably grew up explaining how radios worked to *their* older relatives. What is it about our society that leads us to repeat these same patterns again and again?

Sociologists are interested in two core questions about media and technology: (1) How do people interact with media and technology? and (2) How do media and technology influence society? As Kevin Klose stated in the opening article, print has begun to decline in popularity with the growing influence of the Internet. Is this a change we should embrace as progress, or a sign that our society is sacrificing quality for convenience? As we'll discuss in this chapter, the answer can differ depending on a person's cultural, political, and even financial views on the world.

get the topic: HOW DO EXPANDING TECHNOLOGIES INFLUENCE SOCIETY?

When I was a kid, I remember preferring eight-track cartridges over the new form of musical technology: cassette tapes. For years I stuck with my cartridges, only to find that by the mid-1980s, no one sold them anymore. To this day, I'm the only person in my family who doesn't own an iPod; instead, I listen to the radio or CDs. I'm still holding out for the next "big thing." I'm convinced that in five years or so, iPods will be obsolete, and we'll all be forced to switch over to a new system if we want to continue listening to music.

Is all this constant upgrading necessary? As the years go by, telephones change to cell phones, cell phones change to iPhones, and sometimes new versions come out that don't seem to change anything at all. Has society run out of great inventors who rely on individual creativity?

The truth is, technological advancements have always tended to focus on improving existing technology. Movies come from photography, computers come from punch card readers, and cell phones are the distant progeny of telegraphy. These advances become part of a society that develops new, widespread ways to use and for-

Technology and Media

mat the technology. This adoption, or social institutionalizing, enhances the new technologies and allows them to grow and develop into new media.[2] In other words, a technology that can't engage society doesn't have much of a purpose.

What Is Technology?

Is a pair of pliers technology? Is a cell phone technology? Are instruction manuals from IKEA technology? The answer to all three of these questions is yes. **Technology** consists of all processes, inventions, and methods used to advance society.[3]

Technological Development

Whether you consider the Clovis spear point designed to kill woolly mammoths or the electric light by which I type this sentence, you'll find examples of technological advancement throughout human history. Our species' ability to constantly create new technologies to help us perform necessary tasks distinguishes us from our fellow animals. To put it simply, humans use technology to make their lives easier. There's no doubt that new technologies are constantly improving our lives, but it's important to realize, too, that these same new technologies can lead to social problems. The technological developments themselves are not the problem; rather, problems develop when humans determine how a technology should be used and who gets to use it.

Back in Chapter 1, we learned about sociologist Max Weber, who theorized that society runs like a well-organized bureaucracy. Modern conflict theorist George Ritzer adapts Weber's ideas, suggesting that the United States runs like an efficient business, a process he calls McDonaldization. **McDonaldization** refers to applying the famous restaurant's corporate model to other businesses by following rules of efficiency, calculability, predictability, and technology.[4] Specifically, Ritzer suggests that technology drives the process of McDonaldization because it helps businesses replace human worker who are slower than machines and more likely to make errors. Machines, however, are predictable and efficient. They do not get tired, and they do not get sick. Henry Ford learned this when he mechanized his production line. Today, whether it's the self-checkout at the grocery store or the check-in kiosk at the airport, we use technological tools to replace human beings and reduce the opportunity for human error. Replacing people with machines may increase efficiency and reduce error, but it is very much a social problem for those who lose their jobs and those who believe that society becomes less humane and more isolated as a result.

Who Has Access to Technology?

Technology use varies greatly from country to country, and even people living within the same country can have vastly different access to technological services. For example, does your part of the country have access to FiOS? If your town or city does not provide this service, you have firsthand knowledge of the **digital divide**—a gap between areas that have access to certain technologies and those that do not. Generally, there is a correlation between a geographic location's technological access and its socioeconomic status; in other words, poorer areas are less likely to have technological services than wealthier areas are. Consider the data at the right that the U.S. Department of Commerce released in 2004 when they examined Internet usage across the United States.

These data show some striking trends in the digital divide of the United States. Notice how income and race predict access to the Internet. The higher a family's income, the more likely that family is to use the Internet. In the United States, where socioeconomic status is often determined at least in part by race, white and Asian American individuals tend to have more financial resources than their black and Hispanic peers do. Therefore, it's not surprising that in 2003, whites and Asian Americans used the Internet at a higher rate than black and Hispanic people did. Education is another factor linked to both socioeconomic status and Internet use: More than 80 percent of college graduates used the Internet in 2003, compared to only 15 percent of those who didn't complete high school. Because a college degree has become a tool for boosting one's earning potential in the United States, these data support the idea that wealth and access to technology are closely linked.

The Internet and other innovative technologies grant plenty of advantages to their users, allowing people to work more efficiently, network with friends and colleagues, find bargains, and get information

TECHNOLOGY consists of all processes, inventions, and methods used to advance society.

MCDONALDIZATION refers to applying the business model of McDonald's to other businesses.

DIGITAL DIVIDE is the gap between high-income countries and low-income countries that influences their access to current technology.

from around the world. But as we've discussed, not everyone has access to these tools. Is the digital divide perpetuating—or even increasing—social inequality in the United States? If so, what can be done to ensure that people across the country have the technological tools they need for success?

Internet Users (Percent)		
	Sept. 2001	**Oct. 2003**
TOTAL POPULATION	55.1	58.7
Gender		
Male	55.2	58.2
Female	55	59.2
Race/Ethnicity		
White Alone	61.3	65.1
Black	41.1	45.6
Asian Amer. & Pac. Isl.	62.5	63.1
Hispanic (of any race)	33.4	37.2
Family Income		
Less than $15,000	25.9	31.2
$15,000–$24,999	34.4	38
$25,000–$34,999	45.3	48.9
$35,000–$49,999	58.3	62.1
$50,000–$74,999	68.9	71.8
$75,000 & above	80.4	82.9
Educational Attainment		
Less Than High School	13.7	15.5
High School Diploma/GED	41.1	44.5
Some College	63.5	68.6
Bachelor's Degree	82.2	84.9
Beyond Bachelor's Degree	85	88
Age Group		
Age 3–4	17.6	19.9
Age 5–9	41	42
Age 10–13	66.7	67.3
Age 14–17	76.4	78.8
Age 18–24	66.6	70.6
Age 25–49	65	68
Age 50 +	38.3	44.8

By the author, from the U.S. Department of Commerce, "A Nation Online: Entering the Broadband Age," http://www.ntia.doc.gov/reports/anol/nation onlinebroadband04.htm, Accessed August 16, 2009.

The link between wealth and technological access is strong outside of the United States as well. The infographic at the bottom of the page will give you an idea of cell phone usage internationally. Countries with large populations (such as China and India) and relatively wealthy countries (such as Japan, the United States, and the countries in the European Union) are home to the highest number of cell phones, whereas smaller countries and countries with fewer financial resources don't have many at all. In Western Sahara, in fact, not one of the 405,210 residents has a cell phone. Not only oceans and mountain ranges separate countries from their global neighbors; the digital divide separates nations, too.

How Does Technological Development Affect Society?
CULTURAL LAG

Sometimes, technology changes faster than society can follow. This gap between technological ability and society's willingness to embrace it is known as **cultural lag**. Cultural lag isn't just a "macro level" phenomenon that affects entire nations and societies; on a smaller scale, cultural lag can affect individuals. For example, if you had a classmate from the Marshall Islands, he might not know or care much about sending text messages because cell phones are not abundant in his home country. Many K-12 classrooms are mired in a cultural lag, because of the large number of teachers who didn't grow up in a computerized world, and aren't comfortable relying on technology in their classrooms. These teachers will continue to experience cultural lag until they become literate in the new technology.[5] I frequently see the effects of cultural lag when I teach classes online. Often, a student who has enrolled in the course calls me on the phone to ask, "Do I need to understand the computer to take this class?" A question like this would seem ridiculous to some people—how can a person hope to take an online course without computer skills?—but to the people who are unfamiliar or uncomfortable with the concept of taking courses online, it's a valid concern.

Countries Ranked

United States
Cell phones: 255,000,000
Population: 307,212,123
Cell phone users per capita: 83%

#4

Source: Central Centrral Intelligence Agency, World Factbook, "Country Comparison: Telephone—Mobile Cellular," https://www.cia.gov/library/publications/the-world-factbook/rankorder/2151rank.html?countryCode=xx#xx, Accessed August 12, 2009.

TECHNOLOGY AND CULTURAL CHANGE

Can technology change culture? It's certainly possible. Consider how the technology of the wheel or the electric lightbulb influenced culture. Without these tools, you couldn't drive your car to the movies at night. Or take the example of one of the most influential technological innovations of the recent past: the television. Neil Postman, author of *Amusing Ourselves to Death: Public Discourse in the Age of Show Business*, argues that unlike newspapers and magazines, television is a passive media source that trains us to accept simplistic solutions to complex problems. This leads to a decrease in original thinking that, in the long run, can only harm us.[6]

Postman also suggests that technology can become the driver of culture in and of itself. In his book *Technopoly*, Postman points out that the point of technology is to make life easier for people, and yet it is increasingly driving the culture, rather than serving it.[7] When your cell phone vibrates in class, can you resist checking and responding to your mes-

CULTURAL LAG refers to a situation in which members of society can't keep up with technology.

sages? One student in my class could not: Despite multiple warnings to stop texting, she continued. It was almost like she was one of Pavlov's dogs, conditioned to salivate at the buzz of her phone.

Of course, technology is useful, but using it has a price. Has the computer made you smarter or craftier? Do you actually learn more, or have you just gotten better at using search engines to find what you need to know? Postman argues that our dependence on the computer creates a cultural void in which people lose the ability to learn, making us a nation of idiots. Recently, I made a purchase at a convenience store; my bill was $1.89. I pulled out $2.00 and the cashier immediately punched in the number. While she was opening the drawer, I found four pennies in my pocket and put them on the counter. She looked at me and said, "What am I supposed to do with those?" After a long pause,

by Number of Cell Phones

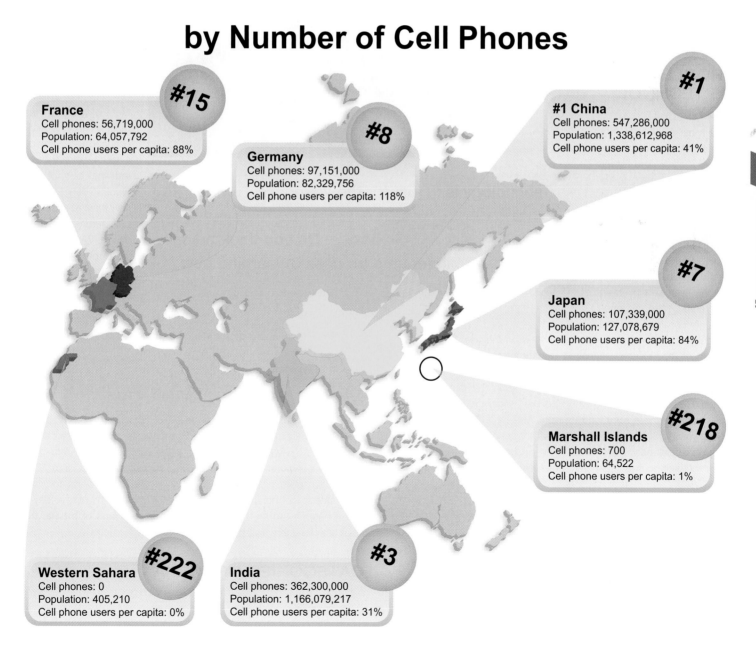

#15

France
Cell phones: 56,719,000
Population: 64,057,792
Cell phone users per capita: 88%

#8

Germany
Cell phones: 97,151,000
Population: 82,329,756
Cell phone users per capita: 118%

#1

#1 China
Cell phones: 547,286,000
Population: 1,338,612,968
Cell phone users per capita: 41%

#7

Japan
Cell phones: 107,339,000
Population: 127,078,679
Cell phone users per capita: 84%

#218

Marshall Islands
Cell phones: 700
Population: 64,522
Cell phone users per capita: 1%

#222

Western Sahara
Cell phones: 0
Population: 405,210
Cell phone users per capita: 0%

#3

India
Cell phones: 362,300,000
Population: 1,166,079,217
Cell phone users per capita: 31%

I said, "Just give me 15 cents." The cashier was so used to conducting transactions through her cash register that the idea of doing arithmetic in her head to make change seemed completely foreign to her.

Of course, not everyone agrees with Postman. In *Culture and Technology*, Andrew Murphie and John Potts argue that society is actually better off because of technology. Yes, our culture is changing, and the days of people sitting and reading the newspaper may be coming to an end, but that does not mean things are necessarily worse. For example, the authors argue that television and the Internet have vastly changed society for the better, inspiring creativity and allowing opportunities for endless innovation. Murphie and Potts see technology as an intertwined part of current culture.[8]

PROBLEMS OF TECHNOLOGY

While most of us enjoy the benefits of computers, cell phones, cars, and other recent technologies, these handy tools have certain drawbacks, too. When you swipe your credit card at the gas station, life is easier for you, but it's also easier for the criminal who hacks into the system and steals your credit card information. According to the Federal Trade Commission, identity theft is on the rise. In 2005, 3.7 percent of Americans experienced identity theft, much of it through computer fraud and credit card scams.[9]

Privacy issues also abound. Many people in my family and my friends use social networking Web sites like Twitter and Facebook regularly, but can these sites lead to problems? Do potential employers look at your MySpace profile to see what they can find out about you? Through social networking sites, many people divulge information about themselves that could create problems with friends, employers, or the law.

Have you ever used the Google Maps "street view" function to see a recent photographic image of your house, dorm, or apartment building? Does it bother you that anyone with a computer can have a picture of your home? Questions abound as to whether there is too much information about individual citizens on the Internet. Google defends its "street view" feature, arguing that its photos are equivalent to pictures anyone could take while driving down any public street.[10] By offering instant, worldwide access to these photos, is Google merely providing a public service, or is it invading people's privacy? When it comes to issues of technology, safety, and the freedom of information, clear lines between right and wrong can be difficult to draw.

TECHNOLOGY AND THE GLOBAL VILLAGE

Despite its pitfalls, rapid technology can facilitate connections between people around the world and bring us together as a global society. In 2003, Peter Dodds and his colleagues at Columbia University conducted an experiment to determine whether the Internet made connecting to strangers around the world any easier. Through e-mail, Dodds sent over 60,000 people on an Internet mission to find 18 specific strangers.[11] Surprisingly, he found that using online social networks made reaching the strangers no easier or faster than when Stanley Milgram carried out the same study by mail in 1967.[12] Together, both studies suggest that we do indeed live in a **global village**, a world reduced in size by increased technological communication.[13] However, it seems that our plugged-in world is no smaller than Milgram's. Has rapid technology really changed us? Perhaps it hasn't radically affected the size of our global village, but it may have affected our *perspective* of that village. Whether we're video-chatting with our friends across the country or combing blogs and Web sites for the latest news developments in Washington, D.C., Iran, China, or Sudan, technology allows us to feel closer to each other than ever.

> ∧∧∧ **Technology isn't just for the young;** many people from older generations welcome the digital age and the possibilities it brings. **Do you think being older helps or hinders the process of learning new technology?**

Media and Technology

You drive home from your afternoon class, flipping through radio stations idly. When you get to your apartment, you turn on the TV for some background noise and skim a novel you're supposed to have read for last week's lecture. After a while, you sit back and log onto MSN Messenger while watching Daily Show reruns and waiting for your roommate to get home from work. All in all, it's a pretty normal day—and it happens to be filled with many different types of **media**, the channels through which we store and receive information.

CATEGORIES OF MEDIA

Although we may not realize it, media play a large part in our everyday lives. Whether you're reading a newspaper on the subway or simply listening to a podcast on your morning jog, you need to consider the role of media in your life. Because media outlets are some of the largest and most influential groups utilizing rapid technology today, it's important to understand exactly what media are and how they influence society. At present, there are four main categories of media: print, television, radio, and Internet.

Print

Print media include newspapers, magazines, and books. After almost six centuries of an ever-increasing global presence, print media may now be on the decline. As you read in the chapter opener, the future for newspapers and other tangible forms of media looks grim. However, the decline of print media doesn't mean that authors will stop writing or that paparazzi will stop snapping photos. The popularity of new inventions like Amazon's e-book reader, the Kindle, suggests that our society still values the written word, though that word may not always be printed on paper.

Television and Radio

Television and radio are continually evolving to meet society's changing demands. During the war in Iraq, for example, dozens of TV shows from *ER* to *Arrested Development* jumped to incorporate the current combat into their plots. Radio has changed drastically since the first half of the century, developing to fill the niches that TV and other media cannot. These days, radio is a form of transportable media, available in cars, on computers, and even in alarm clocks. The popularity of talk radio has encouraged listeners to create communities centered on a variety of topics, from sports to politics to religion.

Keep in mind that, apart from the few publicly funded TV and radio stations in this country, both radio and TV are funded by advertisers.

Because most advertisers want big audiences, these forms of media are often accused of chasing ratings at the expense of content. In other words, they sensationalize the news to keep viewers and listeners hooked.

The Internet

Internet and other electronic media are growing rapidly worldwide. The Internet makes ongoing global communication quick and easy for both business-related and personal matters. The truly interesting thing about the Internet is that, unlike other types of media, it's easily accessible to anyone who wants to make their opinions known. From bloggers, to Wikipedia, to MySpace, to 4chan, the Internet is the first truly open form of media. After the contested election in Iran in the summer of 2009, the Internet became a vital source of information for protesters. State-controlled TV and radio stations were censored, but the Internet allowed protestors to communicate and gather for demonstrations.[14]

Each of these forms of media has the ability to transmit information directly to us, and people often use media to inform the general public of social problems. Recall from Chapter 1 that social movements begin with people who make claims and gain attention for those claims. What would happen to these movements for change if they couldn't make use of media sources to spread their message?

ADVERTISING

Not all media are created by reporters and news organizations. Advertisements, for example, are media created by businesses and corporations. You may think that ads about headache cream or auto insurance

▶▶▶ GO GL🌐BAL

Gurupa

What is television's influence on society? The community of Gurupa, Brazil, offered a unique opportunity to research this question when the first televisions began to appear in the town in 1982. Located in the rainforests of northeastern Brazil, Gurupa is sheltered from much of the world; no roads lead to it, and air transportation is uncommon. The primary means of access to the town is by riverboat, as it sits directly on the lower bank of the mighty Amazon River. The majority of the people in Gurupa live in thatched homes without electricity or running water. The wealthy elite have houses of wood and brick. They receive running water for 12 hours a day and electricity for 6.

When television first arrived in Gurupa, only the wealthier residents of the town could afford to buy a TV. However, the community felt strongly that those people who had televisions should position them so that they were visible from the street; this way their less affluent neighbors could watch TV as well. This arrangement was beneficial to both Gurupa's

wealthier residents and its poorer ones: Television owners were proud to display their status symbols, and poorer residents were able to access mass media through their neighbors' windows. Although this custom might seem segregating to us, the people of Gurupa saw time spent in front of television as social time, an experience to share not only

with family and friends but with the entire community as well.[16]

The introduction of TV technology to Gurupa created new norms and rules for the community. Would Neil Postman most likely classify this development as positive or negative? What do you think—has life in Gurupa changed for better or for worse?

>>> The town of Gurupa is located along the Amazon River in the Brazilian state of Para. **Until the arrival of television, the members of the community spent their evening hours socializing in the streets.** Do you think that their quality of life has gotten better, worse, or stayed the same?

are annoying or goofy, but advertising is big business. As we've already discussed, advertising dollars run the show in American media. Ads on TV, radio, and even the Internet pay the freight. Every day, we're bombarded by thousands of attempts to convince us to buy or do something, and plenty of these attempts are effective. When I go to the grocery store and I can't decide which brand of juice or coffee to buy, I usually pick up the brand I know or the brand I've heard of. Often, I've heard of that brand through advertisements. Advertisers are obviously convinced that ads can influence human behavior. Are they right? Perhaps more importantly, does their influence actually hurt the media's ability to provide objective and accurate information?

MEDIA INFLUENCE

As you'll remember from Chapter 1, data come in two forms: *quantitative* data, which are numerically measurable, and *qualitative* data, which are not numerically measurable. Although the dollars spent on advertising are quantitative data, the influence of advertising on our lives is often studied in a qualitative method. One significant social concern in the ad realm is the influence that advertising has on children and adolescents. Some countries, including Sweden, Norway, Greece, Denmark, and Belgium, have enacted guidelines to protect children from this form of media. These protections include restrictions that limit the amount of commercials that sell child-targeted products, regulations that specify the time of day when such ads can start, and laws forbidding child advertisement at all. In the United States, advertising during children's shows is limited to 12 minutes per hour on weekdays, but 16 minutes per hour on Friday evenings and Saturday mornings—prime time. Obviously, due to school and sleep schedules, children watch the most television during prime time. Between TV and other ad sources, children are targeted with more than 3,000 ads every day, and they view more than 40,000 ads a year.[15] As anyone who's been around a child during the holidays knows all too well, these ads have influence. (I can remember a time when I felt like if I didn't find a "Tickle Me Elmo" doll, the world would end for my daughter.)

Media Bias

Students in my classes often talk about it as if it were a fact: the media are liberal. Other people in other parts of the country argue that the media are conservative. If you believe that a newspaper, television station, or other form of media is not presenting objective facts in a truthful manner without an underlying agenda, you are accusing that source of **media bias**. Plenty of people see media bias as a disturbing social problem. After all, if you can't trust your main source of information to give you the straight facts about the world, it's nearly impossible for you to discover what's really going on. But does media bias actually exist?

MEDIA BIAS RESEARCH

In 2003, William Eveland and Dhavan Shah published a study arguing that the only biases that exist are in our own heads, and that they mostly come from those around us. According to their research, an individual's personal network plays a huge role in his or her sense of media bias. In other words, your views are shaped by the people you hang around with. If you only share your political ideas with like-minded people, you're more likely to perceive bias outside the group. If your social network is diverse, however, you're less likely to perceive bias around you.[17]

Further research has also weakened allegations of political media bias. In a recent study, Covert and Wasburn compared *National Review* and *Progressive*, two popular partisan magazines, with *Time* and *Newsweek*. The researchers found no differences in the magazines' discussions of key issues such as crime, poverty, gender, and the environment.[18] Of course, these findings are not always publicized by some in the media who love to suggest that bias exists.

Media bias, when it does exist, doesn't always have to do with politics. Sometimes, media organizations are so eager to report a certain story that they distribute information that's misleading or downright false. University of California researcher Christopher Kollmeyer found that during a recent low point in the economy, newspapers ran stories on the monetary crisis of big businesses despite these companies' upward financial trends. According to Kollmeyer, not only did newspapers fail to mention the actual prosperity of these corporations, but they also declined to report on the real economic hardships experienced by members of the working class.[19]

The good news is that, according to economist Daniel Sutter, big businesses aren't interested in promoting their political opinions through the media. Non-partisan businesses, he argues, have greater public support since they don't alienate groups of people from either side. His research supports what an experienced entrepreneur I know has always said: "Never put a political sign on your yard; you might lose a customer." Sutter also notes that although corporations may have monetary control over the media, they don't wield absolute power. Instead, the two enjoy a symbiotic relationship: When a media outlet is popular, businesses get the biggest bang for their advertising buck, and newspapers, networks and stations get more money from new advertisers.[20]

MEDIA AND POLITICS

Editorial slant is thought by some to be the same as media bias, but the difference between slant and bias is that bias is not acknowledged by the media outlet, whereas slant is. Anyone watching the *Ed Show* on MSNBC knows the host is a Democrat, just as anyone who watches *Hannity* on Fox knows the host supports Republican ideals. Both shows slant the stories to support their own ideologies.

The goal of editorial slant is to gain support for stated opinions. In 2005, a study was conducted by Druckman and Parkin to study the impact that print media has on voters' perceptions. The researchers focused on a Seattle Senate campaign, each editorially supporting one of the candidates in an area with two major newspapers. Using exit polls on Election Day, they asked voters whether they read either or both of the different newspapers and who they voted for. The results showed that frequent readers were more likely to support the candidate that their newspaper supported, indicating that editorial slant does indeed impact voter decisions.[21] But this slant has mediating effects. The ability of media slant to be communicated to the public is influenced by many factors, all of which make it less likely that bias will enter into the reporting. For example, the collective nature of editorial decision making means that individual reporters often do not have the ability to make reports on their own. Audience size also influences a news organization's ability to lead the public; if an organization has a small audience, it will have difficulty making a big impact. And even if a news organization's owner has strong personal beliefs, those ideologies are likely to become watered down as his or her employees report the news. I don't mean to suggest that media bias never occurs, but I do believe that allegations of media-bias conspiracies are difficult to support.[22]

Media effects don't just apply to newspapers and television shows. In *Deep Democracy, Think Citizenship: The Impact of Digital Media in Political Campaign Strategy*, Philip Howard notes that the digital capabilities of the last decade have significantly changed campaign procedures. Thanks to the far-reaching capabilities of the Internet, campaign consultants can easily collect data on voters, including voter registration records and credit card purchase information. One of the main ways that digital information can be anonymously gathered is through spyware, intrusive software that can be automatically installed on computers without the individual's knowledge. These programs send feedback, allowing your personal information and Web page history to be seen by others. It's a faster, more accurate way to collect data than any traditional survey method. Armed with this information, campaign leaders can organize volunteers and raise money much more effectively than they could 20 years ago. They can also use this information to better predict political outcomes and determine the points that they might want to address.[23]

THE EFFECT OF MEDIA

In 1948, Lazarfeld and Merton coined the phrase "narcotizing" to describe an effect that television can have. They noticed that television has the power to mesmerize people as if they're drugged.[24] Have you ever had to yell at your roommate to get him to answer you during the fourth quarter of an important game? Has your sister ever agreed to lend you her car when *Lost* was on? As a child, was the best time to ask your parents for money while they were watching the nightly news? When what we're watching is engaging, television can definitely be mesmerizing.

On the other hand, massive media overloads can "numb" us to the information. For example, there is so much suffering in the world that when you see another murder on the 6 o'clock local news, do you really pay attention? Probably not. In fact, if you're watching the news, you're probably waiting to see the segment on the dancing koala. As well as desensitizing us to violence and sadness, Postman points out that television also has the potential to function as mindless entertainment, which can create a population that focuses on trivial issues at the expense of paying attention to important ones.

think social problems: HOW DO MEDIA AND TECHNOLOGY CREATE OR ALLEVIATE SOCIAL PROBLEMS?

Conflict Theory and the Media

Several years ago, scholars Edward S. Herman and Noam Chomsky wrote a groundbreaking analysis of media in the United States. In *Manufacturing Consent*, they suggest that mass media follow a "propaganda model," which involves an interaction between government and special interests. Since all national media primarily get their information from government sources, the media tend to serve the needs of the elite, who either hold political office or have power and influence over government. Herman and Chomsky argue that there are five important filters through which information must pass before it gets to your television, newspaper, or radio, and each of these filters influences the outcome you consume:

1 The mass media's size, limited ownership, and profit motive dominate their decisions. In the time that's passed since Herman and Chomsky wrote their book, media concentration has actually increased. These days, there are a small handful of very large corporations that control what you read, see, and hear.[25]

2 The media stay in business primarily through advertising. Therefore, are they likely to raise issues that are in opposition to their advertisers? Herman and Chomsky say no.

3 Media sourcing generally comes from government and "experts" who are often connected to the issue being discussed. For example, when political appointees go on TV to discuss the latest policy issue, they generally "spin" their point of view to show that their ideas are the best. Most news sources take this spin without critical reflection, leading to bias in reporting.

4 If reporters independently attack corporate or government influences in their work, they often get flak from their companies and are labeled as troublemakers or crackpots. Their sources of information will also quickly dry up.

5 Finally, Herman and Chomsky suggest that the media use fear as a control mechanism to silence their critics. Think about the reporting of former President George W. Bush's "war on terror" in the months leading up to the United States' 2003 invasion of Iraq. How often did media actually critically review the claims that supported that invasion?

Herman and Chomsky suggest that media in the United States are little more than propaganda tools used by the elites to control those in the lower classes who tend to be passive receivers of information.[26]

Feminist Perspectives on Media

Since media and technology serve essential functions in society, they have the capacity to affect many different aspects of our day-to-day lives—sometimes for the better and sometimes for the worse. Feminist theorists point out that the media often help promote gender inequalities. As long as women are underrepresented in high-profile media positions and stereotyped on TV shows, media and technology are worsening a social problem.

WRAP YOUR MIND AROUND THE THEORY

Technology helps us stay in constant communication with each other, no matter where we are. **Has constant communication become a norm in our society?**

Most of the U.S. media are controlled by a handful of large businesses.[30] What messages do you think these corporations want to get across to the American public?

FUNCTIONALISM
Functionalists see media as a socialization tool essential for society. These theorists point to AIM, Twitter, and other social networks as examples of how media play a crucial role in our daily lives. Functionalists also see advertising as a way for media to promote the values and norms of a society.

FEMINIST THEORY
Feminist theorists contend that women are often not hired for positions they're qualified for. As you've probably noticed, the amount of men that hold top news anchor and talkshow host positions greatly outnumbers that of women. Feminist theorists also suggest that television's stereotypical placement of women in traditional, subordinate roles furthers the problem and keeps women from experiencing equality within society.

HOW DOES THE TRANSFER OF INFORMATION AFFECT SOCIETY?

CONFLICT THEORY
Conflict theorists point out that information is power; therefore, corporations that control the media hold immense power. To a conflict theorist, media in the United States are neither liberal nor conservative, but driven by corporate interests. Funding presents many potential conflicts of interest. For example, if a local television station uncovers corruption in its largest advertiser, will it broadcast that information?

SYMBOLIC INTERACTIONISM
Symbolic interactionists study the manner in which symbols occur in media. For example, they might consider the subtle messages sent by images in a print ad. The next time you see a "Got Milk?" advertisement, consider this: Are celebrities the only people who drink milk? Of course not, but by associating the beverage with power and esteem, the California Milk Processor Board implies that users of the product will likewise be happy and successful.

In 2006, after 15 years of hosting the light morning show *Today*, **Katie Couric became the first solo anchorwoman of a major network evening news program.** How might a feminist theorist view Couric's promotion?

In our culture, milk has come to symbolize attributes like health, strength, and youth. **How have these symbolic relationships been developed and reinforced by the "Got Milk" media campaign?**

THE UNDERREPRESENTATION OF WOMEN

Women are underrepresented in news shows and talk show positions. Although it seems like more women should hold high-profile media positions today than they did a few decades ago, is that really true? When I watch television, I notice that most of the famous talk show hosts and news anchors are still men. Of *Forbes'* list of the most powerful celebrity personalities (compiled using income and media popularity data), hosts David Letterman, Dr. Phil McGraw, Jay Leno, Howard Stern, and Rush Limbaugh are all well ahead of Tyra Banks and Ellen DeGeneres, who hold the next two slots. A notable exception to the rule that media is a "man's world" is Oprah Winfrey, who tops the charts in terms of her income ($275 million a year) and her TV popularity.[27]

STEREOTYPES

Unfortunately, the television media often portray men and women in stereotypical ways. In family sitcoms such as *Everybody Loves Raymond* and *According to Jim*, men are often the buffoons of the family, while the women of the household are portrayed as controlling shrews. And consider how gender roles are portrayed on the classic game show *Wheel of Fortune*: For 26 years, Pat Sajak has dressed in a professional suit and acted as the game show host, while Vanna White has stayed mostly silent and worn sexually revealing clothing. At the height of his career, Sajak won two Emmys and a People's Choice Award. White has won neither, but she did appear in the Guinness Book of World Records as "Television's Most Frequent Clapper."[28] White surely has several talents in addition to clapping and turning letters, but the format of *Wheel of Fortune* doesn't exactly allow her to show the world what else she can do.

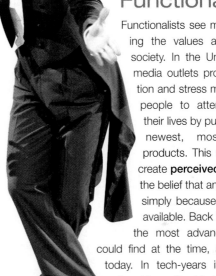

> Even though we're sometimes blind to it, **stereotypes exist quite frequently in the media.** The next time you watch a TV show such as *Dancing with the Stars,* **be on the lookout for gender differences in costume.**

TRADITIONAL PORTRAYALS

Television depictions of male–female roles are significantly traditional in nature. Consider popular TV shows like *The Simpsons*. Although roles may change temporarily depending on the plot of certain episodes, Marge Simpson is portrayed as the traditional housewife, while Homer plays the part of a working man. Marge's primary concerns center around her husband and children, and episodes featuring her usually include stories of past romances or plots involving her mother or sisters. Episodes focusing on Homer usually revolve around his life at work (whether at the nuclear plant or in outer space) and his interactions with the community. It's clear from *The Simpsons* that even progressive TV shows can slip into traditional portrayals of gender; both *Family Guy* and *South Park* share the same role dichotomy.

PERCEIVED OBSOLESCENCE is the belief that an item is outdated because a new model is available.

PLANNED OBSOLESCENCE is the practice of adding technical improvements to make upgrading to the next model a necessity.

Functionalism

Functionalists see media as promoting the values and norms of a society. In the United States, our media outlets promote consumption and stress modernity, leading people to attempt to improve their lives by purchasing only the newest, most cutting-edge products. This media focus can create **perceived obsolescence**, the belief that an item is outdated simply because a new model is available. Back in 2003, I bought the most advanced computer I could find at the time, and I still use it today. In tech-years it's ancient, and since I haven't added RAM or updated my graphics card, it sometimes has trouble loading images or downloading large files. Still, I'm able to use it perfectly well to write this book. The newest technology isn't always strictly necessary. Sometimes, however, **planned obsolescence** makes upgrading a necessity. Did the salespeople already know that Blu-ray was on the way two years ago when they sold me regular DVDs, hoping that I'd replace my movie collection with newer, arguably better, discs in the future? Technological improvements may result in higher-quality products, but they also frequently result in additional income for media companies.

Given that all media are controlled by a small number of corporations,[29] functionalists question if such businesses can actually serve the information needs of a population. Since information is vital to our democratic society, can a limited number of companies provide the diversity of information that we need? Try watching the news on a variety of different channels. You'll quickly notice that all stations provide the same information; the only difference is who is providing it.

discover solutions to social problems:
WHAT IS THE ROLE OF THE GOVERNMENT IN MEDIA?

Do you think it's important for us to have news sources with diverse points of view? Or do you believe that since the news is all straight facts, it wouldn't matter whether the media were owned by a single company or controlled by the government?

Media Ownership

Before 1996, corporations had to get permission from the Federal Communications Commission (FCC) to purchase media outlets. This process stopped businesses from controlling all sources of media in one area of the country. If Viacom owned the local radio station, for instance, it wasn't allowed to own the major TV station as well.

The Telecommunications Act of 1996 changed all this, however. Most restrictions on media ownership were eliminated, allowing big businesses to quickly take control of radio, newspaper, and TV outlets in the United States. Today, only a handful of large media companies remain, and the

majority of our media outlets are owned by these corporations. For example, The Walt Disney Company owns a variety of networks, from the Disney Channel to ABC to ESPN.

Now that the Internet has become a significant media source, though, the future of media ownership is difficult to predict. Since no one company can essentially "own" the Internet, it may prove to be a democratic force that ultimately breaks the monopolies' hold. However, some people argue that by waiting for the Internet to topple monopolies, we're only letting the major companies tighten their control. The only way to truly access diverse points of view, these people claim, is to let the government force big business out and take control of the media itself.

What do you think? How involved should the government be in our media? Would we receive more diverse points of view from government-run media, or would we simply encounter different biases? Keep these questions in mind as we discuss politics in further detail in the next chapter.

Media Monopoly

Except for public radio and television, media outlets in the United States are for-profit businesses.

In 1983, there were 50 large media conglomerates in the United States. Because of consolidations, today there are five: Time Warner, Disney, Murdcoch's News Corporation, Bertelsmann of Germany, and Viacom.

The Internet is now the only major media source in the United States not under the control of the Big Five media conglomerates.

All information systems owned by the Big Five (satellites, airwaves, etc.) were put into place using public money.

Many countries have successful public and private media systems. But the United States keeps decreasing funding for non-commercial media outlets such as NPR and PBS.

By the time a child is 18, he or she has seen around 16,000 simulated murders on television. Local news programs support the violence by using sensationalist reporting techniques.
What will our media be like in 10 years?

Influencing

YOU

∧ At the present, **only a handful of companies own the majority of U.S. media outlets.**
∧ Known as **the Big Five,** these business conglomerates control most of what we hear, read, and see.

The Media's Role in Politics

As you no doubt witnessed in the last presidential election, the media plays a huge role in politics. As we saw in 2004, it can even make or break a candidate. Howard Dean, a contender for the Democratic nomination, was leading the polls until his fateful speech in Iowa, where he uttered a rallying cry to his supporters. Members of the media portrayed his emotional outburst as the ranting of an unstable man and turned a majority of the public against him. As a result, John Kerry won the primary even though many felt he was too "stale" to win the actual election. Indeed, he lost the 2004 race to former president George W. Bush. As we discuss politics in more detail in Chapter 7, keep in mind that the media (and thus, big business) has power over what we see and don't see in the political arena. How might things have been different if, instead of calling him crazy, the press had admired Dean's passion and enthusiasm for the presidency?

As mentioned briefly in Chapter 2, the realities of economic inequality aren't portrayed in the media. Take for example, the group of reality shows called *The Real Housewives*. Starting in 2006 with *The Real Housewives of Orange County*, the shows depict groups of affluent women around the United States. The "housewives" live in luxury, many working high-class jobs they enjoy, and others spending their days primping, shopping, and attending social events. Obviously there is nothing "real" about these women, just like there is nothing "real" about reality TV, since few of us live like those we see on these shows. If the media were to show how the majority of people in the U.S. live, programs would feature middle and working class families earning hourly wages and receiving moderate incomes. The adults might work as electricians or salespeople, and the children would attend public schools and hope to go on to college. This might not be as exciting to watch as the lives of socialites, but it's a realistic representation of our society.

Pro & Con

New Technology in the Workplace

Some people can't wait to get their hands on the latest gadgets; they find it difficult to imagine surviving without up-to-date technological tools. Other people believe that new technology is a gimmick, a waste of time, or even a destructive social force. What are a few of the benefits and drawbacks of introducing new technology into the workforce?

Pro

- New technology leads to increased productivity and eliminates the need for companies to hire countless numbers of employees.
- Increased productivity leads to higher profits.
- New technology also improves communication between people and reduces the amount of waste in our society.

Con

- It can take time to learn new technology, decreasing productivity until the necessary skills are taught.
- The cost of maintaining technology can be greater than if employees were hired to do the same work.
- Preoccupation with instant communication tethers us to technology, leading our society to obsess over the need for constant technological change.

From Classroom to Community | Freedom of the Press?

As a journalism major and a staff writer for the university's alumi magazine, Jordy loved digging up facts. In her sophomore year, Jordy was assigned to write a profile of a prominent alumna who'd single-handedly financed the construction of the school's new music center.

"To be honest, I wasn't too excited about the assignment at first. I set up a phone interview with the alum and asked her about her college days, her experiences in the business world . . . the usual stuff. But I wanted to get some information from other sources, too."

Jordy used the Internet to do more research on the donor's background and the company she'd founded. Most of her search results didn't yield much new information, but on one Web page, Jordy found something she hadn't expected.

"I discovered that the alum and her company had invested millions of dollars in corporations that did business with the Sudanese government, indirectly supporting the genocide in Sudan. A lot of students here believe that it's important for influential people and companies to divest from Sudan, and they care a lot about what's happening in Darfur. I knew that what I'd found out was relevant to our community, and I wanted it to be printed in my article."

Jordy submitted her final article with a paragraph included about the donor's questionable financial ethics. When the editor of the alumni magazine read Jordy's draft, however, he called Jordy into his office.

"Our editor's a good guy, but he told me that he'd talked with the Board of Directors and there was no way he could print my article in the magazine. It would alienate the alumna, and she was too wealthy and influential for us to offend. I understood why the school didn't want to run my article, but their decision to censor factual reporting still made me furious. I decided to resign from the alumni magazine and start my own independent paper on campus so I could make sure that our school community got the real facts, not just sugarcoated ones."

get the topic: HOW DO EXPANDING TECHNOLOGIES AFFECT SOCIETY?

Theory

CONFLICT THEORY   90

- information is power
- five corporations control information in U.S. media
- funding media through advertisement may be a conflict of interest, as corporate interests may drive the media

SYMBOLIC INTERACTIONISM   90

- images in the media contain inaccurate information; even though the actress on the screen is gorgeous, you will not become beautiful by drinking Coke

FEMINIST THEORY   90

- females are largely underrepresented in the media
- television contributes to gender inequality by depicting traditional gender roles and stereotyping both men and women

FUNCTIONALISM   90

- media is a socialization tool that serves an essential function in society
- advertisements create our society's values and norms

Key Terms

technology consists of all processes, inventions, and methods used to advance society.   82

McDonaldization refers to applying the business model of McDonald's to other businesses.   83

digital divide is the gap between high-income countries and low-income countries that influences their access to current technology.   83

cultural lag refers to a situation in which members of society can't keep up with technology.   84

global village is a term referring to the "shrinking" of the world through immediate electronic communications.   86

media are the channels through which we store and receive information; they consist of print, television, radio, and the Internet.   86

media bias occurs when members of the media favor one group over another and let it affect their rendition of the truth.   88

editorial slant appears in arguments that openly present opinions that favor one side over another.   88

perceived obsolescence is the belief that an item is outdated because a new model is available.   91

planned obsolescence is the practice of adding technical improvements to make upgrading to the next model a necessity.   91

Sample Test Questions

These multiple-choice questions are similar to those found in the test bank that accompanies this textbook.

1. Which situation below is most likely to cause a cultural lag?

   a. A person spends a lot of time sending text messages, but not reading books.

   b. A person refuses to learn to drive a motorcycle.

   c. A person resists learning to use new cell phone features.

   d. A person travels two or three hours by car each week.

2. Neil Postman's argument about television is that

   a. it's a passive medium.

   b. people always want the newest model.

   c. it inspires creativity.

   d. it shows too many ads.

3. Which form of media is declining the fastest?

   a. television

   b. print

   c. radio

   d. Internet

4. What ethical problems arise from the current system of advertisement? (Choose one)

   a. Corporations are often controlled by the media.

   b. Big businesses take cuts from local advertisers.

   c. Ads are often strictly censored by media conglomerates.

   d. Media outlets are presented with conflicts of interest.

5. Which statement best describes the results of the Gurupa, Brazil, study?

   a. Their TV-watching etiquette is very different from ours.

   b. The economic gap between the upper and lower class decreased dramatically with the introduction of technology.

   c. Only the rich could afford access to TVs; because of this, crime increased as the months went by.

   d. The poor continued to socialize in the evenings while the wealthy secluded themselves in front of their TVs.

ESSAY

1. Is the field of journalism obsolete? Explain the need, or lack there-of, to "reinvent" journalism.

2. The inhabitants of Gurupa have strict social norms associated with watching television. What are some of our society's "rules" for watching TV? How might a functionalist explain the differences between the two cultures?

3. Do you perceive a political bias in the U.S. media? Back up your argument with at least one of the studies mentioned in this chapter.

4. Which would you rather see controlling the U.S. media: the government or large corporations? Why?

5. Explain this statement: In U.S. society, media has reached the status of "functionalism." Include personal examples.

WHERE TO START YOUR RESEARCH PAPER

To learn more about communications in different countries, go to
https://www.cia.gov/library/publications/the-world-factbook/

To learn more about women in media, go to http://www.iwmf.org/

For more information on the effect of advertising on children, go to
http://www.aap.org/advocacy/releases/dec06advertising.htm

To see a bird's eye view of the town of Gurupa, go to
http://www.maplandia.com/brazil/para/gurupa/gurupa/

To learn more about current bias in the media, visit http://www.fair.org

To read an article on the results of employer access to Facebook, see
http://news.bbc.co.uk/2/hi/uk_news/england/essex/7914415.stm

For more information on media stereotyping, check out
http://www.media-awareness.ca/english/issues/stereotyping/

ANSWERS: 1. c; 2. a; 3. b; 4. d; 5. a

Remember to check www.thethinkspot.com for additional information, downloadable flashcards, and other helpful resources.

POLITICS AND ECONOMY

HOW DO WE GOVERN TO GET WHAT
   WE NEED?
HOW ARE GOVERNMENT AND ECONOMY
   RELATED?
HOW DOES THE ECONOMIC SYSTEM
   INFLUENCE THE POLITICAL?

President

Obama acknowledged that a severe recession has brought "incredible pain and hardship" to millions of families, but said he is confident that his policies will revive the economy and help the nation avoid future calamities.

Though the jobless rate is rising, Obama urged patience while federal efforts to stabilize the financial system and boost economic activity take effect. He also offered a vigorous defense of his decision to pursue an ambitious social agenda in the midst of the crisis, saying he is laying the foundation for "a post-bubble economic growth model."

"The days when we are going to be able to grow this economy just on an overheated housing market or people spending—maxing out on their credit cards—those days are over," Obama told reporters after meeting with economic advisers at the White House. "What we need to do is go back to fundamentals. And that means driving our health care costs down. It means improving our education system so our children are prepared and we're innovating in science and technology. And it means that we're making this transition to the clean-energy economy."

Obama's remarks, tinged with optimism, came as the administration launched a broader campaign to build support for its initiatives and to combat what National Economic Council Director Lawrence H. Summers said yesterday was "an excess of fear" blocking the path to recovery. Over the past week, Obama and other top administration officials have fanned out across Washington to publicly discuss the economy, take questions, and offer reassurance.

On Monday, Christina Romer, chairman of the president's Council of Economic Advisers, told an audience at the Brookings Institution that the current crisis, while severe, "pales in comparison" with the Great Depression. On Thursday, Obama told the Business Roundtable, an association of executives, that things "are not as bad as we think they are." And yesterday, as Obama met with his economic advisers, Summers told another Brookings crowd that he sees glimmers of hope amid the economic gloom.

"It is surely too early to gauge the broader economic impact of the president's program," Summers said. "But it is modestly encouraging that since it began to take shape, consumer spending in the U.S., which was collapsing during the holiday season, appears, according to a number of indicators, to have stabilized."

The campaign continues tomorrow when Summers and Romer are scheduled to appear on the Sunday talk shows.

Republicans, meanwhile, noted that the administration is selling a sense of hope even as the jobless rate has spiked to 8.1 percent and economic advisers to House Speaker Nancy Pelosi (D-Calif.) have warned that another big stimulus package might be needed.

"Their newfound optimism is definitely a tactical shift," said Antonia Ferrier, a spokeswoman for House Minority Leader John A. Boehner (R-Ohio). "For the sake of American families and small businesses, we hope they are right."[1]

---Sack lunches of peanut butter sandwiches, summer "stay-cations," and homemade birthday gifts—recent economic problems have prompted many to tighten their belts and cut expenses wherever possible.

Why, at a time when the public is cutting back, is the government spending even more? How do other nations run their economies? What exactly are the connections between the economic and political systems, and how do they affect our lives? This chapter seeks to answer these and other questions.

get the topic: HOW DO WE GOVERN TO GET WHAT WE NEED?

> **SOCIAL INSTITUTIONS** are organizations that provide a framework for individuals to communicate with the larger society.
>
> **ECONOMIC SYSTEM (OR ECONOMY)** is a social institution that helps a society organize what it produces, distributes, and consumes, including goods and services.
>
> **CAPITALISM** is an economic system in which individuals or private corporations can own and operate the production of goods, make decisions about the price of those goods, and distribute them as they deem appropriate.

Historically, governments have always been involved in their nations' economies, whether they were printing money, generating coins from precious metals, or creating a central bank to control interest on loans. At times, I've had students who've wondered why two different systems don't exist. One student even argued that economic and government systems should be totally separate. My reply was simple: "How?" Governments make laws that protect economic systems, and economic systems provide the resources that people and governments need to continue. The dual systems of government and economy have been, and will always be, connected.

Of course, the nature of this relationship creates a source of political debate. Consider the most recent economic crisis in the United States. In 2008, even before Barack Obama became President, he was pressured to address his plans for "growing" the economy. Over the years, a deep hole had been dug by subprime mortgage lenders, Wall Street executives, and people who felt they could live better—and consume more—than they could afford.

Shortly after Obama was sworn into office, Congress passed an extensive stimulus package of $789 billion.[2] The idea was that if more goods and services were purchased, it would be less likely for demand to fall and companies to lay off workers. The chart on the

next page shows this firsthand example of the interaction of the political and economic systems of a nation.

Economic Systems

As you can see, politics and economics have similar effects on social order. This chapter will focus on politics and economics as **social institutions**—systems within a society that provide frameworks for individuals. In the United States, our government is a system with three branches; as citizens, we're allowed to vote two of those branches into office. However, if you moved to Great Britain, the system would be different and you wouldn't immediately know your place in it.

There are two basic types of **economic systems** (or **economies**): capitalism and socialism. No country has an economy that is entirely capitalist or entirely socialist; all systems will have a mixture of both, although the degrees may vary.

Capitalism is an economic system in which individuals and private corporations can own and operate the production of goods, make decisions about the price of those goods, and distribute them as they deem appropriate.[3] Capitalism is characterized by three main components: private ownership of property, profit motivation, and competition in a free market.

Private ownership of property allows me to own my home, car, and television set. In general, this is a good thing. If I work hard and save money, I can acquire lots of "stuff," and that stuff is mine until I die and pass it to my children. It sounds like a pretty good idea, at least in theory.

Unfortunately, social problems arise because of this, the first being the question of resources. Are there enough homes, cars, and TVs to go around? Does the amount of "stuff" grow as fast as the population? Usually not. Allowing someone to hold onto objects creates a system that breeds inequality. If I inherit property from my uncle and rent it to someone else, I effortlessly profit from the ownership. Such a system allows for the wealth—and lack thereof—of one generation to continue to the next.

Profit motivation in capitalism can help people rise from poverty

>>> **U.S. labor laws,** which regulate matters such as pay rate, hours, and working conditions, **are created by the government to protect workers.** All business, public and private, must follow these laws.

to wealth. It can also create problems in society. A seller wants the highest price he can get, and a buyer wants the cheapest price. As a seller, the best way for me to profit would be to corner the market. If I had the only sociology textbook in print, I could raise the price as high as I wanted. For this reason, the U.S. government has organizations that exist to curb the development of **monopolies**—companies with exclusive control of the production or trade of a product.

Because profit is the underlying motive of capitalism, employee-related problems can occur as well. There is always a danger of companies exploiting workers, paying them as little as possible to keep profits high. It was for this reason that the government established a minimum wage in the 1930s. Even in white-collar jobs, most employers seek to pay their workers only as much as they have to in order to keep them around (and not have to pay to train new ones).

Capitalism needs a **free market** in which it can create competition. This provides consumers with more goods while keeping prices low. In a free market, the "law of supply and demand" rules the day. If there's too much supply and too little demand, prices will drop. If there's a huge demand and too few products, prices will rise. Recently, as I walked through the mall, I was struck by the massive disparities in pric-

MONOPOLY is the exclusive control of the production or trade of a product in the market.

FREE MARKET is an economic market that operates without government control.

ELASTICITY OF DEMAND explains the fact that demand for the product changes when the price changes.

ing between stores. Some "exclusive" boutiques sold men's shirts for upward of $150, while in a discount store, I could buy a similar shirt for $12. This type of variety occurs because the United States operates under a free market.

Some products have a strong **elasticity of demand**, meaning that the demand for them doesn't change much when the prices go up. If you needed a car to get to work and the price of gas went up to $10 a gallon, you would still have to buy it. You might refrain from taking long trips on the weekends, but you couldn't avoid driving completely. A number of products such as electricity, health care, and prescription drugs have a strong price elasticity of demand in the U.S. economy. Generally, the price for these products doesn't matter—if you need them, you'll pay for them.

Economic Stimulus Package:
How it Works and Whom it Helps

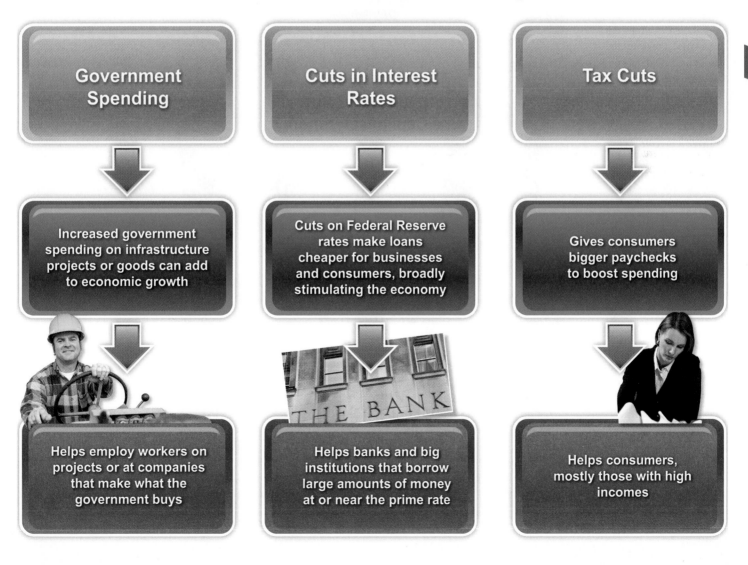

Government Spending	Cuts in Interest Rates	Tax Cuts
Increased government spending on infrastructure projects or goods can add to economic growth	Cuts on Federal Reserve rates make loans cheaper for businesses and consumers, broadly stimulating the economy	Gives consumers bigger paychecks to boost spending
Helps employ workers on projects or at companies that make what the government buys	Helps banks and big institutions that borrow large amounts of money at or near the prime rate	Helps consumers, mostly those with high incomes

As mentioned before, no system can be purely one-sided, which is why in a capitalist economy such as the United States there has always been some degree of government intervention. Policies such as minimum wage and Social Security are put in place by the government so that the welfare of workers is not overshadowed by corporate bottom lines. The government also controls unavoidable monopolies in order to avoid price gouging. For example, where I live, we have only one electric company. Therefore, the state regulates the price of electricity so the citizens aren't extorted.

You may recall that Karl Marx, one of the first and most vocal critics of capitalism, argued that this economic system eventually leads to the exploitation of the common people. Why? A small, elite portion of the population generally gains control over the business aspects of society, leaving lower- and middle-class individuals at their mercy.[4] Under capitalism, the "haves" keep their positions and gain even more control, while the "have-nots" continue to lose ground. Of course, there's no such thing as unfettered capitalism in the United States, nor has there been since the early 1800s. That does not stop many of my students from believing we are a purely capitalist nation. Currently, as President Obama strives to expand access to health care, many of my students complain that the United States is becoming "socialist." Is it really? A clearer definition of the term will shed some light on this argument.

As an alternative to capitalism, Marx proposed **socialism**, an economic system by which resources and means of production are owned collectively by the citizens. In a pure socialist economy as imagined by Marx, the government regulates all property to avoid any possibility of exploitation. This is quite similar to a pure democracy in which the government is literally "ruled by the people" (more on this topic later), except in this case, it's the economy that's ruled by the people. Socialism is based on the idea that goods and services are produced and distributed to meet the needs of society, not to generate a profit.

Of course, socialist economies can create social problems as well. If individual gain isn't possible, why would anyone strive to create new and innovative things? Some argue that socialism stifles individuals. Without the ability to generate personal wealth, people lack the motivation to

improve their lives. The history of planned economies seems to support this notion because, historically, socialist consumers have had fewer choices of goods and services. In almost all countries that have experimented with Marxist socialism, there have generally been a small group of elites who take advantage of society and work to keep their profits from others. One problem not solved by socialism is how to keep people with power from using that power for their own benefit.

Generally speaking, pure forms of capitalism and socialism don't exist in the world today. Most countries, at least in the West, have some variation of what is known as **democratic socialism**. This type of economic system involves a blend of free market capitalism and government regulation of the economy. The concept of democratic socialism has gained ground particularly in Europe and is often associated with the labor movement in countries such as France, Germany, Finland, and Spain.[5] Tax rates in these countries can be anywhere from 40 to 50 percent of a worker's income, with those funds being used to provide public services such as health care and unemployment coverage to the less fortunate. In such a system, the government takes an active role in redistributing the wealth of the nation to decrease inequality.

Of course, the government in the United States does this as well, but to a much lesser degree. The highest tax bracket in the nation is around 38 percent. Yet, the United States does take wealth from some and give it to others. For example, public schools are funded by everyone in society. Whether or not you have children, you still pay to educate the next generation.

People in European countries typically view the role of government and social welfare differently than people in the United States. For example, in a study of eight industrialized nations, researchers found that the people in the United States have the most negative views toward the government's redistribution of wealth, whereas people in Norway are the most likely to accept such disbursement.[6] That's not to say that Americans don't want to help the less fortunate, but they generally distrust the government's ability to do this well.

With the recent federal takeover of mortgage lenders Freddie Mac and Fannie Mae, the two largest lending institutions are now government sponsored. This serves as a real-life example of the way that capitalism and socialism tend to blend together, an idea known as **convergence theory**.[7] This convergence works both ways throughout the world with. Just as democratic socialism is becoming more popular in Europe, many other countries worldwide are moving away from exclusive socialism. In China, for example, the market (rather than the government) determines what goods and services are sold. Although the government still owns many of the major business, individuals are now allowed to own land. This blending of private and public ownership shows convergence as well.

Cycle of Wealth in a Capitalist Economy

Sucessful company

Increased production

More jobs

More income

Increased purchasing

Global Economy

As technology improves our ability to communicate, it becomes difficult for economic systems to remain self-contained. Business deals between companies on two separate continents can be transacted with a click of a mouse, and many corporations are establishing international satellite offices around the globe. A **corporation** is a legal entity that has an objective—typically to make a profit for its owners. Although shareholders own the company and employees run the day-to-day operations, a corporation can purchase property, acquire debt, participate in legal contracts, and enjoy most of the rights and privileges of an individual person. The people who make up international corporations are often a mixture of diverse nationalities. This is especially true for **transnational corporations** (also known as **multinational corporations**), businesses that operate in at least two countries and have the interests of their company at heart rather than the interests of their country of origin. As a dominant force in the global economy, transnational corporations generate huge profits and possess international political power.

Trends in the U.S. Economy

Layoffs, downsizings, production suspensions . . . no matter what it's called, job loss slowly renders an economy powerless. Unfortunately, we can all witness the real-life results of the credit crisis that began in September 2008. In that year alone, 2.6 million jobs were lost in the United States, the largest amount in more than six decades. To put it in perspective, that's as many jobs as states such as Wisconsin and Maryland have *in total*.[9]

As of June 2009, the unemployment rate was 9.7 percent.[10] If your college has around 2,000 students, imagine 194 of them being told to pack up and leave, without warning. Such could actually be the case as universities are forced to cut costs to make ends meet. A friend of mine who teaches for a public college in California told me that the school expects to eliminate 40 percent of the possible sections in sociology this year, due to economic cutbacks. All adjuncts have been fired, and full-time faculty members are required to increase their teaching loads to keep their jobs. The effects of the recession can be felt everywhere.

The economy can be fickle—what's needed one year may be insignificant the next. (Think of fashion: Are Crocs still cool? Even if they are on your campus, they won't be by the time you finish college.) Shifts in the economy affect society. Some industries shrink, while others expand. In the economic crises of 2008, many jobs in manufacturing and construction were lost, while those in health care and social assistance grew.[11] How might this shape the future of society?

Society is also influenced by **demographics**—statistical characteristics of human populations, such as age or gender—of workers. For example, in 1980, whites had the highest participation rate in the labor force. By 2006, Hispanics overtook them, increasing their participation to 68.7 percent. By 2014, the participation rates for whites, blacks, and Asians are all predicted to decrease, while Hispanic participation is expected to increase even further.[12] Why? Is it due to the general increase in age of certain groups, driving many out of the workforce and into retirement? Is it due to immigration, with high rates of young Hispanics entering the United States? Perhaps it's both of these factors, or maybe it's neither.

As we discussed in Chapter 2, individuals may not be participating in the labor force for reasons other than laziness. Some are too ill to work; others suffer with a disability, have retired, or are simply unable to find a job. Although these people may not hold jobs, not all individuals who refrain from working are considered unemployed. By U.S. government standards,

people are classified as **unemployed** if they do not have a job, have actively been looking for work, and are currently available to start employment. "Actively looking for a job" includes sending out resumés, searching employment registrars, or even asking friends and family members for assistance. People classified as *not* "currently available" for work include full-time students, workers on strike, and those who are absent from their regular jobs because of illness, vacation time, or personal reasons.[13] So, when you see U.S. unemployment numbers, remember that you're not being presented with the actual number of people without work.

Many people work for private corporations or government institutions, but some are self-employed, meaning that they operate a business as a sole proprietor or a partner. An agricultural worker (farmer) is one of the most common occupations for a self-employed individual. But as many family farms become corporately owned, the self-employed farmer is becoming a dying breed. This trend is one of the major causes for the decrease in self-employment over the last 50 years. In 2003, only 7.5 percent of the workforce was self-employed, down from 18.5 percent in 1948.[14]

∧
∧ **Furniture store IKEA originally started in**
∧ **Sweden,** but quickly became a multi-national corporation. **Today, IKEA operates in 36 different countries worldwide, from Slovakia to the United Arab Emirates,** and earns over 20 billion euros in sales per year.[8]

ENTREPRENEURSHIP is the creation of new organizations in response to economic and social opportunities.

ENTREPRENEUR is a person who establishes, organizes, manages, and assumes all risks of an organization.

EMBARGO is a restriction on trade that is enforced by a government.

TARIFFS are taxes placed on traded items.

NORTH AMERICAN FREE TRADE AGREEMENT (NAFTA) is an agreement established in 1994 to allow free trade on agricultural products between the United States, Mexico, and Canada.

TRADITIONAL SYSTEMS are organizations in which social power is gained by respect for patterns of government.

CHARISMATIC SYSTEM is a political organization in which power is gained because a leader has extraordinary personal attributes.

RATIONAL-LEGAL AUTHORITY is a system in which power stems from rules and standards that are agreed upon by society.

Even though self-employment in farming is decreasing, individuals haven't stopped forming new businesses. The spirit of the entrepreneur is still alive in the United States. **Entrepreneurship** refers to the creation of new organizations in response to economic and social opportunities. An **entrepreneur** is a person who establishes, organizes, manages, and assumes all risks of an organization. Donald Trump is one of the most well-known entrepreneurs of our time. As a modern business mogul, Trump has built his real estate corporation from the ground—and filed for bankruptcy no less than three separate times.[15]

One in four people in the United States will try his hand at entrepreneurship at some point in his lifetime. Certainly the decision to found a company depends on personal qualities such as motivation and individual drive. But what makes a new company successful? There's an old saying that describes the three most important aspects of business: "Location, location, location." This may be true, but research suggests that social networks and levels of competition in the marketplace play just as strong a role.[16]

Free Trade and Political Objectives

Politics and economics go hand in hand when discussing trade with other nations. International conflicts and national health regulations have created the need to place certain restrictions on transactions. These restrictions are typically in the form of embargos or tariffs. An **embargo** is a restriction on trade that's enforced by the government. The United States imposed a trade embargo on Cuba in 1962. It's still enforced today, which is why Cuban cigars are illegal in the United States.

Tariffs, on the other hand, are taxes placed on traded items. High tariffs limit the amount of trade that occurs because the added tax makes the cost too high for consumers. Not all foreign trade involves tariffs. The **North American Free Trade Agreement (NAFTA)** was established in 1994 to allow free trade on agricultural products between the United States, Mexico, and Canada. Removing all tariffs provided a major economic boost for these countries. Free trade policies such as NAFTA benefit both developing and developed nations; they allow developing countries the opportunity to sell their products at a fair price, as well as provide a wider variety of products with competitive pricing to wealthy countries. Of course, such policies also create controversy and lead to other social problems. For example, what might result from allowing companies to pursue cheaper labor in Mexico without having to fear import tariffs? If even more factory jobs are outsourced could this increase rates of unemployment in the United States?

Political Systems

Free trade policies are a perfect example of economic involvement in political systems. The power of economics is what holds a government together; without at least some authority over the market, a government is not able to create or enforce policies. Sociologist Max Weber believed that political systems are based on three forms of authority: traditional, charismatic, and rational-legal authority.

In a **traditional system**, social power is achieved through general respect for patterns of government. For example, English monarchs such as Charles I and Henry IV gained and held power because of family lineage and the tradition of monarchy. Modern examples include the government of Saudi Arabia, a traditional monarchy backed by a consultative body of officials. In 2005, King Fahd died, leaving the throne to his brother, Crown Prince Abdullah; in return, Abdullah pledged to leave the throne to another brother in the event of his death.[17] Countries that follow traditional systems are generally made up of people who share similar world views and, often, religious principles.

What do Nelson Mandela, Bill Clinton, and Aung San Suu Kyi have in common? All are known to be charismatic leaders. In **charismatic systems**, power is gained by a leader who has extraordinary personal attributes. Such leaders inspire their followers and often initiate influential movements. In the mid-1900s, Fidel Castro sparked revolution in Cuba when he openly protested the existing dictatorial regime. Many contribute Castro's rise in power to his powerful public speaking skills and charismatic personality. **Rational-legal authority** stems from the rules and standards officially sanctified by a

∧
∧ In 1975, 20-year-old **Bill Gates co-founded**
∧ **a company based on the development of microcomputer software.** Eleven years later, the college dropout and Microsoft CEO became the youngest billionaire in American history. It's important to note that **after working together for a number of years, Apple and Microsoft became, and still remain, fierce competitors. How might this have affected both organizations?**

The Benefits of Free Trade

Goods come into a country

No tariffs added, prices stay the same

$19⁹⁶ Competitive prices for consumers

More profits for manufactures

∧
∧
∧
∧ **Free trade allows for an increased exchange of goods between countries.** Without the addition of tariffs, consumers can afford to buy products at competitive market prices. **The more products consumers buy, the more money countries who export those products can make.**

society. For example, American citizens have a written set of rights and regulations in the Constitution. If a U.S. president were to declare himself king, it would go against agreed-upon rules and be fiercely rejected by society. However, if a woman were to walk into a voting booth on Election Day, most people would find it completely rational, in concurrence with the 19th Amendment. Likewise, a U.S. president has the constitutional authority to make executive decisions, such as deploying U.S. troops, but cannot "declare war." Authority and power are important components of any government; social problems in the political realm often occur when the authority of a government conflicts with societal rules. In the summer of 2009, Iranians took to the streets to protest manipulated election results that violated their nation's rational-legal authority.

The amount of power that a leader has is often dependent on the type of government under which a nation operates.

TYPES OF GOVERNMENT

All nations are governed in different ways. At the present, three main types of government exist: monarchy, authoritarianism, and democracy.

A **monarchy** is a political system based on the idea that leaders are selected by heritage or divine right. Monarchies are usually run by a single family that passes power down through generations. Many ancient societies were ruled by this type of government, but today only a handful of nations still use this system in its pure form. In some European countries, kings and queens still sit on a recognized throne, but they have limited power and are acknowledged merely as symbols of cultural tradition. Queen Elizabeth II, for example, is still seen as a figure of authority, but it's the British Parliament and Prime Minister that truly govern the country.

MONARCHY is a political system in which leadership is based on the idea that leaders are selected by divine right or heritage.

AUTHORITARIANISM is a form of government that gives citizens very little say in how the nation is run.

DICTATOR is a single person with complete control in a government system.

OLIGARCHY is a small group of influential people with complete control of the government.

TOTALITARIANISM is an authoritarian government that controls every aspect of citizens' lives.

Authoritarianism is a form of government that gives citizens very little say in how the nation is run and encourages absolute submission to authority. Although these governments can be lead by a king or queen, more often they are ruled by a **dictator**—a single person with complete control—or by an **oligarchy**—a small group of influential people who rule the nation together. Contrary to what you may think, not all authoritarian governments rule through use of power and fear. In 1999, General Pervez Musharraf, in reaction to the country's current political system and stressed relations with India, took control of Pakistan in a bloodless coup. During his nine-year reign as leader, Musharraf worked to decrease Islamic fundamentalism in the region and build, as he stated, a more tolerant and democratic Pakistan. His popularity among the nation's citizens rose steadily until 2006, and in 2008, President Musharraf resigned as leader and gave the government back to the people.[18]

When an authoritarian government controls every aspect of citizens' lives, it becomes **totalitarianism**. In this type of system, the government can tell people how many children to have, what jobs to hold, and where

DEMOCRACY is a political system that is run by the citizens.

VOTER APATHY is a phenomenon in which citizens with the right to vote choose not to.

DEMOCRATIC PARTY is a political party in the United States that supports increased regulation of private institutions and a larger government.

REPUBLICAN PARTY is a political party in the United States that supports a decreased regulation of private institutions and reduced government involvement communicate with the larger society.

they can live. Countries such as Cuba, China, and Russia have a history of totalitarian rule. Regardless of the degree of freedom, however, the average citizen's voice is not heard in authoritarian regimes.

In contrast, a **democracy** is a political system in which power is held by citizens and exercised through participation and representation (literally "rule by the people" in Greek). By definition, pure democratic societies allow citizens to make every decision, but this type of government is difficult to maintain. Can you imagine all 300 million Americans having to vote on everything the government does? Nothing would get done.

The U.S. government is an example of a representative democracy; we choose officials through state-run elections, and these officials are given the authority to make decisions for us. Of course, the problem is that not every citizen takes advantage of the right to elect leaders. In the 2008 presidential election, only 64 percent of qualified citizens voted, the highest percentage since 1968.[19]

So, why don't people vote? Explanations vary. When I ask my students, answers include "What's the point? Leaders do what they want anyway;" "No one in my family votes, so I guess I never thought about it;" "I don't really care about politics;" and the tried and true "I'm only one person, my vote doesn't matter." When citizens with the right to vote chose not to, it's known as **voter apathy**. In a democracy, such apathy poses a real problem to society, because not everyone's voice is heard. Unfortunately, this tends to affect racial minorities the most.

Historically, the percentage of minority voters has been less than white voters. In the 2000 election, as you can see in the chart on the next page, 61.8 percent of eligible white citizens voted, while only 56.8 percent and 43.4 percent of eligible black and Asian American citizens voted, respectively.[20] One of the reasons that minorities have low election turnouts may be because they feel that, as a smaller segment of the population, their opinions will not have as large an impact on politics.

No matter what the cause for voter apathy, recent elections have shown that U.S. citizens are becoming more excited about and involved in the political process. Nearly 132 million people voted in the 2008 presidential election, with previously apathetic voting groups such as young adults and ethnic minorities showing renewed interest.[21] Voter apathy may have been combated by the desire for change in the country, or the affirmation that minorities do indeed hold a prominent place in politics.

POLITICAL PARTIES

Politics in the United States is essentially based on a two-party system: the **Democratic Party** and the **Republican Party**. Smaller parties exist, such as the Green Party or the Constitution Party, but Democrats and Republicans dominate the political landscape. Both parties agree that social issues such as unemployment, unequal education, and problems in health care exist. However, they differ in the solutions that they propose.

Although political platforms change from year to year, Democrats tend to prefer having the government solve social problems, while Republicans prefer to have the private sector deal with them. Because of this, Democrats generally support expanded government services. Republicans, on the other hand, encourage independence from the government, suggesting that individuals can solve social issues if the government simply gets out of the way.[22] Republicans tend to focus on individual morality, such as sexual morality, whereas Democrats tend to talk about social morality, such as a lack of equality for the poor.

Types of Government

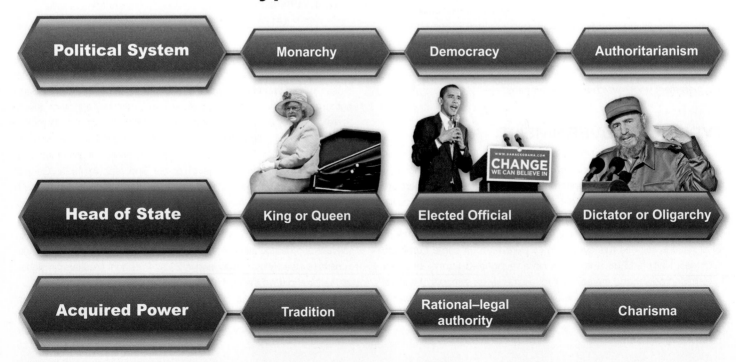

Political System	Monarchy	Democracy	Authoritarianism
Head of State	King or Queen	Elected Official	Dictator or Oligarchy
Acquired Power	Tradition	Rational–legal authority	Charisma

Percentage of Minority Voters (Compared to White Voters)

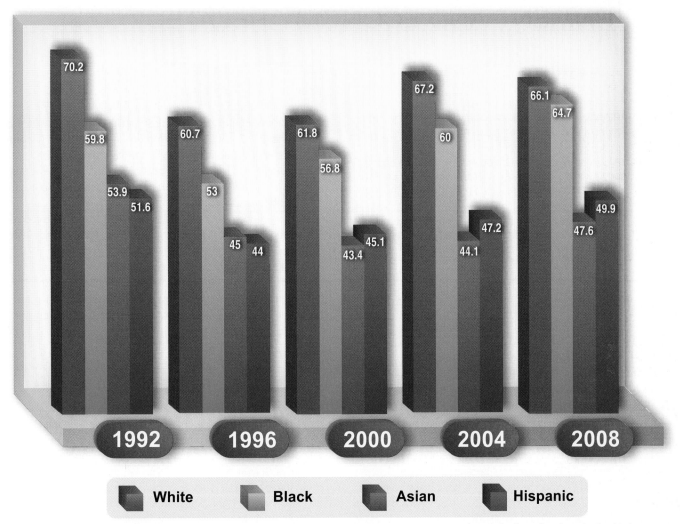

1992 — White 70.2, Black 59.8, Asian 53.9, Hispanic 51.6

1996 — White 60.7, Black 53, Asian 45, Hispanic 44

2000 — White 61.8, Black 56.8, Asian 43.4, Hispanic 45.1

2004 — White 67.2, Black 60, Asian 44.1, Hispanic 47.2

2008 — White 66.1, Black 64.7, Asian 47.6, Hispanic 49.9

■ White   ■ Black   ■ Asian   ■ Hispanic

Source: U.S. Census Bureau, "Voting and Registration Data." Accessed July 29, 2008. http://www.census.gov/population/www/socdemo/voting.html

∧
∧ On the whole, **the percentage of minorities voting in presidential elections has been less
∧ than the percentage of whites.** What causes this discrepancy in voter turnout?

▶▶▶ GO GL🌐BAL

Controlling the Global Economy: A Job for Everyone

Shortly after the dust settled on the disastrous economic crisis of 2008, President Obama had to address more than 20 heads of state at a global summit in London. His plan for economic recovery was much anticipated by major world leaders; however, the most contentious part of President Obama's speech revolved around what the United States could do rather than what it would do. The president announced that the United States could no longer be the sole engine of global growth. During past global economic downturns, the United States had been able to take the lead and increase spending to jump-start the international economy. This time, however, the mounting national debt had overwhelmed the nation's balance sheet. President Obama noted that the latest credit crisis wasn't caused by United States institutions alone; many faulty financial regulations in Europe and Asia also contributed to the crumbling economy. Recovery, he argued, had to be a combined effort.

Although the United States will have to take a less dominate role in managing the global economy this time around, it won't become completely passive. Even though the United States can't play the part of the international financier, it shouldn't miss an opportunity to help lead the way out of the global crisis. "If there's going to be renewed growth, it cannot just be the United States as the engine," stated Obama. "Everybody is going to have to pick up the pace." Many global economists agreed with this decision. "We cannot rely on the U.S. being the global locomotive," said Professor Willem H. Buiter, former member of the Bank of England Monetary Policy Committee. "Those days are gone." Now, acting as partners rather than pupils, leaders of industrialized powers such as Britain and Japan, and emerging powers such as China, India, and Brazil, are working in collaboration with the United States to formulate a solution to the global economic crisis.[23]

think social problems: HOW ARE GOVERNMENT AND ECONOMY RELATED?

ECONOMIC BEHAVIORISM states that people don't make decisions based on what is rational, but what is easiest or most popular.

COMMUNITARIANISM suggests that for society to function properly, it must have communal values and set social policies according to those values.

POWER ELITE is a group comprised of top military officials, heads of major corporations, and high-ranking political leaders; this select group of people pulls the strings that control both the economy and the politics of American society.

INTERLOCKING DIRECTORATES is a practice in which the same people are placed on a variety of corporate boards, allowing separate companies to be controlled by a small, elite group.

Functionalism

Functionalists find political systems naturally balanced. According to political scientist Robert Dahl, power is distributed widely enough in democracies that groups are driven to compete *and* work with each other in order to achieve their goals. These two forces—competition and alliance—lead groups to temper their ideals, leaving society solidly in the middle, balancing between extremes.[24]

The ideas of Richard H. Thaler and Cass R. Sunstein, authors of the book *Nudge: Improving Decisions about Health, Wealth, and Happiness*, hold a similar belief. When left to our own devices, we often make wrong decisions. Do you choose Chinese takeout because it's easy or because it's healthy? Thaler and Sunstein argue that we have many competing choices in an economy such as ours, yet people don't make decisions based on what's rational, but based on what's easiest or most popular. This theory is known as **economic behaviorism**.[25] Like nudging a friend toward a salad instead of takeout, society functions best when we help people make good choices.

Contemporary sociologist Amitai Etzioni acknowledges the interrelation betweens social structures and individual choices. As one of the founders of **communitarianism**, he suggests that for society to function properly, it must have a communal set of values that guide social policies. According to communitarianism, society is made up of three components: the community, the market, and the government. Each sector has an essential role to play, but all three interact with each other constantly. Etzioni also notes that a crucial part of society is being able to see ourselves not only as individuals, but also as part of a community.[26] In this way, decisions are made with the best interests of all in mind.

> >>> **According to economic behaviorism, we make decisions based on what's easiest to do.** The most convenient way is often not the best.

Conflict Theory

About the same time that Dahl was espousing the benefits of a balanced democratic system, sociologist C. Wright Mills was suggesting something else entirely. Mills suggested that a **power elite** runs the United States. Who are these people? According to Mills, the power elite comprises top military officials, heads of major corporations, and high-ranking political leaders. This select group of people pulls the strings that control both the economy and the politics of American society.[27]

A more modern theorist, William Domhoff, has suggested a similar idea: The United States is ruled by those with the most societal power. Consider corporate boards of directors. A common practice known as **interlocking directorates** involves placing the same people on a variety of corporate boards, allowing separate companies to be controlled by a small, elite group. Domhoff points out that this group often interacts with political leaders in exclusive clubs, directing (or at least strongly influencing) the course of the U.S. government.[28]

Symbolic Interactionism

Symbolic interactionists focus on how people define issues, and how those definitions influence our actions. If you were on the classic show *Who Wants to Be a Millionaire*, who would you trust more—a college friend that you called, or the members of the audience? According to James Surowiecki, author of *The Wisdom of Crowds*, you should trust the audience. This is because large groups have a better chance of being right. Surowiecki notes that groups of people are smarter than small clusters, or even individuals, no matter how intelligent those people may be. Large crowds are effective because they think collectively and therefore can easily influence change. They do this through a process of interaction that is often not even recognized by the group. Have you ever attended a football game where you felt that the crowd helped change the outcome? Large groups have an amazing ability to predict and affect the outcomes of their environments.

Justin Bergner remembered the first time he heard David Flores speak. He was at a neighborhood block party, listening to the man discuss politics with a small group of people. Justin had been interested in politics since he joined his high school's student council two years ago, and his awareness had expanded into local politics when he started to notice some of the growing problems in his neighborhood.

"When David began to talk about the changes he wanted to make around the city, I got interested in what he was saying. He mentioned that we needed more funding for after-school programs, and more green space inside the city boundaries. He also said it was crazy how few working-class people were involved in our city's politics."

These were all issues that troubled Justin as well. "I thought it was really cool when he said he'd be running for city council in the fall. After everyone left, I went up to him and introduced myself. I wanted to see if I could help with his campaign. He told me sure; it would be an honor to have me onboard."

David knew the chips were stacked against him. He only had $500 to support his campaign, and the incumbent candidate had thousands of dollars in corporate contributions. Rather than investing what little money he had in signage and advertising, David and his small group of volunteers focused on talking directly to the people. Justin remembered that summer well.

"I must've stood outside fifteen different movie theaters over the course of three months. We'd each go around on the weekends when it was crowded and talk to people as they were coming and going. We'd poll them on different things, like what changes they wanted to see in the city, and David would come up and talk to them personally. He went to as many community events as possible, and always made friends with the people there, letting them know he was running for office. I think the opponent started getting scared, since a week before the election all these new signs with his name appeared on lawns, and he ran this huge full-page ad in the newspaper. David didn't have those kinds of funds, of course, but he believed that the voters would make the right decision."

David's only worry, in fact, was that enough voters wouldn't make it to the polling booths. To combat this problem, Justin suggested that the team travel door-to-door on Election Day and remind residents to vote.

"All five of us walked around from 7am to 8pm, trying to cover as much of the city as we could. After polls closed, all we could do was wait."

In the end, it was announced that David Flores had won the election by only 55 votes. "All of us were jumping up and down and cheering like crazy. It was great. It felt so good to see someone we believed in make it so far, and I think we proved to everyone that politics is about more than just money."

<<< **"David would come up and talk to them personally.** He went to as many community events as possible, and always made friends with the people there, letting them know he was running for office."

WRAP YOUR MIND AROUND THE THEORY

Many of our economic decisions are made based on what is easy or popular rather than what is logical. How does this type of decision making affect society as a whole?

FUNCTIONALISM

Functionalists study how systems interact to affect individuals. Dahl notes that the American form of democracy works because power is diffused enough to be shared by competing groups. Sociologist Amitai Etzioni suggests that the role of the government and the community is to balance the self-centered drive for wealth inherent in a capitalist economy. Because of these balances, our society runs smoothly.

CONFLICT THEORY

Conflict theorists identify how members of society struggle for what is scarce. According to Marx, Mills, and Domhoff, access to wealth and power is scarce in any society. This is largely because those who have it are unwilling to let it go. Generally, they seek short-term rewards to increase their power and wealth, while ignoring the long-term societal consequences.

HOW IS POWER DISTRIBUTED IN ECONOMIC AND POLITICAL SYSTEMS?

SYMBOLIC INTERACTIONISM

Symbolic interactionists are interested in the wisdom of groups. Large groups of people make better choices than individuals and can more easily influence the world around them. Interactionists also study leaders' use of personality and charisma to gain power over groups. Weber suggests that the defining mark of a leader is that he or she has the charisma to get others to follow. Charisma is a powerful tool that can be used to unite people to achieve a common goal.

According to conflict theory, those with power often use it to dominate others. **How do the economic elite dominate the lower class?**

Many people believe that Barack Obama won the 2008 presidential election because of his charismatic way of speaking. **How do speakers use diction, facial expressions, and body language to emphasize their point?**

discover solutions to social problems:
HOW DOES THE ECONOMIC SYSTEM INFLUENCE THE POLITICAL?

Political Funding

In the United States, most political campaigns are not self-funded. When a friend of mine ran for city council, he personally paid for the yard signs and flyers he passed out. However, in a major election, few people have the wealth to pay for national TV ads or print advertising. In our country, funding comes from individuals and groups that have a vested interest in the candidate or the political party that the candidate represents. For example, the National Rifle Association (NRA) might offer funds to a candidate that opposes restrictions on personal firearms, and gun owners might also support this person with smaller individual donations.

A great deal of party donations come from **political action committees (PACs)**. PACs might allocate money to both parties, but are often

POLITICAL ACTION COMMITTEES (PACs) are interest groups that allocate money to political parties.

associated with either Democrats or Republicans. Because money can have such a profound effect on the outcome of an election, many rules and regulations are placed on how political contributions can be allocated. The McCain-Feingold-Cochran Bipartisan Campaign Reform Bill was proposed and enacted in 2002 to prevent contributions from being distributed through unethical means. Among other things, the bill involves a ban on so-called "soft money"—onetime cash contributions to national political parties from corporations, labor unions, and wealthy individuals.[29]

Pro & Con

Does the U.S. democracy actually represent "the people"?

Pro

- According to Dahl, democracy disperses power so that no one group can be in complete control.
- Shared power guarantees that everyone's voice will be heard. Those who don't vote do so of their own free will.
- Politicians seek to please voters in order to be re-elected; therefore, the public's voice is always heard.
- Those who are disenfranchised need only to properly organize and they can change the system.

Con

- Plato suggested thousands of years ago that democracy was doomed to fail because not all people are intelligent enough to choose what's best for everyone. Basing a government on self-interest ultimately leads to societal collapse.
- Marx, Mills, and Domhoff all agree that power corrupts government; when left to its own devices, a government will seek short-term economic rewards.
- Corporate interests fund political campaigns, leading politicians to represent the interests of big businesses as opposed to the voting public.
- Democracy can work, but only if it's kept out of the hands of the power elite. So far in the United States, this has not happened.

MAKE CONNECTIONS

Politics and Money

In Chapter 2 we discussed wealth and poverty. A great deal of political and economic debate centers on the issue of poverty. It would be wonderful to have a nation of wealthy people, but as conflict theorists point out, there just aren't enough resources to go around.

In Chapter 6, we discussed the media and how they appeal to different demographics. Politics are similar. Individuals in certain income brackets tend to side with one particular party because that party caters to the needs of their group. Because Democratic candidates tend to endorse government-run programs that provide services to the indigent, they gain the support of individuals with lower incomes.

HOW **DO WE GOVERN TO GET WHAT WE NEED?** 98

by creating a government that allows individuals to control their financial growth through a capitalist economy

HOW **ARE GOVERNMENT AND ECONOMY RELATED?** 106

through economic behaviorism, the wisdom of crowds, and communitarianism

HOW **DOES THE ECONOMIC SYSTEM INFLUENCE THE POLITICAL?** 109

through campaign funding from PACs and other special interest groups, especially through the use of soft money

get the topic: HOW DO WE GOVERN TO GET WHAT WE NEED?

Theory

FUNCTIONALISM   106

- people make decisions based on what's easy, not on what's logical
- power in the United States is balanced, which helps keep society functioning smoothly

CONFLICT THEORY   106

- individuals struggle for what is scarce in society

- in the United States, members of the elite work to keep their power and wealth, regardless of the outcome for others

SYMBOLIC INTERACTIONISM   106

- large groups are better at making decision and influencing the world around them than individuals or smaller groups are
- leaders use their charismatic personalities to gain power and achieve goals

Key Terms

social institutions are organizations that provide a framework for individuals to communicate with the larger society.   98

economic system (or economy) is a social institution that helps a society organize what it produces, distributes, and consumes, including goods and services.   98

capitalism is an economic system in which individuals or private corporations can own and operate the production of goods, make decisions about the price of those goods, and distribute them as they deem appropriate.   98

monopoly is the exclusive control of the production or trade of a product in the market.   99

free market is an economic market that operates without government control.   99

elasticity of demand explains the fact that demand for the product changes when the price changes.   99

socialism is an economic system by which resources and means of production are owned collectively by the citizens.   100

democratic socialism is a type of economic system involving a blend of free market capitalism and government regulation of the economy.   100

convergence theory describes the tendency for capitalism and socialism to converge.   100

corporation is a legal entity that has some objective, typically to make a profit for its owners. It can purchase property, acquire debt, and participate in legal contracts.   101

transnational corporations operate in at least two countries and have the interests of their company at heart over the interests of their native land.   101

demographics are statistical characteristics of human populations, such as gender and age.   101

unemployed describes people who do not have a job but have actively looked for work in the prior four weeks and are currently available for employment.   101

entrepreneurship is the creation of new organizations in response to economic and social opportunities.   102

entrepreneur is a person who establishes, organizes, manages, and assumes all risks of an organization.   102

embargo is a restriction on trade that is enforced by a government.   102

tariffs are taxes placed on traded items.   102

North American Free Trade Agreement (NAFTA) is an agreement established in 1994 to allow free trade on agricultural products between the United States, Mexico, and Canada.   102

traditional systems are organizations in which social power is gained by respect for patterns of government.   102

charismatic system is a political organization in which power is gained because a leader has extraordinary personal attributes. *102*

rational-legal authority is a system in which power stems from rules and standards that are agreed upon by society. *102*

monarchy is a political system in which leadership is based on the idea that leaders are selected by divine right or heritage. *103*

authoritarianism is a form of government that gives citizens very little say in how the nation is run. *103*

dictator is a single person with complete control in a government system. *103*

oligarchy is a small group of influential people with complete control of the government. *103*

totalitarianism is an authoritarian government that controls every aspect of citizens' lives. *103*

democracy is a political system that is run by the citizens. *104*

voter apathy is a phenomenon in which citizens with the right to vote choose not to. *104*

Democratic Party is a political party in the United States that supports increased regulation of private institutions and a larger government. *104*

Republican Party is a political party in the United States that supports a decreased regulation of private institutions and reduced government involvement communicate with the larger society. *104*

economic behaviorism states that people don't make decisions based on what is rational, but what is easiest or most popular. *106*

communitarianism suggests that for society to function properly, it must have communal values and set social policies according to those values. *106*

power elite is a group comprised of top military officials, heads of major corporations, and high-ranking political leaders; this select group of people pulls the strings that control both the economy and the politics of American society. *106*

interlocking directorates is a practice in which the same people are placed on a variety of corporate boards, allowing separate companies to be controlled by a small, elite group. *106*

political action committees (PACs) are interest groups that allocate money to political parties. *109*

Sample Test Questions

These multiple-choice questions are similar to those found in the test bank that accompanies this textbook.

1. Which of the following is an opinion *best* associated with socialist economics?

   a. After working his way up to a high-powered corporate job, Charles becomes resentful of the amount of taxes he has to pay.

   b. Kate thinks believes that people shouldn't have to pay high prices for essentials such as food and water.

   c. Aidan is motivated by a program on TV and joins the labor movement to promote democracy and the interests of the general public.

   d. Priya drops her philosophy class after deciding that Sartre's thoughts on Marx are too existential for her tastes.

2. It's Thursday, and Carl is at the local office filing for unemployment. Which of the following *shouldn't* he mention?

   a. On Monday his union went on strike.

   b. Last weekend he asked his buddies at the bar if they knew of any job openings.

   c. On Sunday he found a $50 bill lying on the ground.

   d. A couple of weeks ago he filled out applications to Wendy's and McDonald's, but got rejected both times.

3. In Tigrania, the government is run by a council of five, selected by the king and queen who otherwise act as figureheads. What kind of political system do the Tigranians have?

   a. monarchy

   b. totalitarianism

   c. democracy

   d. oligarchy

4. Nora recently moved to Seattle, and she needs to open a new bank account. If she bases her decision on economic behaviorism, which is she *most likely* to do?

   A. Do research online to find the best local banking options

   B. Find the five most popular banks and visit each one

   C. Put her money in the bank most convenient to her house

   D. Pick the bank she saw on a bus ad while driving to work

5. Rational-legal authority would allow the President of the United States to send troops into Albania without the approval of Congress or the nation.

   a. True

   b. False

ESSAY

1. Compare and contrast capitalist and socialist economic systems. Do you think one is more successful than the other?

2. What steps can the government take to combat voter apathy?

3. What political party do you associate yourself with? Explain, making reference to at least one of the three sociological theories.

4. Consider the idea of economic behaviorism. Do you think large groups make decisions based on what is easy and popular or what is logically correct? How does this decision-making behavior validate or invalidate the theory of group wisdom?

5. Do you think political candidates should be able to take monetary campaign contributions from PACs or other interest groups? Why or why not? You may want to reference **From Classroom to Community** in your answer.

WHERE TO START YOUR RESEARCH PAPER

To learn more about socialism, visit the Socialist Labor Party of America's web site at http://www.slp.org/

For more information about President Obama's 2009 economic stimulus package, see http://useconomy.about.com/od/candidatesandtheeconomy/a/Obama_Stimulus.htm

For facts about unemployment, go to the Bureau of Labor Statistics at http://www.bls.gov/bls/unemployment.htm

To learn more about the benefits of free trade, visit http://www.freetrade.org/

To read an excerpt from C. Wright Mills' *The Power Elite*, go to http://www.marxists.org/subject/humanism/mills-c-wright/power-elite.htm

ANSWERS: 1. b; 2. a; 3. d; 4. c; 5. a

Remember to check www.thethinkspot.com **for additional information, downloadable flashcards, and other helpful resources.**

PROBLEMS IN EDUCATION

Math can

be hard enough, but imagine the difficulty when a teacher is just one chapter ahead of the students.

It happens, and it happens more often to poor and minority students. Those children are about twice as likely to have math teachers who don't know their subject, according to a report by the Education Trust, a children's advocacy group.

Studies show the connection between teachers' knowledge and student achievement is particularly strong in math.

"Individual teachers matter a tremendous amount in how much students learn," said Ross Wiener, who oversees policy issues at the organization.

The report looked at teachers with neither an academic major nor certification in the subjects they teach. Among the findings, which were based on Education Department data:

- In high-poverty schools, two in five math classes have teachers without a college major or certification in math.
- In schools with a greater share of African American and Latino children, nearly one in three math classes is taught by such a teacher.

Math is important because it is considered a "gateway" course, one that leads to greater success in college and the workplace. Kids who finish Algebra II in high school are more likely to get bachelor's degrees. And people with bachelor's degrees earn substantially more than those with high school diplomas.

The teaching problem is most acute in the middle grades, 5–8, the report said. That's a crucial time for math, said Ruth Neild, a research scientist at Johns Hopkins University.

"This is a time when kids are making a really important transition from arithmetic to mathematics," Neild said. "It takes careful instruction, and if kids can't get that, and really get it, they're not going to succeed in math in high school."

Yet it can be tougher to find qualified teachers for middle schools, especially in low-income areas, said Neild, who studied the problem in Philadelphia public schools. She did not work on the Education Trust report.

Teachers should not be blamed for out-of-field teaching, the report said. It can happen anywhere there is a teacher shortage in a particular discipline. It can also happen where there is no shortage but where school administrators have planned poorly.

Congress tried to fix the problem in the sweeping 2002 No Child Left Behind Law. The law insisted that all teachers in core academic subjects be "highly qualified" by 2006.

But the most well-known aspect of No Child Left Behind is its requirement for annual state tests in reading and math, and the penalties it imposes on schools that fail to make progress.

The teacher requirement is less well-known, and also less onerous. States were allowed to come up with their own definitions of "highly qualified." As a result, most teachers in the U.S. today are deemed highly qualified.

When it comes to out-of-field teaching, state officials may be understating the problem, the report said.

Researchers compared two different sets of Education Department data, reports from state officials and a survey of teachers themselves. Teachers said out-of-field teaching happens far more often than states reported for highly qualified purposes.

Wiener, the Education Trust official, said teaching is the key to fulfilling the goal of No Child Left Behind — that every student will be able to read and do math on grade level by 2014.

"We cannot meet our goals for increasing student achievement unless and until we focus on improving teaching quality and the effectiveness of teachers in front of the classroom," Wiener said.[1]

CHAPTER 08

---It's hard to imagine that in 21st-century America, the richest nation in the world, children in public schools are failing to learn basics such as reading and writing.

The federal government has tried allocating more money to education and reworking curricula, but still many children are not succeeding in the classroom. What is the recourse?

As Americans, most of us would agree that a free and public education is the right of every citizen. With this said, how can education be a social problem? In this chapter, we will discuss issues related to quality and access of education in the United States, as well as how these factors are linked to problems of race, social class, and gender.

get the topic: WHAT ARE THE SOCIAL PROBLEMS IN EDUCATION?

EDUCATION is the process by which people gain or develop knowledge.

HIDDEN CURRICULUM refers to lessons taught in schools that are unrelated to academic learning.

Education in Society

Over the years I've spent teaching in the classroom, I have experienced many different things: students making out in the back of the room, others answering cell phones in the middle of class, and of course those wanting to know if they "missed anything" on a day they were absent. All faculty have their favorite student horror story, and as a former student, I have my favorite faculty horror story too. But although these experiences take place in an academic setting, can they be considered "education?"

Education is the process by which people gain or develop knowledge. Throughout most of human history, education was informal, usually passing from elders to the next generation. Since the industrial revolution, education has become a more formal system by which society passes on its information and has been linked to economic advancement.

In this way, schools connect to the job system because they often train individuals for specific types of work. For example, to become a nurse, you have to go to nursing school. When you complete school,

you have the benefit of a high salary and a sure career path, and the community benefits from your medical knowledge. Other types of degrees are not as specific. For example, with a sociology degree, a person can do many different types of jobs, from working at a bank to analyzing social services. However, the key point is that the individual has achieved an educational milestone in reaching his or her degree.

Education levels vary slightly by gender. As you can see in the chart below, more women have some college experience but more men complete higher education degrees.

It's also worth noting that the status dropout rate—the percentage of 16- to 24-year olds who are not enrolled in school and do not have a high school credential, whether a diploma or GED—has declined severely over the last 30 years. In 1980, the percentage of dropouts in the United States was 14.1 percent. By 2007, it was down to 8.7 percent. This rate varies significantly by ethnicity. Hispanics have the highest dropout rate—21.4 percent in 2007—while blacks and whites have lower rates, at 8.4 and 5.3 percent, respectively.[2]

History of Education
HISTORY OF PUBLIC EDUCATION IN THE UNITED STATES

When colonists first arrived in the "New World" from England, they brought with them their form of education and educational institutions. Rich in tradition, these educational settings were frequently attended only by the elite. They provided classical education for religious purposes.

In 1647, Massachusetts was the first colony to require compulsory schooling, opening education to everyone. Most other colonies left education in the hands of parents or private organizations, which required individuals to pay their own tuition. After the Revolutionary War, the states began to form four key beliefs regarding education: It should be free to the user, publicly run, nonreligious, and universal (compulsory). In time, these schools expanded their focus. In addition to teaching students the basics of reading, writing, and arithmetic, they sought to teach new immigrant children to be "good citizens" and to develop proper morals.

During the era of westward expansion, American schools often took the form of one-room school houses, with one teacher presiding over children who varied greatly in age and ability. The one-room school presented problems. If, for example, your teacher was not good at math, your math education would be limited. In rural areas particularly, textbooks were nearly unheard of; rather, students would bring with them whatever books could

Educational Attainment of the Population 25 Years and Older, 2007		
Highest Educational Level Achieved	Male Students (%)	Female Students (%)
Less than High School	16.1	15.0
High School Graduate	30.1	30.2
Some College	25.6	28.1
Bachelor's Degree	17.6	17.2
Graduate or Professional Degree	10.7	9.6

Source: Data from the U.S. Census Bureau, *2007 American Community Survey*, Table SE:T22.

>>> **One-room schoolhouses** are a part of public school history. **Some contemporary Amish schools still make use of them today.**

be found in their homes and learn to read those. By today's standards, these early publicly funded schoolhouses provided the equivalent of an elementary education. It wasn't until the mid-1800s that secondary schools began appearing, and these were generally only attended by those seeking college entrance. High schools were not publically funded until the 1900s, and they still only educated a small percentage of the population. For example, when I was a child, I vividly remember my grandmother proudly telling me that she had completed the eighth grade, which at her time was as far as a girl was likely to go in school.[3]

Higher education did not look like it does today, either. Early on, college education and development was not much different from elementary education. For example, Harvard University was first and foremost a school to train ministers. Created in the 1600s, it primarily served the elite, and the recruitment of faculty there and elsewhere was based on the piety of the professors rather than their expertise. In early colleges, there were few faculty members and almost no specialized fields of study. Over time, this changed as faculty became more focused on specific disciplines.[4]

EDUCATION: SPREADING THE FIVE "MYTHS" THROUGHOUT SOCIETY

Education is no longer just about teaching the three Rs—reading, 'riting, and 'rithmetic. Education has expanded into a social movement, stemming from the ideas of building a nation and its ideology. In elementary school, did you start the day with the pledge of allegiance? If so, what did that teach—reading or patriotism? Scholars suggest that the U.S. educational system spreads five "myths" throughout society.[5]

1 **Myth of the individual.** This myth supports the belief that the primary unit in society is the individual—not the family, clan, or ethnic group. Therefore, it is up to the individual to learn in order to improve his or her place in society.

2 **Myth of the nation as a group of individuals.** In this myth, the nation is no longer the property of a king or some group of elites. Instead, individuals make up society and the nation. Therefore, by developing your skills and knowledge, you are bettering yourself and, by extension, the nation.

3 **Myth of progress.** This myth proposes that society's goal is to improve the status of both current and future residents. Thus, childhood education can support the idea that a nation is working toward self-improvement.

4 **Myth of socialization and life cycle continuity.** This myth supposes that childhood socialization leads to adult character. Therefore, if children are socialized properly, this will lead to good character that ultimately benefits the nation in the long run. Might the pledge of allegiance lead some to enter the military later in life?

5 **Myth of the state as the guardian of the nation.** This final myth encourages the belief that it is the state's job to raise good, loyal, and patriotic children who will become the next generation of good, loyal, and patriotic adults. In this way, socializing children is not the role of the family but the job of the nation.[5]

It's important to note that not all groups of people enter into the state education system, in part because they do not believe in these myths. For example, the Amish refuse to participate in state-sponsored education in order to keep their children socialized in their group. Instead, they established and continue to run their own schools.[6] Many friends of mine choose to homeschool their children out of a desire to keep the state out of their business. Is it a social problem for the state to raise our children? Is it good for the long-term health of the nation? Let's look at this further.

HIDDEN CURRICULUM IN SCHOOLS

Many schools have taken to fund-raising through their students. From lemonade stands on the front sidewalk to multi-thousand-dollar school-wide fund-raisers selling wrapping paper or pizzas, children learn the value of hard work and service to obtain a goal outside the school's curriculum. Whether you realize it or not, all of those fund-raising efforts *you* may have been involved in during your grammar and high school years taught you things about capitalism and goal-setting that really had nothing to do with reading, writing, or arithmetic.

The transfer of academic knowledge to the next generation is a primary goal, but schools also socialize students in what some call the "hidden curriculum." The term **hidden curriculum** refers to lessons taught in schools that are unrelated to academic learning. Schools teach students about citizenship when they have "mock" elections; through healthy competition and contests, they teach the use of

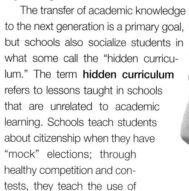

 Fund-raisers teach the **hidden curriculum of capitalism.**

LITERACY RATE is the percentage of people in a population who can read and write.

planning, goal-setting, training, and teamwork; they teach children to follow orders, routines, and other seemingly arbitrary regulations, which ultimately result in our following real laws that sometimes seem senseless. These all help make us a part of the community and thereby make the community run more smoothly.

The hidden curriculum also applies to how students socialize one another. Students take what they've learned in the hallways, playgrounds, and cafeterias at school and apply it to the outside world. One of the most important lessons we learn in school is how to get along with our peers. It helps us negotiate our way through life and has almost nothing to do with knowing how to read.[7]

EDUCATION THROUGHOUT THE WORLD

Every nation has some type of educational system; however, not all educational systems are equal. The amount of resources, funding, and worth placed on education varies, which in turn creates the social problem of inequality in global education. A country's socioeconomic status has a huge effect on its education system. Systems in developing countries often

Regional Literacy Rates for Adults (aged 15+), 2005–2007

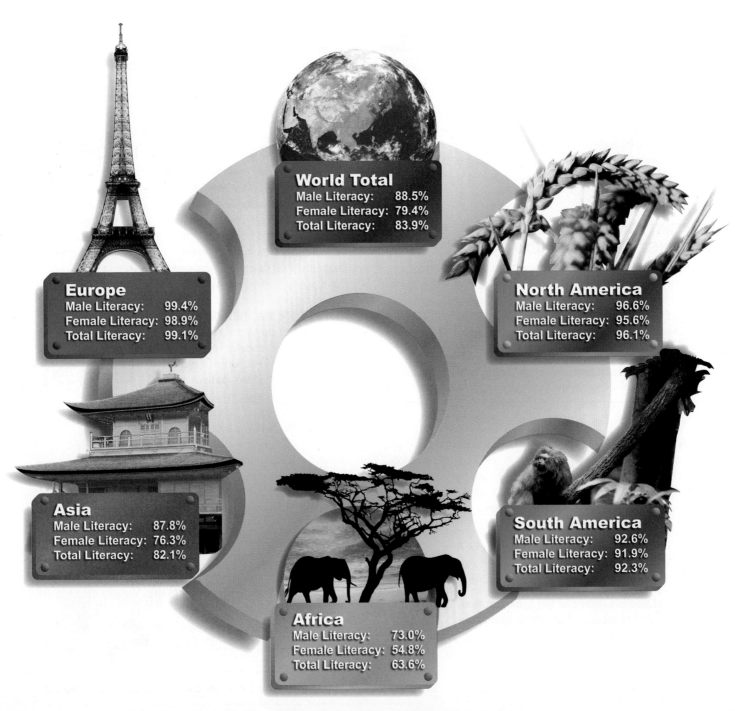

World Total
Male Literacy: 88.5%
Female Literacy: 79.4%
Total Literacy: 83.9%

Europe
Male Literacy: 99.4%
Female Literacy: 98.9%
Total Literacy: 99.1%

North America
Male Literacy: 96.6%
Female Literacy: 95.6%
Total Literacy: 96.1%

Asia
Male Literacy: 87.8%
Female Literacy: 76.3%
Total Literacy: 82.1%

South America
Male Literacy: 92.6%
Female Literacy: 91.9%
Total Literacy: 92.3%

Africa
Male Literacy: 73.0%
Female Literacy: 54.8%
Total Literacy: 63.6%

Source: Data from United Nations Educational, Scientific, and Cultural Organization (UNESCO) Institute for Statistics.

College Participation vs. College Completion

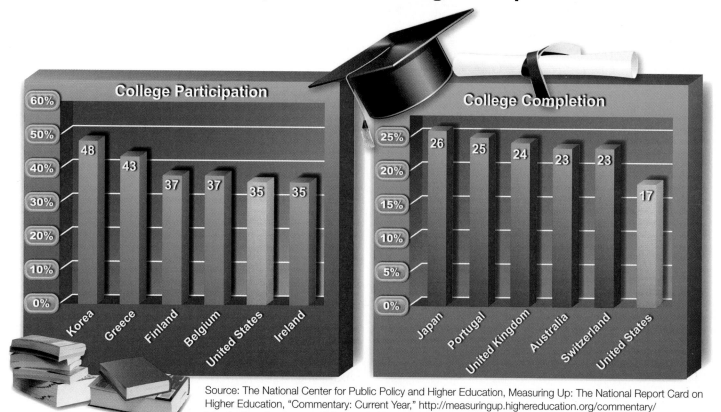

Source: The National Center for Public Policy and Higher Education, Measuring Up: The National Report Card on Higher Education, "Commentary: Current Year," http://measuringup.highereducation.org/commentary/introduction.cfm, Accessed August 7, 2009.

The United States ranks within the top five countries when it comes to college participation of young adults aged 18 to 24. **But the United States ranks much lower—16th of the 27 countries compared—in terms of college completion.**[20]

fail to provide students with basic educational needs and struggle to sustain stable educational institutions. Paraguay, Sri Lanka, and the Philippines are all countries in which one in five students goes to a school with no running water.[8] How might such a situation affect their ability to learn?

In general, poorer nations often have low **literacy rates**, or low percentages of people in the population who can read and write. When you consider the lack of education in some nations, it becomes apparent why some countries seem mired in the same problems year after year. In Sierra Leone, for example, only 47 percent of men and 24 percent of women older than 15 are literate. This falls far below the world literacy rate of 88 percent of men and 79 percent of women.[9] These numbers also demonstrate another facet of social inequality of education throughout much of the world: Women and girls are rarely treated equal to their male counterparts. Note that the number of literate women is almost half the number of educated men in Sierra Leone. Likewise, as you can see in the literacy rates shown on the previous page, male literacy rates are higher than female literacy rates in every region of the world. You learned about gender stratification in Chapter 4, and these data illustrate a social problem in patriarchal societies—that of unequal educational access. Knowledge is power, but women continue to be left out of the knowledge loop in many areas of the globe.

Education provides the ability for a nation to compete globally. You can see from the data that Europe and North America have the strongest literacy rates, and yet the literacy rate for Europe is almost 100 percent, while in North America, it is not nearly that high. This trend is consistent with another social problem in the U.S. education system.

For the last two decades, the United States has had no noticeable increase in college participation rates. Meanwhile, many nations have increased their college ranks and now surpass the United States.[10] Why might this be occurring? One reason may be a lack of funding for college. The United States ranks 57th in the world in educational spending as a percentage of gross domestic product.[11] This ranking is below nations like France, Norway, and the United Kingdom—all nations that have surpassed the United States in graduation rates.[12]

Let's look further at the issue of higher education. Of 27 countries measured, the United States ranks fifth in college participation, yet it is 16th in the number of degrees issued to college students.[13] In fact, the graduation rate for incoming freshmen in the United States is about 56 percent when measured over a six-year period.[14] High school graduation rates have also decreased, although those who do graduate are more likely to attend a two- or four-year college today than a few years ago. The social problems of low educational attainment can lead to long-term problems for a nation by limiting its potential for economic growth.[15]

A country's wealth plays a central role in education, so lack of funding and resources from a nation-state can weaken a system. Governments in sub-Saharan Africa spend only 2.4 percent of the world's public resources on education; however, many of them spend a higher percentage of their entire wealth on it than the United States does. For example, Sudan ranks 42nd in spending as a percentage of GDP, while the United States ranks 57th.[16]

PRESTIGE GAP is the divide between those who have the privilege of attending elite schools and obtaining success in the job market, and those who don't.

TEACHER EXPECTANCY EFFECT is the impact of a teacher's expectations on a student's performance.

GRADE INFLATION is the trend of assigning higher grades than previously assigned to students for completing the same work.

So, is educational spending a social problem? Clearly, the United States spends a lot of money, and yet as a percentage of our total wealth, we rank rather low. Furthermore, the facts indicate that we are losing ground to many nations in number of college degrees. However, between 1997 and 2007, the number of degrees issued by higher education U.S. institutions increased from 24 to 29 percent.[17] So, the number of degrees is increasing, just not as fast as in many European nations. But who exactly is receiving these degrees? Does one's race, gender, or socioeconomic status affect his or her educational attainment? You bet it does.

Problems with Higher Education

The cost of college can have a strong influence on educational attainment. In the United States, the government only pays for primary and secondary education. For higher education, people have to pay their own way—on average $6,595 a year for in-state tuition at a four-year university—which often deters low-income individuals from seeking advanced educations.[18] In other industrialized countries, education at all levels is free. For example, in Sweden, primary, secondary, and postsecondary schools are free of tuition, courtesy of the Swedish government and taxpayers. This allows all students who meet certain academic standards to attend any school regardless of economic status.[19]

In stark contrast is the quest for an Ivy-league education in the United States. It has become increasingly evident to students that in order to obtain one of society's top-paying jobs, they must first attend an Ivy-league school where they'll make the contacts and receive the education that employers require. This is not to say that state or non-Ivy schools prepare students any less vigorously for the rigors of the elite workforce. However, there is a general belief in the United States that by attending and succeeding in a prestigious school, your ticket will be written to whatever employment you so desire.[1]

Unfortunately, as these top-performing students are choosing to attend elite schools, they are creating what is known as the **prestige gap**.

Students who may be equally able to perform but unable to foot the bills of an elite education will be unable to compete in vying for jobs available in an ever-more-competitive market. When "great minds" are pooled together into certain schools, the give-and-take of classroom discussions in other schools may be less provocative. And it follows that excellent faculty will be sought to teach at elite universities, widening the prestige gap even further.[2]

Problems in Education
EDUCATIONAL DISCREPANCIES IN RACE

Hollywood movies such as *Dangerous Minds*, *Lean on Me*, and *Freedom Writers* focus on the efforts of students who are not expected to succeed because of their environment and socioeconomic status. For millions of students around the United States, though, this is more than a movie—it's a real-life trend. A 2007 U.S. Census survey revealed that 31.8 percent of the white population and 52.1 percent of the Asian population ages 25 and older have completed four years of college or more, whereas only 18.5 percent of African Americans and 12.7 percent of Hispanics showed similar attainment.[26] What accounts for this discrepancy? Consider that poor and undereducated people are segregated into inner-city schools. It is here that students are most likely to encounter teachers and administrators with very low expectations for student attainment and extremely limited resources. With the inequality between rich and poor, racial minorities from poor areas are being left behind by the education system. In this way, some suggest that society is locking them out of the competition for empowerment from the very beginning.[27]

TEACHER EXPECTANCY AND ATTAINMENT

Perhaps another part of the problem for racial minorities and poor children has to do with teacher expectation. This is referred to as the **teacher expectancy effect**—the impact of a teacher's expectations on a student's performance—and it doesn't just apply to poor and minority students.[28] The idea is that if a teacher expects that a student will love the class and do well, the student generally does. Of course, measuring teacher expectations is a difficult thing to do.

Some studies show that expectancies influence not only individual student performance, but also the performance of the entire school.[29]

▶▶▶ GO GL◉BAL

The South Korean Educational System

Since the 1960s, education has become the most valuable resource to the South Korean people. Living in a country that lacks exportable natural resources, families have made educating their children the number-one priority.

The South Korean system enforces a national curriculum and spreads the resources much more equitably than the United States does. The South Koreans also allocate a greater amount of their national budget to educational spending.[23]

The country's commitment to education reaps rewards—93 percent of South Korean students graduate from high school, compared to 75 percent of U.S. students.[24]

To be sure, there are valid criticisms of the South Korean educational system: The conformist regimen and relentless workload requires the students to study for eight or more hours per day *outside* of school; the endless push to study and learn stifles creativity; classes average about 40 students; and there are few national universities to choose from, driving students to study abroad.[25]

<<< South Korean students attain lofty goals through **a work ethic that is unmatched worldwide.**

Top Ten Universities Worldwide

Rank	School	Tuition (in $)
1	Harvard University	37,012
2	Yale University	36,500
3	University of Cambridge	5,145*
4	University of Oxford	5,145*
5	California Institute of Technology	34,584
6	Imperial College London	5,145*
7	University College London	5,145*
8	University of Chicago	39,381
9	Massachusetts Institute of Technology	37,782
10	Columbia University	41,316

*converted from pounds

Sources: U.S. News & World Report, "National Universities Rankings," http://colleges.usnews.rankingsandreviews.com/best-colleges/national-universities-rankings, Acessed August 31, 2009; O'Leary, John, Nunzio Quacquarelli, and Martin Ince. *Top Universities Guide*. London: Quacquarelli Symonds Limited, 2009, http://www.topuniversities.com/top-universities-guide, Accessed August 31, 2009; "Universities," Guiardian.co.uk, http://www.guardian.co.uk/education/list/educationinstitution, Accessed August 31, 2009; Graeme Paton, "University tuition fees 'need to rise to £6,500,'" Telegraph.co.uk, March 16, 2009, http://www.telegraph.co.uk/education/universityeducation/5001170/University-tuition-fees-need-to-rise-to-6500.html, Accessed August 31, 2009.

Generally speaking, the more prestigious the school, the more it costs to attend in the United States. **In contrast, universities in the United Kingdom only charge up to $5,145 for an undergraduate education.**

Other studies suggest less obvious findings, which propose that teachers may indeed influence students' self-perception, but it is that perception that influences academic achievement.[30] Regardless, it seems obvious that teachers have great power to influence students, both positively and negatively. In inner-city schools where teacher turnover is often quite high, this becomes a significant problem.

ACADEMIC ACHIEVEMENT

There is an increase in the practice of grade inflation in American high schools and universities. **Grade inflation** is the trend of assigning higher grades than previously assigned to students for completing the same work. Students' grade point averages over the last 20 years have increased by roughly one third of a letter grade.[31] It is unlikely that student performance alone could have contributed to this trend.

Students have begun to see the default grade as an A. Professors nationwide are noticing a sense of entitlement from their students, which results in arrogant assumptions regarding a student's "right" to a superior grade for work that was just average.[32]

To combat this growing trend, universities have begun offering seminars integrated into introductory courses for freshmen. The seminars encourage students to think differently about their work and their lives, so that they can relearn what education truly is.[33]

HUMAN CAPITAL is a person's combination of skills, knowledge, traits, and personal attributes.

CREDENTIALISM is an emphasis on educational degrees as a prerequisite for advancement.

Theories Behind Education

There are several theories put forth by sociologists regarding what criteria students use when evaluating whether or not to attend college.

FUNCTIONALISM

Functionalists tend to look at how structures in a society work to support the society. Recall the literacy data shown earlier in the chapter. In general, when you look at regions of the world, the higher the literacy rate, the wealthier and more advanced that region. Why? Because education helps a student improve his or her **human capital**—a combination of skills, knowledge, traits, and personal attributes. Education also helps integrate the student into society by teaching him or her about the nation's history, government, and social norms. Finally, a public education provides parents a place to occupy their children, allowing adults to work and perform other needed tasks in society.[34]

∧
∧ Obtaining **a college degree is**
∧ **the first step in finding success**
in the marketplace.

SYMBOLIC INTERACTIONISM

Having a degree opens doors for people. In the United States, many students choose to go to college because of the reality of **credentialism**—an emphasis on educational degrees as a prerequisite for advancement. In today's global economy, many of the "good jobs" are now service and white-collar jobs. In short, they require a college degree, but this was not always true. Neither of my parents had college degrees, but with hard work they held white-collar jobs in business management and accounting. This was attainable at the time because hard work, intelligence, and ability were enough to climb from a labor job to a white-collar job. Not anymore. Employers use education as a type of litmus test to determine who is and who is not qualified.[35]

CONFLICT THEORY

Have you ever noticed how the power structure of a school mimics the power structures of society? Samuel Bowles and Herbert Gintis (1976) believe that schools follow a capitalist structure. Administrators control teachers, teachers control students, and students control other students. This pecking order, in a sense, trains students to understand the hierarchy of capitalism. Just like workers who fear for their jobs and must provide labor to their bosses, students must respond to the whims of their teachers.[36]

Conflict theorists also point out the inequality built into the system as well. If education is the doorway to opportunity, then conflict theorists would be interested in how those opportunities are distributed in society. As we have already discussed, public education is not the same in all places; wealthy neighborhoods have better educational outcomes than poorer ones. Conflict theorists point to the problems of the inner cities and the lack of funding to combat such ills as part of the reason.

The hidden curriculum, on the other hand, serves to re-enforce an ideology of fairness and equality within the United States, the validity of which is certainly debatable. Patriotism, capitalism, and even democracy are all reinforced in schools today. Conflict theorists raise the question as to whether this is in students' best interests.

Throughout the world, governments spend more on education of the elite than they do on the education of the poor. This is particularly true in higher education, where there is a strong link between social class and the ability to attend college. If you attend a state college, you're receiving tax assistance to go to school. But even though this funding allows some of the less fortunate to get a degree, less-educated people from wealthier homes continue to dominate society.[37] Even in locations that have tried to create equity between rich neighborhoods and poor ones, the outcomes continue to favor those with the higher social class.[38]

Should I attend college?

No
- My teachers don't expect any of us to go anywhere or accomplish anything.
- College costs too much.
- Even if I get into college, what's the point unless it's an Ivy?

Yes
- I want to improve my knowledge and expand my skills and personal traits.
- I need a college degree to get a good job.
- Going to college will improve my social status in the long run.

discover solutions to social problems:
WHAT CAN WE DO TO ENCOURAGE EDUCATIONAL EQUALITY?

No Child Left Behind

The *No Child Left Behind Act of 2001* (NCLB) is a bipartisan act of Congress that was proposed by President George W. Bush. Generally speaking, the NCLB Act requires states to test students in particular grades, with the results determining the state's eligibility to receive federal funds. Schools that fall behind run the risk of having their funding cut. Where possible, parents are given the choice to transfer their child to a better school. NCLB is designed to reform the way we view education with a four-pronged approach: stronger accountability, increased freedom for states and communities, expanded use of proven education methods, and increases in educational choices for parents.[39]

States measure progress in schools by testing every student in grades 3 through 8 in reading and math by administering annual tests.

Although this Act seems like a much-needed overhaul to make schools and states accountable for student achievement and dropout and illiteracy rates, some have seen it as one of the most controversial pieces of legislation in the history of federal educational policy-making.[40] What's the trouble?

Some sociologists believe that the gaps observed in the educational system are mistaken as educational malfunctions. We know that poor children often fail to receive the same quality of education as wealthier ones. We also know that test results tend to show a strong correlation between schools in poorer areas and schools that fail to achieve the standards of accountability.[41] Certainly, school structures can affect a child's ability to learn. Is it fair to set up national standards and apply them equally, regardless of the location, funding, and social setting? Sociologists tend to say no. Race, social class, and geographic location mean that a one-size-fits-all approach is unlikely to work well.[42]

Furthermore, NCLB expects parents to effectively negotiate the education system, which is problematic especially when parents are themselves not well educated. It seems dubious that the current system will work equally well for everyone, especially racial minorities, immigrants, and the poor.[43]

CHARTER SCHOOLS

Charter schools are nonsectarian public schools of choice that operate with freedom from many of the regulations that apply to traditional public schools. The name "charter school" may have originated in the 1970s when Ray Budde, an educator in New England, suggested that small groups of teachers be given charters (contracts) by their local school boards to explore new educational approaches in a smaller, less bureaucratic setting.[44] From there, this idea blossomed and spread, as various states enacted charter school laws, and President Clinton called for the creation of 3,000 new schools by 2002; President George W. Bush followed that up by dedicating $200 million to charter schools in 2002.

∧
∧ The No Child Left
∧ Behind Act has
changed the way schools are held accountable for helping students succeed.

> **CHARTER SCHOOLS** are nonsectarian public schools of choice that operate with freedom from many of the regulations that apply to traditional public schools.

The "charter" that establishes such a school is a performance contract detailing the school's mission, program, goals, number of students served, methods of assessment, and ways to measure success. Charters are typically granted for three to five years, after which the group who granted the charter will review the goals of the school and determine whether the contract should be renewed.

Charter schools are responsible for producing positive academic results and adhering to the charter contract. These schools are accountable to several groups: the sponsor who grants them, the parents who choose them, and the public that funds them.[45]

Charter schools remain much smaller in population than regular public schools, and they recruit students with demographic characteristics that are similar to the surrounding population in terms of socioeconomic status and race.[46]

One problem that has occurred in offering school choice is a phenomenon known as "white flight." Whites tend to flee an area and its schools as the level of non-white enrollment increases.[47] Research suggests that charter schools tend to segregate students by race, because white students enroll in them in higher percentages than racial minorities. In short, charter schools are creating a further segregated educational system. In the end, both race and parents influence who attends a charter school.[48]

Despite the drawbacks, charter schools have demonstrated an improved alternative to the mainstream public education. Charter schools can re-enroll dropout students, replace failing public schools, create parent/learning centers, and pilot innovative learning models.[49] Critics still wonder, however, whether charter schools will improve opportunities for academically or economically advantaged students if separation by choice continues to encourage isolation and segregation.[50]

The city of New Orleans has attempted a unique experiment with charter school education. After the devastation of Hurricane Katrina in 2005, some public schools were destroyed and many students were displaced. As the city started to rebuild itself, it set up an unprecedented number of charter schools. Now 53 percent of students are enrolled in charter schools, as opposed to just 2 percent before the hurricane.[51]

Some administrators have revamped the structures and curricula that were used at New Orleans public schools. The hope is that these charter schools will help improve the education system in New Orleans, which was in bad shape even before Katrina.[52] So far, the results are mixed. Some studies show that the new schools have improved education in the area, while others show no significant difference.[53] It will be interesting to see the outcome of the charter school chapter in New Orleans as well as in American educational history.

WRAP YOUR MIND AROUND THE THEORY

Functionalism holds that **education helps socialize young people into society.** How have **your experiences** with education **affected the way you interact with peers, professors, and authorities?**

FUNCTIONALISM

Functionalists believe that education fulfills several functions of society. It allows parents to work, knowing that their children are safe and learning. It also provides a place to socialize children into society. This strengthens the human capital of the student and provides a firm foundation for society to expand and prosper.

CONFLICT THEORY

Conflict theorists believe that education serves as a vehicle to keep the social classes separate. For example, higher education is generally most available to children from the upper classes, thereby guaranteeing that they will be able to gain high-paying jobs and maintain their positions in society. This can serve as a stratification tool to maintain and justify inequality. When poor children are not privy to the same opportunities for high-quality education as their wealthier counterparts, no one should be surprised that they remain in the lower classes throughout their lives.

HOW DOES EDUCATION AFFECT SOCIETY?

SYMBOLIC INTERACTIONISM

Symbolic theorists focus on labeling things. Credentials may or may not mean anything about your superiority over another candidate to do a particular job; however using a college degree as a prerequisite provides a social definition that can be useful to an employer and society. It opens doors to the college graduate and closes them to those without formal education.

Conflict theorists suggest that education maintains the separation of social classes. How do the **success and opportunities given to the upper class** contrast with the **inequalities suffered by lower classes?**

Interactionists believe that **a college degree is a social definition** that makes someone more likely to get hired for a job, even if that person is not necessarily more qualified. **How do disciplines such as medicine or physics widen the gap between people who have or have not pursued a formal education?**

School Choice via Charters or Vouchers

There are determined and well-researched arguments flowing from both sides of the debate over school choice. What does each side have to say?

Pro

- Competition in anything breeds improvement.
- Choice offers a way out of a low-performing school for those interested.
- Choice supports educational innovation because it supports alternatives to the traditional school setting.
- School choice can match child and parent needs; both will be more involved and committed to the school.
- School choice can improve the idea of outcome-based education, whereby measurable outcomes become the standard of quality.

Con

- Schools of choice create inequities by taking the more desirable students and abandoning the weaker ones. This results in a two-tier system: the haves and the have-nots.
- Students in schools of choice have fewer opportunities to learn from students of different backgrounds.
- Accessing these schools requires motivated, informed parents, which not all students have.
- School choice changes the focus from education for the public good to education for the private good. Education is no longer being seen as providing "some common experiences in common settings." Will those without children in schools continue to support education in light of this change?

MAKE CONNECTIONS

Social Class, Race, and Gender Outcomes

As you have seen in this chapter, many factors play key roles in the attainment of an equitable and appropriate education. Simply based on family, geography, or gender, some students may not have a fighting chance to achieve the one thing that might free them from the bondage of biases—a worthwhile education.

Chapter 2 challenged your thinking of social inequalities and compared those who live with great poverty to those with great wealth. In this chapter you've learned that

students who live in poverty are often forgotten by the educational system. They are the lowest achievers from whom the least is expected, receiving the barest of educations with the fewest methods and resources. There have been some efforts to level the playing field for these students, including charter schools and the No Child Left Behind Act. Though not perfect, these programs attempt to remedy some of the egregious oversights regarding the students who so easily fall through the cracks of the educational system.

In Chapter 4 we discussed how gender influences the social problems a person

experiences. Throughout the world there remain many women who are denied opportunities for education based solely on their gender.

In Chapter 3, you learned that racial and ethnic inequality still exists in the United States. It is true that many racial groups are disproportionately poor, and that students in poverty-stricken neighborhoods receive a worse education because their schools receive the least tax benefits. Charter schools offer some families an alternative to public schools; however, that often does little more than segregate students further.

From Classroom to Community } High-Quality Schools and Faculty

My mom is an elementary school teacher, so it was natural for me to gravitate to an elementary school for a fall semester internship. I worked as a teacher's aide, helping out two days a week in Ms. Alvary's second-grade classroom. The students, although obviously poor, were so sweet and eager to be in the classroom. Many of them came from unstable homes and bad neighborhoods, and I often wondered if they preferred being at school because of this.

During my third week there, I began to take notice of Ms. Alvary's teaching style. Now, I know I was still a student myself, but I'd been in school a long time, and I knew something wasn't adding up. The teacher was disorganized and

often let the students wander from learning station to learning station for an hour or more without instruction. Written assignments were almost never given, and lessons seemed mostly to consist of arts and crafts that the children could do independently. Although the kids were content to cut and color, they also seemed to know that something was missing.

I asked Ms. Alvary one day how she became a teacher. She told me that this was her first real teaching job and that she was hired two years ago out of an ESL program at the local community center. She said that the school was desperate to fill the position, and although

she wasn't certified, she was—as she put it—"at the right place at the right time."

In this day and age, how can it be that an American public school could hire someone totally unqualified? It's no wonder that students aren't learning the basics of language or math.

How much worse will it get for my little second graders as they progress through the system, and who will speak out and help them? All through the fall, I tried to convince myself to approach the principal and speak to him about firing Ms. Alvary, or call the school board to complain about a poor hiring choice. But in the end, what good would it have done?

WHAT ARE THE SOCIAL PROBLEMS IN EDUCATION?   114

the five myths of education, the hidden curriculum, poor performance compared with global education attainment, inequality in race and gender, grade inflation, and entitlement

WHAT THINKING DRIVES EDUCATION IN SOCIETY?   120

helping students who seek to improve their human capital and credentials and who desire to hold an elite job, teaching the norms and values of society, and maintaining the stratification of inequality in the social classes

WHAT CAN WE DO TO ENCOURAGE EDUCATIONAL EQUALITY?   121

implement social policies such as the No Child Left Behind Act and school choice via vouchers or charters

get the topic: WHAT ARE THE SOCIAL PROBLEMS IN EDUCATION?

Theory

FUNCTIONALISM   120

- education fulfills several functions of society
- education teaches dominant norms and values to better a society

CONFLICT THEORY   120

- higher education is most available to students from the upper classes
- separation of social classes by the availability of education maintains and justifies inequality

SYMBOLIC INTERACTIONISM   120

- credentials such as a college degree provide opportunities for some and eliminate them for others

Key Terms

education is the process by which people gain or develop knowledge.   114

hidden curriculum refers to lessons taught in schools that are unrelated to academic learning.   115

literacy rate is the percentage of people in a population who can read and write.   117

prestige gap is the divide between those who have the privilege of attending elite schools and

obtaining success in the job market, and those who don't.   118

teacher expectancy effect is the impact of a teacher's expectations on a student's performance.   118

grade inflation is the trend of assigning higher grades than previously assigned to students for completing the same work.   119

human capital is a person's combination of skills, knowledge, traits, and personal attributes.   120

credentialism is an emphasis on educational degrees as a prerequisite for advancement.   120

charter schools are nonsectarian public schools of choice that operate with freedom from many of the regulations that apply to traditional public schools.   121

Sample Test Questions

These multiple-choice questions are similar to those found in the test bank that accompanies this textbook.

1. What group of learners suffers *most* as a result of inequitable tax-receipt distribution to schools?

   a. females
   b. upper class
   c. lower class
   d. immigrants

2. Which of the following is a myth associated with education?

   a. The nation is the property of a group of elites.
   b. Childhood socialization leads to adult character.
   c. The family is the primary unit.
   d. Society's goal is to improve the morality of the nation.

3. Which is *not* an objective of the No Child Left Behind Act of 2001?

   a. Implementing stronger accountability will produce results.
   b. Schools will use proven educational methods.
   c. Parents will have more choices in where and how their children are educated.
   d. Greater restraints will be placed on states and communities.

4. Why might parents choose to send their child to a charter school?

   a. The child is in a low-performing school that shows no sign of improvement.
   b. Their family is transient.
   c. The larger class sizes promote lively debate.
   d. The oversight by the federal government will ensure successful learning.

5. An example of hidden curriculum is

   a. spelling bees.
   b. reciting the pledge of allegiance.
   c. field trips to art museums.
   d. cafeteria food choices.

ESSAY

1. What are your thoughts about the lack of certified math teachers in schools, particularly middle schools? Who is responsible, and how can it be remedied?

2. Describe the difficulties in attaining an education if you were a student in a high-poverty school. What would be the greatest obstacle?

3. Consider the pros and cons of the No Child Left Behind Act of 2001. Has this legislation helped or hindered education for the children it was written to include? How?

4. Why do some believe that society is locking racial minorities out of the competition for empowerment from the very beginning?

5. Given the trend that fewer American students are obtaining college degrees while other countries are increasing their numbers, discuss how the global economy will be affected, particularly the world status of the United States.

WHERE TO START YOUR RESEARCH PAPER

For U.S. Census facts and information, go to http://www.census.gov

To view educational statistics, go to
http://nces.ed.gov http://www.uis.unesco.org

To learn more about grade inflation, go to
http://www.gradeinflation.com/

For more information about No Child Left Behind, visit
http://www.ed.gov/nclb/landing.jhtml

To learn more about charter schools, go to
http://www.uscharterschools.org/pub/uscs_docs/index.htm

ANSWERS: 1. c; 2. b; 3. d; 4. a; 5. b

Remember to check www.thethinkspot.com **for additional information, downloadable flashcards, and other helpful resources.**

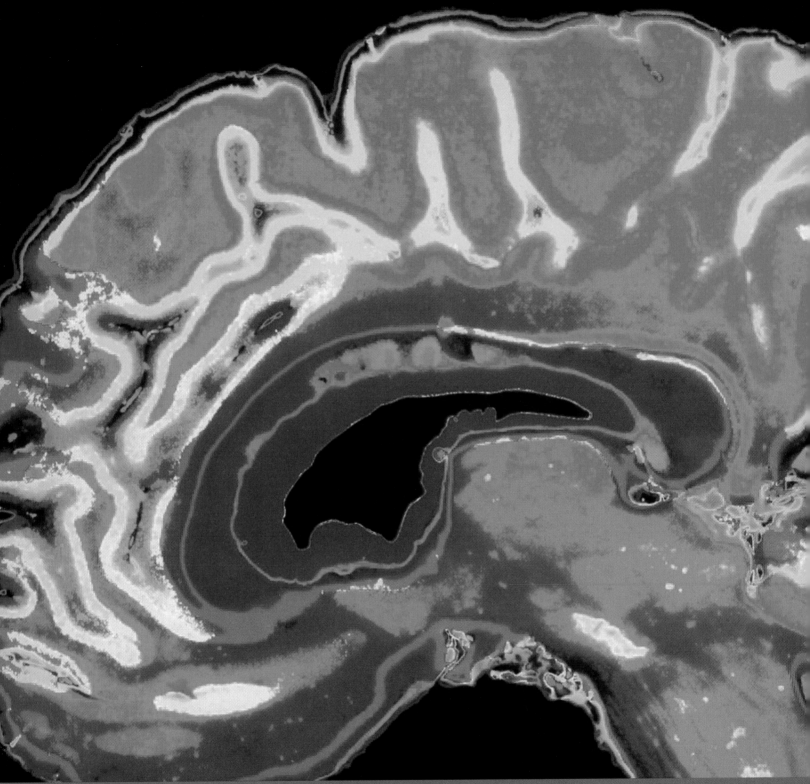

PHYSICAL AND MENTAL HEALTH CARE

WHAT ARE THE SOCIAL PROBLEMS
RELATED TO HEALTH AND AGING?
HOW DO SOCIOLOGISTS VIEW PROBLEMS
RELATED TO MENTAL AND PHYSICAL
HEALTH?
HOW DO SOCIETIES DEAL WITH HEALTH?

For American

children, the state they live in and their family's income and education may help determine how healthy they are, a new survey shows.

Among children aged 17 and younger, 16 percent are in less than optimal health, according to the state-by-state survey from the nonprofit Robert Wood Johnson Foundation.

But that rate ranged widely by state: from 22.8 percent of children in Texas to only 6.9 percent of children in Vermont.

"Child health is a foundation for his or her health throughout life," Dr. Paula Braveman, director of the Center on Social Disparities in Health at the University of California, San Francisco, and co-author of the report, said during a Tuesday teleconference. "So, the health of our children is not only an important concern in itself, it's a very important indicator of the health of the nation."

The report, America's Health Starts With Healthy Children: How Do States Compare?, provides new evidence that children in the United States are not as healthy as they could be, Braveman said."This report shows how much healthier kids in each state could be if we narrow the gap between the children of the wealthiest, most educated families and everyone else," she said.

"The report spotlights poverty as a cause of ill health in kids, and downplays the role of health insurance," said Steffie Woolhandler, an associate professor of medicine at Harvard Medical School and co-founder of Physicians For A National Health Program. "Poverty, however, is a lack of access to resources, and one resource that many poor children cannot access is health care. Lack of adequate health insurance forces parents to go without care for themselves and their kids. While figuring out how to end poverty is complex, figuring out how to achieve universal access to health care is simple—nonprofit national health insurance."

Children's health improves along with increasing levels of family education and income, Braveman noted, "children in poor and less-educated families generally have the worst health, but even children in middle-class families fare worse than those at the top," she said.

Sue Egerter, co-director of the University of California, San Francisco, Center on Social Disparities in Health, and another of the report's authors, noted that in the United States a full third of children in the poorest households are in less than very good health, compared with 7 percent of children in more affluent households.

"These children are not simply suffering from earaches, these are kids with much higher rates of chronic medical conditions including asthma, respiratory allergies, and learning disabilities," Egerter said during the teleconference. "These are kids who, quite simply, have more health problems than most other kids."[1]

127

CHAPTER 09

---Health care in the United States is a hotly contested issue, as it's often argued that the rich reap the benefits of the system, while the poor get left behind. There are public health programs in place, but expensive health insurance still provides the best access to care.

Even children in middle-income families can experience shortfalls compared with children in higher-income families, and stark differences in health are seen across racial and ethnic groups. Despite these gaps in access, the United States has a relatively high standard of health care. In this chapter we'll study the history of health care, compare health care systems internationally, and discuss the often overlooked role of mental health in our nation and society.

get the topic: WHAT ARE THE SOCIAL PROBLEMS RELATED TO HEALTH AND AGING?

HEALTH is a state of complete physical, mental, and social well-being, not merely the absence of disease or infirmity.

MENTAL DISORDERS are patterns of mood, thought, or behavior that cause distress and decrease the ability of a person to function.

Health Defined

So, what makes a person healthy? Eating three square meals a day and taking vitamins? Running a marathon every year? Just feeling good and being relatively disease-free? The term "health" gets tossed around a lot, and it rarely has a clear definition attached to it. According to the World Health Organization, **health** is "a state of complete physical, mental, and social well-being and not merely the absence of disease or infirmity."[2] Health is the sum of several different factors, not only physical and mental, but also social.

Mental health has become a much bigger concern to the medical community in recent years. People have suffered from mental ailments throughout human history, but only now do the medical treatments of these issues make up a major part of the health care system. **Mental disorders** are patterns of mood, thought, or behavior that cause distress and decrease the ability of a person to function. Modern psychology and psychiatry use a wide variety of techniques and medicines in an attempt to treat mental disorders and offer some relief to those who suffer.

HISTORY OF HEALTH CARE

Throughout the history of the United States, medical care has been at the center of many social problems. U.S. health care has always been seen as a luxury, sparking debate over who should have access to it. Other arguments involve quality—what constitutes "good" medical care? Does the answer change over time? To understand the importance of these questions today, we must first look at these issues in a historical context.

Practice vs. Profession of Medicine

Early medical practice involved little more than folk remedies and home cures. In the early U.S. colonies, boys who wished to become physicians generally apprenticed with a medical practitioner in their teen years. In Europe, the system was more established, leaving many to feel that the U.S. medical system was in the hands of "quacks." It wasn't until the mid-1700s that northern colonies began to enact laws and licensure for medical professionals. The first medical school was established in 1765 in Philadelphia to train doctors for the region.

Early American professors strongly believed that doctors needed to dissect human corpses in order to learn about the human body; however, laws were in place that prevented access to cadavers. Thus, many medical students became grave robbers, digging up the bodies of poor citizens from the mass graves of potters' fields to dissect them. Eventually, this practice became so widespread that the public became outraged enough to launch what is now known as the April 13, 1788 Anti-Dissection Riot. This led to new legislation that allowed professionals' legal access to cadavers for medical purposes.[3]

Causes and Cures of Illness and Disease

In the 18th century, medical science was still based on the notion that the body was a system with balanced amounts of blood, phlegm, and bile; if a person was sick, his or her system was obviously out of balance. Bloodletting, use of leeches, and forced vomiting were all means of purging the body of impure fluids. George Washington himself was bled when he became ill and died from a loss of blood.

<<< What makes a person **healthy?**

Four different schools of thought arose in contrast to orthodox medical science at this time. Unorthodox practitioners usually fell into one of four categories:

1 Hydropaths: They believed that the body could be cleansed internally and externally by the use of water, natural foods, good hygiene, and exercise. Special bathhouses and drinks were advocated by hydropathic physicians, and current medicines were eschewed.

2 Osteopaths: These physicians also rejected the use of drugs, but prescribed a different cure than hydropaths. Because the body was thought to be a unified system, they believed that manipulation of the skeleton could improve health. Osteopathic doctors used baths, massage, and even surgery to correct problems in their patients. Although there is an osteopathic branch of medical science today, chiropractic therapy is a closer descendent of this school of thought.

3 Christian Scientists: Founded by Mary Baker Eddy, Christian Scientists believed that all illness was an illusion of the mind and did not really exist. Sickness, like everything in life, was a spiritual matter, and a person could heal himself simply by healing his mind. Similar beliefs can be found in our modern world, as Christian Science reading rooms continue to exist today.

4 Homeopaths: Homeopathic doctors argued that orthodox medical practices overmedicated and overtreated people, making them even more ill. Instead, they insisted, the key to healing could be found in prevention and treatment with small doses of medicine that supported the body's own ability to heal itself. Today, many homeopathic medicines still exist, often referred to as "alternative" forms of treatment in our society.[4]

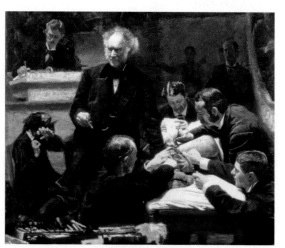

∧
∧ Many **medical breakthroughs**
∧ such as the defibrillator were designed and perfected through the **use of laboratory cadavers.**

Evolution of the Hospital

Historically, care for sick colonists was the responsibility of the family. Almshouses (places for the poor) would eventually become the first hospitals in America. This wasn't planned, but came about naturally because many of the poor were both physically and mentally ill. The first true hospital for the sick was created in Philadelphia in 1752. It was built and funded by voluntary donations, but was rarely used.

It was not until after the Civil War that almshouses were closed, and hospitals were built to take their place. For the most part, however, people still preferred to be cared for at home, and hospitals were often used by those who had no families or were homeless and poor. It wasn't until medical training began to include hospital rotations that the status of doctors was elevated, and over the years the increased professionalization of the medical field, as well as an increased use of surgery, led to increased use of hospitals.[5]

Although we'd like to think that our health care system has improved since the 19th century, many of the same social problems exist in the United States today. Who should have access to medical care? How do

> SOCIAL EPIDEMIOLOGY is the study of the distribution of diseases and health throughout a society's population.

we assess the quality of care? Who decides the answers to these two questions—the government or the people? These difficult issues within the current system remain as we continue to search for ways to expand high-quality health care across America.

SOCIAL EPIDEMIOLOGY

As you learned in the introduction to this chapter, an individual's health seems to be connected with his or her social status. **Social epidemiologists** study the distribution of diseases and health throughout a population and assess the social problems that occur. They might ask questions such as "How does gender affect childhood illness?" or "Do social classes differ in rates of depression?" Their goal is to find links between certain social factors and physical and mental well-being.

AGE AND HEALTH

In the United States, death is rare among the young. Less than 7 infants die per 1,000 births,[6] and the average American can expect to live well into his or her mid-70s.[7] Compare that to developing countries such as Nigeria, where only 1 of every 3 children will live to be a year old, and the average adult lifespan is only 48 years.[8] With the improved life expectancy and longevity in the United States, however, elderly people face a wide variety of health problems that were not as prevalent in the past. Chronic conditions such as arthritis, diabetes, heart and lung disease, and mental illness plague the elderly. These conditions limit activity, making work, socialization, and exercise difficult for seniors to pursue.

Childhood Obesity

Little kids typically seem full of energy, bouncing around the house, running through the playground, and being unable to sit still for long periods of time no matter where they are. If children are this active, they should be skinny, right? This might have been the case in the past, but the United States is witnessing a disturbing trend in children's health in recent years: a rapid increase in childhood obesity. A 2006 study determined that the rise in obesity was a direct result of the availability of energy-dense foods and drinks combined with a lack of energy expenditure.[9] In other words, kids are simply eating more calories than they're burning.

Gender and Health

Gender plays a significant role in life expectancy and types of health problems. The life expectancy for women in the United States is an average of 80.4 years, while the expectancy for men is 75.2 years.[10] Sociologists look for social factors to explain this disparity. Some suggest that males are more likely to take risks, abuse alcohol, drive aggressively, and perform a host of other behaviors that can lead to their early deaths. Men are also more likely to accept dangerous work and make up a greater portion of the armed forces in wartime.[11]

Women are generally more concerned with preventive maintenance of their health than men are—for example, they're twice as likely to get regular medical checkups.[12] Because of this, they're less likely to experience life-threatening illnesses and health problems.[13] Women are also more likely to discuss personal health issues with their doctors.[14] Perhaps men should take notice of the health practices of women and try to take better care of their health in order to live longer lives.

Social Class and Health

As we saw in the opening article, social class has a major effect on health in the United States. In the U.S., the quality of health care is often connected to one's ability to pay for it. The lack of access continues to be a serious social problem for the poor. Back when I worked in hospitals, every day included a session with an uninsured person to discuss how he or she would be able to pay the medical bills. Although there are programs that help some get access to health care, they are often poorly funded. Higher social class means greater access to health care, and having more money allows for more basic needs to be met. Lower socioeconomic status leads to a lower likelihood of access to health care and a poorer standard of life as a result. In fact, studies show that the

higher one's socioeconomic status, the more likely a person is to live longer, healthier, and happier.[15]

People who live in poor neighborhoods are less likely to have access to health care in general, but the neighborhoods themselves can also have serious effects on health as well.[16] Neighborhoods that house many poor, unemployed, uneducated, and single mothers adversely affect the health of people living there.[17] Areas with a high crime rate and drug problems also have negative effects on the health of inhabitants. Dangerous environments like these cause stress, which leads to more serious health problems.[18] Pollution and unsanitary conditions are also an issue; in the Bronx and upper Manhattan, minority children suffer from a high rate of chronic health problems such as asthma as a result of living in areas with high rates of air pollution.[19] As it stands, the urban poor are disproportionately affected by health problems.

Many school lunch programs offer high-calorie foods and drinks, with a lack of healthier options. We have not yet achieved a national standardization of healthy school lunches.

Parents are often too busy to cook healthy food on a regular basis, leaving children to rely on fast food or pre-packaged meals. Busy parents also fail to monitor snacking habits, and unsupervised children can get carried away with junk food consumption.

The popularity of television, video games, and computers has led to a decrease in active outdoor play. Whereas children once relied on running around the neighborhood playing games with other kids for fun, they now turn to electronic entertainment, a majority of which is sedentary.

Race and Health

Racial and ethnic inequality in health care is another serious social problem in the United States. Differences between races in terms of health are tied to the social class issue. In 2005, the average life expectancy of whites was 78.3 years, while African Americans were expected to live 73.2 years.[20] Bear in mind that 24.9 percent of African Americans live below the poverty level, while only 8.3 percent of American whites are impoverished.[21] We have already learned that people who have low incomes and live in poorer neighborhoods are at an increased risk for health problems.

Both access to and quality of health care are repeatedly shown to be affected by race.[22] Infant mortality rates are higher in minority communities, and the quality of care offered is not as high as that provided to whites.[23] Blacks perceive this difference and see it as primarily driven by discrimination.[24]

The Rise in Childhood Obesity in the United States

Source: Pamela M. Anderson and Kristin F. Butcher, "Childhood Obesity: Trends and Potential Causes," *The Future of Children*, 2006. 16: 19–45.

▶▶▶ GO GL🌐BAL

The Best Places to Have Cancer

Is there really a good place to have cancer? The obvious answer to this question is no, but if you were to be diagnosed, your geographical location could be a major factor in your chances of surviving this disease. A recent worldwide study of cancer survival rates provided some interesting results. Data was collected from 31 countries across five continents, looking at men and women separately. The background mortality rate in each country was taken into consideration,

and the study team attempted to calculate "relative survival rates" to account for these differences.

For women suffering from breast, colon, or rectal cancer, Cuba is the best place to live for a high chance of recovery, and Algeria is one of the worst. Generally, people in highly developed countries like the United States and those of Western Europe have a better rate of survival than people in Africa, South America, and Eastern Europe. Researchers suggest that these results are due to higher levels and increased access to health care in certain areas of the globe.

The study also took a look at several subpopulations within the United States and found that New York City was the worst place to live in terms of cancer survival rate, despite the fact that it hosts many of the most advanced medical centers in the world. If this is true, how could Cuba be a better place to live? Generally, the data suggest that early access to health care is one of the most important factors in rates of survival. Because most other nations offer some form of universal health care, it shouldn't be surprising that the United States isn't the best place to receive treatment for cancer.

Health Care

The American health care system is great—if you can afford it. The American Medical Association states that people without health insurance "tend to live sicker and die younger than people with health insurance."[25] Unfortunately, there are a high number of uninsured people living in the United States who fall into this category.

HEALTH CARE: AN INTERNATIONAL COMPARISON

Health care varies greatly from country to country. The system is run by the government in some, and privatized in others. Access can be equal to all or dependent upon money. The fairness of the United States' system has been brought into question many times, but how does it compare to other health care systems around the world?

The World Health Organization (WHO) came up with a set of five criteria for a "good" and "fair" health system in the year 2000. According to this list, a proper health system should have:

1. Low infant mortality rates and high life expectancy
2. A fair distribution of good health (relatively even mortality and life expectancy rates across the country)
3. A high level of health care responsiveness
4. A fair distribution of responsiveness
5. A fair distribution of financing health care (health care costs are evenly distributed based on a person's ability to pay)

The WHO performed a comparison of the health systems in 191 countries across the world and found that the United States was first in responsiveness. Responsiveness includes respect for patients as well as prompt attention to their needs. Although the United States was high in one area, it ranked relatively low overall compared to other similarly wealthy nations. The United States is the only wealthy, industrialized, capitalist nation that doesn't provide some form of universal health care. This caused it to score lower than other countries in fairness of financing and citizen satisfaction. In fact, the United States health care system ranked 37th overall.[26]

National Scorecard on Health Care Performance

We've discussed a number of social problems related to health care, including gender and race differences, as well as connections to social class and age. But how does the U.S. system fair overall? *Health Affairs* magazine did a report called the National Scorecard on Healthcare Performance that uncovered some interesting data on the U.S. health care system. What did it find?

1. The United States spends 16 percent of gross domestic product on the health care system, but doesn't provide universal access. Compare this to the 4.1 percent spent on primary and secondary education, which is accessible to everyone.[27]
2. Only 49 percent of American adults receive the recommended preventive screening tests for their age and sex.
3. Only half of patients with congestive heart failure receive written discharge instructions regarding follow-up care after hospitalization.

Assessment of the World's Health Systems (by the World Health Organization)

Total Rank	Nation	Life expectancy (in years)	Infant Survival Rate	Fairness of financial contribution to health care system (ranked 1–191)	Responsiveness (ranked 1–191)
1	France	79.3	97.8%	26	16
2	Italy	78.8	97.8%	45	22
6	Singapore	78	97.1%	101	20
7	Spain	78.7	97.8%	26	34
10	Japan	81	99.9%	8	6
18	United Kingdom	77.2	99.9%	9	26
30	Canada	79	97.7%	18	7
37	United States	76.8	96.6%	54	1
155	Zimbabwe	40.5	78.5%	175	122
173	Afghanistan	46.3	47.0%	103	181
180	Ethiopia	42.3	51.0%	138	179
186	Liberia	43.7	24.5%	84	175
187	Nigeria	47.5	33.6%	180	149
189	Central African Republic	44.1	30.1%	166	183
190	Myanmar	58.8	57.9%	190	151
191	Sierra Leone	34.3	43.3%	191	173

Source: World Health Organization "World Health Organization Assesses the World's Health Systems," http://www.who.int/whr/2000/media_centre/press_release/en/, Accessed August 28, 2008.

MAJOR DEPRESSIVE DISORDER is a mental disorder characterized by persistent, chronic feelings of sadness, hopelessness, worthlessness, guilt, or pessimism lasting for weeks at a time.

BIPOLAR DISORDER is characterized by drastic shifts in mood and behavior; victims often fluctuate between being overly high and energetic and feeling depressed and hopeless.

SCHIZOPHRENIA is a mental disorder with symptoms including hallucinations, delusions, disordered thinking, movement disorders, flat affect, social withdrawal, and cognitive deficits.

OBSESSIVE COMPULSIVE DISORDER (OCD) is a mental disorder in which the sufferer is subjected to recurring thoughts and feelings that cause distress and anxiety and lead to habitual behaviors.

ANXIETY/PANIC DISORDERS arise when normal anxiety is exceeded and everyday situations become difficult for victims to cope with.

EATING DISORDERS are characterized by extreme behavior regarding food, whether drastically under- or overeating, connected with feelings of concern about body image and weight.

4. Nationwide, preventable hospital admissions for patient with chronic health conditions such as diabetes and asthma were twice as high as the level achieved by the best performing nations.

5. One-third of all adults under 65 have problems paying their medical bills, and many are in serious debt due to health problems.

Percent of the Population Under 65 with Health Insurance

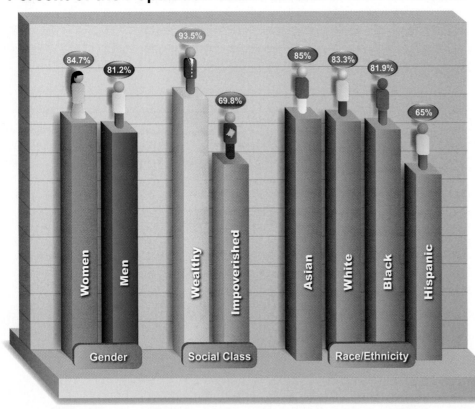

Source: U.S. Department of Health & Human Services, "2008 National Healthcare Quality and Disparities Reports," http://www.ahrq.gov/qual/qrdr08, Accessed August 25, 2009.

∧
∧ As we discussed before, there are **great disparities in health**
∧ **insurance coverage.** How might **different portions of the population vary in mental health as a result?**

6. Only 17 percent of U.S. doctors use electronic medical records, compared with 80 percent of doctors in the top three countries.

7. When measuring quality of care and access to care, there is a wide gap between those with low incomes who are uninsured and those with higher incomes and good insurance. On average, measures for low income and uninsured people in these areas would have to improve by one-third to close the gap.

8. As a part of total health care expenditures, insurance administrative costs in the United States were more than three times the rate in countries with integrated payment systems.[28]

Mental Health

As we discussed earlier, mental health disorders have become increasingly recognized and professionally treated over time. Classifications of specific mental illnesses are relatively new and subject to constant change and adjustment. There are different subcategories of mental disorders, but some of the most common and well known are presented below.

1 **Major depressive disorder**: Victims suffer persistent, chronic feelings of sadness, hopelessness, worthlessness, guilt, and pessimism lasting for weeks at a time.

2 **Bipolar disorder**: Often incorrectly referred to as manic depression, bipolar disorder is characterized by drastic shifts in mood and behavior. Those who suffer from this illness fluctuate between being overly euphoric, agitated, or energetic, and feeling depressed, irritable, or hopeless. The periods of highs and lows are called mania and depression, respectively.

3 **Schizophrenia**: Although multiple subtypes exist, general symptoms of schizophrenia may include auditory or visual hallucinations, mental delusions, disordered thinking, movement disorders, emotional flatness, social withdrawal, and cognitive deficits. This is a severe and often disabling disorder, but modern therapeutic and medicinal treatments offer hope to sufferers and their loved ones.

4 **Obsessive compulsive disorder (OCD)**: People with obsessive compulsive disorder are subjected to recurring thoughts and feelings that cause them extreme distress and anxiety and lead them to carry out certain behaviors. Victims of OCD may find themselves excessively cleaning, counting, or organizing objects to relieve obsessive thoughts.

5 **Panic/anxiety disorders**: A little bit of anxiety is normal and even crucial to react to stressful situations effectively. Anxiety disorders arise when normal anxiety is exceeded, and it becomes difficult for those afflicted to cope with everyday life. Suffering from intense, acute anxiety attacks is known as panic disorder.

6 **Eating disorders**: These illnesses are characterized by extreme behavior regarding food, connected to

feelings of concern about body image and weight. There are several varieties of eating disorders in which victims drastically under- or overeat, the most famous of which include anorexia, bulimia, and binge-eating disorder.

7 **ADHD: Attention deficit hyperactivity disorder** is one of the most common mental disorders in children, although it affects adults as well. Children who suffer from ADHD often have difficulty paying attention in school, misbehave more than usual at home, and have poor relationships with their peers. Symptoms include impulsiveness, hyperactivity, and inattention.

GENDER AND RACE IN MENTAL HEALTH

Are their structural trends that influence mental health? Research shows that men and women tend to suffer from differing types of mental disorders. Females tend to experience more internalizing problems such as anxiety and/or depression. Meanwhile, males tend to externalize problems, leading to aggression, substance abuse, and delinquency. These trends vary somewhat by race. Although the same trends continue for men, white women tend to have much higher rates of internalizing disorders than do minority women. Why? The simple explanation is socialization. Men are socialized early in life to express both dominance and power over others. This results in increased levels of externalization. At the same time, women tend to be socialized early into subordination. This results in higher levels of depression and anxiety in response to this difference in power. The fact that white women tend to have higher rates of internalization problems than women of color seems to show that white women are socialized into stricter subordinate roles.[30]

> ∧
> ∧ According to the United States
> ∧ Department of Health and Human
> Services, about **26.2 percent of the American population suffers from mental health disorders** such as anorexia.[29]

INCOME AND MENTAL HEALTH

Income and social class affect mental health in much the same way as they affect physical health. Longitudinal research shows that children who come from low-income homes experience higher rates of childhood depression as well as antisocial behavior disorders. Furthermore, children who live their entire childhood in poverty have much higher rates of developing *both* of

attention deficit hyperactivity disorder (ADHD) symptoms include impulsiveness, hyperactivity, and inattention.

these mental health issues. There are a number of possible causes for these results, including long-term deprivation, the general stress of living in poorer neighborhoods, or a lack of access to mental health care.[31]

MENTAL HEALTH CARE

There are several different categories of mental health practitioners, including psychiatrists, psychologists, and social workers/counselors. The primary difference among these practitioners is level of education; psychiatrists have an MD, psychologists have a PhD, and social workers/counselors must have at least a bachelor's and in some cases a master's degree. Another key difference is that only psychiatrists are allowed to prescribe medication. In many practices, psychiatrists work in tandem with psychologists or counselors to provide patients with well-rounded, complete treatment.

Psychologists and counselors provide psychotherapy, which is treatment without drugs. Therapy can be used alone or in combination with medication to treat a wide range of disorders, including anxiety/panic disorder, substance abuse, and depression. Psychologists also provide diagnostic testing to determine patients' levels of functioning, and assess whether there is improvement or deterioration of their conditions. Despite Hollywood portrayals of conniving psychologists, establishing a comfortable, honest relationship with patients is the primary goal of therapists. Psychotherapy is designed to help patients develop coping strategies and healthy behaviors, which can reduce the possibility of future illness and improve the quality of life. Patients with chronic diseases often turn to psychologists to help them deal with mental issues that can arise as a result of life-threatening illnesses.[32] Dealing with chemotherapy treatments and the general stress of cancer, for instance, is just as hard on the mind as it is on the body. Depression and anxiety are common reactions to the uncertainties and hardships of experiencing health problems, and psychotherapy can be an effective means of coping with these issues.

> <<< Many people imagine therapy sessions to be scenes out of a Hollywood movie. **In reality, mental health professionals seek to make patients feel comfortable and at ease,** both in conversation and environment.

PERCEPTIONS OF MENTAL ILLNESS

For most of history, the mentally ill have had to endure harsh treatment. Mental illness has been widely misunderstood and misinterpreted, leading some cultures to kill mentally ill people, and others to lock them away for life. In the 1950s, American social scientists began to study the public's perception of the mentally ill. They found that the general community was largely uninformed about current psychiatric medical knowledge and still based much of their opinions on negative stereotypes and misinformation. The prevailing view was that mental problems were not uncontrollable illnesses, but rather some sort of character flaw.

Over time, the public perception of mental illness has shifted from one of fear and disdain to something more closely resembling tolerance and understanding. Most people

∧
∧ Those confined by chains
∧ and bars were often the
lucky ones; **in the mid-1900s, quick and cheap transorbital lobotomies were the trend.**

probably still don't want to live next door to an inpatient facility for mentally ill and violent offenders, but there's a general level of understanding toward people suffering from mental illnesses that wasn't present before.[33] It might not be complete acceptance, but at least society recognizes mental illness as a disease and not an outright moral deficiency.

THE MYTH OF MENTAL ILLNESS

There is some dispute about the diagnosis and treatment of mental illness, with the argument that Americans are so caught up in medically treating every problem that we have greatly misdiagnosed the mental problems themselves. In *The Myth of Mental Illness*, Dr. Thomas Szasz argues that these illnesses are often misdiagnosed and used as a means of social control.[34] Paula Caplan, who served on the committee to update the **DSM (Diagnostic and Statistical Manual of Mental Disorders**—the standard text used by health professionals in the United States to classify mental illnesses), agrees. From her experience, she found that the DSM relies heavily on personal ideology and political maneuvering.[35] Caplan was the only woman on the committee that met to revise the DSM when premenstrual dysphoric disorder (known to most as PMS) was included as a "mental illness," despite the lack of evidence to support such a conclusion. Even if PMS had research supporting its existence, it would still be the only mental illness to happen monthly for a set number of days. Caplan suggests that men would never accept such a diagnosis for themselves.

think social problems: HOW DO SOCIOLOGISTS VIEW PROBLEMS RELATED TO MENTAL AND PHYSICAL HEALTH?

We've discussed how the medical community and the public view health problems. Now let's take a look at the issues from the perspective of a sociologist.

Functionalism: The Medicalization of the American Society

The functionalist perspective examines how health and health care affect people's lives. The late sociologist Talcott Parsons believed that a physical or mental illness could become a social role.[36] The **sick role**, as he called it, is made up of the expected behaviors and responsibilities appropriate for someone who is ill. An ill person is expected to see a doctor to try to rid him- or herself of the afflicting disease. The doctor, therefore, has a powerful position in society, as he controls the labels of sickness and health.

The control and respect that doctors are given has led to the **medicalization** of America. This is the idea that the medical community

is at the center of many aspects of society.[37] There seems to be a prevailing belief in the United States that we can find a pill for every problem. Ads for prescription drugs such as Viagra or Paxil only make the problem worse; research has shown that many consumers go to their doctors requesting pills they've seen on television.[38]

Conflict Theory: Making a Profit

It is easy to see how inequality influences health care. Conflict theorists point to the lack of access, noting that at any given time, 1 in 6 people in the United States do not have health care insurance. Because the United States is the only Western nation not providing some form of government-funded health care, conflict theorists seek to understand why. Sociologist Jill Quadagno (2004) suggests that a number of structural barriers exist. First and foremost is the reality that American medical care

WRAP YOUR MIND AROUND THE THEORY

A little competition can be a good thing. Are some medical professionals right in saying that a national health care system could harm our country?

FUNCTIONALISM

How the does the health care system best function? Some medical professionals define health care as a privilege and not a right because they argue that this introduces competition into the system. From their point of view, competition is necessary because it increases innovation and quality of care.[40] Talcott Parsons, however, would argue that doctors and medical insurance companies support this view solely to retain their positions of power in society.

CONFLICT THEORY

Those who feel that health care is a right suggest that it's for the good of society to provide medical care to all people. Because we ration health care in America to those who can pay, people with money have no desire to make it a right; they keep it as their own special privilege. It may be a privilege to grow up in a family that can vacation in Europe, but should being able to go to the doctor depend on the size of your checkbook?

IS HEALTH CARE A RIGHT OR A PRIVILEGE?

SYMBOLIC INTERACTIONISM

Terms such as "right" and "privilege" make all the difference when it comes to the method of health care. If health care is a *right*, then the government must do something to make sure that it's fairly and equally provided to all citizens. If it's a *privilege*, the government doesn't need to do anything; health care can be entirely privatized. Right now, American health care is established more as a privilege than a right.

In the United States, the rich reap the benefits of the health care system. How might some deal with a lack of access to professional medical care?

In America, health is a privilege. If only the rich can afford health care, what will the population of our country look like in 50 years?

is a for-profit business. Any invasion of the government is not welcome by those who make their living off of the current system. Two groups have the most to lose from government-run health care: insurance companies, and medical professionals themselves. Both reap high profits and hold secure markets for their businesses under the current system. Of course, they make this money at the expense of that 1 person in 6 who cannot afford to go to the doctor.[39] In a sense, the poor pay these professionals' salaries with their lives.

discover solutions to social problems:
HOW DO SOCIETIES DEAL WITH HEALTH?

United States Health Care Spending

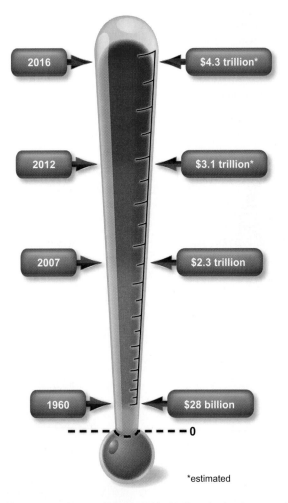

2016	$4.3 trillion*
2012	$3.1 trillion*
2007	$2.3 trillion
1960	$28 billion
	0

*estimated

Source: World Health Organization "World Health Organization Assesses the World's Health Systems," http://www.who.int/whr/2000/media_centre/press_release/en/, Accessed August 28, 2008.

Different societies have taken different approaches to health care. More affluent societies tend to have better access to care, but there are still universal conflicts over whether health care should be considered a basic human right or a privilege to those who can afford it.

Health Care in the United States

So, why exactly does the United States view health care the way it does? Could anything be done to change it? According to a recent study, only 40 percent of Americans are satisfied with their health care system.[41] The United States spends more money per person on health care than any other country, but not everyone has health insurance. National insurance, which would cover all children and the millions of adults who can't afford to pay, doesn't exist. Fewer employers are offering health benefits, and private insurance premiums are going up, pushing nearly 15 percent of the U.S. population out of health insurance.[42]

Why has the U.S. government been so resistant to provide universal health care? Jill Quadagno offers several possible reasons:

1. The Constitution states that the power of the government must be limited. Providing national health care is viewed as a form of welfare, which threatens our freedom.

2. The working class and labor unions fail to support legislation that would provide universal health care.

3. Private health insurance companies strongly oppose the idea of national health care.[43]

Most of the health insurance industry is set up through the work place and medical unions; however there are some public forms of health care that do exist in America.

NATIONAL HEALTH CARE FOR THE ELDERLY: MEDICARE

There is one segment of the population that is guaranteed governmental health care—the elderly. As you learned in Chapter 5, Medicare is a

MAKE CONNECTIONS

Physical and Mental Health Care

In Chapter 2, you learned about poverty and wealth. As we've mentioned, the poor have less access to health care, and as a result, tend to suffer from a lower standard of health. Infant mortality rates are much higher in impoverished communities, and life expectancy is generally tied to income levels.

In Chapter 10, you will learn about alcohol and substance abuse. Although these issues often lead to severe physical health issues, mental health problems are often closely related as well. It's difficult to say whether depression leads to drug use or drug use leads to depression (or a little bit of both), but mental health problems and substance abuse tend to go hand-in-hand.

government-run social insurance program that provides health coverage for elderly Americans. This insurance is available to citizens over the age of 65 who have paid Medicare taxes for at least 10 years or to the spouses of people who have paid Medicare taxes. Medicare coverage is also available to disabled people under the age of 65 who have been receiving Social Security payments for at least 24 months. The program has different sections that cover hospital, doctor, and prescription drug costs; however, like any other insurance program, not all costs are covered. There are premiums, deductibles, and co-insurance that must be paid out-of-pocket.

Medicaid is designed to provide insurance for low-income individuals and families who meet certain qualifications. Income determines eligibility,

> **MEDICAID** is a government-run program designed to provide insurance for low-income individuals and families who meet certain qualifications.

and the program is funded partially by the federal government and partially by each individual state. Not every person with low income is eligible for Medicaid. There are a variety of other requirements, some of which include age, pregnancy, physical disabilities, and citizenship status. Some individuals, known as "Medicare dual eligibles," qualify for both Medicare *and* Medicaid. Medicaid can fill in the gaps of Medicare coverage, handling some of the out-of-pocket costs for elderly people who live in extreme poverty.[44]

Pro & Con

National Health Care vs. Private Health Care

It's no secret that high-quality health care is extremely expensive in the United States. But who should cover the expense? Is it the responsibility of the government to provide for sick citizens, or should care be dependent on an individual's ability to pay for it? What are the pros and cons of strictly government-provided health insurance?

Pro

- Everyone has equal access to care.
- Sick people who live in poverty are not forced to fend for themselves.
- Children who were born into poverty have access to care.
- If everyone has access to proper health care, it can help control the spread of disease, and national life expectancy rates will improve.

Con

- Taxes will increase in order to cover health expenses.
- A nationalized system is much busier; waiting lists and times for procedures will be extended.
- Upper-class citizens who want to pay for premium health care will not have the option to, unless the system allows for private care as well as government-funded care.
- Non-emergency treatments will not take precedence; in fact, not all conditions will be treated due to the huge volume of patients.

From Classroom to Community 〉 Mental Health Facilities

Mental illness used to be a major social stigma. Even as late as the 1960s and '70s, the mentally ill were often locked away at home or in facilities, and treated as burdens on society. Fortunately, modern science has shown us a different view of mental illness, and treatment for these debilitating health problems is rapidly getting better and better.

As part of her clinical psychology degree, Brooke volunteered at a local mental hospital to work firsthand with patients and their caretakers. She was nervous about what she might encounter there, but ended up being pleasantly surprised.

"On my first day, I was really worried about what I might see in the hospital. I'd never been to a mental health facility before, and had these images in my head of a dark stone building like you might see in a horror movie. It couldn't have been further from the truth."

Brooke found the hospital to be a comfortable, therapeutic environment for patients. She worked closely with a doctor who was in charge of the adolescent ward, which housed teenage patients suffering from severe bipolar disorder, depression, and substance abuse problems.

"The doctor seemed to be at ease with the teenagers, and most of the patients seemed comfortable talking to her. Some of them actually called her 'cool,'" Brooke remembered.

While volunteering at the hospital, Brooke filed paperwork, observed several group therapy sessions, and got to talk with some adolescent patients one on one. "I'm glad I got a chance to volunteer there. I got to know some of the teens really well, and I missed them when the semester was over. I know now that I chose the right degree; I want to be able to help people who suffer from mental illness."

WHAT ARE THE SOCIAL PROBLEMS RELATED TO HEALTH AND AGING? 128

in a privatized health care system, health care is available to those who can afford it; upper-class citizens have access to better medical care than lower-class citizens, and they live in healthier, less stressful environments; elderly people face a variety of health problems that weren't as prevalent in the past; youth activity levels have dropped causing childhood obesity to increase at a staggering rate.

HOW DO SOCIOLOGISTS VIEW PROBLEMS RELATED TO MENTAL AND PHYSICAL HEALTH? 134

symbolic interactionists: if health care is a right, it should be available to everyone; if it's a privilege, it can be completely privatized; conflict theorists: the wealthy have no desire to make health care a universal right because once all have it, it will no longer be their privilege; functionalists: America is centered around the medical system; citizens seem to think that for every problem, there's a pill to solve it.

HOW DO SOCIETIES DEAL WITH HEALTH? 136

by providing some form of universal health care (except in the United States); in America, systems like Medicaid and Medicare are available for elderly and poor citizens to help them get by.

get the topic: WHAT ARE THE SOCIAL PROBLEMS RELATED TO HEALTH AND AGING?

Theory

FUNCTIONALISM   134

- Sickness has become a social role. People playing the "sick role" are perceived differently than those who are healthy.
- The medicalization of American society refers to the idea that every ailment can be fixed with some kind of pill or medicinal cure.

SYMBOLIC INTERACTIONISM   135

- The determination of whether health care is a privilege or a right is central to how the government should treat health care.
- A system that is based on the ability to pay considers health care a privilege; a government-funded system considers health care a right.

CONFLICT THEORY   134

- There is an ongoing conflict between those who believe in government-funded health care and those who believe in private health care.

Key Terms

health is a state of complete physical, mental, and social well-being, not merely the absence of disease or infirmity.   *128*

mental disorders are patterns of mood, thought, or behavior that cause distress and decrease the ability of a person to function.   *128*

social epidemiology is the study of the distribution of diseases and health throughout a society's population.   *129*

major depressive disorder is a mental disorder characterized by persistent, chronic feelings of sadness, hopelessness, worthless-

ness, guilt, or pessimism lasting for weeks at a time.   *132*

bipolar disorder is characterized by drastic shifts in mood and behavior; victims often fluctuate between being overly high and energetic and feeling depressed and hopeless.   *132*

schizophrenia is a mental disorder with symptoms including hallucinations, delusions, disordered thinking, movement disorders, flat affect, social withdrawal, and cognitive deficits. *132*

obsessive compulsive disorder (OCD) is a mental disorder in which the sufferer is subjected to recurring thoughts and feelings that cause distress and anxiety and lead to habitual behaviors. *132*

anxiety/panic disorders arise when normal anxiety is exceeded and everyday situations become difficult for victims to cope with. *132*

eating disorders are characterized by extreme behavior regarding food, whether drastically under- or overeating, connected with feelings of concern about body image and weight. *132*

attention deficit hyperactivity disorder (ADHD) symptoms include impulsiveness, hyperactivity, and inattention. *133*

Diagnostic and Statistical Manual of Mental Disorders (DSM) is the standard classification of mental illnesses used by mental health professionals in the United States. *134*

sick role is the expected behaviors and responsibilities appropriate for someone who is ill. *134*

medicalization of America is the idea that the medical community is at the center of many aspects of American society; we feel that there is a pill or some sort of medical cure to fix everything. *134*

Medicaid is a government-run program designed to provide insurance for low-income individuals and families who meet certain qualifications. *137*

Sample Test Questions

These multiple-choice questions are similar to those found in the test bank that accompanies this textbook.

1. Which of the following is the *most likely* reason life expectancy in the United States has increased since the 1700s?

   a. Government-funded health care has risen slowly in the last few decades.

   b. The vaccine for polio was discovered by Albert Camus in 1967.

   c. There have been advances in medical science and greater access to health care.

   d. The past century has seen a rapid decrease in air pollution.

2. Which of the following schools of thought believed that illness was created by the human mind and that spiritual healing was the only necessary medicine?

   a. Christian Scientists

   b. Homeopaths

   c. Osteopaths

   d. Psychopaths

3. Which of the following *best describes* the cause(s) of the child obesity epidemic in America?

   a. There is a lack of healthy, standardized school lunch options.

   b. Single-parent families and dual-income families often consist of parents who are too busy to cook healthy food for their children on a regular basis.

   c. There is an increased reliance on computers and video games for entertainment instead of physical activity.

   d. All of the above are true.

4. Which of the following is *not* one of the World Health Organization's criteria for a good and fair health system?

   a. Low infant mortality rates and high life expectancy

   b. A fair distribution of financing health care

   c. A high level of health care responsiveness

   d. Low rates on privatized health care

5. What was the cause of the 1788 Anti-Dissection Riot?

   a. Members of the community were outraged at the government's strict policies on medical dissection.

   b. Doctors went on strike in Philadelphia over their right to perform medical research.

   c. Civilians protested the unauthorized grave robbing and dissection of their loved ones.

   d. Medical students objected to the unethical killing of animals for dissections.

ESSAY

1. After reading the debate about government-funded vs. private health care, what is your opinion about the best health care system?

2. Do you think that U.S. society is overly "medicalized," relying too heavily on medicine and pill-popping to solve problems?

3. Judging by the fact that medicine has continued to evolve and change over the years, do you think that modern psychology's views on treating mental illness will be the same or different 100 years from now? If it will be different, what kind of changes do you think will be made?

4. Which 1800s school of medical thought do you most agree with: Orthodox, Hydropathic, Osteopathic, Christian Science, or Homeopathic? Which do you think is closest to our general medical practice today?

5. Take a look at the graph on page 131. What could account for such disparities in health between races?

WHERE TO START YOUR RESEARCH PAPER

For U.S. Census facts and information, go to http://www.census.gov

For more information about types of mental illnesses, go to http://www.nimh.nih.gov/health/publications/the-numbers-count-mental-disorders-in-america/index.shtml

For more information about the DSM, go to http://www.psych.org/MainMenu/Research/DSMIV.aspx

To learn more about the current Administration's stance on U.S. health care, visit the official government site at http://www.healthreform.gov/

For up-to-date articles on the latest psychiatric research, visit http://pn.psychiatryonline.org/

ANSWERS: 1. c; 2. a; 3. d; 4. d; 5. c

Remember to check www.thethinkspot.com for additional information, downloadable flashcards, and other helpful resources.

DRUG AND
ALCOHOL ABUSE

IS SUBSTANCE ABUSE A SOCIAL
PROBLEM?
HOW DO SOCIOLOGISTS VIEW DRUG AND
ALCOHOL USE?
WHAT CAN WE DO ABOUT DRUG AND
ALCOHOL ABUSE?

Despite

investing $1 billion in a massive anti-drug campaign, a controversial new study suggests that the push has failed to help the United States win the war on drugs.

A congressionally mandated study released today concluded that the National Youth Anti-Drug Media Campaign launched in the late 1990s to encourage young people to stay away from drugs "is unlikely to have had favorable effects on youths."

In fact, the study's authors assert that anti-drug ads may have unwittingly delivered the message that other kids were doing drugs, inadvertently slowing measured progress that was being made to curb marijuana use among teenagers.

"Youths who saw the campaign ads took from them the message that their peers were using marijuana," the report suggests as a possible reason for its findings. "In turn, those who came to believe that their peers were using marijuana were more likely to initiate use themselves."

The study's authors called the findings, published in the December edition of the *American Journal of Public Health*, "particularly worrisome because they were unexpected."

The widespread anti-drug campaign, which sprang from the efforts of The Partnership for a Drug-Free America and supervised by the White House Office of National Drug Control Policy, targeted 12- to 18-year olds starting in 1998. It has since pervaded American households via commercials, Web sites, advertisements in movie theaters, and other platforms.

According to the study, 94 percent of young people surveyed reported being exposed to the government campaign, on average seeing about two to three messages per week.

"Overall, the campaign was successful in achieving a high level of exposure to its messages; however, there is no evidence to support the claim that this exposure affected youths' marijuana use as desired," the report said.[1]

CHAPTER 10

---Drugs—we use them constantly. From the coffee we sip in the morning to the Tylenol PM we take before bed, they help us get through our day. But this kind of drug use is rarely a social issue.

Drug and alcohol abuse, however, can create many devastating problems for families and individuals, and those problems frequently bleed over into the greater society. Despite the millions of dollars spent every year on combating this matter, drug abuse continues to persist.

Most of my students can name a host of social problems related to substance abuse. Aside from the obvious issues associated with imprisonment, other problems abound. Whether it's dropout and pregnancy rates for teens, or domestic violence and divorce rates for adults, it's easy to see the harmful effects on society. But is substance abuse itself a problem? In the following pages we'll discuss the social concerns that stem from the use and abuse of these substances. Why do certain people abuse drugs? What are some of the results of drug abuse? Are current drug laws effective? Remember these questions as you read on.

get the topic: IS SUBSTANCE ABUSE A SOCIAL PROBLEM?

DRUGS are substances that have psychological or physical effects.

NARCOTICS are drugs that are considered illegal today.

DRUG USE is the act of internally processing chemical substances other than food that have physical effects.

History of Drug Abuse

Drug use is nothing new to the human race. As long as fruit has fermented and been consumed, our species has experienced the effects of **drugs**, substances that have psychological or physical effects. For example, aspirin heals headaches, opiates relieve muscle tension, birth control pills block ovulation, and so forth. Intentional fermentation—the process used to make alcohol—dates back to the Stone Age. Beer jugs from the Neolithic period serve as evidence that alcoholic beverages were produced as early as 10,000 B.C.E. **Narcotics**, drugs that are considered illegal today, also date back thousands of years.

DRUG USE IN ANCIENT TIMES

Citizens of Sumer, the first true civilization, used opium for medical and recreational purposes as early as 3000 B.C.E.; early tablets reveal that Sumerians referred to the substance as "Gil Hul" or "joy plant."[2] Ancient texts such as the Torah describe the early origins of winemaking in the Middle East, and the Ebers Papyrus, a medical document from ancient Egypt, outlines the many medicinal uses of opium.[3]

DRUG USE IN THE 18TH CENTURY

Although opium was originally used as a medicine, it was also one of the first drugs to be abused for recreational purposes. Opium addiction became a serious social problem in China during the 18th century. Initially, it was used to sedate patients and relieve tension and pain. However, by 1729, opium use became so rampant that the emperor outlawed the cultivation, sale, and use of the drug. These laws failed to impede trafficking or abuse, as opium production was still legal in Western Europe. The opium trade was lucrative to nations such as Great Britain, which used profits from opium sales to purchase popular Chinese luxury goods such as silk, porcelain, and tea.[4] Clearly, making something illegal and attempting to punish it out of existence doesn't always work.

EARLY DRUG USE IN THE UNITED STATES

During the Civil War in the United States, both opium and its derivative morphine were regularly given to soldiers to relieve the pain of battle wounds. But dependence on the drugs lasted long after the wounds were healed, leading the addiction to become known as "army disease." In 1898, Bayer, the German company known for producing aspirin, developed heroin. Ironically, this drug was marketed as a non-addictive substitute for morphine, as well as a cough suppressant. Heroin was in fact stronger than morphine, and by 1900, approximately 1 percent of the U.S. population was addicted to some form of opiate.[5]

In the early 1900s, harmful and addictive drugs were readily available to consumers. Drugstores were free to sell virtually anything they wished as long as a person had a prescription, and many over-the-counter drugs contained heroin, morphine, and other opiates. Even Coca-Cola—a seemingly harmless product—contained cocaine until the company switched to caffeine in 1906.[7]

However, around the same time, temperance movements for alcohol and drugs began to arise. The first federal law to restrict the sale, manufacturing, and distribution of drugs was the Harrison Narcotic Act of 1914.

Since that time, a host of laws to restrict, control, and punish drug abuse and alcoholism have been on the books in the United States. However, the social problem of addiction continues. The U.S. Centers for Disease Control and Prevention estimates that about 8 percent of the population over 12 years of age have used illegal drugs in the last month.[8] Meanwhile, about half of the population has used alcohol in the last month, with 5 percent drinking heavily, and another 15 percent binge drinking.[9]

Drug Use and Abuse

Drug use is the act of internally processing chemical substances other than food that have physical effects. A person uses drugs when she takes an aspirin to relieve a headache at the end of a long day. Even consuming a caffeinated beverage in the morning is considered drug use. Illegal or legal, over-the-counter or prescription, it's safe to say that most Americans have used some type of drug in their lifetimes.[10]

Of course, there are no social problems that result from your morning cup of tea, but drug abuse is a serious issue. **Drug abuse** is the use of drugs despite adverse consequences. Adverse consequences are typically associated with street drugs such as cocaine or heroin, which can cause severe nerve and tissue damage. Seemingly harmless drugs, however, can also damage a person's health when they are used frequently and in large quantities. There was a period in my life when I used to drink more than two pots of coffee each day. I began to develop heart palpitations and blood pressure problems. When I tried to kick the caffeine, my body went through withdrawal; I developed headaches and felt lethargic all the time. It seemed that I was hooked on the caffeine. However, I didn't think that I was "addicted."

Addiction is a chronic condition that can include both a psychological and/or physiological compulsion toward drug seeking and use.[11] Addicts feel

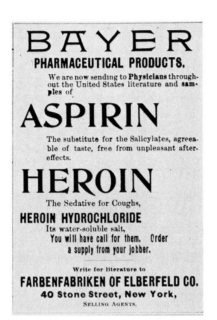

a *need* for a certain drug. They may know that using it will result in adverse consequences; however, they also sense that there will be adverse consequences if they don't. They believe that they can't do certain things such as relax, focus, or energize without the drug in their system. I was able to kick my caffeine habit with a little willpower and tolerance for discomfort, so it's likely that I wasn't truly addicted to the substance, just a little dependent.

Types of Drugs

What type of behavior do you expect from a person on drugs? You might expect him to be erratic and hyperactive or maybe you'd expect her to be mellow and unresponsive. A person's reaction to a drug largely depends on the type of drug that is being used. As you can see in the chart below, there are three main categories of drugs: **stimulants**, which excite the body and stimulate the brain and central

<<< **It's believed that the name "heroin" is derived from the German word** *heroisch*, **or "heroic."** People who use the drug often feel "heroic" while under its influence.[6]

Types of Drugs and Their Effects

Type of Drug	Form	Method of Use	Immediate Effects	Potential Effects of Long-term Abuse
Stimulants	Tobacco	smoke, chew	increased heart and pulse rate	heart and lung disease, cancer, high blood pressure
	Speed	swallow, snort, inject	large amounts of stimulation, increased activity	mental and emotion disturbance, neurological problems
	Crack Cocaine	swallow, snort, inject	increased energy, feelings of power	loss of concentration, aggression, mental disturbances
	Ecstasy	swallow, inject	sensation of floating, paranoia	convulsions, irrational behavior, depression
Depressants	Alcohol	oral	slurred speech, loss of inhibitions	damage to the brain, heart, stomach, and liver
	Opioids	oral, inject, smoke	relief of pain, decreased awareness	damage to the brain and nervous system, high risk of overdose
	Cannabis	oral, smoke	relaxation, decrease in coordination	repertory problems, loss of memory or concentration
	Inhalants	inhalation	relaxation, drowsiness	liver, kidney, and brain damage, vomiting
Hallucinogens	LSD	swallow	hallucinations, anxiety, panic	severe mental disturbances, nerve damage
	Mushrooms	swallow	hallucinations, nausea	severe mental disturbances, nerve damage

Source: "Office of National Drug Control Policy- Drug Facts," Office of National Drug Control Policy, http://www.whitehousedrugpolicy.gov/DrugFact/index.html

nervous system, **depressants**, which slow the activity of vital organs in the body to create a relaxed, sleepy feeling, and **hallucinogens**, which distort the senses and cause hallucinations.

Basics of Drug Use in America

As you can imagine, drug use and abuse creates a plethora of social problems for society, not only because of the extra costs associated with trying to help people "kick the habit" but also due to the lost productivity, destroyed relationships, and personal injury that such abuse can cause. Of all the drugs available in the United States, tobacco and alcohol are the two most commonly used. Recent surveys have shown that 20.6 percent of Americans over 18 are current smokers.[12] In addition, 23 percent of adults drink alcohol at a dangerous level, and even among youth, 91 percent of drinkers 12 to 14 years old admit to binge drinking.[13] College students in particular fall into the binge-drinking scene, as many students view inebriation as a rite of passage. This attitude has created a serious issue for schools, as alcohol-related hospitalizations and deaths are regular occurrences on many college campuses. In fact, numerous colleges are now making it illegal for anyone to consume alcohol on campus, regardless of their age.[14]

CHARACTERISTICS OF DRUG USERS

Age

If you think teenagers and college students make up the majority of "users," you're mistaken. It's true that almost 20 percent of 18- to 25-year olds frequently use illegal drugs, compared to 5.8 percent of those 26 and older.[15] However, a 2007 survey on drug use showed that 42 percent of Americans over 26 have used marijuana, while only about 16 percent of young adults have tried this drug.[16] Researchers attribute this pattern to the aging baby boomer population who grew up in a culture of drug use.[17]

Even if the researchers from the opening article are correct in saying that anti-drug ads have been counterproductive, teen drug use has been steadily decreasing since the turn of the millennium. In 1999, it was estimated that more than half of high school seniors used illicit drugs, mostly marijuana. Even pre-teen drug use was high, as one fourth of eight graders admitted to having been drunk at least once, and 44 percent reported that they smoked cigarettes.[18] Compare those numbers to the current ones in the chart on page 146.

Race

Although drug abuse occurs among all races in the United States, it is more prevalent in some races than others. As you can seen in the graph on the opposite page, Asians currently show the lowest rate of drug use among persons 12 and older (3.6 percent); Native Americans and Alaska Natives have the highest percentage of drug use in the United States (13.7 percent).[19]

Socioeconomic Status

How does drug use effect socioeconomic status? Certainly, there are many studies that show the connection between illegal drug use and dropping out of school, lower educational attainment, unemployment, and low rates of advancement in one's career. However, in terms of earnings, research suggests that lower incomes for drug users takes time to manifest itself. In other words, the effect of drug use has little impact on the individual when he or she is younger, but increases over time. This is in part due to the fact that early in their work lives, drug users tend to take jobs with little potential for growth. Over time, that choice keeps them from advancing, unlike their non-user peers.[20]

PRESCRIPTION DRUG USE

As government and private organizations work to thwart current forms of drug use, Americans are finding new ways to get high. The most current trend in drug abuse is the misuse of prescription drugs. According to the Centers for Disease Control and Prevention, more than 1.8 billion prescription drugs were ordered or provided in 2006, the most frequent prescribed drug being analgesics, or painkillers. Although these drugs are created and prescribed with the intention of healing or providing relief, they are sometimes abused rather than used appropriately.

The three types of prescription drugs that are most commonly abused are opiates (medically prescribed to treat pain), central nervous system depressants (prescribed to treat anxiety and sleep disorders), and stimulants (prescribed to treat disorders such as narcolepsy and attention deficit disorder). Although the use of these types of drugs can help an individual, abuse of these drugs can be extremely harmful to a user's body.

Amphetamines, such as Adderall or Ritalin, are some of the most widely abused prescription drugs, especially among teens. Ritalin, a drug prescribed to individuals with attention deficit disorder, has been used without a prescription by as many as 1 in 10 teenagers.[21] As you may already know, some of the most frequent abuse of amphetamines occurs on college campuses. Whereas some students might drink a can of Red Bull to stay alert for a long night of studying, others might turn to amphetamines. One student even admitted to me that he took Adderall to stay awake when he needed to pull all-nighters.

Why Do We Use Drugs?

Our bodies have natural defenses against infection and disease; when we're in pain, our brains produce chemicals that dull the ache and make us feel happy. So, why do we need drugs? Some suggest that this is the wrong question. People have always used drugs and will likely continue to use them. Most of society's legal efforts to control drug use fail; the issue becomes how to control use while avoiding the harmful aspects of drug abuse.[22] The causes of drug abuse are difficult to determine and often involve claims that abusers cannot delay gratification and have low self-control.[23] However, many people do not agree that addiction is a sign of moral or psychological weakness. Treating addiction as a medical condition—as opposed to a moral failure—arose in the 20th century and resulted in a number of treatment programs and models. In general, these models hold two common beliefs: (1) Individuals have biological predispositions to addiction, and (2) these predispositions can be overcome through treatment.[24]

SOCIALIZATION

Sociological theory and medical research are aware that determining why people use drugs is a complex issue. Researcher Denise Kandel suggests that there is an interaction between how a person is socialized and with whom they interact. Recall that we are socialized by a variety of individuals. Parents provide long-term values, and their use of drugs has the potential to influence their children. However, one's peers provide even more powerful socialization. Teens who get involved

Percent of Persons in the United States (12 Years and Older) Who Have Used an Illicit Drug* in the Past Month

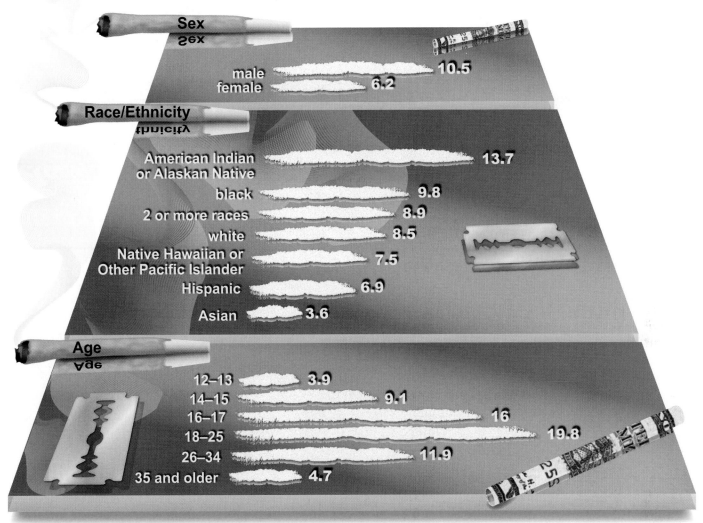

Sex

male	10.5
female	6.2

Race/Ethnicity

American Indian or Alaskan Native	13.7
black	9.8
2 or more races	8.9
white	8.5
Native Hawaiian or Other Pacific Islander	7.5
Hispanic	6.9
Asian	3.6

Age

12–13	3.9
14–15	9.1
16–17	16
18–25	19.8
26–34	11.9
35 and older	4.7

* illicit drugs include marijuana/hashish, cocaine (including crack), heroin, hallucinogens (including LSD and PCP), inhalants, or any prescription-type psychotherapeutic drug used non-medically.

Source: U.S. Department of Health and Human Services. "Use of selected substances in the past month among persons 12 years of age and over, by age, sex, race, and Hispanic origin: United States, 2002, 2005, and 2006" *Health, United States, 2008: With Special Feature on the Health of Young Adults*," 315, http://www.cdc.gov/nchs/data/hus/hus08.pdf#066\

in drugs and/or alcohol generally have peers who are users. The selection of one's peer group provides the foundation for the likelihood of use by adolescents. This happens in part because they bond to users and learn to share their values and behaviors. Of course, we choose our friends not merely based on who we live near, but also by who interests us. In this way, people who get into drug-using groups in a sense choose their path, although, at the same time, they are being steered toward this path by their group. This is a dynamic process that usually starts with minor alcohol use, such as beer or wine, moves to cigarettes and hard alcohol, then to marijuana, and possibly to harder drugs. To put it simply, people can drift into drugs through a process of being socialized into their use.[25]

Another part of drug socialization stems from the fact that the United States is increasingly becoming a medicalized society. Medicalization is the process by which we expand the use of medical terms and solutions to non-medical problems. Medical personnel often claim that certain social components are diseases in need of treatment. Such an attitude expands the power of the medical community, but also increases the public's desire for medical solutions.[26] This leads us to seek a pill to solve our problems. In 2006 alone, more than 1.8 billion prescription drugs were ordered or provided.[27] Does that necessarily make things better? It's clear that what it *does* do is help socialize us into a mind-set whereby drug use is common.

At what point do we change from a culture of drug users to a culture of drug abusers? When so many people seem motivated to abuse substances and modify their behavior with drugs, it's easy to see how this problem can spread to the greater society. A student of mine who had an alcoholic husband put it this way: "Living with an addict is like living with an elephant in your house. It stinks up the place, makes lots of messes, and it's too big to simply act like it's not there because doing that will destroy your family, your children, and your sense of reality." The social problems of substance abuse are not just individual issues.

Substance Use Among High School Seniors*

		1980	1990	2000	2007
Cigarettes	All high school seniors	30.5%	29.4%	31.4%	21.6%
	Male	26.8%	29.1%	32.8%	23.1%
	Female	33.4%	29.2%	29.7%	19.6%
	White	31.0%	32.5%	36.6%	25.2%
	Black	25.2%	12.0%	13.6%	10.6%
Marijuana	All high school seniors	33.7%	14.0%	21.6%	18.8%
	Male	37.8%	16.1%	24.7%	22.3%
	Female	29.1%	11.5%	18.3%	15.0%
	White	34.2%	15.6%	22.0%	19.9%
	Black	26.5%	5.2%	17.5%	15.4%
Cocaine	All high school seniors	5.2%	1.9%	2.1%	2.0%
	Male	6.0%	2.3%	2.7%	2.4%
	Female	4.3%	1.3%	1.6%	1.5%
	White	5.4%	1.8%	2.2%	2.3%
	Black	2.0%	0.5%	1.0%	0.5%
Inhalants	All high school seniors	1.4%	2.7%	2.2%	1.2%
	Male	1.8%	3.5%	2.9%	1.5%
	Female	1.0%	2.0%	1.7%	0.9%
	White	1.4%	3.0%	2.1%	1.2%
	Black	1.0%	1.5%	2.1%	0.9%
Alcohol	All high school seniors	72.0%	57.1%	50.0%	44.4%
	Male	77.4%	61.3%	54.0%	47.1%
	Female	66.8%	52.3%	46.1%	41.4%
	White	75.8%	62.2%	55.3%	49.4%
	Black	47.7%	32.9%	29.3%	27.9%
Binge drinking**	All high school seniors	41.2%	32.2%	30.0%	25.9%
	Male	52.1%	39.1%	36.7%	30.7%
	Female	30.5%	24.4%	23.5%	21.5%
	White	44.6%	36.2%	34.4%	30.5%
	Black	17.0%	11.6%	11.0%	11.0%

**5 or more alcoholic drinks in a row

*(percent of population that used selected substances in the 2 weeks prior to the survey)

Source: By the author, data from the National Center for Chronic Disease Prevention and Health Promotion's *Youth Risk Behavior Survey*, 1991–2007.

The Mexican Drug War

The real Mexican–American War ended in 1848, but lately a new, covert war has begun. Like any other war, this conflict has resulted in casualties: 6,300 bodies in 2008 alone.[28] This time, however, the Mexican and U.S. governments are working together, battling the rampant drug trafficking that goes on at the border.

It's not just drugs that officials are worried about. According to the Federal Bureau of Alcohol, Tobacco, Firearms and Explosives, roughly 90 percent of guns seized in raids of Mexican dealers are traced back to the United States. Drug traffickers cross the border on three-day shopping visas, purchase large quantities of assault weapons and ammunition from local merchants, then return home. It's estimated that nearly 2,000 firearms cross the border into Mexico daily.[29]

Americans aren't just providing drug cartels with guns; they're also providing them with money. The majority of drugs cultivated in Mexico are sold to Americans, and Mexican drug dealers generate profits of $15 billion to $25 billion a year solely from the United States.[30]

Mexico's drug war isn't only an issue south of the border. The U.S. Justice Department has stated that Mexican drug trafficking organizations represent the greatest organized crime threat to the United States. President Obama has been working with Mexican President Felipe Calderon to build a more aggressive offense against drug lords. "We are absolutely committed to working in partnership with Mexico to make sure that we are dealing with this scourge on both sides of the border," Obama said after meeting with Calderon. "You can't fight this war with just one hand. You can't have Mexico making an effort and the United States not making an effort."[31]

So far, the President has sent Congress a war-spending request for $350 million to increase security along the United States–Mexico border.[32] More efforts from the U.S. government are expected to be initiated as violence from the Mexican drug war continues to spread.

>>> According to local authorities, **United States retailers provide more than 3 million rounds of ammunition per year to dealers in Mexico.**[33] Because of this, drug raids are often deadly.

think social problems: HOW DO SOCIOLOGISTS VIEW DRUG AND ALCOHOL USE?

So far in this chapter, you've learned about the harmful effects of drug and alcohol abuse. Although some facts and figures may have been enlightening, the idea that "drugs are bad" is probably not a new concept to you. Most of us have seen the ads advising "don't do drugs" and both our teachers and parents have warned us against the dangers of illegal substances. But how do sociologists view alcohol and drug use? Let's consider some theoretical points of view.

DON'T LET DRUG DEALERS CHANGE THE FACE OF YOUR NEIGHBOURHOOD.
Call Crimestoppers anonymously on 0800 555 111.

Symbolic Interactionism

As we established earlier, most of us have used a drug at some point in our lives, whether it was tobacco, alcohol, caffeine, marijuana, or some type of prescription medicine. Nevertheless, we tend to view the act of popping some Advil differently than popping some speed, even though they're both drugs. It could be because a normal dose of Advil would translate to a potentially lethal dose of amphetamines; however, symbolic interactionists argue that it's not the effects of a drug, but how we perceive the drug that affects our opinions.

<<< **Many campaigns such as drugfree.org's "Faces of Meth" use shock value to get their message across to young teens.** From what you've learned about media influences, do you think these methods are appropriate?

Generally speaking, the social acceptability of a drug is linked to how society defines it. For example, if you consider both alcohol and marijuana, you'll see that both are harmful to the person, both create changes in mood, and both can result in dangerous driving and other criminal behaviors. But one is legal and the other is not. Why? In society the social perception of a drug is linked to who uses it. When CEOs have a three-martini lunch, it's considered a normal part of "doing business." But when a construction worker smokes a joint after work with his friends, it's viewed as a dangerous activity. We see the alcoholic differently than we see the "pothead," usually because they come from different social classes.[34]

Functionalism

Drugs have both manifest and latent functions in society. For example, morphine helps alleviate pain, but it can also be addictive. A few years ago, I worked with cancer patients and noticed that many were afraid of

WRAP YOUR MIND AROUND THE THEORY

"Soft" drugs such as cannabis are legal and socially acceptable in the Netherlands. "Coffeeshops," like the one pictured here, offer a wide selection of hash and marijuana, and allow their customers to smoke inside with friends or take their product home to enjoy.[42] Should these establishments be allowed in the United States?

FUNCTIONALISM

Functionalists are interested in how the intended use of a drug differs from its actual use. People use drugs for different purposes—80 mg of OxyContin can ease a sore back or cause a euphoric high. According to sociologist Robert Merton, drug abuse is an adaptation to societal impediments. If a person no longer believes that success is available to him, he will fall into retreatism and eschew the goals and norms of society.

CONFLICT THEORY

Conflict theory focuses on racial and economic divisions among drug abusers. According to conflict theorists, race and income can affect a person's susceptibility to drug use and likelihood of arrest. Studies have shown that black neighborhoods are more closely patrolled than white neighborhoods, and raided more often despite that fact that drug use among blacks and whites is nearly equal.[44]

WHY DO PEOPLE ABUSE DRUGS AND ALCOHOL?

SYMBOLIC INTERACTIONISM

Symbolic interactionists are interested in the micro interactions of daily life and how they influence our view of the world. In the United States, we consider some drugs to be legal and "OK," whereas others are defined as illegal and "bad" (at least by those in authority). But we know that the legality of a drug does not necessarily have anything to do with its effect. For example, two of the most dangerous drugs available in the United States are alcohol and tobacco, but these are legal. Why? Because these substances are deemed acceptable by society.[41]

As of 2008, 13 states allow the use of marijuana for medical purposes.[43] **Does an unhappy teen have the same right to the drug as a patient with bone cancer?**

Low-income, urban areas are often patrolled more than affluent, suburban ones. **Do you think law enforcement officers are protecting citizens in poorer communities or doing them a social disservice?**

overusing their pain medicines. Of course, the obvious manifest function of such a drug is to relieve pain. And yet, some people who experience chronic pain do become addicted. Such prescription drug addictions illuminate the latent consequences of narcotic use in our society.

Functionalists believe that most drugs have both positive and negative potential and therefore must be controlled. The job of social structures such as family, courts, or churches is to support the proper use, but not the abuse, of such drugs. Efforts to educate the public against illegal drug use are efforts to control use; however, as the opening article of this chapter points out, often they have the opposite effects. One such program is the famous DARE campaign, which was designed to have police officers enter public schools to teach school children how to avoid drugs. Subsequent research on the program showed that DARE had no effect.[35] Clearly, the intended function of the program was not met.

Sociologist Robert Merton suggests that drug use is the result of an individual reaction to social forces. In his theory of anomie, he suggests that some individuals are blocked from attaining certain societal goals, and thus fail to achieve them. In a sense, the cultural norm of a successful life is not available to them. One way such a person may choose to adapt is through **retreatism**. This is the response of a person who has essentially given up trying to achieve the goals of society because he or she believes the means to those goals have no merit. Such individuals may retreat into addictive patterns of drug and alcohol use.[36]

Conflict Theory

In a perfect social system, all humans would be treated equally. Similarly, in a perfect legal system, all criminals would be a treated

RETREATISM is the response of a person who has given up on trying to achieve the goals of society because he or she believes that the means to those goals have no merit.

ALCOHOLICS ANONYMOUS is one of the oldest and most well-known substance treatment programs in the United States.

equally; Cocaine User A and Cocaine User B would be given the same sentence. In reality, if Cocaine User A is a minority living in an impoverished neighborhood, and Cocaine User B is white living in the suburbs, the equality is often not there. Underprivileged minorities, especially blacks, are far more likely to be arrested for drug use and given harsher sentences than middle-class whites.[37] Despite the fact that blacks and whites engage in possession and sale of drugs at similar rates, blacks are arrested on drug charges at 2.8 to 5.5 times the rate of whites. This trend is likely due to the more frequent police patrols in different neighborhoods.[38]

Inequality does not stop at booking and sentencing. Because many of these arrests involve the possession of crack cocaine—a drug that has been the focus of the "war on drugs" for the past decade—sentencing tends to be harsher than on individuals who are found with powdered cocaine. In fact, a convicted individual with 1 mg of crack will receive a similar sentence as someone caught carrying 100 mg of powdered cocaine. Criminologists such as Jeffrey Reiman suggest that race and ethnicity have something to do with this discrepancy, as large amounts of minority drug abusers use crack (90.2 percent of African American and Hispanic abusers, compared to 8.8 percent of white abusers[39]), whereas white addicts tend to prefer snorting powdered cocaine.[40]

discover solutions to social problems: WHAT CAN WE DO ABOUT DRUG AND ALCOHOL ABUSE?

Treatment or Punishment?

Drug abuse is a legal issue and a social issue, and society is faced with a fundamental question: What should we do about it? Some promote jail time; others suggest that users need to be rehabilitated for the greater good. In the end, which should be the main priority: treatment or punishment?

Treating addictions can be a difficult task; it takes both knowledge and skill of trained professionals as well as honesty and willingness from abusers. **Alcoholics Anonymous**, commonly referred to as AA, is one of the oldest and most well-known substance treatment programs in the United States. The organization was formed in the 1930s by Bill W. (last names are never used in the program for the purpose of maintaining members' anonymity). The organization is known for its Twelve-Step Program, which outlines the steps a person must take to fully understand his or her addiction and move on to a life of sobriety. It uses community support, self-reflection, and prayer (or meditation) to combat the powerful pull of alcohol.

Narcotics Anonymous follows a similar design; however, these two programs are not the only forms of treatment available. Effective methods have a variety of components that include the notion that no single type of treatment works for everyone. The most successful ones include individual plans that are designed to meet the needs of a person using a variety of methods. Counseling and behavioral modification are vitally important components to effective treatment, as is medically supervised detoxification. This can occur on an inpatient or outpatient basis.[45]

However, in the United States, the largest category of criminal behavior for which people are incarcerated is related to drugs. The incarceration boom of the 1980s and 1990s was largely fueled by the war on drugs and the increased penalties for drug offenders.[46] Prisons have seen the benefits of providing inmates with drug and alcohol treatment, and today it is quite

Substances that Result in Admission to Rehabilitation Facilities

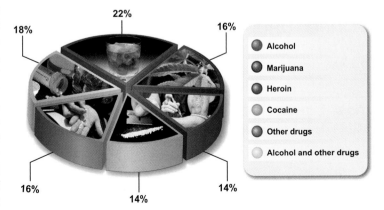

22%
18%
16%
16%
14%
14%

● Alcohol
● Marijuana
● Heroin
● Cocaine
● Other drugs
● Alcohol and other drugs

Source: "Admissions to Publicly Funded Substance Abuse Treatment Programs" National Institute of Drug Abuse, 2006

Social Benefits of Treatment Programs

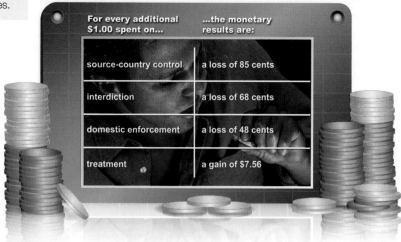

For every additional $1.00 spent on...	...the monetary results are:
source-country control	a loss of 85 cents
interdiction	a loss of 68 cents
domestic enforcement	a loss of 48 cents
treatment	a gain of $7.56

Source: "Treatment vs. Incarceration" Drug Policy Alliance, http://www.drugpolicy.org/library/factsheets/treatment_v_incarceration_nm.cfm#5

common. Such treatment can be effective even if it isn't voluntary. Treated inmates have lower rates of future drug abuse, as well as decreased risks of further criminal activity and future arrests.[47]

So, which solution is more cost-effective? Treatment in the community and/or in prison is effective, but can treatment prevent incarceration? The Center for Substance Abuse recorded an average savings of three to one; every $1 spent on treatment saved society $3. The savings were a result of reduced crime, increased earnings from productive individuals, and lower health care costs that would otherwise be absorbed by society.[48]

SOCIAL AND FINANCIAL BENEFITS

Even though drug treatment programs are not successful 100 percent of the time, many individuals experience successes. The National Treatment Improvement Evaluation Study found that individuals served by federally funded treatment programs were able to reduce their drug use by nearly 50 percent within a year after completing treatment. Treated individuals' use of their primary drug (the one that put them in treatment) declined from 73 percent to 38 percent in the same time period.[49] Additionally, the study showed that addicts' quality of life improved by 53 percent, whereas their alcohol- and drug-related medical visits declined.

Substance abuse treatment programs also help improve the quality of life for everyone in society. The same survey found that drug sales decreased by 78 percent in areas that provided adequate drug treatment programs. Assaults also decreased by 78 percent, and shoplifting declined by nearly 82 percent. Researchers theorized that these trends were associated with the 48 percent decline in individuals who largely supported themselves through illegal activity.[50]

Drug treatment programs not only make neighborhoods safer, but they save the residents money as well. A study by the RAND Corporation found that for every dollar invested into a treatment program, taxpayers save $7.56 in criminal prevention costs. Taxpayers in Arizona found this to be true after a 1996 vote that required nonviolent drug offenders to be sentenced to probation and treatment rather than jail. After the first year, the Arizona Supreme Court reported that taxpayers had saved $2.6 million dollars. What's more, 77.5 percent of drug offenders tested negative for drugs one year after they completed treatment.[51]

THE WAR ON DRUGS AND ASSET FORFEITURE

"Drug dealer" is an occupation of sorts, and we do not want it to be a financially successful one. In reality, most drug dealers are small-time and not wealthy at all; in fact, many still live at home.[52] In 1984, the U.S. government instituted a policy in an effort to make sure that people didn't profit from the drug trade. Its goal was to take profits made from illegal drugs out of the hands of those involved in the trade. It was believed that this would cause the number of drug traffickers to decrease, which would lower the availability of drugs in society. This policy is known as **asset forfeiture**, which allows the government to seize any item that is believed to have been purchased with proceeds from illegal activities. Items can include cars, houses, electronics, and even businesses. Additionally, if authorities suspect that any assets are being used in illegal activity, these assets can be seized immediately.[53]

However, like many policies designed to deal with social problems, asset forfeiture is controversial. Why? Because the burden of proof rests on the accused. The individual suspected of possessing property purchased with illicit funds must provide evidence that it was not associated with illegal activity. For example, if the police suspected that your Camry had been purchased with money you made selling pot around campus, they could seize your car based solely on that suspicion. *You* would need to provide the financial records to show that the car was purchased legally. This practice deviates from the civil rights standard of "innocent until proven guilty." In reality, you can have your property seized and experience no criminal charges at all. Police are not required to arrest—or even charge—individuals whose assets are seized. In fact, a 10-month national study found that over three quarters of the people who were required to forfeit property were never charged with a crime.[55]

>>> Up until their eventual death or arrest, powerful drug lords often lead affluent lifestyles, owning large estates, marrying multiple wives, and sometimes even controlling fleets of aircraft to move drugs around the continent. **In 2009, the famous kingpin Joaquin "El Chapo" Guzman was included on Forbes' list of richest people in the world, with a net worth of $1 billion.**[54]

Drug Use and Crime

As we'll see in Chapters 13 and 14, crime and drug use are closely related trends. According to the White House Office of National Drug Control Policy, 62.4 percent of inmates used drugs regularly before incarceration, and 35.6 percent were using drugs at the time of the offense.[56] Drugs cloud a person's judgment, which can lead individuals to engage in illegal behaviors. Many theories about why individuals commit crimes can be applied to why people use drugs. We will also detail more fully how deviant and criminal behavior get passed on through our associations with peers. Finally, many crimes such as negligence, assault, and driving under the influence are crimes that occur because drugs lower inhibitions. When we're drunk, do we do things we'll regret later? At times, yes, and some of those things lead to crime.

In the previous chapter, we discussed the "medicalization" of America; as we've seen, that applies to the use of drugs as well. In our society, we have a pill for everything, from curing headaches to experiencing wild hallucinations. It seems to be a cultural habit to look for help in a bottle, whether it's a bottle of Jack Daniels or a bottle of Viagra.

Pro & Con

Should Marijuana Be Legalized?

The debate over the legalization of marijuana in the United States has been raging for over a century. Both sides have passionate points of view. Where do you stand?

Pro

- Recreational marijuana use may decrease, as it will no longer be a form of rebellion.
- Like tobacco, the government could tax the sale of cannabis and use this income to lower the national debt.
- In moderation, the health risks of marijuana and hash are no greater than other legal drugs such as cigarettes or alcohol.
- Many "potheads" are functional adults who have good jobs and engage in no other illegal behavior.[57]
- Legalization would reduce profits for organized crime.
- Evidence shows that marijuana is not the first drug used by hard drug users. In fact, the natural progression of drug use starts with legal drugs, such as alcohol and tobacco.[58] The quality and safety of marijuana could be regulated by the FDA, decreasing the health risks associated with low-grade street cannabis (often cut with henna, turpentine, or crushed animal feces to save the dealer money).

Con

- By legalizing marijuana, its use may increase and become mainstream.
- Dangerous social habits, such as driving while under the influence of marijuana, could appear.
- Cannabis users may develop increased health problems such as high blood pressure, hormonal changes, and even schizophrenia.[59]
- Legalization would raise the chances of marijuana falling into the hands of children.
- Some feel that using marijuana is not just legally but morally wrong.
- As a "gateway drug," marijuana may lead to the use of harsher drugs. Twin studies show the appearance of such a connection. Even though data haven't yet been conclusive, the potential pleasure is not worth the risk.[60]

From Classroom to Community | Working on a Drug Prevention Council

Cassandra didn't do drugs or drink alcohol, but she did know a lot of kids in her junior high school who did. Concerned about the path many of her friends were taking, Cassandra decided to join a drug prevention council that met monthly at a local community center. The council was mostly comprised of adults, but Cassandra and a few other young teens served as junior members. At Cassandra's first meeting, the president of the group announced that the council had been awarded a $3,000 grant to form a drug prevention program for the neighborhood.

One woman thought that they should produce an ad campaign showing the mug shots of celebrities who were arrested on drug or alcohol charges and include the line, "Even the brightest stars burn out on drugs."

Most of the people at the meeting thought this was a great idea, but Cassandra wasn't so sure. She thought that showing pictures of celebrities, in any context, might make young people think that drugs were cool.

Another person thought that the council should use the funds to perform unannounced drug tests on random selections of students at the two local high schools.

This time Cassandra wasn't the only one to reject the idea. Many people felt that this measure was too extreme and would make teenagers feel that their privacy was being invaded, engendering a greater desire for rebellion.

After a bit of thinking, Cassandra suggested that they use the funds to start a program that wouldn't just tell teenagers about the evils of drugs, but show them alternative ways to have fun. She suggested that they start a Web site called "MyHigh.com." The site would be a place for teenagers to post videos, blogs, and pictures of fun, drug-free ways they got "high." It could be clips of homemade music videos, blogs of daily poetry, or pictures of personal art. Money could be used to create the Web site and support classes or equipment that would help students create postings.

The group loved the idea. They were happy to have a young person's perspective, and many congratulated her after the meeting. The president of the council even came over to shake Cassandra's hand and tell her that he hoped she would come back next month as a full, voting member.

IS SUBSTANCE ABUSE A SOCIAL PROBLEM?   142

undeniably yes; substance abuse impacts everyone in society, not just those directly affected by it; the medicalization of America has caused us to seek a pill for every problem

HOW DO SOCIOLOGISTS VIEW DRUG AND ALCOHOL USE?   147

the difference between popping aspirin and popping codeine is smaller than you'd think; some uses of drugs are socially acceptable, although the "acceptability" of substances change over time

WHAT CAN WE DO ABOUT DRUG AND ALCOHOL ABUSE?   149

substance abuse treatment is more effective than incarceration; treatment saves the state and taxpayers money and increases addicts' quality of life

get the topic: IS SUBSTANCE ABUSE A SOCIAL PROBLEM?

Theory

SYMBOLIC INTERACTIONISM   147

- it's not the effects of a drug, but how we perceive the drug that determines our opinions
- the social acceptability of a drug is linked to how society defines it

FUNCTIONALISM   147

- functionalists are interested in how the intended use of a drug differs from its actual use
- drugs have both manifest and latent functions in society
- most drugs have both positive and negative potential and therefore must be controlled

CONFLICT THEORY   149

- there are racial and ethnic inequalities in the war on drugs
- minorities are more likely to be arrested and given harsher sentences
- this is due in part to increased amounts of police patrol in poor neighborhoods and harsher drug laws placed on substances that minorities users tend to abuse

Key Terms

drugs are substances that have psychological or physical effects.   *142*

narcotics are drugs that are considered illegal today.   *142*

drug use is the act of internally processing chemical substances other than food that have physical effects.   *142*

drug abuse is the use of drugs despite adverse consequences.   *143*

addiction is a chronic condition that can include both a psychological and/or

physiological compulsion toward drug seeking and use.   *143*

stimulants are a type of drug that excites the body and stimulates the brain and central nervous system.   *143*

depressants are a type of drug that slows the activity of vital organs in the body to create a relaxed, sleepy feeling.   *144*

hallucinogens are a type of drug that distorts the senses and causes hallucinations.   *144*

retreatism is the response of a person who has given up on trying to achieve the goals of society because he or she believes that the means to those goals have no merit.   *149*

Alcoholics Anonymous is one of the oldest and most well-known substance treatment programs in the United States.   *149*

asset forfeiture allows the government to seize any item that is believed to have been purchased with proceeds from illegal activities.   *150*

Sample Test Questions

These multiple-choice questions are similar to those found in the test bank that accompanies this textbook.

1. Which drug was one of the first to be abused?

   a. caffeine
   b. Adderall
   c. opium
   d. Bayer

2. What do stimulants do to the body?

   a. fool the senses
   b. excite the brain and central nervous system
   c. slow down body functions
   d. multiply existing brain cells

3. In what way(s) is the United States responsible for the Mexican Drug War?

   a. American citizens buy the drugs from traffickers.
   b. U.S. gun manufacturers supply traffickers with assault rifles.
   c. Border merchants supply ammunition to traffickers.
   d. All of the above

4. What type of drug use is on the rise among teens and young adults?

   a. spiked street drugs
   b. over-the-counter medication
   c. prescription medication
   d. nicotine

5. In asset forfeiture, on whom does the burden of proof fall?

   a. the owner of the seized property
   b. the state
   c. the law enforcement agency
   d. the owner of the drugs

ESSAY

1. Do you think anti-drug campaigns discourage or encourage drug use? Why?
2. In what way is the opium trade from the 1700s similar to the drug trade today?
3. Do you think Americans are overmedicated? Are advancements in pharmacology helpful or harmful to society?
4. What are your thoughts on asset forfeiture? Is this policy unconstitutional?
5. Do you think drug abusers should be imprisoned, or do you think they should be placed in treatment programs? Are both "punishments" for drug crimes?

WHERE TO START YOUR RESEARCH PAPER

For U.S. Census facts and information, go to http://www.census.gov

For more information about teen drug use, visit
http://www.drugfree.org/

For facts and statistics on marijuana use, see
http://www.nida.nih.gov/infofacts/marijuana.html
http://www.marijuana-info.org/

For information about the National Institute on Drug Abuse, go to
http://www.drugabuse.gov/infofacts/treatmenttrends.html

For statistics on illegal drug use, go to
http://www.cdc.gov/nchs/FASTATS/druguse.htm

For information on how alcohol use affects public health, visit
http://www.cdc.gov/alcohol/index.htm

ANSWERS: 1. c; 2. b; 3. d; 4. c; 5. a

Remember to check www.thethinkspot.com for additional information, downloadable flashcards, and other helpful resources.

SEX AND SEXUALITY

HOW DO AMERICANS VIEW ISSUES OF
SEX AND SEXUALITY?
HOW DO THE DIFFERENT SOCIOLOGICAL
PARADIGMS VIEW SEXUALITY?
HOW DOES SOCIETY DEAL WITH SEXUAL
DIFFERENCES?

Thomas

Beatie, the transgender man who bore a daughter in June 2008, has become the public face of an issue for many other transgender people: having their roles as parents legally recognized . . .

After the birth of their baby girl, Susan, in June, Thomas Beatie, 34, and his wife, Nancy, 46, of Bend, Ore., found themselves in a legal thicket that serves as a cautionary tale for other transgender families.

Thomas Beatie is legally male. But as the parent who gave birth, he was listed by the state of Oregon on the birth certificate as the "mother." His spouse was then listed as their baby's "father."

Later, those designations were scrapped by the state for the gender-neutral term "parent," which is commonly used on the birth certificates of children of same-sex couples. For the Beaties, this was still upsetting.

"In essence, they are invalidating our marriage," Thomas Beatie said. "It is very upsetting to me. I feel that it's a flawed document." . . .

"It just goes to prove that mother and father are social terms," he said. "You don't have to be biologically related to your child to be a mother or a father."

Suzanne Goldberg, who directs the Sexuality and Gender Law Clinic at Columbia University in New York City, sympathizes with the Beaties' frustrations but says they should not be overly concerned about how they are listed on the birth certificate.

"It's hard to imagine a birth certificate being used as a basis to challenge a marriage," Goldberg said.

"What matters is that the adults involved are designated as 'parent.' It doesn't matter legally whether one adult is called 'mother' or 'father.' Those are social categories. They don't have legal meaning in this context." . . .

As the biological parent, Thomas Beatie has legally secure rights. His wife, on the other hand, is not biologically related to their baby but is granted parental rights by virtue of her marriage to Thomas Beatie.

So if the validity of their marriage were challenged, experts say, Nancy Beatie's parental rights could be in jeopardy . . .

In order to secure Nancy Beatie's parental rights, lawyers advise the Beaties to do what many same-sex couples with children do—have Nancy Beatie, as the nonbiological parent, adopt their baby.

"When there is a slight question whether the marriage will be upheld by a court if it's challenged, the nonbiological parent will take the step of adopting the child, not because it's always necessary but just to make absolutely sure that the parent-child relationship is legally protected," Columbia's Goldberg said . . .

The Beaties agree that adoption would protect them, but they don't want to do that as a matter of principle. They see themselves as a legally married heterosexual couple. They note that they file taxes jointly as husband and wife.

"We shouldn't have to adopt our own daughter," Thomas Beatie said.

The Beaties are seeking legal representation to pursue a change in the birth certificate.

"I feel that it's a flawed document," he said. "We'd like to see this process remedied for the next child, for the next pregnant man."[1]

155

CHAPTER 11

---The idea of a man giving birth to a baby was fodder for Hollywood's *Junior*, but America's lukewarm reception to this comedy was only a precursor to the negative public reaction following the announcement of the first pregnant transgender man.

Through the innovations in science and medicine, the terms "mother" and "father" have been brought under the microscope within the state and federal court systems and around the nation in classrooms and living rooms.

Families, school systems, legal systems, and religious organizations are grappling with uncharted territories regarding sexuality and reproduction. When you have so many different voices struggling to define what is "normal," it's not hard to see that sex and sexuality have become a huge social problem for our society. Is it our modern sexuality that's the problem, or is society's reaction the only issue? Who decides what's right, what's wrong, and what should be kept private? As stories like Thomas Beatie's become more mainstream, we must examine the changing ways in which we deal with sexual differences on an individual and national scale.

get the topic: HOW DO AMERICANS VIEW ISSUES OF SEX AND SEXUALITY?

Sex and Gender

Even in this day and age, discrimination toward those with different sexual orientations remains a key issue. In order to speak intelligently about the variety of ideas surrounding sex and sexuality, we need to define the related terms clearly.

Sex refers strictly to the biological makeup of a male or female. In other words, the term refers to whether you have male or female reproductive organs. Sex also refers to activities that lead to sexual gratification and the possibility of reproduction. The appropriateness of sexual interaction differs by culture and includes prescriptions about the proper age, race, and status of possible partners.

As I'm sure you've realized by watching TV, listening to the radio, and surfing the Internet, sex is a powerful device in the United States. Attitudes toward sex and sexual orientation have changed a great deal over time. For example, the median age of acts of first pre-marital sex in the U.S. decreased from 20.4 years to 17.6 years between 1954 and 2003. Only 4 percent of 15-year olds reported having pre-marital sex from 1954–1963; that number jumped to 14 percent between 1994 and 2003.

At virtually every age cohort over this 50-year period, Americans' involvement in pre-marital sex increased, while the age of sexual activity steadily decreased. However, in 2004 the rate of teen age sex began to dip somewhat, suggesting that more teens are waiting, and thereby avoiding some of the common social problems associated with sex, such as sexually transmitted diseases, unwanted pregnancies, and/or increased responsibilities. During the same time period, contraceptive use increased slightly, the most common of which being the oral contraceptive pill. Nearly all modern women of reproductive age have used contraception at some point in their lives; in fact, 98 percent of women who have had intercourse have been found to use at least one method, and more than 80 percent of women have used "the pill."[2]

Gender, as we learned previously, is the personal traits and position in society connected with being a male or female. For instance, in the United States, wearing skirts or dresses is associated with female gender. The biological differences between men and women tend to correlate with some behavioral differences. For example, boys are more likely to roughhouse, and girls tend toward domestic play. However, sociologists suggest that socialization, rather than biology, usually influences what we see as appropriate behaviors for different genders.

GENDER IDENTITY

As you can see, sex and gender are not interchangeable terms. As we discussed in Chapter 4, gender identity is the psychological sense of one's self as male or female. **Transgender** refers to people whose gender identity or gender expression differs from that associated with their birth sex. Of course, gender identity may or may not have anything to do with how a person dresses, or presents him- or herself. Furthermore, a person's sexual attraction to others may not always be clear. There are heterosexual men who find cross-dressing to be appealing, but at the same time have no desire to permanently be a woman. Some suggest that anyone whose identity, appearance, or behavior falls outside conventional gender norms can be described as transgender. On the other hand, not everyone whose appearance or behavior is gender-atypical will consider himself or herself transgender.[3]

<<< **Men who dress up as women,** such as the famous drag queen RuPaul, **provide a difficult case in categorization.** RuPaul, for example, is comfortable being referred to as either gender.

Sexual Orientation

Related to, but different from sex, gender, and gender identity, is sexual orientation. According to the American Psychological Association, **sexual orientation** refers to "an enduring pattern of emotional, romantic, and/or sexual attractions to men, women, or both sexes."[4] People express their sexual orientation through behaviors with others, including such actions as holding hands or kissing.[5] Drawing toward others who have the same need for love, acceptance, and intimacy is part of sexual orientation, and, in addition to romantic attraction, people of the same sexual orientation often share similar goals, values, and mutual support. In this way, you can see that sexual orientation goes beyond an individual characteristic; rather, it defines those with whom you find the comfort and romantic satisfaction that are essential to your personal identity.[6]

Generally speaking, sexual orientation is divided into three key categories: heterosexual, homosexual, and bisexual. **Heterosexual** orientation refers to those who have emotional, romantic, or sexual attractions to members of the opposite sex. **Homosexual** (gay or lesbian) orientation refers to those who have emotional, romantic, or sexual attractions to members of their own sex. **Bisexual** orientation includes those who have emotional, romantic, or sexual attractions to both men and women.

All of these sexual orientations are witnessed in societies and cultures worldwide, with various levels of acceptance.[7] Although there is no definitive evidence of how a person's sexual orientation is determined, researchers believe that many factors may contribute to it, including genetic, hormonal, developmental, social, and cultural influences.[8]

RACE AND SEXUAL IDENTITY

Researchers have attempted to find out whether race plays a role in sexual identity. Patricia Hill Collins suggests that the intersection of race, gender, and sexuality negatively affects blacks in the United States. The

TRANSGENDER refers to people whose gender identity or gender expression differs from that associated with their birth sex.

SEXUAL ORIENTATION refers to an enduring pattern of emotional, romantic, and/or sexual attractions to men, women, or both sexes.

HETEROSEXUAL orientation refers to those who have emotional, romantic, or sexual attractions to members of the opposite sex.

HOMOSEXUAL orientation refers to those who have emotional, romantic, or sexual attractions to members of their own sex.

BISEXUAL orientation includes those who have emotional, romantic, or sexual attractions to both men and women.

stereotypes of black sexuality presented in music videos, songs, and films generally support racism and homophobia, resulting in negative outcomes not just for black homosexuals but for all. For example, some men live on the "down low," meaning they live heterosexual, married lives, and yet engage in homosexual behaviors.[9]

Generally, blacks hold more negative attitudes toward homosexual behavior than do whites. However, researchers found that blacks are slightly more supportive of gay civil liberties, meaning they are more likely to accept issues such as gay marriage and/or child rearing as well as laws that serve to protect gays from employment discrimination.[10] These findings seem to suggest that while stereotypes about homosexuals may be held within the black community, blacks oppose discrimination against other groups.

DISCRIMINATION AND VIOLENCE BASED ON SEXUAL ORIENTATION

Americans once had mostly negative feelings about homosexuality, leading to a number of social problems. For example, in the 1970s, I had a friend in high school who was gay, and he was frequently ridiculed and occasionally threatened with physical violence. Some homosexual men will continue to identify themselves as heterosexual or bisexual to avoid the stigma attached to the label of homosexuality.[11] When a recent survey asked heterosexuals to rank their attitude about different types of people, the issue of bisexuality scored lower than issues relating to race, ethnicity, religion, and political affiliation. Only intravenous drug users scored lower.[12]

Starting around 1973, society has become more accepting of homosexuality due to a couple of factors. First, education typically leads to more accepting attitudes, and the level of educational attainment has increased in the United States. Second, the country has become more culturally diverse, leading people to become more accepting of different lifestyles as well. With each passing year, fewer people believe that homosexuality is morally wrong while more people support civil liberties for homosexuals.[13]

Despite the growing acceptance of homosexuality, violence based on sexual orientation is still a major problem. In 2005, hate crimes related to sexual orientation impacted 1,213 victims, accounting for about 14 percent of the total hate crimes committed that year.[14]

Gay and lesbian youth are at higher risk for poor health, depression, suicide attempts, and suicides. Researchers believe that these tendencies result

Attitudes Toward Homosexuality: 1973–2008*

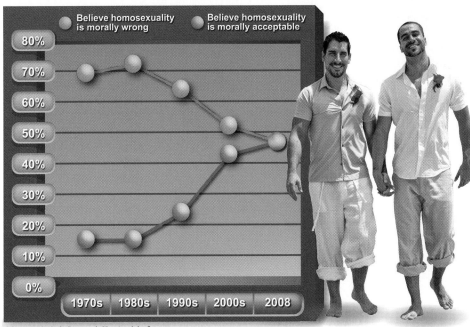

- Believe homosexuality is morally wrong
- Believe homosexuality is morally acceptable

80% 70% 60% 50% 40% 30% 20% 10% 0%

1970s 1980s 1990s 2000s 2008

*does not include "unsure/without opinion"

Sources: Jeni Loftus, "America's Liberalization in Attitudes toward Homosexuality, 1973 to 1998," *American Sociological Review*, 2001. 66(5): 762–782; Lydia Saad, "Americans Evenly Divided on Morality of Homosexuality," June 18, 2008, Gallup, http://www.gallup.com/poll/108115/americans-evenly-divided-morality-homosexuality.aspx, Accessed August 14, 2009.

from feelings of being "different," along with discriminatory experiences that they suffer at the hands of their peers.[15]

The Equal Employment Opportunity standards mean that sexual orientation or perceived orientation cannot be included in decisions related to hiring, promoting, or firing.[16] However, in comparing salaries, homosexual men earn 15 percent less than equally qualified married heterosexual men and 2.4 percent less than equally qualified single heterosexual men.[17] Many suggest the reason is clear: discrimination.

PREVALENCE OF GAYS IN THE UNITED STATES: WHAT ARE THE NUMBERS?

Although heterosexuality is the dominant sexual orientation, homosexuality is the second-most claimed orientation. Edward Lauman's

research shows that approximately 9 percent of men and 4 percent of women have engaged in some form of homosexual activity in their lives. However, only 2.8 percent of men and 1.4 percent of women in his survey claimed a homosexual identity.[18] Why might this be the case? People are not always forthcoming or honest about private sexual matters, regardless of whether the survey is confidential. We can safely assume that homosexual behavior is underreported rather than overreported, given the stigma that surrounds it.

The largest government study on sexual orientation occurred in the 1990 census. The findings estimated that 2.5 percent of American males are gay, and 1.4 percent of women are lesbians. The census also showed that the 20 cities with the largest homosexual populations are home to 60 percent of the nation's homosexuals.[19] Within this population, gays and lesbians are found to be highly educated, and a greater percentage have college degrees than their married heterosexual counterparts.[20]

Reproduction and Controlling Births

The study of social problems relating to sex involves more than sexual orientation; controlling reproduction is another hotly contested issue. For example, the United States has the highest teen pregnancy rates in the developed world. This leads to a number of social problems, including low educational attainment of young mothers and an increased risk of child abuse.[24] What can be done about this?

Since the mid-1980s, the government has sponsored a number of sex-education programs and most recently has focused on abstinence-only education, which urges youth to wait to have sex and warns them of possible pitfalls of early sexual activity.[25] In a review of abstinence-only education, researchers found significant errors, including misleading data about the failure rates of condoms.[26] Furthermore, research shows that participation in abstinence-only programs actually increases the likelihood of becoming a teen parent. One explanation for this unintended effect is that students in these programs lack the correct information to protect themselves from pregnancy and disease when they decide to become sexually active. On the other hand, researchers found that students who attended schools with a comprehensive sexuality program, which included proper use of condoms and other birth control practices, were less likely to become teen parents themselves.[27]

The Centers for Disease Control and Prevention found that contraceptive use in the United States is nearly universal, meaning most people will use some form of contraception at some point.[28] The most common methods are the oral contraceptive pill—used by more than 11 million women—and sterilization, used by 10 million women.[29] Approximately 7 million peo-

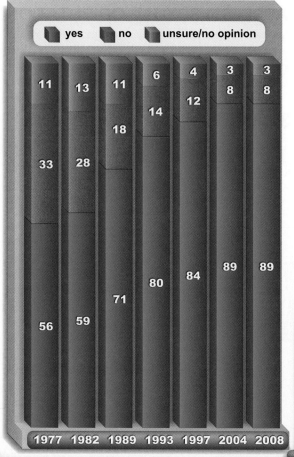

Should homosexuals have equal rights in terms of job opportunities?
(opinions, by percent)

	yes		no		unsure/no opinion

Year	unsure/no opinion	no	yes
1977	11	33	56
1982	13	28	59
1989	11	18	71
1993	6	14	80
1997	4	12	84
2004	3	8	89
2008	3	8	89

Sources: Lydia Saad, "Americans Evenly Divided on Morality of Homosexuality," June 18, 2008, Gallup, http://www.gallup.com/poll/108115/americans-evenly-divided-morality-homosexuality.aspx, Accessed August 14, 2009; "Self-Reported Sexual Orientation and Earnings: Evidence from California" Christopher S. Carpenter *Industrial and Labor Relations Review*, Vol. 58, No. 2 (Jan., 2005), pp. 258–273.

Gay Marriage Around the World

Same-sex marriage is a hot topic in the United States, gaining national attention in 2004 when many states voted on whether or not to ban the practice. But what about the rest of the world?

Many countries in Europe began recognizing "registered partnerships" as early as 1989. In that year, Denmark was the first to grant same-sex couples the same rights as married couples. Norway, Sweden, Iceland, and Finland followed suit over the next 13 years.[21] In 2005, Spain legalized gay marriage and permitted gay couples to adopt children. Other countries around the globe, including Canada and South Africa, have legalized gay marriage. Great Britain gives same-sex partners financial and property rights that are similar to those of married partners.[22]

Germany has taken a more conservative route, allowing same-sex couples to register for "life partnerships" since 2001. This law gives couples the same inheritance and tenants' rights as heterosexual married couples. France and Luxembourg have similar civil partnership laws, which do not extend full marriage rights. Some countries, such as Argentina and New Zealand, recognize civil unions between gay partners.[23] The issue of gay rights is spreading around the globe, though in many places around the world, the pursuit of equality for same-sex couples remains a struggle.

---

ple use the male condom alone or in combination with some other form of birth control such as spermicidal foam.[30] Notice that of these three most common contraceptives, two are predominantly the responsibility of women. As one student put it, "If I don't want to get pregnant, my husband says it's my job to make sure that doesn't happen." This sexist attitude is prevalent. Placing the responsibility for pregnancy solely on women can lead to other problems. For example, the number and percentage of women who were not using any method of birth control actually increased from 1995 to 2002, which may have resulted in larger families and more unintended pregnancies.

ABORTION

One of the most controversial issues of our time is abortion. **Abortion** is the termination and removal of a fetus from a woman's uterus before birth. Cultural stances on abortion have shifted over the years, and although it is currently legal in the United States, it continues to be an issue of intense debate.

Brief History of Abortion in the United States

In early American history, abortion was completely legal. Laws restricting abortion first arose in the early 1800s to protect women from unsafe abortion practices. These laws were mostly levied against midwives and doctors who were performing dangerous abortions, often resulting in the death of the woman undergoing the procedure.[31]

The most important court case concerning abortion law in the United States is *Roe v. Wade*. In 1973, the Supreme Court deemed that abortion was a fundamental right of a woman protected under the constitution and that a woman's right to privacy allowed her to decide for herself whether to terminate her pregnancy, without any external force from the government. Even now, arguments about methods and appropriate time periods for abortion are under constant scrutiny. The debate continues between those who are pro-choice (for abortion rights) and pro-life (against abortion rights).[32]

Abortion Statistics

Although abortion is still legal in the United States, the rate of abortions has shown a steady decline. From 1990 to 2004, the rate decreased from 27.4 per 1,000 women to 19.7 per 1,000 women. The increased availability of birth control and greater education about contraceptive practices could be potential contributing factors to the decline in abortions. The age group with the consistently highest rate of abortions was 20- to 24-year olds, although the rate for women 15 to 24 years of age halved. Over the same time period, black women had a higher rate of abortion than white women, and, not surprisingly, unmarried women had a much higher rate of abortion than married women.[33]

Abortion Rates
Number of Abortions per 1,000 Women

27 | 24 | 21 | 18 | 15 | 12 | 9 | 6 | 3 | 0

1990 | 2000 | 2004

Source: U.S. Census Bureau, Table 98 "Abortions by Selected Characteristics: 1990 to 2004," http://www.census.gov/compendia/statab/tables/09s0098.pdf, Accessed July 21, 2009.

think social problems: HOW DO THE DIFFERENT SOCIOLOGICAL PARADIGMS VIEW SEXUALITY?

> **QUEER THEORY** refers to a body of theory and research that seeks to neutralize the heterosexual bias in the United States.

Queer Theory

Queer theory is a critical analysis of gay and lesbian culture that started in the early 1990s. The main focus of queer theory is to counteract the perceived heterosexual bias in the United States. The theory questions the assumption that we are all "straight" unless proven otherwise. According to queer theory, sexuality exists along a continuum. Sexual identity is constantly developing and changing, as the value and cultural significance ascribed to it changes over time.

To support their theory, queer theorists often reread historical literature, keeping an eye out for any examples of non-normative sexualities and gender constructions. In his work *The History of Sexuality*, Michel Foucault identifies homosexuality as a recent (late 19th-century) phenomenon. Because the historical record is replete with references to sodomy, Foucault believed that same-sex sexuality was once merely considered a sinful behavior instead of an identity construction. Foucault theorized that sexual identity is given form and substance by the society in which it develops.[34] This was in sharp contrast to the prevailing belief that sexual identity was essential; that is, a homosexual in 2009 would be recognizable and compatible with a homosexual in 1789, 1503, or any other year. Another theorist, Eve Sedgwick, analyzed aspects of Western culture, reading the literary works of Herman Melville, Henry James, and other notable authors. Through her research, Sedgwick found that sexual categories and specification came into vogue in Europe and the United States during the late 1800s. Sedgwick identifies a distinct moment when sexuality became as important as gender in social identification and worth.[35] It is interesting to note that the word "homosexual" predates the use of the word "heterosexual," suggesting that before the 1890s, sexuality was not an important factor of an individual's life or worth.

Not everyone agrees with queer theory. Critics find it too dependent on past texts. When scrutinizing past publications for nuances of sexual overtones, modern researchers may misinterpret what they're reading. Without being able to talk to the writer directly, analysts cannot fully understand the point the author was trying to make, leading them to the wrong conclusions. Critics also point out that since most literature is written only by the middle and upper classes, the writings don't provide the most complete perspective of society. Many opponents find it hard to believe that sexuality is constantly changing. Sexual identity might be socially constructed, but sexual desires are timeless.

The inequality and oppression against non-heterosexuals is a social problem, and queer theory suggests that our society tends toward a "heterosexist" distortion: Heterosexuality is set as the norm, and anything that deviates from that is judged as "queer." Although it has its objectors, queer theory introduces the idea that there may be more to what we witness, read, and hear than the heterosexual interpretation of it.

Conflict Theory

Conflict theory and feminist theory view the issue of sexuality similarly. Men often oppress women because they wish to dominate them both physically and sexually. Heterosexual sex is one way in which men can dominate women and maintain their principle position in society.[36] Conflict theorists suggest that sexual oppression has led to social oppression, and women are indeed an oppressed group.[37]

discover solutions to social problems: HOW DOES SOCIETY DEAL WITH SEXUAL DIFFERENCES?

Government on both the state and federal level is bombarded with proposed legislation regarding civil unions, same-sex marriage, and the definition of marriage. As society has increased its acceptance of sexual diversity, law and policy have been slow to follow. What progress is being made in addressing sexual differences in our society?

Homosexual Unions

Same-sex marriage is illegal in most states. In 2004, Massachusetts became the first state to allow gay and lesbian couples to marry. Since then, gay marriage has been legalized in Connecticut, Iowa, Vermont, Maine, and most recently New Hampshire.[38] Thirty-six states have statutes on the books prohibiting gay marriage, including some that also have constitutional bans.[39]

Several states offer marriage alternatives that provide same-sex couples with the same legal rights as heterosexual couples. In eight states—California, Connecticut, Hawaii, Maine, Nevada, New Jersey, Oregon, and Washington—same-sex partners can be recognized in domestic partnerships. In California, Oregon, and Washington, the domestic partnerships share identical legal rights as those who partake in traditional marriage, including tax breaks, rights to hospital visits, approval of organ donations, and inheritance without a will.[40]

So, why do same-sex couples want to marry in the traditional sense? They seek many of the legal and financial covenants that traditional marriage ensures, such as the right to pass property at death, legal issues of child-care and parenting in the event of a death, spousal benefits for retirement and health insurance, and even social acceptance. Many employers already extend the same terms to domestic partners that are given to married partners, including health care and life insurance benefits. There are simple logistical issues for desiring marriage as well; nobody wants to live in or move to a state where their union isn't recognized.

Perhaps the most important question is why the government is involved in sanctioning marriage at all. Up until the early 20th century,

Same-Sex Marriage by State

Source: Christine Vestal, "Gay Marriage Legal in Six States," Stateline.org. http://www.stateline.org/live/details/story?contentId5347390, Accessed July 15, 2009.

marriages were not regulated by the government. It was the Uniform Marriage and Marriage License Act of 1909 that attempted to unify and codify marriage in the United States.[41] The government tacked on fees for marriage licenses, but its goal was to keep track of those who married for the sake of census data, parental obligations, and property rights. Legalization of marriage simplifies taxation and the passing of property to significant others. Some states have as many as 350 rights and responsibilities connected with marriage.

There is no perfect answer yet to the debate over same-sex marriage, but there are many people on both sides of the argument who believe strongly in how it should be handled. See the Pro & Con feature for details outlining the two sides of the issue.

MAKE CONNECTIONS

Sexual Orientation and Families

Throughout this chapter, you've seen how biases affect the day-to-day lives of citizens who hold sexual orientations other than heterosexuality. Queer theory even goes so far as to suggest that we have such a heterocentric society that anything *but* heterosexuality is "queer." This bias is similar to the gender bias we discussed in Chapter 4. Through history, women have had to fight to gain voting rights, obtain equality in the workplace, overcome domestic violence, and defend their choice to conceive, marry, or stay single. Non-heterosexuals are fighting a similar fight today.

We've also discussed the quest for same-sex marriage rights in the United States and the various laws and legislation that have gone into accepting, rejecting, and limiting these types of unions. Civil unions and domestic partnerships, which ultimately strive to be recognized as traditional marriages, will inevitably involve the adoption, fostering, and even conception of children who will become a part of these non-traditional families. In Chapter 14, we'll explore the definition of a "family" and discover how the landscape of families is changing in the 21st century. For instance, now that civil unions are allowed in several states, they present unique legal challenges when it comes to children. If a minor is either adopted or biologically related to one of the partners, parental rights can become complicated. As we saw in the opening article, in some cases the other parent needs to adopt the child to ensure that he or she cannot be taken away if something happens to the biological parent.

WRAP YOUR MIND AROUND THE THEORY

According to queer theory, heterosexuality is favored and **is considered the norm.** How can non-heterosexual groups receive equal respect in society?

Functionalists believe that the purpose of sexuality is for procreation, unification, or both. What role should society have in determining which unions lead to procreation?

QUEER THEORY

Queer theory challenges the heterosexual bias that permeates American society. According to queer theorists, the United States has a heterosexual-minded way of judging, classifying, and presenting everything, from historical art and literature to current red-carpet Oscar nominees. Queer theorists would point out that an assumed heterosexual public figure who has had a homosexual tryst is vilified, whereas a similar figure who finds himself entangled in an extra-marital (but heterosexual) affair is not as harshly condemned. Queer theory considers not just homosexual behavior, but anything outside the realm of heterosexuality: sadism, masochism, prostitution, transgender, bisexuality, asexuality, and other relationships that are deemed "queer."

SYMBOLIC INTERACTIONISM

Symbolic interactionists often question the meaning of sexuality in a person's life. For example, does one sexual encounter with a person of the same sex mean a person is bisexual, gay, or lesbian? Labeling theorists suggest that it is the self-definition of sexuality that's truly important. If you consider the data by Laumann discussed earlier in the chapter, it becomes clear that many people have same-sex encounters but do not consider themselves gay.

HOW DO SOCIOLOGISTS VIEW GENDER DIFFERENCE?

FUNCTIONALISM

Sexuality functions in society to unify people through coupling. Often, functionalists debate the purpose of sexuality. Some view it as merely a vehicle to procreate and continue the species. This is considered a clinical approach. Others view sexuality as a way to unify and improve the lives of people in a society. Still others combine the two approaches and believe that both functions are equally important.

CONFLICT THEORY

Conflict theory and feminist theory often view the issue of sexuality similarly. Recall that conflict theorists focus on inequalities. When society fosters a heterosexual bias by assuming that everyone is straight, those with different sexual identities are cast into the discriminatory category of "abnormal." At the same time, some see heterosexual sex as just another way in which men dominate women and maintain their control over society. Conflict theorists suggest that the continued domination of women over time has resulted in them being an oppressed group.[44]

Symbolic interactionists are concerned that without self-definition, sexual orientation may be muddled by outside influences. How can a person know his or her sexual orientation for sure?

Conflict theorists believe that sexuality is used by the dominant group to oppress others. Do "gentleman's clubs" perpetuate the domination of women?

Same-Sex Unions

The pros and cons of gay marriage in the United States have been greatly debated recently—even in the beauty pageant arena. In 2009, Carrie Prejean, who was later crowned Miss California, was asked whether she believed in gay marriage. When she stated that she was raised to believe that marriage is between a man and a woman, the contestant set off a firestorm on both sides of the argument.

Pro

- Equal opportunities and rights are all that matter. Just as interracial marriage was once illegal and then was overturned, so too should follow same-sex marriage.

- Negative perceptions of gay families seem unmerited. Generally, their satisfaction levels are similar to those of heterosexual relationships.[42] For instance, their love and commitment is equal to that of heterosexual couples. Also, relationship conflicts and sexual intimacy are markedly similar to heterosexual couples.

- Children raised in homes of gay parents are no more likely to grow up to be gay than children raised in homes of straight parents. Furthermore, they are less likely to suffer from abuse, and they show no differences in their sense of self-esteem or psychological health.[43]

Con

- Traditionally, marriage has always been between men and women; gay marriage ratifies a non-normative lifestyle.

- The definition of family will be permanently altered for the sake of a minority of the total population.

- There is no logical stopping point once marriage is redefined: It could extend to polygamy, for example.

- Children may be more likely to be gay themselves.

∨ **Same-sex unions** continue to be a **contentious**
∨ **issue around the world.** Where do you stand?

163

Sex and Sexuality

From Classroom to Community ⟩ The Right to Adopt

In many states, same-sex couples are still fighting for recognition by their local governments. Among the inequities, the restrictions on who can care for children via the foster system and other state-run organizations include same-sex couples.

The summer before college, Ginny spent several weeks shadowing social workers, men and women working tirelessly to help the less fortunate find ways out of difficult situations. Although sometimes emotionally draining, the opportunity solidified Ginny's determination to go into the field of social work herself. But there was one case she couldn't get out of her mind.

"I met this wonderful little girl who was full of life. Her mom had been down on her luck for a few years, and was a recovering alcoholic as well as a cocaine user. While she was working on getting clean, Sadie was in a group home waiting for a foster family to look after her for a bit. Those group homes can be scary for the young ones, and Sadie was only 7."

"I was in the office later that week when a young woman stopped by. I had the chance to talk to her a bit while she was waiting for my supervisor, and she seemed annoyed.

She had received a letter that said she wasn't viable as a foster parent because she wasn't part of a heterosexual couple. She was a lesbian, and she and her partner had a domestic partnership."

"She had come down to talk to someone in charge because she didn't understand why she couldn't bring a child into a warm and loving home just because she wasn't married to a man.

When she put it that way, it did seem ridiculous. And all I could think of was Sadie, who was sleeping another night in a room full of other kids, being bullied and picked on because she was small, and missing her mother. Instead, she could be sleeping in a safe, loving home. It wasn't fair."

"I guess the woman's conversation with my supervisor didn't go well, because she left looking frustrated. I guess there's nothing that can be done, but something *should* be done. After all, who is really losing here? It's Sadie."

11 HOW DO AMERICANS VIEW ISSUES OF SEX AND SEXUALITY? 156

the sexual orientations of heterosexuality, homosexuality, and bisexuality encompass the sexual continuum; Americans can still be quite secretive and judgmental about their own and others' sexual orientation

HOW DO THE DIFFERENT SOCIOLOGICAL PARADIGMS VIEW SEXUALITY? 160

queer theory: society is too slanted toward the heterosexual; functionalism: sexuality functions in society to bring people together through coupling; conflict theory: men use sexuality as a means to dominate others; symbolic interactionism: the meaning of sexuality in a person's life is questioned

HOW DOES SOCIETY DEAL WITH SEXUAL DIFFERENCES? 160

the legality of civil unions, gay marriage, and domestic partnerships varies from state to state; there is a great divide regarding gay adoption, gay marriage, and the definition of marriage

get the topic: HOW DO AMERICANS VIEW ISSUES OF SEX AND SEXUALITY?

Theory

QUEER THEORY   160
- American society is heterocentric on every level
- focuses on literature as a source of research

FUNCTIONALISM   162
- sexuality exists to improve the lives of people
- sexuality exists for the purpose of procreation

CONFLICT THEORY   160
- sexuality is used to dominate or control others
- heterosexual bias, homophobia, and hate legislation are ways of dominating homosexual people

SYMBOLIC INTERACTIONISM   162
- questions how sexual encounters can dictate a person's sexuality and sexual orientation
- a lack of sexual self-definition can lead to confusion about one's sexuality

Key Terms

transgender refers to people whose gender identity or gender expression differs from that associated with their birth sex.   156

sexual orientation refers to an enduring pattern of emotional, romantic, and/or sexual attractions to men, women, or both sexes.   157

heterosexual orientation refers to those who have emotional, romantic, or sexual

attractions to members of the opposite sex.   157

homosexual orientation refers to those who have emotional, romantic, or sexual attractions to members of their own sex.   157

bisexual orientation includes those who have emotional, romantic, or sexual attractions to both men and women.   157

abortion refers to the termination and removal of a fetus from a woman's uterus before birth.   159

queer theory refers to a body of theory and research that seeks to neutralize the heterosexual bias in the United States.   160

Sample Test Questions

These multiple-choice questions are similar to those found in the test bank that accompanies this textbook.

1. What have studies found regarding discrimination based on sexual orientation?

   a. Homosexual men earn less than equally qualified heterosexual men.

   b. Although often perceived as "outsiders" by their peers, bisexual and homosexual children show normal levels of happiness and satisfaction in their lives.

   c. Bisexuals are discriminated against more frequently than lesbians, but less frequently than gay men.

   d. Homosexual and heterosexual men both dominate and discriminate against lesbian and heterosexual women.

2. What state performed the first gay marriages?

   a. Massachusetts

   b. New York

   c. California

   d. Vermont

3. Transgender individuals

   a. consider themselves gay or lesbian.

   b. are more likely than same-sex partners to adopt children.

   c. tend to come from broken homes.

   d. typically fall outside conventional gender norms in dress, behavior, and appearance.

4. A *majority* of U.S. states

   a. allow same-sex civil unions.

   b. have legalized same-sex marriage.

   c. allow same-sex couples to register as domestic partners.

   d. do not allow marriage or marriage alternatives for same-sex couples.

5. Queer theory revolves around the belief that

   a. Americans are bent toward homosexuality.

   b. any orientation outside of heterosexuality is considered odd.

   c. homosexuality is ingrained from birth.

   b. oddities in U.S. culture can be traced to homosexual influences.

ESSAY

1. What are your thoughts about Thomas Beatie's pregnancy, birth, and quest for equality? Is he doing transgender individuals a disservice? Why or why not?

2. Consider the repercussions for society if the requirement for a marriage license was eliminated. Would society be better for it? Take into consideration both queer theory and functionalism in your answer.

3. Where do you stand in the debate over gay adoption? Why?

4. How would the United States be different economically, socially, and culturally if greater limitations were placed on abortion? Keep in mind what you've learned from the chapters on gender, inequality, and economy and politics.

5. In your opinion, what is the ideal solution to the controversy over same-sex unions? Should federal or state laws govern the decision-making? What measures should be taken?

WHERE TO START YOUR RESEARCH PAPER

To learn more about Thomas Beatie, see
http://www.nytimes.com/2008/06/22/fashion/22pregnant.html

For more information about sexual orientation, go to
http://www.apa.org/topics/sorientation.html

To find more detailed information on the rate of abortion in America, visit http://www.census.gov/compendia/statab/tables/09s0098.pdf

For information and articles on Queer Theory, check out
http://www.theory.org.uk/ctr-quee.htm

Remember to check www.thethinkspot.com **for additional information, downloadable flashcards, and other helpful resources.**

SEXUAL DEVIANCE

WHAT KINDS OF SOCIAL PROBLEMS ARE
CAUSED BY SEXUAL DEVIANCE?
HOW DO SOCIOLOGISTS SEE DEVIANCE?
SHOULD CONSENSUAL ACTS BE ILLEGAL?

In the

continuing effort to clear his name, Sen. Larry Craig, R-Idaho . . . filed an appeal to withdraw his guilty plea in connection with an arrest in an airport men's rest room sex sting. But many Republicans are furious that he's still around at all, drawing media attention and, in their view, embarrassing the Republican Party.

The four-page appeal does not explain under what basis Craig is filing his appeal to the order issued Oct. 4, 2007, by Hennepin County District Court Judge Charles Porter for Craig's original guilty plea not to stand. Craig must prove that Porter committed an "abuse of discretion" in his ruling.

"The facts in the case speak for themselves, and we are confident the senator's guilty plea will stand," said Patrick Hogan, spokesman for the Metropolitan Airports Commission.

In an interview with Idaho's KTVB to air this evening, Craig said he is merely exercising the same rights available to any citizen.

"It is my right to do what I am doing," Craig said, suggesting that since he is retiring from the U.S. Senate at the end of his term, "I am no longer in the way. I am no longer blocking the political process of Idaho, but I am pursuing my constitutional rights."

The senior senator pleaded guilty to a misdemeanor charge of disorderly conduct after he was arrested in a gay sex sting in a men's room at the Minneapolis-St. Paul International Airport.

Craig told NBC that he "was very proud of my association with Mitt Romney," the GOP presidential candidate, "and he not only threw me under his campaign bus, he backed up and ran over me again."

But Republican officials seem to have little sympathy for Craig. They watch late-night television too, and they see how Craig has become a punch line.

"The Democrats may have control of the House, but the Republicans have control of the bathroom," "The Tonight Show's" Jay Leno cracked.

And when the public health group Physicians Committee for Responsible Medicine wanted to depict Washington sleaze, it used images from the Craig affair as shorthand for it. In the group's new TV ad, called "Dirty Little Secret," a politician in a bathroom stall tap-tap-taps his foot as a secret signal that he wants to receive money from the pork industry that's represented in the commercial by a large pink pig.

"It's their dirty little secret, members of Congress taking PAC money from corporations producing bacon, burgers, and other fatty foods," says the narrator, describing the disconcerting relationship between Congress and companies that make unhealthy food that ends up in school lunches. The Craig scandal is the quick way to mock D.C. corruption and deviance"[1]

---When sociologist Laud Humphreys, author of the book Tearoom Trade, set out to study deviant sexual behavior among men, he did so by observing those who engaged in public, homosexual encounters, usually in men's restrooms. One of his most surprising findings was that most of the men participating in these encounters were not openly gay.

Throughout the course of his research, he found that 54 percent of the men in his study were "family men," married and still living at home with their wives and children; only 14 percent of the men identified themselves as being homosexual. Humphreys found that what all of these men shared was a desire to have a sexual encounter without commitment.[2] Although others share this desire, many people don't regard these acts as "normal."

In this chapter, we'll focus on sexual deviance and the social problems that arise from two specific issues: prostitution and pornography. In general, these two behaviors raise the most controversy and create a variety of social problems because they conflict with the dominant norms and values of American society. To begin, let's explore the nature of deviance as well as these widely-accepted social "norms."

get the topic: WHAT KINDS OF SOCIAL PROBLEMS ARE CAUSED BY SEXUAL DEVIANCE?

> **DEVIANCE** is a behavior, belief, or condition that is a violation of social norms.
>
> **PROSTITUTION** is the unlawful promotion of or participation in sexual activities for profit.

What Is Deviance?

Deviance is a behavior, belief, or condition that is a violation of social norms. There are many types of deviant behaviors: criminal deviance (Chapter 13), deviant use of drugs and alcohol (Chapter 10), and mental illness (Chapter 9).

Society establishes social norms. When someone violates one of these norms, we consider that behavior deviant. Even so, social norms are often surprisingly flexible. At one time in U.S. history, it was considered deviant behavior for African Americans to sit at the front of a bus. Now, such behavior is unlikely to be given a second thought. Sociologists must consider the following when exploring what is and what is not deviant.

- Definitions of deviance are relative to the values and beliefs of society. Women in a number of Middle Eastern countries—in accordance with their society's values and beliefs—leave their homes with their heads covered by veils. In most of the Western world, this type of behavior is not the norm.

- Defining deviance is a social and historical construct. What is deviant at one point in history may not be in another. For example, once it was considered deviant for men to wear earrings; now this is common. Time affects the way in which society defines its norms and deviances.

- Deviance is a cultural universal. No matter where you are in the world, you will find a subset of the culture that deviates from the established norms.

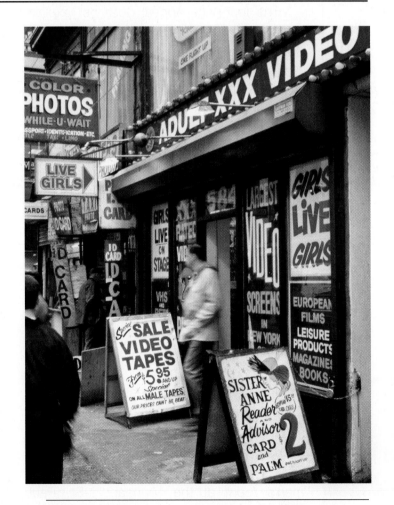

∧
∧ Patrons of adult stores use **coping**
∧ **mechanisms** to **avoid feelings of shame.**

Sociologist Emile Durkheim, while studying deviance and crime, concluded that deviance is needed to establish societal norms. Without people pushing the boundaries, there is no way to tell exactly where the boundaries are. Deviant behavior can lead to a social solidarity that has the potential to unite people in opposition to a particular behavior. He also found that deviant behavior can be a strong catalyst for change. In relation to crime, legislators will often create laws that are designed to prevent certain deviant behaviors.[3]

SHAME, STIGMA, AND DEVIANCE

Sociologist John Braithwaite found that shame, or negative internal feelings about an action that's been committed, is often associated with deviant behavior. Shame can, at times, result in a stigma—a label given to an individual for an act—and such a label can lead the individual to repeat the same behavior. He further concluded that without the presence of stigma, shame can sometimes have a beneficial effect; shame is an undesirable result of a deviant behavior, and it makes the behavior something that would be unpleasant to repeat.[4]

In studying the habits of those who visit adult bookstores, sociologist Kristen Hefley found that many of the patrons she witnessed employed certain methods to avoid feelings of shame or the stigma attached to visiting such a store. Most of these behaviors involved maintaining a degree of privacy and anonymity. Patrons would remain silent while they were in the store, avoid eye contact with others, keep a certain distance between themselves and other customers, and maintain indifferent facial expressions. Customers would disguise their appearance with hats and sunglasses and even wear long coats in warm weather. Some would enter quickly and directly, while others would linger outside before entering. Almost all of the customers paid with cash. Could these all be efforts to avoid feelings of shame for actions that appear sexually deviant?[5]

Sexual Behaviors as Social Problems

PROSTITUTION

Often referred to as "the world's oldest profession," few sexually deviant behaviors create as much controversy as prostitution. This practice can be traced back to the earliest points of recorded history. In ancient Rome and throughout the Mediterranean, it was not uncommon to find temples that housed prostitutes. Joining with them was seen as a way of joining with the gods. Visitors to the temples were able to have the ultimate religious experience through these relations.[7]

Unlike the temple prostitutes of long ago, the modern form of prostitution carries a completely different connotation. In the United States, **prostitution** and commercialized vice are defined as "the unlawful promotion of or participation in sexual activities for profit, including attempts. To solicit customers or transport persons for prostitution

> ∨ Although **prostitution today** is an **illicit and**
> ∨
> ∨ **deviant behavior,** it served a **religious**
> **purpose in some ancient societies.**

purposes; to own, manage, or operate a dwelling or other establishment for the purpose of providing a place where prostitution is performed; or to otherwise assist or promote prostitution."[8] Prostitution is generally seen as an urban blight and an unqualified problem for modern society.[9]

Prostitution in the United States

In the United States, prostitution is only legal in certain areas of the state of Nevada, and even then, not all forms of prostitution are legal. Prostitution in brothels is permitted in a select number of areas, but street prostitution is not allowed anywhere.[10]

Prostitution is as much about the customers as it is about the prostitutes. After all, prostitutes need customers to stay in business. In his research on prostitution, Kingsley Davis identified four distinct motives for men to use prostitutes. Davis suggests that these men have difficulty with sexual relationships, have difficulty finding long-term partners, have broken relationships, or want sexual gratification that is seen as being immoral or that their normal sex partner is unwilling to provide.[11] Sociologist Martin Monto interviewed men who frequented prostitutes and found that the most common activity requested was fellatio. In that case, men were able to hire prostitutes to perform sexual acts that their wives or regular sex partners would refuse to perform.[12]

Others, like feminist scholar Meda Chesney-Lind, suggest that prostitution provides access to non-emotional sex that can benefit both parties involved in the transaction, although the benefit manifests in distinctly different forms for each party. The prostitute earns income without the constraints of a typical, nine-to-five job. The customers, on the other hand, gain the opportunity to have sex with no strings attached. Many argue that this analysis is largely one-sided; they point out the fact that prostitutes are often runaway girls who resort to prostitution as a means of survival. Their need for survival leads them to be exploited by men, whether they are pimps or customers.[13]

In a detailed ethnographic study, Wendy Chapkis interviewed a number of prostitutes and found that sex work for women involves far more than the act of "selling themselves" to customers. Prostitution, like many jobs that women hold, involves emotional labor—that is, regulating one's emotions in accordance with the guidelines of a job. If you are an emergency department doctor, for example, you can't let your sympathy for a patient get in the way of your surgical work. In this way, prostitutes aren't much different from other employees in the workforce. Sex workers provide an intimate service to customers but must control their emotions, maintain boundaries, and separate their work life and their personal life.[14]

Why Prostitution?

So, who is the typical female prostitute? This portrait can vary a great deal, depending on race, social class, physical appearance, and personal attributes.[15] Young prostitutes, for example, are generally girls who are convicted of crimes and status offenses, such as truancy or running away from home. Prostitution is often the only job that a runaway can get. Because of punishments related to prostitution, female delinquents tend to have more status offenses than their male counterparts.[16] A study of adolescent prostitutes in Taiwan found that 71 percent came from a broken home, 73 percent of those studied were physically abused at home, and 57 percent reported being sexually abused. Many of these girls were involved in behaviors that some might see as deviant; 80 percent were truant from school and 78 percent had run away from home. The majority had engaged in sexual activity before turning to prostitution, and were users of alcohol and/or tobacco.[17] These numbers mirror similar findings in the United States.[18]

There are three distinct stages of becoming a prostitute. First, there is **drift**, which occurs when there is a switch from casual sex to the first incident of exchanging sex for money. Many situations can lead to drift, including running away from home, dropping out of school, becoming pregnant, developing drug addictions, or having a juvenile record. In almost every case, prostitutes have had sexual experiences early in life. In one study, prostitutes were found to have had sex, on average, by the age of 13.5.

The second stage is **transition**. It is during this period, lasting six months or so, that the women experience ambivalence toward their new role as prostitutes and consider whether they want to continue along this path. This stage is also the time during which they try to rationalize their behavior as being normal. The third stage is **professionalization**. At this stage, women identify themselves as prostitutes and no longer feel the need to rationalize their behavior.[19]

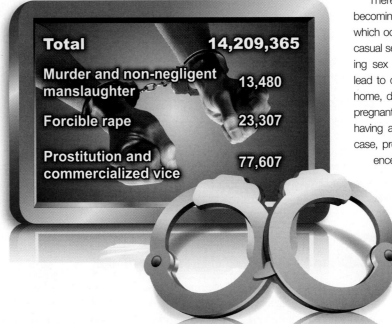

Number of Arrests, 2007

Total	**14,209,365**
Murder and non-negligent manslaughter	**13,480**
Forcible rape	**23,307**
Prostitution and commercialized vice	**77,607**

Source: Data from Table 29, "Estimated Number of Arrests," U.S. Department of Justice, Federal Bureau of Investigation. *Crime in the United States, 2007.* Accessed September 2008, http://www.fbi.gov/ucr/cius2007/data/table_29.html.

In 2007, **more people were arrested for prostitution** and commercialized vice **than murder and rape combined.**

Sex Tourism

As we've seen, prostitution isn't always a personal choice—structures of society can have an impact as well. Globalization, wealth distribution, migration, and tourism all contribute to the recruitment and enslavement of young women into prostitution throughout the world. Wonders and Michalowski studied how globalization has influenced **sex tourism**, the practice of people from wealthy nations traveling to less developed countries to experience sexual acts. These acts may or may not be illegal in their home countries. Sex tourism is seen by tourists as a pleasurably novel experience, not unlike taking a gondola ride in Venice or trying sushi in Japan. Not surprisingly, this aids in the spread of **objectification**, the treating of a person as an object or "thing" without concern for his or her personal characteristics. Sex tourism also drives structural changes in cities, as seen in Havana and Amsterdam, and creates an industry that views the human body as a commodity to be bought and sold for the pleasure of the purchaser.[20] This trend of **commodification**, the transformation of relationships formerly unrelated to commerce into

∧
∧ **The section of Amsterdam known as the**
∧ **Red Light District caters to sex tourists.** Is it
better to have prostitution legal and
regulated or illegal and underground?

SEX TOURISM is the act of people from wealthy nations traveling to less developed countries for sexual acts that may or may not be illegal in their home nation.

OBJECTIFICATION involves treating a person as a thing or object, without concern for his or her personal characteristics.

COMMODIFICATION is the transformation of relationships that were formerly unrelated to commerce into economic relationships built on buying and selling.

economic relationships, is particularly problematic when one considers the vast number of young girls throughout the world who are lured into cities where they are then abused and forced into sex slavery.[21]

Although prostitution creates a number of potential social problems, particularly related to the objectification and commodification of women, it is not the only social problem related to sexual deviance. Let's turn our attention to pornography, another topic that creates a great deal of controversy in society.

PORNOGRAPHY

What is and is not considered pornography is at the center of the debate on this form of sexual deviance. From a legal perspective, this relativity has caused problems in the past. The 1957 case *Roth v. United States* defined pornography as something that appeals to a lust-oriented interest in sex, is in opposition to accepted community standards, and has no redeeming social value. On the other hand, some feminists define pornography as any graphic, sexually explicit medium that diminishes women.[22] Notice how both of these definitions contain value-laden terms. What exactly is something with "no redeeming social value," and how does one decide what "diminishes women"? One of the problems that societies must face when dealing with pornography is how to define it in the first place.

Like prostitution, the roots of pornography can be traced back thousands of years. Ancient cave drawings have been found that depict people engaged in sexual acts. Even though the drawings are often looked upon from an academic distance, the question remains: Are they art, or are they an early form of pornography?

Today, many types of pornography thrive on the Internet, due in no small part to the additional levels of anonymity provided by the medium. No matter what turns you on, you're likely to find a Web site that caters to it.

What Is Classified as Pornography?

In the 1973 case, *Miller v. California*, the United States Supreme Court determined that pornography was not protected by claims of free speech and reaffirmed the rights of the community to determine what was acceptable. Since pornography was not an expression of free speech, it could be eliminated. Those who felt that pornography objectified women and made them more likely to become victims of abuse and domination applauded this decision.

Every state in the United States has statutes related to pornography, and most follow the Roth case in defining it as something that is in opposition to community standards. Thus, what is illegal in one community could be legal in another. This lack of distinction did not stop President George W. Bush's administration from conducting federal pornography prosecutions, which increased dramatically during his time in office.[23]

Controversy and Research on Pornography

If pornography objectifies women, what social problems may result? In the mid-1980s, President Ronald Reagan called for a study on the effects of pornography. Dubbed the Meese Commission, the researchers came to many controversial conclusions, the foremost of which being that exposure to sexually violent materials causes men to act more aggressively toward women. Of the 411 sex offenders studied, the average offender had 336 victims. The Commission also found that rape rates were higher where laws related to pornography were more liberal, and that states with higher porn sales had more instances of rape. They also asserted that rapists were more likely to have been exposed to hard-core pornography as children and that pornography serves to legitimize this violent act. Furthermore, the Meese Commission found that males who were exposed to porn that featured images of sexual violence, such as slasher films, became desensitized and viewed rape victims as being less worthy of sexual rights and less injured than they actually were. In their final analysis, the commissioners stated that understanding the fact that porn caused acts of sexual violence was simply a matter of common sense.[24]

Of course, the Meese report was not widely accepted. Among the problems with the report is that it is difficult to prove that watching porn causes sexual violence in every case. In fact, to disprove the assertion that pornography causes sexual violence, you only need to find one instance where this does not happen. In an industry that makes $10 billion to $14 billion or more per year, it's clear that a rather large clientele exists.[25] Is the size of the industry a sign that pornography is a social problem? With an audience in the millions, it becomes increasingly apparent that not everyone who watches porn resorts to acts of sexual violence. Is porn merely a free expression of society's interest in sex? Or is it deviant?

A more recent study found that during the period between 1995 and 1999, when porn was becoming increasingly available on the Internet, reports of forcible rape actually declined.[26] It is this sort of contradictory evidence that calls into question any claims of a clear-cut connection between pornography and violent sexual behavior. Many of the studies that attempt to show a causal relationship between pornography and behavior offer inconclusive results that only open the door to more questions.

Federal Pornography Prosecutions, 1995–2006

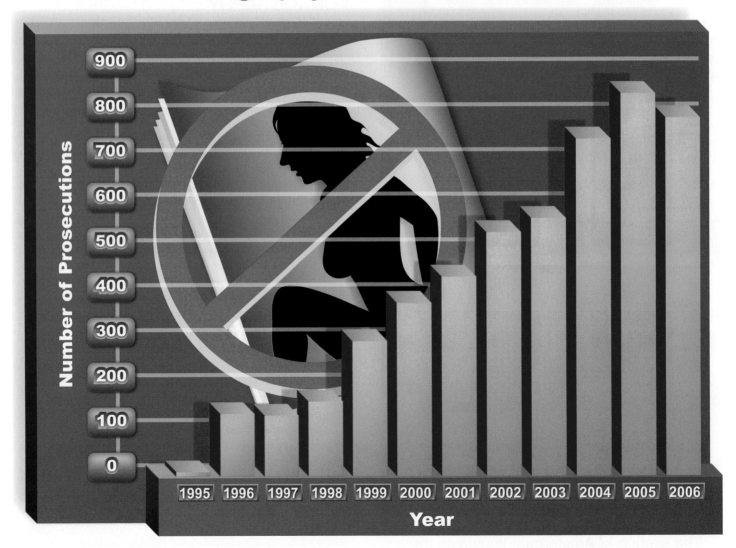

Source: FBI Enforcement Trends by Program Area, Prosecutions Filed FY 1986–2006. TRAC FBI. http://trac.syr.edu/cgi-bin/tracslides2.pl?id=fbi2005&slide=13

∧
∧ Despite the lack of a clear definition of "pornography," **federal prosecutions more than**
∧ **doubled from 2000 to 2006.**

Reported Cases of Forcible Rape, 1995–1999

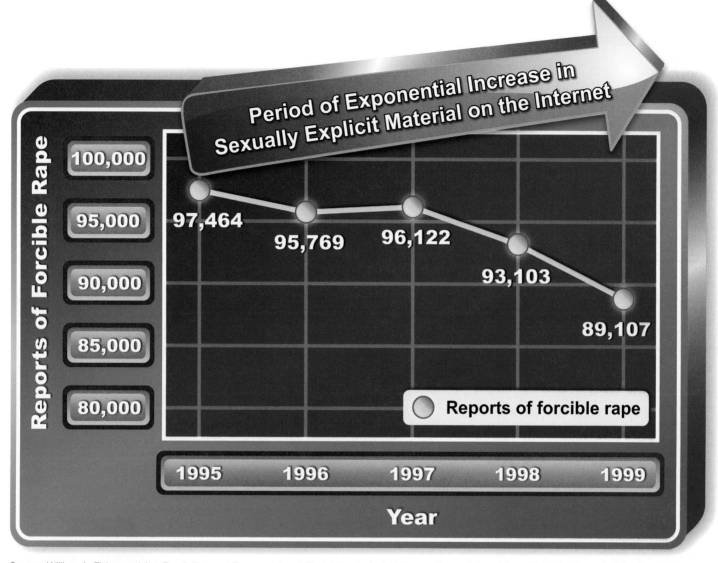

Period of Exponential Increase in Sexually Explicit Material on the Internet

Reports of Forcible Rape

100,000

95,000

90,000

85,000

80,000

97,464

95,769

96,122

93,103

89,107

○ Reports of forcible rape

1995   1996   1997   1998   1999

Year

Source: William A. Fisher and Azy Barak "Internet Pornography: A Social Psychological Perspective on Internet Sexuality." *The Journal of Sex Research*, Vol. 38, No. 4 (Nov., 2001), pp. 312–323

∧
∧ Does pornography lead to acts of sexual violence? Fisher and Barak found that **as the amount**
∧ **of pornographic material** on the Internet **increased, the number of rapes** actually **decreased.**

think social problems: HOW DO SOCIOLOGISTS SEE DEVIANCE?

Symbolic Interactionism: Techniques of Neutralization

When people behave in a deviant fashion, they often seek ways to justify their behavior and eliminate feelings of guilt. These are what Sykes and Matza call "techniques of neutralization," or methods used to rationalize or justify acts that are considered deviant.[27] This type of rationalization is not limited to delinquents and, in fact, was shown to be a common behavior of men who engage in public sex or anonymous sex in tearooms.[28]

One popular tactic is denial of responsibility, or "I didn't do it!" The most widely known delinquent to use this tactic is probably Bart Simpson, who famously uses this method to neutralize his behavior on the show, *The Simpsons*. This denial of responsibility enables a person to repeat the same behavior in the future. Another tactic that is frequently employed is the denial of harm to victims, or "I did it, but it didn't hurt anyone!" By stating that no harm has been done, the person is able to feel better about his or her behavior and can also repeat it in the future. A shoplifter might rationalize her theft of a sweater by arguing that the

WRAP YOUR MIND AROUND THE THEORY

Functionalism promotes the idea that **pornography and prostitution serve as replacements for intimacy.** Does the availability of pornography lead to a decrease in crime?

FUNCTIONALISM

Prostitution and pornography assist men who seek sexual intimacy. Davis suggests that these outlets are mutually beneficial to both men and women; men have their needs met while women gain income. According to Monto, such an outlet allows men to achieve desires that their wives or sexual partners are unwilling or unable to provide. Prostitution also enables them to fulfill their sexual longings without seeking out such intimacy by force or crime. Both forms of deviance are simply means of allowing men to get what they desire.

WHY DO PEOPLE ENGAGE IN SEXUAL DEVIANCE?

CONFLICT THEORY

Sexual deviance is often defined by those with the power to do so. The exploitation of women in the industries of prostitution and pornography, as well as sex tourism, shows that men continue to dominate society and use sexual deviance as a way to keep women objectified. Despite the fact that prostitution and pornography intensify the spread of commodification and objectification of women, both are generally tolerated or even ignored by authorities.

SYMBOLIC INTERACTIONISM

How do people justify their behaviors? According to Sykes and Matza, most people, including deviants, seek to avoid feelings of guilt and shame through rationalization and justification of their actions. By denying responsibility, condemning the condemners, appealing to a set of higher loyalties, and denying harm to victims, we use techniques of neutralization to avoid negative labels.

Conflict theory suggests that **prostitution and pornography lead to the continued subjugation of women.** Would eliminating these deviances change society's attitudes toward women?

People try to avoid shame and guilt. **How might sexual deviants, such as porn star Memphis Monroe, justify their behavior?**

loss of one piece of clothing doesn't affect a huge department store. A third method that is often used is condemning the condemners, or "Who are you to tell me anything? You do the same or worse!" This method serves to make the person feel better by changing the focus from his or her actions to the actions of another. Again, this allows the individual to repeat the same behavior in the future. An alcoholic confronted by his friends may angrily bring up the fact that they themselves smoke cigarettes. The fourth method is an appeal to higher loyalties, or "I study business, not sociology. I don't cheat on my *business* exams!" This tactic serves to neutralize the behavior by diminishing its importance.

You can see how individuals may sometimes reply with one of these justifications when labeled negatively as a "sexual deviant." Think about the opening article. Senator Craig initially pled guilty to the charges he faced and only later decided to claim, "I didn't do it." Was he a sexual deviant merely trying to use a technique of neutralization, or is he an innocent man? It's left to the courts to decide.

Research suggests that prostitutes also use these techniques. In a study that focused on one particular prostitute's attitudes toward her profession, the woman was found to employ several methods to justify her behavior regularly. When a close relation condemned her for being a prostitute, she validated the experience by saying, "Well I made 50 bucks. That's good."[29]

Conflict Theory

Recall that conflict theorists suggest that those in power have the ability to assert their will against others. In our review of both prostitution and pornography, one can clearly claim that men tend to use their power over women for sexual gratification. Turning women into a commodity can justify all kinds of negative treatment of women, including forced prostitution. Sex tourism shows that making money takes precedence over the desire to treat people fairly and justly. In this way, markets turn sex into a service to be bought and sold, and prostitution becomes a way for some to reap wealth from the work of others.[30]

Techniques of Neutralization

The Tactic	The Argument
Denial of Responsibility	"I didn't do it!"
Denial of Harm to Victims	"I didn't hurt anyone!"
Condemning the Condemners	"Who are you to say that?"
Appeal to Higher Loyalties	"This isn't what's important!"

Source: Sykes, Gresham, and David Matza. 1957. "Techniques of Neutralization: A Theory of Delinquency." *American Sociological Review* 22: 664–670.

∧∧∧ What **deviations** might **lead a person to use** each of **these techniques?**

discover solutions to social problems:
SHOULD CONSENSUAL ACTS BE ILLEGAL?

Criminalization of Consensual Acts

More often than not, prostitution and pornography—acts that are consensual in nature—are considered victimless crimes. The logic goes something like this: If all parties involved want the same thing and are willing participants, then what's the harm? In the case of Senator Larry Craig, the question remains whether what he did should be considered illegal. Is it enough to arrest someone for simply soliciting an encounter—especially if it is consensual?

The incident with Senator Craig is complicated by the fact that the encounter was solicited in a public space. On those grounds, there could be an argument made for his arrest. On the other hand, was the behavior considered illegal because it was sexual in nature and implied a deviance from the norm?

Alternatives to Criminalization

In the present day, prostitution and pornography are still illegal. Even so, criminalization of these acts has not proven to be an effective measure in preventing their practice. Prostitution is a fixture in almost every city in the United States, and, with estimated annual earnings that total billions of dollars, pornography remains a profitable business. If such acts are decriminalized, they would be removed from the legal system, and the social stigma attached to them would likely decrease as a result.

The Nevada model is example of how such acts could be legalized, licensed, taxed, and controlled. Prostitutes in brothels must pass safe-sex training courses as well as submit to regular health screenings to avoid the transmission of sexually transmitted diseases. Furthermore, the acts are regulated through taxation. Of course, anyone who has been to Las Vegas knows that even though prostitution is legal only in brothels doesn't mean that it's not available on the streets as well. When we debate this issue in my classes, students often suggest that legislature could create "red-light" districts (such as the famous one in Amsterdam) in all cities, where prostitution and pornographic material would be made available. Creating these districts would ensure that those uninterested in such things would not be forced to encounter them, while at the same time eliminating the thousands of man-hours and millions of dollars spent each year trying to control these sexual acts.

Pro & Con

Legalizing Prostitution

Prostitution, or some form thereof, is permitted in places such as the Netherlands and Nevada. Should it be legalized throughout the entire United States? What does each side have to say?

Pro

- If prostitution is legalized, states will be able to earn income from the practice. In times of economic hardship, this income may very well keep states afloat. The concept may seem far-fetched, but consider the fact that California Governor Arnold Schwarzenegger has recently suggested taxing the sale of marijuana to generate income for the cash-strapped state.[31]

- Legalized prostitution could be restricted to certain red-light districts, similar to the one that exists in Amsterdam. By localizing prostitution, it could be kept away from people who don't want to be exposed to it.

- From a health standpoint, medically licensing prostitutes will help increase safe-sex practices and decrease the chances that STDs will be transmitted during encounters. This monitoring would be a benefit to prostitutes, their customers, and the public at large.

- Legalizing prostitution will enable law enforcement to focus on more serious crimes. Police would be able to stop patrolling the streets in search of prostitutes and their customers and redirect their attention to crimes without willing and consensual participants. This shift in police attention would especially benefit cities in which violent crime and drug trafficking are prevalent.

- From the judicial perspective, legalizing prostitution could offer relief to an already strained legal system. Those who work in the justice system would be able to dedicate more of their time to handling weightier cases. Women who resort to prostitution for survival would no longer develop criminal records that will later stigmatize them.

Con

- Prostitution is illegal because it is a social problem that has a corrosive effect on society—it has widespread implications that go beyond prostitutes and their customers. Prostitution keeps pimps and madams (who are constantly on the lookout for new employees) in business and can corrupt police officers who are bribed to look the other way. Most importantly, it can feed into larger, more harmful organized crimes, such as the drug trade.

- Any neighborhood with the presence of prostitution will be hurt. Property values will decrease substantially. Not only will the prostitution activity be unwanted, but it will also attract undesirable people to the neighborhood. Residents who have children will relocate, and prospective home buyers will look elsewhere.

- Prostitution can rapidly spread disease and is an enormous health risk. Because of the many sexual partners that a prostitute encounters on a regular basis, one prostitute who carries an STD could infect dozens of people. If the disease goes undetected and those clients have other sexual partners, more could be infected as well.

- Prostitution is immoral and undermines an accepted sense of decency. The selling of sex and the sex acts that are performed by prostitutes violates long-held beliefs about intimacy and sexuality. Prostitution ruins marriages, tears families apart, and leads to corruption in the home and community.

- Women are often treated in a manner in which they are objectified, and prostitution only serves to continue—and even enhance—this mind-set. The profession itself is degrading to women, and because of the stigma attached to prostitution, women are often seen and treated as second-class citizens.

<<< Deviant behaviors violate social norms. **If prostitution were legalized, would it become a social norm?**

Sexuality and Deviance

As you've read in this chapter, there are many instances in which sexuality can be linked to deviant behavior. From prostitution to pornography to homosexuality, there can be a negative stigma attached to a person's sexual behavior, and this stigma can apply even when members participate freely and willingly. In the previous chapter we saw that it's often hard to define what constitutes moral sexual behavior; attitudes toward certain behaviors change over time, and what was once considered deviant can gain social acceptance.

In Chapter 13 you will learn that not all deviant behavior is linked to sexuality and that criminal behavior also serves to stigmatize individuals. In many cases, the implications of criminal deviance can be much worse.

Chapter 4 described the role that gender plays in society. As we've seen, prostitution and pornography are often seen as gender exploitation; much of sexual deviation is based on perceptions of gender and the expectations placed on both men and women.

From Classroom to Community | Human Trafficking

Although we've already discussed the deviant acts of sex tourism and prostitution earlier on in this chapter, there is another social problem that carries elements of both: human trafficking. Human trafficking is a form of modern-day slavery: Traffickers target poor individuals, particularly women and children, luring them with false promises of good jobs and pay, then use force, fraud, or coercion to subject their victims to prostitution, debt bondage, and involuntary servitude. Even when these trafficking victims are not forced into prostitution, they suffer sexual abuse and rape as well as torture, beatings, death threats, and starvation. Human trafficking is a major problem around the globe. Even in the United States, approximately 50,000 women and children are trafficked every year.[32]

Like many of his fellow college students, David was unaware of the issue of human trafficking, and was shocked that slavery of any sort existed in the United States. He learned about these issues for the first time when his girlfriend invited him to attend a meeting of the Human Trafficking Awareness Organization on campus.

At the meeting, the president announced an upcoming seminar series to spread awareness to the community. David learned that the organization fought trafficking and prostitution in the United States through education, outreach, and fund-raising. A petition was passed around that called for an update of the current federal Trafficking & Violence Protection Act to further protect victims' rights. Volunteer schedules were then handed out so that members could lend a hand at shelters that housed former child sex slaves.

Near the end of the meeting, a tired-looking young woman who had been sitting in the corner came forward to speak at the front of the room. The president of the organization introduced her as a previous victim of sex trafficking. The students listened in silence as the woman told her story.[33]

She had been homeless at 15 when a man approached her, offering her a place to live and a high-paying job. Instead, she was forced into prostitution. The man kept her and six other women under tight watch in his home, and didn't allow them to leave or communicate with the outside world unless given permission. She was driven six or seven times a day to different addresses and forced to engage in sexual acts with the men there; upon arriving home, she had to give her captor all the money she'd earned. Often, he would beat one of the women in front of the others as an example, and once he had poured boiling water on her for being disobedient. She and the others were too terrified to leave—they had no money or family and friends to contact. Even worse, they were addicted to the cocaine that their pimp gave them as payment.

For six years she lived as sex slave, until the police discovered the women during a drug raid.

Her story moved David, and he was outraged to find that her abuser had appealed his sentence and would probably end up avoiding life imprisonment. In his opinion, the exchange of sex for money among consenting adults had always been a moral gray area, but forced prostitution was entirely wrong.

David joined the awareness organization right then and there. He has since become active in initiating fund-raisers, volunteering time at shelters for victims, and spreading awareness to other campuses across the nation.

12

shame and stigma, which serve to isolate individuals and perpetuate deviant behavior

functionalism: deviance acts such as prostitution are mutually beneficial to men and women and serve as an outlet for society; conflict theory: sexual deviance is men's way of dominating women; symbolic interactionism people rationalize deviant actions through techniques of neutralization to avoid feelings of guilt and shame

this question is at the heart of the debate; some argue that there is no harm in these acts since both parties are consenting; others point out that these behaviors affect society as a whole—for example, the act of prostitution objectifies women

get the topic: WHAT KINDS OF SOCIAL PROBLEMS ARE CAUSED BY SEXUAL DEVIANCE?

Theory

FUNCTIONALISM   174

- pornography and prostitution prevent men who seek sexual intimacy from obtaining it through force or crime

CONFLICT THEORY   174

- sexual deviance is defined by those with the power to do so
- the exploitation of women is another way in which men maintain their dominance in society

- both prostitution and pornography are tolerated even though women are exploited by both

SOCIAL INTERACTIONISM   173

- people seek to eliminate feelings of shame and guilt by rationalizing deviant behaviors through techniques of neutralization

Key Terms

deviance is a behavior, belief, or condition that is a violation of social norms.   168

prostitution is the unlawful promotion of or participation in sexual activities for profit.   169

drift is the first stage of becoming a prostitute and the change from casual sex to the first incident of exchanging sex for money.   170

transition is the second stage of becoming a prostitute and is the six-month period in which women try to rationalize their behavior as normal.   170

professionalization is the third and final stage of becoming a prostitute and the point at which women identify themselves as prostitutes.   170

sex tourism is the act of people from wealthy nations traveling to less developed countries for sexual acts that may or may not be illegal in their home nation.   171

objectification involves treating a person as a thing or object, without concern for his or her personal characteristics.   171

commodification is the transformation of relationships that were formerly unrelated to commerce into economic relationships built on buying and selling.   171

Sample Test Questions

These multiple-choice questions are similar to those found in the text bank that accompanies this textbook.

1. Which of the following is *not* a technique of neutralization?
   a. Denial of responsibility
   b. Condemning the condemner
   c. Acceptance of responsibility
   d. Denial of harm to victims

2. What are the three stages that most women go through in becoming prostitutes?
   a. Draft, translation, personalization
   b. Denial, rejection, acceptance
   c. Disinterest, interest, extreme interest
   d. Drift, transition, professionalization

3. Prostitution and pornography are both seen by sociologists as
   a. deviant sexual behavior.
   b. defiant sexual behavior.
   c. righteous social behavior.
   d. All of the above

4. Sociologists must keep which of the following in mind when examining deviance?
   a. Deviance is relative to the beliefs and values of a culture.
   b. Deviance is a recent social construct.
   c. An act of deviance is recognizable as such in any historical context.
   d. Deviations bring cultures together in ways that social norms aren't able to.

5. According to current research, pornography
   a. has led to a steep increase in rates of forcible rape.
   b. has no clear relationship to violent sexual behavior.
   c. has been legalized in most other first-world countries.
   d. is slowly decreasing in production due to increased female rights around the globe.

ESSAY

1. Did Senator Larry Craig's actions warrant the type of treatment he received? Why or why not? Do you think that he received this type of treatment because he pursued a homosexual encounter, because he pursued a public encounter, or both?

2. Do you believe that either prostitution or pornography cause harm to society as a whole? If so, which do you think causes the greater harm? If you don't think that they harm society, why?

3. If activities such as prostitution and pornography should be legalized on the basis that they are consensual in nature, should the same type of logic be applied to the drug trade? Why or why not?

4. Is it fair to hold politicians accountable for their sexual behaviors while they are in office? Should their personal actions remain private and free of public scrutiny?

5. Give an example of labeling that you have witnessed and explain how it served to validate behavior and enable future deviant acts.

WHERE TO START YOUR RESEARCH PAPER

For an analysis of street prostitution, visit
http://www.cops.usdoj.gov/pdf/e05021552.pdf

For more on the pros and cons of legalized prostitution, see
http://www.prostitution.procon.org

For a profile of America's porn industry, go to
http://www.pbs.org/wgbh/pages/frontline/shows/porn/business/

To see an assessment of whether porn is addictive, check out
http://men.webmd.com/guide/is-pornography-addictive

For an analysis of the effects of pornography on men, visit
http://nymag.com/nymetro/news/trends/n_9437/

To learn how you can get involved in preventing human trafficking, see
http://www.humantrafficking.org/

ANSWERS: 1. c; 2. d; 3. a; 4. a; 5. b

Remember to check www.thethinkspot.com for additional information, downloadable flashcards, and other helpful resources.

CRIME

What's the

murder capital of the nation? That depends on who does the counting.

Until this month, that dubious distinction for 2008 fell on Baltimore. But then, Detroit's police department conceded the city had 339 murders in 2008 rather than 306—making Detroit the deadliest city in the nation.

The disclosure followed newspaper reports that the city had consistently underreported its murder rate, leading to accusations that Detroit, along with other cities, was gaming the system to make the city appear safer.

"Figures don't lie, but liars sure do figure," former North Carolina Attorney General Rufus Edmisten, who used to announce that state's crime statistics, told ABC with a chuckle.

Was Detroit gaming the numbers to avoid an unpopular title? It's a common practice, Edmisten said.

"You have a lot of numbers manipulated, depending on what you want to achieve," he said. "If you need more help you say how bad things are. On the other hand no public official wants to say we're No. 1 in the number of murders."

According to the FBI, the total number of murders Detroit reported last year is 306. That put Detroit behind Baltimore in per-capita murders, at 36.9 murders per 100,000 residents. But Detroit Police Department spokesman Rod Liggons says that number undercounts the total.

"Three-thirty-nine is our actual number," Liggons, who did not immediately return a call from ABC, told The Baltimore Sun.

The higher number pushes Detroit's rate to 37.4 murders per 100,000 residents, making Detroit the deadliest city with more than 500,000 residents in the nation.

Abbe Smith, director of the Criminal Justice Clinic at Georgetown University Law School, agreed.

"I'd bet you this is highly politicized," Smith told ABC News, "especially that in places like Detroit, that are hard-hit by the recession, would do what they could to interpret the statistics in ways that are not quite so damning."

But experts say homicide statistics are harder to game because there are few alternatives in a violent death, such as suicide or accidental death.

"Homicide is one of the more accurate crime statistics versus sexual assault, versus prop crimes, etc," said ABC News Consultant Brad Garrett, a former FBI agent. . . .

Detroit's disclosure came after an analysis of homicide cases by The Detroit Free Press found the city was undercounting homicides, in violation of FBI standards. The Free Press analysis found that among the deaths not considered a homicide were a fatal stabbing and a fatal beating.

City officials have acknowledged that the department uses a different standard than the FBI, based on prosecutors' reports—which are generally stricter because they assign intent—rather than medical examiners' conclusions.

FBI guidelines say that "agencies must report the willful killing of one individual by another, not the criminal liability of the person or persons involved."

That is the standard cities should use, ABC's Garrett said.

"It should be uniform," Garrett said of homicide statistics. "They should be following the same rules to make it accurate."[1]

---What do you think of when you hear the word "crime"? Do you picture a sinister assailant robbing a pedestrian at gunpoint, a drug deal going down in a darkened alley, or young teens spray-painting their initials on a road sign?

Do you think of Bernie Madoff cheating investors out of their retirement funds or a Jewish synagogue being vandalized? Clearly, crime is a social problem, however, people often associate the word "crime" with different acts that vary in style and degrees of severity. In this chapter, we'll focus primarily on types of street crimes, because these tend to be the ones that people fear the most; yet, as we'll see later on, you're more likely to be hurt by someone like Bernie Madoff than a serial killer.

As you read on, we'll discuss the definition of "crime" as well as the statistics and demographics of crime in the United States. What type of person is most likely to commit a crime? Are offenders morally deficient? Do victims sometimes "have it coming"? We'll also focus on sociological factors that motivate criminal behavior, and examine ways to prevent social issues that stem from this problem.

get the topic: HOW IS CRIME A SOCIAL PROBLEM?

CRIME is the violation of norms that have been written into law.

VIOLENT CRIME is an illegal act committed against another person.

NONVIOLENT CRIME is an illegal act committed against property.

CRIMINOLOGY is the scientific study of crime, deviance, and social policies that the criminal justice system applies.

UNIFORM CRIME REPORTS (UCR) include data from official police statistics of reported crimes gathered from police reports and paperwork.

CRIME INDEX is made up of eight offenses used to measure crime: homicide, rape, robbery, aggravated assault, burglary, larceny-theft, motor vehicle theft, and arson.

NATIONAL CRIME VICTIMIZATION SURVEY (NCVS) is the measurement of crime victimization based on contact with a representative sample of over 70,000 households in the United States.

As the opening article suggests, cities such as Detroit have tried to "game the numbers" to protect their reputations and downplay their struggles with crime. In reality, though, crime remains an ongoing issue, especially in urban areas. Big cities such as Detroit, Memphis, Miami, Las Vegas, and Orlando have the highest percentages of violent crime in the United States. How do you think this affects the urban population?

Measuring Crime: Crime Statistics

Before we get too far into the sociology of crime, however, let's first take a step back and examine what crime really is. Simply put, **crime** is the violation of norms that have been written into law. There are two basic types of street crime: violent and nonviolent crimes. **Violent crime** is an illegal act committed against another person. This includes acts such as murder, robbery, forcible rape, and aggravated assault. **Nonviolent crime** is an illegal act committed against property.

Major offenses include burglary, larceny-theft, arson, and motor vehicle theft.

Nobody wants crime in their neighborhood, but it seems that a lot of people like crime in their TV programming, especially when the crime is solved by charismatic detectives with high-tech devices. Shows such as *CSI: Crime Scene Investigation* and *Bones* may make crime sexy and interesting, but they don't quite capture the complicated process of solving and preventing crime as done by real-life officers and public officials. Paperwork is one piece of the process that is rarely seen in fictional crime shows; that task is usually left to the people with desk jobs (i.e., the less important characters). But paperwork is an incredibly important aspect of detective work, especially when it comes to tracking and analyzing crime statistics.

In **criminology**—the scientific study of crime, deviance, and social policies that the criminal justice system applies—criminologists use two primary sources of data to measure the quantity and frequency of street crime. One of these sources is the **Uniform Crime Reports (UCR)**. UCR data come from official police statistics of reported crimes and are collected by the Federal Bureau of Investigation (FBI). For example, a stolen credit card becomes a UCR statistic once the theft is reported to the police.

The UCR **crime index** uses eight major offenses to measure crime. Four of these are violent crimes: homicide, rape, robbery, and aggravated assault. The other four are property crimes: burglary, larceny-theft, motor vehicle theft, and arson.[2]

Because many crimes go unreported, the **National Crime Victimization Survey (NCVS)** is also an important source of crime statistics. The NCVS is one of the nation's largest ongoing household surveys. It calculates how many violent and nonviolent crimes U.S. residents aged 12 and older experience each year. The survey reaches nearly 70,000 households in the United States, and will typically report higher rates of crime than the UCR; for example, in 2002, the NCVS reported approximately twice as many crimes as the UCR did (23 million compared to 12 million).[3] This trend supports the rule of thumb that about half of the crimes committed in the United States go unreported. Criminologists (sociologists who study crime) often use both UCR and NCVS data.

UCR data are useful as a source for reliable and timely statistics on crimes reported to law enforcement agencies nationwide (especially homicides), and NCVS data are useful as a source for information on the characteristics of criminal victimization and the details behind unreported crimes.[4]

Crime Demographics

Who are criminals? Are they mainly men or women? Are they typically teenagers or middle-aged adults? Do they generally belong to a certain social class or race? Criminals, of course, come in all different ages, classes, and colors, but some are more common than others. Crime demographics can give law enforcement officials some insight into who is committing what kinds of crimes.

AGE

The majority of criminal behavior occurs when a perpetrator is between the ages of 15 and 25. After the age of 25, criminal behavior becomes less and less likely to occur throughout life.[5] The age/crime relationship is important to consider when developing target audiences for crime prevention programs. In fact, this demographic factor may be the most important aspect in predicting the rise and fall of crime rates in the United States. For example, Steffensmeier and Harer showed that the majority of the decline in crime rates in the early 1980s could be directly related to one factor, namely a lower percentage of 15- to 25-year-old men in the population.[6]

Of course, the type of crime correlates to the age of those who are most likely to commit it. For example, white-collar criminals who are caught tend to be older. Why? If you consider a crime such as embezzlement, it becomes clear. Generally speaking, it takes a number of years for a person to gain access to money on the job. Therefore, a new hire directly out of college is unlikely to have the ability to steal from an employer, whereas a person with a few years of work experience has the specialized

America's 10 Most Dangerous Cities
(ranked by number of violent crimes per 10,000 people)

Rank	City	Crimes
1	Detroit, MI	1,220
2	Memphis, TN	1,218
3	Miami, FL	988
4	Las Vegas, NV	887
5	Stockton, CA	885
6	Orlando, FL	845
7	Little Rock, AR	831
8	Charleston, SC	824
9	Nashville, TN	817
10	Baltimore, MD	791

Source: Zack O'Malley Greenburg, "America's Most Dangerous Cities," *Forbes*, April 23, 2009. Rankings are based on violent crime statistics from the FBI's latest uniform crime report, issued in 2008.

∧
∧ **Why might crime rates be greater in some
∧ cities** than in others?

access needed to commit this type of crime.[7]

GENDER

Historically, crime has been a male-dominated activity. In fact, 77 percent of people arrested are men, as are 90 percent of inmates in U.S. state and federal prisons.[8] When you consider that men make up less than half of the population in the United States, these statistics are even more startling.[9] Of course, these differences are fluid; the number of female inmates in the United States is growing steadily. According to the Bureau of Justice statistics, 2007 showed a 1.2 percent increase in the number of incarcerated women, whereas the number of incarcerated males only increased by 0.7 percent.[10]

RACE

More so than with any other demographic, the relationship between race and crime has been very controversial. Due to a long history of racial inequality in the United States, many questions can be raised regarding the legitimacy of statistics. For example, African Americans represent approximately 12 percent of the population, yet they account for 27 percent of the arrests in the United States.[11]

Minorities certainly hold more negative views of the police and criminal justice system than do whites. They are more likely to be victims of police brutality, and also much more likely to perceive police actions as racially motivated.[12]

Is this because minorities see something that whites don't see, or do they simply perceive the system to be unfair? Criminologists suggest that this statistic may be skewed due to the practice of

United States: Low on Theft, High on Murder

The United States prides itself on being the land of freedom and opportunity, but does more freedom result in more opportunity for violent crime? Out of all modern and industrialized nations, the United States consistently has the highest murder rate. Some say this is due to Americans' comparatively easy access to guns or our lenient legal system. Others argue that the history of inequality in the United States has fueled violent behavior. Regardless of the reason, the startling statistic remains: U.S. citizens are three times more likely to be murdered than Canadians, and 10 times more likely to be murdered than people in Japan.[18]

However, murder aside, the United States has relatively lower crime rates. The United States does not lead the world in violent crimes such as robbery, assault, and rape, and has fewer instances of nonviolent crimes than several other developed countries. Theft, for example, is more common in Germany, France, and England, and there are more motor vehicles stolen in England, France, and Canada.

All in all, when it comes to crime, the United States is a mixed bag. Compared to other developed countries, a U.S. citizen is more likely to be murdered, but less likely to have his or her possessions stolen.[19] Unfortunately, crime is common in all industrial societies, due, in part, to the spread of high-value, portable goods that can be stolen and easily sold.[20] To put it simply, the more possessions people have, the more can be taken away.

∨
∨ **The United States has the highest murder rate of all modern industrialized nations.**
∨ What factors might play a role in this?

Homicide* Rates (per 100,000 people)

Country	Rate
Canada	1.86
Egypt	0.59
England and Wales	1.41
Germany	0.88
India	2.82
Italy	1.06
Lebanon	0.57
Netherlands	0.97
Singapore	0.39
United States	5.62

*Homicide is defined as "death deliberately inflicted on a person by another person, including infanticide."

Source: "Tenth United Nations Survey of Crime Trends and Operations of Criminal Justice Systems, covering the period 2005–2006" United Nation Office on Drugs and Crime. Accessed September 28, 2009, http://www.indexmundi.com/blog/index.php/category/crime/

racial profiling—the act of using race to determine whether a person is likely to have committed a crime. In the book *No Equal Justice: Race and Class in the American Criminal Justice System*, author David Cole cites a report from a Florida county that revealed that although 95 percent of residents were white, 70 percent of drivers stopped by the police were African American and, in some cases, Latino. The statistic was developed from over 148 hours of police videotape.[13] These findings give support to the claim that "driving while black" is considered a criminal offense in some areas. In addition, minorities tend to be poorer and may live in neighborhoods where crime is more frequent. Such areas also attract more police surveillance.[14]

SOCIOECONOMIC STATUS

Just as race can be linked to crime, so can social class. Sociologists have been studying the relationship between crime and social class for many years. In general, one can find a direct correlation between those who are caught and a lower social class. Why? Author Jeffrey Reiman suggests that there are more crimes reported in deprived areas due to the fact that poor people are easier to catch and convict and lack access to the same resources that the affluent do. Furthermore, at every step of the criminal justice system, the wealthy are weeded out by a system of bail, public defenders, and plea bargains that all work in their favor.[15] For example, in the case of a criminal trial, a wealthy man can afford to hire an experienced—and expensive—lawyer who has the time and resources to provide an exceptional defense. An indigent man may need to rely on the legal services of a court-appointed attorney who has a full caseload and very little time to develop an adequate defense.

∧ ∧ ∧ The phrase "driving while black" refers to the **disproportionate number of African Americans** who get **pulled over by traffic police.**

Media and Crime

Crime is sensational; it scares, enrages, and intrigues people; that is why it can be so entertaining. CBS crime dramas (*NCIS*, *The Mentalist*, *CSI: Miami*, and *CSI: New York*) dominate Nielsen's list of top 10 TV programs week after week.[16] These TV shows, however, do not usually portray an accurate depiction of crime or crime solving. Television police shows add exaggerated details that make viewers think that most crime is dangerous, tense, and provocative. Criminologist Marcus Felson refers to this trend as the "dramatic fallacy" of crime because the offenses most publicized by the media are far more dramatic than those typically found in real life, leading viewers to develop a misperception of crime. This is particularly true when it comes to murder. Murders account for less than 1 percent of violent crimes and an even smaller percentage of overall crime, yet murder is the offense most commonly portrayed in television shows.

Even when a real-life crime occurs, media outlets tend to use it as a ratings boost to entertain the public and keep them watching.[17] In 2008, for example, news media outlets dedicated significant amounts of airtime to cover the investigation of Caylee Anthony, a toddler from Orlando, Florida, who was thought to have been murdered by her young mother. The media's constant use of Caylee's heart-wrenching picture and the continuous coverage of the horrific details generated public interest in the story, but also provided a very unrealistic view of crime. Real crime, such as when someone steals your iPod from your car or shoplifts from the local 7-Eleven, isn't much of a story.

think social problems: WHAT MOTIVATES CRIMINAL BEHAVIOR?

Psychological Perspectives on Crime

Are people who commit crimes mentally ill? Stanton Samenow proposes that criminals think differently than noncriminals. They tend to engage in chronic lying (even to themselves), view others' property as their own, and have an inflated self-image.[21] The American Psychiatric Association claims that criminals are antisocial and unable to conform to the norms of society.[22] Criminals are impulsive, aggressive, and irritable; they deceive often and feel no remorse for their actions.

THEORY OF ANOMIE suggests that criminal activity results from an offender's inability to provide his or her desired needs by socially acceptable or legal means; therefore, the individual turns to socially unacceptable or illegal means to fulfill those desires.

SOCIAL DISORGANIZATION THEORY proposes that poor neighborhoods with weak social institutions have higher rates of crime.

DIFFERENTIAL ASSOCIATION THEORY claims that criminal activity is a learned behavior and that the people with whom we interact influence this learning process.

SOCIAL LEARNING THEORY suggests that learning is the key component to criminality.

SOCIAL CONTROL THEORIES suggest that people are self-interested, and these natural traits can prompt criminal activity.

CONTAINMENT THEORY argues that criminals cannot resist the temptations that surround them.

SOCIAL CONFLICT THEORIES typically focus on issues of social class, power, capitalism, and their relation to crime.

GENERAL STRAIN THEORY suggests that people experience strain from different sources, which results in criminal activity.

Sociological Explanations for Crime

FUNCTIONALIST THEORIES

French social scientist Emile Durkheim noted that crime is always present in society and therefore must serve some function. He suggested that crime provides a clear moral contrast between what is right and what is wrong, which helps unify society. After the September 11th attacks on United States, Americans banded together; as Durkheim noted, crime unites people in the fight against it. Of course, crime can also bring about social revolution. When civil rights leaders broke the law by sitting in "whites only" restaurants, they helped society make necessary, overdue changes.

>>> From a psychological perspective, **isolation from society and inability to conform to the behavior of one's peers can cause criminal behavior.**

American sociologist Robert K. Merton suggests that social factors play a role in criminality. His **theory of anomie** argues that criminal activity results from an offender's inability to achieve certain goals. Americans, he claims, have universal goals, and when a person has little or no access to legitimate means of achieving these, he or she may turn to crime. As poor people tend to be arrested the most, Merton suggests there is a structural problem in America—namely that poor people are blocked from achieving goals they believe they should be able to reach. The individual then turns to socially unacceptable or illegal means to fulfill those desires.[23] For instance, if a person can't afford to purchase a new laptop computer, he or she might steal one.

Structural theories also include **social disorganization theory**, which proposes that poor neighborhoods with weak social institutions have higher rates of crime. In other words, neighborhoods with few social structures such as schools, churches, businesses, and youth centers tend to be the areas where crime is most prevalent.[24] Often, residents of those areas live in poorly maintained rental properties, and there are few opportunities for legitimate work. The combination of these factors leads to social disorganization, and social disorganization leads to crime.[25]

SYMBOLIC INTERACTIONIST THEORIES

The **differential association theory**, developed by American criminologist Edwin Sutherland, claims that criminal activity is a learned behavior that stems from the people with whom we interact. This theory was developed to explain why some juveniles become criminals, and others don't. Sutherland suggests that the more a person associates with delinquents, the more likely it is that the person will learn criminal behavior because he or she is surrounded by an excess of definitions that favor violation of the law. For example, if a teenage boy has friends who shoplift, they are likely to tell him that stealing is OK. The more he hangs out with those friends, the more likely the boy is to participate in similar criminal activity.[26]

Social learning theory, as described by criminologist Ronald Akers, combines these ideas with the teachings of psychologist Albert Bandura, and suggests that learning is the key component of criminality. People learn all kinds of things, from aggression and violence to kindness and peace. Children learn to be aggressive because this behavior has been modeled for them.[27] Akers notes that social learning comes about in the same way as other types of learning—from being enforced.

Potential "learning experiences" can come from those closest to us, such as our parents or peer group, but from other interpersonal interactions as well, such as media.

SOCIAL CONTROL THEORIES

Social control theories claim that people are self-interested, and that these natural traits can prompt criminal activity. According to Walter Reckless, criminality is influenced by both internal and external forces. Internal forces include a sense of morality and knowledge of right and wrong. External forces are factors such as police presence. His **containment theory** argues that criminals cannot resist the temptations that surround them. Since they have low levels of internal control, there is nothing to prevent their illegal behavior.

Criminologist Travis Hirschi tends to agree with Reckless, but

∧
∧ **Everyday responsibilities** such as going to work or school
∧ make us less likely to commit crimes.

suggests that there is more complexity to the internal controls. He theorizes that there are four social bonds that affect personal restraint: attachment, commitment, involvement, and belief. People who lack these social bonds often become involved in criminal behavior.

Attachment, the first bond described by Hirschi, refers to our relationship with others. A teenager with law-abiding friends is not as likely to become involved in criminal behavior as a teenager whose friends often get into trouble. Strong attachments to social conformity lead to low likelihoods of criminal activity.

The second bond, commitment, refers to our dedication to live a socially acceptable life. By showing up to a job every day, a person is behaving in a socially responsible way. People tend to become more socially responsible as they age, which explains why young people tend to commit more crimes than older people.

Involvement, the third of Hirschi's bonds, refers to participating in conventional activities. As you'll continue to see later in this chapter, teens who participate in extracurricular activities are less likely to become involved in criminal behavior. The final bond, belief, refers to a person's dedication and conviction. People who believe that living a conventional life is good will continue to do so, making them less likely to resort to criminal behavior.

CONFLICT THEORY

Social conflict theories typically focus on how issues of social class, power, and capitalism relate to crime. Dutch criminologist Willem Bonger believes that capitalism causes crime because it encourages people to be egoistic and selfish. Since capitalism runs on competition that pits citizens against one another, winners and losers are inevitable, creating a conflict in society that the poor cannot win. Some will enter this struggle

with clear resentment for the rich, and will turn to crime as a way to combat social injustice.[28]

Jeffrey Reiman points out that capitalism creates a system in which actions of the rich are not considered criminal, yet actions of the poor are. For example, consider the obvious fact that it's illegal to murder someone. A poor man who kills a coworker in a fight may receive a death sentence; however, if a mine owner is warned about unsafe working conditions but chooses to do nothing, causing the mine to eventually collapse and kill workers, no one is considered to have been "murdered." Reiman points out that white-collar crimes often work exactly this way. In reality, you are far more likely to die in a work accident or during an unnecessary medical procedure than you are to be murdered. To put it bluntly, your boss and/or your doctor are more likely to kill you than a stranger, and yet whom do you fear?[29] Bernie Madoff swindled thousands of investors, and his victims willingly handed their money to him. Why? Because they perceived him as an expert, and he used that perception to perpetrate one of the biggest frauds in U.S. history. Bonger suggests that such things happen because capitalism creates egoism, whereby people do not care about others, and the ends (obtaining wealth) justify the means.

GENERAL THEORIES OF CRIME CAUSATION

In 1985, Robert Agnew proposed a theory that that stems from Merton's concept of anomie. According to Agnew's **general strain theory**, strains from society lead people to perform criminal activity. A person experiences strain from three sources: First, from individual goals or needs. As Merton argues, if a person is not able to achieve her goals in

Sociological Theories of Criminal Behavior

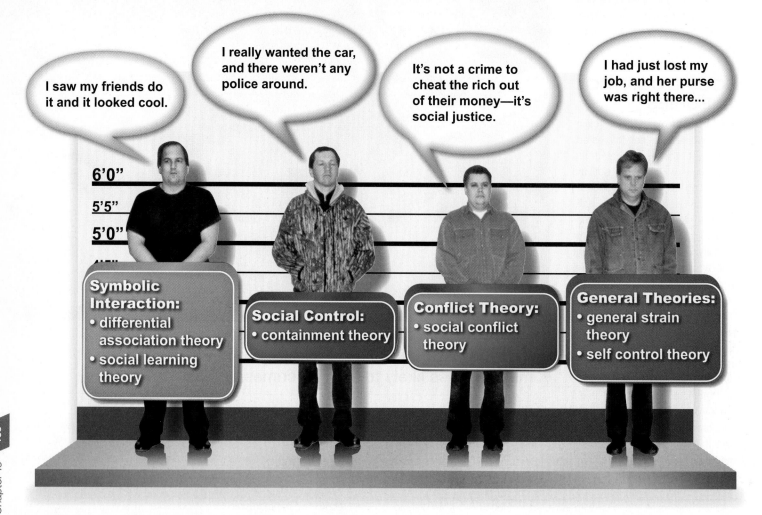

Sociologists differ in their opinions on the cause of crime. Which view do you favor?

MAKE CONNECTIONS

Crime and Society

In this chapter we discussed some of the possible reasons why people commit crimes. Socioeconomic status certainly plays a role. Think back to Chapter 2 and the discussion of inequality, poverty, and wealth. As the disparity between the upper class and the lower class continues to grow in the United States, more and more people from impoverished backgrounds might turn to criminal behavior.

As we've mentioned, crime is a male-dominated activity. Statistically, 77 percent of people arrested are men, and criminal behavior is most likely to occur between the ages of 15 and 25. Therefore, countries with a larger percentage of young men in their population tend to have higher crime rates. Chapter 18 will explore population and demographics and how these factors affect a country's economy and society.

In this chapter we also discussed how criminal behavior might be prevented before it begins. But the truth of the matter is that we can't always head off criminal behavior at the pass. So, once a person has committed a crime, what are some ways to prevent him or her from doing it again? In the next chapter we will explore other ways to control crime, with a focus on deterring criminal behavior through harsh sentencing practices.

life, she is more likely to turn to crime. Second, strain can result from unpleasant life events, such as the loss of a job or the death of a loved one. Finally, a person might suffer strain from negative experiences such as abuse and pain. All or any of these strains can cause a person to engage in criminal behavior if he or she does not have sufficient coping skills. People who learn to cope with stress, on the other hand, are less likely to turn to crime.[30]

Another general theory of crime, proposed by Michael Gottfredson and Travis Hirschi, states that criminals simply lack self-control. Often referred to as self-control theory, it suggests that criminals are not able to delay gratification, so they seek short-term rewards at the expense of long-term consequences. Most crimes involve spur-of-the-moment decisions; a criminal sees a chance to rob you because you're walking alone late at night in a dark parking lot. The thought that you might be an armed police officer or have a black belt in karate never enters his mind. In short, criminals lack the ability to consider the "what ifs." Most people learn this form of self-control from their parents. Thus, according to Gottfredson and Hirschi, criminals are raised by people who fail to teach the importance of rejecting short-term, brief rewards in favor of more pleasurable long-term ones.[31]

discover solutions to social problems:
HOW CAN WE PREVENT CRIME AMONG YOUTH?

As crime statistics have noted, many lawbreakers are young—most street criminals are between 15 and 25 years old. That's why keeping children out of trouble is an important part of preventing crime. But how can we do this?

After-school programs or other extracurricular activities have been shown to be effective. Author Ralph McNeal investigated the effects of extracurricular activities and found that these activities help students increase their personal skills, personal traits, personal achievement, and knowledge. In addition, students learn more about culture by becoming involved in art, sports, and music. Finally, these activities help students gain social skills by allowing them to extend their social network, as well as their access to various adults who supervise. In all of these ways, students become a part of something constructive and find that they are better able to connect with the people around them, making them less likely to get involved in criminal behavior.[32]

However, before we attempt to use extracurricular activities as a method to prevent crime, we must consider who is likely to participate in these activities. Youth from higher socioeconomic status homes are more likely to be involved, but race has no effect at all.[33] In fact, racial minorities have the same participation rates as their white classmates. Both genders are also equally involved in extracurriculars; boys are more likely to participate in athletics, but girls are more commonly found in all other types of activities. Thus, the findings present a mixed picture. Although socioeconomic status does play a role, race and gender do not.

Other studies have found that school size and safety have a significant effect on extracurricular activities. Students from small schools are more likely to participate in activities than students from big schools, because there's less competition. Think about it—if you're in a school of 90 people, it's a lot easier to make the baseball team than if you are in a school with 900 students. In addition, schools with high rates of violence usually have less extracurricular participation. This makes sense—students are less likely to take part in after-school activities if they're worried about their safety.[34]

Pro & Con

Gun Control

The issue of gun control is extremely controversial. Many people feel that it is their personal right to protect themselves with a weapon, whereas others believe that guns are the source of crime. As you know, the United States is the leader in murder rates in the industrialized world, and guns provide an effective and efficient way to kill another person. What do you think—should we have stricter gun control?

Pro

- There is no obvious constitutional right allowing individuals to carry guns. The U.S. Constitution guarantees states' rights of militia, which is a significantly outdated clause.

- Crime has not decreased in states with concealed weapons laws.

- Other similar countries with strict gun controls have lower homicide rates.

- Most gun homicides occur among family members during heated disputes.

Con

- The Constitution grants "the right of the people" to bear arms, not merely militia.

- People who are armed can defend themselves from crime. As the saying goes, "If guns are outlawed, only the outlaws will have guns."

- It would be nearly impossible to confiscate all the guns in the country if personal firearms were made illegal.

- Guns themselves aren't responsible for violence; if they were seized, those who used them hostilely would simply find other weapons.

WRAP YOUR MIND AROUND THE THEORY

According to conflict theory, people's socioeconomic status affects how the law treats them. Do you feel that wealthy individuals get away with committing crimes because of their social class?

CONFLICT THEORY

Criminologist Willem Bonger contends that capitalism encourages crime because it endorses self-serving behavior and creates a culture in which people do what is best for them instead of what's best for society as a whole. Because of capitalism, certain people have more wealth and power than others. This leads some to feel justified in participating in criminal activity in an attempt to balance out the wealth.

FUNCTIONALISM

Functionalists point out that crime is and always has been a part of society. Therefore, crime must serve some social function. According to Merton, crime occurs because some people are not able to attain all of their needs and desires through legal means; the theory of anomie suggests that they then try to attain those things through illegal means.

HOW CAN YOU PREVENT CRIME?

SYMBOLIC INTERACTIONISM

Symbolic interactionism suggests that crime is learned through a process of socializing with others. Delinquent peers teach criminal behavior to their friends by providing both justification for breaking the law and the means by which to do it. By interacting with criminals, people learn that criminality is OK.

The American dream is not easily attainable for some. Is it ever acceptable for people to fulfill their needs through illegal means?

Symbolic interactionists suggest that people learn criminal behavior from those around them. Children can be influenced by their parents and peers. What can our society do to stop the cycle of crime?

Calvin had always been a pretty average kid; he lived with his mother in a small neighborhood in the suburbs, did fairly well in school, and was the goalie for his middle school ice hockey team. During the middle of eighth grade, however, Calvin found himself getting into a lot of trouble. Many of his crimes were petty: curfew violation, public disturbance, and minor vandalism. But one evening, Calvin and his friends broke into a neighbor's garage and stole two bicycles and $500 worth of tools. The kids were caught for the crime, and when the police asked Calvin why he did it, all he could say was "I don't know. I was bored." That was Calvin's answer every time he got in trouble for something.

As punishment, the court ordered Calvin to participate in 100 hours of community service. He was assigned to work in a community garden where he spent a few hours after school weeding, watering, and organizing produce that was donated to local food banks.

After a few months, Calvin's court-ordered time was complete, but that didn't stop him from working in the garden—he'd come to enjoy it. His time spent there made Calvin realize that having something to do after school kept him out of trouble and made him feel like he was helping society, even if only in a small way.

Realizing that his old friends and a lot of other kids could stay out of trouble if they had something to do after school, Calvin decided to contact his school board administrators and ask about developing an after-school volunteer program for students. Calvin proposed a no-cost program that paired kids with local charities for a few hours each week. Calvin explained that this would give students something productive to do after school and help the community at the same time.

The school board liked Calvin's idea. They had wanted to initiate a community service program for many years, but could never find funds in the budget. The school kicked off the program, appropriately named Calvin's Volunteer Corps, the following semester. Its inaugural year was a success; more than one third of the student body and a few faculty members signed up, and local police reported a 25-percent drop in complaints and citations involving school-aged children.

>>> **Extracurricular activities** keep children occupied, making them **less likely to participate in criminal activity.**

HOW IS CRIME A SOCIAL PROBLEM?   182

characteristics such as gender, race, age, and ethnicity do not make people predisposed to criminal activity, but they can affect the level of influence crime has in their lives

WHAT MOTIVATES CRIMINAL BEHAVIOR?   185

there are several schools of thought that explain the motivation behind criminal behavior; they include internal influences, such as a lack of self-control, as well as external influences, such as social class and peer groups

HOW CAN WE PREVENT CRIME AMONG YOUTH?   189

extracurricular activities allow children to occupy themselves with legal and productive interests, giving them less time and motivation to participate in illegal behaviors

get the topic: HOW IS CRIME A SOCIAL PROBLEM?

Theory

SYMBOLIC INTERACTIONISM   186

- social learning theories propose that the criminal behaviors of family and peers condone criminal behavior in younger generations
- people are riotous and self-interested, and these natural traits can prompt criminal activity

CONFLICT THEORY   187

- the mind-set behind capitalism inherently leads to crime
- individuals from lower social classes may feel they need to commit crimes to fulfill their basic needs

FUNCTIONALISM   186

- crime is a permanent fixture in society, and therefore must serve some function
- crime occurs because some people are not able to attain all of their needs and desires through legal means, so they try to attain those things through illegal means

Key Terms

crime is the violation of norms that have been written into law.   182

violent crime is an illegal act committed against another person.   182

nonviolent crime is an illegal act committed against property.   182

criminology is the scientific study of crime, deviance, and social policies that the criminal justice system applies.   182

Uniform Crime Reports (UCR) include data from official police statistics of reported crimes gathered from police reports and paperwork.   182

crime index is made up of eight offenses used to measure crime: homicide, rape, robbery, aggravated assault, burglary, larceny-theft, motor vehicle theft, and arson.   182

National Crime Victimization Survey (NCVS) is the measurement of crime victimization based on contact with a representative sample of over 70,000 households in the United States.   182

racial profiling refers to the act of using race to determine whether a person is likely to have committed a crime.   185

theory of anomie suggests that criminal activity results from an offender's inability to provide his or her desired needs by socially acceptable or legal means; therefore, the individual turns to socially unacceptable or illegal means to fulfill those desires.   186

social disorganization theory proposes that poor neighborhoods with weak social institutions have higher rates of crime.   186

differential association theory claims that criminal activity is a learned behavior and that the people with whom we interact influence this learning process.   186

social learning theory suggests that learning is the key component to criminality.   186

social control theories suggest that people are self-interested, and these natural traits can prompt criminal activity.   187

containment theory argues that criminals cannot resist the temptations that surround them.   187

social conflict theories typically focus on issues of social class, power, capitalism, and their relation to crime.   187

general strain theory suggests that people experience strain from different sources, which results in criminal activity.   187

Sample Test Questions

These multiple-choice questions are similar to those found in the test bank that accompanies this textbook.

1. Which of the following is considered a nonviolent crime?

   a. Murder
   b. Assault
   c. Auto theft
   d. Armed robbery

2. What is the primary difference between the UCR and NCVS?

   a. The UCR records violent crimes; the NCVS records nonviolent crimes.
   b. The NCVS records violent crimes; the UCR records nonviolent crimes.
   c. The UCR records unreported crimes; the NCVS records reported crimes.
   d. The NCVS records unreported crimes; the UCR records reported crimes.

3. Which theory suggests that neighborhoods cause delinquency?

   a. Social disorganization theory
   b. Theory of anomie
   c. Violent crime theory
   d. General strain theory

4. According to social conflict theories, why does capitalism cause crime?

   a. It encourages racial segregation.
   b. It allows for too much government control.
   c. It creates a competitive system that can be unfairly balanced.
   d. It does not allow citizens to act on free will.

5. Students are more likely to participate in extracurricular activities if they are in a(n)

   a. large school.
   b. small school.
   c. urban school.
   d. rural school.

ESSAY

1. Between age, gender, race, and social class, which characteristic do you feel influences criminal activity the most? Why?

2. Why do you think the media focus so much on violent crimes such as murder?

3. Do you agree with social learning theory? Do you think that you can learn criminal behavior from an external source, such as television?

4. What are your thoughts on gun control? In your opinion, what are the pros and cons of gun ownership?

5. Think about a criminal activity you witnessed in real life or saw on the news. What do you feel influenced the behavior? What could have prevented it?

WHERE TO START YOUR RESEARCH PAPER

For U.S. Census facts and information, go to http://www.census.gov

To gather statistics from the Uniform Crime Reports, go to http://www.fbi.gov/ucr/ucr.htm

To read about Bernie Madoff and the motives behind similar crimes, visit http://www.nytimes.com/2009/01/25/business/25bernie.html

To learn more about the (un)reliability of criminal justice reporting, see http://www.jjay.cuny.edu/cmcj/x.asp

For more on the National Crime Victimization Survey, go to http://www.ojp.usdoj.gov/bjs/pub/html/ntcm.htm#ncvs

For more information on the concept of "driving while black," check out http://www.nytimes.com/2009/06/15/opinion/15mon4.html

ANSWERS: 1. c; 2. d; 3. a; 4. c; 5. b

Remember to check www.thethinkspot.com for additional information, downloadable flashcards, and other helpful resources.

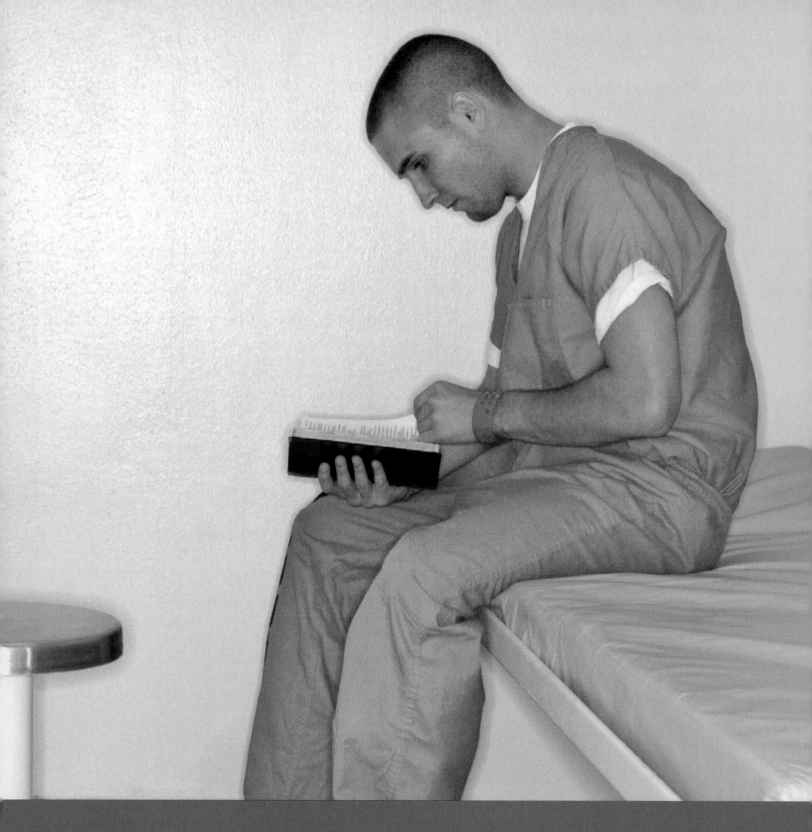

CRIMINAL JUSTICE

New

measures aimed at reducing prison rapes are in the works—and states that fail to take steps to protect their inmates could see their federal money cut.

The new standards were proposed . . . by the National Prison Rape Elimination Commission, a bipartisan panel that spent five years studying the issue. It's estimated that about 60,000 inmates are sexually abused each year.

With more than 7.3 million people behind bars or on parole and probation in the United States, the report said jails and prisons should take a series of steps to eliminate sexual abuse of inmates. Those steps include the adoption of zero-tolerance policies, better staff training, and improved screening to identify prisoners vulnerable to abuse.

"Individuals who are incarcerated have basic human rights," said U.S. District Judge Reggie Walton, chairman of the commission. "Just because they've committed a crime and they're incarcerated does not mean that their human dignity can be abused."

The proposed standards are being sent to Attorney General Eric Holder, who has a year to write national standards. States will be notified of the finalized standards and then must adopt them or risk losing 5 percent of any federal prison grant money.

Some of the report's key findings:

- Inmates who are short, young, gay, or female were more likely to be victimized than other inmates.

- Even when inmates are willing to report abuse, their accounts are not always taken seriously and reported to appropriate officials.

. . . The study found that 4.5 percent of those surveyed reported being sexually abused in the previous 12 months.

That study also said more prisoners reported abuse by staff than by other prisoners: 2.9 percent to about 2 percent, respectively.

The commission's report recommended that prison authorities adopt more internal monitoring, such as video cameras, as well as external oversight by review boards . . .

James Gondles Jr., executive director of the American Correctional Association, said he's optimistic that "we can get something that's workable." But Gondles said he's concerned that county jails, which have fewer resources than prisons, may not have the money to implement some proposals, such as adding staff for mental health treatment of abuse victims.

At the commission's news conference Tuesday, Hope Hernandez told a crowded room of her ordeal in a Washington D.C. jail in the late 90s when the then-23-year old was awaiting trial on drug charges.

After begging for a shower for two weeks, Hernandez said a corrections officer showed up one night with a towel and shampoo to take her for a shower. She said he led her to the shower, where he raped her.

"Rape must never be part of the penalty," said Hernandez, a mother of two who later earned a master's degree in social work.

His punishment, she said, was a seven-day suspension with pay before being returned to duty.[1]

195

CHAPTER 14

---Laws are necessary for society. When a law is broken, a punishment must be served, or the law is meaningless.

The type of punishment, its duration, and its severity draws much debate. Is it "justice" for a small-time drug dealer to experience rape in prison? Does the amount of money we spend on incarceration actually make our communities safer? Should the legal system focus on rehabilitation or discipline? In this chapter, we will investigate some of the social problems that result from the United States' criminal justice system.

get the topic: HOW DO SOCIETIES RESPOND TO CRIME?

> **CONSENSUS MODEL OF LAW** suggests that laws arise because people see a behavior they do not like, and agree to make it illegal.
>
> **CONFLICT MODEL OF LAW** proposes that powerful people write laws and, in doing so, tend to protect their own interests.
>
> **SHAMING** is a deliberate effort to attach a negative meaning to a behavior.

Creation of the Law

Clear expectations of behavior are essential for a functioning society, so it's not surprising that all societies have created laws. The purpose of a legal code is universal: to define illegal actions and outline penalties for those acts.

CONSENSUS AND CONFLICT MODELS

There are two primary models describing how laws are created: consensus and conflict. The **consensus model of law** suggests that laws arise because people see a behavior they do not like and agree to make it illegal. For example, most people believe that murder is wrong, so they support laws against it; however, what is considered "murder" is not that clear-cut. Some believe that any form of killing is wrong, while others suggest that acts of self-defense or war are exceptions. The consensus model does not require complete assent by everyone, but certainly by most.

The **conflict model of law** proposes that powerful people write laws, and in doing so, tend to protect their own interests. Often these laws punish the actions of those without much power. For example, in 2000, a man named Gary Ewing stole three golf clubs and, because of California's Three Strikes law, he was convicted of felony grand theft and sentenced to 25 years to life.[3] However, when a white-collar criminal—such as someone who engages in insider trading—receives a sentence, it is often much lower.[4] "When New York stock broker Joseph Nacchio, was found guilty of fraud totaling

$52 million, he was given a sentence of 6 years—a sentence that recently has been overturned and will soon be decreased because it was seen as too harsh. The conflict approach suggests that this disparity in justice is linked to a perpetrator's wealth or position in society.

PUNISHMENT

Historically, punishments for crimes were often harsh, resulting in physical torture, exile, forced slavery, or death. Sometimes, offenders were shamed in the pillory and stocks in a town square. **Shaming** is a deliberate effort to attach a negative meaning to a behavior. John Braithwaite suggests that shame can either stigma-

∧ Developed between 2100 and 1800 BCE, **The Code of Hammurabi is the first known written legal system.** It contains more than 200 laws and **describes the requirements for behavior** as well as **punishments for violations.**[2]

tize or reintegrate.[5] **Stigmatized shame** is a permanent label given to an offender, which actually increases the likelihood of reoffending because the guilty person is labeled forever. In the United States, former inmates must admit to prior convictions on job and housing applications, and those convicted of sexual offenses must register as sex offenders. Although these regulations are in the interest of public safety, this stigmatized shame means that those people can never escape the negative label, no matter what they do. On the other hand, **reintegrative shaming** allows the offender to reconnect to society after punishment without further stigma. Such a system can include punishments such as restitution, community service, and prison. Our criminal justice system accommodates both types of shaming.

Overall, the criminal justice system relies on **deterrence**, which prevents a person from doing something out of fear of the consequences. There are two types of deterrence: specific and general. **Specific deterrence** seeks to prevent a particular offender from committing that crime again. **General deterrence** seeks to prevent others from committing crimes by making an example of a particular offender.

The U.S. Criminal Justice System

There are three branches of the criminal justice system: police, courts, and corrections. Certain individuals within each branch may differ in opinions and exercise individual measures of discretion, leading to social problems such as racial profiling, unequal sentencing, and increased costs for the community.

POLICE

Today, there are more than 18,000 law enforcement agencies in the United States.[6] Within these agencies, there are more than 800,000 full-time sworn law enforcement officers.[7] TV programs such as *COPS* show police officers on the frontlines fighting crime; however, real police work is rarely like what is portrayed on television. In reality, an officer's job is best described as "hour upon hour of boredom, interrupted by moments of sheer terror."[8] Although you may feel as though a policeman's primary job is to protect you, studies show that police directly protect society less than 1 percent of the time. In fact, studies of increased police numbers show very little impact on crime rates. Instead, researchers find that techniques such as **target hardening**, making an objective less attractive to a possible criminal, are more likely to have positive effects on crime rates. Thus, putting an alarm on your house is more likely to decrease the odds of your being a victim of crime than the city hiring more police officers.[9]

Police officers have the initial **discretion**, or the ability to make decisions, on whether or not a crime has occurred. Police often use their discretion when they frequent so-called "hot-spots"—areas they regularly patrol because they believe they will find criminal activity there.[10] Usually these neighborhoods are poor areas, thereby increasing the odds that poor people will be caught.[11] This kind of discretion perpetuates inequality in the system, as does racial profiling, which occurs when police target certain groups based on race. Racial profiling increases the odds that minority criminals will get caught and makes it less likely that white criminals will be brought to justice.[12]

STIGMATIZED SHAME is a permanent label given to an offender.

REINTEGRATIVE SHAMING is a punishment that allows the offender to reconnect to society after punishment without further stigma.

DETERRENCE is a measure that prevents a person from doing something out of fear of the consequences.

SPECIFIC DETERRENCE is a type of criminal sentencing that seeks to prevent a particular offender from committing that crime again.

GENERAL DETERRENCE is a type of criminal sentencing that seeks to prevent others from committing crimes by making an example of an offender.

TARGET HARDENING makes an objective less attractive to a possible criminal.

DISCRETION is the ability to make decisions.

JUDGE is an elected or appointed public official who presides over the court of law.

PROSECUTING ATTORNEY is an attorney whose official duty is to conduct criminal proceedings on behalf of the state or the people against those accused of committing criminal offenses.

PLEA BARGAINS are out-of-court agreements between the prosecutor and defense attorney that often involve concessions by the prosecution to obtain a guilty plea.

DEFENSE COUNSEL consists of attorneys hired or appointed by the court to provide a legal defense for the accused.

COURTS

After an arrest is made, the individual enters the court system. A **judge** is an elected or appointed public official who presides over a court of law. The court system consists of two opposing camps, prosecutors and defendants, and the judge's role is to ensure that the proceedings are held in accordance with the legal system. Judges exercise discretion over what should and should not be admitted into the case; they may also have power over the outcome, depending on the state and situation.

The **prosecuting attorney**'s official duty is to conduct criminal proceedings on behalf of the state or the plaintiffs. This attorney is often elected or works for an elected district attorney. In the court system, no one has more discretion than the prosecuting attorney. After a person is arrested, it is the district attorney's office that decides what the official charges are. For example, they can change an attempted rape charge into an assault merely by looking at the evidence and deciding that there is not enough proof to prove rape. They also have the greatest amount of power to accept **plea bargains**, which are out-of-court agreements between the prosecutor and defense attorney that often involve concessions by the prosecution to obtain a guilty plea. Approximately 89 percent of cases end with a plea bargain, and often the concession is a reduced sentence.[13]

On the opposite side of the courtroom sits the **defense counsel**, attorneys hired or appointed by the court to provide a legal defense for the accused. The right to a defense attorney is part of a suspect's Miranda rights and guaranteed by the court. There is a great disparity among the types of defense counsels, however. Private attorneys who specialize in criminal law and provide good results for their clients are often costly, whereas public defenders who are paid to provide defense services to indigent people tend to have large caseloads. Data show that conviction rates, including plea bargains, are much higher for public

AGGRAVATING CIRCUMSTANCES are circumstances relating to the commission of an act that increase the degree of liability or responsibility of the person committing the act.

MITIGATING CIRCUMSTANCES are circumstances in the commission of an act that decrease the degree of criminal responsibility of the person committing the act.

INDETERMINATE SENTENCING is a model of criminal punishment that allows the judge and the corrections system a great deal of discretion in the length of the sentence.

STRUCTURED SENTENCING is a model of criminal punishment in which the legislative system of a state enacts constraints on judicial discretion in determining criminal sentences.

GOOD TIME is the amount of time deducted from a prison sentence for good behavior.

GAIN TIME is the amount of time deducted from a prison sentence for participation in special programs.

TRUTH IN SENTENCING is legislation that is aimed at abolishing or limiting parole so that inmates serve a set majority of their sentence.

MANDATORY SENTENCING is a structured sentencing strategy that allows for no discretion on the part of the judge.

defenders versus private attorneys. Therefore, the poor, who usually end up with public defenders, are more likely to be convicted than the rich, who can afford private attorneys.[14]

Sentencing

Assuming that the accused is either convicted or pleads guilty, that person must now be sentenced. A judge or jury can take circumstance into account when sentencing. **Aggravating circumstances** describe a crime in which the gravity is greater than that of the average instance of the offense. For instance, an offender charged with sexual assault would face a more severe sentence if the victim was found to be underage. On the other hand, **mitigating circumstances** are circumstances surrounding the commission of a crime that may reduce the blameworthiness of the defendant. In many cases, young defendants or defendants with impaired mental capacities are considered under mitigating circumstances.

There are several models of sentencing. The first, **indeterminate sentencing**, is a model of criminal punishment that allows the judge and the corrections system a great deal of discretion in the length of the sentence. For example, a defendant may be sentenced to prison for a term of 1 to 10 years. As you can imagine, this model often leads to social problems involving inequality in sentencing, since subjective biases against social class, race, or gender can influence judicial decisions.

In cases of **structured sentencing**, the legislative system of a state enacts constraints on judicial discretion in regards to determining criminal sentences. The proportionality sentencing principle states that the severity of sanctions should bear a direct relationship to the seriousness of the crime. Under this model, the offender is given a fixed-term sentence that may be reduced by **good time**, time deducted from a prison sentence for good behavior, or **gain time**, time deducted for participation in special programs.

So-called "**truth in sentencing**" laws are aimed at abolishing or limiting parole so that inmates serve a set majority of

their sentences. In my own state, inmates convicted of a violent offense must serve 80 percent of their sentence; regardless of their behavior in prison, they are not allowed good time or gain time.

Mandatory sentencing is perhaps the most rigid of the sentencing models. This is a structured sentencing strategy that allows for no discretion on the part of the judge. In cases such as these, a judge merely looks at the offense and the number and types of previous crimes and finds the required sentence on a grid. The Three Strikes law, in which a third felony results in a life sentence, is an example of mandatory sentencing.

Each of these sentencing strategies is used within the United States. However, state and federal governments have become increasingly more restrictive and harsher with sentencing over time. The U.S. prison system has grown mostly because individuals serve longer sentences and have little chance of getting out early for good behavior. Prisons are overcrowded and increasingly dangerous places, as evidenced by violence and rape discussed in the opening article.[15] Furthermore, mandatory sentencing regulations such as the Three Strikes law raise serious questions as to whether or not the justice system is fair. Recall Mr. Ewing, who is serving a life sentence for stealing three golf clubs.

Finally, there continues to be a racial and social class element to sentencing. One example is the 100:1 ratio, in which federal law requires a mandatory five-year sentence for crimes involving 500 grams of powder cocaine or 5 grams of crack. At every level of the sentencing grid, a person can have 100 times more powder cocaine than crack cocaine, and the sentence is the same. Generally, powder cocaine is a drug of the wealthy, whereas crack is a drug of the poor and has a disproportionately high level of users among minorities. Approximately 90 percent of those convicted of crack offenses are black and/or poor, and the average federal sentence for a black person is 40 percent longer than the sentence for a white person.[16]

∧
∧ **Sentencing** is an opportunity for a **judge to exercise**
∧ **judicial discretion.**

THE CORRECTIONS SYSTEM

The corrections system is the third leg of the criminal justice system. It includes probation, parole, and prison. **Probation** is a sentence given in lieu of prison and requires conditions that must be met by the offender. For example, the offender might be required to attend counseling or drug treatment as a condition of their probation. If he or she fails to go, he or she may be sent to prison. Research supports increasing use of probation, since probationers have lower rates of re-offense compared to those who have been sent to prison.[17] **Parole** is a correctional strategy that releases inmates from prison early but supervises them in the community. Parole conditions are often similar to probation conditions, and violating the conditions of parole can result in prison as well.

Prison

Prison, the last resort in the criminal justice system, is where an offender is incarcerated for a period of time as punishment for a crime. In 2007, more than 7.3 million Americans were under some form of correctional supervision.[18] Of today's prison inmates, 64 percent belong to racial or ethnic

PROBATION is a sentence given in lieu of prison and requires conditions that must be met by the offender to avoid going to prison.

PAROLE is a correctional strategy that releases inmates from prison early but supervises them in the community.

minorities, 57 percent of inmates are younger than 35 years old, and 21 percent are serving time for a drug offense.[19] According to the Bureau of Justice Statistics Correctional Surveys, one of every 15 people in the United States will be incarcerated in his or her lifetime, although the likelihood of prison is higher for certain populations.[20] Blacks are three times more likely to be imprisoned than Hispanics and five times more likely than whites. Nearly nine out of ten inmates are male, but the rate of female inmates is increasing.[21]

Various regions in the United States deal with crime differently. Southern states have higher incarceration rates not only because they have more crime, but also because they sentence offenders to prison more often and with longer sentences. The idea that incarceration naturally decreases crime is difficult to support with criminological data.[22] Jeffrey Reiman suggests that as crime rates increase, politicians often use "tough-on-crime" strategies to

The Increase in Adult Correctional Populations

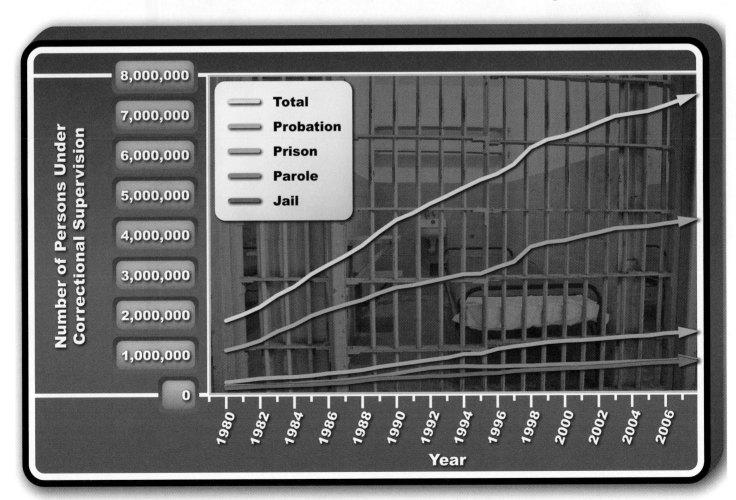

Source: Bureau of Justice Statistics Correctional Surveys (The Annual Probation Survey, National Prisoner Statistics Program, Annual Survey of Jails, and Annual Parole Survey), 2007.

 The **number of adults in the correctional population** has been **increasing dramatically** since 1980.

The United States in the Crosshairs

The rate of incarceration in the United States vastly exceeds the rate in comparative areas such as Canada and the European Union with 751 inmates per 100,000 people.[27] To put this number in a global perspective, the United States comprises less than 5 percent of the world's population, but it incarcerates nearly 25 percent of the world's prisoners.[28] Some people believe that harsher drug laws and policies such as the Three Strikes law have led to much higher incarceration rates. We are the only industrialized nation without strong gun-control laws, and the high rates of violent crime and murder are often blamed on easy access to guns. In addition, the United States is one of the few countries to incarcerate people for minor property crimes, like writing bad checks.[29] The war on drugs has certainly contributed to the bulging prisons as the rate of incarceration for petty offenders, often related to drug charges, is greater than 50 percent.[30]

One alternative to imprisonment is reintegrative shaming. In New Zealand, police officers use family conferencing with young offenders and their parents instead of juvenile detention. The goal is to heal the problems in the family and avoid labeling the teen as an offender. Although its effectiveness is still being evaluated, a survey of officers has shown that they strongly support the program and they feel they are making a difference in the lives of families and youth. Furthermore, they report that this method discourages repeat offending.[31]

Incarceration Rates in Industrialized Nations
(per 100,000 people)

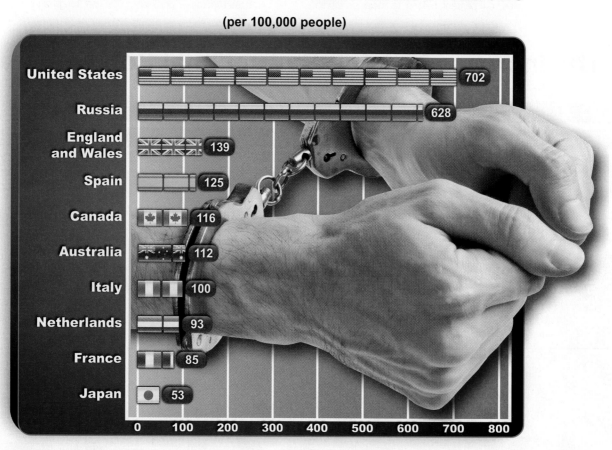

United States	702
Russia	628
England and Wales	139
Spain	125
Canada	116
Australia	112
Italy	100
Netherlands	93
France	85
Japan	53

Source: International Centre for Prison Studies, King's College London, *World Prison Brief*, www.prisonstudies.org

∧
∧
∧ **The United States is home to nearly 25 percent of the world's prisoners.** Do we have more crime, or do we simply have harsher laws?

entice voters. However, such policies have problems being funded since incarceration turns offenders from taxpayers into tax drains.[23]

Recidivism

Most inmates are eventually released from prison, but what happens to them when they return to society? More than 50 percent of all inmates return to prison within three years of their release.[24] This tendency for former inmates to return to prison is called **recidivism**. During the current period of "get tough" policies, recidivism rates have actually gotten worse.[25] Many of my students suggest that recidivism rates would decrease if prisons were harsher. Few of these students have ever visited the overcrowded and dangerous environment of a prison. Inmates have highly restricted freedoms, no privacy, and limited access to friends and family. In addition, prisons limit medical treatment and educational programs.[26] The increases of prison violence and rape discussed in the beginning of this chapter and in the literature call into question whether harsher prisons could even be possible.

Costs of Incarceration

Even though states report a set cost per inmate, these reported numbers often underestimate of the cost of incarceration. The hidden costs

associated with incarceration make determining the actual numbers difficult. For example, when a parent goes to prison, the family may fall into poverty and need public assistance. These social costs are almost never factored into the prison budget because other government departments pay for them, but taxpayers foot the bill either way. Sociologists James Austin and John Irwin calculated these hidden expenses and determined that it actually costs $30,000 per year to incarcerate a single inmate, which is significantly higher than what most states report.[32] The federal government reported paying almost $26,000 per inmate in federal facilities in 2008, and the community corrections center costs were estimated at nearly $24,000 per inmate; however, neither figure includes "social costs."[33]

<<< The **invisible costs of incarceration include the families left behind** to find health care, work, and shelter.

The Rate of Incarceration in Federal and State Facilities (per 100,000 persons)

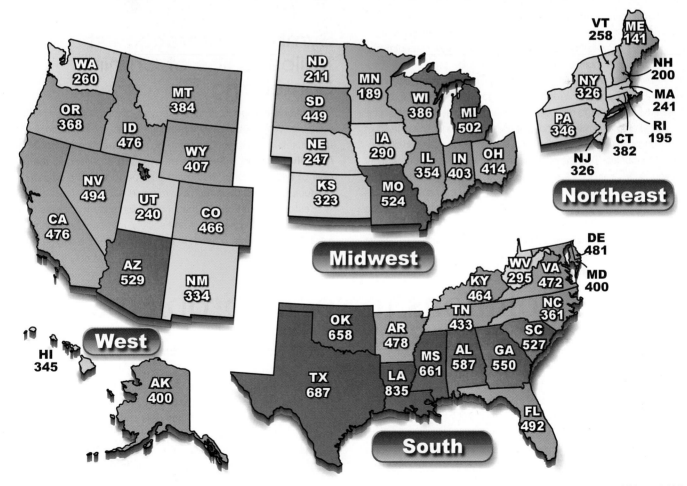

Source: Data from the U.S. Department of Justice, Office of Justice Programs, Bureau of Justice Statistics, Prison and Jail Inmates at Midyear 2006, Appendix Table 1: *Sentenced prisoners under the jurisdiction of State or Federal correctional authorities, June 30, 2005, to June 30, 2006.*

think social problems: HOW DO WE
JUSTIFY PUNISHMENT?

Conflict Theorist Philosophies of Criminal Sentencing

Conflict theorists focus on issues of inequality and power relationships. From their point of view, laws aren't written with the interest of society in mind, but with the interest of the wealthy. If you consider the fact that income and incarceration are linked, it does seem as though the system benefits the rich. Take, for instance, the current system of bail—people who are not yet convicted of crimes are arrested and held in jail unless they can "make bail." This process involves putting up money to be released. If the person does not show up for trial, the bail is forfeited. However, not everyone can afford the amount of money being asked. Because of this, thousands of people remain in jail while awaiting trial, receiving punishment before ever being convicted. Wealth affords good lawyers and bail money, while poverty affords public defenders and plea bargains. Such institutional discrimination clearly harms the poor at greater rates than it does the rich.[34]

In the criminal justice system, power is exercised under certain sentencing philosophies. The philosophy of **retribution** calls for punishment predicated upon a need for revenge. If you feel that you have been wronged, you can "get even" and exact a price from the person who has wronged you. Under this philosophy, the power of the state is used to punish the offender.

Closely aligned to the idea of retribution is a philosophy known as **just deserts**, a model of criminal sentencing that holds that criminal offenders

deserve the punishment they receive at the hands of the law, and that punishments should be appropriate to the type and severity of the crime committed. This philosophy is similar to retribution because they both value equity in sentencing.

Both of these philosophies contend that the primary goal of the criminal justice system is to exert power over the offenders and punish them for their crimes. Since it's a well-documented fact that the poor are more likely than the rich to be incarcerated, the inequality of punishment falls firmly on the indigent.[35]

Functionalist Philosophies of Criminal Sentencing

Functionalists see the world as interconnected and propose **incapacitation**, the use of imprisonment or other means to reduce the likelihood that an offender will be capable of committing future offenses. By sending a person to prison, a society ensures that the only possible people he or she can hurt is other inmates. Functionalists suggest that incapacitation will naturally decrease crime rates because inmates will be off the streets. Sentences relying on this theory are usually harsh and lengthy to ensure that an offender's chance of victimizing someone outside prison walls is nonexistent.

Symbolic Interactionist Philosophies of Criminal Sentencing

Interactionists suggest that the power of a symbol is linked to its meaning. What is the meaning of incarceration? Interactionists argue that prison is not for punishment, but for correcting antisocial behavior. **Rehabilitation** is the attempt to reform an offender; the ultimate goal of any correction method should be to turn the offender into a productive, contributing member of society.

Restorative justice is a model of punishment that strives to restore the bond between perpetrator and society. Perpetrators might pay restitution to their victims or work in the community as a way to reconnect with the public.

discover solutions to social problems:
CAN SOCIETY PUNISH TOO MUCH?

How much regulation, control, and punishment is too much? A glance at the overcrowded prison system and the increase of violence and rape within its walls shows that we clearly have a problem in our society. Frankly, the incredible costs associated with the rising incarceration rates in America should stop policymakers and legislators in their tracks; we are currently imprisoning people at a rate six times greater than Canada and thirteen times greater than Japan.[37] But what are the alternatives? Should we punish more leniently? Can we punish more effectively?

Let's take a look at Finland. In Finland, prisons look significantly different than they do in the United States. First, the fences with razor wire have been rejected in favor of cameras and electronic networks. Cells do not exist; inmates live in areas that look more like college dorms than prisons hallways. Finally, guards are unarmed and do not wear uniforms. Instead they interact with inmates in an effort to get to know them as fellow citizens. The results of this? The Finnish rate of incarceration is 0.05 percent in comparison to the United States' 0.7 percent

WRAP YOUR MIND AROUND THE THEORY

Functionalists suggest that **the criminal justice system exists to bring society together.** How would our lives be affected if the Three Strikes law were upended?

FUNCTIONALISM

Functionalists see the criminal justice system as essential for society. As Durkheim pointed out, all societies have crime, and part of crime prevention involves integrating people more closely into society. The more integrated a society, the less chance deviance will occur.[36] The justice system serves to punish those who violate moral boundaries, thus increasing the solidarity of everyone else.

CONFLICT THEORY

Reiman's statement that "The rich get richer, and the poor get prison," points out that laws are written to benefit the wealthy. Because the rich make the laws, illegal acts of the wealthy are often not considered crimes, and business executives who break the law receive little more than a slap on the wrist. The wealthy can afford private attorneys and lengthy trials, whereas the poor are assigned public defenders who urge them to accept plea bargain regardless of their guilt.

HOW DO SOCIETIES MAINTAIN SOCIAL CONTROL?

SYMBOLIC INTERACTIONISM

Braithwaite suggests that shame can either stigmatize or reintegrate an offender. A person who is subjected to stigmatized shaming is more likely to repeat or commit another offense because they've been labeled forever. Reintegrative shame will help an offender become comfortable in society, and there are no lasting labels that will inhibit his or her productivity.

According to conflict theorists, laws favor the wealthy. If Chris Brown were a working-class sales-clerk, would he still be smiling?

According to symbolic interactionists, **reintegrative shaming allows an offender to reconnect with society, while stigmatized shaming leads to re-offense.** Are these offenders likely to repeat their crimes?

MANDATORY MINIMUMS are fixed sentences for specific crimes.

and yet, their crime and recidivism rates are both lower.[38] Are the sentencing policies in the United States too severe?

Mandatory Minimums

Despite the existence of judicial discretion, state and federal governments have limited its use by passing laws that mandate sentences. **Mandatory minimums** force judges to hand out fixed sentences for spe-

cific crimes, eliminating the possibility of using mitigating circumstances to decrease a sentence. Not surprisingly, these mandates tend to increase the length of time people serve in prison. Such longer sentences result in overcrowding, health care issues, and greater expense, as we've discussed. Some states have built nursing homes within prison walls to care for an increasingly aging inmate population who are too weak to care for themselves but cannot be released due to these laws.[39] Looking at the cost-benefit analysis, the Rand Corporation found that mandatory minimum sentences for drug offenders are not an efficient use of tax dollars, compared to drug treatment. As we learned in Chapter 10, drug treatment is more efficient than prison at reducing drug consumption and drug-related crime, while costing the taxpayers less money.[40]

Number of Inmates Awaiting Execution on Death Row in the United States

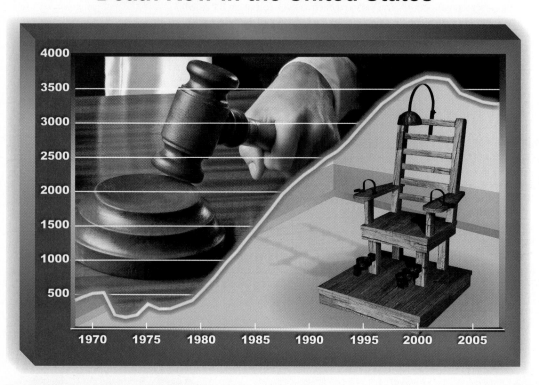

Source: Bureau of Justice Statistics: "Capital Punishment," 1968–2007; NAACP Legal Defense and Educational Fund, Inc., "Death Row USA," http://www. deathpenaltyinfo.org/death-row-inmates-state-and-size-death-row-year#year

The Death Penalty

We reserve the death penalty (capital punishment) for offenders who commit the most serious crimes, such as murder or treason. The United States is the only modern, industrialized democracy on Earth that still makes use of this form of punishment. Many states now include rape or sexual assault of a minor (under 14 years of age) under the umbrella of crimes warranting capital punishment.[41] Thirty-eight states have death penalty sentences on their books, but in the last five years, three states have abolished this practice altogether.[42]

Supporters of the death penalty argue that it is the ultimate deterrent

<<< The **size of death row has increased nearly seven times over** in the past 40 years.

MAKE CONNECTIONS

Crime and Poverty

The link between crime and poverty is seen throughout the criminal justice system. From lower-income areas being more highly saturated with drugs and violence, public defenders being assigned to the indigent, and plea bargains forcing innocents into sentences that they don't deserve, the poor are constantly fighting an uphill battle against the criminal justice system.

In Chapter 13 you saw that crime leads people down a declining slope into the criminal justice system. In Chapter 16, you'll learn about urbanization and how and why crowded cities tend to have more crime. This tendency is more than a function of population; it stems from the geography, stratification, and services available to the citizens. Those who fall below the poverty level are often found in

these crowded cities, and violent crimes such as homicide tend to occur at higher frequencies.

In Chapter 2, you learned that those living in poverty have fewer resources for help and support. They are also more likely to be caught and prosecuted for a crime and often find themselves alone in facing their arrest, trial, and conviction.

Pro & Con

Professional Jurors

Professional jurors are members of society who are educated and trained in law and whose full-time jobs consist of sitting on a courtroom jury. We do not have professional jurors in the United States, but some suggest that they would make trials run more quickly and smoothly. There are strong opinions about this on both sides of the fence.

Pro

- Professional jurors would be dependable; they would show up as required and be there on time.
- These professionals would know about the legal process and could be trained in certain types of cases, such as fraud.
- Professional jurors understand due process and would be more likely to make fair and just decisions.

Con

- Because professional jurors would be government employees, they would inevitably be beholden to their employer; a juror who voted against the government too often might risk losing his or her job.
- Jurors could become jaded after hundreds of trials, acting with the prejudice that a defendant "fits the type."
- There would be no "common man" left on the jury, widening the gap and making the battle for equality even more difficult for those who are at the lower extremes of society.

to crime. However, states with the penalty actually have higher rates of murder than states without it.[43] Not only has recent DNA testing revealed the unjust conviction of several deceased prisoners, but research has found that the cost of prosecuting and executing offenders is actually higher than lifetime incarceration costs.[44] Opponents of the death penalty also criticize its biased applications. Levine and Montgomery studied 6,000 murder cases and found that when the victim was white, black offenders were twice as likely to receive a death sentence as white offenders. Furthermore, blacks convicted of killing whites were four times more likely to receive a death sentence than blacks whose victims were of the same race.[45]

From Classroom to Community | Volunteering in a Detention Facility

The general population has a skewed view of prison life, as a result of both Hollywood's depictions and their own vivid imaginations. Few of us will ever know someone in prison, and even fewer will be prisoners themselves. It's the rare volunteer who gets a glimpse into the halls of a penitentiary, and for Ashley, the experience would not soon be forgotten.

"I grew up in what I guess would be considered an upper-middle class community outside of L.A. My sisters and I went to a private school where everyone was pretty much cut from the same cloth. By the time I got to college, I'd already decided that I needed to step beyond my comfort zone.

"It was during my second week of classes that my Intro to Sociology professor passed around flyers looking for volunteers to assist with visitor paperwork at the minimum-security prison the next county over. The professor said that it would be good experience for students interested in pursuing criminology, and that he would offer extra credit to any volunteers. I figured, minimum security, that was practically the high school cafeteria some days! I took a flyer and called the number that night.

"My first day, I was taken on a brief tour, partly as a courtesy, but also so that I could have a better understanding of the emotional and psychological background of the inmates that I would encounter in the visitor's room. I found myself on a dank, noisy cell block. The inmates were below us in a common area, heading toward the lunchroom. I observed the tiny, public cells that lined the walls and shuddered to see that in some there were four or more beds, housing twice as many prisoners as was intended. I commented to my guide that my dog had a carrying case bigger than the cells. I said it jokingly, but she didn't laugh. I wondered if, inwardly, she was as appalled as I was.

"Suddenly below us, a scuffle began between two men. Immediately, several more joined in, and the guards began swarming the area to break it up. I watched in horror as one bloodied and unconscious man was dragged out of the space and two guards removed the instigator. My guide quickly led me away.

"I asked her what would happen to the guy who started the fight. She said that no one would see him for a while, until he 'got the message.' I didn't realize that solitary confinement was part of the modern jail system, at least not in minimum-security prison. I was afraid to ask what would happen to the injured inmate; the infirmary had been cut back to bare bones due to budget reductions. My guide must have seen the look on my face. 'Don't be afraid,' she said, leading me back into the visitor's room. 'You're safe, and so are they. This is a good prison.'

"I've always believed that how you treat someone is how you'll be treated in return; if you treat them with dignity, they'll act with dignity; if you treat them with respect, respect will be repaid. When caged like rats, it's no wonder that these men were turning on each other, the guards, and themselves. How was this humane? Even now, I still think about what my guide told me; if this is a 'good' prison, what must the bad ones be like?"

HOW DO SOCIETIES RESPOND TO CRIME? 196

by agreeing upon laws to rule the people and punishments to penalize those who break the laws

HOW DO WE JUSTIFY PUNISHMENT? 202

with the philosophies that sentences should be based on the offender being repaid for his or her crimes; that he or she should be incapacitated so that no additional crimes are committed; using deterrence to encourage fear of punishment for wrongdoing; attempting to reform the offender through rehabilitation; and restorative justice that makes an offender a positive, responsible member of the community

CAN SOCIETY PUNISH TOO MUCH? 202

as a result of mandatory minimums, three-strikes laws, the war on drugs, lifetime sentences, and the death penalty, prisons in the United States are overcrowded, sometimes with innocent or unfairly represented inmates who face violence and fear every day

get the topic: HOW DO SOCIETIES RESPOND TO CRIME?

Theory

FUNCTIONALISM   202

- the criminal justice system is essential for society
- for society to function optimally, this system must work smoothly, and criminals must be kept off of the streets

CONFLICT THEORY   202

- laws are written in the interests of the wealthy
- the rich go free and the poor go to prison
- wealth affords good lawyers and bail money, whereas poverty affords public defenders and plea bargains

SYMBOLIC INTERACTIONISM   202

- shame can either stigmatize or reintegrate an offender
- labeling an offender will likely land him or her back in jail
- reintegrative shaming provides support and encourages offenders to return to society without labels

Key Terms

consensus model of law suggests that laws arise because people see a behavior they do not like, and agree to make it illegal.   *196*

conflict model of law proposes that powerful people write laws and, in doing so, tend to protect their own interests.   *196*

shaming is a deliberate effort to attach a negative meaning to a behavior.   *196*

stigmatized shame is a permanent label given to an offender.   *197*

reintegrative shaming is a punishment that allows the offender to reconnect to society after punishment without further stigma.   *197*

deterrence is a measure that prevents a person from doing something out of fear of the consequences.   *197*

specific deterrence is a type of criminal sentencing that seeks to prevent a particular offender from committing that crime again.   *197*

general deterrence is a type of criminal sentencing that seeks to prevent others from committing crimes by making an example of an offender.   *197*

target hardening makes an objective less attractive to a possible criminal.   *197*

discretion is the ability to make decisions.   *197*

judge is an elected or appointed public official who presides over the court of law. *197*

prosecuting attorney is an attorney whose official duty is to conduct criminal proceedings on behalf of the state or the people against those accused of committing criminal offenses. *197*

plea bargains are out-of-court agreements between the prosecutor and defense attorney that often involve concessions by the prosecution to obtain a guilty plea. *197*

defense counsel consists of attorneys hired or appointed by the court to provide a legal defense for the accused. *197*

aggravating circumstances are circumstances relating to the commission of an act that increase the degree of liability or responsibility of the person committing the act. *198*

mitigating circumstances are circumstances in the commission of an act that decrease the degree of criminal responsibility of the person committing the act. *198*

indeterminate sentencing is a model of criminal punishment that allows the judge and the corrections system a great deal of discretion in the length of the sentence. *198*

structured sentencing is a model of criminal punishment in which the legislative system of a state enacts constraints on judicial discretion in determining criminal sentences. *198*

good time is the amount of time deducted from a prison sentence for good behavior. *198*

gain time is the amount of time deducted from a prison sentence for participation in special programs. *198*

"truth in sentencing" is legislation that is aimed at abolishing or limiting parole so that inmates serve a set majority of their sentence. *198*

mandatory sentencing is a structured sentencing strategy that allows for no discretion on the part of the judge. *198*

probation is a sentence given in lieu of prison and requires conditions that must be met by the offender to avoid going to prison. *199*

parole is a correctional strategy that releases inmates from prison early but supervises them in the community. *199*

recidivism is the tendency for former inmates to return to prison. *200*

retribution is model of criminal sentencing predicated upon a felt need for revenge. *202*

just deserts is a model of criminal sentencing that holds that criminal offenders deserve the punishment they receive at the hands of the law and that punishments should be appropriate to the type and severity of the crime committed. *202*

incapacitation is the use of imprisonment or other means to reduce the likelihood that an offender will be capable of committing future offenses. *202*

rehabilitation is the attempt to reform an offender. *202*

restorative justice is a model of punishment that strives to restore the bond between perpetrator and society. *202*

mandatory minimums are fixed sentences for specific crimes. *204*

Sample Test Questions

These multiple-choice questions are similar to those found in the test bank that accompanies this textbook.

1. An effective form of punishment still in use today is

- **a.** the Code of Hammurabi.
- **b.** mitigating circumstances.
- **c.** reintegrative shaming.
- **d.** exile.

2. A public defender would most likely be assigned to

- **a.** a black offender.
- **b.** a wealthy offender.
- **c.** a female offender.
- **d.** a working-class offender.

3. One probable reason for America's high rate of incarceration is

- **a.** the unrestricted democratic freedoms enjoyed by the population.
- **b.** the severity of the war on drugs
- **c.** a politically motivated judicial system.
- **d.** judges who exercise liberal discretion.

4. Reiman argues that

- **a.** the criminal justice system favors the wealthy.
- **b.** the legalization of drugs will reduce incarceration rates.
- **c.** three-strikes laws are improving the national crime rate.
- **d.** prisons require greater regulation and oversight to ensure safety and rehabilitation.

5. The death penalty

- **a.** is an effective deterrent to capital crimes.
- **b.** has reduced the number of homicides in America.
- **c.** is still on the books in most states.
- **d.** involves a streamlined appeals process.

ESSAY

1. As noted in the opening article, research has found that rape in prisons is often perpetrated by the guards. What should be their punishment? How can the system be fixed to protect basic human rights?

2. How would the criminal justice system differ if *every* offender was assigned a public defender?

3. What are your thoughts on the appointment of professional jurors? How might a conflict theorist view this option?

4. Think about Braithwaite's ideas on shaming and the ways in which judicial discretion could put this into practice. What are the pros and cons of public shaming?

5. Which hidden cost of incarceration is most troubling to you? In your opinion, who ultimately pays the greatest price for acts of criminal behavior?

WHERE TO START YOUR RESEARCH PAPER

To learn more about crime in the United States, go to
http://www.fbi.gov
http://www.justice.gov/

To read more on the death penalty, see http://www.deathpenaltyinfo.org

To view justice statistics, go to http://www.ojp.usdoj.gov/bjs

To read insider stories of life in prison, check out
http://www.insideprison.com

To learn more about the U.S. prison system, go to http://www.bop.gov

For more information on restorative justice programs, visit
http://www.restorativejustice.org/

ANSWERS: 1. c; 2. d; 3. b; 4. a; 5. c

Remember to check www.thethinkspot.com for additional information, downloadable flashcards, and other helpful resources.

SOCIAL PROBLEMS OF MARRIAGE AND FAMILY

The line

between actual reality and virtual reality has become more blurred with the advent of the popular online game "Second Life."

The virtual world provides a place for individuals to create an avatar and engage in most everyday activities, including attending concerts, conducting meetings, meeting new friends, and apparently having virtual extramarital affairs.

Amy Taylor, 28, and David Pollard, 40, expect to have their divorce finalized next week. Their three-year marriage came to a crashing end after Pollard was caught by his wife e-snuggling with another Second Life female avatar lover.

"I caught him cuddling a woman on a sofa in the game. It looked really affectionate," Taylor told Sky News.

When Taylor confronted her husband about the matter and asked to see his chat history, he quickly turned off both the monitor and the computer to erase any evidence of his interaction.

The incident was the last straw for Taylor, since it wasn't the first time Pollard had strayed digitally.

After the couple met and were smitten with each other in an Internet chat room in 2003, they decided to get married and held an online wedding in Second Life in 2005. But the honeymoon didn't last long—Pollard's avatar was caught having sex with an online prostitute in Second Life.

"I went mad . . . I was so hurt," Taylor told Sky News. "I just couldn't believe what he'd done."

Dr. Cynthia McVey, Head of Glasgow Caledonian University's Psychology Department, told ABCnews.com that Taylor's emotions reflect her feelings that she "may not be exciting enough" to her husband and even though Pollard may not have committed physical infidelity it still signaled a "step away from her."

Second Life serves as a meeting place for friends and a virtual marketplace, and some countries have even set up embassies on the platform. . .

But what makes one go beyond those public activities and pursue more intimate relationships in Second Life?

McVey told ABCnews.com that people hope to "present themselves as they want others to see them and how they want to be."

McVey explains that Second Life can be a safe haven for individuals who are "shy and lonely," and can be a place where "appearance is no longer a concern" and where people can "connect with someone" without the worry of being judged. Those factors may have played a role in this situation where the couple's avatars clearly did not match up with their real-life physical appearance.

"There is a novelty value associated with it . . . you can be anything you want to be," McVey said, and says in some ways it is "an emotional representation of yourself."

The "other woman" involved in the affair, 55-year-old Linda Brinkley, who lives in Arkansas, was first attracted to Pollard after her online character began work as a hostess at a nightclub run by Pollard on Second Life, the Daily Mail reported. Brinkley claims the relationship between her and Pollard was that of just friends until he split with his wife.

The timing of the affair doesn't matter to Taylor.

"It's cheating as far as I'm concerned," Taylor told Sky News.[1]

---With every generation, society's opinions on marriage and family develop and change. A generation ago, who could have imaged that "virtual affairs" would lead to divorces?

Ideas about marriage and family in the 1950s seem worlds apart from the relationships and family structures we experience in the United States today. Is this a positive or a negative change? Are issues such as divorce, cohabitation, and child abuse "new" or merely current manifestations of deep-rooted social problems?

In this chapter, we will take a look at the issues surrounding and stemming from marital relationships in our society. We will also observe various forms of the family unit and discuss how changes in this aspect of the American society have affected other areas as well. Do different cohabitation patterns result in varied levels of fulfillment? How are children influenced by their parents' life choices? In the end, should we all strive for a utopian family out of *Leave it to Beaver*, or accept the rising divorce and abuse rates as inevitable results of our changing society?

get the topic: WHAT SOCIAL PROBLEMS RELATE TO MARRIAGE AND FAMILY?

MARRIAGE is the union of two people that is typically recognized by law or cultural norms.

FAMILY is two or more people who are related by blood, marriage, or adoption.

NUCLEAR FAMILY is a household consisting of a husband, wife, and children.

EXTENDED FAMILY is a household consisting of a nuclear family and additional relatives.

In order to investigate the social problems that affect marriage and family, it's important to consider some basic questions. What defines a family? What is the purpose of marriage? What role do children play in a family unit? We'll begin with a discussion of the first.

Background of a Family

You've been a part of your family for your entire life. You've spent time with your friends' families. You've even seen depictions of families on television and in the news. Chances are, none of those families look the same as your family. Some may seem more like the Simpsons, while others seem more like the Flanders.

Every year, many new families are created by marriages. A **marriage** is the union of two people that is typically recognized by law or cultural norms. Recently, many gay Americans have been fighting to have their unions recognized by law and to change the cultural perception of same-sex marriage.[2] Is this a social problem in and of itself, or does the problem stem from the reaction of some to this effort? Regardless of your opinion, it raises a sociological issue we may not often consider: how to define family. Generally, a **family** is two or more people who are related by blood, marriage, or adoption. Often, sociologists consider different types of families. A **nuclear family**, for example, is a household consisting of a husband, a wife, and their children. Several popular TV shows from the 1950s such as *The Adventures of Ozzie and Harriet* portrayed nuclear families. But there can be many other variations of the family. Perhaps your grandmother has been having health problems and moves in with you. Maybe your favorite uncle lost his job and needs a place to stay. Maybe everyone in your family just likes living in the same house. These variations are but a few examples of an **extended family**, a structure that includes a nuclear family plus one or more additional relatives. A famous example of an extended family is the Obamas, who began their time in the White House as a nuclear family, but became an extended family when Barack Obama's mother-in-law came to live with them.[3]

MYTHS ABOUT THE FAMILY

There are many misconceptions about what the family is and what it isn't. According to family researcher Stephanie Coontz, there are a number of myths about the family that persist in the United States. First, there is the belief that all families are structured like a nuclear family.[4] The reality is that there are many types of families that can and do exist. In fact, the nuclear family only arose during the industrial revolution as many people left their old land and moved to urban areas seeking work.

Second, there is the myth that family units are self-reliant.[5] This is not as true as you may think. Throughout history, families have had to rely on the government, local community members, and other families to ensure their stability and survival. The old saying, "No one is an island," applies to the family as well. This reliance and help from others allow families to survive.

The third myth is that within each family, there is a predetermined and different set of roles and responsibilities for men and women.[6] Most people believe that, traditionally, women's jobs were cooking, cleaning, and raising the children, whereas men were supposed to work to ensure food, shelter, and protection. However, this is not necessarily so. Throughout history, men and women have shared these responsibilities more often than not, blurring the lines between gender roles. Nowadays, this is true as well. In my own family, we have many tasks that may not seem traditionally assigned. For example, I do the yard work (stereotypically assigned to the male), but I also make the morning lunches and cook about half the meals (not stereotypical). When we

Median Age of First Marriage in the United States

Source: U.S. Census Bureau, "Estimated Median Age at First Marriage, by Sex: 1890 to the Present,"
http://www.census.gov/population/www/socdemo/hh-fam.html#ht, Accessed August 27, 2009.

Modern couples are waiting longer to marry. Is this due to a change in values in the United States?

recently bought a new car, my wife did the negotiating, mostly because she's a *much* better businessperson than I am (not stereotypical). It was funny to see the salesmen at the dealership trying to figure out whom to address with their numbers.

The fourth myth is that the nuclear family of the 1950s is the ideal family.[7] This myth is also difficult to defend. The supposed "perfect" 1950s family was popularized in television shows such as *Leave it to Beaver* and *Father Knows Best*, in which the fathers went to work and the mothers stayed home and cooked and cleaned in pearls and full makeup. But in reality, many of these families were far from perfect. Although divorce rates of the 1950s were low, other family issues such as abuse and addiction were also present and much more common than most people today suspect.

Coontz suggests that the perfect family is more a product of our imagination than of reality. Could this be a continuation of the perception that we have a "problem" with family life in the United States? Or is it simply a result of ever-changing societal patterns that cause us to cling to an image of perfection?[8]

The American Family: A Work in Progress

The idea of the typical American family is constantly changing, and what might seem like the norm today may or may not be the norm tomorrow. As you can see in the diagram above, the median age at which a person gets married has changed considerably over time. Although the modern median age for men is nearly the same as in 1900, the modern age for women is much greater. Why the delay before marriage? It's been spec-

ulated that part of the reason is because more couples today are living together without legally tying the knot. Furthermore, the economic and educational opportunities for women have expanded greatly since 1900, leading some to postpone marriage in favor of starting careers. This delay may also be due to a change in values on the nature of marriage, family, and what one seeks from life. Regardless, the rate of first marriage has continued to decline since the 1960s.[9]

NEW FAMILY STRUCTURES
Cohabitation

Perhaps one of the most significant changes in recent times is the increase in cohabitation in the United States. In 1970, less than 1 percent of U.S. households consisted of unmarried couples. With each decade, this percentage has increased: 2.2 percent in 1980, 3.6 percent in 1990, and almost 5 percent in 1998, with a total of 4.9 million unmarried-couple households.[10]

Researchers have several different theories as to why the rate of cohabitation has increased significantly over the past 40 years. Some theorists propose that because of the rise in divorces over the past few decades, young adults today are all too aware of the realities of divorce. If you're living with your partner and the relationship ends, you can go your separate ways; if you're in a marriage that doesn't work out, you'll have to endure a divorce. Other researchers cite changing societal norms about cohabitation and sexual relationships outside marriage. Because the stigma associated with having sex outside marriage has been greatly reduced, more couples today view cohabitation as an option, whereas 40 years ago, they may not have considered it.[11]

BLENDED FAMILIES are families composed of children and some combination of biological parents and stepparents.

>>> Some high-profile stars are opting to cohabit instead of getting married.

Estimates show that roughly 40 percent of all children will live in a cohabiting family at some point before their 16th birthday.[14]

Additionally, different couples may have different reasons for choosing cohabitation over marriage. For example, some see it as a trial period before marriage; others see it as a substitute. Still others may view living together as a logical step in a serious relationship. As you can see in the table below, these different reasons for cohabiting can affect the success of a relationship.[12]

How does the trend of cohabitation affect families? Without the legal recognition of their union, researchers have noted that couples that opt to remain unmarried maintain a striking resemblance to families of the past. This is particularly true if the couple brings children into the relationship. Parental roles remain rather typical in these instances.[13]

Blended Families and Single-Parent Homes

In this day and age, it's common to see **blended families**, which consist of children and some combination of biological parents and stepparents. At the same time, there are many single-parent households in which children are typically raised by a mother who is either divorced or who never married the father of her children.

Blended families share a number of possible problems that are quite similar to single-parent households, although single-parent households tend to have the lowest incomes of all forms of the family. For example, approximately 48 percent of all single mothers live below the poverty line. In fact, an employed single mother's per capita income is 13 percent lower than per capita income in two-parent households in which the father is the only one employed outside the home.[15] Children raised in single-parent families have increased risk for poor academic performance, low self-esteem, substance abuse, delinquent behavior, and a host of other social problems. Some researchers have suggested that this results from being stigmatized by other children. Others suggest that it is due to a lack of clear and consistent parenting roles. Still others maintain that because family processes in these families are different from those of a nuclear family, the well-being of individuals suffers. Research tends to support the idea that these differences have less to do with family structure and more to do with family processes. In other words, children who come from families with little conflict and low levels of stress tend to do equally well regardless of the structure of the family.[16]

Gay and Lesbian Families

Research on gay and lesbian families is difficult to find and is often controversial.[17] Data on same-sex couples is not widely available; however, census data from the 1990s show that approximately 60 percent of gay families and 45 percent of lesbian families live in urban areas and are concentrated in certain regions of the United States. However, only small percentages of gay and lesbian couples have children. More than 50 percent of heterosexual couples have children, whereas only 5 percent of gay couples and 22 percent of lesbian couples do. How does growing up in a gay household affect a child?[18]

Children raised in gay/lesbian homes are no more likely to grow up to be gay than children raised in straight homes. They are less likely to suffer abuse and tend to have more opportunities because their parents are generally better educated and better off financially than their peers. Additionally, data show that children raised by same-sex couples don't exhibit any adverse effects on self-esteem or self-worth related to the fact that their homes are "different."[19]

ISSUES IN THE FAMILY

Married couples have to confront a wide range of issues that can have a lasting impact on their union. Two of the most important things that they have to consider are marital satisfaction and child rearing.

Marital Satisfaction

Marital satisfaction is difficult to measure. In general, we know that people who are married tend to be happier, have better health, and enjoy a higher standard of living because their incomes tend to be higher.[20] Research on life satisfaction supports the notion that men tend to benefit more from being married than do women, perhaps due to the fact that married men live more stable lives than their single peers. They are less likely to

Outcome of Cohabitation Relationships

Reason for Cohabitation	Couples Still Cohabiting 5 to 7 Years Later (%)	Couples Married 5 to 7 Years Later (%)	Couples No Longer Cohabiting 5 to 7 Years Later (%)
Substitute for marriage	39	25	35
Precursor to marriage	17	52	31
Trial marriage	21	28	51
Co-residential dating	21	33	46
Total for all couples	**21**	**40**	**39**

Source: Data from Suzanne M. Bianchi and Lynne M. Casper, "American Families," *Population Bulletin*, vol. 55, no. 4 (Washington, DC: Population Reference Bureau, December 2000).

become involved in dangerous activities and more likely to experience contentment in their lives.[21]

Having children can also affect marital satisfaction. Studies show that parents report lower levels of satisfaction compared to nonparents. Mothers of infants, however, show the greatest difference in martial contentment when compared to women with no children at all. In general, the data show that satisfaction for both men and women decreases after the birth of the first child. Researchers suggest this is, in large part, due to conflicts that come about from parenting and decreased levels of personal freedom. Children demand attention and force a shift in roles from husband/wife to father/mother.[22] Regardless of the form of family, adult participants exhibit lower levels of a sense of well-being while expressing more frequent negative emotions than do their peers who are without children.[23]

Child Rearing and Child Care

Child rearing can be another point of conflict for some families. For one thing, raising children is expensive. In 2006, raising a child until the age of 17 was $289,000.[24] For couples with limited funds, these expenses can become a major point of tension.

One of the main issues in child rearing is making decisions about child care. This may involve deciding whether one parent will stay home to care for the children or, in families where both spouses are employed, making arrangements for their children during work hours. Working parents have several different options, including day care centers, family day cares, hiring babysitters, or having the children stay with other relatives during the day. Over the last few decades, the increased number of women in the workforce has corresponded with changes in child care arrangements. In 1965, 15 percent of mothers who were employed cared for their pre-school children while they worked; by 1994, that number had dropped to 6 percent. In contrast, the percentage of working fathers who cared for their young children increased from 14 percent to 19 percent. Overall, the percentage of preschool children in day care centers increased from 7 percent in 1965 to 29 percent in 1994.[25]

Divorce

Another social problem associated with the family is divorce. Despite

Popular TV Shows Featuring Non-Traditional Families

1950s	I Love Lucy
1960s	My Three Sons
1970s	Sanford and Son
1980s	Diff'rent Strokes
1990s	Full House
2000s	The Bernie Mac Show
Present	Keeping Up with the Kardashians

the best intentions, some families eventually wind up in divorce court. Some couples see divorce as their only alternative, as expressed by Amy Taylor in the opening article. It didn't matter to her whether her spouse's cheating occurred in real life or within the confines of an online game; to her, cheating was cheating and, in the case of many failed marriages, it constitutes grounds for divorce. Some seek to escape domestic violence, while other couples divorce because they just can't seem to get along anymore. Over the past 100 years, changes in attitudes about the family have made it easier to obtain a divorce in the United States. As family roles have changed, so has the stigma surrounding divorce. Since the 1950s, the divorce rate has increased considerably. Perhaps it is because more women are now able to pursue their own careers and earn a successful living, removing the economic concerns many single women faced in the past.[33] Regardless, people today are far more supportive of divorce than they have been in the past and, because of this, getting divorced seems much more common.[34]

As Bob Dylan noted, the times, they are a-changing—in the 1950s, more than 85 percent of marriages lasted 10 years or more. Now, only about 70 percent of marriages last that long.[35] With such a high divorce rate, why aren't people taking more precautions before marriage? It may surprise you that factors such as cohabitation can increase the chances of getting a divorce by 35 percent.[36] Why that is so is a complicated and often unanswerable question. In general, it appears that people who are willing to cohabit have different values and attitudes about the meaning of marriage, which hurts their changes of creating a lasting relationship.

DECREASING THE ODDS

Of course there are also features that decrease the likelihood of divorce. Some risk factors can be controlled; others are based on

<<< Catholics are 11 percent less likely to get a divorce than couples of other Christian denominations. **Do they value marriage more, or does that the fact that the Catholic Church does not recognize divorce influence their choice?**

Divorce Rates Around the World

Is divorce leading to the decline of family? The United States isn't the only country that has experienced an increase in divorce rates—countries around the world are experiencing similar trends. By 1990, the divorce rates in several developed countries had nearly doubled from 20 years before. Even in less developed countries, 25 percent of marriages end by the time a woman has reached her 40s.[26]

There are exceptions to this trend, however. Countries that have considerably fewer women than men experience lower rates of divorce. Also, the divorce rate is lower in countries where women get married at a later age.[27] As we'll see, waiting to get married increases the odds that a person will select a partner wisely. Surprisingly, even now that Americans are waiting longer to get married, they still tend to marry younger than other people in the developed world. Nearly half of the first-time marriages that occur in the United States happen at age 25. In Italy, people typically wait until age 29. In France, nearly half of all marriages occur at age 31. In Sweden, the average couple ties the knot at 32.[28]

Some suggest that the divorce rate can be attributed to culture. In the United States, for example, there is a heavy cultural emphasis placed on individuality, which can come into conflict with the concept of marriage. After all, marriage is a shared experience, and people aren't always able to express their individuality under such circumstances. In a culture in which self-fulfillment is of great importance, some people will be inclined to leave a marriage if they find that it is no longer fulfilling to them.[29]

The American way of life has become popular in many parts of the world, and some researchers attribute the increase in divorce rates to the adoption of Western cultural values. Others see the increased rates as a function of socioeconomic development; in general, countries that are more economically developed tend to have higher divorce rates.[30]

No matter where in the world divorce occurs, the consequences are detrimental to all involved, especially children. Divorce leads to transitional states within the home; the more transitions that a child experiences, the more likely he or she is to exhibit harmful behavior and become vulnerable to a variety of social problems. Research has found that children who experience multiple transitions are more likely to have difficulties in school and experience sexual relations at an early age.[31] These scenarios lead to increased risks of high school dropout, unplanned teen pregnancies, and contraction of sexually transmitted diseases.

The dissolution of the family can also place a heavy burden on single mothers who often have to shoulder a greater portion of the responsibility of caring for a child. Personal time becomes limited, as does money. Deadbeat dads exist around the world; in the United States, 40 percent of divorced fathers do not pay child support. In Malaysia, this number is closer to 50 percent. In Argentina, the number grows to 66 percent, whereas Japan tops them all at 75 percent.[32]

>>> The divorce rate around the world is increasing. **How does this affect children of all nationalities?**

circumstance. For example, people who share similar educational and religious backgrounds are more likely to remain married than those who do not. In addition, those who get married in their mid-20s or older and wait to have children until they tie the knot are more likely to stay with their spouse. Last, coming from a family that hasn't been through a divorce decreases your likelihood of experiencing one.[37]

CHILDREN AND DIVORCE

Spouses aren't the only people who are affected by divorce, however—children are also heavily impacted by the decision. In many cases, a couple can ease the blow by delivering the message together and in a way that does not focus on conflict. Parents may prevent some trauma by taking responsibility for the decision, avoiding the blame game, and encouraging their children to ask questions.[38]

As mentioned previously, children whose parents divorce may experience a great many social problems. They sometimes encounter difficulties at school due to both emotional drain and loss of time while the parents are in transition. In contrast to the belief that modern-day kids are becoming used to the idea of divorce, research indicates that in the United States, a child loses close to 70 percent of a full school year due to divorce—and the number is increasing.[39] In fact, it has been found that children who experience particularly intense divorces have extreme difficulty in coping with the situation.[40]

Research has shown that children who come from families with divorced parents are more likely to get a divorce themselves. Children of divorce were also found to have more negative attitudes about marriage and the possibility of sustaining a long-term relationship. As adults, this can result in diminished levels of marital commitment and a lack of confidence in their ability to maintain relationships.[41]

think social problems: HOW DO WE VIEW MARRIAGE?

Symbolic Interactionism

Symbolic interactionists examine how marriage relates to society. They start off with basic questions such as "What is marriage?" and "What is family?" They then consider these topics on a larger scale, studying their meaning and roles in society. Based on their observations, interactionists then ask questions such as "Is the importance of family diminishing?"[42]

By exploring the various interpretations of marriage and family that have existed over time, researcher Stephanie Coontz suggests that family structure has always changed. In previous eras, extended families were common, whereas divorce and unmarried coupling were rare. Definitions of family would have reflected the social norms of those times. In the present day, the definition of family has grown to include the nuclear family, blended families, and many other variations. Given enough time, these definitions are also likely to change.[43]

Conflict Theory

Part of what conflict theorists focus on is competition over limited resources. Even in marriage—an institution that is supposed to be based on mutual affection and a desire to ensure the happiness of both parties— conflict theorists see the potential for a struggle over time and energy. In many cases, this conflict revolves around household duties and child care.

Studies have shown that in terms of hours spent on these tasks, men's and women's responsibilities at home are not equal. As you can see in the table below, between 1965 and 1995, the amount of time men spent on household labor actually increased, but still remained much lower than women's.[44] Although the dynamic changed somewhat over this 30-year period, women today still do more total household chores than men.[45] Note the gender stereotypes contained in these data as well. On average, men do more outdoor chores, whereas women do more inside tasks, such as cooking, housecleaning, and laundry. Conflict theorists claim that this is a way for men to use their advantage to keep busy and create a better life for themselves. Some suggest it is clearly oppression.

Functionalism

Functionalists see the family as a means of ensuring that people are able to function successfully in society. Sociologist Emile Durkheim claims that learning to function in a family is the first step in preparing individuals to function in society.[46] In a family unit, children are taught which types of behavior are acceptable and which types of behavior are frowned upon.

Living in a family environment helps children develop skills related to tolerance and cooperation. In this way, children become prepared to operate in the larger world. The skills acquired by living in a family indirectly lead to a person's ability to make friends, maintain a job, and interact with others on a daily basis. Without such a family environment, successful integration into society would be more difficult.

According to sociologist David Popenoe, the traditional American nuclear family has eroded over time, particularly in the past 25 years. As a result, the strengths that make up family institutions—cohesion, the performance of familial functions, and power over other social institutions—have weakened.[47] This change has occurred as family members have become more autonomous and less connected to one another. Without cohesion, families are unable to perform their proper functions. For example, after the industrial revolution, children no longer grew up to work the family farm. Instead, they left home to find jobs working for someone else, meaning their families were no longer providing for them.[48] Years ago, parents also were responsible for educating their children; with the advent of public education, only a small number of parents homeschool their children today. Furthermore, modern families are smaller than they were 100 years ago, which has also weakened traditional functions. Based on these reasons, Popenoe argues that the family, as an institution, is becoming less important in society.

Hours per Week Spent on Household Chores		
Task	Hours per Week 1965	Hours per Week 1995
Cooking and meal cleanup (women)	13.8	5.3
Cooking and meal cleanup (men)	1.6	1.7
Housecleaning (women)	7.2	6.7
Housecleaning (men)	0.5	1.7
Laundry and ironing (women)	5.8	1.9
Laundry and ironing (men)	0.3	0.3
Outdoor chores, gardening, and animal care (women)	0.9	1.6
Outdoor chores, gardening, and animal care (men)	0.6	2.9
Repairs and maintenance (women)	0.4	0.7
Repairs and maintenance (men)	1.0	1.9
Bills, other (women)	1.8	1.3
Bills, other (men)	0.9	1.5
Total time spent per week on household chores (women)	30.0	17.5
Total time spent per week on household chores (men)	4.9	10.0

Source: Data from Suzanne M. Bianchi and Lynne M. Casper, "American Families," *Population Bulletin*, vol. 55, no. 4 (Washington, DC: Population Reference Bureau, December 2000).

WRAP YOUR MIND AROUND THE THEORY

Families exist to provide companionship, affection, and recreation. What happens to children who don't have access to these types of relationships?

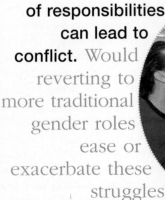

FUNCTIONALISM

The family establishes and maintains order; in addition, it serves five primary functions. First, it acts as a means of creating offspring and socializing them. For humanity to continue, there have to be new generations, and families serve not only to create them, but to condition them as well. This means teaching children how to function in society. Second, it acts as an outlet for affection, companionship, and recreation; families are often the first line of support. Third, it serves to provide sexual regulation; that is, it helps determine lineage and thereby prevents conflicts that might result from the absence of such distinctions. Fourth, it allows for economic cooperation; family members are able to combine their resources in order to survive with greater ease. Fifth, it provides care for the ill and elderly. If a member of society gets sick or has age-related difficulties, he or she has a place to turn for help and support.

CONFLICT THEORY

Husbands and wives often come into conflict over the performance of household duties. Bickering about things such as who will take out the trash might seem like a minor obstacle in a healthy relationship, but it has the potential to make or break a marriage. Household duties require time and energy and reduce amounts of leisure. Because of pre-established social norms, women are often seen as the ones who perform a majority of the work around the home, leading to feelings of resentment. Some see this conflict as having socioeconomic roots. In a change from the past, many families now need two income earners instead of just one; this means that housewives, whose sole job was to maintain the home, are steadily becoming a thing of the past. But even though men spend an increasing amount of time doing household chores, women still spend *more* time on these tasks each week.[49] With both partners working outside the home, intense conflicts can arise when couples can't agree on who will perform household chores in addition to their daily jobs.

IS THE FAMILY IN DECLINE?

SYMBOLIC INTERACTIONISM

Understanding family dynamics and the problems that can arise requires an understanding of the meaning of marriage. Interactionists suggest that in every marriage, there are really two meanings: his and hers. In other words, if you were to ask me and my wife about our marriage, you would get two different answers, because we have different perceptions of what is and is not happening in it. To interactionists, a marriage is really the result of two people who happen to share similar enough definitions in order for it to be maintained. In general, men are found to receive greater benefits from marriage and therefore are generally happier in it.[50]

Uneven distribution of responsibilities can lead to conflict. Would reverting to more traditional gender roles ease or exacerbate these struggles?

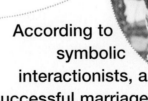

According to symbolic interactionists, a successful marriage is the result of two people who share similar definitions (and therefore **similar expectations) of marriage.** When spouses aren't on the same page in terms of their expectations, how is the family as a whole affected?

discover solutions to social problems:
WHAT ARE SOME PROBLEMS IN THE FAMILY?

Child abuse and divorce are two major problems that can arise in the family. Fortunately, there are various social policies that have been created to prevent these problems from occurring.

Preventing Child Abuse

Child abuse is defined by federal law as "any recent act or failure to act on the part of a parent or caretaker, which results in death, serious physical or emotional harm, sexual abuse, or exploitation, or an act or failure to act which presents an imminent risk of serious harm."[51] In 2007, there were 1,760 child fatalities as a direct result of an injury related to neglect or physical abuse. The most vulnerable children in these instances are also the youngest—children under the age of 4 accounted for about 75 percent of the child abuse-related fatalities in 2007.[52]

There are, however, preventive measures that can be taken. Most states now require immediate notification to authorities if a person suspects that a child is being abused—more rapid responses lead to fewer children being murdered. Complications arise over the definition of "abuse," however. Some parents who use violence on their children believe that they are using physical punishment as a just form of discipline. Methods of punishment such as spanking blur the line, however, as some suggest that this form of chastisement is related to an increased likelihood of child abuse.[53]

Of course, with more than 7 million cases of child abuse and/or neglect each year, the fact that there is a problem is obvious. Children in the United States are at the greatest risk of being abused by someone who is responsible for their care. This social problem is one most often faced by schools, courts, and a host of social service agencies.[54] Therapy and family intervention may help parents identify and understand their triggers and develop ways of coping with and avoiding situations that have previ-

ously resulted in abuse.[55] Still, children die every day in America at the hands of someone who is supposed to take care of them.

No-Fault Divorce and Covenant Marriage

A no-fault divorce is a divorce in which both parties in a marriage are granted a divorce without having to prove fault. Prior to these types of divorces, at least one party had to be found guilty of some form of wrong-doing in order for a couple to be allowed to divorce. Between 1953 and 1987, most fault-based divorce laws were eliminated in the United States, enabling spouses to split without legally establishing blame. Some view the elimination of these laws as devastating to the family institution. The relative ease of obtaining a divorce under no-fault laws leads some to believe that these laws provide incentives for divorce rather than providing incentives to solve marital problems. As you can see in the graph on the next page, during the year that the no-fault divorce legislation was enacted, the divorce rate increased in almost every state.[56]

One alternative to these laws is covenant marriage, which places conditions on the circumstances in which a divorce will be permitted. The specific terms of a covenant marriage vary by state, but the intention is to put a roadblock between a couple and an "easy divorce." This does not mean that couples cannot divorce in states with covenant marriages—only that for those who agreed to enter into one, divorce is more difficult. There has been some debate over the benefits of covenant marriage; some argue that this will decrease divorces, while others claim that it can trap people in unhappy marriages.[57] Should society spend effort attempting to lower divorce rates? Is divorce really a social problem, or does it merely reflect a change in the way we construct families?

Child Abuse and Neglect Fatality Victims by Age

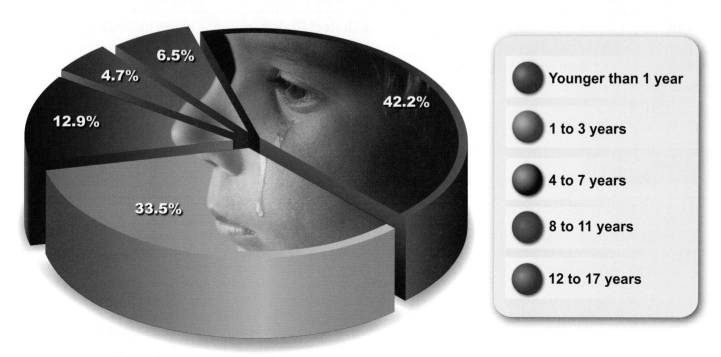

- Younger than 1 year
- 1 to 3 years
- 4 to 7 years
- 8 to 11 years
- 12 to 17 years

42.2%
33.5%
12.9%
4.7%
6.5%

Source: Child Welfare Information Gateway, "Child Abuse and Neglect Fatalities: Statistics and Interventions," 2008, http://www.childwelfare.gov/pubs/factsheets/fatality.cfm, Accessed August 27, 2009.

Changes in Divorce Rate Following the Passage of No-Fault Divorce Laws

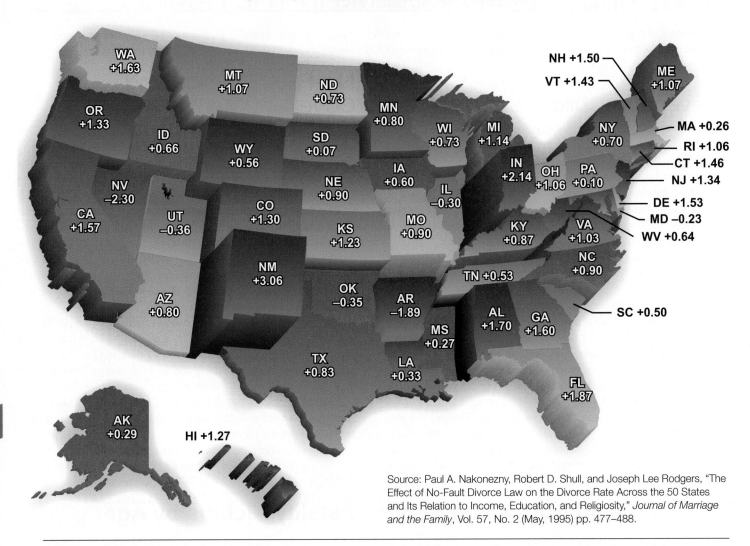

Source: Paul A. Nakonezny, Robert D. Shull, and Joseph Lee Rodgers, "The Effect of No-Fault Divorce Law on the Divorce Rate Across the 50 States and Its Relation to Income, Education, and Religiosity," *Journal of Marriage and the Family*, Vol. 57, No. 2 (May, 1995) pp. 477–488.

∧
∧ **After no-fault divorce laws were enacted in the United States, divorce rates increased** in
∧ almost every state. Does this represent a breakdown of family values, or a chance for
many to escape unhappy marriages?

MAKE CONNECTIONS

The Family and Society

Problems in the family are closely related to other social problems. As you learned in Chapter 13, crime is a social problem that affects many people around the world, and child abuse is no exception. By enacting social policies to prevent this abuse, we can reduce its negative impact on society.

Changing family structures can also have an impact on population. In Chapter 18, you'll discover that families are having fewer children now than they did a few decades ago. In some countries, this "birth dearth" has resulted in a population decline. However, raising fewer children has effects on the definition of marriage as well. If people are no longer marrying with the intention of having children and start-ing their own families, has the purpose of marriage changed?

In addition to the change in family struc-tures, ideas about marriage are changing as well. As you learned in Chapter 11, mar-riage relationships are no longer strictly lim-ited to those that exist between men and women. Same-sex unions are also likely to have an impact on our future perceptions and definitions of marriage and family.

Does Covenant Marriage Help or Harm Families?

Pro

- Covenant marriages prevent couples from jumping into divorce too quickly, which helps keep families intact. The establishment of a covenant marriage prevents either spouse from making hasty decisions and can, over time, lead to the resolution of marital difficulties.

- People entering into covenant marriages require counseling before getting married and before considering a divorce. Forcing couples to address marriage in a realistic way through premarital counseling will lead to stronger marriages and families, because both parties will have fewer unmet expectations. Research shows that couples who receive some form of counseling to address their issues before considering a divorce are less likely to separate.

- These strict limitations for divorce lead to stronger families with two parents who are able to provide a stable environment for their children. In this type of atmosphere, children are able to thrive in a way that children in single-parent homes cannot.

- If one spouse wants to get a divorce and bypass the stipulations of the covenant marriage, he or she only has to file for divorce in a state that does not legally recognize covenant marriage. At present, there are 47 such states.

Con

- The fact that covenant marriages prevent couples from getting quick divorces leads to prolonged agony, stress, and dissatisfaction within the home. The entire family will be affected, leading to extended trauma for both the spouses and the children.

- Even though covenant marriages require counseling, there is no guarantee that such an intervention will produce positive results. Counseling before marriage is relatively useless because both parties expect to have a successful marriage as they begin their lives together.

- Under the rules outlined in covenant marriages, a divorce can only be granted through one of three circumstances: (1) spousal abuse, (2) adultery, or (3) the commission of a felony that results in jail time. If one spouse does not want a divorce, counseling is recommended, even under one of these three circumstances. In some cases, even if abuse is proven, there is still a mandatory two-year separation period. Some argue that these strict limitations serve to trap unhappy spouses, leading to further deterioration of the family and the relationship.

- Covenant marriages are only recognized in three states: Louisiana, Arizona, and Arkansas. Because covenant marriages are recognized in so few states, any couple interested in pursuing such a marriage would have to do so in a select area. These factors can make a covenant marriage exceptionally inconvenient and costly to pursue.

From Classroom to Community | Helping Children of Divorce

During her four years at college, Diana volunteered as an aide in a local elementary school's after-school program for kids whose parents weren't able to pick them up immediately when school ended. She spent most of her days helping with homework, playing games, or talking to the kids about what was going on in their lives. In most cases, these kids came from single-parent families.

Diana found that although many of the children were there under different circumstances, they all had some things in common as well. Most of them were visibly withdrawn and depressed. They would participate in the activities she arranged, but Diana could tell it was only because they had to. Many of them needed extra attention paid to their homework as well.

One of the parents Diana spoke with was concerned because her son had gotten excellent grades before the divorce, but now he seemed disinterested and found it difficult to focus on his schoolwork. Other children seemed overly anxious or shy. They were so afraid of messing up that Diana almost hated to call on them to participate in activities.

After seeing the same sorts of behaviors time and time again, Diana realized that the kids in the after-school program might benefit from talking to each other about the issues they faced as children from single-parent families. Once a week, she held a discussion group in which the children could air their worries and concerns, as well as their anger and other emotions associated with the changes most of them had gone through.

In less than a month, Diana saw results. Some of the quietest children became outgoing, leading the discussions and volunteering to participate in other activities as well. A couple of them started a study group, and she would often find a circle of children sitting on the floor working on assignments together.

Now, Diana is one of the community center administrators and heads the after-school program.

"Volunteering was really a great experience for me. It's wonderful to see the way the kids have improved. Some have gone from being really anxious and withdrawn to being really friendly and open about their feelings. I think it's important that these children have others to talk to who understand what they're going through. They need to know that they're not alone. I look forward to seeing the day when some of the kids who have benefited from this program come back to guide other kids who are dealing with the same issues."

WHAT SOCIAL PROBLEMS RELATE TO MARRIAGE AND FAMILY? 210

marital satisfaction, child rearing, and divorce

HOW DO WE VIEW MARRIAGE? 215

symbolic interactionism: looking at marriage on a micro level, the expectations and roles of men and women help determine the success of a marriage; as these roles change and couples adjust to these changes, the structure of the family also changes
conflict theory: when both spouses must work outside the home, conflict can arise in determining who will take on certain household chores
functionalism: the purpose of marriage is to have children and provide a safe environment in which to raise them to become productive members of society

WHAT ARE SOME PROBLEMS IN THE FAMILY? 217

child abuse and divorce

get the topic: WHAT SOCIAL PROBLEMS RELATE TO MARRIAGE AND FAMILY?

Theory

FUNCTIONALISM 215
- the family serves the purpose of ensuring that people are able to successfully function in society
- by living in a family unit, children are taught which types of behavior are acceptable and which types of behavior are frowned upon, and develop skills related to tolerance and cooperation

SYMBOLIC INTERACTIONISM 215
- it's important to think about how marriage relates to society
- asking questions about marriage and what it means to people will lead to a better understanding of the importance of family in everyday life

CONFLICT THEORY 215
- in marriage, there is competition over the limited resources of time and energy
- in many cases, this conflict revolves around household duties and child care

Key Terms

marriage is the union of two people that is typically recognized by law or cultural norms. *210*

family is two or more people who are related by blood, marriage, or adoption. *210*

nuclear family is a household consisting of a husband, wife, and children. *210*

extended family is a household consisting of a nuclear family and additional relatives. *210*

blended families are families composed of children and some combination of biological parents and stepparents. *212*

Sample Test Questions

These multiple-choice questions are similar to those found in the test bank that accompanies this textbook.

1. A nuclear family consists of
   a. a husband and a wife.
   b. a single parent.
   c. a husband, a wife, and children.
   d. a boy and his dog.

2. Which of the following is *not* a myth about the family?
   a. All families are nuclear families.
   b. Nuclear families are outdated.
   c. Families are self-reliant.
   d. Nuclear families are ideal.

3. One of the observations that conflict theorists make about marriage is the potential for struggle over
   a. time and energy.
   b. food and resources.
   c. child affection.
   d. interior decorating.

4. Sarah and Jason are thinking of marriage. Which of of these factors might increase their chance of a divorce?
   a. Sarah comes from a wealthier background than Jason does.
   b. Jason's parents separated when he was fifteen.
   c. Neither plan on raising children.
   d. They both have Second Life accounts.

5. Covenant marriages
   a. allow spouses to split without legally establishing blame.
   b. limit the circumstances under which a divorce can be granted.
   c. are sexist in nature, favoring men over women.
   d. have recently been abolished in all 50 states.

ESSAY

1. In your opinion, is an online flirtation with a member of the opposite sex grounds for divorce? How might an interactionist explain Amy Taylor's reaction to her husband's online "cheating"?

2. Is the nuclear family the "ideal" family arrangement? If not, which arrangement is ideal?

3. Do you think that same-sex unions pose a challenge for defining family? Why or why not?

4. In your opinion, is a covenant marriage likely to build stronger unions, or does it serve to trap individuals in their marriages? What effect might such a marriage have on children?

5. From the point of view of a functionalist, how does child abuse affect a child in the long run? Taking this into consideration, do you believe that parents who abuse their children should receive jail time or treatment (or both)?

WHERE TO START YOUR RESEARCH PAPER

For information on marriage and divorce rates in the United States, go to http://www.cdc.gov/nchs/fastats/divorce.htm

To learn more about the characteristics of families in the United States, visit http://www.census.gov/population/www/socdemo/hh-fam.html

To read an article on various types of marriages, go to http://www.redbookmag.com/love-sex/advice/types-of-marriages

For child abuse and neglect statistics, see
http://www.childwelfare.gov/preventing/
http://www.childhelp.org/resources/learning-center/statistics

To learn more about covenant marriage, visit
http://www.covenantmarriage.com

ANSWERS: 1. c; 2. b; 3. a; 4. b; 5. b

Remember to check www.thethinkspot.com **for additional information, downloadable flashcards, and other helpful resources.**

URBANIZATION:
SOCIAL PROBLEMS FROM THE GROWTH OF CITIES

HOW DO CITIES AFFECT SOCIETY?
DO CITIES CREATE SOCIAL PROBLEMS
FOR SOCIETIES AND INDIVIDUALS?
CAN PLANNING PROVIDE SOLUTIONS TO
PROBLEMS CREATED BY
URBANIZATION?

It's easy

to get lost in the maze that is Beidian. The small village on the outskirts of Beijing is a network of alleyways, some so tight that a couple can barely walk hand in hand, others just wide enough for a farm truck loaded down with cabbages to squeeze by. Homes, shops, and tiny eateries jam up against each other.

Similar enclaves have sprung up in the Chinese capital's rural northeast in recent years as a steady flow of people makes their way from poorer provinces in search of higher-paying jobs. In Beidian, the population of permanent residents has grown to about 1,000 people from 800 in 2003.

At the same time, communities are being gobbled up by urban sprawl and many people have lost their fields and homes to development. The struggle to make a living is continuous.

By day, the paved but dusty streets of Beidian are buzzing with a chaotic mix of people, bicycles, and roadside vendors. There is simple, hearty fare to be found at almost every corner, from hand-cut noodles to crisp and flaky variations of fried dough to roasted-on-the-spot popcorn and pumpkin seeds.

When the sun sets, pockets of fluorescent, neon, and yellow lights flicker on as hair salons, mom-and-pop grocery stores and small eateries continue to operate. In winter, the smell of burning coal fills the air as residents cook dinner and keep warm.

They live in rented rooms—averaging about 13 by 13 feet (4 by 4 meters)—in partitioned one-story brick and concrete buildings with corrugated tin roofs and courtyards filled with drying clothes, mops, and empty paint cans. The compounds are sealed off with big metal gates. The cheapest is just under 200 yuan ($28) a month and the price goes all the way up to about 500 yuan ($70).

Many of the tenants are women from the poor, central province of Anhui who have come to Beijing to secure jobs as maids to support their families at home. Some come with their husbands, mostly laborers, and have stayed for many years, cleaning the homes of foreigners and other Chinese. It's an existence vastly different from the farm life they are used to.

"Sure we make a little more money here but life is also more expensive," said Shi Yulian, 37, who came to Beijing 10 years ago with her husband. "In the end, the benefits aren't that great but we have no choice. There are still more opportunities in the city than where I'm from."

As the sun lowers in the sky, it's time to shop at the markets and cook meals for their families. Oil sizzles as cut-up vegetables are thrown into coal blackened woks. Windows steam up as rice cookers bubble away. A bit of dried salt pork, hanging from a wire, is cut to round off a meal.

Families sit down to eat as a stillness settles over Beidian.

Soon it will be time for bed.[1]

---The bright lights, the busy streets, the constant hustle and bustle—these aspects of city life sound exciting to some and unpleasant to others.

No matter what your opinion on urban living, however, the fact remains that cities have become a necessary hub for modern finance, industry, and government. As Beijing resident Shi Yulian mentioned in the opening article, cities offer more opportunities than small villages because housing and commerce are centrally located.

Although the United States has no city as crowded as Beijing, the problems created by urban growth occur here as well. Certainly, as populations around the world continue to expand, more and more people are likely to live in cities. What types of social issues might arise when people move from rural to urban areas?

How do cities deal with their growing populations? What effect do you think this has on both the citizens of cities and the citizens of rural areas?

As we broach these topics, we will primarily focus on urbanization in the United States. Keep in mind, however, that these issues do not affect just one country. No matter where they live, urban citizens share many of the same problems.

get the topic: HOW DO CITIES AFFECT SOCIETY?

Urban and Rural

Do you live in an urban area or a rural one? Your answer, of course, depends on how you define those terms. The term **urban** is used when referring to a city with a population density of at least 1,000.[2] **Population density** indicates the number of humans per square mile. For example, the density of New York City (which has approximately 8.2 million people living within 300 square miles) is 27,000 people per square mile.[3] Meanwhile, Calumet City, Illinois is 7 square miles large and is home to 37,000 people, making its population density about 5,300 people per square mile.[4] Both cities fit the definition of "urban" according to the United States Census Bureau. How might the lives of residents differ based on population density?

The term **rural** is used to refer to areas not considered urban.[5] Throughout most of human history, even though many ancient cities existed, a majority of the people lived in rural areas where they could hunt, farm, and live off the land. Even as late as 1800, estimates suggest that only about 3 percent of the world's population lived in urban areas. It's only in the last two centuries that populations and cities have begun to grow rapidly. In 1935, there were almost 6.8 million farms in the United States; by 2008, there were just 2.1 million.

In that same time period, the number of Americans nearly tripled from 127 million to 300 million.[6] Over time, the population has shifted from rural to urban areas, so much so that now more than 80 percent of U.S. residents live in cities.[7] The process by which individuals or groups migrate from rural areas to urban areas is known as **urbanization**.

Urbanization Around the World

Globally, this trend continues as well. In fact, 2008 was the first time in known human history that the world's population was split evenly between those living in rural and those living in urban areas. Currently, there are more than 400 cities with over 1 million people worldwide. Estimates suggest that by 2050, approximately 70 percent of the world's population will be urban.[8] Throughout the planet, the number of **megacities**—cities with 10 million residents or more—has grown significantly, especially in the poorer regions of the world. In 1980, there were three megacities; in 2000, there were over 15.[9]

>>> **The San Fernando Valley,** commonly called "The Valley," **is a metropolitan area made up of five cities:** Los Angeles, Burbank, Glendale, San Fernando, and Calabasas, with Los Angeles as the central city.

Rapid urbanization can introduce many social problems. The population boom increases the demand for public services, housing, and infrastructure, as well as the need for clean water, sewage, and solid waste disposal. Still, the opportunity for work is enough to lure individuals to the city, even if the city is not yet prepared to satisfy those individuals' basic needs.[10] Some point out that urban areas can be efficient vehicles for growth. For example, by hosting large pools of low-skilled laborers, cities can attract foreign investors seeking cheaper manufacturing prices. Furthermore, if planned well, cities can actually be an efficient way to support a large population. If a city builds up, instead of out, farm land can remain relatively unaffected.[11]

How can a city in a poor nation, such as Dhaka, Bangladesh, be able to support a population almost the size of Los Angeles? In short, it often can't. Dhaka is the fastest growing megacity in the world, and its problems continue to mount. Many residents live in low-lying areas prone to flooding, which promotes disease; in these slums, crime, and poverty abound. Imagine the issues associated with trying to provide something simple, such as clean water, to a city of this size and poverty level. In Dhaka, 70 percent of the poor do not have access to this basic necessity, and 90 percent do not have means to proper sewage disposal. Schools are few and far between, leaving most children illiterate. Employment is difficult to find, and many beg and steal for survival. The city grows because people migrate there to seek jobs and because population control measures have failed to curb increasing birth rates. Dhaka is just one of thousands of cities throughout the developing world where urbanization and population growth combine to create serious social problems.[12]

Urbanization in the United States

During the early stages of urbanization in the United States, cities often experienced many of the same types of problems that are present in Dhaka and other parts of the developing world. As population and immigration expanded, cities in the United States became centers for filth, disease, and crime. Urban ghettos in the late 1800s may have resembled the modern day megacities around the globe. However, a great deal has changed since then; as public health in the United States has expanded, the average U.S. city provides clean water and sewage systems, as well as an extensive police and fire service.[13]

Today, almost every household in the United States has electricity and water, and 99.9 percent have a refrigerator.[14] Problems in U.S. cities revolve around sprawl, suburbanization, and segregation. Before we address these issues, however, let's consider some facts about urbanization in the United States.

The table below lists the most populated cities in the United States. The significantly larger number in the fourth column represents the **metropolitan area**, a city that is inclusive of the surrounding areas. For example, the Washington, D.C., metropolitan area consists of the main city of Washington as well as Alexandria, VA, Arlington, VA, Bethesda, MD, and other urban areas in a 20-mile radius. When the land between cities becomes completely filled with people, houses, and businesses, a metropolitan area becomes known as a **megalopolis**.

For a town to be considered part of a metropolitan area, it needs to be connected to the main city by more than proximity; according to the United States Office of Management and Budget, the community must

> **URBAN** is a term used when referring to a city.
>
> **POPULATION DENSITY** is a measure of the number of humans per square mile.
>
> **RURAL** is a term used when referring to the countryside.
>
> **URBANIZATION** is a process by which individuals or groups migrate from rural areas to urban areas.
>
> **MEGACITIES** are cities with 10 million residents or more.
>
> **METROPOLITAN AREA** is a metropolis, or city, that is inclusive of the surrounding areas.
>
> **MEGALOPOLIS** is an extensive metropolitan area.

U.S. Cities with the Largest Populations

City	State	Population	Metropolitan Population	Cities Included in Metropolitan Area
1. New York City	New York	8,214,426	18,323,002	New York City, Northern New Jersey, Long Island
2. Los Angeles	California	3,849,378	12,365,627	Los Angeles, Long Beach, Santa Anna
3. Chicago	Illinois	2,833,321	9,098,316	Chicago, Naperville, Joliet
4. Houston	Texas	2,144,491	4,715,407	Houston, Baytown, Sugarland
5. Phoenix	Arizona	1,512,986	3,251,876	Phoenix, Mesa, Scottsdale
6. Philadelphia	Pennsylvania	1,448,394	5,687,147	Philadelphia, Camden, Wilmington
7. San Antonio	Texas	1,296,682	1,711,703	San Antonio
8. San Diego	California	1,256,951	2,813,833	San Diego, Carlsbad, San Marcos
9. Dallas	Texas	1,232,940	5,161,544	Dallas, Fort Worth
10. San Jose	California	929,936	1,735,819	San Jose, Sunnyvale, Santa Clara

Source: U.S. Census Bureau, Population Division, Annual Estimates of the Population for Incorporated Places over 100,000, Ranked by Population: April 1, 2000 to July 1, 2006, http://www.census.gov/popest/cities/SUB-EST2007.html

The 10 Most Populated Urban Areas

2000 Urban Area	Population (in thousands)	2015 Urban Area	Population Estimate (in thousands)
1. Tokyo (Japan)	26,444	1. Tokyo (Japan)	27,190
2. Mexico City (Mexico)	18,066	2. Dhaka (Bangladesh)	22,766
3. São Paulo (Brazil)	17,962	3. Mumbai (India)	22,577
4. New York City (USA)	16,732	4. São Paulo (Brazil)	21,229
5. Mumbai (India)	16,086	5. Delhi (India)	20,884
6. Los Angeles (USA)	13,213	6. Mexico City (Mexico)	20,434
7. Calcutta (India)	13,058	7. New York City (USA)	17,944
8. Shanghai (China)	12,887	8. Jakarta (Indonesia)	17,268
9. Dhaka (Bangladesh)	12,519	9. Calcutta (India)	16,747
10. Delhi (India)	12,441	10. Karachi (Pakistan)	16,197

Source: United Nations, World Urbanization Prospects: The 2001 Revision, Accessed January 15, 2008,
http://www.un.org/esa/population/publications/wup2001/WUP2001_CH6.pdf

have a high degree of social and economic integration with the center city. For example, a large number of residents of Bethesda, MD, work in Washington, D.C., and regularly take the Metro transit system into the city to shop and dine.[15]

The crowded nature of urban life holds both advantages and disadvantages. For individuals who want to reap the benefits of city living such as job opportunities and commerce, but don't want to deal with the dense population and limited dwelling space, settling in a city suburb is a sensible compromise. A **suburb** is an area that is near a central city but beyond the political boundaries of that city. For example, Norwood, Ohio, is a suburb of Cincinnati. Norwood is only a few miles away, so individuals can live in Norwood and work, shop, and do business in the city. However, since they are not residents, they cannot vote in Cincinnati elections.

Suburbs and smaller towns around central cities have been growing rapidly in the past decades, a process known as **counterurbanization**. This term refers to the new trend in which city growth has slowed as more rural areas and suburban areas have grown.[16] Such growth is driven by a number of factors, one of which is income segregation. Research shows that higher-income households are more likely to occupy newer houses while lower-income households are likely to live in older houses. These newer, larger homes are in expensive suburban areas outside central cities, which deny the cities the tax revenue from these wealthy, suburban citizens.[17]

In addition to the loss of revenue, when individuals move to the suburbs, their absence puts a strain on the central city. Although these individuals live outside the border, they still use city resources such as parks and transit systems. They also contribute to problems in the city such as crime, pollution, and traffic, without contributing fiscally to the police, fire department, or other city services used to control these problems.

When people leave the central city, they take their political power as well. This migration creates a transfer in authority from central government to local government, known as **decentralization**. To combat this dilemma, many cities have created an umbrella structure. The city of Miami, for example, created a **metropolitan federation**—a collaborative form of government across a metropolitan area—with Dade County in 1957. The "metro" government includes Miami and 27 suburban towns. The city and individual suburbs retain control of local utilities, while the federation controls the area-wide utilities such as police departments and transportation. Other major metropolitan areas such as Nashville and Davidson County, Tennessee, and Jacksonville and Duval County, Florida, have similar systems.[18]

The Problems of Urbanization
URBAN SPRAWL

A sea of interconnected cul-de-sacs with uniform homes and manicured lawns forms the suburban utopia portrayed in television shows such as *Desperate Housewives* and movies such as *Pleasantville*. However, due

>>> **Suburban developments,** typically in the form of subdivisions, **threaten the** livelihood of farmers and the entire **agricultural industry.**

to urban sprawl, suburban life is not pleasant for everyone, particularly farmers, environmentalists, and urban planners. **Urban sprawl** refers to the spreading of a city and its neighboring suburban areas over rural land along the borders of the metro area. This phenomenon happens when city or suburban dwellers move to the fringes of an urban region in search of larger homes or more serene surroundings. Although modern transportation enables urban sprawl, suburban dwellers contribute to traffic jams, pollution, and diffusion of the economic base.[19] Low population density—a small number of residents in a large space—is a marker of a sprawl area. This trend started to gain popularity after World War II. In 1950, nearly 70 million Americans lived in the nation's urbanized regions, which, at the time, covered some 13,000 square miles. By 1990, the population in urban and suburban neighborhoods had more than doubled, yet the area occupied by that population nearly quintupled to more than 60,000 square miles.[20]

Levittown, NY, which sits a few miles outside New York City, was the first mass-produced community and has come to represent the stereotypical sprawl suburb. The development company Levitt and Son was one of the first to introduce the mass-produced home, which made housing cheap and development fast. The company also built three other Levittowns in Pennsylvania, New Jersey, and Puerto Rico.[21]

Developments like Levittown are controversial because the expansion of urban areas can fragment and destroy wildlife habitats. People who reside in these areas typically live in single-family homes and drive to work; they therefore tend to emit more pollution per person than city dwellers because they do not have access to mass transit systems or the option to walk or bike.[22] A suburban family with two vehicles makes 10 car trips a day on average. A commuter who lives an hour from work spends the equivalent of 12 workweeks, or 500 hours, in a car annually. This commute is usually met with traffic delays that create more than 72 billion dollars in wasted fuel and subsequent pollution.[23]

SUBURB is an area near a central city but beyond the political boundaries of that city.

COUNTERURBANIZATION refers to the process by which city growth has slowed as more rural areas and suburban areas have grown.

DECENTRALIZATION is the transfer of authority from a central government to a local government.

METROPOLITAN FEDERATION is a collaborative form of government across a metropolitan area.

URBAN SPRAWL is the spreading of a city and its neighboring suburban areas over rural land along the borders of the metro area.

Urban sprawl also threatens farming by invading farmland or inflating property taxes that render the land too expensive to farm. Currently, urban sprawl is taking over farmland at the rate of 1.2 million acres a year; factoring in forest and other undeveloped land, the net annual loss is nearly two million acres.[24] According to a U.S. Census Bureau survey that measured metro area growth from 2006 to 2007, urban sprawl is also happening in smaller cities, such as Austin, Texas, and Raleigh, North Carolina.[25]

Urban planners hope to curb urban sprawl by growing more efficient communities, a process sometimes referred to as "smart growth." Plans include fixing up and filling in old communities that are sandwiched between cities and suburban sprawl areas, and extending mass transit systems. "Smart growth" efforts also try to preserve open spaces by creating zoning laws that prevent development. The National Aeronautics and Space Administration (NASA) uses their satellite systems to document urban growth from a bird's-eye view, so that urban planners can get a better understanding of the impact of a sprawl.[26]

Chicago's Growth and Decline

1850 — 29,963 people

Urbanization

1950 — 3,620,962 people

Urban Sprawl

2009 — 2,853,114 people

Source: "Chicago Growth 1850–1990" from Chicago Imagebase, by the University of Illinois at Chicago, Accessed Sept. 28, 2009, http://tigger. uic.edu/depts/ahaa/imagebase/chimaps/mcclendon.html; U.S. Census Bureau , 2008 Population Estimates, Census 2000, 1990 Census

> **Urban sprawls,** such as that of Chicago, **place monetary strains on cities, decentralize political power, and damage the natural environment.**

INDEX OF DISSIMILARITY (D) indicates the percentage of people that would need to be relocated in order to have a perfectly even distribution of race and ethnicity in a city.

P* INDEX FOR INTERACTION calculates the amount of contact an average person of one group has with an average person of another group on any given day.

ETHNIC GROUPING is the tendency for members of particular ethnic groups to want to live in close proximity to one another.

WHITE FLIGHT is the departure of Caucasian individuals from neighborhoods increasingly or predominantly populated by minorities.

DISINVESTMENT is a deliberate pattern whereby banking and lending institutions make decisions about where they will and will not support investments.

REDLINING is a practice in which home lenders draw red lines on a map, indicating to which sides of a city they will and will not lend money.

GRIDLOCK is a series of traffic jams.

SEGREGATION

As you learned in Chapter 3, segregation is the process by which racial or ethnic groups are kept separate from each other. Although segregation is technically illegal in the United States, that does not mean that individuals aren't separated by race within cities. Sociologists often use a variety of measures to calculate segregation.[27] The **index of dissimilarity (D)** indicates the percentage of people that would need to be relocated to have a perfectly even distribution of race and ethnicity in a city. Sociologists use data from census blocks to calculate how people in an area are actually distributed. Massey and Denton, using these techniques, found that blacks across all income levels experience similar levels of segregation from whites. In other words, the index of dissimilarity is equally high regardless of socioeconomic status (SES).[28]

Another important measure is known as the **P* index for interaction**. This formula calculates the amount of contact an average person of one group has with an average person from another group on any given day. Instead of simulating an even distribution of individuals, this calculation simply provides a measure for the amount of interaction between people.[29]

Cities are typically composed of a heterogeneous population—a melting pot that includes people of different racial and ethnic backgrounds. However, in many instances that pot is not stirred well, and pockets of racially segregated areas develop, decreasing the opportunities for interaction. Chicago, for instance, is America's most racially segregated city. Many neighborhoods have populations that are made up of 75 percent of one particular ethnic group.[30] Such ethnic and racial segregation can create social problems for a city, especially when a disparity of wealth between groups exists. Does residential segregation occur primarily because of socioeconomic differences among racial groups?

Massey notes that the disparity between the rich and the poor has been increasing in the United States. This trend affects the distribution of people, creating a situation in which the poor are increasingly concentrated in poor areas and the rich in rich areas. Such economic segregation is linked to race, but cannot be totally explained by such. One thing is certain: Economic segregation reduces contact between the two groups and the subsequent benefits that come from such interaction. Reduced interaction can lead to lower political representation, fewer job opportunities, and deteriorating schools.[31] Research shows that high-SES racial and ethnic groups are less segregated from whites than low-income groups; this tendency is especially true for Hispanics and Asians. However, as mentioned before, African Americans, regardless of their SES, are more segregated from whites than other groups.[32] Thus, both race and income determine levels of segregation.

These racial lines have been established and maintained by **ethnic grouping**, the tendency for members of particular ethnic groups to want to live in close proximity, as well as prejudice and racism, particularly in the case of white flight. **White flight** is the departure of Caucasian individuals from neighborhoods increasingly or predominantly populated by minorities. Some minorities also engage in "flight" from primarily white neighborhoods. Still, whites have a higher likelihood of outmigration when their neighborhoods become integrated, regardless of the minority's race or ethnicity.[33] Although there is no denying that "flight" of any kind is motivated by prejudicial beliefs, some might argue that the migration is a matter of economics, as the racial demographics of a neighborhood can affect the value of real estate.

Residential segregation is one of the reasons that racism still persists in the United States. Would a decline in segregation change attitudes? Microresearch among students yields some interesting results. Using longitudinal data, researchers were able to show correlations between in-school friendships and residential segregation. Many friendships are segregated by race, but this research showed that a decline in residential segregation mitigated friendship segregation. In other words, those who lived in mixed neighborhoods had a greater chance at overcoming racial segregation of friendships.[34]

Social policies that lead to economic and racial segregation can result in structural problems as well. **Disinvestment** is a deliberate choice made by banking and lending institutions on where they will and will not support investments. This behavior is also known as **redlining** because home lenders used to literally draw lines on a map with a red pen to denote on which sides of a city they would or would not lend money. This practice is now illegal, but still occurs in subtle ways, and goes beyond home loans. Other important social services and access to jobs, health care, and stores are sometimes denied simply because

>>> So-called **redlining** is illegal today, although it **continues through subtle biases.**

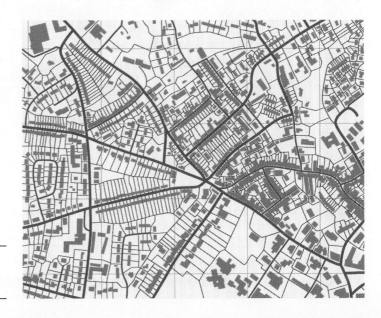

a neighborhood is on the "wrong side" of the tracks, highway, or river. This denial causes already disadvantaged areas to remain disadvantaged and to deteriorate further.[35]

TRANSPORTATION

Transportation issues naturally develop in a city; after all, with an increase in population comes an increase in cars. In major metro areas, the combined length of the morning and evening rush hours has doubled from three hours to six hours in the last 25 years. The average driver spends the equivalent of almost a full workweek each year stuck in traffic. People in the Los Angeles area lose the most amount of time due to traffic (56 hours per year), followed by commuters in Atlanta and Seattle (53 hours per year).[36]

Unclogging this **gridlock**, or series of traffic jams, has been a puzzle for urban planners and governments. The expansion of highways and mass transit systems has been a common solution to urban traffic problems, but these types of infrastructure take a lot of time and tax dollars to build.[38] Some government programs help make a city's current transportation system more efficient. For example, in Los Angeles drivers who carpool have an exclusive lane on the highway, and in New York City, individuals use tax-free income to pay for mass transit fares. Other initiatives such as bike- or walk-to-work programs also clear more cars from the road.

The Benefits of Mass Transit

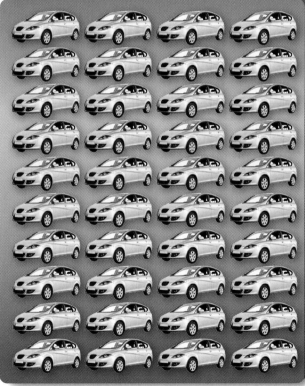

Sources: Peter J. Pantuso, President & CEO, American Bus Association, *Testimony, Surface* Transportation Policy & Revenue Commission, March 19, 2007, http://transportationfortomorrow.org/pdfs/commission_meetings/0307_field_hearing_washington/031907_fh_aba_testimony.pdf; Moving Beyond Congestion, *Mass Transit Capital Funding: The Need to Maintain, Enhance, and Expand* http://www.rtachicago.com/CMS400Min/uploadedFiles/Bklt-Web.pdf

 **= 20 cars**

∧
∧ Ninety percent of cars on the highway are only carrying one person.[37] **Public transportation**
∧ **provides a much more efficient way to move large numbers of people.**

City Dwellers

Some city dwellers can look past problems of crime, segregation, and congestion and see the liveliness that makes a city more than just a location. For example, the character of Carrie Bradshaw from *Sex and the City* often referred to New York City as her significant other. Sociologist Louis Wirth has a more critical view of the urbanite. He contends that urban life isolates individuals and leaves them with fewer interpersonal relationships and less connection to society. Urbanites develop impersonality and self-interest and tend to put off marriage and have fewer children.

City dwellers are more socially diverse and less unified than those who live in rural areas, and this diversity disrupts traditional social structures, which in turn creates instability and insecurity. This unstable social structure is connected to higher rates of suicide, mental breakdown, delinquency, crime, and a host of other problems.[39] Poor urban areas often develop a separate culture, in which toughness, strength, and self-centered existence rule, and roughness and violence are more acceptable than kindness and tolerance.[40]

Profile of an Urbanite

Has few personal relationships

Experiences more stress than peers who live in rural areas

Does not connect with the people around him or her

Is overly concerned with money

Puts off marriage

Places more emphasis on what he or she does for a living than on the type of person he or she is

Source: Louis Wirth, "Urbanism as Way of Life." 1938. *American Journal of Sociology* 434.1, July 1938. 1–24.

According to Louis Wirth, **urban individuals live more isolated lives** with fewer personal relationships and connections to society **than their rural and suburban peers.**

UN-HABITAT

Urbanization is occurring around the world. Some of the problems associated with urbanization may be unique to a particular city and require a specific action plan to solve. However, a global approach to urbanization can improve the overall standard of living for citizens around the world, and prevent possible international crises. This international response needs to happen soon, as the number of people living in urban areas has already reached 50 percent. Every year, 20 new cities reach the population size of Washington, D.C.

This projected growth is due to the rapid urbanization of developing countries. By the end of the 21st century, it's estimated that there will be more people living in the dense cities of developing countries than there are people alive in the entire world today. The urbanization of developing countries can have a destructive effect on the global economy because workers are leaving the agriculture sector in rural areas for industrial jobs in the city. Governments often see this movement as a sign of progress and sophistication, but the devaluing of agriculture can affect a country's ability to provide the products needed to sustain city dwellers. For example, approximately 30 years ago, Algeria was able to export surpluses of wheat; due to urbanization in the country, today it does not have enough to feed its own population and must import the crop from other nations.[41]

The United Nations Human Settlements Programme (UN-HABITAT) hopes to develop global initiatives that will solve the problems related to urbanization, such as crime, agricultural shortages, and lowered standards of living. The UN General Assembly has authorized this program to promote socially and environmentally sustainable cities with the objective of providing adequate shelter for all urban dwellers. The primary goal of UN-HABITAT is to improve "the social, economic, and environmental quality of human settlements and the living and working environments of all people." Current UN-HABITAT programs that address water, sanitation, and housing rights are already starting to increase the standard of living in urban areas around the globe.[42]

think social problems: DO CITIES CREATE SOCIAL PROBLEMS FOR SOCIETIES AND INDIVIDUALS?

Functionalism

Does the size of the city influence how people live within it? German sociologist Ferdinand Tonnies divided society into two distinct groups based on the concept of *Gemeinschaft* (community) and *Gesellschaft* (society).[43] ***Gemeinschaft*** refers to community connections involving personal relationships based on friendship and kinship ties. People in rural areas have direct face-to-face contact with one another that often involves genuine and spontaneous emotions. Thus, the smaller the community, the greater the chance that people will care for their neighbors and become personally invested in their lives. Urban dwellers tend to live a different way. ***Gesellschaft*** refers to social connections that are more formal and impersonal. People in cities tend to be focused on personal interests and act more distant toward others.

Tonnies suggested that as societies grow more complex, interactions invariably become more impersonal. This is not always negative. To survive in urban areas, one must tend toward *Gesellschaft* relationships. Trying to get involved in everyone's life would be impossible if only because of the sheer size of the group.[44]

French sociologist Emile Durkheim agreed that the size of society and the form of society influences the way in which people live. He argued that solidarity is an important component that holds society together. Durkheim divided solidarity into two different types: mechanical and organic. **Mechanical solidarity** refers to the state of community bonding in traditional societies in which people share beliefs and values and perform common activities. Because of this homogeneity, each member of the society is directly and equally attached to the other members. An example of mechanical solidarity is a small farming co-op, which is a modern-day version of a hunting and gathering society.[45]

As societies become more complex, their type of solidarity changes from mechanical to organic. **Organic solidarity** occurs when people live in a society with a diverse division of labor. In urban areas, organic solidarity

GEMEINSCHAFT refers to community connections involving personal relationships based on friendship and kinship ties.

GESELLSCHAFT refers to social connections that are more formal and impersonal.

MECHANICAL SOLIDARITY is the state of community bonding in traditional societies in which people share beliefs and values and perform common activities.

ORGANIC SOLIDARITY is a state that occurs when people live in a society with a diverse division of labor.

is more likely because people become interdependent. A diverse division of labor means that people have different types of jobs, and they are tied to each other out of a need for survival. While rural citizens such as farmers may be tied together by the mechanisms of their day, city dwellers live as constant interdependent organisms.[46]

Conflict Theory

As we have discussed, segregation in U.S. cities is increasingly influenced by socioeconomic status. Such an idea relates to Marx's theory, which suggests that those with an advantage tend to work in ways to keep that advantage. When suburbanites flee the central city, they take their tax money with them. However, they often return to the city for entertainment, such as sporting and cultural events. Clearly, those with advantages and access to transportation can take their tax dollars out of the city and use them to build up the suburbs in which they live. Furthermore, segregation based on race and economic status tends to favor those who have the greatest access to wealth and power, contributing to expanding racism and economic deprivation of the poor. Conflict theorists suggest that such shortsightedness can lead to the death of the central city, hurting suburban dwellers in the long run as well.[47]

WRAP YOUR MIND AROUND THE THEORY

Urban areas are said to offer more opportunities, but in cases such as Calcutta, cities cannot provide all residents with adequate accommodations and services. **How do such circumstances affect people's social relationships?**

FUNCTIONALISM

Tonnies' and Durkheim's theories address how population density affects society's interactions and solidarity. The industrial revolution spurred on urbanization and changed the way in which people related to one another. While rural dwellers could afford to maintain their sense of community, urban dwellers developed a new way to coexist. In areas of rapid urbanization, inhabitants may struggle to adjust to the changes, and some may be left behind. Calcutta, India, is one of the largest cities in the world. Of the approximately 16 million people, more than 5 million are classified as slum dwellers, or individuals who live in well below average conditions.[48]

CONFLICT THEORY

The process of revitalizing an urban neighborhood isn't simple. What looks like a run-down slum to one person is home to another. Renewing struggling neighborhoods is often seen as positive because it beautifies a city and increases property value; however it also displaces residents who can no longer afford the new developments that have popped up to replace low-income housing. While developers make money from such transactions, others lose their homes. Those with wealth and power can use the process of revitalization to expand their fortunes at the expense of the poor.

HOW DO SOCIETIES DEAL WITH RAPID URBAN GROWTH?

SYMBOLIC INTERACTIONISM

Louis Wirth views urban life as a form of social organization that can be harmful and dehumanizing to the individual. In his words, the effects of urban life include a "substitution of secondary for primary contacts, the weakening of bonds of kinship, the declining social significance of the family, the disappearance of neighborhoods and the undermining of traditional basis of social solidarity."[49] Symbolic interactionists point out that urban residents are generally more isolated than those who live outside of cities, and they suffer from higher rates of depression, stress, and mental breakdowns.

Because individuals who live in low-income neighborhoods typically rent their homes, they are limited in their ability to fight new developments. **Do you think that laws should be enacted to stop developers from "renewing" certain neighborhoods, or do the benefits of revitalization outweigh the costs?**

Wirth suggests that even though urbanites are surrounded by thousands of people, they're actually more isolated than their peers outside of the city. **What aspects of urban life might cause a city dweller to isolate him- or herself?**

discover solutions to social problems:
CAN PLANNING PROVIDE SOLUTIONS TO PROBLEMS CREATED BY URBANIZATION?

Urban Renewal

A run-down neighborhood reflects poorly to the outside community, so urban renewal initiatives focus on fixing such eyesores. **Urban renewal** is the process of purchasing, clearing, and replacing neglected properties with newer, more appealing developments. The logic is that clearing run-down neighborhoods and relocating an unsavory population or industry will improve the overall city. These areas may have many problems, but they do provide affordable housing.

Urban renewal generally results in **gentrification**, which involves renovating and redeveloping a dilapidated neighborhood so that it meets middle-class standards, and subsequently displacing the original low-income residents. As a neighborhood gentrifies, its taxes and rents increase; low-income families are soon priced out of their neighborhood, sometimes even becoming homeless.[50] Research on the homeless shows that many are indeed employed, but they cannot afford housing on their wages.[51]

> **URBAN RENEWAL** is the process of purchasing, clearing, and replacing run-down properties with newer, more appealing developments.
>
> **GENTRIFICATION** is a trend that involves renovating and redeveloping a run-down neighborhood so that it meets middle-class standards, and subsequently displacing the original low-income residents.

The Pros and Cons of Urban Renewal

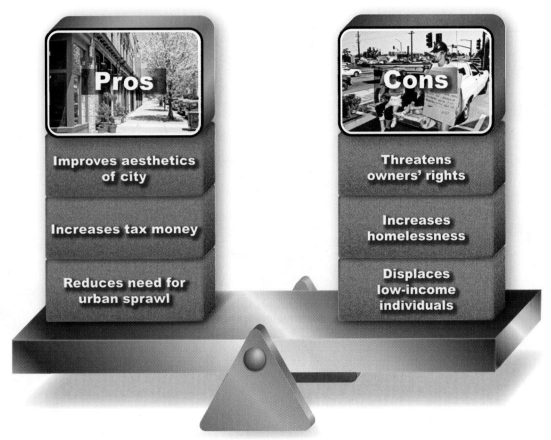

Pros
- Improves aesthetics of city
- Increases tax money
- Reduces need for urban sprawl

Cons
- Threatens owners' rights
- Increases homelessness
- Displaces low-income individuals

MAKE CONNECTIONS

Population Growth

In Chapter 19, we'll discuss the social problems involved with our treatment of the environment. Urbanization can create even greater strains on our ecosystem. Some of the issues facing cities revolve around the need for clean water, waste disposal, and reduction of air pol-lutants. As you learned in this chapter, cities around the globe are expanding their boundaries to encompass smaller towns and villages, while at the same time, citizens are moving to more urban places to increase their opportunities in life. Is there a future for the rural lifestyle?

Chapters 17 and 18 discuss the effects of population growth and globalization in the world today. As you saw in the opening article, the rural population is beginning to decrease as the population of the world increases. Cities that are well-planned can build up instead of out, handling the increasing population efficiently.

Funding Urban Renewal

From the standpoint of the city, low-income individuals pay fewer taxes and contribute less to the city's economy than middle-class residents do and, in some cases, are a drain on the city's resources. To encourage urban renewal, cities have started to use public funds to support private development. **Tax increment financing (TIF)** enables cities to use tax revenues generated by a development project (usually an urban renewal project) to help finance the construction of the new project through bonds given to developers and/or direct tax incentives. Ideally, the new construction project will generate new taxes, which will then support the project.

With the goal of urban renewal, sometimes the government takes property from individuals—often against the owner's will—for public use, a policy known as **eminent domain**. The Supreme Court supports eminent domain as long as four key elements are present:

1. Land must be private property. It cannot be taken from other government property such as public schools.

2. Land must be taken from private individuals.

3. Land must have a public use.

4. Owners must receive just compensation.

These four elements can be rather broadly interpreted. For example, how do you set a fair price on a property in poor condition? What if it's located in a high-traffic area that would be perfect for a new shopping center? Shouldn't it be worth more? What about its sentimental value to the owner? A fair compromise is usually made between the government and owners of the property, but ultimately the government has more authority and the owner may be shortchanged.

∧
∧
∧ If **the government** wanted to build a new school, highway, or hospital, it **could obtain your home** for a fair purchase price **under eminent domain.**

Urban Renewal Through Tax Funding

There are strong proponents and opponents of the government's use of TIF to encourage urban renewal. What does each side have to say?

Pro

- More tax dollars will be generated than spent, thereby increasing total revenue.
- Urban renewal benefits all citizens by eliminating unsightly and dangerous areas and reinvigorating them.
- Redevelopment draws higher-income individuals back into the center city, thereby increasing tax revenues.
- Such development serves the public good.
- Eminent domain keeps the costs of development down, making urban renewal more likely, compared to having to buy out property owners who are reluctant to sell their properties.

Con

- Renewal eliminates affordable housing for low-income individuals, increasing homelessness and decreasing quality of life for many.
- TIF often benefits land developers at the expense of other areas of city government, taking funds away from parks, roads, and other public areas to fund private enterprise.
- TIF is unfair to existing businesses, which do not receive this tax break but have supported the local economy with their tax dollars.
- Taking private property from one citizen to sell it to another by force of the government is unfair and unjust, especially since those taking the property have wealth and political power while those losing their property tend to be poor and powerless.

From Classroom to Community } Urban Renewal

At 18, Alex Ramos had lived in Houston his entire life. His parents had rented their house from the same company for 15 years. When it was time to go to college, he didn't think twice before applying to the University of Houston. Most of his high school friends were still nearby, and Alex knew he was lucky to save money on housing by living at home.

"I knew that we never had much money. Growing up, I was never the kid with the PlayStation or the guy who rented a limo for the prom. But everyone in the neighborhood was pretty much in the same boat, so I learned to just ignore the people at school who tried to make an issue out of it."

During his first year of college, Alex noticed a few new developments popping up in his neighborhood. A new pharmacy opened, and a row of rundown homes were rehabbed with top-of-the-line features. To Alex's amazement, a sign in one of the empty lots announced that the space would be turned into a park through a government-sponsored program called "Neighborhoods Alive!" Alex wondered if the city government had initiated the program because it thought the neighborhood was dead.

"It was only a few days later that we got the phone call. The housing company was raising the rent because, as they said, there had been 'an increase in property taxes.' The new price was crazy. It was more than double the amount we were paying before!"

Already on a fixed budget, the Ramos family could not afford to stay in their home. In fact, they soon realized that they couldn't afford to stay in the same neighborhood.

"The next year or so was rough. We ended up living with relatives until my dad's friend found him a better job in San Antonio. We'd all been chipping in to get by, and at that point, I didn't have enough money to return to UH. I would have felt bad leaving my parents anyway; we were all each other had."

After the move, the family worked hard to get back on its feet. They spent 18 months renting a small apartment before they had enough savings to consider a bigger townhouse in a better part of town.

"It's not the same as before, but it'll have to do. I work on the UT campus now, and I'm hoping to start taking classes there this spring. I'm glad things worked out for us, but what I still don't understand is why our old neighborhood had to change. Don't they realize that we all would have rather lived in our 'dead' neighborhood than be at the mercy of urban renewal?"

16

HOW DO CITIES AFFECT SOCIETY? 224

poor living conditions and crime result from overpopulation; loss of habitat and farmland result from urban sprawl

DO CITIES CREATE SOCIAL PROBLEMS FOR SOCIETIES AND INDIVIDUALS? 231

where we live affects our behavior and social interactions: urbanities tend to make impersonal *Gesellschaft* connections, which lead to an increase in isolation, depression, and stress; rural dwellers tend to make *Gemeinschaft* connections, which are friendly and personal, causing them to feel less isolated than their urban peers

CAN PLANNING PROVIDE SOLUTIONS TO PROBLEMS CREATED BY URBANIZATION? 233

yes, by preventing urban sprawl and protecting habitat and farmland; by redeveloping urban neighborhoods through urban renewal programs, which push low-income families out of run-down but affordable neighborhoods in an attempt to improve the overall aesthetics of a city and increase tax revenues

get the topic: HOW DO CITIES AFFECT SOCIETY?

Theory

FUNCTIONALISM 231

- where we live affects how we interact with other people
- cities offer individuals more opportunities than can be found in rural areas, but rapid population growth results in problems regarding lack of space and resources

- increased urban population results in fewer resources for current city dweller
- urban sprawl threatens the livelihood of the agricultural industry and has adverse effects on the environment

CONFLICT THEORY 231

- the displacement of low-income families is often overlooked by improved aesthetic and economical status brought about by urban renewal

SYMBOLIC INTERACTIONISM 232

- urban life weakens the bonds of kinship in a community
- urbanites are self-involved and care more about status than substance when it comes to personal relationships

Key Terms

urban is a term used when referring to a city. 224

population density is a measure of the number of humans per square mile. 224

rural is a term used when referring to the countryside. 224

urbanization is a process by which individuals or groups migrate from rural areas to urban areas. 224

megacities are cities with 10 million residents or more. 224

metropolitan area is a metropolis, or city, that is inclusive of the surrounding areas. 225

megalopolis is an extensive metropolitan area. 225

suburb is an area near a central city but beyond the political boundaries of that city. 226

counterurbanization refers to the process by which city growth has slowed as more rural areas and suburban areas have grown. 226

decentralization is the transfer of authority from a central government to a local government. 226

metropolitan federation is a collaborative form of government across a metropolitan area. 226

urban sprawl is the spreading of a city and its neighboring suburban areas over rural land along the borders of the metro area. 227

index of dissimilarity (D) indicates the percentage of people that would need to be relocated in order to have a perfectly even distribution of race and ethnicity in a city. 228

P* index for interaction calculates the amount of contact an average person of one group has with an average person of another group on any given day. 228

ethnic grouping is the tendency for members of particular ethnic groups to want to live in close proximity to one another. *228*

white flight is the departure of Caucasian individuals from neighborhoods increasingly or predominantly populated by minorities. *228*

disinvestment is a deliberate pattern whereby banking and lending institutions make decisions about where they will and will not support investments. *228*

redlining is a practice in which home lenders draw red lines on a map, indicating to which sides of a city they will and will not lend money. *228*

gridlock is a series of traffic jams. *229*

Gemeinschaft refers to community connections involving personal relationships based on friendship and kinship ties. *231*

Gesellschaft refers to social connections that are more formal and impersonal. *231*

mechanical solidarity is the state of community bonding in traditional societies in which people share beliefs and values and perform common activities. *231*

organic solidarity is a state that occurs when people live in a society with a diverse division of labor. *231*

urban renewal is the process of purchasing, clearing, and replacing run-down properties with newer, more appealing developments. *233*

gentrification is a trend that involves renovating and redeveloping a run-down neighborhood so that it meets middle-class standards, and subsequently displacing the original low-income residents. *233*

tax increment financing (TIF) is a program that enables cities to use tax revenues generated by a development project to help finance the construction of the new project through bonds given to developers and/or direct tax incentives. *234*

eminent domain is a policy that allows the government to take property from individuals, often against the owner's will, for public use. *234*

Sample Test Questions

These multiple-choice questions are similar to those found in the test bank that accompanies this textbook.

1. How did the industrial revolution influence urbanization?

   a. It brought jobs to rural areas.
   b. It brought jobs to urban areas.
   c. It dispersed the workforce.
   d. It decreased the workforce.

2. Which of the following is a problem associated with urban sprawl?

   a. Populations are too crowded in urban sprawl areas.
   b. Housing is expensive in urban sprawl areas.
   c. Urban sprawl areas consume land that is needed for farming.
   d. Urban sprawl areas do not pay enough taxes to the center city.

3. What is involved in the process of redlining?

   a. Unequal treatment of individuals based on the areas in which they live
   b. Inflated housing prices in urban sprawl areas
   c. The granting of subprime home loans in low-income areas with larger minority populations
   d. The displacement of middle-class families due to the practice of "white flight"

4. Gentrification typically has adverse affects on

   a. middle-class individuals.
   b. government programs.
   c. low-income individuals.
   d. rural dwellers.

5. The primary goal of urban renewal is to increase the size of a metro area.

   a. True
   b. False

ESSAY QUESTIONS

1. Is urban sprawl a problem in your area? At what point do you feel that urban sprawl needs to be controlled?

2. In major U.S. metro areas, the length of the combined morning/evening rush hour commute has doubled since 1982. What do you think has contributed to this change? Explain your answer.

3. If estimates are correct and urbanites will account for 80 percent of the population in 20 years, what social problems do you foresee?

4. Do you agree with the classification of *Gemeinschaft* and *Gesellschaft* communities? Which category would a suburban population fall under?

5. What are the advantages and disadvantages of urban renewal? In general, do you think urban renewal programs have a positive or negative effect on cities?

WHERE TO START YOUR RESEARCH PAPER

For facts and information on all U.S. cities, visit
http://www.city-data.com/

For statistics on international cities, as well as future predictions, see
http://www.citymayors.com/sections/rankings_content.html

To view maps of urban sprawl, go to
http://science.nasa.gov/headlines/y2002/11oct_sprawl.htm

For a discussion on the future of gentrification, see
http://www.forbes.com/2009/06/02/real-estate-panel-intelligent-investing-fitch.html

To learn more about UN-HABITAT programs, go to
http://www.unhabitat.org/

To read about the international effects of "shrinking cities," visit
http://www.forbes.com/2007/06/11/ghost-cities-future-biz-cx_21cities_ee_0611ghostcities.html

Remember to check **www.thethinkspot.com for additional information, downloadable flashcards, and other helpful resources.**

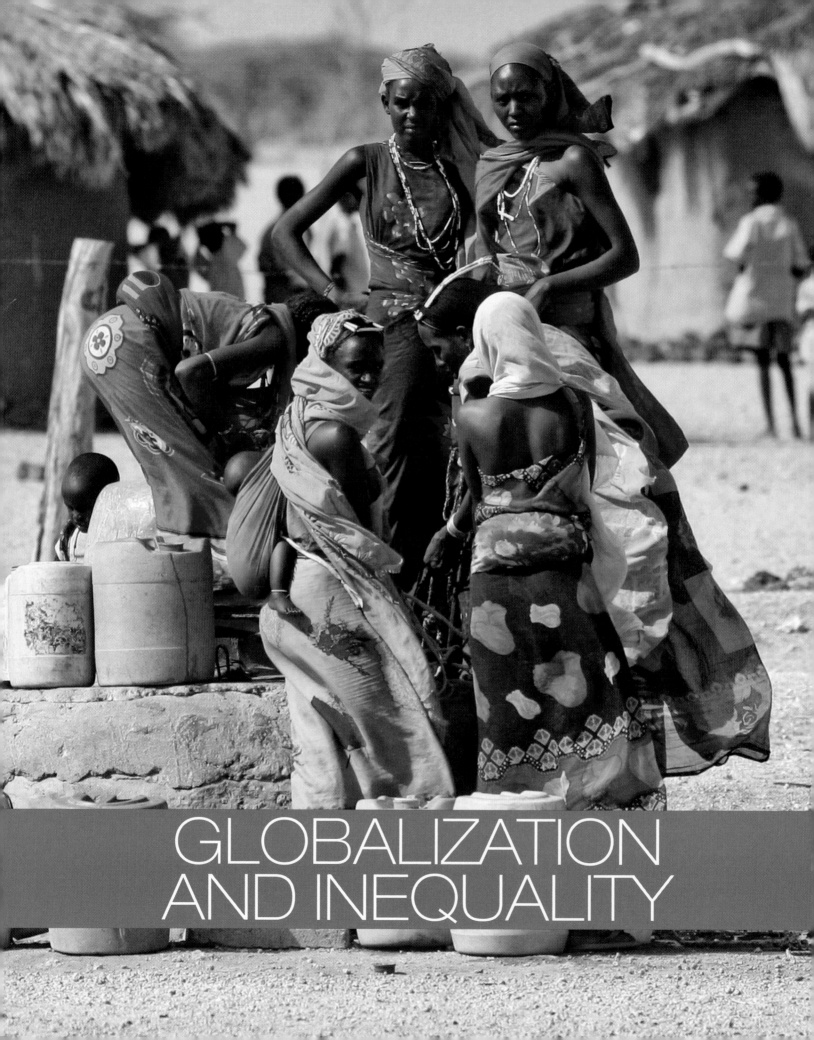

GLOBALIZATION AND INEQUALITY

WHAT IS GLOBALIZATION AND HOW
DOES IT AFFECT THE WORLD?
WHAT THEORIES EXIST ABOUT
GLOBALIZATION?
HOW DOES SOCIETY DEAL WITH
GLOBALIZATION?

Leaders of

21 nations that represent half the global economy fear a raft of new protectionist barriers will strangle commerce as the world slides into a frightening recession.

There are growing signs that developing countries will erect protectionist barriers to weather the crisis, partly because they have seen that time after time, "free trade" agreements have focused chiefly on beating rivals to market.

Even free-trade disciples say many trade deals have been mishandled, limiting their ability to spread wealth and level the competitive playing field.

"These are not free trade agreements in any sense of the term," said Joseph Stiglitz, the Nobel Prize-winning economist. "They're really advantage-trade agreements. They're worse than NAFTA, which Obama says he wants to - renegotiate.". . .

Economists generally concur that truly free trade erases inefficiencies and inequalities, rewarding innovation and benefiting everyone with cheaper goods and services. President George W. Bush and other leaders unanimously endorsed it at the Asia-Pacific Economic Cooperation conference this past weekend.

But many say that what the APEC leaders tout as "free trade" devalues and distorts that admirable goal.

Since the early 1990s, nearly 400 free trade agreements have been reached, covering about a third of global trade. . .

Most such agreements have been nation-to-nation and, invariably carry exemptions that protect domestic industries that politicians decided were vital.

All Canadian pacts, for example, protect Canada's milk, poultry, and egg industries. The Peru-China pact signed last week exempts 10 percent of the Andean nation's industries, including clothing and shoes.

Even the 15-year-old North American Free Trade Agreement doesn't promote truly free trade. Among its protectionist provisions: 62.5 percent of an automobile's total parts must be made within the three member states—Canada, the United States and Mexico—in order for the car to cross a border.

President Felipe Calderon of Mexico has treated Obama's vow to renegotiate NAFTA like a sack of rotten fish, warning in Lima that if Obama is crazy enough to do it, it would set loose a tide of job-starved Mexicans that no U.S. border fence could possibly hold back.

Still, the agricultural subsidies by the United States and European nations represent huge infidelities to the free trade religion, and have paralyzed global trade talks since 2001. . .

International food aid groups blame these subsidies—along with a conversion of farmland from food to biofuel—for increasing hunger across the developing world, where local food producers gave up growing crops that couldn't compete against subsidized imports. The imports then soared in price along with fuel costs, putting essential staples like rice and soy out of reach for the poor. . .

"Full-scale trade liberalization with insufficient safeguards is the last thing these countries should be signing up for," Oxfam advocacy officer Romain Benicchio said of countries where subsistence farmers struggle to compete with subsidized food imports.

Since the global financial crisis struck in September, a few protectionist measures have been announced. . .

The biggest fear at the APEC summit was of a return to the huge trade barriers of the Great Depression, when some U.S. import duties reached 70 percent and world trade contracted by some 66 percent between 1929 and 1934.

Free-trade disciples wish the world had managed these treaties better.

"People now look at the financial crisis and the lesson they learn is, 'See, globalization doesn't work,'" Aggarwal said. "It's an unfortunate lesson but that's how they see it."[1]

---When I look at the clothes in my closet, what do I see? There are shirts made in Pakistan, shoes made in China, jeans from Mexico, and so forth.

In fact, my world is interconnected to all parts of the world through the products I own. Look in your closet; you'll see that most of your clothes come from different countries as well.

This is because of globalization, which we'll discuss in detail in this chapter. In the 1960s, Marshall McLuhan declared the world a "global village" because of the impact of immediate communications.[2] Technology helps us interact with the world, and it helps the world interact with us. For example, let's say a typhoon hits the coast of China, an event that you watch on TV. But do you notice when the price of shoes rises? That occurrence may be a direct result of the typhoon and its effect on Chinese manufacturing. Today, this international trend continues not just because of rapid communication, but also because of globalization.

The world is more interconnected than we might think. Go to the grocery store and look around: The strawberries are from Mexico, the bananas are from Ecuador, and both types of fruit are presented to us on metal racks that are made with Brazilian steel. Although this interconnection can help nations such the United States acquire more goods at lower prices, how does it affect poorer countries? What social problems might occur when developing nations sell off their resources or their labor to build manufacturing plants that employ low-paid workers to produce these goods? How does society respond to the social problems that are linked to globalization? We'll explore these questions and more throughout this chapter.

get the topic: WHAT IS GLOBALIZATION AND HOW DOES IT AFFECT THE WORLD?

GLOBALIZATION is a complex process by which the world and the international economy are becoming more and more intertwined.

GLOCALIZATION occurs when countries seek to combine the local and the global into a unique structural blend to maintain their native customs while fitting into the global environment.

BRAIN DRAIN occurs when the best talent leaves poor countries and thereby provides an even greater advantage to wealthy countries.

Globalization

Today, nations are becoming much more closely linked through business, travel, immigration, health issues, and the production of goods.[3] **Globalization** is a complex process by which the world and its international economy are growing more and more intertwined. As a result, the consequences of one nation's actions become shared by all. This can, in theory, bring about a convergence in the world as people from different areas become increasingly alike and have more and more shared experiences. On the other hand, globalization can also create a backlash against external forces, increasing the strength of the local community.[4] For example, across the globe, the English language is expanding, mostly as a language of commerce. This is in large part because of the colonial history of Great Britain, but more recently because of the economic power of the United States. Those who wish to engage in international business generally learn the English language, which allows the world to converge even more. At the same time, some nations are placing great emphasis on saving their native languages, in fear that these dialects will be eliminated by this trend. **Glocalization** occurs when countries seek to combine the local and the global into a unique structural blend to maintain their native customs while fitting into the global environment.[5]

What exactly drives globalization is a debated issue. Is it the force of capitalism, causing some nations to seek cheaper labor so that prices can remain low? Is it a desire to spread political principles throughout the world? Is it a product of greed and consumption, causing countries to need more and more "stuff," even if these products are not available locally? The truth is that all of these notions are interrelated in the motivation toward globalization; no one cause can explain this trend.[6]

PROBLEMS ASSOCIATED WITH GLOBALIZATION

Sometimes, the lean toward globalization can have negative effects. Different countries have different natural resources to offer, and they may sell these resources to become part of the global game. Furthermore, many poor nations have rapidly growing populations, which results in large numbers of young people seeking work. Having an abundant supply of workers allows employers to pay less and less for the labor. There has been a great deal of controversy over exploitation and "sweatshop" labor as big manufacturers outsource work to poorly managed factories in developing countries.[7]

Additionally, as the opening article explained, increasing globalization has also encouraged trade between nations, although existing trade agreements do not always promote free trade. Instead of leveling the playing field between nations, these agreements sometimes have the opposite effect—they benefit wealthy nations and put poorer nations at a greater disadvantage. For example, the United States and European nations provide subsidies to agribusinesses, making it cheaper to produce crops. These foods are then exported to developing countries, where local farmers are unable to compete with the lower prices of these goods. As a result, local farmers stop producing certain foods, and when prices rise for imported goods—due to fuel costs or other reasons—the local poor are unable to afford basics such as rice and soy.[8]

Another problem that has arisen from globalization is **brain drain**. This occurs when individuals with the greatest talents leave poor countries, thereby providing an even greater advantage to wealthy countries.[9] This occurs throughout the world as developing nations send their best and brightest to the developed world where work, education, and other opportunities abound. These men and women are able to enjoy better standards of living and higher salaries than they would otherwise. But how does this affect the countries that they left?[10]

One concern with brain drain is that developing nations who send their best and brightest generally receive nothing in return; while they lose those with the most ability and talent, the receiving nations reap the benefits of having even more talented and intelligent people in their society. This is particularly true for small nations, which have much higher likelihoods of losing their most educated individuals.[11] In this way, brain drain only helps widen the gap between wealthy and less fortunate nations.

∧
∧ **Many of the best and brightest from**
∧ **foreign nations have relocated to**
wealthier nations. What are the worldwide effects of brain drain?

GLOBALIZATION AND CULTURE

As previously discussed, one of the questions surrounding globalization is whether it unites the world culturally. It's not uncommon to see citizens in other countries eating Big Macs or wearing Dallas Cowboy shirts and Nike tennis shoes. Certainly, globalization influences the spread of material culture throughout the world. Some suggest that because of this expansion of common influences, our differences will eventually become nonexistent; in the future, all cultures may meld into one large homogenous society.[12]

GLOBALIZATION AND MIGRATION

Globalization influences migration patterns in ways that do not only involve brain drain. Recently there has been a rapid increase in international migration. The influx of people—both legal and illegal—is associated with various social problems. For example, foreign workers represent increased competition for jobs. As you saw in the opening article, Mexican President Felipe Calderon has warned the United States that renegotiating NAFTA will cause many more Mexicans to cross the U.S. border desperately seeking jobs. With unemployment on the rise, a number of American workers view this as a significant problem. As a result of this and other issues, many developed nations are now seeking policies to slow the rate of immigration. In the United States, for example, the government has built fences along the Mexican border in an effort to minimize undocumented entry. Migration can also create a backlash against the people who enter a new country, resulting in issues of violence, victimization, and abuse.[13]

Globalization has resulted in roughly 3 percent of the world's population living outside their nation of birth. As I write this, two of my family members are living in other countries, while at least two others are considering taking jobs in New Zealand and India. This increase in interaction and travel means that diseases can also spread more easily. West Nile virus—an illness that infects mosquitoes and birds—came to the United States from Africa, most likely transported here by travelers or in containers with agricultural products.[14] Recent fears over the spread of avian flu (H5N1) and swine flu (H1N1) are influenced by the migration of people around the world. Clearly, interconnectedness is not always a positive thing for our health.

Are these issues social problems? It probably depends on which side of the globe you're sitting. When capitalist nations use developing countries as a source of cheap labor, it can have negative effects on the poor citizens of those nations while at the same time benefiting consumers in the wealthy nations. In a sense, the price of cheap clothing in the United States is borne on the backs of the underpaid workers in Bangladesh and elsewhere.[15]

But some see it a different way. The opposing point of view suggests that globalization is a major opportunity for poorer nations to improve their economic status. Another interesting question raised in the debate is whether cultures around the world are becoming more similar as a result of working together more closely. Some suggest that the world's cultures are adopting more Western values. On the flip side, others feel that globalization is causing local groups to work harder to maintain their own customs, religions, and languages.[16]

How Did the World Become Stratified?

Exactly how human societies arose is beyond the scope of this chapter. However, globalization is related to how the world is divided between the rich and the poor. At the earliest point in human history, all humans were on equal footing, and yet we know that some societies advanced technologically, whereas others did not.

There are a lot of factors that contribute to how quickly a society develops. In his book *Guns, Germs, and Steel,* author Jared Diamond explains why the Western world advanced so quickly and other regions of the world did not. Climate, geography, and available natural resources all played a role, as did the ability to use trade and interaction for the citizens' own advantages. Gunpowder, for example, was developed in China but the use of it for weapons was perfected by Europeans, who learned the power of this material through the process of trade—a precursor to globalization today. An increase in trade results in an increase in knowledge, which allows civilizations to flourish through an improved quality of life.[17]

> **GLOBAL STRATIFICATION** is the categorization of countries based on objective criteria, such as wealth, power, and prestige, which highlight social patterns and inequality throughout the world.
>
> **PER-CAPITA INCOME** is calculated by dividing a country's total gross income by the number of people in that country.

Over many centuries, Europeans became powerful by using the information they gained from other parts of the world, as well as those they developed themselves to increase their relative wealth. Intercontinental struggles led to the development of alliances, technologies, increased trade for goods, and the spread of knowledge into Europe. These trends continue today through globalization.[18]

Global Stratification

Poverty exists in all parts of the world, but the biggest gaps in social inequality are not within nations, but between them. **Global stratification** is the categorization of countries based on objective criteria such as wealth, power, and prestige, which highlight social patterns and inequality throughout the world. For instance, although the United States still struggles with social problems related to poverty, the standard of living is extremely high in a global context.

INCOME

Income is difficult to use to measure the standard of living of an entire population, as it is not evenly distributed, and not all countries are the same size. However, sociologists often use a country's **per-capita income** as a marker. This is calculated by dividing the country's total gross income by the number of people in that country. The majority of top income-producing countries are in Europe, and most of the bottom income-producing countries are in Africa. The wealthiest U.S. citizens have a larger share of the national income than wealthy citizens in other nations. Beneficial taxation policies allow affluent U.S. citizens to keep more of their income by paying less in taxes than their counterparts in other developed nations.[19]

UNDERDEVELOPED NATIONS AND STRATIFICATION

A country is considered an underdeveloped nation if it is relatively poor and has not yet been industrialized. The United Nations provides some assistance to underdeveloped countries based on three criteria: (1) The country must have a low gross national income; (2) the population must meet health and education criteria; and (3) population size and proximity to other developed nations must be taken into consideration.

>>> **Camel racing** is a popular sport in many Middle Eastern countries. Because of their light weight, **children are traditionally used as jockeys,** and over the years, this has led to a profitable child trafficking industry. It's estimated that, because of this sport alone, **over 40,000 children are currently living as slaves** in the Middle East and South Asia.

Asian Human Rights Commission, "Child Jockeys: 40,000 children on slave labour as 'child camel jockeys' in Middle East and Arab countries," Accessed November 13, 2009, http://acr.hrschool.org/mainfile.php/0205/390; UNICEF, "Child camel jockeys return home," Accessed November 13, 2009, http://www.unicef.org/infobycountry/pakistan_27517.html.

Some countries are considered developing or in the process of becoming industrialized. Issues such as poverty and hunger still affect these countries, though not as greatly as in underdeveloped countries.

The sub-Saharan region of Africa is the most disadvantaged area in the world. Infant mortality, childhood death, hunger, and poverty rates are worse there than anywhere else. Poor sanitation also leads to high rates of illness and death.[20] Those living in impoverished areas have control over their lives but are certainly limited by the low standards of living. It is difficult to get ahead when food and resources in your country are scarce. Does globalization aid these people? The consensus is no. Generally, development in these areas is rare. Add to this the reality that many of these countries have unstable political environments, and you can see that globalization may take a long time to help these nations climb out of poverty.[21]

Two major dividing factors between modern developed and underdeveloped nations are communication and literacy. You probably don't stop to think when you use these throughout your day—communication through e-mail, text messaging, and more is common in the United States. Access to these forms of technology is low in underdeveloped countries, however, which provides a distinct disadvantage in communication. Literacy is more or less taken for granted in the United States, but not in all parts of the world. When people lack the ability to read, they are forced to take unskilled, labor-intensive jobs to support their families. For example, the United Nations estimates that literacy rates for adults in the developed world stand at about 95 percent, whereas those same rates are only about 62 percent in sub-Saharan Africa.[22]

Modern-Day Slavery?

One serious problem related to globalization and the extension of capitalism throughout the world involves increasing levels of slavery around the globe. In his book *Disposable People: New Slavery in the Global Economy*, sociologist Kevin Bales estimates that 27 million people are currently enslaved around the world. In some parts of the world, human trafficking

Gross National Income Per-Capita, 2008

NORWAY

GNI: $87,070

3

Rank: #3

UNITED STATES

GNI: $47,580

14

Rank: #14

BURUNDI

GNI: $140

210

Rank: #210

Source: Data from the World Development Indicators database, World Bank, July 1, 2009,
http://siteresources.worldbank.org/DATASTATISTICS/Resources/GNIPC.pdf

∧ **The per-capita income of a nation is often used to measure the nation's standard of living.**
∧ Norway and the United States rank relatively high, while Burundi comes in last at
number 210.

CONTRACT SLAVERY is a form of slavery in which a person signs a work contract, receiving food and shelter from an employer, but is threatened when he or she tries to leave.

GROBALIZATION refers to the idea that capitalist countries use their corporate interests to expand their power and influence throughout the world.

includes individuals (often women) sold into prostitution by family members.[23] This modern form of slavery does not quite fall into the same category as slavery in the past. Slavery in the past was legal, and owners viewed slaves as long-term investments. Today, however, slaves are disposable; once they are used up, they are released.[24] Although they may be given their freedom, the physical and mental condition in which most slaves are released is poor. In Thailand, female prostitutes are often HIV positive, mentally ill, or both. When given their freedom, they are essentially left to die on the streets.[25]

Even though slavery is illegal everywhere, it is common for companies to use slave laborers in their factories around the world. **Contract**

slavery is a form of slavery in which a person signs a work contract, receiving food and shelter from an employer, but is threatened when he or she tries to leave.

Although you may think that these workers' difficulties do not affect you directly, you're wrong. Even if you avoid buying certain clothing or shoe brands, you may still unknowingly buy products that are indirectly related to slave labor. According to Bales, most of the products available on the market today were either produced under or are somehow related to slave labor.[26] Globalization, the pursuit of cheap labor, rapid population growth, weak local governments, and consumer desires for cheap goods all contribute to the fact that we now have more slaves on the planet than at any other time in history. Bales asks the question, "Are we willing to live in a world with slaves?"[27] For most of us, the knee-jerk reaction to this question is "no!" even though our spending habits indicate otherwise. But how do we abolish this new form of slavery? Our system of living seems to encourage it.

One reason slavery is so difficult to eradicate is because of an idea Ritzer calls grobalization. **Grobalization** refers to the idea that capitalist countries use their corporate interests to expand their power throughout the world. These groups seek to constantly increase their influence, until

▶▶▶ GO GL🌐BAL

Poor Countries and the World's Economy

Throughout late 2008 and 2009, the state of the world's economy was a hot topic. The United States faced the worst economic downturn since the Great Depression, and other countries suffered in the wake of that loss. The recession had the greatest impact on developing countries. The growth forecast for developing nations was 7.7 percent in 2007, but fell to 1.2 percent in 2009.[29] Leaders of these countries were, in many ways, powerless to do anything about the world's economic problems. Since their nations were already relying on aid from the wealthier countries of the world, they were unable to offer a financial contribution to the solution. However, leaders of developing countries were quick to point out the necessity of their role in economic reform. "Reforms are needed to enhance productivity and capacity to cope with risks," said Bangladesh's Foreign Minister Dipu Moni on behalf of the world's poorest nations.[30]

After drafting a plan, the United Nations held a three-day summit to discuss possible reforms that would turn the economy back around. During their talks, the UN attempted to find solutions that would aid developing countries, where a continued economic crisis could mean an additional 200,000 infants dying each year from malnutrition or disease.[31] Nobel Laureate in Economics Joseph Stiglitz suggested that the plan set out in the draft was inadequate. The plan called for the World Bank, as well as lenders across the globe, to be flexible with developing countries, an idea that Stiglitz said limited the power of change to the richest nations. The 20 key economic powers represented in the UN account for 80 percent of the global economy; however, Stiglitz insisted that all 192 members of the UN should be included in the decision-making process.[32]

Stiglitz further called for a change in how wealthier countries provide aid

to developing countries. Grants, rather than loans, should be used for aid, Stiglitz argued, in order for countries to avoid a debt crisis. China's Foreign Minister Yang Jiechi presented the plan to keep exchange rates stable. He said that taking this action would further aid developing countries, allowing them to "make more effective use of external funds for their development."[33]

>>> As **Joseph Stiglitz notes,** although globalization has proceeded at a staggering rate, **we have yet to create a global financial institution.**[34] What issues might arise from an attempt to form a universal economy?

Poverty Rates of Developed Countries

Country	Percent of total population in poverty	Percent of children in poverty	Percent of children in poverty after taxes and welfare transfers	Percent of elderly in poverty
United States	17.0	26.6	21.9	24.7
Ireland	16.5	24.9	15.7	35.8
United Kingdom	12.4	25.4	15.4	20.5
Canada	11.4	22.8	14.9	5.9
Denmark	9.2	11.8	2.4	6.6
Germany	8.3	18.2	10.2	10.1
France	8.0	27.7	7.5	9.8
Belgium	8.0	16.7	7.7	16.4
Austria	7.7	17.7	10.2	13.7
Switzerland	7.6	7.8	6.8	18.4

Source: Data from Lawrence Mishel, Jared Bernstein, and Sylvia Allegretto, *State of Working America 2004/2005* (Ithaca, New York: Cornell University Press, 2005).

∧
∧ Although **the United States ranks high in per-capita income, a large percentage of its**
∧ **citizens are living in poverty.** Why do you think this is the case?

expanded influence becomes an end in and of itself. Grobalization increases profits for companies as well as control. Of course, this influence often comes at the expense of the environment and the freedom of the people who live in the nations that are exploited.[28]

DEVELOPED NATIONS AND STRATIFICATION

We have discussed underdeveloped nations, but what exactly qualifies a nation as "developed"? Some characteristics of developed nations are a well-educated population, regular elections, abundant industry, and free enterprise. The United States, Germany, Japan, and Great Britain are all examples of developed countries. Living in a developed nation is certainly a privilege compared to living in an underdeveloped nation, but it's not a guarantee that one will *be* privileged. As you can see in the chart above, a large percentage of citizens in developed countries still live in poverty.

The United States is a good example—it may have a high per-capita income, but the huge gap between the rich and the poor leaves many in poverty. In fact, the United States has the highest percentage of people living in poverty of any developed nation, with 17 percent of the total population below the poverty line, even after taking into account government-sponsored programs such as welfare. Of the 21 wealthiest nations in the world, the distance between the top 10 percent of incomes and the bottom 10 percent of incomes is the greatest in the United States. In the 1990s, the incomes of the top 10 percent were 5.64 times higher than incomes in the bottom 10 percent. This means that if the bottom 10 percent made an average of $20,000 a year, the top 10 percent made 5.64 times more, or $112,800! This is a sizable gap, to say the least. In contrast, Sweden has the lowest ratio, with the top 10 percent earning 2.59 times more than the bottom 10 percent. In Sweden, if the average income for the bottom were $20,000, the average income for the top would be $51,800.[35]

QUALITY OF LIFE

What characteristics make a country a desirable place to live? One way to measure quality of life in a country is to measure health and longevity. A country with a low infant mortality rate and a long life expectancy

>>> According to Kai Müller, **Norway ranks top in quality of life,** whereas the United States doesn't even make it into the top 20.[39]

seems as though it would have a high quality of life. Andorra, a small nation in Europe, has the highest life expectancy in the world at 83.5 years, while Swaziland in southern Africa has the shortest at 31.9 years.[36] Singapore has the lowest infant mortality rate at 2.3 deaths per 1,000 babies born, whereas the impoverished nation of Angola has 80 times that rate, with 184.4 deaths per 1,000 births.[37] So, does this mean that Andorra and Singapore are the best places to live? Not necessarily. There are many other factors to consider in quality of life.

As we discussed earlier, income is an important measure. Other measures include access to telephones, televisions, and newspapers. Sociologists and economists also take measures such as debt ratio and gross national product into consideration. Kai Müller created a ranking system based on all of these criteria.[38] Using this system, Müller determined that Norway is the best country in the world in which to live and the Democratic Republic of Congo is the worst.

With the exceptions of Japan, New Zealand, Australia, and Canada, all of the top 20 ranked countries are located in Western Europe. The bottom 20 countries are all in Africa. You may be surprised to learn that the United States is not considered one of the 20 best countries in which to live.

Of course, this a subjective study, and results can vary greatly depending on how you weigh different factors. Daniel Slottje conducted a different study using older data but similar variables. Slottje found the United States to be the 13th best country to live in and Switzerland to be the first.[40] Regardless of the criteria used, it's clear that every country does not boast the same quality of life, and some countries are better places to live in than others.

think social problems: WHAT ARE THE THEORIES ABOUT GLOBALIZATION?

NEOCOLONIALISM is a process by which powerful nations use loans and economic power to maintain control over poor nations.

Conflict Theory

WALLERSTEIN'S WORLD SYSTEMS THEORY

When I was in college, we learned that the world was divided into three parts: the first, second, and third worlds. The first world was made up of the United States and our allies, the second was made up of the Soviet Union and their allies, and the third contained everyone else. Sociologists do not use this system today for a number of reasons. First, this system is based on political and economic ideologies, and is largely ethnocentric, placing the Western world first. Second, the Soviet bloc has largely dissolved. Third, putting 60 percent of the world into one category fails to provide an accurate description of the differences among these nations.

Immanuel Wallerstein's world systems theory, however, provides an alternative to the old theory. He suggests that the world is divided by connections to economic power. The core is made up of nations that are constantly trying to expand their markets, decrease costs, and increase profits. These nations are at the core because their economies largely influence the actions of the rest of the world.[41]

Because these core nations are constantly seeking expansion, they find ways to enter periphery countries. As we discussed, colonization was the popular method in the past, but is no longer practiced in the same way. Today, core nations use multinational corporations and loans to tap into the periphery nations. Periphery nations, in turn, seek to benefit by generating wealth through these arrangements. Nigeria and Iraq are examples of desirable periphery nations, as they have abundant natural resources such as natural gas and oil.

If a periphery nation can generate enough wealth to stabilize its economy, select members of that society will begin to develop industries of their own. When a country reaches this level, it is considered semi-periphery—a developing nation that uses its raw materials to create goods that can be sold to core nations to generate more wealth. Continued industrial advancement will improve the economy, giving the nation a chance to move closer to the core. Brazil and South Korea are current examples of semi-periphery nations.

External nations are located outside this sphere. These are underdeveloped nations that have little interaction with the rest of the system. A lack of natural resources often makes it difficult for these countries to attract investors or interest from the core nations. Examples of external nations are Burundi, Chad, and many of the countries of sub-Saharan Africa. External nations have little to no economic impact on other nations.

NEOCOLONIALISM

The United States is no stranger to conquest and colonization. As you know, the U.S. developed from a series of colonies settled by Europeans. Sociologist Michael Harrington asserts that a new kind of colonialism exists in the modern world. He calls it **neocolonialism**, a process by which powerful nations use loans and economic power to maintain control over poor nations.[42] Poor nations become dependent on wealthier nations for food, weapons, and development through the use of loans. This debt is often too great for the poor nations to repay, so they have to agree to alliances, sale of natural resources, and trade agreements that mostly benefit the wealthier nations.

The idea of neocolonialism extends to wealthy nations that use multinational corporations to control poorer nations. These corporations provide jobs and income to the poorer nations, and benefit greatly by gaining tax-free status in that nation, or by other concessions that are not in the best interest of the poorer country. As we discussed earlier, the conditions in manufacturing plants in poor countries are often disastrous. It's unlikely that executives of these companies want to be involved in slave labor, but they are under pressure to maximize profits.

Through the use of outsourcing, multinational corporations allow wealthy countries to control weaker ones through corporate investment. The jobs provided are often the only opportunities that these workers have, and poor countries are easily enticed to perform hard labor to make money.

For Thomas Friedman, such interconnection means that the world is growing increasingly "flat." Through the interconnection between nations caused by low-cost communications, the world is becoming a place where those with means can win at the expense of those without them. In such a system, the weak will end up falling farther and farther behind. For example, throughout the world, outsourced jobs in the service sector require certain skills: speaking English, understanding accounting, programming computers, etc. In such a setting, American businesses are likely to further outsource jobs to areas of the world where English is

World Systems Theory

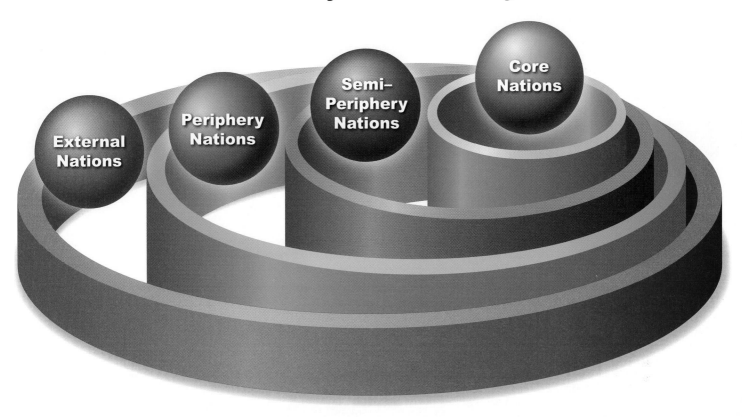

Source: Adapted from Wallerstein's The Modern World Systems, 1974.

> ∧
> ∧ According to Wallerstein, **the world is divided into countries with different levels of**
> ∧ **economic power.**

spoken and workers require lower pay for the same skill set. This is all made possible as the world flattens through use of rapid and cheap inter-communication technologies such as the Internet.[43]

Symbolic Interactionism

At the conclusion of World War II, European nations decided to work together to prevent future wars. Meetings of diplomats led to treaties that ultimately led to the creation of the European Union. The European Union has grown from simple trade relations between six countries to a collection of more than 20 nations.[44]

The countries of the European Union have a weak central government to handle trade disputes among nations, a common currency (the euro), and an increasingly common language (English). There is no military force

exclusive to the European Union, but the North Atlantic Treaty Organization (NATO) has troops that come from a variety of European Union nations and the United States.

If the European Union banded together to form a single nation, it would be the wealthiest, most powerful country in the world. T. R. Reid notes that Europeans are in fact seeing themselves less as members of specific nations and more as members of the European Union. What might such a definition mean for globalization? There have already been considerable results. Many of the world's largest banks and most successful businesses have risen to prominence in the European Union. The E.U. makes more scientific discoveries than any other country. Additionally, E.U. countries have the highest standards of living in the world, and, as you can see in the chart on page 249, Europeans work fewer hours while receiving more paid vacation time than United States workers.[45]

discover solutions to social problems:
HOW DOES SOCIETY DEAL WITH GLOBALIZATION?

Foreign Aid

I have had students up in arms about the issue of foreign aid. The most common argument is "Why should I pay huge amounts of tax dollars to

other nations when there are people in my own country who are in need?" This is a valid question, as the United States certainly has its fair share of poverty. But does this mean that we should adopt a strictly

WRAP YOUR MIND AROUND THE THEORY

Many wealthy countries have corporate interests in underdeveloped nations. **Globalization creates jobs in poorer countries, but at what cost?**

FUNCTIONALISM

Functionalists believe that stratification is mostly a result of geographic conditions. Historically, certain areas thrived while others did not as a result of these differences. Today, globalization benefits not only the countries that have risen to prominence, but also the poorer nations around the world. Globalization brings needed wealth and technology, which helps less-developed nations advance.

CONFLICT THEORY

Conflict theorists feel that the imbalance of power between the rich and the poor creates stratification. This is true on a national as well as domestic scale; in the United States, the gap between wealthy people and poor people is significant. Internationally, this gap exists between rich and poor nations. Recall Wallerstein's world systems theory, in which core nations use periphery nations to get what they need or want. This creates competition and conflict between these nations. As the world "flattens" due to cheap technologies, Friedman suggests that only those with the necessary skills will survive, while others will be left behind. Certainly, each country is trying to get ahead, with its own best interests in mind. The external nations are perceived to have nothing to offer the rest of the world and are left to fall by the wayside.

HOW DOES GLOBALIZATION INFLUENCE THE LIVES OF PEOPLE?

SYMBOLIC INTERACTIONISM

Symbolic interactionists look at how language and symbolic events affect society. T. R. Reid suggests that, since the formation of the European Union, Europeans increasingly identify themselves as citizens of a continent, rather than the individual country of which they were born. If the E.U. were to form a United States of Europe, it would be the world's greatest superpower. What impact might this have on the long-term influence of Europe over the rest of the world?

Conflict theorists believe that stratification is caused by the imbalance of power between the rich and the poor. **What chance do poor nations have to get ahead?**

The European Union has changed the way Europeans view their nationalities. **How would the world be different if they decided to unite further?**

Average Weekly Working Hours

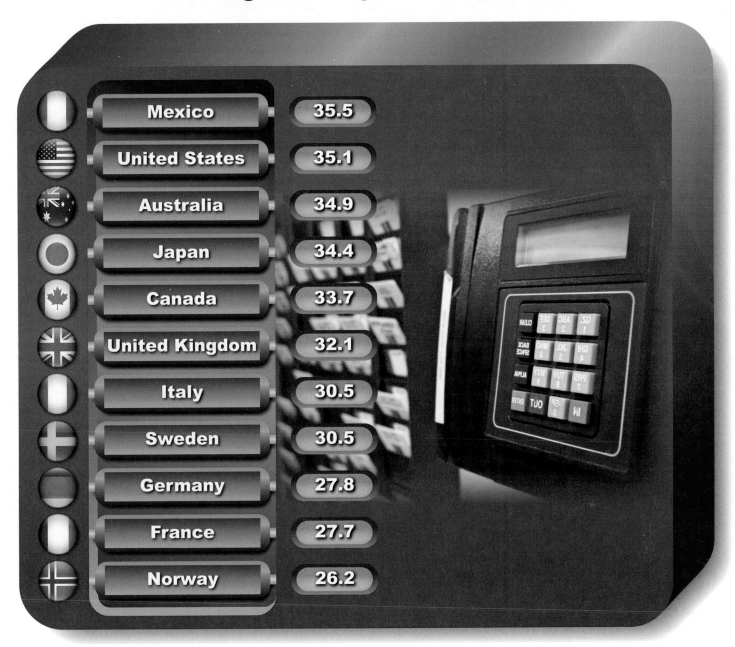

Country	Hours
Mexico	35.5
United States	35.1
Australia	34.9
Japan	34.4
Canada	33.7
United Kingdom	32.1
Italy	30.5
Sweden	30.5
Germany	27.8
France	27.7
Norway	26.2

Source: Data from the Organisation for Economic Co-operation and Development (OECD), 2005.

∧
∧
∧ People in the United States work more hours per week than residents of most other developed countries. **Does this affect quality of life?**

isolationist policy and let the rest of the world fend for themselves? The U.S. government does not think so.

The government's stance on foreign aid is as follows: "Helping the world's poor is a strategic priority and a moral imperative. Economic development, responsible governance, and individual liberty are intimately connected. The United States must promote development programs that achieve measurable results—rewarding reforms, encouraging transparency, and improving people's lives."[46]

This policy sounds good on paper, but does it help or hinder the world in practice?

The stated purpose of foreign aid by the United States is that it aids the strategic interests and safety of the nation while also promoting development and freedom in the underdeveloped parts of the world. This strategy should benefit all countries involved, both those giving aid and those receiving it. Many of the world's wealthiest countries have agreed to donate 0.7 percent of their gross national product

Total Dollar Amount and Percent of GNI Given to Foreign Aid, 2007

Country	Amount (In Millions of U.S. Dollars)	Percent of GNI	Country	Amount (In Millions of U.S. Dollars)	Percent of GNI
Norway	3,728	0.95	Switzerland	1,689	0.37
Sweden	4,339	0.93	United Kingdom	9,849	0.36
Luxembourg	376	0.91	Australia	2,669	0.32
Denmark	2,562	0.81	Canada	4,080	0.29
Netherlands	6,224	0.81	New Zealand	320	0.27
Ireland	1,192	0.55	Portugal	471	0.22
Austria	1,808	0.50	Italy	3,971	0.19
Belgium	1,953	0.43	Japan	7,679	0.17
Finland	981	0.39	Greece	501	0.16
France	9,884	0.38	United States	21,787	0.16
Germany	12,291	0.37	Total of EU countries	61,540	0.39
Spain	5,140	0.37	TOTAL	103,491	0.28

GNI = gross national income, the total amount produced by that nation (GDP) plus incomes received from other countries

Source: Created by the author. Data from the Organisation for Economic Co-operation and Development, "Statistical Annex of the 2009 Development Co-operation Report," http://www.oecd.org/document/9/0,3343,en_2649_34447_1893129_1_1_1_1,00.html, Accessed September 3, 2009.

to foreign aid. However, only the top five wealthiest countries have met this goal.

The table above is sorted by percentage of gross national income given to foreign aid. While the United States ranks first in number of total dollars provided, it falls at the bottom of the list, donating only 0.16 percent of its gross national income to countries in need. This translates into less than one-fourth of what has been promised. You may wonder, perhaps, how private donations compare to official ones. Among these same nations, the U.S. still provides the most dollars in private foreign aid, but ranks 14th in its percentage of GNI (0.70 percent). Austria ranks first in private donations, contributing 5.3 percent of its GNI. So, is the United States really the most generous country? If you consider the matter in terms of total dollars, then the answer is yes. If you're talking about a percentage of income, the answer is no. Which do you think is more important?[47]

MAKE CONNECTIONS

Globalization and Its Links to Population Growth and Environmental Damage

As you will learn in Chapter 18, the population of human beings on Earth is growing rapidly. This issue is connected with today's "new" slavery in poor countries, as an expanding population requires more jobs. If there isn't enough work to go around, people in poor countries cannot make enough money to survive. The expanding population in wealthier countries creates issues as well. These people need to work to feed their families, which leads to greater expansion of industry. The growing population also puts a strain on natural resources, which will further the core nations' need to get involved with periphery nations that have necessary resources. The issues of globalization will only increase with an ever-expanding population.

In Chapter 19, you will learn about environmental issues. As you probably know, the United States creates a great deal of waste. Some of the methods of getting rid of this waste are tied to globalization, as the United States seeks to ship certain toxins for "disposal" to other parts of the world.

Globalization

Across the globe you will find people with differing opinions on globalization. When political, cultural, and economic boundaries blend together, some countries benefit more than others. Globalization can encourage familiarity with cultural norms outside your own personal beliefs. It also allows companies to do business in multiple countries. However, although developed countries often see the benefits of a global economic market, developing countries are less likely to see any profit from the elimination of boundaries. What are the arguments for and against the continuation of this international trend?

Pro

- Globalization is a possible solution to the world's economic crisis.
- Globalization allows for the expansion of business; having a global market allows goods and services to move across borders.
- Globalization creates global standards of living and human rights, and decreases discrimination against minorities by encouraging familiarity with people of different races, ethnicities, and cultures.
- By developing worldwide regulations and standards for working conditions, globalization can end the use of sweatshops and child labor and promote the development of environmentally friendly technologies.

Con

- Globalization creates many of the world's economic hardships.
- Globalization allows industrialized countries to gain control over the economic development of developing countries.
- Globalization spreads disease and increases migration, which, in certain situations, leads to conflict.
- When multinational companies outsource labor and build manufacturing plants in other countries, resources (and therefore profits) are being taken from these poorer countries.

From Classroom to Community } Medical Aid in Botswana

Tamara is a nursing student who spent three months of her summer vacation working as a medical assistant in Botswana. Her job was to aid the doctors in educating the poorer communities on health practices as well as administering medications.

"It was sometime after winter break that I learned Dr. Koeller was making the trip to Africa with his church. I thought I knew what to expect when I signed up, but I was surprised by what I saw when we finally arrived in the first village. Having lived in a large city for most of my life, I was used to seeing the poor and homeless, but this was so much worse. More than half of the town was HIV positive, and some suffered from malaria or typhoid. Since they were far from the city, the people relied on local doctors who traveled between towns, and those who were ill were malnourished due to the parasitic tapeworms that spawned in the river water. I walked two miles with the other missionaries just so we could bring back clean water to wash our hands before seeing patients.

"Dr. Koeller had gotten his hospital to donate vaccines for the children. I was surprised that some children were 12 years old and had never been vaccinated for diseases I'd been inoculated for as a baby. I learned that measles was common in the area, as was Hepatitis A.

"The people I met in these villages taught me a lot about what life is really like in many places outside of the United States. In one of the towns, Dr. Koeller intro-duced me to a five-year-old boy who he knew from previous trips. Kufuo had been born with HIV, and with a lack of health care, wasn't expected to live to his seventh birthday. Dr. Koeller told me it was a miracle he'd made it so far. My heart broke as I saw him playing with the other children, and I couldn't help but think that if we'd been here only a few years earlier, we might have been able to prevent this while he was still in the womb. In a developed country, this would have been a standard practice.

"By the end of the summer I'd made up my mind—I plan on going back to Botswana, and perhaps other countries in need of aid, as soon as I get my nursing degree."

CHAPTER

17

WHAT IS GLOBALIZATION AND HOW DOES IT AFFECT THE WORLD?   240

globalization is the process by which the world and the international economy become more closely intertwined; this results in an increase of shared culture and experiences, as well as glocalization, brain drain, and grobalization

WHAT THEORIES EXIST ABOUT GLOBALIZATION?   246

conflict theory: the imbalance of power between the rich and the poor creates stratification; this is true on a national scale, as exhibited by the gap between the rich and poor in the United States; on an international scale, this gap is between rich and poor nations; wealthy countries use neocolonialism to benefit from poorer countries that have desirable natural resources and cheap labor
symbolic interactionism: the creation of the European Union is an example of how language and symbolic events influence society; members of the European Union identify themselves as Europeans, rather than as members of various smaller nations; the European Union shows how unity and cooperation can drastically benefit a region and its people
functionalism: stratification is a result of geographic conditions; today, globalization bring wealth to less developed nations, benefitting both rich and poor areas of the world

HOW DOES SOCIETY DEAL WITH GLOBALIZATION?   247

foreign aid is offered by countries around the world to poorer nations in order to assist in economic development

get the topic: WHAT IS GLOBALIZATION AND HOW DOES IT AFFECT THE WORLD?

Theory

CONFLICT THEORY   246

- the imbalance of power between the elite and the poor creates stratification
- richer countries exploit poorer countries to preserve and augment their own wealth

SYMBOLIC INTERACTIONISM   247

- Europeans are beginning to view themselves less as members of their individual home countries and more as members of the European Union

FUNCTIONALISM   248

- stratification is mostly a result of geographic differences
- globalization does not solely benefit the countries that have risen to prominence; it also brings needed wealth and technology to poorer nations, which helps them advance

Key Terms

globalization is a complex process by which the world and the international economy are becoming more and more intertwined. *240*

glocalization occurs when countries seek to combine the local and the global into a unique structural blend to maintain their native customs while fitting into the global environment. *240*

brain drain occurs when the best talent leaves poor countries and thereby provides an even greater advantage to wealthy countries. *241*

global stratification is the categorization of countries based on objective criteria, such as wealth, power, and prestige, which highlight social patterns and inequality throughout the world. *242*

per-capita income is calculated by dividing a country's total gross income by the number of people in that country. *242*

contract slavery is a form of slavery in which a person signs a work contract, receiving food and shelter from an employer, but is threatened when he or she tries to leave. *244*

grobalization refers to the idea that capitalist countries use their corporate interests to expand their power and influence throughout the world. *244*

neocolonialism is a process by which powerful nations use loans and economic power to maintain control over poor nations. *246*

Sample Test Questions

These multiple-choice questions are similar to those found in the test bank that accompanies this textbook.

1. Which of the following is a result of globalization?
   a. Countries in the world interact less with one another economically.
   b. Multinational corporations have factories in many poor nations.
   c. Countries with abundant natural resources dominate the world politically.
   d. Worldwide literacy rates have declined.

2. Brain drain
   a. is detrimental to core countries.
   b. demonstrates an unhealthy Western influence in the world.
   c. is a result of migration.
   d. leads to glocalization.

3. Which of the following is *not* part of the criteria for global stratification?
   a. The amount of wealth possessed by a country
   b. The level of prestige a country carries
   c. The amount of power and influence a country has over others
   d. The type of government a country possesses

4. Which of the following is a characteristic of a developed nation?
   a. A well-educated population
   b. A democratic government
   c. A lack of profitable industry
   d. Government-sponsored health care and education

5. Immanuel Wallerstein's world systems theory divides the world into
   a. first, second, and third world countries.
   b. countries that are the most feared by others.
   c. core, semi-periphery, periphery, and external nations.
   d. primary and secondary spheres of influence.

ESSAY

1. How does globalization affect your life? Think about the prices of the things you buy, such as clothing and electronics. Without globalization, what do you think would happen to the prices of these goods?

2. How would your life be different if you lived in an underdeveloped nation? Do you think that you would feel the same as you do now, or would it significantly decrease your level of satisfaction with life?

3. What factors do you believe affect the quality of life in a country? Are these "ranked" lists biased towards a Western point of view, or do they objectively take all factors into consideration?

4. How do you think the world will change over the course of the next 50 years as a result of globalization? Do you believe that the United States will continue to be the most powerful economic influence, or will this position belong to a United States of Europe or another superpower?

5. Do you think that it's possible for nations that are currently underdeveloped to become influential? Does the current system of neocolonialism allow for such a possibility?

WHERE TO START YOUR RESEARCH PAPER

For U.S. Census facts and information, go to http://www.census.gov

To learn more about neocolonialism, visit http://www.postcolonialweb.org/poldiscourse/neocolonialism1.html

For more information about the North Atlantic Treaty Organization (NATO), see http://www.nato.int

For more information on the European Union, go to http://europa.eu

To learn more about U.S. foreign aid policy, check out http://www.usaid.gov/

ANSWERS: 1. b; 2. c; 3. d; 4. a; 5. c

Remember to check www.thethinkspot.com for additional information, downloadable flashcards, and other helpful resources.

POPULATION PROBLEMS

The world's

population will hit 7 billion early in 2012 and top 9 billion in 2050, with the vast majority of the increase coming in the developing countries of Asia and Africa, according to a U.N. estimate released Wednesday.

Hania Zlotnik, director of the U.N. Population Division, said that "there have been no big changes" from the previous estimate in 2006.

"We are still projecting that by 2050 the population of the world will be around 9.1 billion," she said at a news conference. "The projections are based on the assumption that fertility that is now around 2.56 children per woman is going to decline to about 2.02 children per woman in the world."

Zlotnik said if fertility remained about where it is now, then world population would reach 10.5 billion by 2050. If fertility fell even more than expected, to about 1.5, then the population would only increase to 8 billion by mid-century, she said.

Population growth will remain concentrated in the most populous countries through 2050. Nine nations are expected to account for half the projected increase: India, Pakistan, Nigeria, Ethiopia, the U.S., Congo, Tanzania, China and Bangladesh, the report said.

In sharp contrast, the populations of 45 countries or regions are expected to decline at least 10 percent over the same period, including Japan, Italy, and many other countries that were once part of the Soviet Union, the U.N. said.

According to the study, the largest number of migrants will head to the United States—an estimated 1.1 million every year between 2010 and 2050.

The immigrants and the U.S. birth rate will help boost the U.S. population from an estimated 314.7 million in mid-2009 to 403.9 million in 2050, according to Gerhard Heilig, chief of the U.N.'s Population Estimates and Projections Section.[1]

---Even in a developed nation like the United States, the population continues to increase.

In my town, new housing is constantly being built to accommodate the growing number of people. Of course, in a country such as ours, a growing population generally means more economic growth and very few real problems related to providing residents with adequate shelter, water, and sanitation. This is not always true in other parts of the world.

What will it be like to live in a world with 9 billion people, as projected in the opening article?

How will developing nations in Asia and Africa handle the predicted population surges, and how will this change our lives in the developed world as well?

These are just a few of the questions that researchers explore when considering the impact of population growth on a world with limited resources and a fragile environment.

get the topic: IS POPULATION GROWTH A PROBLEM?

DEMOGRAPHY is the study of the size and composition of a population.

POPULATION VARIABLES are the changeable characteristics of a given population.

FERTILITY is the number of births that occur in a population.

CRUDE BIRTH RATE is the number of births for every 1,000 people each year.

AGE-SPECIFIC BIRTH RATE is the number of births for every 1,000 women in a specific age group.

TOTAL FERTILITY RATE (TFR) is the average number of births expected from any woman in a population.

ZERO POPULATION GROWTH is a TFR of two, meaning that each woman has two children to replace the mother and father.

LIFE EXPECTANCY is the average number of years of life for a person of any given age.

LIFE SPAN is the maximum length of time that it is possible for a human being to live.

Population by the Numbers

In graduate school, one of my favorite classes was demography. It taught one simple truth: All societies are influenced by their populations. **Demography** is the study of the size and composition of a population, and as a wise old professor once told me, "It's all in the numbers." If a population of a country is large, the nation can face many problems, such as how to provide its people with the necessary resources. Of course, the country also faces many possible opportunities, because more people allows for more economic growth, more innovation, and greater possibilities for development.

What different characteristics might the population of Sweden have from the population of Afghanistan? To study a population, demographers use **population variables**, changeable characteristics of a given population such as size, racial composition, birth rates, and death rates.

As you may already know, the world's population is unevenly distributed. The number of people in the two most populated countries, China and India, is larger than the next 23 countries combined. The United States is the third greatest populated nation, but is home to just 4.6 percent of the world's people.[2] To get a sense for just how staggering these statistics are, check out the diagram on page 258. How might these figures affect the lives of the people in these countries?

The world's population is constantly changing, as you can see from the graph on the opposite page. Note that the growth of the population is rather slow for a long period of time and then rapidly increases around the time of the industrial revolution. As nations develop, life expectancies increase, largely due to advances is public health and access to other goods we take for granted, such as clean water and sewage disposal. Notice that it took more than 11,000 years for the world's population to grow to 1 billion; however, it more than doubled again 100 years later, and again from 1940 to 1982. It's projected that the number of people will double again by 2042, bringing the world's total population to over 9 billion people.[3] Demographers refer to this span as doubling time, which we will discuss in more detail later on in the chapter.[4]

Tools for Studying Population
FERTILITY

Fertility refers to the number of births that occur in a population. It's often calculated as **crude birth rate**, which is the number of births each year per 1,000 people. There are several factors that can determine fertility rate, including health, wealth, and education, as well as access to birth control and the number of women of child-bearing age. **Age-specific birth rate** measures the number of births per every 1,000 women in a specific age group. The **total fertility rate (TFR)** is the average number of births expected from a woman in a population. **Zero population growth** refers to a TFR of two, meaning that each woman, on average, is expected to have two children to replace the mother and father. Each of these calculations allows demographers to make predictions about a population and can help the society plan ahead for the future. For example, if a community notices that crude birth rate is declining, they may decide to put off building a new elementary school.

LIFE EXPECTANCY

How long will you live? No one knows for sure, of course, but demographers can calculate how long you might expect to live. **Life expectancy** is the average number of years of life for a person of any given age. This figure should not be confused with **life span**, which is the maximum length of time it is possible for a human being to live. So, while a human being may be capable of living well over 100 years, he or she may only live for a portion of that time based on other factors. Over the last century, the life expectancy for many people around the world has increased dramatically, thanks, in large part, to improvements in our standard of living, such as access to clean water and better housing, and expanded availability of health care.[5] Between the 1860s and the 1990s, the human life span increased from 108 years to 116 years.[6]

At the time of birth, all people around the world can expect to live an average of 65 years. This number changes based on other factors that can affect the life expectancy rates in a given area. For example, nations such as France, Italy, and Spain have some of the longest life expectancies at 81, 80.2, and 80.5 years, respectively. On the other hand, countries such as Zimbabwe and Ethiopia have some of the shortest life expectancies, falling in the low 40s. There are 48 other countries with higher life expectancies than the United States, where the life expectancy is 78.1 years. However, when compared to the 10 largest nations on Earth, the United States is second only to Japan. The low life expectancy rate in some African countries is due to a number of factors, including lack of clean water, sewage problems, malaria, and the widespread presence of HIV/AIDS—the leading cause of death in countries such as Angola (in which individuals are only expected to live 38.2 years).[7]

MORTALITY RATES

The **mortality rate** is the number of deaths that occur in a population. Sociologists can examine mortality rates to calculate what is called the **crude death rate**, the number of deaths per 1,000 people each year. Such a number helps in comparisons of nations. A population going through a period of war, disease, or famine would experience an increased mortality rate. One statistic that researchers pay close attention to is the **infant mortality rate**, which is the number of children per 1,000 who are born alive but die before reaching the age of one year.

> **MORTALITY RATE** is the number of deaths that occur in a population.
>
> **CRUDE DEATH RATE** is the number of deaths per 1,000 people each year.
>
> **INFANT MORTALITY RATE** is the number of children per 1,000 who are born alive but who die before reaching the age of one year.
>
> **POPULATION PYRAMIDS** are tools that visually represent data about a specific population in relation to age and sex.

One of the reasons life expectancies are so low in some countries is because of their high infant mortality rates, which are also affected by environment and access to health care. For example, the infant mortality rate in Angola is 180, while it is only 2.75 in Sweden. This means that 18 percent of children born in Angola die within the first year of life while only 0.275 percent of babies born in Sweden are likely to die before their first birthday. The United States' rate of 6.26 is rather high for a developed nation and falls just behind Cuba in world rankings. More than 40 countries have lower rates of infant mortality. Why might this be the case? As we discussed in previous chapters, access to prenatal care tends to lower infant mortality rates. Countries such as Angola have weak health care systems with limited access to services. Meanwhile, nations such as Sweden offer universal coverage. The U.S. system does not assure everyone access to medical care, which may be part of the reason for our relatively high rate of infant death.[8]

POPULATION PYRAMIDS

A **population pyramid** visually represents data about a specific population in relation to age and sex. Population pyramids track changes in a population over time, and this information can help researchers assess

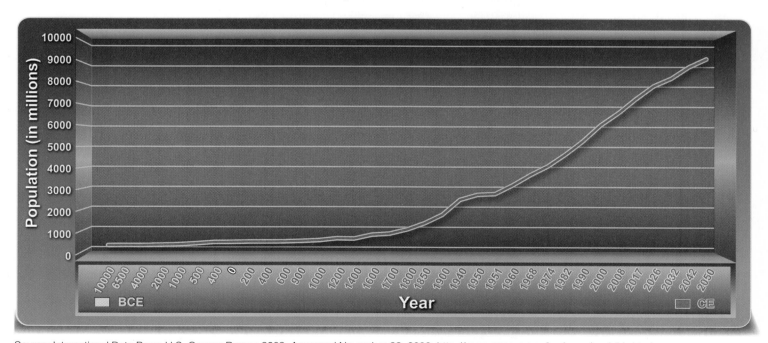

World Population Growth

Source: International Data Base: U.S. Census Bureau 2009, Accessed November 29, 2009, http://www.census.gov/ipc/www/worldhis.html.

∧
∧ The doubling time of the world's population has decreased rapidly. **How long do you predict it will be until the population doubles to 18 billion people?**

the potential needs of a society. The population pyramids on the next page demonstrate how the populations of Mexico and the United States have changed from 20 years ago to the present and how they are likely to change in the next 20 years. Notice that the countries do not have the same shape. As people begin to live longer and birth rates stabilize, a "squaring" of the pyramids occur, and they begin to take on a more rectangular shape. In the United States, this squaring is already happening. In Mexico, the effect is less pronounced. Can you think of possible social problems that might result as the pyramid of the U.S. squares? Will there

be enough young people to care for and financially support the growing number of elderly citizens? As we discussed in Chapter 5, might older workers need to continue working later in their lives to maintain a reasonable standard of living? What would happen to the pyramid if migration to the United States halted? These are just some of the issues that demographers raise when discussing population predictions.

MIGRATION

Demographers know that people have always migrated. Today, as in the past, population increases and global interaction contribute to **migration**, or the movement of people from one area to another. We discussed in more detail the issue of migration in Chapter 3, but remember that migration is usually discussed in terms of immigration and emigration. **Immigration** is the movement of people into a nation-state. **Emigration** is the movement

Distribution of World Population: The Top Five

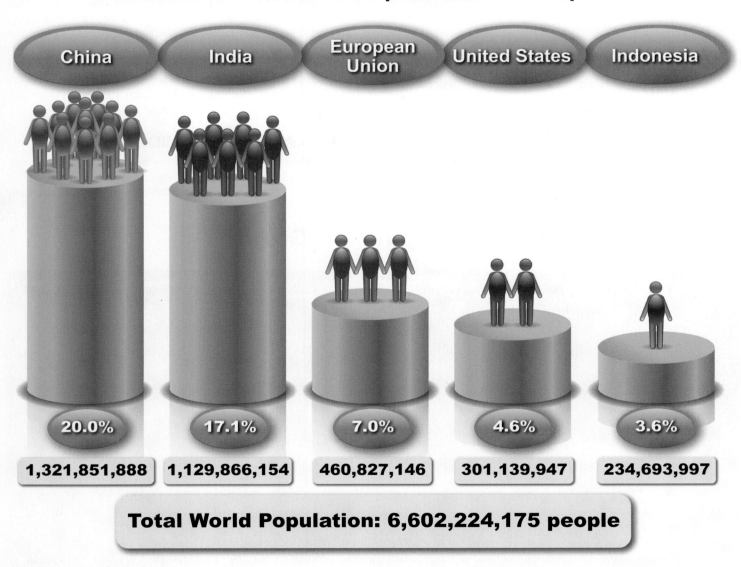

China	India	European Union	United States	Indonesia
20.0%	17.1%	7.0%	4.6%	3.6%
1,321,851,888	1,129,866,154	460,827,146	301,139,947	234,693,997

Total World Population: 6,602,224,175 people

Source: Central Intelligence Agency, "Population 2007," *The World Factbook,* https://www.cia.gov/cia/publications/factbook/rankorder/2119rank.html, Accessed April 20, 2007.

∧
∧ **China and India both contain more people than the next 23 countries combined.** What benefits
∧ might a larger population provide?

of people out of a nation-state. The vast majority of U.S. citizens are either descendants of immigrants or are immigrants themselves.

Issues like infant mortality and life expectancy can play a role in peoples' decisions to emigrate from their country of birth. People from poorer areas of the world often move to more prosperous areas in hopes of improving their lives. For example, my German ancestors came to America due to lack of work in Germany, just as today some Mexican citizens immigrate to the United States for the same reason.[9]

Of course, migration patterns can lead to problems such as those we discussed in Chapter 3. When large numbers of a group migrate to an area, locals may react with discrimination and violence. For example, in the United States, anti-immigrant sentiment is on the rise. Hate groups

Population Pyramids

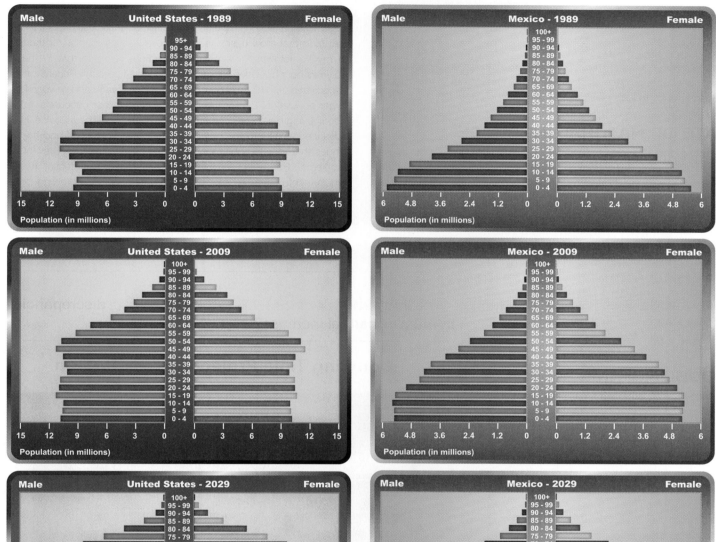

Source: U.S. Census Bureau, Population Division, 2007, www.census.gov/ipc/www/idb/index.php

∧
∧ The populations of both the United States and Mexico are slowly "squaring," but at separate
∧ rates. **What factors may have led to the differences in population between the two countries?**

are cropping up around the country with their focus on recent immigrants. Such groups often scapegoat the new immigrants as the "cause" of their suffering to justify their bigotry and violence.[10]

RATE OF NATURAL INCREASE

The **rate of natural increase (RNI)** is a calculation that demographers use to determine the growth or decline of a population. Populations with a positive RNI are growing, while populations with a negative RNI are in decline. Infant mortality and life expectancy are only two factors that can contribute to a negative RNI. In some cases, citizens in a population are opting not to have children, or are having fewer children than before, leading to **birth dearth**, or declining birth rates. For example, in the early 1990s, the total fertility rate in Japan dropped to 1.46, below the replacement level of two children per woman.[11] The shrinking population of future workers will have a hard time supporting a growing elderly population. Government policies hope to boost birth rates and temper this demographic imbalance.[12]

DOUBLING TIME

As you will recall, **doubling time** is the length of time in which it takes a population to double in size. The doubling time of a population can have a significant and lasting impact on its future. A shorter doubling time means that there will be less time to sufficiently increase available resources. If, for example, a country's doubling time is 50 years, then that country must be able to double its resources in that 50-year period in order to sustain itself. Otherwise, the growing population will put a strain on resources.

A simple way to calculate doubling time is by using the rule of 70. The **rule of 70** estimates doubling time by dividing 70 by the annual RNI for a population, resulting in an approximate number of years in which that population will double. Looking at the table on the right, you can see that the doubling time for the population of South America is 46.6 years (70/1.5), while the doubling time for the population of Oceania is 70 years (70/1). Because the RNI can vary from year to year, it is important to be aware that most populations do not grow exactly as predicted, and in the past, doubling time estimates have rarely been completely accurate.[13] Even so, demographers can use doubling time calculations to show possible population growth trends and to compare populations. Looking back at the table, notice that in many regions of the world the populations are projected to double

within your lifetime. What impact will this have on your life? What social issues will this create for both the young and the old?

POPULATION PROJECTIONS

Fertility rates, life expectancies, mortality rates, population pyramids, migration rates, and rates of natural increase are all taken into consideration when making population projections. Of course, such projections may not be able to predict factors such as war, disease, or changes in birth rates, so they can be incorrect. However, this does not mean that population projections have no value at all. Scientific estimates are important tools that allow businesses and policy makers to plan for the future. In my hometown, for example, projections suggest that in the next 20 years our population will grow by around 14 percent. Recently, the city council began to discuss how to plan for clean water and sewage for this larger population. Even if the projection is not exactly accurate, and the population grows by 13 percent, the services will still be available. Having advance insight into the potential needs of a population and the challenges that they face helps societies prepare for or even prevent such problems. Population projections can determine potential resource requirements, such as schools, homes, and jobs for growing populations, as well as adequate health care facilities for populations with longer life expectancies.

> The population of Africa will double long before that of any other continent. What causes such **discrepancies in rates of natural increase?**

Doubling Time Projections, by Region

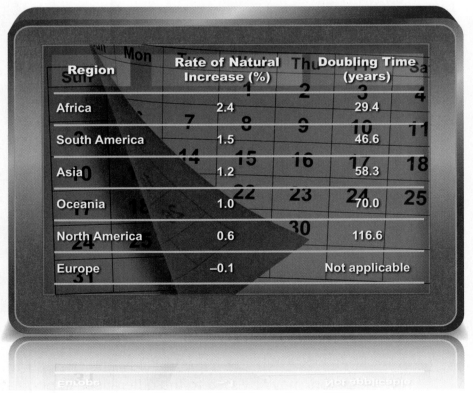

Region	Rate of Natural Increase (%)	Doubling Time (years)
Africa	2.4	29.4
South America	1.5	46.6
Asia	1.2	58.3
Oceania	1.0	70.0
North America	0.6	116.6
Europe	−0.1	Not applicable

Source: *World Population Data Sheet*, Population Reference Bureau, 2007, http://www.prb.org/pdf07/07WPDS_Eng.pdf

China and the One-Child Policy

In the future, do you plan on having a large family? You can do this in the United States, but that's not an option for everyone around the world. Can you imagine being rewarded for having one child, but being penalized for having more? That's the way China's "one-child" policy works. Unlike the United States, where couples are given incentives to have children by way of tax breaks, the Chinese approach offers couples incentives to have only one child. After having their first child, Chinese citizens can be penalized if they decide to have any more.

In 1979, the Chinese government implemented the one-child policy in an effort to address a social problem—that of a rapidly growing population. The government hoped to prevent future problems by eliminating the strain on resources and ensuring that opportunities were available for all of its citizens. If the size of the Chinese population was not kept in check and people were permitted to have families of any size, the government foresaw the potential for starvation, uneven distribution of jobs and resources, and conflict resulting from these factors. Aside from limitations placed on the number of children that couples can have, the Chinese government also promotes the use of birth control and encourages its citizens to marry later in life, thereby reducing the amount of time that couples will have to reproduce.[14]

There are rewards for following the rules. In China, after having their first child, couples vow not to have any more children. If they keep that vow, they may receive higher pay, better health options, and more educational possibilities for their child, and the expecting mother receives an extended maternity leave. On the other hand, if they violate their pledge, they can be penalized by having their earnings taxed. There are exceptions to the one-child rule. The rule is most strictly enforced on people who live in highly populated, urbanized areas. People who live in less densely populated rural areas, however, are permitted to have two children without being penalized.[15]

China's one-child policy is not without its critics, who have accused the country of state-mandated sterilizations and abortions.[16] In Chinese society, males retain more power than females and are held in higher regard by parents for their ability to move upward in society in ways that females cannot. A side effect of the one-child rule is that when families are forced to have only one child, they often opt for male children. Women have been known to abort or abandon children once it is known that the child is female or disabled.[17] This abundance of males in the population can lead to future difficulties with the nation's fertility rate, causing an imbalance in the availability of single women and single men. Having so many males in the Chinese population is also seen by some as increasing the likelihood of internal strife, war, and civic unrest as masses of young, single men are shown to exhibit more aggression, and may be inclined to pursue military careers.[18]

<<< The **Chinese** government instated the **"one-child"** policy as a means of **population control.**

Economic Issues of Population Growth and Decline

The growth rate of a population can have an impact on its economy. Often countries with the weakest economies experience the greatest population growth. Countries in this situation are in a double bind because they can't support the existing population and will have even greater difficulty in trying to support a larger population.

The news isn't all bad, though. Economist Julian Simon found that population growth can improve a country's economy over a span of more than 100 years. When compared to countries with stable population growth, the economies of countries with growing populations saw greater improvement. His explanation was that people living in growing populations need to find jobs to survive, and those jobs slowly help improve the economy over time.[19] In developed countries, population growth leads to greater specialization of labor, increased development of knowledge, and the promotion of innovation, resulting in the generation of income and improved quality of life for many. The same is not true of developing countries, where growing populations lead to reductions in income and put a greater strain on public resources.[20]

think social problems: HOW DO WE MEASURE POPULATION?

Malthusian Theory

Thomas Malthus was an English clergyman known for making one of the earliest population projections. In 1798, he published *An Essay on the Principle of Population* that introduced his observations on population. Now known as the **Malthusian theorem**, he stated that populations grow at a geometric rate (2, 4, 8, 16 . . .), while food grows at an arithmetic rate (1, 2, 3, 4 . . .). Even with advanced technology that increases food production, there will come a time when the population cannot be sustained by the food supply. At that point, food shortages are likely to lead to famine, war, and the spread of disease. However, any famine, war, or disease that occurs *before* that point in history is a positive check on population, because it pushes back the day when the number of people will outgrow the amount of food. Keep in mind that during Malthus's time, measures such as birth control were not widely available. Today, Malthus's thoughts on population remain highly influential, and many of the environmental arguments you will learn about in Chapter 19 are built on the idea that the world has finite resources and populations will eventually overwhelm those resources. If Malthus could see the world today, would he argue that we are close? Some suggest that current famines are due less to shortages of food and more to corrupt governments and poor distribution systems. What do you think?

Demographic Transition Theory

Demographic transition theorists, for example, disagree with Malthus' conclusions. **Demographic transition theory** states that people control their fertility as societies change from being agrarian to industrial, and that this occurs in four basic stages. These findings are based on historical data on population growth trends in Northern Europe, leading critics to point out that this model may not apply to non-European countries.[22]

In the first stage, a society is not industrialized and experiences high birth and death rates. The life expectancy of the population is low, and infant mortality is high. It's beneficial for citizens to have many children because it increases the odds that some will grow into adulthood and be able to assist with labor. The population grows slowly during this stage due to similar rates of birth and death.

In the second stage, a society enters the initial phase of industrialization. New technologies decrease the need for physical labor, and people relocate to urban areas seeking jobs in factories. Along with industrialization comes an increased food supply, improved health care, and a higher standard of living. Birth rates remain high, while infant mortality declines.[23] Life expectancy also increases, leading to a decline in the death rate; because of this, populations see the greatest rates of growth during this period.

In the third stage, as a society establishes its industrialized status, birth rates decline. Death rates also decline and stabilize due to longer life expectancies. Improvements in economic and social conditions affect personal reproductive choices, and people begin to opt for smaller families. Note that the population is still growing at this stage, just at a slower rate.[24]

In the fourth stage, a society becomes postindustrial and experiences either a stable or declining population size. At this point, both birth and death rates are relatively low.

Malthus Curve

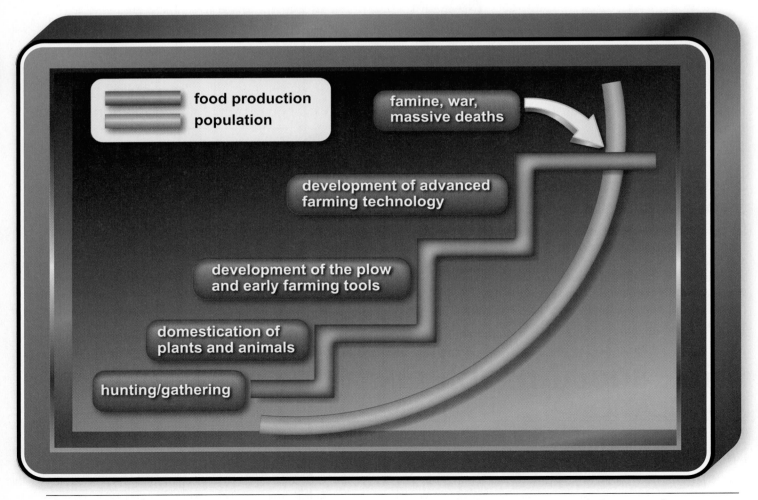

Thomas Malthus argued that food is produced at an arithmetic rate, while populations grow at a geometric rate. **How close do you think we are from expending all of our resources?**

Demographic Transition Model

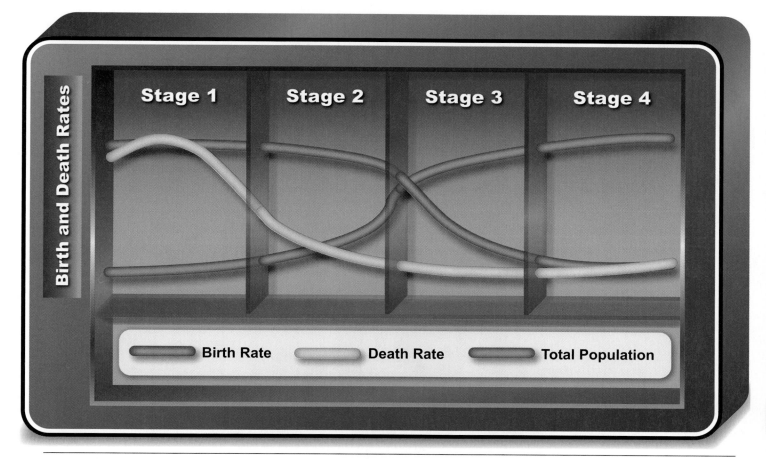

Stage 1   Stage 2   Stage 3   Stage 4

Birth and Death Rates

Birth Rate   Death Rate   Total Population

∧
∧ According to the demographic transition model, population growth is constantly in flux as
∧ a society transitions to an industrialized status. **Where is the United States in this model?**

discover solutions to social problems: HOW DO DEMOGRAPHERS THINK ABOUT THE ISSUE OF POPULATION?

Population Control

Populations grow as a result of both birth rates and death rates. Because managing the death rate is not an acceptable solution, population control programs must focus on the birth rate. As mentioned before, countries like China focus their policies on how many children a couple can have; conversely, the United States does not have a population control policy and rewards large families with more tax breaks. In a way, small American families subsidize large American families. In other countries around the world, the opposite is true.

Although birth control options such as contraceptives and abortion are available in the United States, these decisions are left to individuals and are provided by private sources. In other parts of the world, this is not the case. For example, Mexico provides publicly funded abortions that are free to all citizens.[25] Likewise, in Colombia, contraception is available to adolescents in an effort to prevent unwanted pregnancies.[26]

From a global perspective, the world's population is still growing, but the *rate* at which the population is growing has declined.[27] In most parts of the world now, population control efforts tend to focus on educating women on their reproductive rights and making contraceptives widely available.[28]

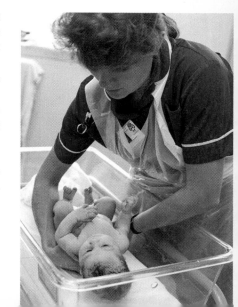

>>> While the rate of population growth has declined, **the world's population** is still growing and **is projected to reach 9 billion by 2042.**[29]

WRAP YOUR MIND AROUND THE THEORY

Overuse of resources can lead to disaster. **Is our way of life putting a strain on the environment?**

FUNCTIONALISM

Functionalists focus on the relationships between different social structures. What role does a growing population play in society? From a functionalist perspective, having children ensures that a population will be able to carry on. Population growth can lead to economic progress, but it can also lead to problems when a society overtaxes its resources. The ancient inhabitants of Easter Island died off due to deforestation and overuse of resources that stemmed from population growth; we must take precautions to avoid these same issues today.[21]

CONFLICT THEORY

A growing population increases competition over resources such as food, water, fuel, and space. Even with the development of new technologies that make necessary resources available to large groups of individuals, a constantly rising number of people will eventually overwhelm our ability to produce and distribute those necessities. Who will "win" this competition? Conflict theorists suggest that the future shortage will divide the population into groups: those with access to resources and those with little or no access to them. Those with access will increase their level of power and influence over society, while those without will have a diminished status. This inequality will lead to conflict not only over resources, but power, influence, and social standing as well. Social problems of this nature have occurred throughout history; a growing population increases the likelihood of similar conflicts occurring in the near future.

HOW DOES POPULATION GROWTH AFFECT SOCIETY?

SYMBOLIC INTERACTIONISM

Symbolic interactionists examine how society itself affects the growth of the population. By examining the culture of a society, symbolic interactionists hope to gain a better understanding of the causes of population growth. A society's overall feelings about children can have an impact on the size of the population, as can changes in male and female roles. Symbolic interactionists study how attitudes regarding marriage, use of birth control, increased education of women, and other shifts in culture can alter the development of a population. Countries in which people delay marriage until they've reached a certain point in their career or education, for example, might see a decline in the growth rate of their population. An increase in the use of birth control could result in similar trends.

Limited resources can lead to conflict. Can our resources support the entire population?

Some men and women postpone marriage until they've finished school. What effects can this have on population growth?

Population and the Planet

Almost every chapter you have read so far in this book has had some connection to issues caused by population. We discussed some of the problems caused by immigration in Chapter 3. In Chapter 5, you learned how an aging population could affect society, while in Chapter 13 you saw how population distribution could influence crime rates. In Chapter 16, we mentioned that urban areas are susceptible to overpopulation, which can challenge sanitary conditions and overtax resources. In Chapter 17, you learned that working conditions on a highly populated, globalized planet could deteriorate into low-wage jobs, sweatshops, and even slavery. As you'll read in Chapter 19, overpopulation can also have negative and lasting impacts on the environment, sometimes damaging the world's resources beyond repair.

Pro & Con

Population Control

To address rapid population growth, some countries have enacted policies and programs to encourage population control. Are these programs ultimately effective or destructive?

Pro

- A controlled population allows for increased opportunities for success. An overpopulated area will have a limited availability of jobs and limited opportunities for education.
- A controlled population benefits women in developing nations who will have increased access to these resources and a greater chance for upward mobility.
- Population control is important for maintaining peace. Conflicts over limited resources are more like to occur as a result of overpopulation.
- Overpopulation can strain the environment beyond its ability to support itself. If too many of the world's resources are used before they can be replaced, the world's population will suffer as a result.

Con

- Overpopulation is a social problem that will take care of itself, as the entire world continues to go through the demographic transition.
- The state has no inherent right to influence a couple's decision to reproduce or to predetermine the size of their family. Trying to control personal decisions that citizens make violates a person's right to think and decide for him- or herself.
- Such policies encourage abortions and infanticide as well as the abandonment of children. In China, for example, people tend to favor male children, which can increase these social problems.
- Claims of the devastating impact of population growth have been greatly exaggerated, and there is no tangible evidence to support such claims. There is no real way to accurately determine whether societal problems occur as a result of population growth.

From Classroom to Community | Clean Water

Christine was accepted into the Peace Corps after her senior year of college. Armed with a BA in education, she assumed that she'd be assigned to teach undereducated children. Instead, she found herself in the small town of Mafi-Dove, Ghana, as a member of a new clean water initiative.

"At first I was disappointed. Working with water didn't seem nearly as exciting as teaching, or even constructing houses. However, after a few days there, I began to see how much of a problem there really was. Since there weren't enough latrines for everyone in the village, many people went near the river. When it rained, waste would be carried into the river, contaminating it. People in Mafi-Dove routinely suffered from Guinea worms and other parasites that were found in the water, and seeing huge boils on the children made me want to cry."

Christine learned that the other Peace Corps members had spent the last year digging shallow wells, but the holes weren't deep enough to reach a clean source of water, or to sustain such a rapidly growing population. "During my second week there, a construction crew was called in by our leader. Using a huge drill, they dug a borehole. It was over a hundred feet deep and, when tested, was found to provide an almost endless supply of sanitary water."

Christine spent the following months overseeing more drilling projects, testing water sources, and educating the residents on sanitary waste practices. "By the time my two years were over, three new boreholes had been dug in the village, and most of the citizens were either getting their water from those pipes or boiling river water before using it. I joined the Peace Corps because I wanted to teach and make a difference—and in a way, I think I did."

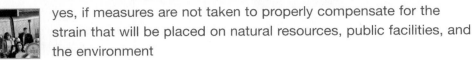

IS POPULATION GROWTH A PROBLEM?   256

yes, if measures are not taken to properly compensate for the strain that will be placed on natural resources, public facilities, and the environment

HOW DO WE MEASURE POPULATION?   261

through the Malthusian theorem, which states that the population grows at a faster rate than the food supply, and the demographic transition theory, which states that people control their fertility as populations make the transition from agrarian to industrial

HOW DO DEMOGRAPHERS THINK ABOUT THE ISSUE OF POPULATION?   263

population control programs are the best methods of preventing destructive population growth

get the topic: IS POPULATION GROWTH A PROBLEM?

Theory

FUNCTIONALISM   264

- a growing population is necessary for the continuation of society and leads to increased opportunities
- a population that grows too large can lead to a scarcity of resources and inhibit the planet's ability to support a population of any size
- it is important for people to know the sustainable limits of the environment that supports them

CONFLICT THEORY   264

- even the development of new technologies will not be able to support a constantly growing population forever, and the result will be an inevitable shortage of resources
- a shortage of resources will lead to two groups of people: those with access to resources who will grow in power and influence as a result, and those without, who will lose power and influence in society

- these divisions will lead to conflict over resources, power, and influence in society

SYMBOLIC INTERACTIONISM   264

- it is important to look at the role society plays in a population, since studying a culture can lead to a better understanding of population growth
- factors such as how a society views children can have an impact on the growth rate of a population
- major shifts in the attitudes and behaviors of a society, like changes in male and female roles, opinions about marriage, the use of birth control, and the education of women can have a lasting impact on how quickly a population grows

Key Terms

demography is the study of the size and composition of a population.   *256*

population variables are the changeable characteristics of a given population.   *256*

fertility is the number of births that occur in a population.   *256*

crude birth rate is the number of births for every 1,000 people each year.   *256*

age-specific birth rate is the number of births for every 1,000 women in a specific age group.   *256*

total fertility rate (TFR) is the average number of births expected from any woman in a population.   *256*

zero population growth is a TFR of two, meaning that each woman has two children to replace the mother and father.   *256*

life expectancy is the average number of years of life for a person of any given age.   *256*

life span is the maximum length of time that it is possible for a human being to live.   *256*

mortality rate is the number of deaths that occur in a population.   *257*

crude death rate is the number of deaths per 1,000 people each year.   *257*

infant mortality rate is the number of children per 1,000 who are born alive but who die before reaching the age of one year.   257

population pyramids are tools that visually represent data about a specific population in relation to age and sex.   257

migration is the movement of people from one area to another area.   258

immigration is the movement of people into a nation-state.   258

emigration is the movement of people out of a nation-state.   258

rate of natural increase (RNI) is a calculation that demographers use to determine the growth or decline of a population.   260

birth dearth refers to declining birth rates.   260

doubling time is the length of time in which it takes a population to double in size.   260

rule of 70 estimates doubling time by dividing 70 by the annual rate of natural increase for a population.   260

Malthusian theorem states that populations grow at a geometric rate, while food grows at an arithmetic rate.   261

demographic transition theory states that people control their fertility as societies change from being agrarian to industrial.   262

Sample Test Questions

These multiple-choice questions are similar to those found in the test bank that accompanies this textbook.

1. According to Malthus
   a. populations grow at arithmetic rates.
   b. doubling time is calculated by the rule of 70.
   c. population control is primarily a method of maintaining peace.
   d. famine, war, and disease can be beneficial to a population.

2. Getting married and having children later in life is likely to
   a. increase the size of the population.
   b. decrease the size of the population.
   c. have no effect on the size of the population.
   d. only be an effective means of population control in first-world countries.

3. The average age to which a member of a population can expect to live is called
   a. life expectancy.
   b. life span.
   c. life term.
   d. life trajectory.

4. Doubling time is
   a. a technique used to determine the original size of a population.
   b. a calculation of the number of people born between two dates in time.
   c. the length of time it takes for a population to increase twofold.
   d. a comparison of the length of time taken by two separate societies to become industrialized.

5. One of the criticisms of China's One Child Policy is that it favors women over men and may lead to a predominantly female population in the future.
   a. True
   b. False

ESSAY

1. Do you think that government should have any involvement in controlling population size? Why or why not?
2. Which model best describes global population growth: the Malthus Curve or the Demographic Transition Model (or neither)? Explain your answer.
3. Do you think that it would be a good idea for the United States to implement population control policies?
4. Which resources have you seen diminish as a result of population growth? How has it affected you?
5. With careful planning, can a population continue to grow for an unlimited amount of time? Explain your conclusion using one or more of the sociological theories.

WHERE TO START YOUR RESEARCH PAPER

For information and statistics on the world's population, go to http://www.census.gov/ipc/www/idb

For information on China's one-child policy, see http://www.ncbi.nlm.nih.gov/pmc/articles/PMC1116810

To see a presentation about the effects of overpopulation, go to http://www.nationalgeographic.com/eye/overpopulation/overpopulation.html

To read about possible solutions to overpopulation, go to http://www.overpopulation.org/solutions.html

To see a map of the world with countries sized by population, visit http://www.worldmapper.org/countrycartograms

To view a running population clock, check out http://www.worldometers.info/population/

ANSWERS: 1. d; 2. b; 3. a; 4. c; 5. b

Remember to check www.thethinkspot.com **for additional information, downloadable flashcards, and other helpful resources.**

ENVIRONMENT

Governments

are failing to stem a rapid decline in biodiversity that is now threatening extinction for almost half the world's coral reef species, a third of amphibians and a quarter of mammals, a leading environmental group warned Thursday.

"Life on Earth is under serious threat," the International Union for Conservation of Nature said in a 155-page report that describes the past five years of a losing battle to protect species, natural habitats, and geographical regions from the devastating effects of man.

IUCN, the producer of the world's Red List of endangered animals, analyzed over 44,000 species to test government pledges earlier this decade to halt a global loss in biodiversity by 2010.

That target will not be met, the Gland, Switzerland–based body said, describing the prospects of coral reefs as the most alarming. It also said slightly more amphibians, mammals, and birds were in peril compared to five years ago, with species most prized by humans for food or medicine as disproportionately threatened.

"Biodiversity continues to decline and next year no one will dispute that," said Jean-Christophe Vie, the report's senior editor. "It's happening everywhere."

Vie told The Associated Press that biodiversity threats need to be highlighted and combated, even at a time when many world leaders are preoccupied by economic recession and financial instability. Unlike markets and debts, animal extinction is an irreversible element of today's "wildlife crisis."

He urged governments to usher in major changes to society, such as reducing energy and overall consumption, redesigning cities and reassessing the environmental consequences of globalization—producing goods in one part of the world and sending them thousands of miles to be sold.

Vie said climate change only threatened to make the situation worse.

Governments pledged in 2002 at a meeting of the U.N. Biodiversity Convention and the World Summit on Sustainable Development to halt biodiversity decline by the end of the decade. European governments have set a similar goal among themselves. In Europe, "about 50 percent of species are under threat or vulnerable," said Barbara Helfferich, a European Union spokeswoman. "Habitats are shrinking and a lot needs to be done. We are doing a lot, but it's not enough as promised to halt biodiversity loss."

Helfferich said a report last year suggested a number of steps for European governments to better protect biodiversity. They included expanding conservation sites, cutting down on overfishing, expanding protection to marine environments, and better incorporating ecological concerns in government decisions.[1]

---From the disappearance of the dodo bird in 1681 to the death of the last passenger pigeon in 1914, man-made extinction has threatened the future of Earth's natural habitats. There are more than 1,200 types of animals on the U.S. government's endangered species list, which includes not just animals that are "endangered" but also those that are threatened with extinction as well.

Some animals on the list are as famous as the California condor, while you've probably never heard of others, such as the Mexican long-nosed bat. If we include plant life, the list gets even longer. For example, there are more than 700 different types of endangered flowering plants. What do these threats mean for human societies?[2]

The truth is, the problems associated with the destruction of the environment extend far further than concern over the loss of one type of animal or plant. Like all life on this planet, human beings are organisms struggling to sustain themselves on the resources around them; like all organisms, when those resources vanish, so do we. What social issues might arise over a newly contaminated water supply? A shortage of fuel? A lack of clean air?

In this chapter, we'll discuss the impact of the environment on societies around the world. Who is more at risk of developing health problems from air pollutants—a child from inner-city Chicago or a woman from a rural village in Nepal? Can the rising sea levels wipe away entire civilizations? How large can the U.S. population continue to grow before the resources can no longer support the people? The answers to these questions may surprise you.

We'll also examine the social problems inherent in environmental policies. How can societies maintain the ecosystem while still providing resources for their citizens? What can we do to combat the rise of illness and disease as industrialization increases around the world? Are the poor at an environmental and medical disadvantage? We must take all of these questions into consideration when studying the social problems surrounding the environment.

get the topic: IS THE ENVIRONMENT IN DANGER?

In the 1970s, scientists began to investigate what is now considered a new sociological paradigm—**environmental sociology**. Within this field of study, researchers evaluate how the environment influences society, and vice versa.[3] Do people live differently due to differences in the environment? Who is most affected by changes in the ecosystem? Will these changes impact certain social classes differently?

Environmental sociology arose out of a feeling that something was wrong with the common belief of human exemptionalism. We'll take a look at this model first.

>>> **When rivers and lakes become polluted** due to industry or human activity, **we create advanced filtering systems to make the water suitable for drinking again.** Lake Ontario, considered the most polluted of the Great Lakes, is a prime example.[5] But despite these advances, **can humans truly remain exempt from the damage they cause?**

Human Exemptionalism

When an entire species becomes extinct, it is of great concern to conservationists and other members of the scientific community but, at least in my classes, most students don't see how it directly affects them. They don't know it, but their opinions are that of human exemptionalism. **Human exemptionalism** considers humans to be different from other species on Earth, and therefore not affected in the same way by changes in the environment. According to this notion, humans have the ability to innovate and adapt to a changing environment through the use of technology and cultural flexibility. Because this ability allows us to expand how we fit into the environment, environmental factors don't influence us in the same way that they do other organisms. In many ways, human exemptionalism suggests that we are exempt from the limitations of nature. For example, if salmonella destroyed the entire crop of corn and wheat in the Midwest, the people there would not starve to death; they'd simply import corn and wheat from someplace else, or eat other grains and vegetables that weren't affected.

Although our species shows great levels of flexibility, are we really exempt from the damage we cause to the environment? Perhaps humans are just the last ones on the "hit list."

Environmental Sociology

Unlike human exemptionalism, environmental sociology considers human beings just one species within a global ecosystem that is interdependent on other species.[6] Although human beings have a greater brain capacity than other animals, the forces of nature still affect us. As author Jared Diamond notes in his book *Collapse*, several societies such as the Vikings in Greenland, the Rapa Nui society of Easter Island, and the Anasazi of the American Southwest have collapsed because their populations exceeded what the ecosystem could handle.[7]

Like other species, humans have a **carrying capacity**, a term that refers to how many members of a specific species can exist in a given environment. For example, the entire U.S. population could not move to Hawaii's Big Island because the environment would not be able to provide for that large a population—i.e., humans would be living above

> **ENVIRONMENTAL SOCIOLOGY** is the study of how the environment influences society, and vice versa.
>
> **HUMAN EXEMPTIONALISM** is the belief that considers human beings different from other species on Earth.
>
> **CARRYING CAPACITY** is the number of a specific species that can exist in a given environment.
>
> **OVERPOPULATION** occurs when a species' population lives beyond the carrying capacity, resulting in too few resources.
>
> **UNDERPOPULATION** occurs when a species' population lives under the carrying capacity, resulting in abundant resources.

their carrying capacity. When a species lives above its carrying capacity, it experiences **overpopulation**. In instances of overpopulation, resources (particularly food and water) are limited, and the entire population suffers. Conversely, when a species lives below its carrying capacity, it experiences **underpopulation**. In instances of underpopulation, resources are abundant and the species thrives.[8]

The population of the United States is estimated to grow by approximately 1.1 percent per year, which could cause the population to double by 2100.[9] Will we be able to sustain our current standard of living with a population of more than 600 million?[10] Yes, we can physically fit that number of people into the borders of the country, but will the land still be able to adequately provide the resources we need to survive? This issue of sustainability is particularly important as we watch our finite resources such as coal and oil continue to dwindle. Some conservationists may argue that we have already passed the tipping point, the point at which we are beyond our ability to recover. According to this idea, it's only a matter of time before the United States and the entire world reaches carrying capacity and massive social problems result in disease, war, and the general destruction of society. Land area is limited, and eventually we will run out of it—under such a line of thinking, human initiative is merely a temporary method by which we can expand the carrying capacity of the planet. Without population control, the demand for resources will eventually expand past the ability of the ecosystem to provide.[11]

Of course, there is another side of this coin. Some scientists argue that the world has plenty of space and, while carrying capacity may

The World's Most Polluted Cities

City	Type of Pollution	Source of Pollution
Linfen, China	Coal and particulates	Cars and industrial emissions
Tianying, China	Lead and other metals	Mining and processing
Sukinda, India	Hexavalent chromium and other metals	Chromite mines and processing
La Oroya, Peru	Lead, copper, zinc, and sulfur dioxide	Heavy metal mining and processing
Dzerzhinsk, Russia	Chemicals and toxic byproducts	Cold War–era chemical weapons manufacturing
Norilsk, Russia	Particulates, sulfur dioxide, heavy metals, phenols	Metal mining and processing
Chernobyl, Ukraine	Radiation	Nuclear meltdown
Sumgayit, Azerbaijan	Organic chemicals, oil and heavy metals	Petrochemicals and industrial complex
Kabwe, Zambia	Lead and cadmium	Lead mining processing

Source: "The World's Most Polluted Places," *Time.* 2007. Retrieved at http://www.time.com/time/specials/2007/0,28757,1661031,00.html

indeed become a problem, it is a long way off. Consider the infographic below. Although population certainly influences carrying capacity, one of the greatest skills available to humanity is the ability to change and adapt. This notion parallels human exceptionalism, suggesting that we can adapt to less space and still survive. As discussed in the opening article, other members of the animal kingdom do not have that luxury. When there is a prolonged power outage in an area, residents change their behavior and learn to deal with the darkness. When the water is too polluted to sustain a food supply, fish die. But, even among human populations, there are differences in how much groups can adapt.

ENVIRONMENTAL JUSTICE

How would you like to live in Hell, Michigan, or Disappointment, Kentucky? The people who live in these towns have a sense of humor about the unfortunate names of their cities. Unfortunately, the residents of Cancer Alley, Louisiana, can't join in the laughter. Cancer Alley isn't the official name of the 100-mile stretch between Baton Rouge and New Orleans, but with roughly 176 factories and refineries dumping more than 8 billion pounds of industrial waste into the region each year, Cancer Alley seems an appropriate nickname.[12] In 1987, in the small community of St. Gabriel, Louisiana, 15 cases of cancer were confirmed in a two-block radius. Just one mile down the road, another seven cancer victims lived on the same block. The high level of vinyl chloride—a known human carcinogen—found in the Mississippi River, which outlines most of this region, is the suspected culprit. To compound the problem, most people who live in the area have low incomes and limited access to health care. As you learned in Chapter 2, many poorer areas of the United States have high minority populations. Cancer Alley isn't much different; most of the residents in this area are African American.[13]

This case illustrates a major social problem: Generally, environmental damage affects the poor more adversely than the rich.[14] Because the poor

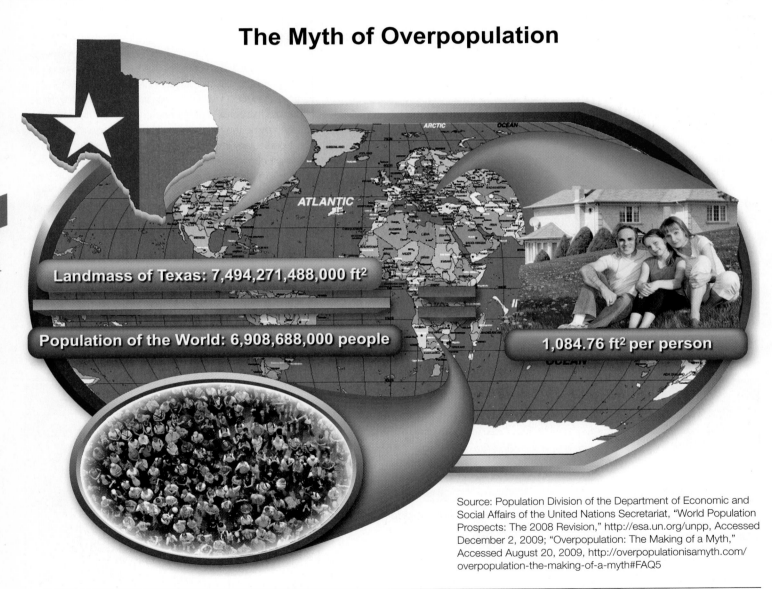

The Myth of Overpopulation

Landmass of Texas: 7,494,271,488,000 ft²

Population of the World: 6,908,688,000 people

1,084.76 ft² per person

Source: Population Division of the Department of Economic and Social Affairs of the United Nations Secretariat, "World Population Prospects: The 2008 Revision," http://esa.un.org/unpp, Accessed December 2, 2009; "Overpopulation: The Making of a Myth," Accessed August 20, 2009, http://overpopulationisamyth.com/overpopulation-the-making-of-a-myth#FAQ5

Some researchers note that **if the entire world's population was forced to live in** a space the size of **Texas, there would still be 1,085 square feet per person**—room for a townhouse. **A family of four would have** enough space for **a moderately sized house with a yard.** Of course, having enough space doesn't necessarily mean that the eco-system can support all those people.

often don't have access to information about pollution or a means of moving away from polluted communities, they tolerate toxic gas emissions and contaminated water. This is often seen as a form of environmental classism or racism, especially in poorer areas with high minority populations.[15] Sociologists explore issues like these by examining **environmental justice**, the impact of environmental factors on social classes. The Environmental Protection Agency (EPA) defines environmental justice as "fair treatment and meaningful involvement of all people regardless of race, color, national origin, or income with respect to the development, implementation, and enforcement of environmental laws, regulations, and policies."[16] Although it is the EPA's goal is for environmental justice to be implemented in every community across the United States, that goal is not easily achieved. For example, Atlanta has a total of 94 abandoned toxic waste sites, and approximately 83 percent of African-American residents live in zip codes in which these sites are found.[17] Is this an oversight, or racism? One thing is certain: Someone somewhere is not managing these resources very well.

Ecosystem Management

I often ask my classes, "How we can go about creating a 'clean world'?" Students favor ideas ranging from banning any form of carbon emissions to requiring people to eat only locally grown foods. Of course, when I point out that humans exhale carbon emissions (CO_2) and that eating only locally grown foods would mean an end to enjoying strawberries in January, many of them start to change their minds. Figuring out a way to manage our natural resources so that we can sustain our ecosystem and meet human needs is a critical part of achieving harmony for human societies. Let's look at some of the major environmental problems facing the world today.

WATER

Water is a vital element of human survival. Whether it is in the sky, below the ground, or coming out of the tap, water is one of our most precious resources, so water pollution naturally has a serious effect on humans. For most Americans, finding clean drinking water is as simple as turning on a faucet (and for those who are a little more particular, it's as easy as picking up a few bottles at the nearest grocery store). The EPA regulates the quality of our water by enforcing drinking water standards and safeguarding our nation's watersheds from pollution.[18] Not all nations have the natural or municipal resources to supply citizens with an abundance of clean drinking water. I remember being warned not to drink tap water when I lived in Mexico. Why? Because developing nations tend to have problems supplying citizens with clean water due to the lack of freshwater sources (rivers, streams, lakes), the inability to reach clean groundwater, or the absence of water filtration systems that prevent contamination. Water contamination is a major concern of the World Health Organization (WHO) because water-borne infectious diseases caused by viruses, bacteria, protozoa, and other microorganisms are linked to outbreaks of other diseases in developing countries.[19]

One of the leading sources of water pollution is nonpoint source (NPS) pollution, or polluted runoff water, specifically from farms and other forms of agriculture. This type of pollution occurs when rainwater, snow, or excess irrigation runs off into lakes, streams, or rivers or seeps into the groundwater. This runoff can be contaminated with excess soil (sedimentation), plant nutrients, pesticides, fertilizers, or pathogens from animal waste. Once in a freshwater supply, these pollutants can either contaminate the water immediately, as in the case of pesticides, fertilizers, and pathogens, or harm the freshwater ecosystem by preventing or intensifying plant growth. If you drink the contaminated water, you also ingest the fertilizer; if you eat the fish from the lake, you ingest some of the toxins.[20]

Agricultural Pollution

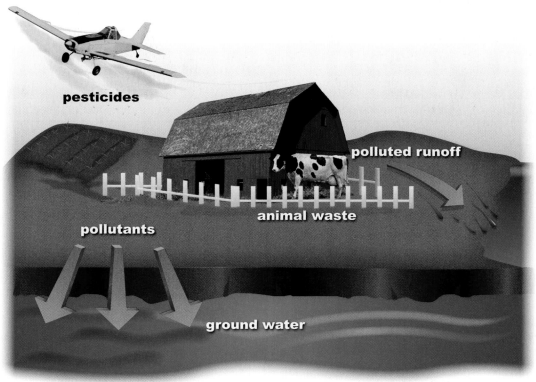

pesticides

polluted runoff

animal waste

pollutants

ground water

Not all pollution comes from factories or refineries. **A great deal of water contamination stems from agricultural sources.**

AIR

Certain types of pollution affect some societies more than others, but air pollution is not something that people can ignore because it surrounds us— literally. Air pollution is made up of gases, finely divided solids, and thinly dispersed liquid droplets; it includes well-known pollutants such as mercury and asbestos, as well as lesser-known materials such as chlorofluorocarbons and refrigerants.[21] Air pollution is typically associated with big, dirty cities and industrial hubs, but even in Hawaii, the quintessential picture of paradise, there are major air pollution problems due to volcanic gases, fumes from controlled burns, and elevated radiation from suspected depleted uranium that may have been used by the military.[22]

<<< **Air pollution in Beijing, China, is** such **a concern** that the U.S. Embassy monitors it every day and reports its findings via Twitter.[26]

You're probably already aware that poor air quality can cause or exacerbate health problems—particularly asthma and other respiratory disorders. But how is this a social problem? It becomes a social problem when certain groups are affected more than others. For example, active children are at the highest risk for health problems associated with poor air quality. Children as a whole are more likely than adults to suffer from asthma or other respiratory problems, and active kids typically spend a lot of time outdoors, where poor air quality can aggravate these conditions.[23] Consider the following case in Boston. In one poor area, Roxbury, 44 percent of families had at least one member with asthma. Researchers found that 64 percent of Boston's 74 trash transfer stations were located in this area. There were also 15 truck and/or bus depots located in the same area. Concerns among the residents regarding diesel emissions and a possible link to the high rates of asthma began to mount. Students at a local elementary school, along with law students from Boston College, worked to convince the city to replace an old fleet with cleaner buses. Such an effort in environmental justice illustrates the importance of community involvement in combating such inequality.[24]

Of course, environmental justice is not only an issue in the United States. Pollution, especially indoor air pollution, can occur in the small rural villages of developing nations. Villagers in China and Nepal use rudimentary stoves or fire pits to cook in poorly ventilated huts, causing them to inhale large amounts of hazardous smoke. According to a study from the University of California, Berkeley, a woman cooking for three hours in an unventilated space inhales amounts of benzoapyrene and benzopyrene (carcinogens) that are equal to smoking two packs of cigarettes. Knowing that this type of cooking is harmful may not stop many individuals from using it, as this is sometimes the only method available, factoring in both limited resources and the need to stay shielded from adverse weather.[25]

CLIMATE CHANGE

During discussions involving human impact on the environment, the topic of global climate change typically hits the table. My students often have diverse points of view. For example, one student recently argued, "This has been the coldest summer in recorded history. How can the globe be warming?" A detailed scientific approach to this topic is beyond the scope of this text; however, we do know one thing for certain: The climate is changing, and many suspect that it is, in part, related to human beings' activities.

In 2008, NASA's Surface Temperature Analysis reported that the global average surface temperature had increased by approximately 1.2° F since 1900.[27] Whether this increase was caused by humans or by

Rank	Source	Social Impact
	**Toxic Top 10: The World's Worst Pollution Problems**	
1	Metals smelting and processing	Leads to chronic health conditions, birth defects, and reproductive damage.
2	Used lead-acid battery recycling	Recycling is typically done by unskilled labors who don't know the risks.
3	Groundwater contamination	Causes a decrease in fresh drinking water and possible health risks.
4	Artisanal gold mining	There are virtually no regulations on mining, so laborers and their families in the nearby communities are often unknowingly exposed to toxic chemicals.
5	Indoor air pollution	Activities such as indoor cooking over open flames cause health risks equal to those associated with chain smoking.
6	Urban air quality	The inhalation of particles can lead to severe respiratory and cardiovascular diseases.
7	Untreated sewage	Sewage that reaches freshwater supplies can cause serious illness and damages to aquatic ecosystems that communities rely on for food production.
8	Contaminated surface water	This type of pollution is common in poor communities where resources to clean the water are limited. This leads to outbreaks of disease.
9	Radioactive waste and uranium mining	By-products of mining and processing pose health risks to humans, particularly children.
10	Industrial mining activities	By-products of mining contaminate groundwater.

Source: Daniel Stone and Karsten Moran, "Toxic Top 10," *Newsweek,* http://www.newsweek.com/id/164813

The Greenhouse Effect

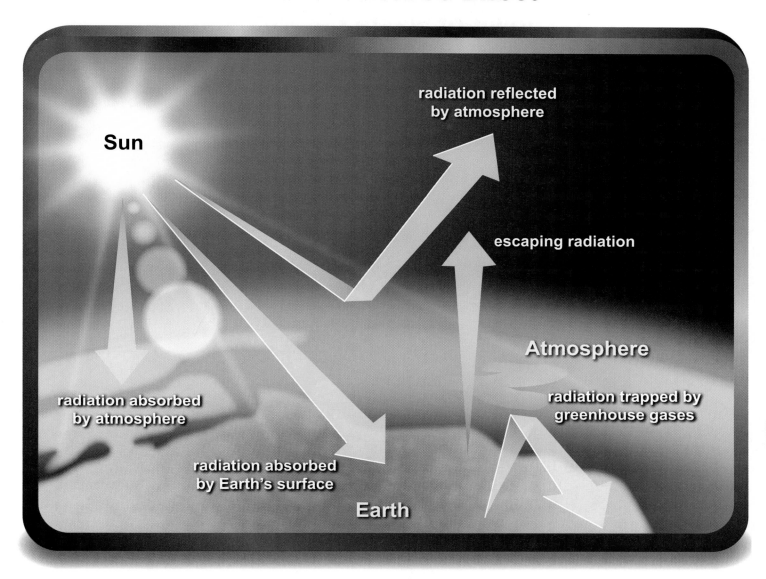

radiation reflected
by atmosphere

Sun

escaping radiation

Atmosphere

radiation absorbed
by atmosphere

radiation trapped by
greenhouse gases

radiation absorbed
by Earth's surface

Earth

∧
∧ **Greenhouse gases include carbon dioxide, methane, and nitrous oxide.** These gases trap
∧ excess radiation in the Earth's atmosphere, making the planet warmer.

Earth's natural climate cycles is a point of argument, but research has shown many connections between human activity and climate change. Dramatic changes have occurred in the world's recent weather patterns. Incidents of drought have increased in the Southern Hemisphere, as well as in areas that have not experienced them previously. Meanwhile, rainfall totals have increased in the Northern Hemisphere. Global climate change has also been linked to the melting of the polar ice caps, which raises sea levels and increases the volume of saltwater in the ocean. When oceans rise, individuals who live in low-lying areas are vulnerable to floods, storm surges, and erosion of the coastland.[28]

How might such change influence society? According to a 2007 study published in *Environment and Urbanization*, rising sea levels threaten 634 million people. More than two thirds of the world's largest cities are in vulnerable coastal areas—those that sit less than 33 feet above sea level. If preventive measures are not taken, major floods and intense storms could sweep away those cities and the millions of people who live in them.[29] This

may seem more like a Hollywood disaster film than a real-life event, but recall what happened when Hurricane Katrina flooded New Orleans. If sea levels continue to rise, more and more cities in the world are likely to face ruin from similar flooding. Such events tax a society's ability to reconstruct and support those who are hurt by such changes.

According to a UN panel of experts, climate change could also result in increased risk of plant and animal extinction. Since humans rely on some of these for food and survival, this is a serious issue. Climate change can influence wind and weather patterns, bringing droughts to regions that once had plenty of rain while at the same time flooding areas that once were dry. As areas that could once produce food turn arid, population shifts may also need to occur to keep societies alive.[30]

Those on one side of the argument point to historical changes in weather and suggest that climate change is merely a natural occurrence. What, if anything, can humans do about it? Consider this. The so-called "Little Ice Age" lasted for 600 years from 1300 to 1850 and followed a

Inside an American Trash Heap:
a breakdown of waste before recycling

Newspapers 32.7%

Grass/yard trimmings 12.8%

Food 12.5%

Plastics 12.1%

Glass 5.3%

Metals 8.2%

Wood 5.6%

Rubber, leather, and textiles 7.6%

Other 3.2%

Source: Data from the Environmental Protection Agency, "Wastes," http://www.epa.gov/waste/facts-text.htm#chart1

∧
∧   **If the amount of waste the United States uses**
∧   **yearly were loaded into a line of garbage**
trucks, those trucks would encircle the world
six times and reach halfway to the moon.[41]
What percentage of this waste could be
eliminated by recycling or composting?

period of apparent warming in the Northern Hemisphere. During this ice age, cold weather led to increased deaths, loss of farm land, and frozen regions that had once been inhabitable. These climate changes clearly occurred before the massive expanse of greenhouse gases. Might we be in such a position today?[31]

Proponents of human-caused climate change suggest that it is due to modern increases in greenhouse gas emissions. These come naturally from humans as well as from the pollution that results when we burn fossil fuels for industry, transportation, and residential purposes.[32] These gases create the greenhouse effect, blocking the release of heat from the planet and making it warmer. Of course, few of us could get by without fossil fuels—from the gas we use to drive our cars to the coal that's burned to power our electricity, our society is reliant on this form of energy to survive. What would happen if we were forced to stop immediately?

In an effort to eliminate the possibility of damage to the atmosphere, more than 180 nations agreed to the Kyoto Protocol in 1997. This legally binding treaty, signed by 37 nations, set targets for reducing emissions of greenhouse gases. With the exception of the United States and Australia, all other developed nations agreed to this goal in an effort to stabilize climate change and reduce the possibility of long-term environmental damage.[33] The United States refused to sign because it suggested that the science backing the climate change treaty was less than clear. However, it's difficult to deny that some form of climate change is occurring.

Can we use increased technology to stabilize and decrease the problem? For example, during a time when the total population and consumption of fossil fuels increased, the air pollution in the state of

California actually decreased. This was, in large part, due to restrictions on emissions from cars as well as new laws designed to promote the use of alternative fuels.[34] Does this show human exemption from pollution problems? Can we continue to live the way we do and not pollute ourselves to death? The answers to these questions may lie in green living.

GREEN LIVING

In high school, I wrote a report on the benefits of solar power, and since then, I have dreamed of the day when my lights would be powered by the sun and the wind. As of yet, there is no windmill at my house, mostly due to the cost. However, new policies show that the U.S. government is becoming more interested in fostering green living. Recently, the government developed the Car Allowance Rebate System (CARS), or Cash for Clunkers, to get gas-guzzlers off the road and get citizens into more fuel-efficient vehicles. This program offers a rebate to those who traded in their "clunkers" for "greener" cars. Compact gas/electric hybrids are increasingly replacing tank-like SUVs, and even luxury carmakers, such as BMW and Lexus, are taking pains to make more fuel-efficient vehicles.

However, living green is about more than the car you drive. We waste energy many times per day, not just during our daily commute. The EPA recommends that people use Energy Star appliances, replace traditional fluorescent lightbulbs with energy-efficient LED bulbs, and seal windows and doors. Some extremely green individuals install solar panels or windmills, but even the simple steps of reducing, reusing, and recycling can help limit greenhouse gases.[35] In a world with environmental problems, cutting down on our use of resources, keeping things as long as possible, and recycling as much as we can may be the simplest and most effective responses to the issues at hand.

Harmful Substances and Resource Efficiency

Our best shot at saving the environment is to stop polluting it in the first place. Think about how much waste you dispose of every day: the Styrofoam coffee cup in the morning, the apple core and sandwich bag at lunch, the product packaging and food scraps used in your dinner preparation, and all the gum wrappers, soda cans, and plastic bags in between. How does all this waste you make impact the environment?

Environmental sociologists have created a method to answer that question. The IPAT formula describes the impact of the population on the environment. IPAT stands for impacts = population × affluence × technology.[36] This formula proposes that these components interact to describe the environmental effects of a society. In simple societies, the environmental impact is small. In hunter and gatherer societies, for example, people live off the land and generally have small populations with limited technologies. The IPAT formula suggests that as a society advances, its impact increases. A complex post-industrial society such as the United States leaves a significant environmental footprint because our wealth, technology, and population size all increase our impact.[37]

On average, each U.S. resident produces 4.6 pounds of trash a day, equaling a total of 251 million tons every year. This mountain of garbage not only creates problems for landfills (and for the air, if burned), but may also influence the global climate change by its very creation.[38] Only about 33 percent of all solid waste is recycled; the bulk of trash in this country finds its way into landfills.[39] Recently, San Francisco passed one of the most stringent trash laws in the United States. Residents are given three separate bins for compostable materials, recyclable materials, and trash; those who refuse to recycle can be fined up to $1,000. In general, most solid waste can be composted, and estimates suggest that if carried out, this would eliminate 90 percent of the trash in landfills. This compost could be used as a natural fertilizer by farmers and residents, eliminating mountains of garbage that pollute water and soil for years.[40]

Will this solve the problem? Certainly, some waste biodegrades and eventually works its way back into the natural cycle, but some waste becomes pollutants that adversely affect the ecosystem. An extreme example occurred in the world's largest ship graveyard, which is located on a beach in the western Indian city of Alang. Large teams of unskilled workers dissect old oil tankers, military ships, and cargo ships so the pieces can be sold as scrap metal. The business of shipbreaking has brought a lot of money to the region, but it has also brought a lot of pollution. Due to a lack of safety regulations on the job site, the workers are exposed to cancer-causing toxins from the metal. The land also suffers from this industry as environmental pollutants leak into the ocean, killing fish and other plant life.[42] Unfortunately, the industry is important to the economic growth of the area, so, as in other places, human and environmental health has taken a backseat to the bottom line.

▶▶▶ GO GL⊕BAL

Environmental Crisis

You're probably familiar with the Indian Ocean tsunami in 2004, the environmental disaster that killed more than 250,000 people. Since then, world leaders have been working to improve risk reduction for environmental crises, but much more still needs to be done. An important step in preventing disasters is to deal with climate change issues. Research indicates that approximately 90 percent of disasters are climate related. The cyclones in Brazil in 2004 and in Oman in 2007 are prime examples; those regions had never seen storms of that intensity before. To mitigate these types of disasters, the Global Platform for Disaster Risk Reduction plans to restore and safeguard ecosystems, as well as build disaster-proof schools and hospitals, generate early-warning systems, and reduce human settlement in disaster-prone areas.[43]

However, in addition to the threat of environmental disasters, there is also the more gradual—and largely ignored—threat of rising sea levels. Inhabitants of the small island nation of Tuvalu have been working to increase awareness of the relationship between greenhouse gas emissions and ocean levels.[44] Tuvalu, located just off the eastern coast of Australia, is home to approximately 9,000 people, but many island residents are migrating to New Zealand and Australia because the ocean is engulfing the island.[45] The highest elevation in Tuvalu is 15 feet, but most of the nation is no more than 3 feet above sea level. Several times throughout the year, the regular lunar cycle of tides brings the Pacific Ocean flowing into the roadways and neighborhoods. Even communities in the center of the island suffer major water damage. As the ocean rises each year, the small island, which has just 26 square kilometers of land area, becomes even more vulnerable to flooding.[46] If industrialized nations fail to significantly reduce greenhouse gas emissions, sea levels will continue to rise, and eventually Tuvalu will be uninhabitable.[47]

WRAP YOUR MIND AROUND THE THEORY

Oil is one of our most valuable resources because it literally and figuratively fuels many of the world's vital industries. **Do you think we are stretching this resource too thin? Should we be looking for other sources of energy** instead of looking for more oil?

Evidence suggests that **minorities and low-income communities suffer the most from pollution** and benefit the least from cleanup programs.[53] **Why do you think this is?**

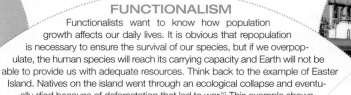

FUNCTIONALISM

Functionalists want to know how population growth affects our daily lives. It is obvious that repopulation is necessary to ensure the survival of our species, but if we overpopulate, the human species will reach its carrying capacity and Earth will not be able to provide us with adequate resources. Think back to the example of Easter Island. Natives on the island went through an ecological collapse and eventually died because of deforestation that led to war.[51] This example shows us that it's unwise to stretch resources too thin. Eventually, we will reach a point of no return. Humans are part of a larger integrated system, and for society to function properly, we must find our place within that system.

ENVIRONMENTAL THEORY

Humans are connected in some way to every living organism on Earth. Although human exemptionalism is based on the idea that human beings are different from other beings on this planet, we are still reliant on the same resources. When we do not take care of those resources, disastrous repercussions can occur. Our overuse of fossil fuels has resulted in global climate change, which has in turn resulted in violent weather patterns and rising sea levels. How to prevent and mitigate these environmental crises is a major issue that our society must deal with in the 21st century.

CONFLICT THEORY

Air is a wonderful thing because it is one of the few resources that is free to everyone; unfortunately, not all air is created equal. Some segments of society are exposed to more unhealthy air than others. From the perspective of a conflict theorist, this means that society does not view a life free from harmful pollutants as a basic human right. A federal EPA report found evidence that racial and ethnic minorities suffer disproportionate exposure to dust, ozone, soot, sulfur, carbon monoxide, and emissions from hazardous waste dumps.[52] This type of issue regarding environmental justice is seen in poor communities in the United States as well as in developing countries around the globe.

HOW DO YOU THINK ABOUT THE ENVIRONMENT?

SYMBOLIC INTERACTIONISM

During a recent trip to the grocery store, I forgot my reusable canvas shopping bags. I saw a neighbor with her cloth bags and felt the sting of her eyes. "I forgot mine," I said, making an excuse for contributing to the mounds of plastic bags filling my local landfill. This is just one example of "green living" habits that have become trendy. Organic clothing, hybrid vehicles, and energy-efficient appliances are all making their way into mainstream society. News of global climate change has motivated society to understand that "reduce, reuse, recycle" is more than just a catchy slogan; it needs to be the instructions we follow in our daily lives.

Global climate change is thought to have **fueled** the forces behind **Hurricane Katrina.**[50] If this is true, **what do you think the government should do to prevent these types of disasters from occurring?**

If every person in New York City used one less plastic grocery bag, it would reduce waste by five million pounds and save $250,000 in disposal costs.[54] What can you do to reduce the amount of waste you produce?

think social problems: HOW DO SOCIOLOGISTS THINK ABOUT ENVIRONMENTAL PROBLEMS?

Environmental Theory

If you visit the World Population Clock on the U.S. Census Bureau's Web site, you can watch as Earth's population grows by the second. The idea that the population increases more than one percent each year is a little scary.[48] Similar to riding an elevator that keeps packing in people, you can't help but wonder if there's going to be enough room for us all. Although it will be quite a while before Earth gets so crowded that we literally run out of room for everyone, there is a legitimate concern that humans will reach their carrying capacity and that the ecosystem will not be able to provide for our species as it has in the past. When this occurs, humans must employ their most valuable resource: the ability to adapt. When we run out of oil, for example, we will have to develop more renewable energy technologies and incorporate them into our lives. Our ability to change our behavior and develop ways to increase our carrying capacity is the backbone of the human exemptionalism theory. I can recall my grandmother telling me how excited she was when they finally had electricity on her family farm. "We didn't need the lanterns anymore!" she said. How might culture change without access to electricity? Although some people who live in temperate climates would survive just fine, who would want to spend their winters in Minnesota without some form of heat?

Many societies, particularly poor ones, have a hard time obtaining the resources needed for survival. Mumbai, India, for example, struggles to get the 33 billion liters of water it needs to service the basic needs of the city, and clean drinking water in the slums is still scarce.[49] Our overexertion of Earth affects more than just quality of life; it affects actual lives. As discussed in the opening article, entire species are wiped out due to the pollutants that human beings introduce into the ecosystem. Even though these changes may not affect *your* daily life, the extinction of any animal will have some effect on the biodiversity of our ecosystem, which will in turn affect our vital resources.

Environmental sociology studies how human lives are also in danger due to pollution and the overexertion of resources. In the case of Easter Island, entire societies can be lost, or in the case of Tuvalu, entire societies may be displaced. The balance between the best interests of our environment and the best interests of the human species can be hard to achieve, especially if it requires us to lower our standards of living. We can only hope that if we do our best to take care of Earth, Earth will do its best to take care of us.

Conflict Theory

One way conflict theorists look at the environment is from a justice point of view. As we've already discussed, environmental justice issues tend to focus primarily on the poor. Why are there certain areas in the country where cancer or asthma rates are so high? Why can we pollute the beaches of India with old ships, and no one seems to care? A conflict theorist would suggest that the answer is simple: Environmental problems mostly affect those who are least able to fight them—the poor. Where are the landfills in your area? I'll bet they're nowhere near the wealthy neighborhoods. On my way to work, I routinely drive by a mountain of trash and notice that only the trailer parks and run-down apartments are near it. In general, conflict theorists argue that environmental disasters are allowed because they serve the interests of those in power, and the negative effects are not immediately felt by the wealthy.

discover solutions to social problems: WHAT CAN WE DO ABOUT ENVIRONMENTAL PROBLEMS?

English economist Thomas Malthus argued in *An Essay on the Principle of Population* (1798) that without the use of moral restraint, a population tends to increase at a rate that is greater than its environment is able to provide for it. This can lead to war, famine, and disease. It is questionable whether our society is using moral restraint when it comes to using our resources. Many of us are guilty of taking an extra long shower, driving to a destination that is within walking distance, and using disposable materials when reusable materials are available. Perhaps using moral restraint is the key to solving our environmental problems.

The Environmental Protection Agency (EPA)

On December 2, 1970, the Nixon administration formed the Environmental Protection Agency. The EPA's goals were to establish and enforce environmental protection standards, conduct research on the adverse effects of pollution, assist other groups in preventing pollution through grants, and develop and recommend new policies for the protection of the environment to the president. One of the first policies to impact the agency was the Clean Air Act of 1970. The act required the EPA to establish national air quality standards and national standards for substantial new pollution sources and for all facilities that emit hazardous substances. Although 1970 may be seen as a golden year of sorts for the environment, past EPA agents state that the agency is far more efficient and influential today. The EPA is currently the nation's leader in environmental science, research, education, and assessment efforts. Now, more than ever, the agency has added resources to achieve its mission of a cleaner, healthier environment for the American people.[55]

MEASURING ENVIRONMENTAL IMPACT

As stated above, the mission of the EPA is to improve lives by improving the environment. The agency also tries to enforce policies that protect Americans during environmental crises. But how does the EPA measure environmental impact? Furthermore, how does it determine which policies are cost-effective to implement and which policies are cost prohibitive?

When deciding whether to implement new policies or regulations, government agencies weigh the costs of implementing regulations against their potential lifesaving benefits. If the benefits outweigh the costs, it's more likely that a particular policy or regulation will be passed. For example, suppose a regulation that prevents toxic dumping costs $16 billion to enforce, but will prevent approximately 2,200 deaths. The government would compare the cost of implementing the regulation to the value of lives saved by the regulation. Using the "value of a statistical life" from five years ago ($7.8 million per person), the lives saved by the regulation are worth more than its $16 billion price tag. Based on these numbers, the regulation is likely to be passed. However, in 2008, the EPA recalculated its estimated value of a statistical life. Using the current value—$6.9 million per person—the cost of the regulation would outweigh the lives that it would potentially save; in this scenario, the regulation might not be adopted. As you can see, what may seem at first like a simple recalculation can have serious consequences when it comes to environmental policy.[56]

"It appears that they're cooking the books in regards to the value of life," said S. William Becker, executive director of the National Association of Clean Air Agencies, the agency that represents state and local air pollution regulators. "Those decisions are literally a matter of life and death."[57] The EPA stresses that the public should not view this value as a price tag on life, but simply as a measurement for statistical purposes, which goes to show that environmental impact is more of a matter of policy decision than the quality of human life.

The Environmental Movement

The idea that only moral restraint is needed to keep society from abusing the environment is nice in theory, but to do that, society needs to accept the idea that protecting the environment is a moral responsibility. Americans, in general, did not begin to accept conservation as an issue until the latter half of the 20th century, although there were plenty of concerned conservationists who existed before then. Many celebrated writers such as Henry David Thoreau and

Theodore Roosevelt played a central role in establishing our country's national park system. His influence on national parks such as **Yellowstone, pictured above,** extended far beyond his presidency.

MAKE CONNECTIONS

Population and the Environment

As you read in this chapter and the previous one, the global population continues to grow. As Malthus's theory suggests, population has a significant effect on the environment; the greater the population, the fewer resources available.

As a collective society, we have yet to exceed our carrying capacity, but large urban cities are feeling the stress of over-population. As you learned in Chapter 16, urbanization causes social problems as masses of people stress the carrying capacity of a city. Resources such as clean drinking water and fresh food are often insufficient, and options for the disposal of waste are limited as well. According to the Clean Air Council, New York City disposes of enough trash each day to fill the entire Empire State Building.[60] For years, New York City garbage has been brought to Fresh Kills Landfill on Staten Island. The landfill is so large that it is one of two man-made structures that are visible from space (the other is the Great Wall of China).[61]

Disposing of this excess waste is not just an urban problem; it has also become linked to globalization. In Chapter 17, you learned that the world is becoming more connected. This growing trend involves importing and exporting goods, outsourcing labor and manufacturing, and now, even trash removal. Recently, the Brazilian newspaper *Correio do Povo* reported that over a four-month period, England shipped off 1,600 tons of domestic and toxic trash to be disposed of on Brazilian soil.[62] This is one example of how globalization does not always bring societies together.

Pro & Con

Combating Global Climate Change

Almost all researchers and world politicians agree that the global climate is changing. What are the pros and cons of working to combat this problem?

Pro

- Thousands of environmental scientists agree that a climate change is happening, and that human beings are causing it.
- Polar ice caps are melting at alarming rates, displacing animals (including human beings) from their natural habitats and causing oceans to rise.
- Warming changes weather patterns; some arid areas are experiencing more rain, whereas other, more fertile areas are experiencing drought.

Con

- This may merely be a cycle of warming caused by a force of nature we do not understand, or one that we cannot control (such as an increase in the temperature of the sun).
- Recent data support the idea that areas are experiencing cooler temperatures, not warmer ones.
- Even if greenhouse gases are causing the globe to warm, human flexibility can combat future problems; prevention methods are unnecessary and distract us from more pressing social issues at hand.

Herman Melville incorporated the power and beauty of nature into their works. At the turn of the 19th century, President Theodore Roosevelt worked to make conservationism popular socially and politically. Roosevelt's desire to preserve the natural resources of our country helped pave the way for important government programs such as the Soil Conservation Service and the Pittman-Robertson Act, which was established to fund fish and wildlife programs.

The urbanization and resulting urban sprawl that occurred in the 1950s created entirely new concerns for conservationists. City growth exposed citizens to the dangers of pollution. As toxic substances from agricultural runoff seeped into cities' water systems and fumes from factories filled the streets, the dangers of chemicals and pesticides was brought to public awareness. The subject of pollution even sparked a heated debate in the 1968 Presidential election between Richard Nixon and Hubert Humphrey.[58]

After Nixon won the election, Congress sent the president a bill that would come to be, according to many lawmakers, the most important piece of environmental legislation in history. The National Environmental Policy Act (NEPA) was created with the purpose to "declare a national policy which will encourage productive and enjoyable harmony between man and his environment." President Nixon signed the bill on New Year's Day, 1970.[59]

From Classroom to Community Every Little Bit Counts

As a student at Oregon State University, Marissa enjoyed spending time outdoors, but never put much thought into environmental issues until the spring of her sophomore year.

"I had heard a lot about problems such as pollution and climate change, but I didn't care very much about them because I felt like they didn't have a direct impact on my day-to-day life. Why should it matter to me if the surface temperature of Earth had increased by a degree or two over the last hundred years?

"But then I saw a program on TV about how volunteers in China were cleaning up trash on Mt. Everest. The program said that there was an unbelievable amount of trash on the mountain—about 120 tons! All of it had

been left by climbers, and now they were recruiting other climbers to help bring it back down. I also learned that climate change has affected the huge Rongbuk Glacier on the northern face of the mountain. As it's melted, the glacier has lost nearly 500 feet in the last 10 years. Without fresh water from this glacier, the Himalayan wildlife will be forced to move elsewhere to survive. The glacier could disappear completely in just 30 years if we don't reduce global carbon emissions.[63]

"That definitely got my attention. As a rock climber, it really hit home when I realized that one of the greatest peaks in the world is in danger due to climate change and human pollution.

"I wanted to get involved but wasn't exactly sure where to start. Then I saw a flyer on campus about a volunteer effort to

pick up trash at illegal dumpsites on Mount Hood. When I told some friends about it, they were interested as well. We've gone climbing there before, and a lot of people from school go skiing and snowboarding there during the winter.

"I wanted to help other people get involved, so I started a group on Facebook to raise awareness about the cleanup effort. By the time the volunteer day rolled around, more than 50 students had signed up to participate.

"It wasn't Everest, but cleaning up Mount Hood made me realize that it doesn't take much to get involved. Pollution and climate change are huge global issues, but these small local efforts are a good start toward tackling such big problems."

CHAPTER

19

IS THE ENVIRONMENT IN DANGER?   270

evidence such as increased pollution and changing global sea levels serve as reminders that our actions have an effect on the health of our environment; humans need to manage their use of Earth's resources before these resources are gone

HOW DO SOCIOLOGISTS THINK ABOUT ENVIRONMENTAL PROBLEMS?   279

humans affect, and are affected by, all aspects of the environment; humans are just one part of the entire ecosystem, and we must find our place in it; we are in conflict with the immediate needs of our current society and the future needs of subsequent generations; society is learning to change its way of thinking and people are beginning to incorporate "green" behaviors into their lives

WHAT CAN WE DO ABOUT ENVIRONMENTAL PROBLEMS?   279

information, education, and application are the key elements to solving our environmental problems; government and private agencies need to do extensive research to discover ways in which we can decrease our carbon footprint; subsidiary agencies need to educate the public on the do's and don'ts of conservation; most importantly, humans need to learn to apply this information to their daily lives even if it results in slight inconveniences

get the topic: IS THE ENVIRONMENT IN DANGER?

Theory

ENVIRONMENTAL THEORY   278
- humans are in some way connected to every living organism on Earth
- we must change our behavior and develop ways to increase our carrying capacity

FUNCTIONALISM   278
- overpopulation can cause the human species to reach carrying capacity, which will result in limited resources
- humans are a part of a larger integrated system; for society to function properly, we must find our place within that larger system

CONFLICT THEORY   278
- society does not view a life free from harmful pollutants as a basic human right
- environmental justice is an issue in low-income and minority neighborhoods

SYMBOLIC INTERACTIONISM   278
- "green living" has become a trend in our society
- conservation is now seen as a moral responsibility

Key Terms

environmental sociology is the study of how the environment influences society, and vice versa. *270*

human exemptionalism is the belief that considers human beings different from other species on Earth. *271*

carrying capacity is the number of a specific species that can exist in a given environment. *271*

overpopulation occurs when a species' population lives beyond the carrying capacity, resulting in too few resources. *271*

underpopulation occurs when a species' population lives under the carrying capacity, resulting in abundant resources. *271*

environmental justice is the impact of environmental factors on social classes. *273*

Sample Test Questions

These multiple-choice questions are similar to those found in the test bank that accompanies this textbook.

1. According to the theory of human exemptionalism,
   a. humans can't be wiped out due to disease.
   b. humans need more resources to survive than do animals.
   c. humans are different from other living organisms.
   d. humans are affected by the limits of nature.

2. When a population is below its carrying capacity, it is
   a. overpopulated.
   b. underpopulated.
   c. subject to exemptionalism.
   d. in danger of disease and famine.

3. Which of the following *best* demonstrates an issue involving environmental justice?
   a. Commercial fishing boats have depleted the ocean's supply of blue fin tuna.
   b. A local government agency gives tax breaks to companies that reduce their carbon emissions.
   c. A predominantly African American community experiences an increase in air pollution due to the presences of a nearby factory.
   d. A university is refused funding because the school has not properly disposed of asbestos in many of the campus buildings.

4. Functionalists support the idea that humans are members of the ecosystem, not the leaders of the ecosystem.
   a. true
   b. false

5. Which of the following is a stated goal of the EPA?
   a. to build American-made, fuel-efficient cars
   b. to cultivate biodiversity in our oceans
   c. to regulate the use of additives in foods
   d. to research the effects of pollution

ESSAY

1. What are your thoughts on human exemptionalism? How are humans different from other living organisms? How are we the same?

2. Why is the ability to adapt a human's most valuable asset?

3. Is global climate change happening naturally, or is it man-made? How might different sociological theorists perceive this trend?

4. What can the government do to combat environmental racism and other environmental justice issues?

5. Why do you think it took the U.S. government nearly 200 years to create a government agency that protects the environment? Do you think our founding fathers were concerned about conservation?

WHERE TO START YOUR RESEARCH PAPER

For more information on United States conservation, visit http://www.epa.gov/

For resources and information on prehistoric and newly extinct animals, see http://www.extinctanimal.com/

To read Malthus's *An Essay on the Principle of Population*, go to http://www.esp.org/books/malthus/population/malthus.pdf

For information on pollution in your community, check out http://www.scorecard.org/

To learn more about the hazardous practice of shipbreaking, visit http://www.greenpeaceweb.org/shipbreak/travelreport_alang.asp

Remember to check www.thethinkspot.com **for additional information, downloadable flashcards, and other helpful resources.**

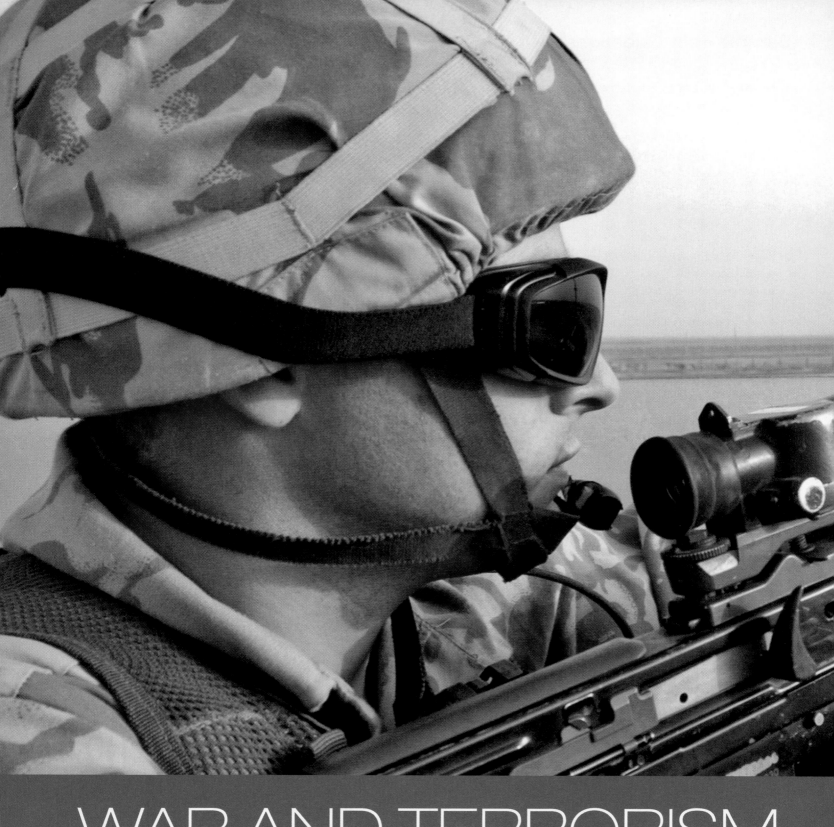

WAR AND TERRORISM

Q

HOW DO COUNTRIES DEAL WITH
CONFLICTS?
WHAT ARE SOME THEORIES OF
CONFLICTS?
HOW DO WE CONTROL CONFLICTS?

It's a

question at the heart of what it is to be human: why do we go to war? The cost to human society is enormous, yet for all our intellectual development, we continue to wage war well into the 21st century.

Now a new theory is emerging that challenges the prevailing view that warfare is a product of human culture and thus a relatively recent phenomenon. For the first time, anthropologists, archaeologists, primatologists, psychologists and political scientists are approaching a consensus. Not only is war as ancient as humankind, they say, but it has played an integral role in our evolution.

The theory helps explain the evolution of familiar aspects of warlike behaviour such as gang warfare. And even suggests the cooperative skills we've had to develop to be effective warriors have turned into the modern ability to work towards a common goal.

These ideas emerged at a conference last month on the evolutionary origins of war at the University of Oregon in Eugene. "The picture that was painted was quite consistent," says Mark Van Vugt, an evolutionary psychologist at the University of Kent, UK. "Warfare has been with us for at least several tens, if not hundreds, of thousands of years." He thinks it was already there in the common ancestor we share with chimps. "It has been a significant selection pressure on the human species," he says. In fact several fossils of early humans have wounds consistent with warfare.

Studies suggest that warfare accounts for 10 per cent or more of all male deaths in present-day hunter-gatherers. "That's enough to get your attention," says Stephen LeBlanc, an archaeologist at Harvard University's Peabody Museum in Boston. Primatologists have known for some time that organized, lethal violence is common between groups of chimpanzees, our closest relatives. Whether between chimps or hunter-gatherers, however, intergroup violence is nothing like modern pitched battles. Instead, it tends to take the form of brief raids using overwhelming force, so that the aggressors run little risk of injury . . . This opportunistic violence helps the aggressors weaken rival groups and thus expand their territorial holdings.

Such raids are possible because humans and chimps, unlike most social mammals, often wander away from the main group to forage singly or in smaller groups, says Wrangham. Bonobos—which are as closely related to humans as chimps are—have little or no intergroup violence because they tend to live in habitats where food is easier to come by, so that they need not stray from the group.

If group violence has been around for a long time in human society then we ought to have evolved psychological adaptations to a warlike lifestyle. Several participants presented the strongest evidence yet that males - whose larger and more muscular bodies make them better suited for fighting—have evolved a tendency towards aggression outside the group but cooperation within it. "There is something ineluctably male about coalitional aggression—men bonding with men to engage in aggression against other men," says Rose McDermott, a political scientist at Stanford University in California.[1]

285

---We may never know its true origins or when and where the first war occurred, but war has been a social problem that humans have faced for ages.

The United States is considered a young country by many standards, and yet it has found itself in the midst of several large-scale conflicts since its founding. It is a pattern, sadly, that most countries follow.

Although you may not notice it in your daily life, war creates social issues that affect us all.

What factors lead to terrorism, and how did the United States react after the attacks in 2001? Did U.S. society become unified, brought together by an outside threat, or disorganized and confused, suspicious of anyone with a foreign name? How was U.S. military spending altered? Did public opinion change over time? What social problems arose from this, and will they affect us in the future? This chapter will explore the nature of war and terrorism and the causes behind conflict. We will discuss how nations confront these challenges, and the consequences these "solutions" have on society. As you read through this chapter, keep in mind that war is a global issue—one whose effects can be felt throughout the world.

get the topic: HOW DO COUNTRIES DEAL WITH CONFLICTS?

WAR is a violent conflict between groups that are organized for such conflict.

If you turn on the evening news on any given day, you're likely to see a conflict going on somewhere in the world. You're aware of the U.S. wars in Iraq and Afghanistan and the threats of war posed by countries such as North Korea or Iran. Beyond that, you've most likely heard of a variety of violent acts that span the globe, from the genocide in Sudan to the kidnappings of civilians by guerrilla groups such as Shining Path in South America. **War** is a violent conflict between groups that are organized for such conflict. Depending on the size and scale of the war, it can lead to the loss of dozens—or sometimes millions—of lives, as well as the damage of land and the destruction of resources.

The Nature of Power and War

In my classroom, I have power—I decide the textbook we use, the subjects to be covered, and all assignments and due dates. Students have less power in a classroom, although they do have the ability to decide whether to stay in a class or withdraw. You'll find that, in any given situation in life, every person has a varying degree of power, and no single individual ever possesses absolute control. This dynamic is true on a larger scale as well. On the national level, those with power are able to influence the direction in which a country moves. According to sociologist C. Wright Mills, the people with the most power in the United States are political leaders, heads of corporations, and high-ranking military officials. As we learned before, he referred to this group as the power elite. Mills noted that members of the power elite have the power to control the flow of information and thus are able to steer the country in the direction of their choosing.[2]

Sociologist G. William Domhoff saw society similarly, but proposed that an elite group of white men hold the majority of power in the country. In his argument he identifies two distinct groups—a corporate coalition and a labor coalition. Both play a major role in determining who runs for office and which positions those people will hold. Domhoff suggests that it is the interaction between these two coalitions that determines, to a large degree, the direction in which the country will move.[3] In some cases, the country moves toward war.

Democratic societies believe that power should not be concentrated in the hands of a few. President

<<< Who makes up the current, past, and future **power elite** in the United States?

Dwight D. Eisenhower was one of the first to recognize the potential danger of such concentration and warned against the influence of what he called the "military-industrial complex," a term that has since become part of the American lexicon. The **military-industrial complex** is a combination of the armed forces and defense industries that provide weapons and other materials to a country and, needless to say, has great influence over the country's policies.

In President Eisenhower's 1961 farewell address, he warned, "In the councils of government, we must guard against the acquisition of unwarranted influence, whether sought or unsought, by the military-industrial complex. The potential for the disastrous rise of misplaced power exists and will persist. We must never let the weight of this combination endanger our liberties or democratic processes. We should take nothing for granted. Only an alert and knowledgeable citizenry can compel the proper meshing of the huge industrial and military machinery of defense with our peaceful methods and goals, so that security and liberty may prosper together."[4]

Eisenhower was a general during World War II, and knew that when an industry benefited from the sale of weapons, it also benefited from war. Because of this, he recognized that prominent members of the military and the weapons industry could be highly influential in setting the country's agenda.

CAUSES OF WAR

Even with the frequency of conflict around the world, war is not always an inevitable outcome. However, there are several factors to look for that can increase the likelihood that a war will occur. One factor that groups often consider is **easy victory**; when conquest is seen as being easy for one side, a war is more likely to take place.[5] The 1983 invasion of Granada by the United States is a good example. Granada was a small country with a very small military, and a victorious outcome for the United States was relatively simple to achieve.

Optimism also plays a role, as states are more likely to engage in war when they are overly confident about the outcome of a potential conflict.[6] Before the outbreak of the most recent war with Iraq, U.S. politicians often stated that the American soldiers would be greeted as liberators. It was discovered only after the war had begun that not all Iraqis felt that way; instead, they saw the American military as an occupying force.

In some situations, there is a perceived advantage in striking first. The factor of **first strike** can increase the chances of war considerably. If a nation's leaders determine that making the initial move will give them an advantage, they are likely to seize the opportunity.[7]

MILITARY-INDUSTRIAL COMPLEX is a combination of the armed forces and defense industries that provide weapons and other materials to a country.

EASY VICTORY is a cause of war when conquest is seen as being easy for one side.

OPTIMISM is a cause of war when a nation is overly confident about the outcome of a potential conflict.

FIRST STRIKE is a cause of war when a nation's leaders determine that making the initial move will give them an advantage.

THREAT is a cause of war stemming from impending danger.

PROFIT is cause of war when a country believes that there is the possibility of monetary gain by either capturing or exploiting the resources of another country.

The recent war in Iraq is also an example of first strike. While trying to generate support for the war, U.S. defense officials often argued that Saddam Hussein and the Iraqi military were harboring weapons of mass destruction and that the United States needed to initiate a pre-emptive strike against Iraq before Hussein could unleash an attack.

When the power structure of a state is in flux, the likelihood of war increases. This is especially true if one nation sees another as a **threat**, or an impending danger.[8] During the Bay of Pigs invasion in 1961, the United States military believed that Cuba's political structure was waning and that a U.S. victory would be easily secured. At the same time, Americans also believed that if action was not taken quickly, Cuba would develop a strong and lasting relationship with Russia. In the end, neither of these assumptions was true, and the invasion of the Bay of Pigs proved to be unsuccessful.

Where there is the potential for financial gain, there is also the potential for war. **Profit** can be a strong motivation for war; when a country believes that there is the possibility of monetary gain by either capturing or exploiting the resources of another country, conflict may ensue.[9] For example, some observers have noted that while the first Gulf War resulted in the liberation of Kuwait, it also helped ensure U.S. access to Kuwait's oil supply.

The Military and the Use of Force

The military is an important part of protecting the safety and interests of any nation. In the period between 1798 and 1993, the United States used its military force a total of 234 times for incidents that either led to combat or had the potential to.[10] In the table below, you can see some of the major conflicts

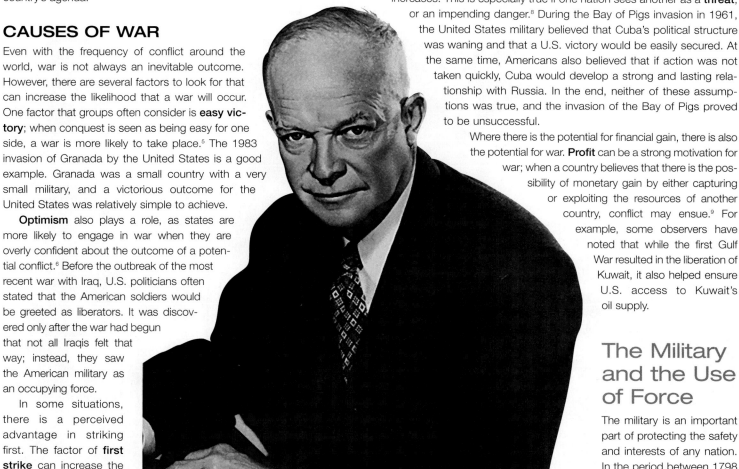

∧
∧
∧ President Dwight D. **Eisenhower warned** the country **of the dangers of military control.**

in which the United States has been involved and the effects that those conflicts have had on human lives.

MILITARY SPENDING

Keeping up military hardware can come with a hefty price tag, and the United States spends more than any other country on its military: $607 billion of the total $1.4 trillion military spending in the world. In terms of actual dollars, the only other country that approaches this level of military spending is China, with an estimated total of $84.9 billion. France comes in third with $65.7 billion dedicated to its military.[11]

The table on the next page highlights the military spending of several countries around the world. Notice that although the United States spends the most money, it does not spend the largest percentage of its GDP. Saudi Arabia spends 9.3 percent, followed by the U.S. at 4.0 and Russia at 3.5. Of the nations listed, Japan dedicates the least amount of its GDP to its military.[12]

The amount of spending in this area has often been attributed to the rise of the military-industrial complex. In the period between 1999 and 2008, military spending around the world increased by 45 percent.[13] Could this money be put to a better use?

Studies show that there is a link between an increase in military spending and a decrease in spending for other publicly funded services, such as education.[14] This equation makes sense—the more money you spend on your car, for example, the less you have for spring break. However, other research has found that when a government increases its spending in one area, the entire economy benefits.[15] Take World War II for example. Increased government spending on the military created more jobs at home and helped pull the United States out of the Great Depression.

So, does increased military spending help or harm an economy? Research has found that timing plays an important role. University of Florida professor Errol Anthony Henderson noted that peacetime military spending increases poverty by increasing inequality and unemployment, while wartime spending has the reverse effect.[16] So, during wartime there seems to be a benefit to military spending, but during times of peace the money would be better allocated elsewhere.

There is recent concern over the increase in the price of machinery and materials that are used by the military, which, since the end of World

Conflicts Involving the United States

War/Conflict	Number Serving	Total Deaths*	Wounds (not mortal)
Revolutionary War 1775–1783	n/a	4,435	6,188
War of 1812 1812–1815	286,730	2,260	4,505
Mexican War 1846–1848	78,718	13,283	4,152
Civil War 1861–1865 (Union only)	2,213,363	364,511	281,881
Spanish–American War	306,760	2,446	1,662
World War I 1917–1918	4,734,991	116,516	204,002
World War II 1941–1946	16,112,566	405,399	671,846
Korean War 1950–1953	5,720,000	36,574	103,284
Vietnam Conflict 1964–1973	8,744,000	58,209	153,303
Persian Gulf War 1990–1991	2,225,000	382	467
Global War on Terrorism: Operation Enduring Freedom and Operation Iraqi Freedom 2003–?	Approx. 1,500,000**	5,115	34,173

*Civilians not included
**As of November 2007

By the author; Navy Department Library, "American War and Military Operations Casualties: Lists and Statistics," http://www.history.navy.mil/library/online/american%20war%20casualty.htm; United States Department of Defense, "DoD Casualty Reports," http://www.defenselink.mil/news/casualty.pdf.

Military Spending

Country	Spending (in billions)	World Share (%)	Share of GDP (%)
United States	$607.0	41.5	4.0
China	$84.9*	5.8*	2.0*
France	$65.7	4.5	2.3
United Kingdom	$65.3	4.5	2.4
Russia	$58.6*	4.0*	3.5*
Germany	$46.8	3.2	1.3
Japan	$46.3	3.2	0.9
Italy	$40.6	2.8	1.8
Saudi Arabia	$38.2	2.6	9.3
India	$30.0	2.1	2.5
South Korea	$24.2	1.7	2.7
Brazil	$23.3	1.6	1.5
Canada	$19.3	1.3	1.2
Spain	$19.2	1.3	1.2
Australia	$18.4	1.3	1.9
World Total	$1,464	100	2.4 (average)

*Estimated Figure

Source: *Military expenditure: SIPRI Yearbook 2008: Armaments, Disarmament and International Security* (Oxford University Press: Oxford, 2008), Appendix 5A. www.sipri.org/research/armaments/milex/resultoutput/15majorspenders

∧
∧ **Although the United States spends the most money on its military, it does not spend the largest**
∧ **percentage of its GDP.** What characteristics does the United States share with other nations that devote above-average percentages of their GDP to military spending?

War II, has greatly outpaced the increase in price of any other product.[17] Companies that produce military-related goods have also seen their business grow considerably—American Body Armor Corporation alone saw a 2,000 percent increase in its income between 2001 and 2006.[18]

Almost all will agree that ensuring the safety and security of a nation and its defenders is worth some expense. However, all of these factors— the strain of military spending on a peacetime economy, the decrease in funding for public services, the increasing price of military products—bring into question the necessity of excessive military spending. What can we do to find the right balance between military spending and the dedication of funds to other programs and resources that benefit society?

WEAPONS

When considering the weapons of war, most picture high-powered weaponry like battleships, tanks, and nuclear warheads. Although such weapons pose a significant danger, the use of small arms and light weapons (SALW) results in the greatest number of deaths during any type of conflict. Used in practically every incidence of armed conflict, SALW also target civilians, aiding in acts of violence such as rape or forced displacement.[19]

Although used less frequently than SALW, weapons of mass destruction (WMD) are a major danger due to their capacity to cause harm on a large scale. WMD include nuclear weapons, chemical weapons, and biological weapons.

A **nuclear weapon** is a device that employs atomic energy to create a large-scale explosion. The bombs dropped on Hiroshima and Nagasaki during World War II were nuclear weapons. After seeing the destruction that they caused, many began to hope that these weapons would never be used again. As of January 2009, nine countries are known to be holding more than 8,000 nuclear warheads.[20] Many people fear that nuclear material could fall into the hands of nations that would choose to use it for arbitrary reasons. Later in this chapter we will discuss efforts to control the numbers of and restrict access to nuclear weapons.

Biological weapons employ organic agents, such as viruses, to cause harm. *Bacillus anthracis*, the bacterium that produces anthrax, is one of the most deadly. An attack using biological weapons can be hard to predict, detect, and prevent, making it one of the most feared terrorist tactics.[22]

Chemical weapons are synthetically created materials. Napalm, a jelly-like acid that was used frequently during the Vietnam War, is an example of a chemical weapon. Because of their ability to cause a great amount of damage over

Number of Deployed Warheads

Country	Total Deployed Warheads
Russia	4,834
United States	2,702
France	300*
China	186*
United Kingdom	160*
Israel	80*
India	60–70*
Pakistan	60*
North Korea	Unknown

*Uncertain/Estimated Figure

Source: Shannon N. Kile, Vitaly Fedchenko and Hans M. Kristensen, 'World Nuclear Forces', *SIPRI Yearbook 2009* (Oxford University Press: Oxford, 2009), pp. 345–379. www.sipri.org/research/armaments/nbc/nuclear

As this table shows, **there are more than 8,000 nuclear warheads deployed around the world** today. However, this number does not take into account the thousands of active warheads that are currently in reserve or the hundreds of inactive warheads that are still intact and deployable.[21]

a wide area, all chemical weapons are considered weapons of mass destruction.

The Nature of Terrorism

On September 11, 2001, most of us experienced the damage that acts of terrorism can inflict. As you know, that day's events were enough to change a nation's policies and lead to war. Even worse than the death and destruction that acts of terrorism cause, its power to affect society makes terrorism a serious social problem. As we continue to witness in countries around the globe, a small group of individuals can bring about large-scale fear and alter the course of nations in a matter of hours.

WHAT IS TERRORISM?

Because not all terrorist organizations are alike, terrorism itself can be difficult to define, making it even more complex to study.[23] Sociologist Austin Turk suggests that terrorism is a social construction. Events are defined as acts of terror after they have occurred, and are classified as such based on how people view them. For Turk, terrorism is a threatening, often illegal, unconventional form of violence that is motivated by a particular belief. For this reason, terrorism is always a political term.[24] You can see this emphasis in the CIA's definition: "**Terrorism** is premeditated, politically-motivated violence perpetrated against noncombatant targets by sub-national groups or clandestine agents."[25] Like war, terrorism involves the desire to exert power over others.

CHARACTERISTICS OF TERRORIST GROUPS

Turk points out that organizations labeled "terrorist" by the United States government tend to be ones that oppose the nation's policies. Other groups throughout the world may behave in a similar manner; however, because they act in accordance with the United States, they are not defined as terrorists.[26]

Although no two groups are the same, terrorist acts and organizations have some common characteristics:

- Terrorist activity involves premeditation, calculation, and planning.[27] As in the case of the September 11th attacks, it can take many years of preparation to carry out one act of terrorism.

- Terrorism involves both governments and civilians.[28] Many terrorist organizations will focus on harming civilians as a means to persuade governments to comply with their demands. The goal in carrying out terrorist activity is not

NUCLEAR WEAPON is a device that employs atomic energy to create a large-scale explosion.

BIOLOGICAL WEAPONS are composed of an organic agent such as a virus that is used to cause harm.

CHEMICAL WEAPONS are composed of synthetically created materials that are used to cause harm.

TERRORISM is premeditated, politically motivated violence perpetrated against noncombatant targets by sub-national groups or clandestine agents.

always to kill but to impact society and generate a reaction from political organizations.

- Terrorists use psychological intimidation and fear.[29] The unpredictable and radical nature of terrorist groups makes them feared among civilians and military forces alike. A society periodically under attack by suicide bombers won't know who to turn to or where to hide—all people become enemies, and all public places become potentially dangerous.

- Terrorists focus on a specific target.[30] Acts of terrorism aim to produce damage to persons, property, or infrastructure such as bridges or public utilities.

- The element of threat is a key element of terrorism.[31] Terrorist groups will often make threats regardless of whether or not they actually intend to follow through with them. This unpredictability adds to the fear and creates a sense of imminent danger for all possible targets.

- Terrorist groups have an agenda that they wish to further.[32] They often align themselves with a political movement in an attempt to gain power or legitimacy.[33]

Along with these components, certain goals are often associated with acts of terrorism. Terrorists generally believe that they are acting on behalf of a moral or just cause. They may feel so strongly that they will die for their beliefs.[34] Terrorist groups sometimes feel that their actions are necessary for change to occur. For example, when Timothy McVeigh bombed the federal building in Oklahoma City, he felt justified in killing 168 people for what he believed was the "just cause" of attacking the federal government.[35] Like many terrorists, he hoped that his actions would arouse a sense of excitement and enthusiasm in others.[36]

Terrorism can also provide a sense of power to those who feel they have very little. By identifying with a larger movement, they are given a sense of importance and purpose. This power and purpose provides a sense of strength and group solidarity to people who might otherwise feel powerless or insignificant.[37]

Type of Terrorist	Motive/Goal	Willing to Negotiate?	Expectation of Survival
"Crazy"	Clear only to perpetrator	Possibly, but only if negotiator can understand motive and offer alternatives	Strong, but not based on reality
"Criminal"	Personal gain or profit	Usually in return for profit and/or safe passage	Strong
"Crusader"	A "higher cause"	Seldom, because to do so is a betrayal of the higher cause	Minimal, because death offers rewards

Source: Crusaders, Criminals, Crazies: Terror and Terrorism in our Time: By Frederick J. Hacker. New York: W. W. Norton. 1976. p. 355.

Terrorist groups are often small and usually have fewer than 100 members. It used to be the case that the majority of terrorist organizations were composed of a tight-knit group of like-minded individuals, but nowadays some are larger, with branches in many different countries. In some ways, these groups are becoming a leaderless resistance. This shift in structure is most likely due to advances in technology that allow for improved communication.[38]

The members of terrorist groups usually share the same ethnic and political backgrounds. In some instances, terrorist groups are composed of people with close ties, such as friends and relatives.[39] This, and the fact that most operate from multiple locations, makes infiltration of such organizations a difficult task. Illegal businesses, foreign political groups, and property crime or drug money often provide funding for terrorist groups.[40]

WHO ARE AMERICAN TERRORISTS?

Domestic terrorism is also a social issue. Although terrorists who come from abroad grab most of the headlines, homegrown terrorists continue to develop and thrive. In the United States, most terrorist organizations develop from right-wing, conservative groups.[41] For example, extremist groups that are opposed to abortion have been known to create hit lists with the names of doctors who perform such procedures.[42] Although the size of domestic terrorist groups has diminished, the number of incidents of domestic terrorism has increased.[43] This is because, like elsewhere, American terrorism has become a fractured, leaderless resistance. When organizations are small in size, they are extremely difficult to identify and stop.[44]

Terrorist Activity

Type	Committed by	Target	Tactics
Mass Terror	political leaders	general population	coercion and violence, both organized and non organized
Dynastic Assassination	individuals or groups	head(s) of state	very selective violence
Random Terror	individuals or groups	anyone	bombs in cafés, markets, businesses, etc
Focused Random Terror	individuals or groups	members of the opposition	bombs in specific locations
Tactical Terror	revolutionary movements	government	political targets

Source: Cindy C. Combs. (2003). *Terrorism in the Twenty-First Century, 3rd Edition*. Upper Saddle River, NJ: Prentice Hall.

Although they share many of the same characteristics, **terrorist groups possess separate motives and goals,** as detailed in the chart above.

Child Soldiers

When you picture armies, you're likely to envision adult men engaged in combat. It's not uncommon to see news segments that feature large masses of uniformed men marching in time with their fellow soldiers in the company of tanks, armed aircraft, or other military machinery. During times of conflict, there are often pieces written about children who suffer on the periphery as a result of war. Most articles describe how war can tear families apart and leave orphans in its wake. However, there is another way in which children can be affected by war: by becoming participants in the conflict.

Many believe that this behavior is rare and only found in select countries. The truth is, child soldiers are present in almost every part of the world, including the Middle East, Asia, Africa, Latin America, and parts of Europe. Recruiters generally target children ages 14 to 18 years old to serve as part of a militia and, in a single stroke, rob them of their innocence and the remainder of their childhood.[45] Some even argue that in the United States, where individuals under the age of 18 are not allowed to serve in the military, the practice of recruitment begins at childhood, long before a person reaches the age of consent.[46]

Although most child soldiers are not usually tied to or associated with any government, they are often put to use for the purpose of enhancing the military strength of armed groups with a political agenda. These groups do not limit their search to young males to fill their ranks, either. Both boy and girl soldiers can serve many purposes for these armed forces. Aside from engaging in actual combat, they can act as scouts, spies, decoys, cooks, manual laborers, and, especially in the case of young girls, sources of sexual gratification.[47]

There has been some debate over Eastern and Western interpretations of adulthood, and whether applying Western standards to other cultures is appropriate in the discussion of child soldiers. Is a 14-year-old boy in Michigan as mature as a 14-year-old boy in Uganda? Despite this dispute, most agree that child soldiers are compelled to witness—or even commit—acts of violence that no person of any age should ever have to experience.[48]

To help diminish the occurrence of child soldiers around the world, the International Criminal Court has decided to prosecute anyone who recruits soldiers under the age of 15. Most organizations that engage in this practice seek international recognition as being legitimate entities; the hope is that the threat of being condemned by the International Criminal Court will be enough to deter them from this crime.[49] In 2009, the first trial began. Thomas Lubanga Dyilo of the Democratic Republic of Congo was accused of war crimes for his recruitment of several thousand children for the purposes of combat. The trial has yet to reach its conclusion, but, if convicted, Lubanga faces life in prison.[50]

<<< "When they came to my village, **they asked my older brother whether he was ready to join the militia.** He was just 17 and **he said no; they shot him in the head.** Then they asked me if I was ready to sign, so **what could I do? I didn't want to die."**

— Ndungutsa, former child soldier, taken when he was 13.[51]

think social problems: WHAT ARE SOME THEORIES OF CONFLICTS?

Functionalism

Functionalists view societies as being bound by solidarity. Because war serves a necessary purpose—defending the nation while at the same time helping it maintain a sense of unity—it can be seen as functional.[52] Most of my students feel that the Revolutionary War of 1776 was functional; after all, violence is a logical means by which a group can overcome its oppression.[53] When people face a common threat, they are more likely to stick together. For example, after the September 11th attacks on the World Trade Center, many of my students joined the military out of a desire to protect their homeland. Ethnic and religious minorities who band together to create their own societies display this same form of solidarity.

From a functionalist point of view, war also offers economic benefits. As mentioned earlier, military spending during wartime benefits a nation financially, and an infusion of government money can advance a stagnant economy. New jobs are created to produce the needed weapons and war-related technology, which aids society and the economy.

Conflict Theory

Both war and terrorism are the result of conflict. Some conflict theorists have noted that rich nations such as the United States use their military power to maintain their dominance over other nations.[54] Despite the assertions of politicians and national leaders, wars are not fought over

Wars can boost job production. **Do the economic benefits outweigh the consequences of war?**

FUNCTIONALISM

Functionalists believe that instead of being a societal ill, war actually serves a function that is both necessary and beneficial to society. Functionalists see war as a way for societies to maintain solidarity; by coming together to combat a common enemy, societies are able to remain unified and intact. War is one way in which people discover that they need each another and decide that it's in their best interests to stick together. Functionalists also believe that war can benefit a nation by inserting government money into the economy and creating jobs that would not exist during times of peace. Because war generates a need for weapons, supplies, and other technologies, new segments of the market are opened or expanded.

CONFLICT THEORY

Conflict theorists believe that war is simply one way that a nation preserves or establishes its dominance over other nations. Regardless of the official reasons given for going to war, conflict theorists believe that all wars essentially stem from a quest for dominance. Conflict theorists also believe that because war benefits certain companies, those companies are likely to try to influence policies in ways that make war a more likely outcome. The end result is an overall increase in the size, strength, and influence of the military-industrial complex. An increase in amount of influence of the military-industrial complex also increases the likelihood of future conflicts, a scenario that President Eisenhower foretold.

WHY ARE THERE WARS?

SYMBOLIC INTERACTIONISM

Symbolic interactionists look at the underlying meaning of war. Why are people fighting? Are they doing it in support of an ideal? Are they doing it out of fear? Are they doing it out of necessity? These are the type of questions that symbolic interactionists consider. Interactionists claim that a society must believe in the reasons for going to war in order for a war to occur; therefore, a nation's leaders must ensure that public opinion is favorable before engaging in the conflict. If the public is not in support, the war is unlikely to be successful and will have negative consequences that can impact the future of that nation and its leaders. Think of the wars in Iraq and Vietnam. As public support for those wars waned, so did support for the presidents who initiated them. Both also negatively affected the image of the United States around the world.

Wars establish dominance. **Is war just the adult version of children's playground games?**

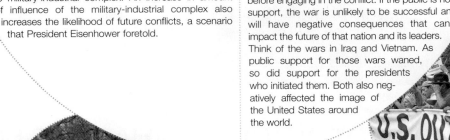

It is important to have public support when considering war. **Why might public support decline?**

ideologies such as peace and democracy. Instead, wars are fought to maintain a position of power in the world system. For conflict theorists, the only true objective in any conflict is to maintain dominance. To them, war is simply a large and deadly game of king of the hill.

Conflict theorists often ask who benefits from a war. Mills and Domhoff suggest that a strong and powerful corporate lobby associated with the military-industrial complex drives most of the decisions of the country. Corporate CEOs do not fight and die in wars; people from the lower and working classes do.[55] Meanwhile, who profits from the use of weapons, ammunition, supplies, and other wartime necessities? The companies that create those necessities can benefit a great deal from a long-term war. As Eisenhower warned, the military-industrial complex influences policy to suit its own interests. Conflict theorists point out that this endangers the liberty of everyone in the nation, because profit reigns over ideals.

On the other hand, research suggests that terrorism rarely occurs as a result of poverty and deprivation. In fact, terrorists generally come from wealthy sections of a population and richer areas of the world. Suicide bombers in particular are typically from the advantaged class and have respectable families and strong religious beliefs. Thus, unlike war, terrorism is generally a pursuit of a political or ideological goal and not an effort in improve one's economic well-being.[56]

Symbolic Interactionism

Symbolic interactionists look at conflict a bit differently. For example, they question the meaning of terrorism. Is the hijacking of a merchant vessel in order to make a political statement (as happened on September 11, 2001) an act of terrorism? If so, how about the Boston Tea Party? That event could also be classified as terrorism.

MUTUALLY ASSURED DESTRUCTION is the idea that the use of nuclear weapons from one side will trigger the use of nuclear weapons from the opposing side and will culminate in the ultimate decimation of both parties.

DETERRENCE STRATEGY aims to limit the spread and use of nuclear weapons.

I often ask my students if there is a difference between being a revolutionary and being a terrorist. This question is usually met with puzzled and angry responses. The truth is that terrorists often claim to be liberators. In fact, Timothy McVeigh, one of the worst domestic terrorists in American history, considered himself a revolutionary.[57] There *is* a subtle difference between a revolutionary and a terrorist, however. Revolutionaries set out with the purpose of overthrowing a repressive regime, whereas terrorists often have goals that are much less clear. Defining the difference between these two groups can be difficult. Is terrorism in the eye of the beholder? Terrorists in the Middle East generally justify their violent acts based on religion and the pursuit of freedom from Western influences. The use of religion to justify violence may seem odd, but all of the world's major religions—Christianity, Judaism, Hinduism, Islam, and even Buddhism—permit violence in response to attacks on faith.[58]

Public support is often necessary before a nation can effectively engage in a war. Symbolic interactionists examine a population's reaction to conflict. When President George W. Bush and his administration advocated the war with Iraq, for example, they cited the looming threat of weapons of mass destruction as justification, even though no evidence of these weapons would ever be found. In addition, the war was linked to terrorism, unifying many people behind the cause through their strong disapproval of terrorist acts.

discover solutions to social problems:
HOW DO WE CONTROL CONFLICTS?

For many nations, the threat of war is always present. In the year 2007 alone, there were 14 major armed conflicts and 61 "peace" operations in which troops were deployed.[59] On top of this, the worldwide production of weapons is increasing.[60] Diplomacy and arms control measures are among some of the strategies used to curb the threat of war.

Nuclear Arms Control

Since their invention, nuclear weapons have been seen as a threat to humanity and to the world. The United States alone has an estimated 5,400 nuclear warheads in its possession.[61] Now that nuclear weapons stockpiles are aging and remain unused, there is the question of what should be done with them.

The Treaty on the Non-Proliferation of Nuclear Weapons was introduced in 1968 in an effort to prevent the creation and spread of more nuclear weapons. The ultimate goal of the treaty was the complete elimination of these warheads. The countries that signed the treaty fell into two categories: countries with nuclear weapons and countries without nuclear weapons. The countries that had already developed nuclear weapons

agreed not to distribute the weapons to other countries and to diminish their arsenals over time until they had no more. The countries that did not have nuclear weapons agreed not to pursue the development of such devices. Excluding India, Pakistan, and Israel, every member state of the United Nations has signed the Treaty on the Non-Proliferation of Nuclear Weapons, making it the most accepted arms agreement in the world.[62]

Another similar agreement is the Comprehensive Nuclear-Test-Ban Treaty that prohibits all nuclear explosions for any purpose. Although not as widely supported as the Treaty on the Non-Proliferation of Nuclear Weapons, it has been signed by 167 of 197 countries.[63]

Have these treaties worked? It's difficult to know for certain. The lack of nuclear attacks could also be attributed to the strategy known as "mutually assured destruction." **Mutually assured destruction** means that the use of nuclear weapons from one side will trigger the use of nuclear weapons from the opposing side, culminating in the ultimate decimation of both parties. As long as no nation pulls the trigger, no others will either. Such a **deterrence strategy** aims to limit the spread and use of nuclear weapons and keep the planet safe from the horrors of another Hiroshima.

Combating International Terrorism

To combat terrorism, organizations around the world have resolved to address many of the underlying issues that can lead to it, such as discrimination, human rights violations, exclusion, marginalization of a particular group, and absence of the rule of law. These organizations promote peaceful solutions and implement programs focused on negotiation, mediation, and conflict resolution.[64] By eliminating the issues that commonly lead to acts of terrorism, people will be less likely to resort to violence to have their needs addressed.

The United Nations also takes measures to prevent terrorist activities and to ensure that terrorists do not have access to the materials needed to carry out violent acts. It also focuses on joining with other states in the war on terror and the apprehension and prosecution of terrorist groups.[65]

MAKE CONNECTIONS

War, Globalization, and Population Growth

As you've learned in Chapter 17, globalization does not affect every nation in the same way; some countries benefit more than others. In Chapter 18 we discussed the impact that population growth can have on a nation's resources. A country experiencing a decline in resources might see war as a possible solution to its problems, as conflicts can offer economic or emotional gain. Rich nations have strong militaries and are better able to protect their own resources. When those rich nations experience a decline in resources, they are in a better position to take resources from a poorer nation because of their strong military power.

Pro & Con

Using the Military to Fight Terrorism

Terrorism plagues many nations worldwide. Tactics to combat terrorism include economic sanctions and criminal prosecutions, as well as preemptive efforts to alleviate issues that can lead to conflict. Some have suggested that military force is the most effective way to fight this global threat. Can a nation's military win a war on terror?

Pro

- Military forces can destroy the weapons, bases, and personnel of terrorist groups and eliminate or significantly diminish the terrorists' abilities to attack. If you eliminate the enemy, you also eliminate the threat posed by the enemy.

- By moving the fight to where the terrorists live, you keep them on the defensive and prevent them from conducting more attacks on your homeland. Terrorist groups have a difficult time initiating more attacks when they are in the midst of being attacked themselves.

- Conquered peoples do not always revolt against their conquerors. During World War II, for example, Japan was considered an enemy. Near the end of the war in 1945, Japan was subjected to the worst attack by a weapon of mass destruction in the history of the world when atomic bombs were dropped on Hiroshima and Nagasaki. Afterward, Japan became a strong ally of the United States, and this relationship continues to the present day.

- Other methods such as economic sanctions and criminal prosecutions do not have the same effect as military force in convincing people to cease terrorist activities. For instance, a population that is already heavily sanctioned is unlikely to be affected by more sanctions. In the same way, criminal prosecutions may not serve as a deterrent if only a few terrorists are captured and brought to justice. Instead, these prosecutions may serve as an incentive for future terrorist activity.

Con

- Addressing the causes of terrorism is more effective than trying to kill terrorists. If the issues that led to the terrorist activity are addressed in a reasonable way, there is a strong chance that the terrorism will cease. If the causes are not addressed, there are likely to be more terrorists that are willing to take up the fight, no matter how many are killed.

- Like any war, the outcome of combating terrorists is uncertain. Military operations are unpredictable and can even result in civilian casualties. In these situations, a military intervention can cause much more harm than good, and can even serve as a way to recruit more terrorists. Those angered by the death of a loved one may blame the invading army and take up arms against it.

- Prosecution in criminal courts places a nation on the moral high ground. It also serves to frame the terrorist activity as being criminal in nature and makes other potential terrorists reconsider whether they want to participate in such activity.

- Economic sanctions are more effective in combating terrorist states than using military force. Placing economic pressure on a nation can induce its leaders and its citizens to pressure terrorist organizations to cease their activities. Leaders will want the sanctions to end so that their nation can thrive. Other members of the population are likely to blame the terrorist outfit for their economic hardships as well, and these negative associations may prevent others from aligning with the organization in the future.

James was young when the bombing occurred, but he still remembered seeing it on the news that day. He didn't know anyone who was hurt or killed in the incident, but he was struck by the fact that something of that magnitude could happen in his own hometown of Oklahoma City.

On April 19, 1995, a truck filled with explosives demolished a federal building in Oklahoma City. The explosion killed 168 people, wounded hundreds of others, and shattered many lives as a result.[66] Later, the Oklahoma City National Memorial & Museum was built on the site of the destruction and was designed to be a place of remembrance and education for generations to come.[67] Visitors today can visit the museum to honor those who lost their lives, learn about the event, and hear from individuals who were personally affected.

While James was a sophomore in college, he decided to volunteer at the memorial. He saw it as a chance to learn about the event that had such an impact on him when he was younger. "I think a lot of people around here were traumatized by the attack. In some sense, I think volunteering was my way of coping with what I witnessed as a kid. I don't understand what could lead someone down such a violent and destructive path; I don't think many people can."

One of the things that stood out to James was that American citizens had carried out the Oklahoma City bombing. "I hadn't really thought of it in that way when I was younger, but what happened was an act of domestic terrorism. Even though you see car bombs and suicide bombings happening all over the world in the news, you don't think of things like that ever happening here in the United States. It really opened my eyes to the fact that America had experienced terrorism before September 11th."

Even with the devastation left in its wake and the uncertainty that still surrounds the event, what left the biggest impression on James was how people dealt with the tragedy. "People from around the country offered support. It didn't matter if they knew anyone involved or not. Even now, people from all over send us donations and tell us how moved they are by the monument."

For James, volunteering was a way for him to do the same. Throughout the summer, he served as a guide and conducted museum tours. He had a chance to interact with people who were directly affected by the event and those who wanted to understand more about it. "I think it's great when people can take a negative event and turn it into something positive. That's exactly what happened with the museum. Now people can become educated and remember the victims of that day; not just those who passed away, but those who live on with the memories. I think it's brought our city together more than ever."

<<< **The Oklahoma City National Memorial & Museum** commemorates the **April 19, 1995 bombing** of the Alfred P. Murrah Federal Building.

HOW DO COUNTRIES DEAL WITH CONFLICTS? 286

in a number of ways, but often through war and acts of terrorism

WHAT ARE SOME THEORIES OF CONFLICTS? 293

functionalism: conflict is necessary to maintain the solidarity of society and boost the economy

conflict theory: conflict is a way for nations to establish or maintain a position of dominance

symbolic interactionism: there are a variety of reasons behind conflict, and each group has its own definition of terms such as war, revolution, and terrorism

HOW DO WE CONTROL CONFLICTS? 295

by initiating treaties and sanctions, addressing the sources of conflicts, and other diplomatic methods that focus on preventing the outbreak of hostility and the use of deadly weapons

get the topic: HOW DO COUNTRIES DEAL WITH CONFLICTS?

Theory

FUNCTIONALISM   293
- conflict is necessary to maintain the solidarity of a society
- conflict can boost a nation's economy

CONFLICT THEORY   293
- conflict is a way for nations to establish or maintain a position of dominance
- conflict promotes the growth of the military-industrial complex

SOCIAL INTERACTIONISM   294
- it is important to examine the social and political meaning behind conflicts
- public support is necessary for a country to succeed at war

Key Terms

war is a violent conflict between groups that are organized for such conflict.   286

military-industrial complex is a combination of the armed forces and defense industries that provide weapons and other materials to a country.   287

easy victory is a cause of war when conquest is seen as being easy for one side.   287

optimism is a cause of war when a nation is overly confident about the outcome of a potential conflict.   287

first strike is a cause of war when a nation's leaders determine that making the initial move will give them an advantage.   287

threat is a cause of war stemming from impending danger.   287

profit is cause of war when a country believes that there is the possibility of monetary gain by either capturing or exploiting the resources of another country.   287

nuclear weapon is a device that employs atomic energy to create a large-scale explosion.   290

biological weapons are composed of an organic agent such as a virus that is used to cause harm.   290

chemical weapons are composed of synthetically created materials that are used to cause harm.   290

terrorism is premeditated, politically motivated violence perpetrated against noncombatant targets by sub-national groups or clandestine agents.   291

mutually assured destruction is the idea that the use of nuclear weapons from one side will trigger the use of nuclear weapons from the opposing side and will culminate in the ultimate decimation of both parties.   295

deterrence strategy aims to limit the spread and use of nuclear weapons.   295

Sample Test Questions

These multiple-choice questions are similar to those found in the test bank that accompanies this textbook.

1. The combination of the armed forces and defense industries that provide weapons and other materials is called
   a. the military-armament industry.
   b. the power elite.
   c. the military-industrial complex.
   d. the industrial defense complex.

2. The country that spends the most money on its military is
   a. Saudi Arabia.
   b. Russia.
   c. India.
   d. The United States.

3. In armed conflict, which type of weapons are responsible for the greatest number of casualties and deaths?
   a. Nuclear weapons
   b. Weapons of mass destruction
   c. Chemical weapons
   d. Small arms and light weapons

4. Functionalists view war as a way in which
   a. nations can maintain dominance.
   b. a country can boost its economy.
   c. public support can be gathered.
   d. a society can spread its ideological and political beliefs.

5. Military spending harms a peacetime economy.
   a. True
   b. False

ESSAY

1. Do you believe that the United States is strongly influenced by an elite group of powerful individuals? Why or why not?

2. From the view of a conflict theorist, do you think that there is a clear distinction between being a terrorist and being a revolutionary?

3. Compare and contrast Mills's power elite with Eisenhower's military-industrial complex. Which seems to influence United States policy more?

4. At what age do you feel it is appropriate for people to be recruited for military service? Should this vary nation by nation, or should it be a global universal?

5. According to functionalists, conflicts serve to bring societies closer together. After the 2001 attacks on the World Trade Center, Americans came together to decry acts of terror. Does the same happen to the offensive group? (for example, after September 11th, did members of Al-Qaeda feel a similar solidarity?) Explain your answer, perhaps making reference to the 2003 war in Iraq.

WHERE TO START YOUR RESEARCH PAPER

For statistics on United States conflicts, go to
www.va.gov/opa/fact/amwars.asp

For more facts on terrorism, visit
www.state.gov/s/ct/rls/crt/2006/82739.htm

To read the Treaty on the Non-Proliferation of Nuclear Weapons, check out www.un.org/events/npt2005/npttreaty.html

For more information on child soldiers, go to
http://www.child-soldiers.org

To see an interactive timeline of the war in Iraq, visit
www.msnbc.msn.com/id/23694433

For an overview of domestic terrorism and information on past events, see
http://www.fbi.gov/page2/sept09/domesticterrorism090709.html

ANSWERS: 1. c; 2. d; 3. d; 4. b; 5. a.

Remember to check http://www.thethinkspot.com/ for additional information, downloadable flashcards, and other helpful resources.

GLOSSARY

Parenthetical numbers refer to the pages on which the term is introduced.

abortion   refers to the termination and removal of a fetus from a woman's uterus before birth. (159)

absolute poverty   refers to poverty so severe that one lacks resources to survive. (30)

activity theory   states that life satisfaction depends on maintaining social involvement by developing new interests, hobbies, roles, and relationships. (74)

addiction   is a chronic condition that can include both a psychological and/or physiological compulsion toward drug seeking and use. (143)

attention deficit hyperactivity disorder (ADHD)   symptoms include impulsiveness, hyperactivity, and inattention. (133)

ageism   is prejudice and discrimination based solely on age. (71)

age-specific birth rate   is the number of births for every 1,000 women in a specific age group. (256)

aggravating circumstances   are circumstances relating to the commission of an act that increase the degree of liability or responsibility of the person committing the act. (198)

Alcoholics Anonymous   is one of the oldest and most well-known substance treatment programs in the United States. (149)

anxiety/panic disorders   arise when normal anxiety is exceeded and everyday situations become difficult for victims to cope with. (132)

asset forfeiture   allows the government to seize any item that is believed to have been purchased with proceeds from illegal activities. (150)

assimilation   is the process by which minority groups adopt the patterns of the dominant culture. (50)

authoritarianism   is a form of government that gives citizens very little say in how the nation is run. (103)

awareness   is the ability of a person or group to bring a problem into public recognition. (7)

biological weapons   are composed of an organic agent such as a virus that is used to cause harm. (290)

bipolar disorder   is characterized by drastic shifts in mood and behavior; victims often fluctuate between being overly high and euphoric and feeling depressed and hopeless. (132)

birth dearth   refers to declining birth rates. (260)

bisexual   orientation includes those who have emotional, romantic, or sexual attractions to both men and women. (157)

blaming the victim   refers to the act of accusing those who suffer from a social problem for that problem. (31)

blended families   are families composed of children and some combination of biological parents and stepparents. (212)

brain drain   occurs when the best talent leaves poor countries and thereby provides an even greater advantage to wealthy countries. (241)

campaigns   are organized and ongoing efforts that make claims targeting a specific authority in the society. (7)

capitalism   is an economic system in which individuals or private corporations can own and operate the production of goods, make decisions about the price of those goods, and distribute them as they deem appropriate. (98)

carrying capacity   is the number of a specific species that can exist in a given environment. (271)

causal relationships   are relationships in which a condition or variable leads to a certain consequence. (14)

causation   is the relationship between cause and effect. (14)

charismatic system   is a political organization in which power is gained because a leader has extraordinary personal attributes. (102)

charter schools   are nonsectarian public schools of choice that operate with freedom from many of the regulations that apply to traditional public schools. (121)

chemical weapons   are composed of synthetically created materials that are used to cause harm. (290)

color-blind racism   is the idea that racism still exists in society in more subtle ways. (46)

commodification   is the transformation of relationships that were formerly unrelated to commerce into economic relationships built on buying and selling. (171)

communitarianism   suggests that for society to function properly, it must have communal values and set social policies according to those values. (106)

conflict model of law   proposes that powerful people write laws and, in doing so, tend to protect their own interests. (196)

conflict theory   is a theoretical framework that views society as being in a constant struggle over scarce resources. (8)

consensus model of law   suggests that laws arise because people see a behavior they do not like, and agree to make it illegal. (196)

containment theory   argues that criminals cannot resist the temptations that surround them. (187)

continuity theory   states that older people seek out familiar areas of their lives and strive to keep those constant as they age, which becomes a strategy for adaptation to the challenges of growing old. (74)

contract slavery   is a form of slavery in which a person signs a work contract, receiving food and shelter from an employer, but is threatened when he or she tries to leave the contract. (244)

control variables are variables that are kept constant to accurately test the impact of an independent variable. (14)

convergence theory describes the tendency for capitalism and socialism to converge. (100)

corporation is a legal entity that has some objective, typically to make a profit for its owners. It can purchase property, acquire debt, and participate in legal contracts. (101)

correlation is an indication that one factor *might* be the cause for another factor. (14)

counterurbanization refers to the process by which city growth has slowed as more rural areas and suburban areas have grown. (226)

credentialism is an emphasis on education degrees as a prerequisite for advancement. (120)

crime is the violation of norms that have been written into law. (182)

crime index is made up of eight offenses used to measure crime: homicide, rape, robbery, aggravated assault, burglary, larceny-theft, motor vehicle theft, and arson. (182)

criminology is the scientific study of crime, deviance, and social policies that the criminal justice system applies. (182)

crude birth rate is the number of births for every 1,000 people each year. (256)

crude death rate is the number of deaths per 1,000 people each year. (257)

cultural lag refers to a situation in which members of society can't keep up with technology. (84)

cultural universal is any aspect of one's social life that is common to all societies. (6)

cycle of poverty is a generational barrier that prevents poor people from breaking into middle and upper classes. (43)

decentralization is the transfer of authority from a central government to a local government. (226)

defense counsel consists of attorneys hired or appointed by the court to provide a legal defense for the accused. (197)

democracy is a political system that is run by the citizens. (104)

Democratic Party is a political party in the United States that supports increased regulation of private institutions and a larger government. (104)

democratic socialism is a type of economic system involving a blend of free market capitalism and government regulation of the economy. (100)

demographic transition theory states that people control their fertility as societies change from being agrarian to industrial. (262)

demographics are statistical characteristics of human populations, such as gender and age. (101)

demography is the study of the size and composition of a population. (256)

dependent variables are the responses to the manipulated variable. (13)

depressants are a type of drug that slows the activity of vital organs in the body to create a relaxed, sleepy feeling. (144)

deterrence is a measure that prevents a person from doing something out of fear of the consequences. (197)

deterrence strategy aims to limit the spread and use of nuclear weapons. (295)

deviance is a behavior, belief, or condition that is a violation of social norms. (168)

Diagnostic and Statistical Manual of Mental Disorders (DSM) is the standard classification of mental illnesses used by mental health professionals in the United States. (134)

dictator is a single person with complete control in a government system. (103)

differential association theory claims that criminal activity is a learned behavior and that the people with whom we interact influence this learning process. (186)

digital divide is the gap between high-income countries and low-income countries that influences their access to current technology. (83)

discretion is the ability to make decisions. (197)

discrimination is the deliberate and unfair treatment of people based on a prejudice. (42)

disengagement theory states that reduced interaction between elderly persons and other members of society is unavoidable, mutual, and acceptable. (74)

disinvestment is a deliberate pattern whereby banking and lending institutions make decisions about where they will and will not support investments. (228)

double consciousness is the sense that a person must keep a foot in two worlds, one in the majority group's world and one in the minority group's world. (42)

doubling time is the length of time in which it takes a population to double in size. (260)

drift is the first stage of becoming a prostitute and the change from casual sex to the first incident of exchanging sex for money. (170)

drug abuse is the use of drugs despite adverse consequences. (143)

drug use is the act of internally processing chemical substances other than food that have physical effects. (142)

drugs are substances that have psychological or physical effects. (142)

easy victory is a cause of war when conquest is seen as being easy for one side. (287)

eating disorders are characterized by extreme behavior regarding food, whether drastically under- or overeating, connected with feeling of concern about body image and weight. (132)

economic behaviorism states that people don't make decisions based on what is rational, but what is easiest or most popular. (106)

economic system (or economy) is a social institution that helps a society organize what it produces, distributes, and consumes, including goods and services. (98)

editorial slant appears in arguments that openly present opinions that favor one side over another. (88)

education is the process by which people gain or develop knowledge. (114)

elasticity of demand explains the fact that demand for the product changes when the price changes. (99)

embargo is a restriction on trade that is enforced by a government. (102)

emigration is the movement of people out of a nation-state. (258)

eminent domain is a policy that allows the government to take property from individuals, often against the owner's will, for public use. (234)

entrepreneur is a person who establishes, organizes, manages, and assumes all risks of an organization. (102)

entrepreneurial immigrants are people who migrate because they seek to own their own businesses. (44)

entrepreneurship is the creation of new organizations in response to economic and social opportunities. (102)

environmental justice is the impact of environmental factors on social classes. (273)

environmental sociology is the study of how the environment influences society, and vice versa. (270)

ethics refers to a system of values or principles that guides one's behavior. (15)

ethnic enclaves are neighborhoods where people from similar cultures live together and assert cultural distinction from the dominant group. (45)

ethnic grouping is the tendency for members of particular ethnic groups to want to live in close proximity to one another. (228)

ethnicity is the classification of people who share a common cultural, linguistic, or ancestral heritage. (40)

ethnocentrism is thinking about or defining another culture on the basis of your own. (45)

exchange mobility is a concept suggesting that, within the United States, each social class contains a relatively fixed number of people. (29)

extended family is a household consisting of a nuclear family and additional relatives. (210)

family is two or more people who are related by blood, marriage, or adoption. (210)

feminism is a philosophy based on the political, social, and economic equality of the sexes, specifically a woman's right to have the same opportunities as a man. (58)

fertility is the number of births that occur in a population. (256)

first strike is a cause of war when a nation's leaders determine that making the initial strike will give them an advantage. (287)

force is a type of power that occurs when you make someone do something against his or her will. (24)

free market is an economic market that operates without government control. (99)

functionalism is a theoretical framework that defines society as a system of interrelated parts. (8)

gain time is the amount of time deducted from a prison sentence for participation in special programs. (198)

Gemeinschaft refers to community connections involving personal relationships based on friendship and kinship ties. (231)

gender refers to the behavioral, cultural, and psychological traits associated with being male or female. (56)

gender identity is the psychological sense of one's self as male or female. (57)

gender-inequality theories focus on sexist patterns that limit women's opportunities for work, education, and other social needs. (10)

gender roles are society's expectations of how males and females should think and act. (58)

general deterrence is a type of criminal sentencing that seeks to prevent others from committing crimes by making an example of an offender. (197)

general strain theory suggests that people experience strain from different sources, which results in criminal activity. (187)

genocide is the attempt to destroy or exterminate a people based on their race and/or ethnicity. (41)

gentrification is a trend that involves renovating and redeveloping a run-down neighborhood so that it meets middle-class standards, and subsequently displaces the original low-income residents. (233)

Gesellschaft refers to social connections that are more formal and impersonal. (231)

global village is a term referring to the "shrinking" of the world through immediate electronic communications. (86)

global stratification is the categorization of countries based on objective criteria, such as wealth, power, and prestige, which highlight social patterns and inequality throughout the world. (242)

globalization is a complex process by which the world and the international economy are becoming more and more intertwined. (240)

glocalization occurs when countries seek to combine the local and the global into a unique structural blend to maintain their native customs while fitting into the global environment. (240)

good time is the amount of time deducted from a prison sentence for good behavior. (198)

grade inflation is the trend of assigning higher grades than previously assigned to students for completing the same work. (119)

gridlock is a series of traffic jams. (229)

grobalization refers to the idea that capitalist countries use their corporate interests to expand their power and influence throughout the world. (244)

hallucinogens are a type of drug that distorts the senses and causes hallucinations. (144)

hate groups are organizations that promote hostility or violence toward others based on race and other factors. (42)

health is a state of complete physical, mental, and social well-being, not merely the absence of disease or infirmity. (128)

heterosexual orientation refers to those who have emotional, romantic, or sexual attractions to members of the opposite sex. (157)

hidden curriculum refers to lessons taught in schools that are unrelated to academic learning. (115)

home-health care is provided for patients who cannot leave their homes but have the possibility of improving. (73)

homosexual orientation refers to those who have emotional, romantic, or sexual attractions to members of their own sex. (157)

horizontal mobility refers to moving within the same status category. (29)

hospice care is short-term care, but only available to patients with six months or less to live. (73)

human capital is a person's combination of skills, knowledge, traits, and personal attributes. (120)

human exemptionalism is the belief that considers human beings different from other species on Earth. (271)

immigration is the movement of people into a nation-state. (258)

incapacitation is the use of imprisonment or other means to reduce the likelihood that an offender will be capable of committing future offenses. (202)

income is the money received for work or through investments. (22)

income gap is the difference in earnings between different demographics. (60)

indeterminate sentencing is a model of criminal punishment that allows the judge and the corrections system a great deal of discretion in the length of the sentence. (198)

independent variables are variables that are deliberately manipulated to test the response in an experiment. (13)

index of dissimilarity (D) indicates the percentage of people that would need to be relocated in order to have a perfectly even distribution of race and ethnicity in a city. (228)

infant mortality rate is the number of children per 1,000 who are born alive but who die before reaching the age of one year. (257)

institutional discrimination maintains the advantage for the dominant group, while providing the appearance of fairness to all. (42)

institutional welfare is a preventive "first line of defense" against poverty. There is no time limit, and no social stigma is associated with receiving this aid. (33)

intergenerational mobility is the change that family members make from one social class to the next through generations. (29)

interlocking directorates is a practice in which the same people are placed on a variety of corporate boards, allowing separate companies to be controlled by a small, elite group. (106)

intragenerational mobility occurs when an individual changes social standing, especially in the workforce. (29)

involuntary immigration is the forced movement of people from one society to another. (44)

judge is an elected or appointed public official who presides over the court of law. (197)

just deserts is a model of criminal sentencing that holds that criminal offenders deserve the punishment they receive at the hands of the law and that punishments should be appropriate to the type and severity of the crime committed. (202)

labor immigrants are those who migrate to a new country because they are seeking work. (44)

life expectancy is the average number of years of life for a person of any given age. (256)

life span is the maximum length of time that it is possible for a human being to live. (256)

literacy rate is the percentage of people in a population who can read and write. (117)

lower class is a social class living in poverty. (27)

macro is a large-scale point of view. (4)

major depressive disorder is a mental disorder characterized by persistent, chronic feelings of sadness, hopelessness, worthlessness, guilt, or pessimism lasting for weeks at a time. (132)

majority group is the group that has the largest population in society and holds significant power and privilege. (41)

Malthusian theorem states that populations grow at a geometric rate, while food grows at an arithmetic rate. (261)

mandatory minimums are fixed sentences for specific crimes. (204)

mandatory sentencing is a structured sentencing strategy that allows for no discretion on the part of the judge. (198)

marginal poverty refers to a state of poverty that occurs when a person lacks stable employment. (30)

marriage is the union of two people that is typically recognized by law or cultural norms. (210)

matriarchy is a social system in which women are the main authority and hold power over men. (57)

McDonaldization refers to applying the business model of McDonald's to other businesses. (83

mechanical solidarity is the state of community bonding in traditional societies in which people share beliefs and values and perform common activities. (231)

media are the channels through which we store and receive information; they consist of print, television, radio, and the Internet. (86)

media bias occurs when members of the media favor one group over another and let it affect their rendition of the truth. (88)

median is the midpoint of a group of numbers ranked from lowest to highest. (23)

Medicaid is a government-run program designed to provide insurance for low-income individuals and families who meet certain qualifications. (137)

medicalization of America is the idea that the medical community is at the center of many aspects of American society; we feel that there is a pill or some sort of medical cure to fix everything. (134)

Medicare is a government-run social insurance program that provides health coverage for people 65 and older. (76)

megacities are cities with 10 million residents or more. (224)

megalopolis is an extensive metropolitan area. (225)

mental disorders are patterns of mood, thought, or behavior that cause distress and decrease the ability of a person to function. (128)

meritocracy argument states that those who get ahead in society do so according to their own merit. (31)

metropolitan area is a metropolis, or city, that is inclusive of the surrounding areas. (225)

metropolitan federation is a collaborative form of government across a metropolitan area. (226)

micro is a small-scale reference. (4)

middle class is a social class that consists of those who have moderate incomes. (26)

migration is the movement of people from one area to another area. (258)

military-industrial complex is a combination of the armed forces and defense industries that provide weapons and other materials to the country. (287)

minority group is a group that has a smaller population and less power than the majority group. (41)

mitigating circumstances are circumstances in the commission of an act that decrease the degree of criminal responsibility of the person committing the act. (198)

monarchy is a political system in which leadership is based on the idea that leaders are selected by divine right or heritage. (103)

monopoly is the exclusive control of the production or trade of a product in the market. (98)

mortality rate is the number of deaths that occur in a population. (257)

multiculturalism is a concept that supports the inherent value of different cultures within society. (49)

mutually assured destruction is the idea that the use of nuclear weapons from one side will trigger the use of nuclear weapons from the opposing side and will culminate in the ultimate decimation of both parties. (295)

narcotics are drugs that are considered illegal today. (142)

National Crime Victimization Survey (NCVS) is the measurement of crime victimization based on contact with a representative sample of over 70,000 households in the United States. (182)

negative correlation occurs when the variables move in opposite directions. (15)

neocolonialism is a process by which powerful nations use loans and economic power to maintain control over poor nations. (246)

nonviolent crime is an illegal act committed against property. (182)

North American Free Trade Agreement (NAFTA) is an agreement established in 1994 to allow free trade on agricultural products between the United States, Mexico, and Canada. (102)

nuclear family is a household consisting of a husband, wife, and children. (210)

nuclear weapon is a device that employs atomic energy to create a large-scale explosion. (290)

objectification involves treating a person as a thing or object, without concern for his or her personal characteristics. (171)

objective condition is any aspect of society that can be viewed without bias. (5)

objectivity refers to the ability to conduct research without allowing personal biases or prejudices to influence them. (12)

obsessive compulsive disorder (OCD) is a mental disorder in which the sufferer is subjected to recurring thoughts and feelings that cause distress and anxiety and lead to habitual behaviors. (132)

oligarchy is a small group of influential people with complete control of the government. (103)

optimism is a cause of war when a nation is overly confident about the outcome of a potential conflict. (287)

organic solidarity is a state that occurs when people live in a society with a diverse division of labor. (231)

overpopulation occurs when a species' population lives beyond the carrying capacity, resulting in too few resources. (271)

P* index for interaction calculates the amount of contact an average person of one group has with an average person of another group on any given day. (228)

paradigms are theoretical frameworks through which scientists study the world. (8)

parole is a correctional strategy that releases inmates from prison early but supervises them in the community. (199)

patriarchy is a social system in which men control a majority of the power and exert authority over women and children. (57)

per-capita income is calculated by dividing a country's total gross income by the number of people in that country. (242)

perceived obsolescence is the belief that an item is outdated because a new model is available. (91)

persuasive power refers to using direct or indirect methods to get what you want. (24)

planned obsolescence is the practice of adding technical improvements to make upgrading to the next model a necessity. (91)

plea bargains are out-of-court agreements between the prosecutor and defense attorney that often involve concessions by the prosecution to obtain a guilty plea. (197)

political action committees (PACs) are interest groups that allocate money to political parties. (109)

population density is a measure of the number of humans per square mile. (224)

population pyramids are tools that visually represent data about a specific population in relation to age and sex. (257)

population variables are the changeable characteristics of a given population. (256)

positive correlation involves two variables moving in a parallel. (14)

power is the ability to carry out your will and impose it on others. (24)

power elite is a group comprised of top military officials, heads of major corporations, and high-ranking political leaders; this select group of people have the power to control both the economy and the politics of American society. (106)

prejudice refers to rigid generalizations, often negative, about an entire category of people. (42)

prestige is the level of esteem associated with one's status and social standing. (25)

prestige gap is the divide between those who have the privilege of attending elite schools and obtaining success in the job market, and those who don't. (118)

probation is a sentence given in lieu of prison and requires conditions that must be met by the offender to avoid going to prison. (199)

professional immigrants are those who migrate to a new country because they possess some skill or profession. (44)

professionalization is the third and final stage of becoming a prostitute and the point at which women identify themselves as prostitutes. (170)

profit is cause of war when a country believes that there is the possibility of monetary gain by either capturing or exploiting the resources of another country. (287)

progressive taxation is a system in which people who earn more pay higher taxes. (34)

prosecuting attorney is an attorney whose official duty is to conduct criminal proceedings on behalf of the state or the people against those accused of committing criminal offenses. (197)

prostitution is the unlawful promotion of or participation in sexual activities for profit. (169)

qualitative data refer to information that may include words, pictures, photos, or any other type of information that comes to the researcher in a non-numerical form. (15)

quantitative data refer to data based on numbers and used for macroanalysis (15)

queer theory refers to a body of theory and research that seeks to neutralize the heterosexual bias in the United States. (160)

race is the division of people based on certain physical characteristics. (40)

racial profiling refers to the act of using race to determine whether a person is likely to have committed a crime. (185)

racism is a prejudice that asserts one race is inferior to another, thus making them less worthy of fair treatment. (41)

rapid assimilation occurs when a minority group completely abandons its previous culture in favor of a new one. (50)

rate of natural increase (RNI) is a calculation that demographers use to determine the growth or decline of a population. (260)

rational-legal authority is a system in which power stems from rules and standards that are agreed upon by society. (102)

recidivism is the tendency for former inmates to return to prison. (200)

redlining is a practice in which home lenders draw red lines on a map, indicating to which sides of a city they will and will not lend money. (228)

refugees are people who migrate because they are seeking safety and freedom. (44)

regressive taxation is a system that taxes everyone the same percentage of money. (34)

rehabilitation is the attempt to reform an offender. (202)

reintegrative shaming is a punishment that allows the offender to reconnect to society after punishment without further stigma. (197)

relative poverty is a state of poverty that occurs when we compare ourselves to those around us. (30)

repertoire is the second element of a social movement. (7)

Republican Party is a political party in the United States that supports a decreased regulation of private institutions and reduced government involvement communicate with the larger society. (104)

research methods are scientific procedures that sociologists use to conduct research and develop knowledge about a particular topic. (12)

residual poverty refers to chronic and multigenerational poverty. (30)

residual welfare is a temporary system of relief when a person's job or family has failed to be enough to support them. (33)

restorative justice is a model of punishment that strives to restore the bond between perpetrator and society. (202)

retreatism is the response of a person who has given up trying to achieve the goals of society because he or she believes that the means to those goals have no merit. (149)

retribution is a model of criminal sentencing predicated upon a felt need for revenge. (202)

rule of 70 estimates doubling time by dividing 70 by the annual rate of natural increase for a population. (260)

rural is a term used when referring to the countryside. (224)

scapegoat means making an unfair accusation against a person or group as the cause of a problem. (42)

schizophrenia is a mental disorder with symptoms including hallucinations, delusions, disordered thinking, movement disorders, flat affect, social withdrawal, and cognitive deficits. (132)

segmented assimilation is the idea that there is more than one way to adopt a new land and become economically and social successful. (50)

segregation is the process by which racial or ethnic groups are kept separate from one another. (49)

sex is the biological makeup of males or females, especially in regard to their reproductive organs and physical structures; refers also to activities that lead to sexual gratification and the possibility of reproduction. (56)

sex tourism is the act of people from wealthy nations traveling to less developed countries for sexual acts that may or may not be illegal in their home nation. (171)

sexism is the belief that one sex is superior to the other. (58)

sexual orientation refers to an enduring pattern of emotional, romantic, and/or sexual attractions to men, women, or both sexes. (157)

shaming is a deliberate effort to attach a negative meaning to a behavior. (196)

sick role is the expected behaviors and responsibilities appropriate for someone who is ill. (134)

social conflict theories typically focus on issues of social class, power, capitalism, and their relation to crime. (187)

social control theories suggest that people are self-interested, and these natural traits can prompt criminal activity. (187)

social disorganization theory proposes that poor neighborhoods with weak social institutions have higher rates of crime. (186)

social epidemiology is the study of the distribution of diseases and health throughout a society's population. (129)

social institutions are organizations that provide a framework for individuals to communicate with the larger society. (98)

social learning theory suggests that learning is the key component to criminality. (186)

social mobility is the ability to change social classes. (29)

social movements are activities that support or protest social issues organized by non-governmental organizations. (7)

social policies refer to deliberate attempts on the part of society to solve social problems. (16)

social problem is an issue that negatively affects a person's state of being in a society. (4)

social stratification is the ranking of people and the rewards they receive based on objective criteria, often including wealth, power, and/or prestige. (22)

socialism is an economic system by which resources and means of production are owned collectively by the citizens. (100)

sociology refers to a systematic and objective science that investigates human behavior in the social environment. (4)

sociological imagination is the ability to look beyond the individual as the cause for success and failure and see how one's society influences the outcome. (4)

specific deterrence is a type of criminal sentencing that seeks to prevent a particular offender from committing that crime again. (197)

spurious correlation occurs when two variables appear to be related, but actually have separate causes. (15)

stereotypes are simplified and extreme perceptions of an entire group of people that are usually based on false assumptions. (42)

stigmatized shame is a permanent label given to an offender. (197)

stimulants are a type of drug that excites the body and stimulates the brain and central nervous system. (143)

structural mobility is when social changes affect large numbers of people. (29)

structural oppression theories refer to the fact that women's oppression is rooted in capitalism; patriarchies keep women on the margins of the social world. (10)

structured sentencing is a model of criminal punishment in which the legislative system of a state enacts constraints on judicial discretion in determining criminal sentences. (198)

subjectivity refers to making judgments based on personal feelings and opinions rather than external facts. (5)

suburb is an area near a central city but beyond the political boundaries of that city. (226)

symbolic interactionism is a theoretical framework that focuses on how individual interactions between people influence their behavior and how these interactions can impact society. (9)

target hardening makes an objective less attractive to a possible criminal. (197)

tariffs are taxes placed on traded items. (102)

tax increment financing (TIF) is a program that enables cities to use tax revenues generated by a development project to help finance the construction of the new project through bonds given to developers and/or direct tax incentives. (234)

teacher expectancy effect is the impact of a teacher's expectations on a student's performance. (118)

technology consists of all processes, inventions, and methods used to advance society. (82)

terrorism is premeditated, politically motivated violence perpetrated against noncombatant targets by sub-national groups or clandestine agents. (291)

theory of anomie suggests that criminal activity results from an offender's inability to provide his or her desired needs by socially acceptable or legal means; therefore, the individual turns to socially unacceptable or illegal means to fulfill those desires. (186)

theories of gender oppression refer to a situation in which men purposefully maintain control over women through discrimination and the use of power, leading to oppression. (10)

threat is a cause of war stemming from an impending danger. (287)

Title IX is a 1972 educational amendment that prohibits the exclusion of any person from participation in an education program on the basis of gender. (63)

total fertility rate (TFR) is the average number of births expected from any woman in a population. (256)

totalitarianism is an authoritarian government that controls every aspect of citizens' lives. (103)

traditional systems are organizations in which social power is gained by respect for patterns of government. (102)

transgender refers to people whose gender identity or gender expression differs from that associated with their birth sex. (156)

transition is the second stage of becoming a prostitute and is the six-month period in which women try to rationalize their behavior as normal. (170)

transitional poverty refers to a temporary state of poverty that occurs when someone loses a job for a short time. (30)

transnational corporations operate in at least two countries and have the interests of their company at heart over the interests of their native land. (101)

triangulation is the process of using multiple approaches to study a phenomenon. (15)

"truth in sentencing" is legislation that is aimed at abolishing or limiting parole so that inmates serve a set majority of their sentence. (198)

underpopulation occurs when a species' population lives under the carrying capacity, resulting in abundant resources. (271)

unemployed describes people who do not have a job but have actively looked for work in the prior four weeks and are currently available for employment. (101)

Uniform Crime Reports (UCR) include data from official police statistics of reported crimes gathered from police reports and paperwork. (182)

upper or **elite class** is a social class that is very small in number and holds significant wealth. (26)

upper middle class is a social class that consists of high-income members of society who are well educated but do not belong to the elite membership of the super wealthy. (26)

urban is a term used when referring to a city. (224)

urban renewal is the process of purchasing, clearing, and replacing run-down properties with newer, more appealing developments. (233)

urban sprawl is the spreading of a city and its neighboring suburban areas over rural land along the borders of the metro area. (227)

urban underclass is a social class living in disadvantaged neighborhoods that are characterized by four components: poverty, family disruption, male unemployment, and lack of individuals in high-status occupations. (27)

urbanization is a process by which individuals or groups migrate from rural areas to urban areas. (224)

values are a part of a society's nonmaterial culture that represent cultural standards by which we determine what is good, bad, right, or wrong. (6)

vertical mobility refers to moving from one social status to another. (29)

violent crime is an illegal act committed against another person. (182)

voluntary immigration is the willing movement of people from one society to another. (44)

voter apathy is a phenomenon in which citizens with the right to vote choose not to. (104)

war is a violent conflict between groups that are organized for such conflict. (286)

wealth is all of an individual's material possessions, including income. (22)

white flight is the departure of Caucasian individuals from neighborhoods increasingly or predominantly populated by minorities. (228)

working class is a social class generally made up of people with a high school diploma and a lower level of education. (26)

WUNC refers to worthiness, unity, numbers, and commitments, which are the characteristics shown by members of a social movement. (7)

zero population growth is a TFR of two, meaning that each woman has two children to replace the mother and father. (256)

ENDNOTES

CHAPTER 1

1. "Is society really broken?" *The Times*, July 14, 2008, http://www.timesonline.co.uk/tol/comment/leading_article/article4326945.ece.

2. American Sociological Association, "Ethics," Accessed February 21, 2006, http://www.asanet.org/page.ww?section=Ethics&name=Ethics.

3. C.W. Mills, *The Sociological Imagination*. New York: Oxford, 1959.

4. United States Department of Labor, Bureau of Labor Statistics, "Economic News Release: Employment Situation Summary," Accessed May 31, 2009, http://www.bls.gov/news.release/empsit.nr0.htm.

5. United States Department of Labor, Bureau of Labor Statistics, "Economic News Release: Mass Layoffs Summary," Accessed May 31, 2009, http://www.bls.gov/news.release/mmls.nr0.htm.

6. W.T. Gallo, E.H. Bradley, and S.V. Kasl, "Health effects of job loss among older workers: Findings from the health and retirement survey," *Association for Health Services Research*, 1999. 16: 388.

7. C.W. Mills, *The Sociological Imagination*. New York: Oxford, 1959.

8. H. Zinn, *People's History of the United States*. New York: Harper Perennial, 1980.

9. R.M. Williams, *American Society: A Sociological Interpretation*. New York: Knopf, 1970.

10. F.J. McVeigh and L. Wolfer, *A brief history of social problems: A critical thinking approach*. Lanham, MD: University Press of America, 2004.

11. C. Tilly, *From Mobilization to Revolution*. Reading, MA: Addison-Wesley, 1978.

12. Jonathan Turner, Leonard Beeghley, and Charles H. Powers, *The Emergence of Sociological Theory*. Albany, NY: Wadsworth Publishing Company, 1998.

13. Emile Durkheim, *The Division of Labor in Society*. New York: Free Press, 1997.

14. Talcott Parsons, *The Social System*. Glencoe, IL: The Free Press, 1951.

15. Ibid.

16. Ibid.

17. W.E.B. Du Bois, "The Philadelphia Negro: A Social Study," in *Readings in Social Theory: The Classical Tradition to Post-Modernism*. New York: McGraw-Hill, 2004.

18. John Bellamy Foster, "The End of Rational Capitalism," *Monthly Review*, 2005. http://findarticles.com/p/articles/mi_m1132/is_10_56/ai_n16126168/pg_1?tag5artBody;col1.

19. Herbert Blumer, "Society as Symbolic Interaction," in *Human Behavior and Social Process: An Interactionist Approach*. Boston: Houghton-Mifflin, 1969.

20. Max Weber, "Class, Status, Party," in *Readings in Social Theory: The Classical Tradition to Post-Modernism*. New York: McGraw-Hill, 2004.

21. Factcheck.org, "Misstatement of the Union: The President Burnishes the State of the Union through Selective Facts and Strategic Omissions," Accessed July 15, 2009, http://factcheck.org/article 376.html#.

CHAPTER 2

1. Chris Bury and Shani Lewis, "In Tough Times, Lottery Offers Hope," *ABCNews.com*, November 12, 2008, http://abcnews.go.com/Business/Economy/story?id=6238473&page=1.

2. "State Governments and Lotteries," *Consumers' Research Magazine*, 1999. 82(8): 12–14.

3. National Gambling Impact Study Commission, "Lotteries," Accessed July 7, 2009, http://govinfo.library.unt.edu/ngisc/research/ lotteries.html.

4. William C. McConkey and William E. Warren, "Psychographic and demographic profiles of state lottery ticket purchasers," *The Journal of Consumer Affairs*, 1987. 21(2): 314–327.

5. Charles T. Clotfelter and Phillip Cook, "On the economics of state lotteries," *The Journal of Economic Perspectives*, 1990. 4(4): 105–119; "State Governments and Lotteries," *Consumers' Research Magazine*, 1999. 82(8): 12–14.

6. Philip Carl Salzman, "Is Inequality Universal?" *Current Anthropology*, 1999. 40: 31–61.

7. Sergio Diaz-Briquets and Jorge Perez-Lopez, *Corruption in Cuba: Castro and beyond*. Austin: University of Texas Press, 2006.

8. Carmen DeNavas-Walt, Bernadette D. Proctor, and Jessica C. Smith, *Current Population Reports, P60–235, Income, Poverty, and Health Insurance Coverage in the United States: 2007*. Washington, D.C.: U.S. Government Printing Office, 2008.

9. U.S. Census Bureau, "Current Population Survey, Annual Social and Economic Supplement, Table HINC-05: Percent Distribution of Households, by Selected Characteristics Within Income Quintile and Top 5 Percent in 2007," Accessed July 15, 2009, http://www.census.gov/hhes/www/macro/032008/hhinc/new05_000.htm.

10. Ibid.

11. Ibid.

12. Carmen DeNavas-Walt, Bernadette D. Proctor, and Jessica C. Smith, *Current Population Reports, P60–235, Income,*

Poverty, and Health Insurance Coverage in the United States: 2007. Washington, D.C.: U.S. Government Printing Office, 2008.

13. Carmen DeNavas-Walt, *Current Population Survey, Annual Social and Economic Supplements.* Washington, D.C.: Government Printing Office, 2006.

14. David Cay Johnson, *Perfectly Legal: The Covert Campaign to Rig Our Tax System to Benefit the Super Rich and Cheat Everybody Else.* New York: Penguin Group Inc., 2003.

15. Ibid.

16. Ibid.

17. Ibid.

18. Ibid.

19. Max Weber, *Readings in Social Theory: The classical tradition to post-modernism.* New York: McGraw-Hill, 2004.

20. Lawrence Mishel, Jared Bernstein, and Sylvia Allegretto, *State of working America 2006/2007.* Ithaca, NY: Cornell University Press, 2007.

21. Mark Haugaard, "Reflections on seven ways of creating power," *European Journal of Social Theory,* 2003. 6(1): 87–113.

22. Elia Kacapyr, "Are You Middle Class? Definitions and Trends of the U.S. Middleclass Households," *American Demographics,* 1996. 18: 30–36.

23. Austin Scaggs, "Paris Hilton," *Rolling Stone,* 2004. 964: 92–94.

24. G. William Domhoff, *Who Rules America?: Power and Politics.* New York: McGraw-Hill, 2002; G. William Domhoff, *The Higher Circles.* New York: Random House, 1970.

25. Harold R. Kerbo, *Social Stratification and Inequality: Class Conflict in Historical, Comparative and Global Perspective, 6th edition.* New York: McGraw-Hill, 2006.

26. Dennis Gilbert, *The American Class Structure in an Age of Growing Inequality.* Belmont, CA: Wadsworth, 2003.

27. Ibid.

28. Ibid.

29. Ibid.

30. Carmen DeNavas-Walt, Bernadette D. Proctor, and Cheryle Hill Lee, "Income, Poverty and Heath Insurance Coverage in the United States: 2005," *Current Population Reports,* 2007. http://www.census.gov/prod/2004pubs/p60–226.pdf.

31. Ibid.

32. Ibid.

33. Ibid.

34. Ibid.

35. Catherine E. Ross, John Reynolds, and Karlyn Geis, "The Contingent Meaning of Neighborhood Stability for Residents' Psychological Well-being," *American Sociological Review,* 2000. 65: 581–597.

36. Jeanne Brooks-Gunn, Greg Duncan, Pamela Klebanove, and Naomi Sealand, "Do Neighborhoods Influence Child and Adolescent Development?" *American Journal of*

Sociology, 1993. 99: 353–395; Catherine L. Garner and Stephen W. Raudenbush, "Neighborhood Effects on Educational Attainment: A Multilevel Analysis," *Sociology of Education,* 1991. 64: 251–262; Gary Solon, Marianne Page, and Greg J. Duncan, "Correlations Between Neighboring Children and Their Subsequent Educational Attainment," *Review of Economics and Statistics,* 2000. 82: 383–393.

37. Jeanne Brooks-Gunn, Greg Duncan, Pamela Klebanove, and Naomi Sealand, "Do Neighborhoods Influence Child and Adolescent Development?" *American Journal of Sociology,* 1993. 99: 353–395.

38. Jonathan Kozol, *Savage Inequalities: Children in America's Schools.* New York: Crown Publishers Inc., 1991.

39. Vincent Roscigno, Donald Tomaskovic-Devey, and Martha Crowley, "Education and the Inequalities of Place," *Social Forces,* 2006. 84: 2121–2145.

40. Carmen DeNavas-Walt, Bernadette D. Proctor, and Jessica C. Smith, *Current Population Reports, P60-235, Income, Poverty, and Health Insurance Coverage in the United States: 2007.* Washington, D.C.: U.S. Government Printing Office, 2008.

41. Ibid.

42. Ibid.

43. Ibid.

44. White House, "Working Toward Independence," Accessed March 11, 2007, http://www.whitehouse.gov/news/releases/2002/02/welfare-reform-announcement-book.pdf.

45. Molly A. Martin, "Family Structure and Income Inequality in Families with Children, 1976 to 2000," *Demography,* 2006. 43(3): 421–445.

46. Ibid.

47. Jonathan Kozol, *Savage Inequalities: Children in America's Schools.* New York: Crown Publishers Inc., 1991.

48. Ibid.

49. Frank J. McVeigh and Loreen Wolfer, *Brief History of Social Problems: A Critical Thinking Approach.* Lanham, MD: University Press of America, 2004.

50. Ibid.

51. Ibid.

52. Ibid.

53. Ibid.

54. Ibid.

55. Ibid.

56. U.S. Department of Health & Human Services, "Frequently Asked Questions Related to the Poverty Guidelines and Poverty," Accessed July 15, 2008, http://aspe.hhs.gov/poverty/faq.shtml.

57. U.S. Department of Health and Human Services, "The Development and History of the U.S. Poverty Thresholds—A Brief Overview," Accessed July 15, 2009, http://aspe.hhs.gov/poverty/papers/hptgssiv.htm.

58. Ibid.

59. Carmen DeNavas-Walt, Bernadette D. Proctor, and Cheryle Hill Lee, "Income, Poverty and Heath Insurance Coverage in the United States: 2005," *Current Population Reports*, 2007. http://www.census.gov/prod/2004pubs/p60-226.pdf.

60. United States Department of Health and Human Services, "Special Populations of American Homeless," Accessed July 15, 2008, http://aspe.hhs.gov/progsys/homeless/symposium/2-Spclpop.htm.

61. Glenn Firebaugh and Brian Goesling, "Accounting for the Recent Decline in Global Income Inequality," *The American Journal of Sociology*, 2004. 110(2): 283-312.

62. Ibid.

63. Kingsley Davis and Wilbert E. Moore, "Some Principles of Stratification," *American Sociological Review*, 1944. 10: 242-249.

64. William Ryan, *Blaming the Victim, revised edition*. New York: Vintage Books, 1976.

65. William Julius Wilson, *More Than Just Race: Being Black and Poor in the Inner City*. New York: W.W. Norton and Company Inc., 2009.

66. Kathryn Edin and Laura Lein, "Stratification Processes: Women, Work, and Wages: Work, Welfare, and Single Mothers' Economic Survival Strategies," *American Sociological Review*, 1997. 62: 253-266.

67. "Dethroning the Welfare Queen: The Rhetoric of Reform," *Harvard Law Review*, 1994. 107: 2013-2030.

68. Kathryn Edin and Laura Lein, "Stratification Processes: Women, Work, and Wages: Work, Welfare, and Single Mothers' Economic Survival Strategies," *American Sociological Review*, 1997. 62: 253-266.

69. U.S. Department of Labor, Bureau of Labor Statistics, "Characteristics of Minimum Wage Workers: 2008," Accessed July 9, 2009, http://www.bls.gov/cps/minwage2008.htm.

70. Marjorie E. Kornhauser, "The Rhetoric of the Anti-Progressive Income Tax Movement: A Typical Male Reaction," *Michigan Law Review*, 1987. 86(3): 465-523.

71. "Warren Buffett: The Rich Need to Pay More Taxes," *ABCNews.com*, November 15, 2007, http://abcnews.go.com/GMA/story?id=3869458&page=1.

72. Marjorie E. Kornhauser, "The Rhetoric of the Anti-Progressive Income Tax Movement: A Typical Male Reaction," *Michigan Law Review*, 1987. 86(3): 465-523.

73. Ibid.

74. "Warren Buffett: The Rich Need to Pay More Taxes," *ABCNews.com*, November 15, 2007, http://abcnews.go.com/GMA/story?id=3869458 &page=1.

CHAPTER 3

1. Alan Fram, "'Mutts Like Me' - Obama Shows Ease Discussing Race," *ABC News*, November 8, 2008, http://abcnews.go.com/Politics/wireStory?id=6211371.

2. Jack E. White, Tamala M. Edwards, Elaine Lafferty, and Sylvestor Monroe, "I'm Just Who I Am," *Time.com*, May 5, 1997, http://www.time.com/time/magazine/article/0,9171,986278-2,00.html.

3. Ibid.

4. Joseph L. Graves, *The Race Myth: Why We Pretend Race Exists in America*. New York: Penguin, 2004.

5. PBS.org, "RACE - The Power of an Illusion," Accessed May 12, 2009, http://www.pbs.org/race/000_General/000_00-Home.htm.

6. U.S. Census Bureau, "Race," Accessed August 14, 2008, http://factfinder.census.gov/home/en/epss/glossary_r.html.

7. Social Explorer, "Demographic Reports," Accessed June 8, 2009, http://www.socialexplorer.com/pub/reportdata/htmlresults.aspx?ReportId=R5940229.

8. Louis Wirth, "The Problem of Minority Groups," in *The Science of Man in the World Crisis*. New York: Columbia University Press, 1945.

9. U.S. Census Bureau, "Population Projections," Accessed May 12, 2009, www.census.gov/ipc/www/usinterimproj.

10. Jeffrey Gettleman and Kennedy Abwao, "U.S. Envoy calls some Kenya violence Ethnic Cleansing," *New York Times*, January 31, 2008; James Hider, "Ethnic cleansing claim as Iraqi hostages found dead," *The Times*, April 21, 2005.

11. Kevin Merida, "Racist Incidents Give Some Obama Campaigners Pause," *The Washington Post*, May 13, 2008, http://www.washington post.com/wp-dyn/content/article/2008/05/12/ AR2008051203014.html?sid=ST2008051301359.

12. Southern Poverty Law Center, "Active U.S. Hate Groups," Accessed April 28, 2009, http://www.splcenter.org/intel/map/hate.jsp.

13. Teresa Watanabe and Christi Parsons, "Marking Armenian genocide, many feel snubbed by Obama," *LATimes.com*, April 25, 2009, http://www.latimes.com/news/local/la-me-armenians25-2009apr25,0,235730.story.

14. Jonathan Kozol, *Savage Inequalities: Children in America's Schools*. New York: Harper Publishing Co., 1991.

15. William J. Wilson, *More Than Just Race; Being Black and Poor in the Inner City*. New York: W.W. Norton, 2009.

16. PBS.org, "Fenceline," Accessed May 15, 2009, http://www.pbs.org/pov/pov2002/fenceline/.

17. John Dollard, *Frustration and Aggression*. New Haven, CT: Yale University Press, 1939.

18. M. Brewster Smith, "The Authoritarian Personality: A Re-review 46 Years Later," *Political Psychology*, 1997. 18(1): 159-163; John Levi Martin, "The Authoritarian Personality, 50 Years Later: What Lessons Are There for Political Psychology?" *Political Psychology*, 2001. 22(1): 1-26.

19. Ellis Cose, *The Rage of the Privilege Class*. New York: HarperCollins, 1993.

20. Corcoran, Mary, "Rags to Rags: Poverty and Mobility in the United States," *Annual Review of Sociology*, 1995. 21: 237-267.

21. NPR.org, "Income Gap Between Blacks, Whites Expands," Accessed May 12, 2009, http://www.npr.org/templates/story/story.php?storyId=16293332.

22. U.S. Census Bureau, "The Big Payoff: Educational Attainment and Synthetic Estimates of Work-Life Earnings," Accessed June 5, 2009, http://www.census.gov/prod/2002pubs/p23-210.pdf.

23. National Center for Education Statistics, "Fast Facts," Accessed April 28, 2009, http://nces.ed.gov/FastFacts/display.asp?id=61.

24. Martin N. Marger, *Race and Ethnic Relations: American and Global Perspectives.* Belmont, CA: Wadsworth Publishing, 1997.

25. Roger Waldinger, *Still the Promised City? New Immigrants and African Americans in Post Industrial New York.* Cambridge, MA: Harvard University Press, 1996.

26. Alejandro Portes and Ruben Rumbaut, *Immigrant America: A portrait.* Los Angeles: University of California Press, 1996.

27. Ibid.

28. Ibid.

29. Ibid.

30. Shelly Lowe, "Census Bureau Data Show Characteristics of the U.S. Foreign-Born Population," *U.S. Census Bureau News*, February 19, 2009, http://www.census.gov/Press-Release/www/releases/archives/american_community_survey_acs/013308.html.

31. George Mason University's History News Network, "What's Scary About the Anti-Immigration Debate," Accessed May 12, 2009, http://hnn.us/articles/40316.html.

32. European-American Unity and Rights Organization, "European-American Unity and Rights Organization (EURO) Principles," Accessed May 12, 2009, http://www.whitecivilrights.com/?page_id=7.

33. NumbersUSA, "'No' to Immigrant Bashing," Accessed May 12, 2009, http://www.numbersusa.com/content/learn/about-us/no-immigrant-bashing/no-immigrant-bashing.html.

34. Elizabeth Arias, PhD, "United States Life Tables, 2004," *Centers for Disease Control National Vital Statistics Reports*, 2007. 56(9): http://www.cdc.gov/nchs/data/nvsr/nvsr56/nvsr56_09.pdf.

35. Jonathan Kozol, *Savage Inequalities: Children in America's Schools.* New York: Harper Publishing Co., 1991.

36. Ibid; Philip Kasinitz, John Mollenkopf, and Mary C. Waters, "Becoming American/Becoming New Yorkers: Immigrant Incorporation in a Majority Minority City," *International Migration Review*, 2002. 36(4): 1020-1036; Mary C. Waters and Karl Eschbach, "Immigration and Ethnic and Racial Inequality in the United States," *Annual Review of Sociology*, 1995. 21: 419-446; Grace Kao and Jennifer S. Thompson, "Racial and Ethnic Stratification in Educational Achievement and Attainment," *Annual Review of Sociology*, 2003. 29: 417-443; Yolanda Padilla, Jason D. Boradman, Robert A. Hummer, and Marilyn Espitia, "Is the Mexican American 'Epidemiological Paradox' Advantage at Birth Maintained Through Early Childhood?" *Social Forces*, 2002. 80(3): 1101-1123; Rory McVeigh, "Structured Ignorance and Organized Racism in the United States," *Social Forces*, 2004. 82(3): 895-936; Ronald Weitzer and Steven A. Tuch, "Race and Perceptions of Police Misconduct," *Social Problems*, 2004. 51(3): 305-325.

37. Eduardo Bonilla-Silva, "The Linguistics of Color Blind Racism: How to Talk Nasty about Blacks Without Sounding 'Racist,'" *Critical Sociology*, 2002. 28(1-2): 41-64.

38. Lawrence Bobo, James R. Kluegel, and Ryan A. Smith, "Laissez Faire Racism: The Crystallization of a Kinder, Gentler, Antiblack Ideology," in *Racial Attitudes in the 1990's.* Westport, CT: Praeger 1997.

39. William J. Wilson, *More Than Just Race; Being Black and Poor in the Inner City.* New York: W.W. Norton, 2009.

40. Catherine Donaldson-Evans, "Elton John: 'American Idol' Is Racist," *FOXNews.com*, April 28, 2004, http://www.foxnews.com/story/0,2933,118432,00.html.

41. Christopher Rocchio, "'American Idol' producer says calling the show racist is 'idiotic,'" *Reality TV World*, March 27, 2007, http://www.realitytvworld.com/news/american-idol-producer-says-calling-show-racist-is-idiotic-4915.php.

42. W.E.B. DuBois, *The Souls of Black Folk.* New York: Penguin, 1996.

43. Craig St. John and Tamara Hearld-Moore, "Fear of Black Strangers," *Social Science Research*, 1995. 24(3): 262-280.

44. Patricia Hill Collins, *Black Feminist Thought.* New York: Routledge, 1990; Darlene Clark Hine, "In the Kingdom of Culture: Black Women and the Intersection of Race, Gender, and Class," in *Lure and Loathing: Essays on Race, Identity and the Ambivalence of Assimilation.* New York: Penguin Press, 1993.

45. Douglas Massey and Nancy Denton, *American Apartheid: Segregation and the Making of the Underclass.* Cambridge MA: Harvard University Press, 1993.

46. U.S. Department of Housing and Urban Development, Office of Fair Housing and Equal Opportunity, "About FHEO," Accessed April 28, 2009, http://www.hud.gov/offices/fheo/aboutfheo/aboutfheo.cfm.

47. U.S. Customs and Border Protection, "About CBP," Accessed April 28, 2009, http://www.cbp.gov/xp/cgov/about/.

48. The 'Lectric Law Library, "ACLU Briefing Paper Number 6: 'English Only,'" Accessed August 12, 2008, http://www.lectlaw.com/files/con09.htm.

49. David Wallace Adams, *Education for extinction: American Indians and the Boarding School Experience.* Lawrence, KS: University of Kansas Press, 1995.

50. Alejandro Portes and Rueben G. Rumbaut, *Immigrant America.* Berkeley CA: University of California Press, 1996; Alejandro Portes and Alex Stepick, *City on the edge: The transformation of Miami.* Berkeley, CA: University of California Press, 1993.

51. U.S. Census Bureau, "Population Projections," Accessed May 12, 2009, http://www.census.gov/ipc/www/usinterimproj.

52. American Civil Liberties Union, "CA's Anti-Immigrant Proposition 187 is Voided, Ending State's Five-Year Battle with ACLU, Rights Groups," Accessed May 12, 2009, http://www.aclu.org/immigrants/gen/11652prs1999 0729.html.

53. Media Matters for America, "Buchanan said immigration will cause the 'complete balkanization of America' create 'a giant Kosovo in the Southwest,'" Accessed May 12, 2009, http://mediamatters.org/items/200606060011.

CHAPTER 4

1. S. Alfonsi, J. Shaylor, and J. Brady, "Public Service Ads Get More Graphic: Actress Keira Knightley Stars in Shocking Ad Against Domestic Abuse," *ABCNews.com*, April 3, 2009, http://abcnews.go.com/GMA/story?id=7245548& page=1.

2. K. Keenan and D. Shaw, "Developmental and social influences on young girls' early problem behavior," *Psychological Bulletin*, 1997. 121(1): 95–113.

3. L. Serbin, D. Poulin-Doubis, K. Colburne, M. Sen, and J. Eichsted, "Gender stereotyping in infancy: Vision preferences for knowledge of gender stereotyped toys in the second year," *International Journal of Behavioral Development*, 2001. 25: 7–15.

4. K. Keenan and D. Shaw, "Developmental and social influences on young girls' early problem behavior," *Psychological Bulletin*, 1997. 121(1): 95–113.

5. J.S. Hagan and A.R. Gillis, "Class in the household: A power-control theory of gender and delinquency," *American Journal of Sociology*, 1987. 92: 788–816.

6. C. West and D.H. Zimmerman, "Doing Gender," *Gender and Society*, 1987. 1(2): 125–151.

7. Ibid.

8. Ibid; M.A. Messner, "Barbie Girls versus Sea Monsters: Children Constructing Gender," *Gender and Society*, 2000. 14(6): 765–784.

9. World Health Organization, "Female Genital Mutilation," Accessed July 28, 2008, http://www.who.int/mediacentre/factsheets/fs241/en.

10. Liverpool Local News, "I Saw Horror of Girl Mutilation," Accessed July 15, 2009, http://www.liverpoolecho.co.uk/liverpool-news/local-news/2008/02/07/i-saw-horror-of-girl-mutilation-100252-20446072/.

11. World Health Organization, "Female Genital Mutilation," Accessed July 28, 2008, http://www.who.int/mediacentre/factsheets/fs241/en/.

12. Ibid.

13. Ibid.

14. Ibid.

15. IMDb.com, "Biography for Fatima Siad," Accessed June 12, 2009, http://www.imdb.com/name/nm2923869/bio.

16. P. Constable, "Afghan Law Ignites Debate on Religion, Sex," *The Washington Post*, April 11, 2009, http://www.washingtonpost.com/wp-dyn/content/article/2009/04/10/AR2009041003638.html.

17. U.S. Census Bureau, "Historical Income Tables—People," Accessed June 24, 2009, http://www.census.gov/hhes/www/income/histinc/p16.html.

18. M.G. Durham, *The Lolita Effect: The Media Sexualization of Young Girls and What We Can Do About It*. Woodstock, NY: The Overlook Press, 2008.

19. Ibid.

20. M.K. Underwood, *Social Aggression Among Girls*. New York: The Guilford Press, 2003.

21. M. Mead, *Sex and Temperament*. New York: Harper Perennial, 1935.

22. Ibid.

23. D. Freeman, *Margaret Mead and Samoa: The Making and Unmaking of an Anthropological Myth*. Cambridge, MA: Harvard University Press, 1983.

24. G.P. Murdock, "Comparative Data on the Division of Labor by Sex," *Social Forces*, 1937. 15: 551–553.

25. A. Roberts and A. Klosowska, *Violence against Women in Medieval Texts*. Gainesville, FL: University of Florida Press, 1998.

26. F.J. McVeigh and L. Wolfer, *Brief History of Social Problems: A Critical Thinking Approach*. Lanham, MD: University Press of America, 2004.

27. University of Miami, "Bell Hooks," Accessed June 12, 2009, http://www.education.miami.edu/ep/contemporaryed/Bell_Hooks/bell_hooks.html.

28. U.S. Census Bureau, "Educational Attainment in the United States: 2008," Accessed July 22, 2009, http://www.census.gov/population/www/socdemo/education/cps2008.html.

29. S. Brzuzy and A. Lind, *Battleground: Women, Gender, and Sexuality*. Santa Barbara, CA: Greenwood Publishing Group, 2007.

30. C. Lukas, "A Bargain At 77 Cents To a Dollar," *The Washington Post*, April 3, 2007, http://www.washingtonpost.com/wp-dyn/content/article/2007/04/02/AR2007040201262.html.

31. Social Explorer, "American Community Survey 2007," Accessed July 22, 2009, http://www.socialexplorer.com/pub/reportdata/htmlresults.aspx?ReportId=R5402380.

32. S.J. Correll, S. Benard, and I. Paik, "Getting a Job: Is There a Motherhood Penalty?" *American Journal of Sociology*, 2007. 112(5): 1297–1338.

33. Congress.org, "Demographics: Gender," Accessed November 13, 2009, http://www.congress.org/congressorg/directory/demographics.tt?catid=gend.

34. The American Political Science Association, "Women Voters and the Gender Gap," Accessed June 12, 2009, http://www.apsanet.org/content_5270.cfm.

35. U.S. Department of Commerce, "Gender and Aging," Accessed July 22, 2009, http://www.census.gov/ipc/prod/ib98-2.pdf.

36. N. Martin, "In Heart Attack, Gender Matters," *ABCNews.com*, December 8, 2008, http://abcnews.go.com/Health/HeartDisease News/story?id=6420282& page=1.

37. T. Parsons, "Age and Sex in the Social Structure of the United States," *American Sociological Review*, 1942. 7(5): 604–616.

38. U.S. Department of Justice, "Extent, Nature, and Consequences of Intimate Partner Violence," http://www.ncjrs.gov/pdffiles1/nij/181867.pdf.

39. DomesticViolence.org, "Violence Wheel," Accessed July 22, 2009, http://www.domesticviolence.org/violence-wheel/.

40. National Women's Law Center, "Title IX and Women's Athletic Opportunity: A Nation's Promise Yet to be Fulfilled," http://www.nwlc.org/pdf/Nation's%20Promise%20July%202008.pdf.

41. Ibid.

42. Ibid.

43. Ibid.

44. Ibid.

CHAPTER 5

1. Dave Carpenter, "Laboring Longer a Growing Trend for Americans," *The Associated Press*, September 1, 2008, http://www.usatoday.com/money/economy/2008-09-01-3794114560_x.htm.

2. Gina Kolata, "So Big And Healthy Grandpa Wouldn't Even Know You," *The New York Times*, July 30, 2006, http://www.nytimes.com/2006/07/30/health/30age.html.

3. U.S. Census Bureau, "Grandparents Living with Grandchildren," Accessed June 14, 2009, http://www.census.gov/prod/2003 pubs/c2kbr-31.pdf.

4. U.S. Census Bureau, "An Older And More Diverse Nation by Mid-century," Accessed June 11, 2009, http://www.census.gov/press-release/www/releases/archives/population/012496.html.

5. Ibid.

6. Centers for Disease Control and Prevention, "Life expectancy at birth, at 65 years of age, and at 75 years of age, by race and sex: United States, selected years 1900–2005," Accessed August 14, 2009, http://www.cdc.gov/nchs/data/hus/hus08.pdf#026.

7. The White House, "About the White House: Presidents," Accessed August 14, 2009, http://www.whitehouse.gov/about/presidents/thomasjefferson/.

8. Dave Carpenter, "Laboring Longer a Growing Trend for Americans," *The Associated Press*, September 1, 2008, http://www.usatoday. com/money/economy/2008-09-01-3794114560_x.htm.

9. American Society of Plastic Surgeons, "2008 Quick Facts," http://www.plasticsurgery.org/Media/stats/2008-quick-facts-cosmetic-surgery-minimally-invasive-statistics.pdf.

10. "Recession means even cheaper reality shows," *The Associated Press*, April 7, 2009, http://www.msnbc.msn.com/id/30093190/.

11. Palmore Erdman, "Ageism," in *Social Gerontology*. Westport, CT: Auburn House, 1998.

12. Thomas R. Cole, *The Journey on Life: A Cultural History of Aging in America.* New York: Cambridge University Press, 1992.

13. Ibid.

14. Ibid.

15. J.S. McKinlay and S. McKinlay, "The Questionable Contribution of Medical Measures to the Decline of Mortality in the United States in the Twentieth Century," *Milbank Quarterly*, 1977. 55(3): 405–428.

16. Thomas McKeown, "Fertility, Mortality and Causes of Death: An examination of issues related to the modern rise of population," *Population Studies*, 1978. 32(3): 535–542.

17. Central Intelligence Agency, "Life Expectancy at Birth," Accessed August 17, 2009, https://www.cia.gov/library/publications/the-world-factbook/fields/2102.html?countryName=World& countryCode=xx&regionCode=oc&#xx.

18. BBC News, "Zimbabweans have 'shortest lives'," Accessed June 11, 2009, http://news.bbc.co.uk/2/hi/africa/4890508.stm.

19. Ibid.

20. Sheila Hoban and Kathleen Kearney, "Elder Abuse and Neglect," *The American Journal of Nursing*, 2000. 100(11): 49–50; Karl Pillemer and David Finkelhor, "The Prevalence of Elder Abuse: A Random Sample Survey," *Gerontologist*, 1988. 28: 51–57.

21. Sandra Sayles-Cross, "Profile of Familial Elder Abuse: A Selected Review Of The Literature," *Journal of Community Health Nursing*. 5(4).

22. Ibid.

23. Ronald J. Manheimer, *Older Americans Almanac: A reference work on seniors in the United States.* Detroit: Gale Research, 1994.

24. Ciaran O'Neill, Charlene Harrington, Martin Kitchener, and Debra Saliba, "Quality of Care in Nursing Homes: An Analysis of Relationships Among Profit, Quality, and Ownership," *Medical Care*, 2003. 41(12): 1318–1330.

25. AARP Public Policy Institute, "The 1987 Nursing Home Reform Act," Accessed June 11, 2009, http://www.aarp.org/research/legis-polit/legislation/aresearch-import-687-fs84.html.

26. Nicholas G. Castle, "Nursing Homes with Persistent Deficiency Citations for Physical Restraint," *Medical Care*, 2002. 40(10): 868–878.

27. Vincent Mor, Gerry Hendershot, and Cynthia Cryan, "Awareness of Hospice Services: Results of a National Survey," *Public Health Reports, Association of Schools of Public Health*, 1989. 104(2): 178–183.

28. J. Lynn, J. Teno, R. Phillips, A. Wu, N. Desbiens, et al., "Perceptions by Family Members of the Dying Experience of Older and Seriously Ill Patients," *Annals of Internal Medicine*, 1997. 126(2): 97–106.

29. Ibid.

30. Elaine Cumming, Lois R. Dean, David S. Newell, and Isabel McCaffrey, "Disengagement—A tentative theory of aging," *Sociometry*, 1960. 23: 23–35.

31. Ibid.

32. Elaine Cumming and William E. Henry, *Growing old, the process of disengagement.* New York: Basic Books, 1961.

33. Robert Crosnoe and Glen H. Elder, Jr., "Successful Adaptation in the Later Years: A Life Course Approach to Aging," *Social Psychology Quarterly*, 2002. 65: 309–328.

34. Jaber F. Gubrium and James A. Holstein, *Aging And Everyday Life.* Malden, MA: Blackwell Publishers Ltd, 2000.

35. Dave Carpenter, "Laboring Longer a Growing Trend for Americans," *The Associated Press*, September 1, 2008, http://www.usatoday.com/money/economy/2008-09-01-3794114560_x.htm.

36. Robert C. Atchley, "A continuity theory of normal aging," *The Gerontologist*, 1989. 29(2): 183–190.

37. Robert C. Atchley, "Continuity, Spiritual Growth, and Coping in Later Adulthood," *Journal of Religion, Spirituality & Aging*, 2006. 18(2–3): 19–29.

38. Dave Carpenter, "Laboring Longer a Growing Trend for Americans," *The Associated Press*, September 1, 2008, http://www.usatoday.com/money/economy/2008-09-01-3794114560_x.htm.

39. Ibid.

40. Soleman H. Abu-Bader, Anissa Rogers, and Amanda S. Barusch, "Predictors Of Life Satisfaction In Frail Elderly," *Journal Of Gerontological Socialwork*, 2002. 38: 3–17.

41. Social Security Administration, "Social Security's Future: FAQs," Accessed June 16, 2009, http://www.ssa.gov/qa/htm.

42. U.S. Census Bureau, "An Older and More Diverse Nation by Mid-century," Accessed June 16, 2009, http://www.census.gov/press-release/www/releases/archives/population/012496.html.

43. Social Security Administration, "Social Security's Future: FAQs," Accessed June 16, 2009, http://www.ssa.gov/qa.htm.

44. U.S. Census Bureau, "World's Older Population Growing by Unprecedented 800,000 a Month," http://www.census.gov/pressrelease/www/releases/archives/aging_population/000370.html.

45. Social Security Administration, "Status of The Social Security and Medicare Programs," Accessed June 16, 2009, http://www.social security.gov/oact/trsum/trsummary.html.

46. Ibid.

47. Maurice A. M. de Wachter, "Euthanasia in The Netherlands," *The Hastings Center Report*, 1992. 22(2): 23–30.

48. Ibid.

49. Ibid.

50. Oregon.gov, "Records and Reports Data on the Act," Accessed June 18, 2009, http://oregon.gov/dhs/ph/pas/index.shtml.

51. Oregon.gov, "2008 Summary of Oregon's Death with Dignity Act," Accessed June 18, 2009, http://oregon.gov/DHS/ph/pas/docs/year11.pdf.

52. Washington State Department of Health, "Washington Death with Dignity Act Forms Received by Department of Health," Accessed June 18, 2009, http://www.doh.wa.gov/dwda/formsreceived.htm.

53. Death with Dignity National Center, "Poll: U.S. Adults Favor Euthanasia and Physician Assisted Suicide," http://www.deathwithdignity.org/voices/opinion/harrispoll04.27.05.asp.

54. "Kevorkian released from prison after 8 years," *msnbc.com*, June 1, 2007, http://www.msnbc.msn.com/id/18974940/.

CHAPTER 6

1. Kinzie, Susan, "New Dean Will Leap Into Journalism's Reinvention," *The Washington Post*, March 1, 2009, http://www.washingtonpost.com/wp-dyn/content/article/2009/02/28/AR2009022801878.html.

2. Rudolf Stöber, "What Media Evolution Is: A Theoretical Approach to the History of New Media," *European Journal of Communication*, 2004. 19(4): 483–505.

3. Langdon Winner, "Trust and Terror: The vulnerability of complex socio-technical systems," *Science as Culture*, 2004. 13: 155–172.

4. George Ritzer, *The McDonaldization of Society: Revised New Century Edition.* Thousand Oaks, CA: Pine Forge Press, 2004.

5. Jean Piaget and Barbel Inhelder, *The Psychology of the Child.* New York: Basic Books, 2000.

6. Neil Postman, *Amusing Ourselves to Death: Public Discourse in the Age of Show Business.* New York: Penguin Books, 2005.

7. Neil Postman, *Technopoly: The Surrender of Culture to Technology.* New York: Vintage Books, 1993.

8. Andrew Murphie and John Potts, *Culture and Technology.* New York: Palgrave McMillian, 2003.

9. Federal Trade Commission, "2006 Identity Theft Survey Report," http://www.ftc.gov/os/2007/11/SynovateFinalReportIDTheft2006.pdf.

10. Miguel Helft, "Google Zooms In Too Close for Some," *The New York Times*, June 1, 2007, http://www.nytimes.com/2007/06/01/technology/01private.html.

11. Peter Sheridan Dodds, Roby Muhamad, and Duncan J. Watts, "An Experimental Study of Search in Global Social Networks," *Science*, 2003. 301(5634): 827–829.

12. Stanley Milgram, "The Small-World Problem," *Psychology Today*, 1967. 1: 61–67.

13. Richard Layard, *Happiness: Lessons from a new science.* Penguin Books, NY, 2005; Marshall McLuhan, *The Gutenberg*

Galaxy: The Making of Typographic Man. Toronto: University of Toronto Press, 1962.

14. Alan Boyle and Suzanne Choney, "Iran's Internet Battle Hits New Heights," *msnbc.com*, June 17, 2009, http://www.msnbc.msn.com/id/31411475/.

15. "Children, Adolescents, and Advertising," *Pediatrics*, 2006. 118: 2563–2569. http://pediatrics.aappublications.org/cgi/content/full/118/6/2563.

16. Richard Pace, "First-time Televiewing in Amazonia: Television Acculturation in Gurupa, Brazil," *Ethnology*, 1993. 32(2): 187.

17. William P. Eveland, Jr. and Dhavan V. Shah, "The Impact of Individual and Interpersonal Factors on Perceived News Media Bias," *Political Psychology*, 2003. 24(1): 101–117. http://www.jstor.org/stable/3792512.

18. Tawnya J. Adkins Covert and Philo C. Wasburn, "Measuring Media Bias: A Content Analysis of Time and Newsweek Coverage of Domestic Social Issues," *Social Science Quarterly*, 2007. 88(3): 1975–2000.

19. Christopher J. Kollmeyer, "Corporate Interests: How the News Media Portray the Economy," *Social Problems*, 2004. 51(3): 432–452. http://www.jstor.org/stable/4148754.

20. Daniel Sutter, "Advertising and Political Bias in the Media: The Market for Criticism of the Market Economy," *American Journal of Economics and Sociology*, 2002. 61(3): 725–745. http://www.jstor.org/stable/3487733.

21. James N. Druckman and Michael Parkin, "The Impact of Media Bias: How Editorial Slant Affects Voters," *The Journal of Politics*, 2005. 67(4): 1030–1049.

22. Gregory L. Bovitz, James N. Druckman, and Arthur Lupia, "When Can a News Organization Lead Public Opinion? Ideology Versus Market Forces in Decisions to Make News," *Public Choice*, 2002. 113(1): 127–155.

23. Philip N. Howard, "Deep Democracy, Think Citizenship: The Impact of Digital Media in Political Campaign Strategy," *Annals of the American Academy of Political and Social Science*, 2005. 597: 153–170.

24. Lyman Bryson, "The communication of ideas: a series of addresses," *New York: Institute for Religious and Social Studies*, 1948.

25. Ben Bagdikian, *The New Media Monopoly.* Boston: Beacon Press, 2004.

26. Edward S. Herman and Noam Chomsky, *Manufacturing Consent: The Political Economy of Mass Media.* New York: Pantheon Books, 1988.

27. Forbes.com, "The Celebrity 100," http://www.forbes.com/lists/2008/53/celebrities08_The-Celebrity-100_Rank.html.

28. Wheeloffortune.com, "Vanna White," http://www.wheeloffortune.com/showguide/bios/vannawhite/.

29. Ben Bagdikian, *The New Media Monopoly.* Boston: Beacon Press, 2004.

30. Ibid.

CHAPTER 7

1. Lori Montgomery, "Obama Team Touts Economic Plans," *The Washington Post*, March 14, 2009, http://www.washingtonpost.com/wp-dyn/content/article/2009/03/13/AR2009031301469.html.

2. *The New York Times*, "Breaking a Barrier to Lending," Accessed June 22, 2009, http://www.nytimes.com/interactive/2009/02/20/business/20090220-lend-graphic.html.

3. capitalism. (2009). In *Merriam-Webster Online Dictionary*. Accessed June 22, 2009, http://www.merriam-webster.com/dictionary/capitalism.

4. Leslie Sklair and Peter Robbins, "Global Capitalism and Major Corporations from the Third World," *Third World Quarterly*, 2002. 23(1): 81–100.

5. Courtney D. Von Hippel, "When People Would Rather Switch Than Fight: Outgroup Favoritism Among Temporary Employees," *Group Processes and Intergroup Relations*, 2006. 9(4): 533–546.

6. Ibid.

7. Charles H. Cooley, *Human Nature and the Social Order.* New York: Schocken Books, 1964.

8. IKEA, "Facts & Figures," http://www.ikea.com/ms/en_GB/about_ikea_new/facts_figures/index.html.

9. David Goldman, "Worst year for jobs since '45 Annual loss biggest since end of World War II," *CNNMoney.com*, January 9, 2009, http://money.cnn.com/2009/01/09/news/economy/jobs_december/index.htm.

10. United States Bureau of Labor Statistics, "Metropolitan Area Employment and Unemployment: June 2009," http://www.bls.gov/news.release/pdf/metro.pdf.

11. U.S. Bureau of Labor Statistics, "January 2008," *Employment & Earnings,* 2008. 55(1): http://www.bls.gov/opub/ee/empearn 200801.pdf.

12. U.S. Bureau of Labor Statistics, "January 2007," *Employment & Earnings,* 2007. 54(1): http://www.bls.gov/opub/ee/home.htm.

13. U.S. Bureau of Labor Statistics, "Labor Force Statistics from the Current Population Survey," Accessed June 23, 2009, http://www.bls.gov/cps/faq.htm#Ques5.

14. U.S. Department of Labor, "Self-employment rates, 1948–2003," http://www.bls.gov/opub/ted/2004/aug/wk4/art02.htm.

15. Wayne Parry, "Donald Trump's Casino Company Files for Bankruptcy," *Huffington Post,* February 17 2009, http://www.huffingtonpost.com/2009/02/17/donald-trumps-casino-comp_n_167474.html.

16. Patricia Thornton, "The Sociology of Entrepreneurship," *Annual Review of Sociology*, 1999. 25: 19–46.

17. *BBC News*, "King Fahd of Saudi Arabia dies," August 1, 2005, http://news.bbc.co.uk/2/hi/middle_east/4734175.stm.

18. Jane Perlez, "In Musharraf's Wake, U.S. Faces Political Disarray," *The New York Times*, August 18, 2008, http://www.nytimes.com/2008/08/19/world/asia/.

ENDNOTES

19. *BBC Online*, "Profile: Pervez Musharraf," August 18, 2008, http://news.bbc.co.uk/2/hi/south_asia/4797762.stm.

20. U.S. Census Bureau, "Voter Turnout Increases by 5 Million in 2008 Presidential Election, U.S. Census Bureau Reports Data Show Significant Increases Among Hispanic, Black and Young Voters," http://www.census.gov/Press-Release/www/releases/archives/voting/013995.html.

21. U.S. Census Bureau, "Voting And Registration," http://www.census.gov/population/www/socdemo/voting.html.

22. U.S. Census Bureau, "Voter Turnout Increases by 5 Million in 2008 Presidential Election, U.S. Census Bureau Reports Data Show Significant Increases Among Hispanic, Black and Young Voters," http://www.census.gov/Press-Release/www/releases/archives/voting/013995.html.

23. Ibid.

24. Anthony Faiola, "U.S. Signals New Era for Global Economy; Urging Nations to 'Pick Up the Pace,' Obama Says U.S. Cannot Go It Alone," *The Washington Post*, April 2, 2009.

25. Robert Dahl, *Who governs?* New Haven, CT: Yale University Press, 1961.

26. Richard H. Thaler and Cass R. Sunstein, *Nudge: Improving decisions about health, wealth, and happiness.* New Haven, CT: Yale University Press, 2008.

27. Amitai Etzioni, *The Spirit of Community: The Reinvention of American Society.* New York: Simon & Schuster, 1994.

28. Wright Mills, *The power elite: A new edition.* New York: Oxford University Press, 2000.

29. William G. Domhoff, *Who Rules America? Power, Politics, and Social Change.* New York: McGraw-Hill, 2006.

30. Federal Election Committee, "Major Provisions of the Bipartisan Campaign Reform Act of 2002," http://www.fec.gov/press/bkgnd/bcra_overview.shtml.

CHAPTER 8

1. Libby Quaid, "Study: Math Teachers a Chapter Ahead of Students," *ABC News,* November 25, 2008, http://abcnews.go.com/US/wireStory?id=6329327.

2. U.S. Department of Education, National Center for Education Statistics, "Fast Facts," Accessed August 26, 2009, http://nces.ed.gov/FastFacts/display.asp?id=16.

3. Frank J. McVeigh and Loreen Wolfer, *Brief History of Social Problems: A Critical Thinking Approach.* Lanham, MD: University Press of America, 2004.

4. Harvey Kantor and Robert Lowe, "Reflections on history and quality education," *Educational Researcher*, 2004. 33(5): 6–10.

5. Francisco O. Ramirez and John Boli, "The Political Construction of Mass Schooling: European Origins and Worldwide Institutionalization," *Sociology of Education,* 1987. 60: 2–17.

6. John Andrew Hostetler, *Amish Society.* Baltimore: The Johns Hopkins University Press, 1993.

7. Annette Hemmings, "The 'Hidden' Corridor Curriculum," *High School Journal*, 2000. 83(2): 1–10.

8. UNESCO Institute for Statistics, "Under-privileged Children Also Disadvantaged in the Classroom," http://www.uis.unesco.org/ev.php?ID57200_201&ID25DO_TOPIC.

9. UNESCO Institute for Statistics, "Literacy Rates," Accessed August 12, 2008, http://stats.uis.unesco.org/unesco/TableViewer/document.aspx?ReportId5121&IF_Language5eng&BR_Country 56940; The Central Intelligence Agency, "Sierra Leone," Accessed July 17, 2008, https://www.cia.gov/library/publications/the-world-factbook/print/sl.html.

10. Organisation for Economic Co-operation and Development, "OECD Briefing Note for the United States," http://www.oecd.org/dataoecd/22/51/39317423.pdf.

11. The Central Intelligence Agency, "Country Comparison: Education Expenditures," Accessed August 26, 2009, https://www.cia.gov/library/publications/the-world-factbook/rankorder/2206rank.html.

12. The Central Intelligence Agency, "Country Comparison: Education Expenditures," Accessed July 17, 2008, https://www.cia.gov/library/publications/the-world-factbook/print/sl.html.

13. Ibid.

14. NCHEMS Information Center, "Graduation Rates," Accessed August 26, 2009, http://www.higheredinfo.org/dbrowser/?level=nation&mode=graph&state=0&submeasure=27.

15. Thomas J. Tierney, "How Is American Higher Education Measuring Up? An Outsider's Perspective," in *American Higher Education: How Does it Measure Up for the 21st Century?* San Jose, CA: The National Center for Public Policy and Higher Education, 2006.

16. The Central Intelligence Agency, "Country Comparison: Education Expenditures," Accessed August 26, 2009, https://www.cia.gov/library/publications/the-world-factbook/rankorder/2206rank.html.

17. Institute of Educational Sciences, "Digest of Education Statistics: 2007," Accessed June 29, 2009, http://nces.ed.gov/programs/digest/d07/.

18. College Board, "2008–2009 College Prices," Accessed June 30, 2009, http://www.collegeboard.com/student/pay/add-it-up/4494.html.

19. Estia in Sweden, "Higher Education," Accessed June 30, 2009, http://www.estia.educ.goteborg.se/sv-estia/edu/edu_sys5.html.

20. The National Center for Public Policy and Higher Education, Measuring Up: The National Report Card on Higher Education, "Commentary: Current Year," Accessed August 7, 2009, http://measuringup.highereducation.org/commentary/introduction.cfm.

21. Philip J. Cook and Robert H. Frank, "The Economic Payoff of Attending an Ivy-League Institution," *The Chronicle of Higher Education,* January 5, 1996.

22. Ibid.

23. David A. Lynch, "USA Could Learn from South Korean Schools," *USA Today*, November 18, 2008, http://abcnews.go.com/Business/story?id=6293334&page=1.

24. Ibid.

25. Ibid.

26. U.S. Census Bureau, "Percent of People 25 Years and Over Who Have Completed High School or College, by Race, Hispanic Origin and Sex: Selected Years 1940 to 2007," Accessed June 30, 2009, http://www.census.gov/population/socdemo/education/cps2007/tabA-2.xls.

27. Jonathan Kozol, *Savage Inequalities: Children in America's Schools*. New York: Crown Publishers, 1992.

28. Robert Rosenthal and Lenore Jacobson, *Pygmalion in the Classroom*. New York: Holt, 1968.

29. Hussain Al-Fadhili and Madhu Singh, "Teachers' Expectancy and Efficacy as Correlates of School Achievement in Delta, Mississippi," *Journal of Personnel Evaluation in Education*, 2006. 19(1-2): 51-67.

30. Margaret R. Kuklinksy and Rhona S. Weinstein, "Classroom and Developmental Differences in a Path Model of Teacher Expectancy Effects," *Child Development*, 2001. 72(5): 1554-1579.

31. The National Center for Educational Statistics, "America's High School Graduates: Results from the 2005 NAEP High School Transcript Study," Accessed June 30, 2009, http://nces.ed.gov/nationsreportcard/pdf/studies/2007467.pdf.

32. Max Roosevelt, "Student Expectations Seen as Causing Grade Disputes," *New York Times*, February 18, 2009, http://www.nytimes.com/2009/02/18/education/18college.html?_r=1&emc=eta1.

33. Ibid.

34. Philo Washburn, "The public school as an agency of political socialization," *Quarterly Journal of Ideology*, 1986. 10(2): 24-35.

35. Randall Collins, *The Credential Society*. New York: Academic Press, 1979; Randall Collins, "Functional and Conflict Theories of Educational Stratification," *American Sociological Review*, 1971. 36: 1002-1019.

36. Samuel Bowles and Herbert Gintis, *Schooling in capitalist America: educational reform and the contradictions of economic life*. New York: Basic Books, 1976.

37. Hilary Metcalf, "Increasing Inequality in Higher Education: The Role of Term-Time Working," *Oxford Review of Education*, 2003. 29(3): 315-329.

38. Pauline Lipman, "Making the Global City, Making Inequality: The Political Economy and Cultural Politics of Chicago School Policy," *American Educational Research Journal*, 2002. 39(2): 379-419.

39. United States Department of Education, "Why NCLB is important," Accessed July 1, 2009, http://www.ed.gov/nclb/overview/importance/list.jhtml?page=2&size=10&sort=date&desc= show.

40. David Karen, "No Child Left Behind? Sociology Ignored!" *Sociology of Education*, 2005. 78: 165-182.

41. Ibid.

42. Ibid.

43. Joyce L. Epstein, "Attainable Goals? The Spirit and Letter of the No Child Left Behind Act on Parental Involvement," *Sociology of Education*, 2005. 78(2): 179-182.

44. U.S. Charter Schools, "History," Accessed July 1, 2009, http://www.uscharterschools.org/pub/uscs_docs/o/history.htm.

45. U.S. Charter Schools, "Overview and Benefits," Accessed July 1, 2009, http://www.uscharterschools.org/pub/uscs_docs/o/index.htm.

46. Robert R. O'Reilly and Lynn Bosetti, "Charter Schools: The Search for Community," *Peabody Journal of Education*, 2000. 75(4): 19-36.

47. Linda A. Renzulli and Lorraine Evans, "School Choice, Charter Schools, and White Flight," *Social Problems*, 2005. 53(3): 398-418.

48. Ibid.

49. George F. Garcia and Mary Garcia, "Charter Schools—Another Top-Down Innovation," *Educational Researcher*, 1996. 25(8): 34-36.

50. Ibid.

51. Jay Mathews, "Charter Schools' Big Experiment," *The Washington Post*, June 9, 2008, http://www.washingtonpost.com/wp-dyn/content/article/2008/06/08/AR2008060802174.html.

52. Ibid.

53. Pamela N. Frazier-Anderson, "Public Schooling in Post-Hurricane Katrina New Orleans: Are Charter Schools the Solution or Part of the Problem?" *Journal of African American History*, 2008. 93(3): 410-429.

CHAPTER 9

1. Steven Reinberg, "Family Income Impacts Children's Health," *ABCnews.com*, October 9, 2008, http://abcnews.go.com/Health/Healthday/story?id=5984822&page=1&page=1.

2. Preamble to the Constitution of the World Health Organization as adopted by the International Health Conference, New York, 19-22 June, 1946; signed on 22 July 1946 by the representatives of 61 States (Official Records of the World Health Organization, no. 2, p. 100) and entered into force on 7 April 1948.

3. Frank McVeigh and Loreen Wolfer, *A brief history of social problems: A critical thinking approach*. Lanham MD: University Press of America, 2004.

4. Ibid.

5. Ibid.

6. National Center for Health Statistics, *Health, United States, 2007 With Chartbook on Trends in the Health of Americans*. Hyattsville, MD: 2007.

7. U.S. Census Bureau, "Births, Deaths, Marriages, & Divorces: Life Expectancy," http://www.census.gov/compendia/statab/cats/births_deaths_marriages_divorces/life_expectancy.html.

8. World Health Organization, "The world health report 2000: Health systems: improving performance," http://www.who.int/whr/2000/en/.

9. Pamela M. Anderson and Kristin F. Butcher, "Childhood Obesity: Trends and Potential Causes," *The Future of Children*, 2006. 16: 19–45.

10. National Center for Health Statistics, *Health, United States, 2007 With Chartbook on Trends in the Health of Americans.* Hyattsville, MD: 2007.

11. John Hagan, A. R. Gillis, and John Simpson, "Class in the Household: A Power-Control Theory of Gender and Delinquency," *American Journal of Sociology*, 1987. 92: 788–816.

12. *CNN.com*, "Women Visit Doctors More Than Men," http://transcripts.cnn.com/TRANSCRIPTS/0606/17/hcsg.01.html.

13. John Knodel and Mary Beth Ofstedal, "Gender and Aging in the Developing World: Where Are the Men?" *Population and Development Review*, 2003. 29: 677–698.

14. Clarian Health, "Healthy Living for Men, The Commonwealth Fund News Release," Accessed August 28, 2008, http://www.clarian.org/portal/patients/healthy living?paf_gear_id5200001&paf_dm5full&paf_gm5content &task_name5articleDetail&articleId59764&section Id59.

15. James B. Kirby and Toshiko Kaneda, "Neighborhood Socio-economic Disadvantage and Access to Health Care," *Journal of Health and Social Behavior*, 2005. 46(1): 15–31.

16. Ibid.

17. Terrence D. Hill, Catherine E. Ross, and Ronald J. Angel, "Neighborhood Disorder, Psychophysiological Distress, and Health," *Journal of Health and Social Behavior*, 2005. 46: 170–186.

18. Ibid.

19. R. Charon Gwynn and George D. Thurston, "The Burden of Air Pollution: Impacts Among Racial Minorities," *Environmental Health Perspectives*, 2001. 109(4): 501–506. http://www.ehponline.org/members/2001/suppl-4/501-506gwynn/EHP109s4p501PDF.pdf.

20. National Center for Health Statistics, *Health, United States, 2007 With Chartbook on Trends in the Health of Americans.* Hyattsville, MD: 2007.

21. Ibid.

22. Brian D. Smedly, Adrienne Y. Stith, and Alan R. Nelson, *Unequal treatment: Confronting racial and ethnic disparities in health care.* Washington D.C.: the National Academies Press, 2003.

23. Jerry Cromwell, Nancy T. McCall, Joseph Burton, and Carol Urato, "Racial/Ethnic disparities in Utilization of life saving technologies by Medicare Ischemic heart disease beneficiaries," *Medical Care*, 2005. 43: 330–337.

24. Jennifer Malat and Mary Ann Hamilton, "Preference for Same-Race Health Care Providers and Perceptions of Interpersonal Discrimination in Health Care," *Journal of Health and Social Behavior*, 2006. 47(2): 173–187.

25. American Medical Association, "Resolutions for a Healthy New Year," http://www.ama-assn.org/ama/pub/category/18240.html.

26. World Health Organization, "World Health Organization Assesses the World's Health Systems," Accessed August 28, 2008, http://www.who.int/whr/2000/media_centre/press_release/en/.

27. National Center for Educational Statistics, "Education Across Levels: Funding for Education Expenditure for Education: 2003, Key Findings: France, Germany, Italy, Japan, United Kingdom, United States," http://nces.ed.gov/surveys/international/Intlindicators/index.asp?SectionNumber=1&SubSectionNumber=3&IndicatorNumber=101.

28. Cathy Schoen, Karen Davis, Sabrina K.H. How, and Stephen C. Schoenbaum, "National Scorecard on Healthcare Performance," *Health Affairs*, 2006. 25(6): w457–w475.

29. National Mental Health Information Center, "Twelve-month prevalence and severity of DSM-IV disorders in the NCS-R," http://mentalhealth.samhsa.gov/publications/allpubs/SMA06-4195/chp15table1.asp

30. Sarah Rosenfield, Julie Phillips, and Helene White, "Gender, Race, and the Self in Mental Health and Crime," *Social Problems*, 2006. 53(2): 161–185.

31. Lisa Strohschein, "Household Income Histories and Child Mental Health Trajectories," *Journal of Health and Social Behavior*, 2005. 46(4): 359–375.

32. American Psychological Association, "Psychologists Promote Health and Well-Being Throughout Our Nation," http://www.apapractice.org/apo/pracorg/legislative/psychology.html.

33. Joe C. Phelan, Bruce G. Link, Ann Stueve, and Bernice A. Pescosolido, "Public Conceptions of Mental Illness in 1950 and 1996: What Is Mental Illness and Is It to be Feared?" *Journal of Health and Social Behavior*, 2000. 41(2): 188–207.

34. Thomas Szasz, *The Myth of Mental Illness: Foundations of a Theory of Personal Conduct.* New York: Harper and Row, 1974.

35. Paula Caplan, *They Say You're Crazy: How the World's Most Powerful Psychiatrists Decide Who is Normal.* New York: Perseus Books Group, 1995.

36. Talcott Parsons, "The Sick Role and the Role of Physicians Reconsidered," *Milbank Medical Fund Quarterly Health and Society*, 1975. 53: 257–278.

37. Ivan Illich, *Medical Nemesis.* New York: Pantheon Books, 1975; Peter Conrad and Joseph Schneider, *Deviance and Medicalization: From Badness to Sickness.* Philadelphia: Temple University Press, 1992.

38. Peter Conrad and Valerie Leiter, "Medicalization, Markets and Consumers," *Journal of Health and Social Behavior*, 2004. 45: 158–176.

39. Jill Quadagno, "Why the United States Has No National Health Insurance: Stakeholder Mobilization Against the Welfare State, 1945–1996," *Journal of Health and Social Behavior*, 2004. 45: 25–44.

40. Frank J. McVeigh and Loreen Wolfer, *A brief history of social problems: A critical thinking approach.* Lanham, MD: University Press of America, 2004.

41. James W. Russell, *Double Standard: Social Policy in Europe and the United States.* Lanham, MD: Rowman & Littlefield Publishers Inc., 2006.

42. Leighton Ku, "Census Revises Estimates of the Number of Uninsured People," *Center on Budget and Policy Priorities*, April 5, 2007, http://www.cbpp.org/4-5-07 health.htm.

43. Jill Quadagno, "Why the United States Has No National Health Insurance: Stakeholder Mobilization Against the Welfare State, 1945–1996," *Journal of Health and Social Behavior*, 2004. 45: 25–44.

44. Centers for Medicare & Medicaid Services, "Medicare & You," Accessed July 13, 2009, http://www.medicare.gov/publications/pubs/pdf/10050.pdf.

CHAPTER 10

1. Kate Barrett and Joanna Schaffhausen, "Study: Anti-Drug Ads Haven't Worked," *ABC News*, October 15, 2008, http://abcnews.go.com/Health/story?id=6041092&page=1.

2. L.D. Kapoor, *Opium Poppy: Botany, Chemistry, and Pharmacology*. New York: Haworth Press Inc., 1997.

3. wine. (2009). In *Encyclopedia Britannica*. Retrieved July 12, 2009, from Encyclopedia Britannica Online: http://www.britannica.com/EBchecked/topic/645269/wine.

4. opium trade. (2009). In Encyclopædia Britannica. Retrieved November 18, 2009, from Encyclopædia Britannica Online: http://www.britannica.com/EBchecked/topic/430160/opium-trade.

5. United Nations Office on Drugs and Crime, "A Century of International Drug Control," http://www.unodc.org/documents/data-and-analysis/Studies/100_Years_of_Drug_Control.pdf.

6. *Sunday Times*, "How aspirin turned hero," September 13, 1998, http://opioids.com/heroin/heroinhistory.html.

7. United Nations Office on Drugs and Crime, "A Century of International Drug Control," http://www.unodc.org/documents/data-and-analysis/Studies/100_Years_of_Drug_Control.pdf.

8. Centers for Disease Control and Prevention, "Illegal Drug Use," Accessed September 14, 2009, http://www.cdc.gov/nchs/FASTATS/druguse.htm.

9. Centers for Disease Control and Prevention, "Alcohol and Public Health," Accessed September 14, 2009, http://www.cdc.gov/alcohol/index.htm.

10. National Center for Health Statistics, *Health, United States, 2007 With Chartbook on Trends in the Health of Americans.* Hyattsville, MD: 2007.

11. National Institute on Drug Abuse, "Drugs, Brains, and Behavior: The Science of Addiction," Accessed September 14, 2009, http://www.drugabuse.gov/scienceofaddiction/sciofaddiction.pdf.

12. American Lung Association, "Smoking 101 Fact Sheet," Accessed September 14, 2009, http://www.lungusa.org/site/c.dvLUK9O0E/b.39853/.

13. U.S. Department of Justice, "Drinking in America: Myths, Realities, and Prevention Policy," http://www.udetc.org/documents/Drinking_in_America.pdf.

14. Barrett Seaman, *Binge: What Your College Student Won't Tell You.* Hoboken, NJ: John Wiley and Sons Inc., 2005.

15. Substance Abuse and Mental Health Services Administration, *Results from the 2007 National Survey on Drug Use and Health: National Findings.* Rockville, MD: Office of Applied Studies, NSDUH Series H-34, DHHS Publication No. SMA 08-4343, 2008.

16. Ibid.

17. Ibid.

18. University of Michigan, "The Monitoring the Future Study, Table 1: Trends in Lifetime Prevalence of Use of Various Drugs in Grades 8, 10, and 12," Accessed September 14, 2009, http://www.monitoringthefuture.org/data/08data/pr08t1.pdf.

19. U.S. Department of Health and Human Services, "Health, United States, 2008: With Special Feature on the Health of Young Adults," http://www.cdc.gov/nchs/data/hus/hus08.pdf#066.

20. Denise Kandel, Kevin Chen, and Andrew Gill, "The Impact of Drug Use on Earnings: A Life-Span Perspective," *Social Forces*, 1995. 74(1): 243–270.

21. Partnership for a Drug Free America, "Getting High on Prescription and Over-the-Counter Drugs Is Dangerous," Accessed September 14, 2009, http://www.drugfree.org/Files/rx%20guide.

22. Jean-Pierre Changeux, "Drug Use and Abuse," *Daedalus*, 1998. 127(2): 145–165.

23. Michael Gottfredson and Travis Hirschi, *A General Theory of Crime.* Stanford, CA: Stanford University Press, 1990.

24. Darin Weinberg, "Out There: The Ecology of Addiction in Drug Abuse Treatment Discourse," *Social Problems*, 2000. 47(4): 606–621.

25. Denise B. Kandel, *Stages and Pathways of Drug Involvement: Examining the Gateway Hypothesis.* Cambridge: Cambridge University Press, 2002.

26. Peter Conrad, "Medicalization and Social Control," *Annual Review of Sociology*, 1992. 18(1): 209–232.

27. E. Hing, D.K. Cherry, and D.A. Woodwell, "National Ambulatory Medical Care Survey: 2004 Summary," *Vital and Health Statistics*, 2006. 374.

28. Todd Bensman, "The Cross-border bullet trade," *Globalpost.com*, March 4, 2009, http://www.globalpost.com/dispatch/mexico/090303/the-cross-border-bullet-trade.

29. *CNN.com*, "Senators want to fight Mexican drug cartels' expanding influence," March 17, 2009, http://edition.cnn.com/2009/POLITICS/03/17/mexican.drug.war/index.html.

30. Mary Beth Sheridan, "Clinton: U.S. Drug Policies Failed, Fueled Mexico's Drug War," *The Washington Post*, March 26, 2009, http://www.washingtonpost.com/wp-dyn/content/article/2009/03/25/AR2009032501034.html.

31. *MSNBC.com*, "Obama: Mexico drug war 'sowing chaos,'" April 16, 2009, http://www.msnbc.msn.com/id/30232095.

32. Ibid.

33. Todd Bensman, "The Cross-border bullet trade," *Globalpost.com*, March 4, 2009, http://www.globalpost.com/dispatch/mexico/090303/the-cross-border-bullet-trade.

34. Jeffrey Reiman, *The Rich Get Richer and the Poor Get Prison: Ideology, Class, and Criminal Justice*. Boston: Allyn and Bacon, 1998.

35. Earl Wysong, Richard Aniskiewicz, and David Wright, "Truth and DARE: Tracking Drug Education to Graduation and as Symbolic Politics," *Social Problems*, 1994. 41(3): 448–472.

36. Robert K. Merton, "Social structure and anomie," *American Sociological Review*, 1938. 3(6): 672–82.

37. Jeffrey Reiman, *The Rich Get Richer and the Poor Get Prison: Ideology, Class, and Criminal Justice*. Boston: Allyn and Bacon, 1998.

38. Human Rights Watch, "Decades of Disparity: Drug Arrests and Race in the United States," http://www.hrw.org/en/reports/2009/03/02/decades-disparity-0.

39. The Sentencing Project, "Federal Crack Cocaine Sentencing," http://www.sentencingproject.org/doc/publications/dp_crack_sentencing.pdf.

40. Jeffrey Reiman, *The Rich Get Richer and the Poor Get Prison: Ideology, Class, and Criminal Justice*. Boston: Allyn and Bacon, 1998.

41. Ibid.

42. Amsterdam.info, "Amsterdam Coffeeshops," http://www.amsterdam.info/coffeeshops.

43. Marijuana Policy Project, "State By State Medical Marijuana Laws: Report 2008," http://www.mpp.org/assets/pdfs/download-materials/SBSR_NOV2008.pdf.

44. Clayton James Mosher and Scott Akins, *Drugs and Drug Policy: The Control of Consciousness Alteration*. Thousand Oaks, CA: Sage Publications Inc., 2007.

45. National Institute on Drug Abuse, "Treatment Approaches for Drug Addiction," Accessed September 14, 2009, http://www.drugabuse.gov/PDF/InfoFacts/Treatment08.pdf.

46. James Austin and John Irwin, *It's About Time: Americans Imprisonment Binge*. Belmont, CA: Wadsworth, 2000.

47. National Institute on Drug Abuse, "Treatment Approaches for Drug Addiction," Accessed September 14, 2009, http://www.drugabuse.gov/PDF/InfoFacts/Treatment08.pdf.

48. Office of National Drug Control Policy, "Drug Treatment in the Criminal Justice System," Accessed September 14, 2009, http://www.whitehousedrugpolicy.gov/publications/factsht/treatment/index.html.

49. U.S. Department of Health and Human Services, "National Treatment Improvement Evaluation Study (NTIES), 1992–1997," Accessed September 14, 2009, https://icpsr.umich.edu/cocoon/SAMHDA/STUDY/02884.xml.

50. Ibid.

51. Drug Policy Alliance, "Treatment vs. Incarceration," Accessed September 14, 2009, http://www.drugpolicy.org/library/factsheets/treatment_v_incarceration_nm.cfm#5.

52. Steven D. Levitt and Stephen J. Dubner, *Freakonomics: A Rogue Economist Explores the Hidden Side of Everything.* New York: Harper Collins, 2005.

53. Drug Policy Alliance, "Personal Liberties and the War on Drugs," Accessed September 14, 2009, http://www.drugpolicy.org/library/factsheets/personallibe/fact_liberties.cfm.

54. Hartley Engel, "Drug Lord Joaquin 'El Chapo' Guzman Loera Makes Forbes' Billionaire List," *Associated Content*, March 13, 2009, http://www.associatedcontent.com/article/1562414/drug_lord_joaquin_el_chapo_guzman_loera.html.

55. Drug Policy Alliance, "Personal Liberties and the War on Drugs," Accessed September 14, 2009, http://www.drugpolicy.org/library/factsheets/personallibe/fact_liberties.cfm.

56. Office of National Drug Control Policy, "Drug Treatment in the Criminal Justice System," Accessed September 14, 2009, http://www.whitehousedrugpolicy.gov/publications/factsht/treatment/index.html.

57. Jacob Sullum, *Saying Yes: In Defense of Drug Use.* New York: Penguin Publishing, 2003.

58. Denise Kandel, "Does marijuana use cause the use of other drugs?" *JAMA*, 2003. 289(4): 482–483.

59. National Institute on Drug Abuse, "NIDA InfoFacts: Marijuana," Accessed September 14, 2009, http://www.nida.nih.gov/infofacts/marijuana.html.

60. Michael T. Lynskey, Andrew C. Heath, Kathleen K. Bucholz, et al, "Escalation of drug use in early-onset cannabis users vs. co-twin controls," *JAMA*, 2003. 289:427–433.

CHAPTER 11

1. Joneil Adriano, "Pregnant Man, Other Transgender Parents Face Legal Questions: Thomas Beatie Tells Barbara Walters About Unique Legal Challenges Faced by Transgender Parents," *ABC News*, November 14, 2008, http://abcnews.go.com/TheLaw/story?id=6246058&page=1.

2. American Psychological Association, "Answers to your questions about transgender individuals and gender identity," Accessed July 13, 2009, http://www.apa.org/topics/transgender.html.

3. Ibid.

4. American Psychological Association, "Answers to your questions for a better understanding of sexual orientation and homosexuality," Accessed July 13, 2009, http://www.apa.org/topics/sorientation.html#whatis.

5. Ibid.

6. Ibid.

7. Ibid.

8. Ibid.

9. Patricia Hill Collins, *Black Sexual Politics: African Americans, Gender, and the New Racism*. New York: Routledge, 2004.

10. Gregory B. Lewis, "Black-White Differences in Attitudes toward Homosexuality and Gay Rights," *The Public Opinion Quarterly*, 2003. 67(1): 59–78.

11. Ibid.

12. Gregory M. Herek, "Heterosexuals' Attitudes toward Bisexual Men and Women in the United States," *The Journal of Sex Research*, 2002. 39(4): 264–274

13. Jeni Loftus, "America's Liberalization in Attitudes toward Homosexuality, 1973 to 1998," *American Sociological Review*, 2001. 66 (5): 762–782.

14. U.S. Census Bureau, "Hate Crimes—Number of Incidents, Offenses, Victims, and Known Offenders by Bias Motivation: 2000 to 2005," http://www.census.gov/compendia/statab/2008/tables/08s0310.pdf.

15. James Lock and Hans Steiner, "Gay, lesbian, and bisexual youth risks for emotional, physical, and social problems: Results from a community-based survey," *Journal of the American Academy of Child and Adolescent Psychiatry*, 1999. 38(3): 297–304; Stephen T. Russel and Kara Joyner, "Adolescent Sexual Orientation and Suicide Risk: Evidence From a Natural Study," *American Journal of Public Health*, 2001. 91(8): 1276–1281.

16. U.S. Census Bureau, "Equal Employment Opportunity," http://www.census.gov/eeo/complaint.html.

17. Sylvia A. Allegretto and Michelle M. Arthur, "An Empirical Analysis of Homosexual/Heterosexual Male Earnings Differentials: Unmarried and Unequal?" *Industrial and Labor Relations Review*, 2001. 54(3): 631–646.

18. Edward Laumann, John H. Gagnon, Robert T. Michaels, and Stuart Michaels, *The Social Organization of Sexuality: Sexual Practices in the United States*. Chicago: University of Chicago Press, 1994.

19. Dan Black, Gary Gates, Seth Sanders, and Lowell Taylor, "Demographics of the Gay and Lesbian Population in the United States: Evidence from Available Systematic Data Sources," *Demography*, 2000. 37(2): 139–154.

20. Ibid.

21. *BBC News*, "Gay Marriage around the Globe," Accessed July 15, 2009, http://news.bbc.co.uk/2/hi/americas/4081999.stm.

22. Ibid.

23. Ibid.

24. Ibid.

25. Karen (Kay) Perrin and Sharon Bernecki DeJoy, "Abstinence-Only Education: How We Got Here and Where We're Going," *Journal of Public Health Policy*, 2003. 24(3–4): 445–459.

26. Alison Jeanne Lin and John S. Santelli, "The Accuracy of Condom Information in Three Selected Abstinence-Only Education Curricula," *Sexuality Research & Social Policy: Journal of NSRC*, 2008. 5(3): 56–69.

27. "New study questions effectiveness of abstinence-only education," *Contemporary Sexuality*, 2008. 42(5): 11; Nancy Kendall, "Sexuality Education in an Abstinence-Only Era: A Comparative Case Study of Two U.S. States," *Sexuality Research & Social Policy: Journal of NSRC*, 2008. 5(2): 23–44; Karen (Kay) Perrin and Sharon Bernecki DeJoy, "Abstinence-Only Education: How We Got Here and Where We're Going," *Journal of Public Health Policy*, 2003. 24(3–4): 445– 459.

28. U.S. Department of Health and Human Services, "Teens Delaying Sexual Activity: Using Contraception More Effectively," http://www.cdc.gov/nchs/PRESSROOM/04news/teens.htm.

29. Ibid.

30. Ibid.

31. Debran Rowland, *The Boundaries of Her Body: The Troubling History of Women's Rights in America*. Naperville, IL: Sphinx Publishing, 2004.

32. Andrea Tone, *Controlling Reproduction: An American History*. Wilmington, DE: Scholarly Resources Inc., 1997.

33. U.S. Census Bureau, "Abortions by Selected Characteristics, 1990–2004," Accessed July 21, 2009, http://www.census.gov/compendia/statab/tables/09s0098.pdf.

34. Michel Foucault, *The History of Sexuality*. New York: Vintage Books, 1990.

35. Eve Kosofsky Sedgwick, *Epistemology of the Closet*. Berkeley: University of California Press, 1990.

36. Andrea Dworkin, *Intercourse*. New York: Free Press, 1987.

37. Engels, Friedrich, *The Origin of the Family: Private Property and the State*. New York: Pathfinder Press, 1972.

38. Christine Vestal, "Gay Marriage Legal in Six States," *Stateline.org*, April 8, 2009, http://www.stateline.org/live/details/story?contentId=347390.

39. Ibid.

40. Ibid.

41. Ibid.

42. National Conference of Commissioners on Uniform State Laws, *American Uniform Marriage and Marriage License Act*. Williamsport, PA: Railway Printing Company, 1911.

43. Charlotte Patterson, "Family relationships of lesbians and gay men," *Journal of Marriage and Family*, 2000. 62: 1052–1069.

44. Ibid; Judith Stacey and Timothy J. Biblarz, "(How) Does the Sexual Orientation of Parents Matter?" *American Sociological Review*, 2001. 66(2): 159–183.

CHAPTER 12

1. Jake Tapper, "Sen. Larry Craig: Liability to Republicans?" *ABCnews.com*, October 16, 2007, http://abcnews.go.com/GMA/story?id=3734906&page=1.

2. Laud Humphreys, *Tearoom Trade: Impersonal Sex in Public Place*. Chicago: Adline Publishing Co., 1970.

3. Emile Durkheim, *The Rules of Sociological Method*. New York: Free Press, 1964.

4. John Braithwaite, *Crime, Shame, and Reintegration*. New York: Cambridge University Press, 1989.

5. Kristen Hefley, "Stigma Management of Male and Female Customers to a Non-Urban Adult Novelty Store," *Deviant Behavior*, 2007. 28(1): 79–109.

6. United Nations General Assembly, "Women's Anti-Discrimination Committee Examines Netherland's Policies On Prostitutions, Domestic Violence, Human Trafficking," http://www.un.org/News/Press/docs/2007/wom1601.doc.htm.

7. Nils Johan Ringdal, *Love For Sale: A World History of Prostitution*. New York: Grove Press, 2004.

8. Federal Bureau of Investigation, "FBI Uniform Crime Report: Crime in the United States, 2007: Offense Definitions," http://www.fbi.gov/ucr/cius2007/documents/offense definitions.pdf.

9. Wendy Chapkis, *Live sex acts: Women performing erotic labor*. New York: Routledge, 1997.

10. State of Nevada, "Prostitution," http://www.nv.gov/Visiting_Nevada.htm.

11. Kingsley Davis, "Sexual Behavior," *Contemporary Social Problems, 2nd ed*. Robert Merton and Robert Nisbet, eds. New York: Harcourt, 1961.

12. Martin A. Monto, "Prostitution and Fellatio," *The Journal of Sex Research*, 2001. 38(2): 140–145.

13. Meda Chesney-Lind, "Girls' Crime and Woman's Place: Toward a Feminist Model of Female Delinquency," *Crime & Delinquency*, 1989. 35(1): 5–29.

14. Wendy Chapkis, *Live sex acts: Women performing erotic labor*. New York: Routledge, 1997.

15. Ibid.

16. Meda Chesney-Lind, "Girls' Crime and Woman's Place: Toward a Feminist Model of Female Delinquency," *Crime & Delinquency*, 1989. 35(1): 5–29.

17. Shu-ling Hwang and Olwen Bedford, "Precursors and pathways to adolescent prostitution in Taiwan," *The Journal of Sex Research*, 2003. 40(2): 201–210.

18. Susan F. McClanahan, Gary M. McClelland, Karen M. Abram, and Linda A. Teplin, "Pathways Into Prostitution Among Female Jail Detainees and Their Implications for Mental Health Services," *Psychiatric Services*, 1999. 50: 1606–1613.

19. Nanette J. Davis, *Prostitution: An International Handbook on Trends, Problems, and Policies*. Westport, CT: Greenwood Publishing Group, 1993; James Henslin and Edward Sararin, *The sociology of sex: An Introductory reader*. New York: Schocken, 1987.

20. Nancy A. Wonders and Raymond Michalowski, "Bodies, borders, and sex tourism in the globalized world: A tale of two cities–Amsterdam and Havana," *Social Problems*, 2001. 48(4): 545–571.

21. Kevin Bales, *Disposable People: New Slavery in the Global Economy*. Berkeley: University of California Press, 2000.

22. C. MacKinnon, *Only Words*. Cambridge, MA: Harvard University Press, 1993.

23. Transactional Records Access Clearinghouse, Syracuse University, "FBI Enforcement Trends by Program Area: Prosecutions Filed FY 1986–2006," Accessed September 29, 2009, trac.syr.edu/cgi-bin/tracslides2.pl?id=fbi2005&slide=13.

24. U.S. Department of Justice, "Attorney General's Commission on Pornography: Final Report, 1986," http://www.porn-report.com.

25. Dan Ackman, "How Big is Porn?" *Forbes.com*, May 25, 2001, http://www.forbes.com/2001/05/25/0524porn.html.

26. William A. Fisher and Azy Barak, "Internet Pornography: A Social Psychological Perspective on Internet Sexuality," *The Journal of Sex Research*, 2001. 38(4): 312–323.

27. Gresham Sykes and David Matza, "Techniques of Neutralization: A Theory of Delinquency," *American Sociological Review*, 1957. 22: 664–670.

28. Laud Humphreys, *Tearoom Trade: Impersonal Sex in Public Place*. Chicago: Adline Publishing Co., 1970.

29. Miyuki Tomura, "A Prostitute's Lived Experiences of Stigma," *Journal of Phenomenological Psychology*, 2009. 40: 51–84.

30. Nancy A. Wonders and Raymond Michalowski, "Bodies, borders, and sex tourism in the globalized world: A tale of two cities–Amsterdam and Havana," *Social Problems*, 2001. 48(4): 545–571.

31. Tom McNichol, "Is Marijuana the Answer to California's Budget Woes?" *Times.com*, July 24, 2009, http://www.time.com/time/nation/article/0,8599,1912113,00.html.

32. United States Department of Justice, Civil Rights Division, "Trafficking in Persons—A Guide for Non-Governmental Organizations," http://www.usdoj.gov/crt/crim/wetf/traffic brochure.php.

33. Adapted from *FBI Alaska*, "Federal Jury Convicts Anchorage Man in the First Sex Trafficking Trial in the District of Alaska," http://anchorage.fbi.gov/doj/pressrel/2008/aksex trafficking020608.htm.

CHAPTER 13

1. John Hendren, "U.S. 'Murder Capital' a Tricky Figure," *ABC News*, June 19, 2009, http://abcnews.go.com/US/story?id=7884362&page=1.

2. Federal Bureau of Investigation, "Crime in the United States 2005," Accessed July 27, 2009, http://www.fbi.gov/ucr/05cius/offenses/ violent_crime/index.html.

3. U.S. Department of Justice, Office of Justice Programs, "The Nation's Two Crime Measures," Accessed July 27, 2009, http://www.ojp.usdoj.gov/bjs/pub/html/ntcm.htm.

4. Ibid.

5. Michael Gottfredson and Travis Hirschi, *A General Theory of Crime.* Stanford, CA: Stanford University Press, 1990.

6. Darrell Steffensmeier and Miles Harer, "Did Crime Rise or Fall During the Reagan Presidency?" *Journal of Research in Crime and Delinquency*, 28(3): 330-359.

7. Marcus Felson and Dr. Rachel L. Boba, *Crime and Everyday Life.* Thousand Oaks, CA: Sage Publications Inc., 2009.

8. Federal Bureau of Investigation, Department of Justice, *Crime in the United States: Uniform Crime Reports.* Washington, D.C.: Government Printing Office, 2002.

9. U.S. Census Bureau, "U.S. Summary 2000," http://www.census.gov/prod/2002pubs/c2kprof00-us.pdf.

10. U.S. Department of Justice, Office of Justice Programs, "Prison Statistics," http://www.ojp.usdoj.gov/bjs/prisons.htm.

11. U.S. Census Bureau, "U.S. Summary 2000," http://www.census.gov/prod/2002pubs/c2kprof00-us.pdf.

12. Ronald Weitzer and Steven A. Tuch, "Race and Perceptions of Police Misconduct," *Social Problems*, 2004. 51(3): 305-325.

13. David Cole, *No Equal Justice: Race and Class in the American Criminal Justice System.* New York: New Press, 1999.

14. Ronald Weitzer and Steven A. Tuch, "Race and Perceptions of Police Misconduct," *Social Problems*, 2004. 51(3): 305-325; Marcus Felson and Dr. Rachel L. Boba, *Crime and Everyday Life.* Thousand Oaks, CA: Sage Publications Inc., 2009.

15. Jeffrey Reiman, *The Rich Get Richer and the Poor Get Prison: Ideology, Class and Criminal Justice.* Needham Heights, MA: Allyn and Bacon, 2007.

16. The Nielson Company, "Measurement: Television," Accessed July 27, 2009, http://www.nielsenmedia.com/nc/portal/site/Public/menuitem.43afce2fac27e890311ba0a347a062a0/?vgnextoid=9e4df9669fa14010VgnVCM100000880a260aRCRD.

17. Marcus Felson and Dr. Rachel L. Boba, *Crime and Everyday Life.* Thousand Oaks, CA: Sage Publications Inc., 2009.

18. J.N. van Kesteren, P. Mayhew, and P. Nieuwbeerta, *Criminal Victimization in Seventeen Industrialized Countries: Key-findings from the 2000 International Crime Victimization Survey.* The Hague: Ministry of Justice, WODC, 2000.

19. Ibid.

20. Marcus Felson and Dr. Rachel L. Boba, *Crime and Everyday Life.* Thousand Oaks, CA: Sage Publications Inc., 2009.

21. Stanton E. Samenow, *Inside the Criminal Mind: Revised and Updated Edition.* New York: Crown Publishers, 2004.

22. *Diagnostic and Statistical Manual of Mental Disorders, 4th edition.* Washington, D.C.: American Psychiatric Association, 1994.

23. Robert K. Merton, "Social Structure and Anomie," *American Sociological Review*, 1938. 3: 672-682.

24. Clifford Shaw and Henry McKay, *Juvenile Delinquency and Urban Areas.* Chicago: University of Chicago Press, 1942.

25. Robert Sampson and John H. Laub, "Crime and Deviance in the Life Course," *Annual Review of Sociology,* 1992. 18: 63-84.

26. Edwin Sutherland and Donald Cressey, *Principles of Criminology.* Philadelphia: Lippincott, 1978.

27. Ronald Akers and Gary F. Jensen, *Social Learning Theory and the Explanation of Crime: A Guide for the New Century.* New Brunswick, NJ: Transaction Publishers, 2003.

28. Willem A. Bonger, *Criminality and Economic Conditions.* Bloomington, IN: Indiana University Press, 1969.

29. Jeffrey Reiman, *The Rich Get Richer and the Poor Get Prison: Ideology, Class and Criminal Justice.* Needham Heights, MA: Allyn and Bacon, 2007.

30. Robert Agnew, "Foundation for a General Strain Theory of Crime and Delinquency," *Criminology*, 1992. 30: 47-66.

31. Michael Gottfredson and Travis Hirschi, *A General Theory of Crime.* Stanford, CA: Stanford University Press, 1990.

32. Ralph McNeal, "Participation in High School Extracurricular Activities: Investigating School Effects," *Social Science Quarterly*, 1999. 80: 291-309.

33. Ralph McNeal, "Extracurricular Activities and High School Drop Outs," *Sociology of Education*, 1995. 68: 62-81.

34. Phil Schoggen and Maxine Schoggen, "Student voluntary participation and high school size," *Journal of Educational Research*, 1988. 81(5): 288-293.

CHAPTER 14

1. Jennifer C. Kerr, "States Could Lose Money Over Prison Rapes," *ABC News,* June 23, 2009, http://abcnews.go.com/Politics/wireStory?id=7904960.

2. W.L. Reese, *Dictionary of Philosophy and Religion: Eastern and Western Thought.* Atlantic Highlands, NJ: Humanities Press Inc., 1987.

3. *Ewing V. California*, 538 U. S. 11 (2003), Accessed July 26, 2009, http://www.law.cornell.edu/supct/html/01-6978.ZS.html.

4. United States Sentencing Commission Office of Policy Analysis, "2005 Datafile, OPAFY05, Post-*Booker* Only Cases (January 12, 2005, through September 30, 2005)," http://www.ussc.gov/JUDPACK/2005/1c05.pdf.

5. John Braithwaite, *Crime, Shame, and Reintegration.* New York: Cambridge University Press, 1989.

6. Joseph J. Senna and Larry J. Siegel, *Introduction to Criminal Justice.* Belmont, CA: West/Wadsworth Publishing Co., 1999.

7. U.S. Department of Justice, Bureau of Justice Statistics, "Law enforcement statistics," Accessed July 26, 2009, http://www.ojp.usdoj.gov/bjs/lawenf.htm.

8. Marcus Felson, *Crime and Everyday Life*. Thousand Oaks, CA: Sage Publishing, 2002.

9. Ibid.

10. Ibid.

11. Jeffrey Reiman, *The Rich Get Richer and the Poor Get Prison: Ideology, Class, and Criminal Justice*. Needham Heights, MA: Allyn and Bacon, 2007.

12. David Cole, *No Equal Justice: Race and Class in the American Criminal Justice System*. New York: The New Press, 1999.

13. Jodi M. Brown and Patrick A. Langan, *State Court Sentencing of Convicted Felons*. Washington, D.C.: Government Printing Office, 1998.

14. Jeffrey Reiman, *The Rich Get Richer and the Poor Get Prison: Ideology, Class, and Criminal Justice*. Needham Heights, MA: Allyn and Bacon, 2007.

15. James Austin and John Irwin, *It's About Time: America's Imprisonment Binge*. Belmont, CA: Wadsworth Publishing Company, 2001.

16. Ibid.

17. Ibid.

18. Ibid.

19. Bureau of Justice Statistics. "Criminal Victimization in the United States," Accessed July 28, 2009, http://www.ojp.usdoj.gov/bjs/gcorpop.htm#CorrPopRace.

20. Ibid.

21. James Austin and John Irwin, *It's About Time: America's Imprisonment Binge*. Belmont, CA: Wadsworth Publishing Company, 2001.

22. Ibid.

23. Jeffrey Reiman, *The Rich Get Richer and the Poor Get Prison: Ideology, Class, and Criminal Justice*. Needham Heights, MA: Allyn and Bacon, 2007.

24. Bureau of Justice Statistics, *Criminal Victimization in the United States*. Washington, D.C.: Government Printing Office, 2002.

25. Bureau of Justice Statistics, "Recidivism of Prisoners Released in 1994," Accessed July 28, 2009, http://www.ojp.usdoj.gov/bjs/pub/ascii/rpr94.txt.

26. James Austin and John Irwin, *It's About Time: America's Imprisonment Binge*. Belmont, CA: Wadsworth Publishing Company, 2001.

27. Adam Liptak, "U.S. Prison Population Dwarfs that of other Nations," *New York Times*, April 23, 2008, http://www.nytimes.com/2008/04/23/world/americas/23iht-23prison.12253738.htm.

28. Ibid.

29. Ibid.

30. James Austin and John Irwin, *It's About Time: America's Imprisonment Binge*. Belmont, CA: Wadsworth Publishing Company, 2001.

31. L. Thomas Winfree, Jr., "New Zealand Police and Restorative Justice Philosophy," *Crime and Delinquency*, 2004. 50: 189–213.

32. Ibid.

33. News Worldwide. "Annual Determination of Average Cost of Incarceration," Accessed July 29, 2009, http://newsworldwide.wordpress.com/2009/07/10/annual-determination-of-average-cost-of-incarceration/.

34. Jeffrey Reiman, *The Rich Get Richer and the Poor Get Prison: Ideology, Class, and Criminal Justice*. Needham Heights, MA: Allyn and Bacon, 2007.

35. Ibid.

36. Emile Durkheim, *The Rules of Sociological Method*. New York: Free Press, 1964.

37. Adam Liptak, "U.S. Prison Population Dwarfs that of other Nations," *New York Times*, April 23, 2008. http://www.nytimes.com/2008/04/23/world/americas/23iht-23prison.12253738.htm.

38. Warren Hoge, "Finnish Prisons: No Gates or Armed Guards," *New York Times*, January 2, 2003, http://www.nytimes.com/2003/01/02/international/europe/02FINL.html?pagewanted=all.

39. Ronald H. Aday, *Aging Prisoners: Crisis in American Corrections*. Westport, CN: Praeger Press, 2003.

40. Rand Corporation: Drug Policy Research Center, "Are Mandatory Minimum Drug Sentences Cost-Effective?" http://www.rand.org/publications/RB/RB6003/.

41. Death Penalty Information Center, "Capital Punishment 2007," Accessed July 30, 2009, http://www.deathpenaltyinfo.org/crimes-punishable-death-penalty#BJS.

42. Ibid.

43. Death Penalty Information Center, "Nationwide Murder Rates, 1996–2007," Accessed July 30, 2009, http://www.deathpenaltyinfo.org/murder-rates-1996–2007.

44. Richard Dieter, "Costs of the Death Penalty: Testimony before Joint Committee on Criminal Justice of the Legislature of Massachusetts," March 27, 2003, http://www.deathpenaltyinfo.org/MassCostTestimony.pdf.

45. Susan Levine and Lori Montgomery, "Large Racial Disparity Found in Study of Maryland Death Penalty," *Washington Post*, January 8, 2003.

CHAPTER 15

1. Philip Victor, "Virtual Affair Ends in Real-Life Divorce," *ABCNews.com*, November 14, 2008, http://abcnews.go.com/International/SmallBiz/story?id=6255277&page=1.

2. John King, "King: Same-sex marriage debate heats up in New York," *CNN.com*, May 22, 2009, http://www.cnn.com/2009/POLITICS/05/29/sotu.same.sex/index.html?iref=newsearch.

3. Rachel L. Swarns, "An In-Law Is Finding Washington to Her Liking," *NYTimes.com*, May 3, 2009, http://www.nytimes.com/2009/05/04/us/politics/04robinson.html.

4. Stephanie Coontz, *The Way We Never Were: American Families and the Nostalgia Trap*. New York: Basic Books, 2000.

5. Ibid.

6. Ibid.

7. Ibid.

8. Ibid.

9. Suzanne M. Bianchi and Lynne M. Casper, *American Families*. Washington, D.C.: Population Reference Bureau, 2000, http://www.prb.org/Publications/PopulationBulletins/2000/AmericanFamiliesPDF458KB.aspx.

10. Ibid.

11. Ibid.

12. Ibid.

13. Larry L. Bumpass, James A. Sweet, and Andrew Cherlin, "The Role of Cohabitation in Declining Rates of Marriage," *Journal of Marriage and the Family*, 1991. 53: 913-927.

14. Urban Institute, "Introduction," Accessed August 27, 2009, http://www.urban.org/publications/310962.html.

15. Suzanne M. Bianchi and Lynne M. Casper, *American Families*. Washington, D.C.: Population Reference Bureau, 2000, http://www.prb.org/Publications/PopulationBulletins/2000/AmericanFamiliesPDF458KB.aspx.

16. Jennifer E. Lansford, Rosario Ceballo, Antonia Abbey, and Abigail J. Stewart, "Does Family Structure Matter? A Comparison of Adoptive, Two-Parent Biological, Single-Mother, Stepfather, and Stepmother Households," *Journal of Marriage and Family*, 2001. 63(3): 840-851.

17. Judith Stacy and Timothy J. Biblarz, "(How) does the sexual orientation of parents matter?" *American Sociological Review*, 2001. 66(2): 159-183.

18. Ibid.

19. Charlotte Patterson, "Family relationships of lesbians and gay men," *Journal of Marriage and Family*, 2000. 62: 1052-1069.

20. Linda J. Waite and Maggie Gallager, *The Case for Marriage: Why Married People Are Happier, Healthier, and Better off Financially*. New York: Doubleday, 2000.

21. Steven L. Nock, *Marriage in Men's Lives*. New York: Oxford University Press, 1998.

22. Jean M. Twenge, W. Keith Campbell, and Craig A. Foster, "Parenthood and Marital Satisfaction: A Meta-Analytic Review," *Journal of Marriage and Family*, 2003. 65(3): 574-583.

23. Ranae J. Evenson and Robin W. Simon, "Clarifying the Relationship between Parenthood and. Depression," *Journal of Health and Social Behavior*, 2005. 46: 258-341.

24. Center for Nutrition Policy and Promotion, United States Department of Agriculture, "Expenditures on Children by Families, 2006," http://www.cnpp.usda.gov/Publications/CRC/crc2006.pdf.

25. Suzanne M. Bianchi and Lynne M. Casper, *American Families*. D.C.: Population Reference Bureau, 2000, http://www.prb.org/Publications/PopulationBulletins/2000/AmericanFamiliesPDF458KB.aspx.

26. "Global Family Decay," *Society*, 1995. 33(1): 3-9.

27. Katherine Trent and Scott J. South, "Structural Determinants of the Divorce Rate: A Cross-Societal Analysis," *Journal of Marriage and the Family*, 1989. 51(2): 391-404.

28. Andrew J. Cherlin, *The Marriage-Go-Round: The State of Marriage and Family In America Today*. New York: Knopf Publishers, 2009.

29. Ibid.

30. Katherine Trent and Scott J. South, "Structural Determinants of the Divorce Rate: A Cross-Societal Analysis," *Journal of Marriage and the Family*, 1989. 51(2): 391-404.

31. Andrew J. Cherlin, *The Marriage-Go-Round: The State of Marriage and Family In America Today*. New York: Knopf Publishers, 2009.

32. Ibid.

33. Ibid.

34. Jay D. Teachman, "Stability Across Cohorts in Divorce Risk Factors," *Demography*, 2002. 39(2): 331-351.

35. Ibid.

36. Ibid.

37. Ibid.

38. Joseph M. Gumina, "Communication of the Decision to Divorce: A Retrospective Qualitative Study," *Journal of Divorce & Remarriage*, 2009. 50(3): 220-232.

39. M.D.R. Evans, Jonathan Kelley, and Richard A. Wanner, "Consequences of Divorce for Childhood Education: Australia, Canada, and the USA, 1940-1990," *Comparative Sociology*, 2009. 8(1): 105-146.

40. Nicole M. Bing, W. M. Nelson, and Kelly L. Wesolowski, "Comparing the Effects of Amount of Conflict on Children's Adjustment Following Parental Divorce," *Journal of Divorce & Remarriage*, 2009. 50(3): 159-171.

41. Sarah W. Whitton, Galena K. Rhoades, Scott M. Stanley, and Howard J. Markman, "Effects of Parental Divorce on Marital Commitment and Confidence," *Journal of Family Psychology*, 2008. 22(5): 789-793.

42. A. Kroska, "The Division of Labor at Home: A Review and Reconceptualization," *Social Psychology Quarterly*, 1997. 60: 304-322.

43. Stephanie Coontz, *Marriage, a History: From Obedience to Intimacy, or How Love Conquered Marriage*. New York: Viking Adult, 2005; Stephanie Coontz, *The Way We Never Were: American Families and the Nostalgia Trap*. New York: Basic Books, 2000.

44. Suzanne M. Bianchi and Lynne M. Casper, *American Families*. Washington, D.C.: Population Reference Bureau, 2000, http://www.prb.org/Publications/PopulationBulletins/2000/AmericanFamiliesPDF458KB.aspx.

45. Ibid.

46. Herbert Bynder, "Émile Durkheim and the Sociology of the Family," *Journal of Marriage and Family*, 1969. 31: 527-533.

47. David Popenoe, "American Family Decline, 1960-1990: A Review and Appraisal," *Journal of Marriage and the Family*, 1993. 55: 527-542.

48. Ibid.

49. Suzanne M. Bianchi and Lynne M. Casper, *American Families*. Washington, D.C.: Population Reference Bureau, 2000, http://www.prb.org/Publications/PopulationBulletins/2000/AmericanFamiliesPDF458KB.aspx.

50. Jessie Bernard, *The Future of Marriage*. New Haven, CT: Yale University Press, 1982.

51. Child Welfare Information Gateway, "Definitions of Child Abuse and Neglect," Accessed August 27, 2009, http://www.childwelfare.gov/systemwide/laws_policies/statutes/define.cfm.

52. Ibid.

53. Murray A. Straus, Richard J. Gelles, and Suzanne K. Steinmetz, *Behind Closed Doors: Violence in the American Family*. New Brunswick, NJ: Transaction Publishers, 2006.

54. U.S. Department of Health and Human Services, "Child Maltreatment 2007," Accessed October 12, 2009, http://www.acf.hhs.gov/programs/cb/pubs/cm07/index.htm.

55. "Ways to Stop Child Abuse," *ABCNews.com*, August 15, 2005, http://abcnews.go.com/GMA/TurningPoints/story?id=1019415&page=1.

56. Paul A. Nakonezny, Robert D. Shull, and Joseph Lee Rodgers, "The Effect of No-Fault Divorce Law on the Divorce Rate Across the 50 States and Its Relation to Income, Education, and Religiosity," *Journal of Marriage and the Family*, 1995. 57(2): 477-488.

57. Ibid.

CHAPTER 16

1. Audra Ang, "Life in a Chinese Village En Route to Beijing," *ABC News*, December 21, 2008.

2. U.S. Census Bureau, "Definition: urban and rural," https://ask.census.gov/cgi-bin/askcensus.cfg/php/enduser/std_adp. php?p_faqid=623&p_created=1092150238&p_sid=iLNdjSHj&p_accessibility=&p_lva=&p_sp=cF9zcmNoPSZwX3NvcnRfYnk9JnBfZ3JpZHNvcnQ9JnBfcm93X2NudD0mcF9wcm9kcz0mcF9jYXRzPSZwX3B2PSZwX2N2PSZwX3BhZ2U9MQ**&p_li=&p_topview=1&p_search_text=urban area definition.

3. U.S. Census Bureau, "State and County QuickFacts," http://quickfacts.census.gov/qfd/index.html.

4. Ibid.

5. Ibid.

6. U.S. Environmental Protection Agency, "Demographics," Accessed Sept. 28, 2009, http://www.epa.gov/oecaagct/ag101/demographics.html.

7. Population Reference Bureau, "Rural America Undergoing a Diversity of Demographic Change," Accessed August 14, 2009, http://www.prb.org/Articles/2006/RuralAmericaUndergoingaDiversityofDemographicChange.aspx.

8. Population Reference Bureau, "Human Population: Urbanization," Accessed August 14, 2009, http://www.prb.org/Educators/TeachersGuides/HumanPopulation/Urbanization.aspx.

9. Population Reference Bureau, "The Urban Demographic Revolution," http://www.prb.org/Articles/2000/TheUrbanDemographicRevolution.aspx.

10. Shaohua Chen, and Martin Ravallion, "How Have the World's Poorest Fared Since the Early 1980s?" *World Bank Research Observer*, 2004. 19(2): 141-170, http://www.prb.org/Articles/2004/UrbanizationAnEnvironmentalForcetoBeReckonedWith.aspx.

11. Population Reference Bureau, "The Urban Demographic Revolution," http://www.prb.org/Articles/2000/TheUrbanDemographicRevolution.aspx.

12. World Bank, "Dhaka: Improving Living Conditions for the Urban Poor," Accessed August 14, 2009, http://www.worldbank.org.bd/WBSITE/EXTERNAL/COUNTRIES/SOUTHASIAEXT/BANGLADESHEXTN/0,,contentMDK:21384826~pagePK:141137~piPK:141127~theSitePK:295760,00.html.

13. Eric H. Monkkonen, *America Becomes Urban: The Development of U.S. Cities and Towns, 1780-1980*. Berkeley: University of California Press, 1988.

14. Energy Information Administration, "Residential Energy Consumption: Special Topics," Accessed August 14, 2009, http://www.eia.doe.gov/emeu/plugs/plrecs01.html.

15. U.S. Census Bureau, "About Metropolitan and Micropolitan Statistical Areas," Accessed August 10, 2009, http://www.census.gov/population/www/metroareas/aboutmetro.html.

16. Brian J.L. Berry, "Urbanization and Counterurbanization in the United States," *Annals of the American Academy of Political and Social Science*, 1980. 451: 13-20.

17. Rachel E. Dwyer, "Expanding Homes and Increasing Inequalities: U.S. Housing Development and the Residential Segregation of the Affluent," *Social Problems*, 2007. 54(1): 23-46.

18. Joseph F. Zimmerman, "Metropolitan Reform in the U.S.: An Overview," *Public Administration Review*, 1970. 30(5): 531-543, http://www.jstor.org/pss/974421.

19. Thomas J. Nechyba and Randall P. Walsh, "Urban Sprawl," *The Journal of Economic Perspectives*, 2004. 18(4): 177-200.

20. John G. Mitchell, "Urban Sprawl," *National Geographic*, July 2001, http://ngm.nationalgeographic.com/ngm/data/2001/07/01/htm/fulltext3.html.

21. Ibid.

22. Howard Frumkin, "Urban Sprawl and Public Health," *Centers for Disease Control and Prevention*, 2002. http://www.cdc.gov/healthyplaces/articles/Urban%20Sprawl%20and%20Public%20Health%20-%20PHR.pdf.

23. John G. Mitchell, "Urban Sprawl," *National Geographic*, July 2001, http://ngm.nationalgeographic.com/ngm/data/2001/07/01/htm/fulltext3.html.

24. Ibid.

25. "U.S. Census Press Release," *U.S. Census Bureau News*, March 27, 2008, http://www.census.gov/Press-Release/www/releases/archives/population/011671.html.

26. "Urban Sprawl: the Big Picture," *Science@NASA*, October 11, 2002, http://science.nasa.gov/headlines/y2002/11oct_sprawl.htm.

27. Sean F. Reardon and Glenn Firebaugh, "Measures of Multigroup Segregation," *Sociological Methodology*, 2002. 32: 33–67.

28. Douglas S. Massey and Nancy A. Denton, "Hypersegregation in U.S. Metropolitan Areas: Black and Hispanic Segregation along Five Dimensions," *Demography*, 1989. 26(3): 373–391; Douglas S. Massey and Nancy A. Denton, "The Dimensions of Residential Segregation," *Social Forces*, 1988. 67(2): 281–315.

29. Sean F. Reardon and Glenn Firebaugh, "Measures of Multigroup Segregation," *Sociological Methodology*, 2002. 32: 33–67.

30. *The Chicago 77*, "Chicago is America's Most Segregated City," January 21, 2009, http://www.thechicago77.com/2009/01/chicago-is-americas-most-segregated-city/.

31. Douglas S. Massey, "The Age of Extremes: Concentrated Affluence and Poverty in the Twenty-First Century," *Demography*, 1996. 33(4): 395–412.

32. John Iceland and Rima Wilkes, "Does Socioeconomic Status Matter? Race, Class, and Residential Segregation," *Social Problems*, 2006. 53(2): 248–273.

33. Jeremy F. Pais, Scott J. South, and Kyle Crowder, "White Flight Revisited: A Multiethnic Perspective on Neighborhood Out-Migration," *Population Research & Policy Review*, 2009. 28(3): 321–346.

34. Ted Mouw and Barbara Entwisle, "Residential Segregation and Interracial Friendship in Schools," *The American Journal of Sociology*, 2006. 112(2): 394–441.

35. *The Chicago 77*, "Chicago is America's Most Segregated City," January 21, 2009, http://www.thechicago77.com/2009/01/chicago-is-americas-most-segregated-city/.

36. Phillip J. Longman, Jim Moscou, Jill Jordan Sieder, Mike Tharp, John Slania, and Mike Tobin, "American Gridlock," *U.S. News & World Report*, 2001. 130(21): 16–22.

37. Surface Transportation Policy & Revenue Study Commission, "Peter J. Pantuso, President & CEO, American Bus Association: Testimony," http://transportationfortomorrow.org/pdfs/commission_meetings/0307_field_hearing_washington/031907_fh_aba_testimony.pdf.

38. "Ways to Unjam Highways," *Christian Science Monitor*, 2001. 93(116), http://www.csmonitor.com/2001/0510/p10s1.html.

39. Louis Wirth, "Urbanism as a way of life," *American Journal of Sociology*, 1938. 434(1): 1–24.

40. Elijah Anderson, *Code of the street: Decency, violence and the moral life of the inner city*. New York: W.W. Norton and Company, 1999.

41. Wally N'Dow, "Cities in crisis: the internationalization of urban problems," *Harvard International Review*, March 22, 1996.

42. UN HABITAT, "Our Mission," Accessed August 13, 2009, http://www.unhabitat.org/categories.asp?catid=10.

43. Ferdinand Tonnies, *Community and Society (Gemeinschaft und Gesellschaft)*. East Lansing, MI: Michigan State University Press, 1887.

44. Ibid.

45. Emile Durkheim, *The Division of Labor in Society*. New York: Free Press, 1997.

46. Ibid.

47. John Iceland and Rima Wilkes, "Does Socioeconomic Status Matter? Race, Class, and Residential Segregation," *Social Problems*, 2006. 53(2): 248–273.

48. Environmental Software and Services, "From Calcutta With Love," Accessed August 12, 2009, http://www.ess.co.at/GAIA/CASES/IND/CAL/CALmain.html#popu.

49. Louis Wirth, "Urbanism as a way of life," *American Journal of Sociology*, 1938. 434(1): 1–24.

50. Christopher Jencks, *The Homeless*. Cambridge MA: Harvard University Press, 1994.

51. Elliot Leibow, *Tell them who I am: The lives of homeless women*. New York: Penguin Books, 1995.

CHAPTER 17

1. Frank Bajak, "After APEC, Free Trade Orthodoxy Questioned," *The Associated Press*, November 25, 2008, http://abcnews.go.com/Business/wireStory?id=6330029.

2. Marshall McLuhan, *The Gutenberg Galaxy: The Making of Typographic Man*. Toronto: University of Toronto Press, 1962.

3. A. Aboubakr Badawi, "The Social Dimension of Globalization and Health," *Perspectives on Global Development and Technology*, 2004. 3(1–2): 73–90.

4. George Ritzer, *The Globalization of Nothing*. Thousand Oaks, CA: Pine Forge Press, 2004; Jeffrey G. Williamson, "Globalization, Convergence, and History: Papers Presented at the Fifty-Fifth Annual Meeting of the Economic History Association," *The Journal of Economic*

History, 1996. 56(2): 277–306; Hugo Radice, "Globalization and National Capitalisms: Theorizing Convergence and Differentiation," *Review of International Political Economy*, 2000. 7(4): 719–742.

5. Chauncy D. Harris, "English as International Language in Geography: Development and Limitations," *Geographical Review*, 2001. 91(4): 675–689; George Ritzer, *The Globalization of Nothing*. Thousand Oaks, CA: Pine Forge Press, 2004.

6. George Ritzer, *The Globalization of Nothing*. Thousand Oaks, CA: Pine Forge Press, 2004.

7. George Ross, "Labor versus Globalization," *Annals of the American Academy of Political and Social Science*, 2000. 570: 78–91.

8. Frank Bajak, "After APEC, Free Trade Orthodoxy Questioned," *The Associated Press*, November 25, 2008, http://abcnews.go.com/Business/wireStory?id=6330029.

9. Jonathan Crush, "The Global Raiders: Nationalism, Globalization and the South African Brain Drain," *Journal of International Affairs*, 2002. 56 (1): 147–173.

10. Donald Lien and Yan Wang, "Brain Drain or Brain Gain: A Revisit," *Journal of Population Economics*, 2005. 18(1): 153–163.

11. Jean-Christophe Dumont and Georges Lemaître, "Beyond the Headlines: New Evidence on the Brain Drain," *Revue économique*, 2005. 56(6): 1275–1299.

12. Manfred B. Steger, "Global Culture: Sameness or Difference?" in *Globalization: The Transformation of Social Worlds,* eds. D. Stanley Eitzen and Maxine Baca Zinn. Belmont, CA: Wadsworth, 2009.

13. Susan F. Martin, "Heavy Traffic: International Migration in an Era of Globalization," in *Globalization: The Transformation of Social Worlds,* ed. D. Stanley Eitzen and Maxine Baca Zinn. Belmont, CA: Wadsworth, 2009.

14. D. Stanley Eitzen, "Dimensions of Globalization," in *Globalization: The Transformation of Social Worlds,* ed. D. Stanley Eitzen and Maxine Baca Zinn. Belmont, CA: Wadsworth, 2009.

15. Harold Kerbo, *World Poverty: Global Inequality and the Modern World System.* New York: McGraw-Hill, 2006.

16. Jonathan Crush, "The Global Raiders: Nationalism, Globalization and the South African Brain Drain," *Journal of International Affairs*, 2002. 56 (1): 147–173.

17. Jared Diamond, *Guns, Germs, and Steel: The Fates of Human Societies.* New York: W.W. Norton & Company, 1997.

18. Ibid.

19. Urban Institute and Brookings Institution, Tax Policy Center, "OECD Taxes as Share of GDP 1999–2005," Accessed September 2, 2009, http://www.taxpolicy center.org/taxfacts/displayafact.cfm?Docid=307&Topic2 id=95.

20. United Nations, "The Millennium Development Goals Report: Statistical Annex 2006," Accessed August 27, 2009, http://unstats.un.org/unsd/mdg/Default.aspx.

21. Harold Kerbo, *World Poverty: Global Inequality and the Modern World System.* New York: McGraw-Hill, 2006.

22. UNESCO Institution for Statistics, "Towards the next generation of literacy statistics," http://www.uis.unesco.org/ev_en.php?ID=7804_201&ID2=DO_TOPIC.

23. Nicholas D. Kristof and Sheryl WuDunn, *Half the Sky: Turning Oppression into Opportunity for Women Worldwide.* New York: Knopf, 2009.

24. Kevin Bales, *Disposable People: New Slavery in the Global Economy.* Berkeley, CA: University of California Press, 1999.

25. Ibid.

26. Ibid.

27. Ibid.

28. George Ritzer, *The Globalization of Nothing.* Thousand Oaks, CA: Pine Forge Press, 2004.

29. Michael Astor, "Poor Countries Want Greater Role in World Economy," *The Associated Press*, June 25, 2009, http://abcnews.go.com/Business/wireStory?id=7923886.

30. Ibid.

31. Ibid.

32. Ibid.

33. Ibid.

34. Ibid.

35. Timothy M. Smeeding and Lee Rainwater, "Comparing Living Standards Across Nations: Real Incomes at the Top, the Bottom, and the Middle," *Social Policy Research Centre*, 2002. 120: 1–39, http://www.sprc.unsw.edu.au/dp/DP120.pdf.

36. Global Policy Forum, "The World Economic and Social Development," http://www.globalpolicy.org/nations/kaiswork. htm.

37. Ibid.

38. Daniel J. Slottje, "Measuring the Quality of Life Across Countries," *Review of Economics and Statistics*, 1991. 73(4): 684–693.

39. Immanuel Wallerstein, *The Modern World System: Capitalist Agriculture and the Origins of the European World-Economy in the Sixteenth Century.* New York: Academic Press, 1974; Immanuel Wallerstein, *The Capitalist World-Economy.* New York: Cambridge University Press, 1979.

40. Michael Harrington, *The Vast Majority: The Journey to the World's Poor.* New York: Simon and Schuster, 1977.

41. Thomas L. Friedman, *The World Is Flat: A Brief History of the Twenty-first Century.* New York: Farrar, Straus & Giroux, 2005.

42. T.R. Reid, *The United States of Europe: The New Superpower and the End of American Supremacy.* New York: Penguin, 2004.

43. Ibid; Jeremy Rifkin, *The European Dream.* New York: Jeremy P. Tarcher/Penguin, 2005.

44. USAID, "New frontiers in U.S. Foreign Aid," Accessed September 3, 2009, http://www.usaid.gov/policy/.

45. Organisation for Economic Co-operation and Development, "Statistical Annex of the 2009 Development Cooperation Report," Accessed September 3, 2009, http://www.oecd.org/document/9/0,3343,en_2649_344 47_1893129_1_1_1_1,00.html.

46. Ibid.

CHAPTER 18

1. Edith M. Lederer, "UN Says World Population to Hit 7 Billion in 2012," *ABCNews.com*, March 11, 2009, http://abcnews.go.com/US/wireStory?id=7061338.

2. Central Intelligence Agency, "Population 2007," Accessed April 20, 2007, https://www.cia.gov/cia/publications/factbook/rankorder/2119rank.html.

3. Ibid.

4. Ibid.

5. Eric Neumayer, "HIV/AIDS and Cross-National Convergence in Life Expectancy," *Population and Development Review*, 2004. 30(4): 727-742.

6. John R. Wilmoth and Jean-Marie Robine, "The World Trend in Maximum Life Span," *Population and Development Review*, 2003. 29: 239-257.

7. Central Intelligence Agency, "Life Expectancy at Birth," https://www.cia.gov/library/publications/the-world-factbook/rankorder/2102 rank.html.

8. Central Intelligence Agency, "Country Comparison: Infant Mortality Rate," Accessed Sept. 21, 2009, https://www.cia.gov/library/publications/the-world-factbook/rank order/2091rank.html.

9. Douglas Massey, Rafael Alarecon, Jorege Durand, and Humberto Gonzalez, *Return to Aztlan: The Social Process of International Migration from Western Mexico.* Berkeley, CA: University of California Press, 1987; Alejandro Portes and Ruben G. Rumbaut, *Immigrant American: A Portrait.* Berkeley, CA: University of California Press, 1996.

10. "Blood on the Border," *Intelligence Report*, 2001. 101: http://www.splcenter.org/intel/intelreport/article.jsp? pid=418; "Anti-Immigration Groups," *Intelligence Report*, 2001. 101: http://www.splcenter.org/intel/intelreport/article.jsp?sid=175.

11. Naohiro Ogawa and Robert D. Retherford, "The Resumption of Fertility Decline in Japan: 1973-92," *Population and Development Review*, 1993. 19(4): 703-741.

12. Cynthia G. Wagner, "Promoting Parenthood in Japan," *Futurist*, 2007. 41(3): 9-13; Hayashi Yuka and Sebastian Moffett, "Cautiously, and Aging Japan Warms to Foreign Workers," *Wall Street Journal*, May 25, 2007.

13. John R. Bermingham, "Exponential population growth and doubling times: Are they dead or merely quiescent?" *Population and Environment*, 2003. 24(4): 313-327.

14. James Lee and Feng Wang, *One Quarter of Humanity: Malthusian Mythology and Chinese Realities, 1700-2000.* Cambridge, MA: Harvard University Press, 1999; Rachel Murphy, "Fertility and Distorted Sex Ratios in a Rural Chinese County: Culture, State, and Policy," *Population and Development Review*, 2003. 29(4): 595-626; Nancy E. Riley, "China's Population: New Trends and Challenges," *Population Bulletin*, 2004. 59(2): 3-36.

15. Rachel Murphy, "Fertility and Distorted Sex Ratios in a Rural Chinese County: Culture, State, and Policy," *Population and Development Review*, 2003. 29(4): 595-626; Nancy E. Riley, "China's Population: New Trends and Challenges," *Population Bulletin*, 2004. 59(2): 3-36.

16. *The International Herald Tribune*, "Report: China's One-Child Policy has Prevented 400 Million Births," November 9, 2006, http://www.iht.com/articles/ap/2006/11/09/asia/AS_GEN_China_One_Child_Policy.php.

17. Ibid.

18. Therese Hesketh and Zhu Wei Xing, "Abnormal sex ratios in human populations: Causes and consequences," *Proceedings of the National Academy of Sciences of the United States of America*, 2006. 103(36): 13271-13275, http://www.pubmedcentral.nih.gov/articlerender.fcgi?art id=1569153.

19. Julian L. Simon, *Theory of Population and Economic Growth.* New York: Basil Blackwell, 1986; Julian L. Simon, "One Aggregate Empirical Studies Relating to Population Variables to Economic Development," *Population and Development Review*, 1989. 15(2): 323-332.

20. Gary S. Becker, Edward L. Glaeser, and Kevin M. Murphy, "Population and Economic Growth," *The American Economic Review*, 1999. 89(2): 145-149.

21. Jared Diamond, *Collapse: How Societies Choose to Fail or Succeed.* London: Penguin Books Ltd., 2005.

22. Kingsley Davis, "The World Demographic Transition," *The Annals of the American Academy of Political and Social Science,* 1945. 237: 1-11; Sarah F. Harbison and Warren C. Robinson, "Policy Implications of the Next World Demographic Transition," *Studies in Family Planning*, 2002. 33(1): 37-48.

23. Dudley Kirk, "Demographic Transition Theory," *Population Studies*, 1996. 50(3): 361-387.

24. Kingsley Davis, "The World Demographic Transition," *The Annals of the American Academy of Political and Social Science*, 1945. 237: 1-11.

25. United Nations Population Fund, "UNFPA Global Population Policy Update," http://www.unfpa.org/parliamentarians/news/newsletters/issue49.htm.

26. Ibid.

27. Carl Haub, "Global Aging and the Demographic Divide," *Public Policy & Aging Report*, 2007. 17(4): http://www.prb.org/Articles/2008/globalaging.aspx.

28. Matthew Conelly, "New perspectives on the international campaign to limit population growth," *Comparative Studies in Society and History*, 2003. 45(1): 122–147.

29. Central Intelligence Agency, "Population 2007," Accessed April 20, 2009. https://www.cia.gov/cia/publications/factbook/rankorder/2119rank.html.

CHAPTER 19

1. Bradley S. Klapper, "Group: World Failing to Halt Biodiversity Decline," *ABC News*, July 1, 2009, http://abcnews.go.com/International/wireStory?id=7982697.

2. U.S. Fish and Wildlife Service, "Threatened and Endangered Species Database System (TESS)," Accessed October 5, 2009, http://ecos.fws.gov/tess_public/.

3. William R. Catton and Riley Dunlap, "Environmental Sociology: A New Paradigm," *The American Sociologist*, 1978. 13: 41–19; Frederick H. Buttel, "New Directions in Environmental Sociology," *Annual Review of Sociology*, 1987. 13: 465–488.

4. William R. Catton, "Foundations of Human Ecology," *Sociological perspectives*, 1994. 37(1): 75–95.

5. Environmental Protection Agency, "Great Lakes Monitoring," Accessed August 19, 2009, http://www.epa.gov/glnpo/monitoring/great_minds_great_lakes/journey_of_lake_guardian/ontario.html.

6. Riley E. Dunlap, "Environmental Sociology: A personal perspective on its first quarter century," *Organization and Environment*, 2002. 15: 10–29.

7. Jared Diamond, *Collapse: How Societies Choose to Fail or Succeed*. New York: Penguin Group, 2005.

8. Julian L. Simon, *Population Matters: People, Resources, Environment, and Immigration*. New Brunswick, NJ: Transactions Press, 1990.

9. U.S. Census Bureau: Public Information Office, "Census Bureau Projects Doubling of Nation's Population by 2100," Accessed October 5, 2009, http://www.census.gov/Press-Release/www/2000/cb00-05.html.

10. Ibid.

11. Riley E. Dunlap, "Environmental Sociology: A personal perspective on its first quarter century," *Organization and Environment*, 2002. 15: 10–29; Riley E. Dunlap and William R. Catton, Jr., "Which function(s) of the environment do we study? A comparison of environmental and natural resource sociology," *Society and Natural Resources*, 2002. 15: 239–249.

12. Pollution Issues, "Cancer Ally Louisiana," Accessed August 23, 2009, http://www.pollutionissues.com/Br-Co/Cancer-Alley-Louisiana.html.

13. Ibid.

14. Robert E. Bullard, *Confronting Environmental Racism: Voices from the Grassroots*. Boston: South End Press, 1993; Robert E. Bullard, "Anatomy of Environmental Racism and the Environmental Justice Movement," *The Environment and Society Reader*. Needham Heights, MA: Allyn and Bacon, 2001

15. Natgan Keyfitz, "Population Growth, Development, and the Environment," *Population Studies*, 1996. 50(3): 335–359; Beverly H. Wright, "Endangered Communities: The Struggle for Environmental Justice in Louisiana's Chemical Corridor," *Journal of Public Management and Social Policy*, 1998. 4: 181–191.

16. Environmental Protection Agency, "Environmental Justice," Accessed August 23, 2009, http://www.epa.gov/oecaerth/environmentaljustice.

17. Ivor Lensworth Livingston, *The Handbook of Black American Health: the mosaic of conditions, issues, policies, and prospects*. Santa Barbara, CA: Greenwood Publishing, 1994.

18. Environmental Protection Agency, "Drinking Water," Accessed August 23, 2009, http://www.epa.gov/ebtpages/watedrinkingwater.html.

19. World Health Organization, "Drinking-water quality and preventing water-borne infectious disease," Accessed August 24, 2009, http://www.who.int/water_sanitation_health/dwq/infectdis/en/index.html.

20. Environmental Protection Agency, "Managing Nonpoint Source Pollution from Agriculture," Accessed August 24, 2009, http://www.epa.gov/nps/facts/point6.htm.

21. Environmental Protection Agency, "Air Pollutants," Accessed Sept. 21, 2009, http://www.epa.gov/ebtpages/airairpollutants.html.

22. Lourdes Salvador, "Hawaii No Panacea, Air Pollution is Everywhere," *Los Angeles Chronicle*, June 1, 2008.

23. U.S. Environmental Protection Agency, "Smog—Who Does It Hurt? What You Need to Know About Ozone and Your Health," http://www.epa.gov/airnow/health/smog.pdf.

24. Pen Loh and Jodi Sugerman-Brozan, "Environmental Justice Organizing for Environmental health: Case Study on Asthma and Disel Exhaust in Roxbury, Massachusetts," *Annals of the American Academy of Political and Social Science*, 2002. 584: 110–124.

25. Daniel Stone and Karsten Moran, "Toxic Top Ten," *Newsweek*, http://www.newsweek.com/id/164813.

26. Austin Ramzy, "Twittering Ban Air Particles in Beijing," *Time*, June 19, 2009.

27. Environmental Protection Agency, "Climate Change: Science," Accessed Sept. 21, 2009, http://www.epa.gov/climatechange/science/index.html.

28. Gerhard K. Helig, "Neglected dimensions of global land-use change: Reflections and data," *Population and Development Review*, 1994. 20(4): 831–859.

29. Thomas Wagner, "Millions at risk from rising sea levels," *USAToday.com*, March 29, 2007, http://www.usatoday.

com/weather/climate/globalwarming/2007-03-27-sea-level-rise_N.htm.

30. United Nations Environment Programme, "Science," Accessed October 28, 2009, http://www.unep.org/climatechange/Science/tabid/234/language/en-US/Default.aspx.

31. Brian M. Fagan, *The Little Ice Age: How Climate Made History, 1300-1850.* New York: Perseus Books, 2000.

32. Environmental Protection Agency, "Climate Change: Basic Information," Accessed Sept. 21, 2009, http://www.epa.gov/climatechange/basicinfo.html.

33. United Nations Framework Convention on Climate Change, "Kyoto Protocol," Accessed October 28, 2009, http://unfccc.int/kyoto_protocol/items/2830.php.

34. Gerhard K. Helig, "Neglected dimensions of global land-use change: Reflections and data," *Population and development review*, 1994. 20(4): 831-859.

35. Environmental Protection Agency, "Learn the Issues," Accessed August 24, 2009, http://www.epa.gov/epahome/learn.htm#green.

36. Richard York, Eugene A. Rosa, and Thomas Deitz, "Bridging environmental science with environmental policy: Plasticity of population, affluence, and technology," *Social Science Quarterly*, 2002. 83(1): 18-34; Richard York, Eugene A. Rosa, and Thomas Deitz, "Footprints on the Earth: The environmental consequences of modernity," *American Sociological Review*, 2003. 68(2): 279-300.

37. Andrew K. Jorgenson and Thomas J. Burns, "The political-economic causes of change in the ecological footprints of nations, 1991-2001: A quantitative investigation," *Social Science Research*, 2007. 36: 834-853.

38. Environmental Protection Agency, "Municipal Solid Waste," Accessed February 3, 2008, www.epa.gov/msw/facts.htm.

39. Ibid; Clean Air Council, "Waste Reduction and Recycling Program," Accessed August 24, 2009, http://www.cleanair.org/Waste/wasteFacts.html.

40. Heather Knight, "No flies on S.F.'s new composting law," *San Francisco Chronicle*, September 9, 2009, http://www.sfgate.com/cgi-bin/article.cgi?f=/c/a/2009/09/09/BAR419IP8A.DTL.

41. Environmental Sustainability Committee, "Nationwide Waste Statistics," Accessed October 28, 2009, http://www.esc.mtu.edu/docs/NationWideStatistics.pdf.

42. Anand Krishnamoorthy, "Behind the Hype, the Real India: Unskilled Workers Stoke Economy as Tech Sector Takes Glory," *The International Herald Tribune*, July 12, 2006; Ken Moritsugu, "Many Environmental Fears: Ship Breaking, Big Industry in India Falters," *The Philadelphia Inquirer*, November 12, 2006.

43. Jonathan Lynn, "World 'Sleepwalking' Into Disasters: U.N. Aid Chief," *ABCNews.com*, June 16, 2009, http://abcnews.go.com/International/WireStory?id=7851163&page=1.

44. Central Intelligence Agency, "Australia-Oceana—Tuvalu," Accessed October 5, 2009, https://www.cia.gov/library/publications/the-world-factbook/geos/tv.html.

45. Intergovernmental Panel on Climate Change, "Climate change 2007: Synthesis Report," http://www.ipcc.ch/.

46. Brad Crouch, "Sinking Tuvalu Wants Our Help As Ocean Levels Rise," *PerthNow*, October 4, 2008, http://www.news.com.au/perthnow/story/0,,24446057-5005369,00.html.

47. World View of Global Warning, "Global Warming, photography, pictures, photos, climate change..."Accessed August 25, 2009, http://www.worldviewofglobalwarming.org/pages/rising-seas.html.

48. SUSPS, "Population Numbers, Projections, Graphs, and Data," Accessed August 20, 2009, http://www.susps.org/overview/numbers.html.

49. Delnaaz Irani, "Mumbai disrupted by water shortages," *BBC News*, August 2, 2009, http://news.bbc.co.uk/2/hi/business/8178729.stm.

50. Jeffrey Kluger, "Is Global Warming Fueling Katrina?" *Time*, August 25, 2005, http://www.time.com/time/nation/article/0,8599,1099102,00.html.

51. Jared Diamond, *Collapse: How Societies Choose to Fail or Succeed*. New York: Penguin Group, 2005.

52. Roberto Suro, "Pollution-Weary Minorities Try Civil Rights Tack," *The New York Times*, January 11, 1993, http://www.nytimes.com/1993/01/11/us/pollution-weary-minorities-try-civil-rights-tack.html.

53. Ibid.

54. ReuseThisBag.com, "Why Use Reusable Grocery Bags," Accessed August 24, 2009, http://www.reusethisbag.com/why.asp.

55. Environmental Protection Agency. "The Birth of the EPA," Accessed August 25, 2009, http://www.epa.gov/history/topics/epa/15c.htm.

56. Seth Borenstein, "AP IMPACT: An American life worth less today," *USAToday.com*, July 11, 2008, http://www.usatoday.com/news/ nation/2008-07-10-796349025_x.htm.

57. Ibid.

58. Environmental Protection Agency, "From Ecology to Environmentalism," Accessed August 25, 2009, http://www.epa.gov/history/publications/origins4.htm.

59. Environmental Protection Agency, "The Birth of the EPA," Accessed September 18, 2009, http://www.epa.gov/history/topics/epa/15c.htm.

60. Clean Air Council, "Waste Reduction & Recycling Program," Accessed August 25, 2009, http://www.nytimes.com/1993/01/11/us/pollution-weary-minorities-try-civil-rights-tack.html.

61. Ibid.

62. Toward Freedom, "The Globalization of Garbage," Accessed August 25, 2009, http://towardfreedom.com/home/content/view/1640/1/.

63. "China Plans to Pick up Trash on Mt. Everest," *Celsias*, August 6, 2008, http://www.celsias.com/article/china-plans-pick-trash-mt-everest/.

CHAPTER 20

1. Bob Holmes, "How Warfare Shaped Human Evolution," *ABC News,* November 13, 2008, http://abcnews.go.com/Technology/story? id=6241250&page=1.

2. C. Wright Mills, *The Power Elite. A New Edition.* New York: Oxford University Press, 2000.

3. G. Williams Domhoff, *Who Rules America? Power, Politics, and Social Change, 5th edition.* New York: McGraw-Hill, 2006.

4. Dwight D. Eisenhower, "Military-Industrial Complex Speech," Accessed August 5, 2008, http://www.yale.edu/lawweb/avalon/presiden/speeches/eisenhower001.htm.

5. Stephen Van Evera, *Causes of war: Power and the roots of conflict.* Ithaca, NY: Cornell University Press, 1999.

6. Ibid.

7. Ibid.

8. Ibid.

9. Ibid.

10. Department of the Navy, Naval Historical Center, "Instances of Use of United States Forces Abroad, 1798–1993," http://www.history.navy.mil/wars/foabroad.htm.

11. Stockholm International Peace Research Institute, "Military expenditure: SIPRI Yearbook 2008: Armaments, Disarmament and International Security," www.sipri.org/research/armaments/milex/resultoutput/15major spenders.

12. Ibid.

13. Stockholm International Peace Research Institute, "Recent Trends in Military Expenditure," Accessed Sept. 22, 2009, http://www.sipri.org/research/armaments/milex/resultoutput/trends.

14. Alex Mintz and Chi Huang, "Guns versus Butter: The Indirect Link," *American Journal of Political Science*, 1991. 35(3): 738–757.

15. Errol A. Henderson, "Military Spending and Poverty," *The Journal of Politics,* May 1998. 60(2): 503–520.

16. Ibid.

17. Benjamin Fordham, "The Political and Economic Sources of Inflation in the American Military Budget," *The Journal of Conflict Resolution*, 2003. 47(5): 574–593.

18. William Hartung and Frida Berrigan, "Top Pentagon Contractors, FY 2006: Major Beneficiaries of the Bush Administration's Military Buildup," *A World Policy Institute Special Report*, 2007.

19. Stockholm International Peace Research Institute, "Small arms and light weapons (SALW)," http://www.sipri.org/research/disarmament/salw.

20. Stockholm International Peace Research Institute, "Nuclear forces development," Accessed Sept. 22, 2009, http://www.sipri.org/research/armaments/nbc/nuclear.

21. Natural Resources Defense Council, "New Estimates of the U.S. Nuclear Weapons Stockpile, 2007 and 2012," Accessed October 30, 2009, http://www.nrdc.org/nuclear/stockpile_2007–2012.asp.

22. A. Carter, J. Deutsch and P. Zelicow, "Catastrophic terrorism," *Foreign Affairs*, 1998. 77: 80–95.

23. Kelly R. Damphousse and Brent L. Smith, "Terrorism and Empirical Testing: Using Indictment Data to Assess Changes in Terrorist Conduct," in *Terrorism and Counter-Terrorism: Criminological Perspectives*. Philadelphia, PA: Elsevier Science, 2004.

24. Austin Turk, "Sociology of Terrorism," *Annual Review of Sociology*, 2004. 30: 271–286.

25. Central Intelligence Agency, "Terrorism FAQs," Accessed October 30, 2009, https://www.cia.gov/news-information/cia-the-war-on-terrorism/terrorism-faqs.html.

26. Austin Turk, "Sociology of Terrorism," *Annual Review of Sociology*, 2004. 30: 271–286.

27. Kelly R. Damphousse and Brent L. Smith, "Terrorism and Empirical Testing: Using Indictment Data to Assess Changes in Terrorist Conduct," in *Terrorism and Counter-Terrorism: Criminological Perspectives*. Philadelphia, PA: Elsevier Science, 2004.

28. Ibid.

29. Ibid.

30. Ibid.

31. Ibid.

32. Walter Laqueur, *The new terrorism: fanaticism and the arms of mass destruction.* New York: Oxford University Press, 1999.

33. Ibid.

34. Ibid.

35. Catherine McNicole-Stock, *Rural Radicals: Righteous Rage in the American Grain*. Ithaca, NY: Cornell University Press, 1996.

36. Ibid.

37. Ibid.

38. Cindy C. Combs, *Terrorism in the Twenty-First Century, 3rd Edition*. Upper Saddle River, NJ: Prentice Hall, 2003.

39. Walter Laqueur, *The new terrorism: fanaticism and the arms of mass destruction.* New York: Oxford University Press, 1999.

40. Ibid.

41. Kelly R. Damphousse and Brent L. Smith, "Terrorism and Empirical Testing: Using Indictment Data to Assess Changes in Terrorist Conduct," in *Terrorism and Counter-Terrorism: Criminological Perspectives*. Philadelphia, PA: Elsevier Science, 2004.

42. Ibid.

43. Ibid.

44. Ibid.

45. The Coalition to Stop the Use of Child Soldiers, "Some Facts," Accessed Sept. 22, 2009, http://www.child-soldiers.org/childsoldiers/some-facts.

46. The Coalition to Stop the Use of Child Soldiers, "Questions & Answers," Accessed Sept. 22, 2009, http://www.child-soldiers.org/childsoldiers/questions-and-answers.

47. Ibid.

48. Ibid.

49. Ibid.

50. The Coalition to Stop the Use of Child Soldiers, "Legal Framework," Accessed Sept. 22, 2009, http://www.child-soldiers.org/childsoldiers/legal-framework.

51. Karen Allen, "Bleak future for Congo's child soldiers," *BBC News*, July 25, 2006, http://news.bbc.co.uk/2/hi/africa/5213996.stm.

52. Austin Turk, "Sociology of Terrorism," *Annual review of sociology*, 2004. 30: 271–286.

53. Ibid.

54. Immanuel Wallerstein, *The capitalist world economy*. New York: Cambridge University Press, 1979.

55. Jonathan D. Glater, "Blue collars in olive drab," *The New York Times*, May 22, 2005, http://www.nytimes.com/2005/05/22/national/class/MILITARY-FINAL.html.

56. Austin Turk, "Sociology of Terrorism," *Annual review of sociology*, 2004. 30: 271–286.

57. Catherine McNicole-Stock, *Rural Radicals: Righteous Rage in the American Grain*. Ithaca, NY: Cornell University Press, 1996.

58. Austin Turk, "Sociology of Terrorism," *Annual review of sociology*, 2004. 30: 271–286.

59. Stockholm International Peace Research Institute, "SIPRI Yearbook 2008: Armaments, Disarmament and International Security," http://www.docstoc.com/docs/5532736/Stockholm-International-Peace-Research-Institute-Press-release-June-Embargo.

60. Ibid.

61. Robert Burns, "US Considering Implications of Nuclear Decline," *ABC News*, Oct. 26, 2008, http://abcnews.go.com/Politics/wireStory?id=6113547.

62. The Norwegian Nobel Institute, "The Development and Proliferation of Nuclear Weapons," Accessed Sept. 22, 2009, http://nobelprize.org/educational_games/peace/nuclear_weapons/readmore.html.

63. Ibid.

64. UN Action to Counter Terrorism, "Resolution: The United Nations Global Counter-Terrorism Strategy," Accessed Sept. 22, 2009, http://www.un.org/terrorism/strategy-counter-terrorism.shtml# poa1.

65. Ibid.

66. *CNN.com*, "CNN Presents Classroom: A Day of Terror: Remembering the Oklahoma City Bombing," Accessed Sept. 22, 2009, http://www.cnn.com/2006/EDUCATION/04/04/cnnpce.oklahoma.city/index.html?iref=newssearch

67. Oklahoma City National Memorial & Museum, "Building and Memorial Site," Accessed Sept. 22, 2009, http://oklahomacitynationalmemorial.org/secondary.php?section=1&catid=49.

PHOTO CREDITS

CHAPTER 1 PAGE 2: © Chris Rank/CORBIS All Rights Reserved; **5:** © Andrew Holbrooke/CORBIS All Rights Reserved; **6:** Zigy Kaluzny/Getty Images Inc. - Stone Allstock; **8:** Courtesy of the Library of Congress; **9 (from left):** Todd Gipstein/National Geographic Image Collection; George Washington by Gilbert Stuart, Museum of the City of New York; **13:** Michael Buckner/Getty Images Entertainment/Getty Images; **11 (from top):** David Young Wolff/PhotoEdit Inc.; A. Ramey/PhotoEdit Inc.; John Moore/Getty Images News/Getty Images; **17:** SW Productions/Photodisc/Getty Images; **18 (from top):** © Andrew Holbrooke/CORBIS All Rights Reserved; Courtesy of the Library of Congress; SW Productions/Photodisc/Getty Images

CHAPTER 2 PAGE 20: AP Wide World Photos; **23:** Louie Schoeman/Shutterstock; **24:** © Ellen B. Senisi; **26 (from top):** Gillian Laub/Getty Images Inc. - Stone Allstock; Ariel Skelley/Getty Images Inc.- Blend Images; Annie Griffiths Belt/CORBIS All Rights Reserved; Robert Van Der Hilst/Reportage/Getty Images; **28 (from left):** cultura/Creative/Corbis RF; Heide Benser/Corbis; Erwin Wodicka/Shutterstock; Christoph Weihs/Shutterstock; Morgan David de Lossy/CORBIS All Rights Reserved; Dhannte/Shutterstock; Gregor Schuster/CORBIS All Rights Reserved; Steve McAlister/Riser/Getty Images; Jean-Yves Ruszniewski/TempSport/CORBIS All Rights Reserved; Artiga Photo/CORBIS All Rights Reserved; Roy McMahon/CORBIS All Rights Reserved; G. Baden/CORBIS All Rights Reserved; Erik Snyder/Stone/Getty Images; **31:** Mark Richards/PhotoEdit Inc.; AGB/Shutterstock; **32 (from top):** LUKE MACGREGOR/Reuters/Corbis; Robert Brenner/PhotoEdit Inc.; AP Wide World Photos; **33:** The Kobal Collection/NBC TV; **34 (from top):** Elnur/Shutterstock; Craig Wactor/Shutterstock; **(background)** xivier/Shutterstock; **35:** AP Wide World Photos; **36 (from top):** © Ellen B. Senisi; Mark Richards/PhotoEdit Inc.; The Kobal Collection/NBC TV

CHAPTER 3 PAGE 38: Obama For America/Handout/Reuters/CORBIS- NY; **40:** Stephen Aaron Rees/Shutterstock; **41 (from top):** Mark Richards/PhotoEdit Inc; Jacques Collet/EPA/Corbis; **44 (from top):** © William P. Gottlieb/www.jazzphotos.com; Rob Brimson/Taxi/Getty Images; **45 (from left):** Joe Sohm/Chromosohm/Stock Connection; U.S. Department of Agriculture; Lewis Hine (American, 1874–1940), "A Carolina Spinner," 1908. Gelatin silver print, 4 3/4 3 7 in. Milwaukee Art Museum, Gift of the Sheldon M. Barnett Family; Brian Yarvin/Photo Researchers, Inc.; Brad Zueroff/CORBIS- NY; **47:** Mark Savage/CORBIS All Rights Reserved; **48 (from top):** Superstock Royalty Free; Bob Daemmrich/PhotoEdit Inc.; A. Ramey/PhotoEdit Inc.; **50 (from top left):** Ramzi Hachicho/Shutterstock; Andrey Zyk/Shutterstock; Andrey Zyk/Shutterstock; maxstockphoto/Shutterstock; Natasha R. Graham/Shutterstock; maxstockphoto/Shutterstock; Andrey Zyk/Shutterstock; Nina Malyna/Shutterstock; dowiliukas/Shutterstock; **(background)** Aquaman/Shutterstock; **52 (from top):** Brian Yarvin/Photo Researchers, Inc.; Mark Savage/CORBIS All Rights Reserved

CHAPTER 4 PAGE 54: Jeff Greenberg/PhotoEdit Inc.; **57:** Zuma/Red World/Newscom; **60:** Strauss/Curtis/Images; **61 (from left):** © Judith Miller/Dorling Kindersley/Sloan's; Hulton Archive/Getty Images; Kean Collection/Hulton Archive/Getty Images; FPG/Getty Images, Inc. - Taxi; Alex Wong/Getty Images News/Getty Images; Bill Pierce/Getty Images/Time Life Pictures; Jeff T. Green/Getty Images News/Getty Images; William Thomas Cain/Getty Images News/Getty Images; **62 (clockwise from top left):** Joe Carini/PacificStock.com; A.B./Getty Images; Jeff Randall/Getty Images - Digital Vision; Joe Raedle/Getty Images News/Getty Images; **64 (from left):** Shawn Frederick/Getty Images; © Bettmann/CORBIS All Rights Reserved; Hulton Archive/Getty Images; Carson Ganci/Design Pics/Corbis RF; **65:** Andy Lyons/Getty Images Sport/Getty Images; **66 (from top):** Zuma/Red World/Newscom; A.B./Getty Images; Jeff Greenberg/PhotoEdit Inc.

CHAPTER 5 PAGE 68: Marcin Balcerzak/Shutterstock; **71:** Gallo Images/Foto24/Alamy; **73:** Thinkstock/Getty Images, Inc./Jupiterimages; **74:** Ariel Skelley/CORBIS- NY; **75 (from top):** Image Source Black/Alamy; Glenda M. Powers/Shutterstock; Jivan Child/Shutterstock; **77:** Jim West/Alamy; **78 (from top):** Marcin Balcerzak/Shutterstock; Glenda M. Powers/Shutterstock; Jim West/Alamy

CHAPTER 6 PAGE 80: © Ed Kashi/CORBIS All Rights Reserved; **82 (from top):** Creative Element Photos/Alamy Images Royalty Free; Photosani/Shutterstock; iStockphoto.com; **84:** Andy Crawford/© Dorling Kindersley; **85:** Andy Crawford/© Dorling Kindersley; **86:** Sakala/Shutterstock; **87:** Olinchuk/Shutterstock; **90 (clockwise from top left):** Tomasz Trojanowski/Shutterstock; iofoto/Shutterstock; Michael Newman/PhotoEdit; stocklight/Shutterstock; **91:** Carol Kaelson/© ABC/Everett Collection; **92 (from top left):** Tiplyashin Anatoly/Shutterstock; Supri Suharjoto/Shutterstock; Supri Suharjoto/Shutterstock; Flashon Studio/Shutterstock; Felix Mizioznikov/Shutterstock; Gina Smith/Shutterstock; **94 (from top):** © Ed Kashi/CORBIS All Rights Reserved; Carol Kaelson/© ABC/Everett Collection; iofoto/Shutterstock

CHAPTER 7 PAGE 96: Laima Druskis/Pearson Education/PH College; **98:** Allyn & Bacon Royalty-Free Collection/Photodisc; **99 (from left):** iStockphoto.com; Foto Factory/Shutterstock; Allyn & Bacon Royalty-Free Collection/Photodisc; **100 (clockwise from top):** Pinchuk Alexey/Shutterstock; INDEXOPEN; Creatas/Jupiterimages/Getty Images, Inc.; C. Jordan Harris/PhotoEdit Inc.; Gary Ombler/Dorling Kindersley; **101:** Andre Maslennikov/AGE Fotostock America, Inc.; **102:** Getty Images, Inc.; **103 (from left):** Steve Gorton/© Dorling Kindersley; Tomislav Forgo/Shutterstock; Ralf-Finn Hestoft/CORBIS- NY; iStockphoto.com; **104 (from left):** Tulchinskaya/Shutterstock; Alan Freed/Shutterstock; Alejandro Ernesto/Landov Media; **106:** C Barnes Photography/Shutterstock; **107:** iofoto/Shutterstock; **108 (from top):** Photolibrary.com; Solaria/Shutterstock; Mike Goldwater/Alamy; **110 (from top):** C. Jordan Harris/PhotoEdit Inc.; C Barnes Photography/Shutterstock; Solaria/Shutterstock

CHAPTER 8 PAGE 112: Allyn & Bacon Royalty-Free Collection/Photodisc; **115 (from top):** Joe Sohm/Chromosohm/Stock Connection; Jupiterimages/Creatas/Getty Images, Inc - Jupiter Images; **116 (clockwise from top):** Photos.com; Mark Kulpers/Shutterstock; Alan Keohane/© Dorling Kindersley; Teb Nad/Shutterstock; Comstock/© 2009 Jupiterimages Unlimited; Patrick Wang/Shutterstock; **117 (from left):** Zoommer/Shutterstock; Tasika/Shutterstock; **118:** Allyn & Bacon Royalty-Free Collection/Photodisc; **119:** Photos.com; **120:** Allyn & Bacon Royalty-Free Collection/Photodisc; **121:** Win McNamee/CORBIS- NY; **122 (from top):** Allyn & Bacon Royalty-Free Collection/Photodisc; Will & Deni McIntyre/Photo Researchers, Inc.; Allyn & Bacon Royalty-Free Collection/Photodisc; **124 (from top):** Jupiterimages/Creatas/Getty Images, Inc - Jupiter Images; Allyn & Bacon Royalty-Free Collection/Photodisc; Win McNamee/CORBIS- NY

CHAPTER 9 PAGE 126: Photos.com; **128:** Allyn & Bacon Royalty-Free Collection/Photodisc; **129:** Thomas Eakins, "The Gross Clinic". 1875. Oil on Canvas. 89 3 6960. Jefferson Medical College of Thomas Jefferson University, Philadelphia; **130:** Scott Cunningham/Merrill Education; **133 (from top):** Photos.com; Lamia Druskis/Pearson Education/PH College; **134:** Jerry Cooke/Photo Researchers, Inc.; **135 (from top):** Allyn & Bacon Royalty-Free Collection/Photodisc; Feng Yu/Shutterstock; S. Rubin/The Image Works; **138 (from top):** Allyn & Bacon Royalty-Free Collection/Photodisc; Feng Yu/Shutterstock; S. Rubin/The Image Works

CHAPTER 10 PAGE 140: Photos.com; **143:** Pearson Education/PH College; **146:** Hutchings Stock Photography/CORBIS All Rights Reserved; **147 (from top):** Allyn & Bacon Royalty-Free Collection/Corbis Royalty-Free; National Picture/Topham/The Image Works; **148 (from top):** Peter Horree/Alamy; Allyn & Bacon Royalty-Free Collection/Corbis Royalty-Free; Jim West/Alamy; **149 (clockwise from top):** Allyn & Bacon Royalty-Free Collection/Corbis Royalty-Free; Desiree Walstra/Shutterstock; Allyn & Bacon Royalty-Free Collection/Corbis Royalty-Free; Allyn & Bacon Royalty-Free Collection/Corbis Royalty-Free; Donna Cuic/Shutterstock; **150 (from top):** Allyn & Bacon Royalty-Free Collection/Corbis Royalty-Free; Guillermo Arias/AP Wide World Photos; **152 (from top):** Allyn & Bacon Royalty-Free Collection/Corbis Royalty-Free; Jim West/Alamy; National Picture/Topham/The Image Works

CHAPTER 11 PAGE 154: Crystal Kirk/Shutterstock; **156:** Getty Images, Inc.; **157:** ArrowStudio, LLC/Shutterstock; **158:** Allyn & Bacon Royalty-Free Collection/Photodisc; **162 (clockwise from top):** Eugene Gordon/Pearson Education/PH College; Allyn & Bacon Royalty-Free Collection/Rubberball Productions; Jan van der Hoeven/Shutterstock; Banana Stock/Jupiter Images - PictureArts Corporation/Brand X Pictures Royalty Free; **163:** Liquidlibrary/Jupiter Images Royalty Free; **164 (from top):** Getty Images, Inc.; Banana Stock/Jupiter Images - PictureArts Corporation/Brand X Pictures Royalty Free; Liquidlibrary/Jupiter Images Royalty Free

CHAPTER 12 PAGE 166: Scott J. Ferrell/Congressional Quarterly/Alamy; **168:** Laima Druskis/Pearson Education/PH College; **169:** Allyn & Bacon Royalty-Free Collection/Corbis Royalty-Free; **170:** Allyn & Bacon Royalty-Free Collection/Corbis Royalty-Free; **171:** Yadid Levy/Alamy; **174 (from top):** Jeff Greenberg/Alamy; Cleve Bryant/PhotoEdit; **175 (from top):** Jason Stitt/Shutterstock; Rudanto Wijaya/Shutterstock; Jason Stitt/Shutterstock; © Dorling Kindersley; **176:** Dan Lee/Shutterstock; **178 (from top):** Laima Druskis/Pearson Education/PH College; Jeff Greenberg/Alamy; Cleve Bryant/PhotoEdit

INDEX

INDEX